Markov Random Fields for Vision and Image Processing

Markov Random Fields for Vision and Image Processing

edited by Andrew Blake, Pushmeet Kohli, and Carsten Rother

The MIT Press
Cambridge, Massachusetts
London, England

For information about special quantity discounts, please email special_sales@mitpress.mit.edu

This book was set in Syntax and Times New Roman by Westchester Books Composition. Printed and bound in the United States of America.

Library of Congress Cataloging-in-Publication Data

Markov random fields for vision and image processing / edited by Andrew Blake, Pushmeet Kohli, and Carsten Rother.
    p.   cm.
Includes bibliographical references and index.
ISBN 978-0-262-01577-6 (hardcover : alk. paper)
1. Image processing—Mathematics. 2. Computer graphics—Mathematics. 3. Computer vision—Mathematics. 4. Markov random fields. I. Blake, Andrew, 1956– II. Kohli, Pushmeet. III. Rother, Carsten.
TAI637.M337   2011
006.3′70151—dc22

                                                                    2010046702

10   9   8   7   6   5   4   3   2   1

Contents

1 Introduction to Markov Random Fields

Andrew Blake and Pushmeet Kohli

This book sets out to demonstrate the power of the Markov random field (MRF) in vision. It treats the MRF both as a tool for modeling image data and, coupled with a set of recently developed algorithms, as a means of making inferences about images. The inferences concern underlying image and scene structure to solve problems such as image reconstruction, image segmentation, 3D vision, and object labeling. This chapter is designed to present some of the main concepts used in MRFs, both as a taster and as a gateway to the more detailed chapters that follow, as well as a stand-alone introduction to MRFs.

The unifying ideas in using MRFs for vision are the following:

- Images are dissected into an assembly of nodes that may correspond to pixels or agglomerations of pixels.

- Hidden variables associated with the nodes are introduced into a model designed to "explain" the values (colors) of all the pixels.

- A joint probabilistic model is built over the pixel values and the hidden variables.

- The direct statistical dependencies between hidden variables are expressed by explicitly grouping hidden variables; these groups are often pairs depicted as edges in a graph.

These properties of MRFs are illustrated in figure 1.1. The graphs corresponding to such MRF problems are predominantly gridlike, but may also be irregular, as in figure 1.1(c). Exactly how graph connectivity is interpreted in terms of probabilistic conditional dependency is discussed a little later.

The notation for image graphs is that the graph $\mathcal{G} = (\mathcal{V}, \mathcal{E})$ consists of vertices $\mathcal{V} = (1, 2, \ldots, i, \ldots, N)$ corresponding, for example, to the pixels of the image, and a set of edges $\mathcal{E}$ where a typical edge is (i, j), $i, j \in \mathcal{V}$, and edges are considered to be undirected, so that (i, j) and (j, i) refer to the same edge. In the superpixel graph of figure 1.1), the nodes are superpixels, and a pair of superpixels forms an edge in $\mathcal{E}$ if the two superpixels share a common boundary.

The motivation for constructing such a graph is to connect the hidden variables associated with the nodes. For example, for the task of segmenting an image into foreground and background, each node i (pixel or superpixel) has an associated random variable X_i that

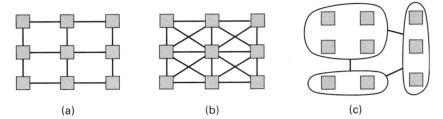

(a)   (b)   (c)

Figure 1.1
Graphs for Markov models in vision. (a) Simple 4-connected grid of image pixels. (b) Grids with greater connectivity can be useful—for example, to achieve better geometrical detail (see discussion later)—as here with the 8-connected pixel grid. (c) Irregular grids are also useful. Here a more compact graph is constructed in which the nodes are superpixels—clusters of adjacent pixels with similar colors.

may take the value 0 or 1, corresponding to foreground or background, respectively. In order to represent the tendency of matter to be coherent, neighboring sites are likely to have the same label. So where $(i, j) \in \mathcal{E}$, some kind of probabilistic bias needs to be associated with the edge (i, j) such that X_i and X_j tend to have the same label—both 0 or both 1. In fact, any pixels that are nearby, not merely adjacent, are likely to have the same label. On the other hand, explicitly linking all the pixels in a typical image, whose foreground/background labels have correlations, would lead to a densely connected graph. That in turn would result in computationally expensive algorithms. Markov models *explicitly* represent only the associations between relatively few pairs of pixels—those pixels that are defined as neighbors because of sharing an edge in $\mathcal{E}$. The great attraction of Markov Models is that they leverage a *knock-on effect*—that explicit short-range linkages give rise to implied long-range correlations. Thus correlations over long ranges, on the order of the diameters of typical objects, can be obtained without undue computational cost. The goal of this chapter is to investigate probabilistic models that exploit this powerful Markov property.

1.1 Markov Chains: The Simplest Markov Models

In a Markov chain a sequence of random variables $\mathbf{X} = (X_1, X_2, \ldots)$ has a joint distribution specified by the conditionals $P(X_i \mid X_{i-1}, X_{i-2}, \ldots, X_1)$. The classic tutorial example [381, sec. 6.2] is the weather, so that $X_i \in \mathcal{L} = \{sunny, rainy\}$. The weather on day i can be influenced by the weather many days previous, but in the simplest form of Markov chain, the dependence of today's weather is linked explicitly only to yesterday's weather. It is also linked *implicitly*, as a knock-on effect, to all previous days. This is a *first-order* Markov assumption, that

$$P(X_i \mid X_{i-1}, X_{i-2}, \ldots, X_1) = P(X_i \mid X_{i-1}). \tag{1.1}$$

This is illustrated in figure 1.2. The set of conditional probabilities $P(X_i \mid X_{i-1})$ is in fact a 2×2 matrix. For example:

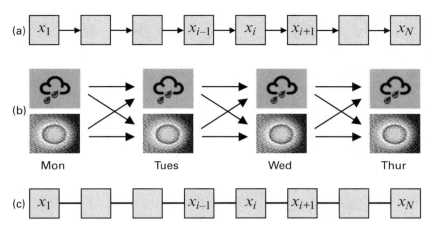

Figure 1.2
A simple first-order Markov chain for weather forecasting. (a) A directed graph is used to represent the conditional dependencies of a Markov chain. (b) In more detail, the state transition diagram completely specifies the probabilistic process of the evolving weather states. (c) A Markov chain can alternatively be expressed as an undirected graphical model; see text for details.

		Yesterday (X_{i-1})	
		Rain	Sun
Today (X_i)	Rain	0.4	0.8
	Sun	0.6	0.2

An interesting and commonly used special case is the *stationary* Markov chain, in which the matrix

$$M_i(x, x') = P(X_i = x \mid X_{i-1} = x') \tag{1.2}$$

is independent of time i, so that $M_i(., .) = M_{i-1}(., .)$. In the weather example this corresponds to the assumption that the statistical dependency of weather is a fixed relationship, the same on any day.

We will not dwell on the simple example of the Markov chain, but a few comments may be useful. First, the first-order *explicit* structure implicitly carries longer-range dependencies, too. For instance, the conditional dependency across three successive days is obtained by multiplying together the matrices for two successive pairs of days:

$$P(X_i = x \mid X_{i-2} = x'') = \sum_{x' \in \mathcal{L}} M_i(x, x') M_{i-1}(x', x''). \tag{1.3}$$

Thus the Markov chain shares the elegance of Markov models generally, which will recur later with models for images, that long-range dependencies can be captured for the "price" of explicitly representing just the immediate dependencies between neighbors. Second, higher-order Markov chains, where the *explicit* dependencies go back farther than immediate neighbors, can also be useful. A famous example is "predictive text," in which probable letters in a typical word are characterized in terms of the two preceding letters—taking just the one preceding letter does not give enough practical predictive power. Predictive text, then, is a second-order Markov chain.

The directed graph in figure 1.2a) is a graphical representation of the fact that, for a Markov chain, the joint density can be decomposed as a product of conditional densities:

$$P(\mathbf{x}) = P(x_N \mid x_{N-1}) \dots P(x_i \mid x_{i-1}) \dots P(x_2 \mid x_1) P(x_1), \tag{1.4}$$

where for simplicity, in a popular abuse of notation, $P(\mathbf{x})$ denotes $P(\mathbf{X} = \mathbf{x})$ and, similarly, $P(x_i \mid x_{i-1})$ denotes $P(X_i = x_i \mid X_{i-1} = x_{i-1})$. This convention is used frequently throughout the book. An alternative formalism that is commonly used is the *undirected* graphical model. Markov chains can also be represented in this way (figure 1.2c), corresponding to a factorized decomposition:

$$P(\mathbf{x}) = \Phi_{N,N-1}(x_N, x_{N-1}) \dots \Phi_{i,i-1}(x_i, x_{i-1}) \dots \Phi_{2,1}(x_2, x_1), \tag{1.5}$$

where $\Phi_{i,i-1}$ is a factor of the joint density. It is easy to see, in this simple case of the Markov chain, how the directed form (1.4) can be reexpressed in the undirected form (1.5). However, it is not the case in general, and in particular in 2D images, that models expressed in one form can easily be expressed in the other. Many of the probabilistic models used in computer vision are most naturally expressed using the undirected formalism, so it is the undirected graphical models that dominate in this book. For details on directed graphical models see [216, 46].

1.2 The Hidden Markov Model (HMM)

Markov models are particularly useful as prior models for state variables X_i that are to be inferred from a corresponding set of measurements or observations $z = (z_1, z_2, \dots, z_i, \dots, z_N)$. The observations z are themselves considered to be instantiations of a random variable Z representing the full space of observations that can arise. This is the classical situation in speech analysis [381, sec. 6.2], where z_i represents the spectral content of a fragment of an audio signal, and X_i represents a state in the time course of a particular word or phoneme. It leads naturally to an inference problem in which the *posterior* distribution for the possible states X, given the observations z, is computed via Bayes's formula as

$$P(\mathbf{X} = \mathbf{x} \mid \mathbf{Z} = \mathbf{z}) \propto P(\mathbf{Z} = \mathbf{z} \mid \mathbf{X} = \mathbf{x}) P(\mathbf{X} = \mathbf{x}). \tag{1.6}$$

Here $P(\mathbf{X} = \mathbf{x})$ is the prior distribution over states—that is, what is known about states $\mathbf{X}$ in the absence of any observations. As before, (1.6) is abbreviated, for convenience, to

$$P(\mathbf{x} \mid \mathbf{z}) \propto P(\mathbf{z} \mid \mathbf{x}) P(\mathbf{x}). \tag{1.7}$$

The omitted constant of proportionality would be fixed to ensure that $\sum_{\mathbf{x}} P(\mathbf{x} \mid \mathbf{z}) = 1$. Often multiple models are considered simultaneously, and in that case this is denoted

$$P(\mathbf{x} \mid \mathbf{z}, \omega) \propto P(\mathbf{z} \mid \mathbf{x}, \omega) P(\mathbf{x} \mid \omega), \tag{1.8}$$

where the model parameters $\omega \in \Omega$ may determine the prior model or the observation model or both. The constant of proportionality in this relation would of course depend on $\mathbf{z}$ and on ω.

The prior of an HMM is itself represented as a Markov chain, which in the first-order case was decomposed as a product of conditional distributions (1.4). The term $P(\mathbf{z} \mid \mathbf{x})$ is the *likelihood* of the observations, which is essentially a measure of the quality of the measurements. The more precise and unambiguous the measuring instrument, the more the likelihood will be compressed into a single, narrow peak. This captures the fact that a more precise instrument produces more consistent responses $\mathbf{z}$, under a given condition represented by the state $\mathbf{X} = \mathbf{x}$. It is often assumed—and this is true of the models used in many of the chapters of this book—that observations are independent across sites. The observation at site i depends only on the corresponding state. In other words:

$$P(\mathbf{z} \mid \mathbf{x}) = P(z_N \mid x_N) P(z_{N-1} \mid x_{N-1}) \dots P(z_1 \mid x_1). \tag{1.9}$$

The directed graphical model for the conditional dependencies of such a first-order HMM is given in figure 1.3a). The figure captures the conditional dependencies both of the underlying

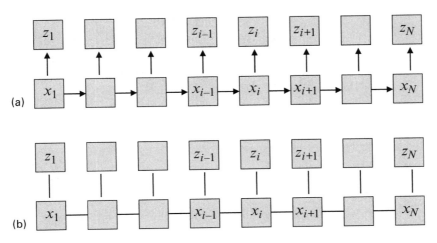

Figure 1.3
A first-order hidden Markov model (HMM). (a) A directed graph is used to represent the dependencies of a first-order HMM, with its Markov chain prior, and a set of independently uncertain observations. (b) Alternatively the HMM can be represented as an undirected graphical model (see text).

Markov chain and of the independence of the observations. Alternatively, an HMM can be expressed as an undirected graphical model, as depicted in figure 1.3(b), in which the prior is decomposed as in (1.5), and the likelihood is

$$P(\mathbf{z} \mid \mathbf{x}) = \Phi_N(x_N)\Phi_{N-1}(x_{N-1})\ldots\Phi_1(x_1), \tag{1.10}$$

where trivially $\Phi_i(x_i) = P(z_i \mid x_i)$.

Discrete HMMs, with a finite label set $\mathcal{L}$, are largely tractable. Rabiner and Juang [382] set out three canonical problems for HMMs, and algorithms to solve them. The problems are the following:

1. *Evaluating the observation probability* $P(\mathbf{z} \mid \omega)$ In this problem there is no explicit state dependence, because it has been "marginalized" out by summation over states:

$$P(\mathbf{z} \mid \omega) = \sum_{\mathbf{x} \in \mathcal{L}^N} P(\mathbf{z} \mid \mathbf{x}, \omega) P(\mathbf{x} \mid \omega). \tag{1.11}$$

The main application of this evaluation is to determine which of a set of known models fits the data best:

$$\max_{\omega \in \Omega} P(\mathbf{z} \mid \omega). \tag{1.12}$$

The quantity $P(\mathbf{z} \mid \omega)$ is also known as the *evidence* [328] for the model ω from the data $\mathbf{z}$.

2. *MAP estimation* Given a model ω and a set of data $\mathbf{z}$, estimate the most probable (maximum a posteriori) sequence $\mathbf{x}$ of states as the mode of the posterior distribution (1.8).

3. *Parameter estimation* Given a set of data $\mathbf{z}$, estimate the parameters $\omega \in \Omega$, a continuous parameter space that best fits the data. This is the problem that must be solved to build a particular model from training data. It is closely related to the model selection problem above, in that both maximize $P(\mathbf{z} \mid \omega)$, the difference being that the model space Ω is, respectively, discrete or continuous.

These three problems are essentially solved by using two algorithms and variants of them.

The first problem requires the *forward* algorithm that computes a marginal distribution node i from the distribution at the previous node $i - 1$:

$$P(x_i, z_1, \ldots, z_i \mid \omega) = P(z_i \mid x_i, \omega) \sum_{x_{i-1}} P(x_i \mid x_{i-1}, \omega) P(x_{i-1}, z_1, \ldots, z_{i-1} \mid \omega). \tag{1.13}$$

This is a special case of *Belief Propagation* (BP) that will be discussed later in this chapter and in various subsequent chapters in the book. In fact there are two forms of BP [367, 46], and this one is an example of *sum-product* BP. (The name derives from the summation and product steps in (1.13).) The other form is described shortly. In the case of the HMM, where the underlying prior model is simply a Markov chain, sum-product belief propagation is quite straightforward and is an exact algorithm for computing the marginal posteriors. After one complete forward pass, the final marginal distribution is $P(x_N, \mathbf{z} \mid \omega)$, and so finally

$$P(\mathbf{z} \mid \omega) = \sum_{x_N} P(x_N, \mathbf{z} \mid \omega) \tag{1.14}$$

can be computed as the evidence for a known model ω that solves problem 1 above. The forward pass (1.13) constitutes half of BP, the remaining part being a backward pass that recurs from node N back to node 1 (details omitted here, but see [382]). Using the forward and backward passes together, the full set of marginal posterior distributions

$$P(x_i \mid \mathbf{z}, \omega), \; i = 1, \ldots, N \tag{1.15}$$

can be computed. This is required for problem 3 above, in order to compute the expected values of the sufficient statistics that are needed to estimate the parameters ω by *expectation maximization* [121]—also known in the speech analysis literature as the Baum–Welch method [381].

The second algorithm is the Viterbi algorithm, a dynamic programming optimization algorithm applied to the state sequence $\mathbf{x}$. It is also equivalent to a special case of max-product belief propagation, which also is mentioned quite frequently in the book. The aim is to solve the second problem above, computing the MAP estimate of the state vector as

$$\hat{\mathbf{x}} = \arg\max_{\mathbf{x}} P(\mathbf{x} \mid \mathbf{z}, \omega) \tag{1.16}$$

via a forward recursion:

$$P_i(x_i) = P(z_i \mid x_i, \omega) \max_{x_{i-1}} P(x_i \mid x_{i-1}, \omega) P_{i-1}(x_{i-1}) \tag{1.17}$$

where P_i is defined by

$$P_i(x_i) \equiv \max_{x_1, \ldots, x_{i-1}} P(x_1, \ldots, x_i, z_1, \ldots, z_i \mid \omega). \tag{1.18}$$

Each forward step of the recursion can be viewed as a message-passing operation. In step $i - 1$ of the computation, node $i - 1$ sends the message $P_i(x_i)$ to node i.

After the forward steps are complete, the final component $\hat{x}_N$ of the MAP solution $\hat{x}$ can be computed as

$$\hat{x}_N = \arg\max_{x_N} P_n(x_N). \tag{1.19}$$

This is followed by a backward recursion

$$\hat{x}_{i-1} = \arg\max_{x_{i-1}} P(\hat{x}_i \mid x_{i-1}, \omega) \, P_{i-1}(x_{i-1}), \tag{1.20}$$

after which all components of $\hat{x}$ are determined.

The purpose of the discussion in this section has been largely to explain the nature of hidden variables in simple Markov models, as a precursor to later discussion of hidden variables in the more complex, two-dimensional kinds of models that are used in vision. However, even in vision the discrete HMM structure has some direct applications. It has proved useful for representing temporal problems that are somewhat analogous to speech analysis, but in which the audio input is replaced by a time sequence of visual features. Well-known examples include the recognition of American Sign Language [449] and the recognition of hand gestures for command and control [522]. This book deals mainly with discrete Markov models—that is, ones in which the states of each X_i belong to a finite set $\mathcal{L}$. However, in vision by far the greater application of timelike HMMs employs continuous state-space to represent position, attitude, and shape in visual tracking [333, 477, 50, 253, 209, 124]. In such continuous settings the HMM becomes a classical or nonclassical form of Kalman filter. Both exact solutions to the estimation problems that arise, and efficient approximate solutions, are much studied, but are outside the scope of this book.

1.3 Markov Models on Trees

In the following section 1.4, Markov Random Fields (MRFs) are defined as probabilistic models over undirected graphs. On the way there, we now consider undirected models on trees as intermediate in complexity between the linear graphs—chains and HMMs—of section 1.2, and graphs of unrestricted connectivity. Clearly the HMM graph (figure 1.3b) is a special case of an undirected model on a tree. Trees appear to be of intermediate complexity but, perhaps surprisingly, turn out to be closer to HMMs, in that inference can be performed exactly. The Viterbi and forward-backward algorithms for HMMs generalize to two different kinds of message passing on trees. However, once the nodes on two leaves of a tree are coalesced into a single leaf—for example, leaves **b** and **d** in figure 1.4—a circuit may be formed in the resulting graph, and message-passing algorithms are no longer an exact solution to the problems of inference.

As with Markov chains and HMMs, in undirected trees the topological structure conveys two aspects of the underlying probabilistic model. First are the conditional independence properties, that:

$$P(x_i \mid \{x_j, \ j \neq i\}) = P(x_i \mid \{x_j, \ (i, j) \in \mathcal{E}\}). \tag{1.21}$$

The set $B_i = \{j : \ (i, j) \in \mathcal{E}\}$ is known as the Markov blanket of i, its neighbors in the tree (or generally graph) $\mathcal{G}$. The second aspect is the decomposition of the joint distribution, the generalization of (1.5) and (1.10). How can a distribution with this independence property be constructed? The answer is, as a distribution that is factorized over the edges of the tree:

$$P(\mathbf{x}) = \prod_{(i,j)\in\mathcal{E}} F_{i,j}(x_i, x_j). \tag{1.22}$$

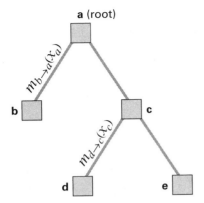

Figure 1.4
Message passing for MAP inference in tree structured graphical models. A graphical model containing five nodes (a, b, c, d, and e) connected in a tree structure.

1.3.1 Inference on Trees: Belief Propagation (BP)

The message-passing formulation of the Viterbi algorithm can be generalized to find marginal distributions over individual variables and the MAP estimate in a tree structured graphical model. The resulting algorithm is known as belief propagation [367] and has two variants: *max-product*, for computing the MAP solution, and sum-product (mentioned earlier), which allows computation of marginals of individual random variables.

Max-product message passing is similar in spirit to dynamic programming algorithms. Like the Viterbi algorithm, it works by passing messages between tree nodes in two stages. In the first stage, messages are passed from the leaf nodes to their parents, which in turn pass messages to their parents, and so on until the messages reach the root node. The message $m_{i \to j}$ from a node i to its parent j is computed as

$$m_{i \to j}(x_j) = \max_{x_i} P(x_j, x_i) \prod_{k \in \mathcal{N}_c(i)} m_{k \to i}(x_i) \tag{1.23}$$

where $\mathcal{N}_c(i)$ is the set of all children of node i. The MAP label of the variable at the root r of the tree can be computed as

$$\hat{x}_r = \arg \max_{x_r} \prod_{k \in \mathcal{N}_c(r)} m_{k \to r}(x_r). \tag{1.24}$$

Given the MAP label $\hat{x}_p$ of a variable X_p, the label of any of its children i can be found as

$$\hat{x}_i = \max_{x_i} P(\hat{x}_p, x_i) \prod_{k \in \mathcal{N}_c(i)} m_{k \to i}(x_i). \tag{1.25}$$

1.3.2 Example: Max-Product BP on a Five-Node Model

Consider the undirected, tree-structured graphical model shown in figure 1.4. The joint distribution factorizes as

$$P(\mathbf{x}) = P(x_a, x_b) P(x_a, x_c) P(x_c, x_e) P(x_c, x_d). \tag{1.26}$$

The messages computed by max-product are

$$m_{d \to c}(x_c) = \max_{x_d} P(x_c, x_d) \tag{1.27}$$

$$m_{e \to c}(x_c) = \max_{x_e} P(x_c, x_e) \tag{1.28}$$

$$m_{c \to a}(x_a) = \max_{x_c} P(x_a, x_c) m_{e \to c}(x_c) m_{d \to c}(x_c) \tag{1.29}$$

$$m_{b \to a}(x_a) = \max_{x_b} P(x_a, x_b). \tag{1.30}$$

The MAP labels can be found as

$$\hat{x}_a = \max_{x_a} m_{b \to a}(x_a) m_{c \to a}(x_a) \tag{1.31}$$

$$\hat{x}_b = \max_{x_b} P(\hat{x}_a, x_b) \tag{1.32}$$

$$\hat{x}_c = \max_{x_c} P(\hat{x}_a, x_c) m_{e \to c}(x_c) m_{d \to c}(x_c) \tag{1.33}$$

$$\hat{x}_d = \max_{x_d} P(\hat{x}_c, x_d) \tag{1.34}$$

$$\hat{x}_e = \max_{x_d} P(\hat{x}_c, x_e). \tag{1.35}$$

The sum product BP algorithm computes the marginal distributions $P(x_i)$ for all variables X_i. It essentially works in a way similar to max-product BP (1.23), except that rather than taking the max, a *sum* is performed over the different labels:

$$m_{i \to j}(x_j) = \sum_{x_i} P(x_j, x_i) \prod_{k \in \mathcal{N}_c(i)} m_{k \to i}(x_i) \tag{1.36}$$

where $\mathcal{N}_c(i)$ is the set of all children of node i. The marginal $P(x_i)$ can be computed by taking the product of the messages sent to the root node i:

$$P(x_i) = \prod_{k \in \mathcal{N}_c(i)} m_{k \to i}(x_i). \tag{1.37}$$

Now, by successively rearranging the tree so that each node i in turn becomes the root node, $P(x_i)$ can be computed for all nodes i.

1.4 MRFs: Markov Models on Graphs

At the start of the chapter, the choice of graphs for image processing was motivated by the need to establish dependencies between pixels that are nearby in an image. The graphs that were proposed for that purpose are not trees, but contain cycles of edges, typically many cycles, as in figure 1.1. The representation of independence in undirected graphs follows the methodology given above for trees (1.21). The random variable at a node is dependent directly only on random variables in its Markov blanket B_i. The Hammersley–Clifford theorem [98] gives the general form for a distribution with these Markov properties:

$$P(\mathbf{x}) = \prod_{c \in C} F_c(\mathbf{x}) \tag{1.38}$$

where C is the set of maximal cliques of $\mathcal{G}$—defined to be the set of maximal subgraphs of $\mathcal{G}$ that are fully connected in $\mathcal{E}$, and maximal in the sense that no further node can be added to a clique without removing the full connectedness property. Note that for a tree the cliques are simply the edges of the graph, and so the decomposition (1.38) simplifies to the decomposition (1.22) for trees, above. Usually the decomposition is expressed in terms of an energy or cost function $E(\mathbf{x})$:

$$P(\mathbf{x}) \propto \exp\left(-E(\mathbf{x})\right) \text{ where } E(\mathbf{x}) = \sum_{c \in C} \Psi_c(\mathbf{x}). \tag{1.39}$$

More generally, there may be a dependence on parameters, so that

$$P(\mathbf{x}) = \frac{1}{Z(\omega)} \exp\left(-E(\mathbf{x}, \omega)\right) \text{ where } E(\mathbf{x}, \omega) = \sum_{c \in C} \Psi_c(\mathbf{x}_c, \omega), \tag{1.40}$$

and now the *partition function*

$$Z(\omega) = \sum_{\mathbf{x}} \exp\left(-E(\mathbf{x}, \omega)\right) \tag{1.41}$$

is included to maintain the normalization condition for the distribution, $\sum_{\mathbf{x}} P(\mathbf{x}) = 1$.

An alternative representation of the undirected graph in figure 1.1 is the *factor graph* [276]. The undirected graph (or *Markov network*) makes conditional dependencies explicit, but factorization properties are somewhat implicit—they need to be computed in terms of maximal cliques. Factor graphs are a little more complex in that they introduce a second type of node, the function node, in addition to the nodes for variables but have the advantage of making factorization explicit. In many of the cases used in this book—for example, figure 1.1a, with 4-way connectivity between pixels—the factorization structure is straightforward. Each edge in that example is a maximal clique, and therefore the factors are functions of the two variables on the nodes belonging to each edge. On the other hand, figure 1.1b, with its 8-way connectivity, has a more complex set of statistical dependencies, and the factors may not simply correspond to edges. The most general factor structure for the Markov model with the statistical dependencies denoted by that graph is a function of the *four variables* in each of the 2×2 squares of variables, which are the maximal cliques of the graph. In computer vision, it is usual to define models directly in terms of their factors, in contrast to normal practice in statistical modeling, where models are defined first in terms of their Markov properties, with factors specified subsequently over maximal cliques, as in (1.38). In the more complex cases of factors involving more than two variables at a time, factor graphs are useful, and are mentioned in chapters 21 and 24. For the most part, though, pairwise factors and simple undirected graphs suffice.

1.4.1 Example: Pseudo-Boolean Energy on a 4-Connected Graph of Pixels

A standard example of an MRF, just about the simplest one that is interesting, is the *Ising* model with the single parameter $\omega = \{\gamma\}$, whose origins are in statistical physics [523]. The state-space consists of Boolean variables $x_i \in \mathcal{L} = \{0, 1\}$, and the energy function $E(\mathbf{x})$ is termed a *Pseudo-Boolean Function* (PBF)—because its input is Boolean but its output is not (the energy is real valued). As for the graph, the maximal cliques are the horizontal and vertical edges of the rectangular graph of pixels shown in figure 1.5a. All cliques in this

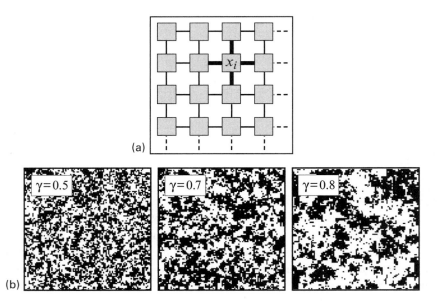

(a)

(b)

Figure 1.5
Simulating a simple model: The Ising model. (a) The horizontal and vertical edges of a rectangular grid form the cliques of the Ising model. (b) Simulations of typical probable states of the Ising model for various values of the coherence parameter γ.

case are of size 2, containing two nodes (pixels). The clique potentials, referred to in this kind of model as *pairwise* potentials because the cliques are pairs of pixels, are

$$\Psi_{ij}(x_i, x_j) = \gamma |x_i - x_j|. \tag{1.42}$$

This represents a penalty γ that increases the energy E wherever adjacent x_i and x_j have different values, and so reduces the joint probability $P(\mathbf{x})$ by a factor e^γ. This enhances the probability of configurations $\mathbf{x}$ in which there is large-scale agreement between the values of adjacent pixels. In fact, a moment's thought will make it clear that the *total* penalty $\sum_{(i,j)\in\mathcal{C}} \Psi_{ij}$ is simply γ times the total perimeter (in the Manhattan metric) of boundaries separating regions of value 1 from regions of value 0. Thus the distribution $P(\mathbf{x})$ favors configurations $\mathbf{x}$ in which that total perimeter is relatively small. The simulations in figure 1.5b show how higher values of γ indeed tend to favor larger regions of 1s and 0s.

It is worth saying at this stage, and this will come out repeatedly later, that algorithms for inference with general graphs that contain loops—many loops in the case of the example above—are hard. Even simulation from the Ising model is hard, compared with the equivalent simulation for a chain or tree, which is straighforward and can be done exactly. The simulations of the Ising model above were done using a form of *Markov chain Monte Carlo*, adapted specifically for the Ising model [165], the Swendsen–Wang iterative sampler [25].

1.5 Hidden MRF Models

A Markov random field $P(\mathbf{X} = \mathbf{x})$, as in the previous section, can act as a prior model for a set of hidden random variables $\mathbf{X}$, under a set of observations $\mathbf{z}$, in direct analogy to the HMM model of section 1.2. As with HMMs, the observations are most simply modeled as random variables that are independent when conditioned on the hidden variables $\mathbf{X}$. This is illustrated in figure 1.6, in which the simple 4-connected graph of figure 1.5a appears as a layer of hidden variables $\mathbf{x}$ with observations $\mathbf{z}$ distributed across sites. Each individual observation z_i depends statistically just on the state x_i of the corresponding pixel. Now the posterior for the state $\mathbf{x}$ of the pixels is obtained from Bayes's formula, just as it was for HMMs (1.6), as

$$P(\mathbf{x} \mid \mathbf{z}, \omega) \propto P(\mathbf{z} \mid \mathbf{x}, \omega) P(\mathbf{x} \mid \omega), \tag{1.43}$$

with the observation likelihood $P(\mathbf{z} \mid \mathbf{x})$ factorized across sites/pixels as it was earlier (1.9), and including the possibility of multiple models as before. It is common also to express this *posterior MRF* in terms of a sum of energies, generalizing the prior MRF (1.40) to include terms for the observation likelihood:

$$P(\mathbf{x} \mid \mathbf{z}, \omega) = \frac{1}{Z(\mathbf{z}, \omega)} \exp{-E(\mathbf{x}, \mathbf{z}, \omega)}, \tag{1.44}$$

where $E(\mathbf{x}, \mathbf{z}, \omega) = \sum_{c \in \mathcal{C}} \Psi_c(\mathbf{x}, \omega) + \sum_i \Phi_i(x_i, z_i). \tag{1.45}$

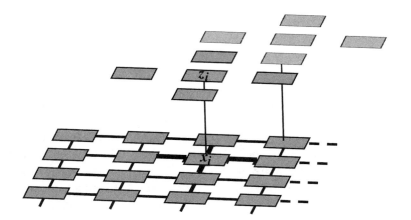

Figure 1.6
Two-dimensional hidden Markov model. An MRF on a regular grid, as in figure 1.5, serves here as the prior over hidden variables in a model that is coupled to an array **z** of observations.

Here $Z(\mathbf{z}, \omega)$ is the partition function for the posterior MRF. Unlike the HMM (1.8), for which Z can in fact be computed quite easily, computing the partition function $Z(\mathbf{z}, \omega)$ for the posterior MRF is intractable.

The most common form of inference over the posterior MRF in vision and image-processing problems, is Maximum A Posteriori (MAP) estimation. MAP inference of **x** is done in principle by computing $\hat{\mathbf{x}} = \arg\max P(\mathbf{x} \mid \mathbf{z})$, or equivalently by minimizing energy:

$$\hat{\mathbf{x}} = \arg\min E(\mathbf{x}, \mathbf{z}, \omega). \tag{1.46}$$

Note that this does not require knowledge of the partition function $Z(\mathbf{z}, \omega)$, which is just as well, given its intractability. The energy functions for many commonly used Markov models (see examples below) can be written as a sum of unary and pairwise terms:

$$E(\mathbf{x}, \mathbf{z}, \omega) = \sum_{i \in \mathcal{V}} \Phi_i(x_i, z_i, \omega) + \sum_{(i,j) \in \mathcal{E}} \Psi_{ij}(x_i, x_j, \omega). \tag{1.47}$$

Algorithms for computing the MAP are discussed in the following sections. Suffice it to say that the MAP can in fact be computed exactly in a time that is polynomial with respect to the size N of the image array, using *graph cut*, at least when the prior $P(\mathbf{x})$ is an Ising distribution.

1.5.1 Example: Segmentation on a 4-Connected Graph of Pixels
Here we give the simplest useful example of a hidden MRF model, for segmenting an image into foreground and background components. The state-space is Boolean, so $x_i \in \{0, 1\}$ denotes background/foreground labels, respectively. The model, originated by Boykov and

Jolly [66], has a number of variants. For tutorial purposes the simplest of them is illustrated here. It uses the Ising model as a prior to encourage the foreground and background components to be as coherent as possible. Thus the Ψ terms in the hidden MRF model (1.45) are the ones from the Ising prior (1.42). The likelihood terms (for details, see chapter 7 on MRF models for segmentation) can be specified by constructing histograms $h_F(z)$ and $h_B(z)$ in color space for foreground and background, respectively (taking care to avoid zeros), and setting

$$\Phi_i(z_i) = \log h_F(z_i) - \log h_B(z_i).$$ \hfill (1.48)

The resulting model specifies a posterior, which is maximized to obtain the estimated segmentation $\hat{x}$, and the resulting method is demonstrably effective, as figure 1.7 shows.

a)

b)

c)

d)

Figure 1.7
MRF model for bilevel segmentation. (a) An image to be segmented. (b) Foreground and background regions of the image are marked so x_i in those regions is no longer hidden but observed. The problem is to infer foreground/background labels in the remaining unlabeled region of the *trimap*. (c) Using simply a color likelihood model learned from the labeled regions, without the Ising prior, the inferred labeling is noisy. (d) Also introducing a pairwise Ising term, and calculating the MAP estimate for the inferred labels, deals substantially with the noise and missing data. (Results of the CRF variant of the Ising term, described below, are illustrated here.)

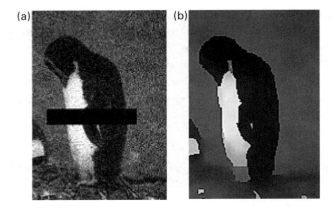

Figure 1.8
MRF model for image reconstruction. (a) An image with added noise, and a portion masked out. (b) Introducing a truncated quadratic prior and calculating (approximately) the MAP estimate of the hidden variables deals much more effectively with the noise.

1.5.2 Example: Image Reconstruction

A classic example of a multilabel MRF problem is image reconstruction, in which a noisy and/or damaged image requires repair. An example is shown in figure 1.8. In this case the state-space may have $x_i \in \{0, 255\}$, corresponding to the possible gray values of pixels in the reconstructed image. A suitable model for reconstruction is to choose the unary as follows:

$$\Phi_i(x_i) = \begin{cases} (x_i - z_i)^2 & \text{if } z_i \text{ observed} \\ 0 & \text{otherwise.} \end{cases} \tag{1.49}$$

The pairwise term is chosen to encourage smoothness in the reconstructed image, but not so strongly as to blur across genuine edges. A suitable choice is a truncated quadratic prior of the form

$$\Psi(x_i, x_j) = \lambda \min((x_i - x_j)^2, \Psi_{\max}). \tag{1.50}$$

(More detail is given in later chapters, particularly chapter 11.) The special case that $\Psi_{\max} = 1$ gives the classic Potts model, which penalizes any nonzero difference between x_i and x_j equally, regardless of magnitude, with λ.

1.5.3 Continuous Valued MRFs

So far we have seen examples of MRFs with discrete label values—either Boolean or multi-valued: for example, integer. Of course it is natural in many cases to regard hidden variables as continuous. For example, the underlying image in an image reconstruction problem is a physical property of the world, and its values are most naturally regarded as continuous. Visual reconstruction is therefore often cast in terms of continuous variables [172, 54], and in this book, chapters 8, 12, and 13 deal with MRFs over continuous variables. One direct approach is to define Gaussian distributions over the variables, so-called GMRFs, as in chapter 13. Nonlinear variations on that basic theme also have interesting and useful properties.

1.5.4 Conditional Random Field

A Conditional Random Field (CRF) is a form of MRF that defines a posterior for variables $\mathbf{x}$ given data $\mathbf{z}$, as with the hidden MRF above. Unlike the hidden MRF, however, the factorization into the data distribution $P(\mathbf{x}|\mathbf{z})$ and the prior $P(\mathbf{x})$ is not made explicit [288]. This allows complex dependencies of $\mathbf{x}$ on $\mathbf{z}$ to be written directly in the posterior distribution, without the factorization being made explicit. (Given $P(\mathbf{x}|\mathbf{z})$, such factorizations always exist, however—infinitely many of them, in fact—so there is no suggestion that the CRF is more general than the hidden MRF, only that it may be more convenient to deal with.) One common application of the CRF formalism in vision is in Boolean (foreground/background) segmentation, where it is natural to think of a modification of the Ising prior (1.42) to incorporate some data dependency [65]:

$$\Psi_{ij}(x_i, x_j, \mathbf{z}) = f(\mathbf{z})\gamma|x_i - x_j|, \tag{1.51}$$

in which the additional term $f(\mathbf{z}) \leq 1$ weakens the penalty γ wherever the image data suggest the presence of a segmentation boundary—for instance, where image contrast is high. This is described in detail in chapter 7. CRFs are also used in scene labeling [284], for example, to label areas of a scene as natural or as man-made. Other applications of CRFs appear in chapters 9, 11, 24, 25, and 27.

1.6 Inference: MAP/Marginals

Given a hidden MRF for some posterior distribution $P(\mathbf{x} \mid \mathbf{z})$, as in (1.44) but omitting the parameters ω, the common inference problems are to estimate either the most probable state

$$\arg \max_{\mathbf{x}} P(\mathbf{x} \mid \mathbf{z}) \tag{1.52}$$

or the marginal distributions at each pixel, $P(x_i \mid \mathbf{z})$, $i = 1, \ldots, N$. This is in direct analogy to MAP inference and inference of marginals for HMMs, as discussed in section 1.2, but closed form algorithms are no longer available for two-dimensional problems. Dropping the explicit mention of the data $\mathbf{z}$, the inference problems are equivalent to estimating the mode and marginals of an MRF $P(\mathbf{x})$, as in (1.39). The remainder of this section outlines various approaches to estimation using this posterior distribution.

1.6.1 Gibbs Sampling

Gibbs sampling is a procedure introduced by Geman and Geman [161] for sampling fairly from an MRF. At successive visits to each site i, the variable x_i is sampled from the local, conditional distribution $P(x_i \mid \{x_j, (i, j) \in \mathcal{E}, j \neq i\})$, and all sites are visited, arbitrarily often, in some random order. Asymptotically, after many visits to each site, the set of samples $(x_1, \ldots, x_N)$ settles down to be a fair sample from the MRF. However, this *burn-in* process may happen very slowly, and this is a problem for practical application. Further details of Gibbs sampling are given in chapter 5.

1.6.2 Mean Field Approximation

Mean field approximation is a form of *variational approximation* in which the distribution $P(\mathbf{x})$ is approximated as a product of factors,

$$P(\mathbf{x}) \approx \prod_i b_i(x_i), \tag{1.53}$$

and the factors become the approximations to the marginals $P(x_i)$ of the distribution. Of course this factorized form cannot represent the posterior exactly, but mean field algorithms choose the b_i in such a way as to approximate the posterior as closely as possible. This is done by minimizing *KL divergence*, a single numerical measure of difference between the true and approximate distributions. Full details of this important approach are given in chapter 5.

Classical Algorithms for MAP Inference   The MAP solution of a hidden Markov model can be found by minimizing an energy function (1.45). A number of algorithms exist for solving these minimization problems defined over discrete or continuous random variables. Some of the best-known of these algorithms will be reviewed in this section. Comparisons of their performance on various test problems will be given in chapter 11.

1.6.3 Iterated Conditional Modes (ICM)

Iterated Conditional Modes (ICM) are one of the oldest and simplest MAP inference algorithms [38, 235]. They belong to the family of local (also called move-making) algorithms that start with an initial solution. At each step these algorithms explore a space of possible changes (also called a move space) that can be made to the current solution $\mathbf{x}^c$, and choose a change (move) that leads to a new solution $\mathbf{x}^n$ having the lowest energy. This move is referred to as the *optimal* move. The algorithm is said to converge when no solution with a lower energy can be found.

ICM works in a coordinate descent fashion. At each step it chooses a variable $X_i, i \in \mathcal{V}$. Keeping the values of all other variables fixed, it finds the label assignment for X_i that leads to the lowest energy:

$$x_i^n = \arg \min_{x_i \in \mathcal{L}} E(\{x_j^c : j \neq i\}, x_i). \tag{1.54}$$

This process is repeated for other variables until the energy cannot be decreased further (i.e., all variables are assigned labels that are locally optimal.) Note that the descent step is efficient in that it need involve only variables in the Markov blanket of i.

1.6.4 Simulated Annealing

The ICM algorithm makes changes to the solution if they lead to solutions having lower energy. This *greedy* characteristic makes it prone to getting stuck in local minima. Intuitively, an energy minimization algorithm that can jump out of local minima will do well in problems with a large number of local optima. Simulated annealing (SA) is one such class of algorithms. Developed as a general optimization strategy by Kirkpatrick et al. [234], simulated annealing allows changes to the solution that lead to a higher energy with a certain probability. This probability is controlled by a parameter T that is called the temperature. A higher value of T implies a high probability of accepting changes to the solution that lead to a higher energy. The algorithm starts with a high value of T and reduces it to 0 as it proceeds. When $T = 0$ the algorithm accepts only changes that lead to a decrease in energy, as, for example, ICM does. Details are given in chapter 5.

1.6.5 Loopy Belief Propagation

We have seen how the sum-product and max-product message-passing algorithms can be used to perform inference in tree structured graphs. Although these algorithms are guaranteed only to find the optimal solutions in tree structured graphs, they have been shown to be effective heuristics for MAP/marginal estimation even in graphs with loops, such as the grid graphs found in computer vision.

The max-product algorithm can be used to minimize general energy functions approximately. Since an energy function is the negative log of posterior probability, it is necessary only to replace the product operation with a sum operation, and the max operation with a min. For the pairwise energy function (4.1) the message $m_{j \to i}$ from a variable X_j to any neighboring variable X_i is computed as

$$m_{j \to i}(x_i) = \min_{x_j} \left(\Phi_j(x_j) + \Psi_{ij}(x_i, x_j) + \sum_{k \in \mathcal{N}(j) - \{i\}} m_{k \to j}(x_j) \right). \tag{1.55}$$

These messages can also be used to compute a (min-sum) analogue of the belief, called the *min-marginal*:

$$M(x_i) = \min_{\mathbf{x} - \{x_i\}} E(\mathbf{x}). \tag{1.56}$$

The min-marginal can be computed from the messages as

$$M^*(x_i) = \Phi_i(x_i) + \sum_{k \in \mathcal{N}(j) - \{i\}} m_{k \to j}(x_j). \tag{1.57}$$

The min-marginal can be used to find an alternative estimate to the MAP assignment of a variable, as follows:

$$x_i^* = \arg \min_{x_i} M^*(x_i). \tag{1.58}$$

Chapter 10 will describe an application of Bayesian belief propagation to quickly find approximate solutions to two-dimensional vision problems, such as image superresolution using patch priors, and for the problem of transferring the style of a picture (e.g., a painting) to another picture (e.g., a photograph). Those results have inspired a lot of work on the theoretical properties of the way in which BP operates in a general probabilistic model [517]. For instance, it was shown that when sum-product BP converges, the solution is a local minimum of the Bethe approximation [539] of the free energy defined by the Markov model. More recently, a number of researchers have shown the relationship between message-passing algorithms and linear programming relaxation-based methods for MAP inference [504, 536]. This relationship is the subject of chapter 6.

1.7 MAP Inference in Discrete Models

Many problems in vision and machine learning give rise to energies defined over discrete random variables. The problem of minimizing a function of discrete variables is in general NP-hard, and has been well studied in the discrete optimization and operations research communities. A number of "greedy" and "approximate" techniques have been proposed for solving these discrete optimization problems. An introduction to these methods is given in this section.

Although minimizing a function of discrete variables is NP-hard in general, there are families of energy functions for which it can be done in polynomial time. Submodular functions are one such well-known family [155, 324]. In some respects they are analogous to the convex functions encountered in continuous optimization, and have played a big part in the development of efficient algorithms for estimating the MAP solution of many image labeling problems. For instance, the Ising energy described earlier (1.42) is an important example in vision and image processing of a submodular function.

It is worth reflecting for a moment that this approach gives an exact solution to inference problems at image scale. This is quite remarkable, given how rare it is that realistic scale information problems in the general area of machine intelligence admit exact solutions. Graph cut was first used to give exact solutions for Boolean MRF problems over images by Greig et al. [176], at a time when the method was so slow that it could be used only to benchmark faster, approximate algorithms. Since then, the progress in understanding and developing graph cut algorithms in general, and for images specifically, allows these algorithms to be regarded as highly practical. Even real-time operation is possible, in which several million pixels in an image or video are processed each second.

1.7.1 Submodular Pseudo-Boolean Functions

The minimization of a Pseudo-Boolean Function (PBF) $E : \{0, 1\}^n \to \mathbb{R}$ is a well-studied problem in combinatorial optimization [215] and operations research [61]. A PBF $f : \{0, 1\}^n \to \mathbb{R}$ is submodular if and only if, for all label assignments $\mathbf{x}_A, \mathbf{x}_B \in \{0, 1\}^n$, the function satisfies the condition

$$f(\mathbf{x}_A) + f(\mathbf{x}_B) \geq f(\mathbf{x}_A \vee \mathbf{x}_B) + f(\mathbf{x}_A \wedge \mathbf{x}_B), \tag{1.59}$$

where $\vee$ and $\wedge$ are componentwise OR and AND, respectively. From the above definition it can easily be seen that all PBFs of arity 1 are submodular. Similarly, any PBF of arity 2 is submodular if and only if

$$f(1, 0) + f(0, 1) \geq f(1, 1) + f(0, 0). \tag{1.60}$$

Another interesting property of submodular functions is that the set of submodular functions is closed under addition (i.e., the sum of two or more submodular functions is another submodular function). This condition implies that the energy of a pairwise MRF (1.47) is submodular if all the pairwise potentials Ψ_{ij} are submodular. For example, the Ising model pairwise potential consists of terms $\Psi_{ij}(x_i, x_j) = \gamma |x_i - x_j|$ (1.42), which are submodular, as is apparent from substituting $f(x, x') = \gamma |x - x'|$ into (1.60). Hence the entire Ising potential function is submodular.

1.7.2 Minimizing Submodular Pseudo-Boolean Functions Using Graph Cut

The first polynomial time algorithm for minimizing submodular functions [215, 427] had high practical runtime complexity. Although recent work has been partly successful in reducing the complexity of algorithms for general submodular function minimization, they are still quite expensive computationally and cannot practically be used for large problems. For instance, one of the best algorithms for general submodular function minimization has a worst case complexity $O(n^5 Q + n^6)$, where Q is the time taken to evaluate the function [358]. This is certainly too expensive for use in computer vision, where n is frequently of the order of millions (of pixels).

However, there is one important subclass of submodular functions that can be optimized much more efficiently: the submodular functions of arity at most 2, corresponding to MRFs with factors that are functions of at most two variables. This is the common case that was illustrated in the graphs in figure 1.1. Optimization over this class is known as Quadratic Pseudo-Boolean Optimization or (QPBO). It turns out to be equivalent to finding the minimum cost cut in a certain graph [61, 68, 211, 421] — the so-called s-t min-cut problem. This is described in detail in chapter 2. It leads to efficient algorithms for finding the MAP solution of many important pairwise MRF models for vision problems, for example, foreground/background image segmentation problems like the one illustrated in figure 1.7.

A general QPB function can be expressed as:

$$
\begin{aligned}
E(\mathbf{x}) = \theta_{\text{const}} &+ \sum_{i \in V} (\theta_{i;1} x_i + \theta_{i;0} \overline{x}_i) \\
&+ \sum_{(i,j) \in E} (\theta_{ij;11} x_i x_j + \theta_{ij;01} \overline{x}_i x_j + \theta_{ij;10} x_i \overline{x}_j + \theta_{ij;00} \overline{x}_i \overline{x}_j),
\end{aligned}
\tag{1.61}
$$

where $\overline{x}_i$ defines the complementary variable $\overline{x}_i = 1 - x_i$. Parameter $\theta_{i;a}$ is the penalty for assigning label a to latent variable x_v, and $\theta_{ij;ab}$ is the penalty for assigning labels a and b

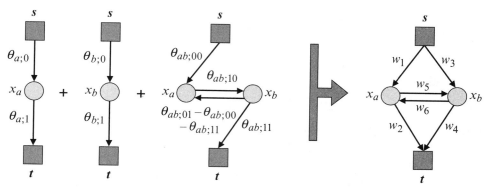

Figure 1.9
Energy minimization using graph cut. The figure shows how individual unary and pairwise terms of an energy function taking two binary variables are represented and combined in the graph. Multiple edges between the same nodes are merged into a single edge by adding their weights. For instance, the cost w_1 of the edge (s, x_a) in the final graph is equal to $w_1 = \theta_{a;0} + \theta_{ab;00}$. The cost of an s-t cut in the final graph is equal to the energy $E(\mathbf{x})$ of the configuration $\mathbf{x}$ the cut induces. The minimum cost s-t cut induces the least-energy configuration $\mathbf{x}$ for the energy function.

to the latent variables x_i and x_j, respectively. To minimize this energy with s-t min-cut, the individual unary and pairwise terms of the energy function are represented by weighted edges in the graph. Multiple edges between the same nodes are merged into a single edge by adding their weights. The graph construction in the simple case of a two-variable energy function is shown in figure 1.9. In this graph an s-t cut is defined to be a curve that separates the source node s from the terminal node t. The cost of such a cut is defined to be the sum of the weights of edges traversed by the cut. The s-t cut with the minimum cost provides the minimum solution $\mathbf{x}^*$ by disconnecting a node x_i either from s, representing the assignment $x_i = 0$, or from t, representing $x_i = 1$. The cost of that cut corresponds to the energy of the solution $E(\mathbf{x}^*)$ modulo the constant term θ_{const}. Algorithms for finding the s-t min-cut require that all edges in the graph have nonnegative weights. This condition results in a restriction that the energy function E be submodular. This is all explained in detail in chapter 2.

1.8 Solving Multilabel Problems Using Graph Cut

Many computer vision problems involve latent variables that can take values in integer spaces. The energy functions corresponding to these problems are defined over multistate variables. Graph cut-based algorithms for minimizing such functions can be divided into two broad categories: transformation methods and move-making algorithms. Transformations methods transform the energy minimization problem defined over multistate variables $X_i \in \mathcal{L} = \{l_1, ..., l_k\}, k \geq 2$ to one that is defined over k binary variables per multistate variable. This is done by encoding different states of the multistate variables by the assignments of a set of Boolean variables—a full discussion is given in chapter 4. Move-making algorithms, on the other hand, work by decomposing the problem into a set of problems defined over Boolean random variables, which, as we have seen, can be solved efficiently using *s-t* min-cut algorithms. In practice, move making has been the dominant approach for multilabel problems.

1.8.1 Graph Cut-Based Move-Making Algorithms

The key characteristic of any move-making algorithm is the number of possible changes it can make in any step (also called the size of the move space). A large move space means that extensive changes can be made to the current solution. This makes the algorithm less prone to getting stuck in local minima and also results in a faster rate of convergence. Boykov et al. [72] proposed two move-making algorithms: *α-expansion* and *αβ-swap*, whose move, space size increases exponentially with the number of variables involved in the energy function. The moves of the expansion and swap algorithms can be encoded as a vector of binary variables $\mathbf{t} = \{t_i, \forall i \in \mathcal{V}\}$. The *transformation* function $T(\mathbf{x}^c, \mathbf{t})$ of a move algorithm takes the current labeling $\mathbf{x}^c$ and a move $\mathbf{t}$, and returns the new labeling $\mathbf{x}^n$ that has been induced by the move.

The expansion algorithm has one possible move per label $\alpha \in \mathcal{L}$. An α-expansion move allows any random variable either to retain its current label or to take the label α. The transformation function $T_\alpha()$ for an α-expansion move transforms the current label x_i^c of any random variable X_i as

$$x_i^n = T_\alpha(x_i^c, t_i) = \begin{cases} \alpha & \text{if} \quad t_i = 0 \\ x_i^c & \text{if} \quad t_i = 1. \end{cases} \tag{1.62}$$

One iteration of the algorithm involves making moves for all α in $\mathcal{L}$ successively in some order.

The swap algorithm has one possible move for every pair of labels $\alpha, \beta \in \mathcal{L}$. An $\alpha\beta$-swap move allows a random variable whose current label is α or β to take either label α or label β. The transformation function $T_{\alpha\beta}()$ for an $\alpha\beta$-swap transforms the current label x_i^c of a random variable x_i as

$$x_i^n = T_{\alpha\beta}(x_i^c, t_i) = \begin{cases} \alpha & \text{if} \quad x_i^c = \alpha \text{ or } \beta \text{ and } t_i = 0 \\ \beta & \text{if} \quad x_i^c = \alpha \text{ or } \beta \text{ and } t_i = 1. \end{cases} \tag{1.63}$$

One iteration of the algorithm involves performing swap moves for all α and β in $\mathcal{L}$ successively in some order.

The energy of a move $\mathbf{t}$ is the energy of the labeling $\mathbf{x}^n$ that the move $\mathbf{t}$ induces, that is, $E_m(\mathbf{t}) = E(T(\mathbf{x}^c, \mathbf{t}))$. The move energy is a pseudo-Boolean function ($E_m : \{0, 1\}^n \to \mathbb{R}$) and will be denoted by $E_m(\mathbf{t})$. At each step of the expansion and swap-move algorithms, the *optimal* move $\mathbf{t}^*$ (i.e., the move decreasing the energy of the labeling by the greatest amount) is computed. This is done by minimizing the move energy, that is, $\mathbf{t}^* = \arg\min_\mathbf{t} E(T(\mathbf{x}^c, \mathbf{t}))$. Boykov et al. [72] showed that for certain families of pairwise energy functions, the move energy is submodular, and hence the optimal move $\mathbf{t}^*$ can be computed in polynomial time using s-t min-cut algorithms. More details on the expansion and swap algorithms can be found in chapter 3.

1.9 MAP Inference Using Linear Programming

Linear programming (LP) is a popular method for solving discrete optimization problems. It has also been extensively used for MAP inference in discrete Markov models. To convert the energy minimization problem into an LP, we will first need to formulate it as an integer program (IP). This is illustrated for the pairwise energy function (4.1). The energy function is first linearized using binary indicator variables $y_{i;a}$ and $y_{ij;ab}$ for all $i, j \in \mathcal{V}$ and $l_a, l_b \in \mathcal{L}$. The indicator variable $y_{i;a} = 1$ if $x_i = l_a$, and $y_{i;a} = 0$ otherwise. Similarly, the variables $y_{ij;ab}$ indicate the label assignment $x_i = l_a, x_j = l_b$. The resulting IP can be written as

$$\text{Minimize} \sum_{i \in \mathcal{V}, l_a \in \mathcal{L}} \Phi_i(l_a) y_{i;a} + \sum_{\substack{(i,j) \in \mathcal{E}, \\ l_a, l_b \in \mathcal{L}}} \Psi_{ij}(l_a, l_b) y_{ij;ab}, \tag{1.64}$$

subject to

$$\sum_{l_a \in \mathcal{L}} y_{ij;ab} = y_{j;b}, \quad \forall (i, j) \in \mathcal{E}, l_b \in \mathcal{L}, \tag{1.65}$$

$$\sum_{l_b \in \mathcal{L}} y_{ij;ab} = y_{i;a}, \quad \forall (i, j) \in \mathcal{E}, l_a \in \mathcal{L}, \tag{1.66}$$

$$\sum_{l_a \in \mathcal{L}} y_{i;a} = 1, \quad \forall i \in \mathcal{V}, \tag{1.67}$$

$$y_{i;a}, y_{ij;ab} \in \{0, 1\} \quad \forall i \in \mathcal{V}, \forall (i, j) \in \mathcal{E}, \forall l_a, l_b \in \mathcal{L}. \tag{1.68}$$

The constraint (1.65) enforces consistency over marginalization, and constraint (1.67) makes sure that each variable is assigned only one label.

Relaxing the integrality constraints (1.68) of the IP leads to an LP problem that can be solved in polynomial time using general-purpose LP solvers. These solvers are relatively computationally expensive, and make this approach inappropriate for vision problems that involve a large number of variables. A number of message-passing and maximum flow-based methods have recently been developed to efficiently solve the LP defined above [270, 277, 504, 520]. See chapters 6 and 17 for more details, including discussion of when the solution to the LP is also a solution to the IP.

1.9.1 Nonsubmodular Problems in Vision

We have seen how submodular pseudo-Boolean functions can be minimized using algorithms for computing the s-t min-cut in weighted graphs. Although this is an extremely useful method, energy functions corresponding to many computer vision problems are not submodular. We give two examples here by way of motivation. The first is the *fusion move* described in chapter 18, in which two trial solutions to a problem such as optimal image denoising are available, and a final solution is to be constructed by combining the two, pixel by pixel. A binary array is constructed that switches each pixel between its values in the first and second solutions. The original denoising functional now induces a functional over the Boolean array that will not, in general, be submodular (see chapter 18 for details). A second example of an important nonsubmodular problem arises in the general case of multilabel optimization, as discussed in the previous section. (Details are given in chapter 3.)

Minimizing a general nonsubmodular energy function is an NP-hard problem. We also saw earlier how general energy minimization problems can be formulated in terms of an IP. Relaxing the integrality constraints of the IP leads to an LP problem, and this is attractive because there is no requirement for the IP energy to be submodular. Chapter 2 will explain a particular relaxation of QPBO called the *roof dual* [61, 261], which leads to an LP that can be solved efficiently using *s-t* min-cut algorithms.

1.10 Parameter Learning for MRFs

Learning the parameters ω of an MRF (or CRF) $P(\mathbf{x}|\mathbf{z}, \omega)$ from labeled training data is an important problem. The alternative is to attempt to select the parameters ω by hand or by experiment; this is known to be difficult, and quite impractical if the dimensionality of ω is at all large. It also proves to be a challenging problem. Note that here the learning problem is rather different from the parameter learning problem for HMMs discussed earlier. It is a little easier in that the data are labeled—that is, the $\mathbf{x}$-values are known for each $\mathbf{z}$ in the training set—those previously hidden variables $\mathbf{x}$ in the model may become observed variables in the context of learning. In contrast, in HMM parameter learning, the state values $\mathbf{x}$ were unknown. But it is a harder problem in that the estimation is done over a graph that is not merely a tree, so the underlying inference problem is not exactly tractable.

1.10.1 Maximum Likelihood
A standard approach to parameter learning is via Maximum Likelihood Estimation (MLE), that is, by solving

$$\max_{\omega} L(\omega) \text{ where } L(\omega) = P(\mathbf{x}|\mathbf{z}, \omega). \tag{1.69}$$

Now, from (1.40),

$$\log L(\omega) = -\log Z(\omega) - \sum_{c \in \mathcal{C}} \Psi_c(\mathbf{x}_c, \omega), \tag{1.70}$$

and differentiating this to maximize the likelihood L w.r.t. ω is entirely feasible for the second term, as it is decomposed into a sum of local terms, but generally intractable for the first term, the log partition function that was defined earlier (1.41). This is well known, and is fully described in standard texts on Markov random fields [523, 309].

As a result, it is necessary to approximate the likelihood function in order to maximize it. Probably the best-known classical approximation is pseudo likelihood in which L is replaced by

$$L^* = \prod_i P(x_i \mid \{x_j, \ (i, j) \in \mathcal{E}\}), \tag{1.71}$$

a product of local, conditional densities. Its log is a sum of local functions, which can tractably be differentiated in order to maximize with respect to parameters. This pseudo likelihood function does not itself approximate the likelihood L, but its maximum is known to approximate the maximum of L under certain conditions [523].

Alternative approximate learning schemes have been proposed by others. For example, Kumar et al. [283] propose three different schemes to approximate the gradients of the log likelihood function in the case of pairwise energy functions, such as the one used for image segmentation (1.47). The derivatives of the log likelihood are easily shown to be a function of the expectations $\langle x_i \rangle_{\omega;\mathbf{z}}$. If we were given the true marginal distributions $P(x_i \mid \mathbf{z}, \omega)$, we could compute the exact expectations:

$$\langle x_i \rangle_{\omega;\mathbf{z}} = \sum_{x_i} x_i P_i(x_i \mid \mathbf{z}, \omega). \tag{1.72}$$

This is generally infeasible, so the three proposed approximations are as follows.

1. *Pseudo Marginal Approximation (PMA)* Pseudo marginals obtained from loopy belief propagation are used instead of the true marginals for computing the expectations.

2. *Saddle Point Approximation (SPA)* The label of the random variable in the MAP solution is taken as the expected value. This is equivalent to assuming that all the mass of the distribution $P_i(x_i \mid \mathbf{z}, \theta)$ is on the MAP label.

3. *Maximum Marginal Approximation (MMA)* In this approximation the label having the maximum value under the pseudo marginal distribution obtained from BP is assumed to be the expected value.

1.10.2 Max-Margin Learning

An alternative approach to parameter learning that has become very popular in recent years is max-margin learning. Similar to ML estimation, max-margin learning also uses inference in order to compute a gradient with respect to the parameters; however, only the MAP labeling need be inferred, rather than the full marginals.

Most margin-based learning algorithms proposed and used in computer vision are inspired from the structured support vector machine (SVMSTRUCT) framework of Tsochantaridis et al. [484] and the maximum margin network learning of Taskar et al. [14, 473]. The goal of these methods is to learn the parameters so that the ground truth has the lowest energy by the largest possible margin Θ or, if that is not possible, that the energy of the ground truth is as close as possible to that of the minimum energy solution. More formally,

$$\max_{\omega:|\omega=1|} \quad \Theta \quad \text{such that} \tag{1.73}$$

$$E(\mathbf{x}, \mathbf{z}; \omega) - E(\hat{\mathbf{x}}, \mathbf{z}; \omega) \quad \geq \Theta \quad \forall \mathbf{x} \neq \hat{\mathbf{x}}, \tag{1.74}$$

where $\hat{\mathbf{x}}$ is the MAP estimate for $\mathbf{x}$. A detailed discussion of max-margin learning for MRFs is given in chapter 15.

This concludes the introduction to Markov random fields. We have tried to set out the main ideas as a preparation for the more detailed treatment that follows. In part I of the book, some of the main algorithms for performing inference with MRFs are reviewed. Then in part II, to reward the reader for hard work on the algorithms, there is a collection of some of the most successful applications of MRFs, including segmentation, superresolution, and image restoration, together with an experimental comparison of various optimization methods on several test problems in vision. Part III discusses some more advanced algorithmic topics, including the learning of parameter values to tune MRF models, and some approaches to learning and inference with continuous-valued MRFs. Part IV addresses some of the limitations of the strong locality assumptions in the small-neighborhood MRFs discussed in this introduction and in many of the earlier chapters of the book. This includes going beyond pairwise functions in the MRF factorization, to ternary functions and higher, and to models that, though sparse, do not restrict neighborhoods to contain pixels that are nearby in the image array. Finally, part V is a showcase of some applications that use MRFs in more complex ways, as components in bigger systems or with multiterm energy functions, each term of which enforces a different regularity of the problem—for instance, spatial and temporal terms in multiview video, or acting over multiple layers of hidden variables for simultaneous recognition and segmentation of objects.

1.11   Glossary of Notation

Some of the basic notation for Markov random fields is listed below. It is the notation used in this introductory chapter, and also is used frequently in later chapters of the book.

Symbol	Meaning
$\mathcal{G} = \mathcal{V}, \mathcal{E}$	graph of MRF nodes (sites) $\mathcal{V}$ and edges $\mathcal{E}$
$i \in \mathcal{V}$	index for nodes/sites
$(i, i') \in \mathcal{E}$ or $(i, j) \in \mathcal{E}$	edges linking nodes of $\mathcal{G}$
$c \in \mathcal{C}$	cliques of $\mathcal{G}$, so each $c \subset \mathcal{V}$
$\mathbf{z} = (z_1, \ldots, z_i, \ldots, z_N)$	image data, pixel value (monochrome or color) at site i
$\mathbf{X} = (X_1, \ldots, X_i, \ldots, x_N)$	random state variables at site (pixel) i

$\mathbf{x} = (x_1, \ldots, x_i, \ldots x_N)$,	values taken by state variables, that is, $X_i = x_i$
$\mathcal{L} = \{l_1, \ldots, l_k, \ldots, l_K\}$	label values for discrete MRF, so $x_i \in \mathcal{L}$
$P(\mathbf{X} \mid \mathbf{z})$	posterior probability distribution for state given data
$P(\mathbf{x} \mid \mathbf{z})$	shorthand for $P(\mathbf{X} = \mathbf{x} \mid \mathbf{z})$
$P(\mathbf{x} \mid \mathbf{z}) = \frac{1}{Z(\mathbf{z})} \exp -E(\mathbf{x}, \mathbf{z})$	Gibbs energy form of the MRF
$Z(\omega)$ or $Z(\omega, \mathbf{z})$	partition function in Gibbs form of MRF
$E(\mathbf{x}) = U(\mathbf{x}) + V(\mathbf{x})$	Gibbs energy: unary and neighbor terms
$E(\mathbf{x}, \mathbf{z}) = U(\mathbf{x}, \mathbf{z}) + V(\mathbf{x}, \mathbf{z})$	Gibbs energy where dependence on data $\mathbf{z}$ is explicit
$\omega \in \Omega, P(\mathbf{x} \mid \mathbf{z}, \omega), E(\mathbf{x}, \mathbf{z}, \omega)$	Parameters ω for MRF model
$\Phi_i(x_i)$	unary potential for MRF, so $U(\mathbf{x}) = \sum_i \Phi_i(x_i)$
$\Psi_{ij}(x_i, x_j)$	pairwise potentials, so $V(\mathbf{x}) = \sum_{ij} \Psi_{ij}(x_{ij})$
$\Psi_c(\mathbf{x}_c)$	higher-order potentials,
$V(\mathbf{x}) = \sum_{c \in \mathcal{C}} \Psi_c(\mathbf{x}_c)$	general form of Gibbs term as a sum over cliques
y_i	auxiliary Boolean variables, for example, for label expansion schemes

I Algorithms for Inference of MAP Estimates for MRFs

Part I of this book deals with some of the fundamental issues concerning inference in the kinds of MRFs that are used in vision. In machine learning generally, inference is often taken to refer to inference of an entire probability distribution $P(\mathbf{x} \mid \mathbf{z})$ or projections of that distribution as marginal distributions [46] over subsets of variables x_i. This is a general view of inference that allows the output of the inference process to be treated as an intermediate result capable of refinement by fusion with further information as it subsequently may become available. In principle this approach can be taken with images where $\mathbf{x}$ is an array of pixels or some other high-dimensional array of image-related variables such as superpixels. In practice, for images the dimension of $\mathbf{x}$ is so high that it is quite infeasible to represent the full posterior distribution. One approach is to use Monte Carlo samplers, as described in chapter 1, but it is unlikely that "burn-in" can be achieved on any practical timescale. For low-dimensional information extracted from images, such as curves, it may be practical to represent the full posterior, either exactly or via samplers [51]. This book, however, is mostly concerned with inferences over the whole image, and the most that can practically be done is to infer (approximate) marginals over individual pixels or, conceivably, small sets of pixels. This idea is mentioned in chapter 1 and, in more detail, in chapter 5. There are some possible applications for pixelwise marginals in parameter learning (discussed in part III), but on the whole they have not been greatly used in vision. This discussion is all by way of explaining why part I, and indeed much of the book, restricts inference to MAP estimation.

As pointed out in chapter 1, maximizing the posterior $P(\mathbf{x} \mid \mathbf{z})$ is equivalent to minimizing energy $E(\mathbf{x}, \mathbf{z})$, so part I begins with chapter 2 explaining in detail the idea, introduced in chapter 1, of solving pseudo-Boolean optimization exactly, using a graph cut algorithm. The basic graph cut mechanism that gives exact solutions for the minimization of submodular, pseudo-Boolean functions can also give exact solutions when even the Boolean domain is replaced by a multilabel domain such as the integers. The conditions under which this can be done place tight restrictions on the objective function $E(\mathbf{x})$, and are detailed in chapter 4. Under less strict conditions on $E(\mathbf{x})$, pseudo-Boolean graph cut can be used as an exact partial optimization step—a *move* (see chapter 1)—to solve a multilabel optimization problem. However, the overall solution will be only approximately optimal, as chapter 3 explains.

Graph cut is one of the dominant approaches for inference in MRFs for vision; two others are Loopy Belief Propagation (LBP) and mean field approximation, which were introduced briefly in chapter 1. Chapter 5 describes both methods and explains that they are related to energy minimization, but with a different kind of objective functions known as a *free energy*. As an alternative to these deterministic methods, stochastic estimation using Markov Chain Monte Carlo (MCMC) is also explained. The final chapter in part I, chapter 6, expands on the idea of Linear Programming (LP) relaxation as a means of embedding an integer-valued optimization problem on a graph in a more tractable, continuous-valued optimization. Interestingly, it turns out that this approach is closely related to BP and that variants of BP can be used as efficient means of solving the LP.

2 Basic Graph Cut Algorithms

Yuri Boykov and Vladimir Kolmogorov

This chapter describes efficient methods for solving an inference problem for pairwise MRF models (equation 1.55) in a simple special case when state variables x_i are binary. Many problems in computer vision can be represented by such binary models (see part III). One basic example is segmentation of an image into object and background pixels, as in chapter 7. The inference problem can be formulated as finding a binary labeling $\mathbf{x}$ in which the energy E defined in chapter 1 (equation 1.47) achieves its minima for some given observations z_i and for some fixed parameter ω. This section describes efficient optimization techniques for binary pairwise models using standard graph cut algorithms from combinatorial optimization.

This chapter uses a different representation of energy E that is more convenient for binary variables x. This representation is common in combinatorial optimization literature in which algorithms for binary pairwise energies have been actively studied for forty years; for example, see the survey in [61]. Without loss of generality, assume that binary state variables x_i take two values, 0 and 1. Then, energy E can be written as a *quadratic pseudo-Boolean function*, as in (2.1):

$$E(\mathbf{x}) = \theta_{\text{const}} + \sum_{i \in \mathcal{V}} (\theta_{i;1} x_i + \theta_{i;0} \overline{x}_i)$$

$$+ \sum_{(i,j) \in \mathcal{E}} (\theta_{ij;11} x_i x_j + \theta_{ij;01} \overline{x}_i x_j + \theta_{ij;10} x_i \overline{x}_j + \theta_{ij;00} \overline{x}_i \overline{x}_j),$$
(2.1)

where $\overline{x}_i = 1 - x_i$ denotes the negation of variable $x_i \in \{0, 1\}$. "Boolean" refers to the fact that variables x_i can take only two values, and "quadratic" means that there are only unary (e.g., $\theta_{i;1} x_i$) and quadratic (e.g., $\theta_{ij;11} x_i x_j$) terms. For binary-valued labelings the $\mathbf{x}$-function (equation 1.47) is equivalent to (2.1) with constants $\theta_{i;1} = \Phi_i(1, z_i, \omega)$, $\theta_{i;0} = \Phi_i(0, z_i, \omega)$, $\theta_{ij;11} = \Psi_{ij}(1, 1, z_i, z_j, \omega)$, and $\theta_{ij;01} = \Psi_{ij}(0, 1, z_i, z_j, \omega)$, $\theta_{ij;10} = \Psi_{ij}(1, 0, z_i, z_j, \omega)$, $\theta_{ij;00} = \Psi_{ij}(0, 0, z_i, z_j, \omega)$, assuming that observations z and parameters ω are known. Note that the energy (2.1) can also be written as

$$E(\mathbf{x}) = \theta_{\text{const}} + \sum_{i \in \mathcal{V}} \theta_{i;x_i} + \sum_{(i,j) \in \mathcal{E}} \theta_{ij;x_i x_j}.$$
(2.1′)

In this chapter we will see that for an important class of pseudo-Boolean functions the minimization problem (equation 1.1) can be reduced to a min-cut/max-flow problem on graphs. This is a classical combinatorial optimization problem with many applications even outside of computer vision. It can be solved in polynomial time, and many efficient algorithms have been developed since 1956 [146]. New fast algorithms for the min-cut/max-flow problem are actively being researched in the combinatorial optimization community [11]. Existing algorithms vary in their theoretical complexity and empirical efficiency on different types of graphs. Some efficient algorithms were developed specifically for sparse grids common in computer vision [68, 120].

This chapter describes the general s-t min-cut problem and standard algorithms for solving it, and shows how they can be used to minimize pseudo-Boolean functions like (2.1). The structure is as follows:

• Section 2.1 covers terminology and other basic background material on the general s-t min-cut problem required to understand this and several later chapters. This section also gives an overview of standard combinatorial algorithms for the s-t min-cut problem, focusing on methods known to be practical for regular grid graphs common in vision.

• Section 2.2 describes how graph cut algorithms can be used to globally minimize a certain class of pseudo-Boolean functions (2.1). This class is characterized by a certain *submodularity* condition for parameters of energy (2.1). Many interesting problems in vision, such as object/background segmentation (as in chapter 7), are based on submodular binary models.

• Section 2.3 concludes this chapter by describing more general graph, cut techniques that can be applied to nonsubmodular binary models. Such methods are not guaranteed to find the solution for all variables, but those variables x_i whose values are determined are guaranteed to be a part of some globally optimal vector x. In many practical problems, such partial solutions cover most of the state variables.

2.1 Algorithms for Min-Cut/Max-Flow Problems

2.1.1 Background on Directed Graphs

Chapter 1 described undirected graphs consisting of a set of vertices $\mathcal{V}$, typically corresponding to image pixels, and a set of undirected arcs or edges $\mathcal{E}$, corresponding to a 4, 8, or any other neighborhood system (see figure 1.1). In this chapter we will use the corresponding *directed* weighted graphs $(\hat{\mathcal{V}}, \hat{\mathcal{E}}, w)$, including two additional terminal vertices, source s and sink t,

$$\hat{\mathcal{V}} := \mathcal{V} \cup \{s, t\}, \tag{2.2}$$

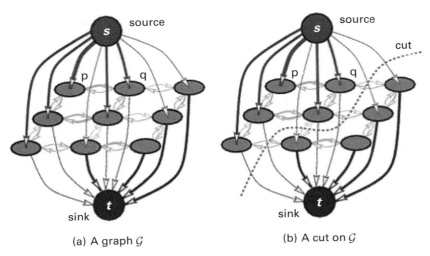

(a) A graph $\mathcal{G}$ (b) A cut on $\mathcal{G}$

Figure 2.1
Example of a directed, capacitated graph. Edge costs are represented by their thickness. Such grid graphs are common in computer vision.

and a larger set of *directed* edges,

$$\hat{\mathcal{E}} := \{(s \rightarrow i), (i \rightarrow t) \mid i \in \mathcal{V}\} \cup \{(i \rightarrow j), (j \rightarrow i) \mid (i, j) \in \mathcal{E}\} \tag{2.3}$$

whose weights (capacities) are nonnegative: $w_{ij} \geq 0$ for $(i \rightarrow j) \in \hat{\mathcal{E}}$.[1]

In the context of vision, terminals often correspond to labels that can be assigned to pixels. In figure 2.1a we show a simple example of a two-terminal directed graph that can be used for optimizing the posterior distribution (equation 1.6) on a 3×3 image in the case of two labels. The structure of graphs representing different problems in computer vision may vary. However, many of them use 2D or 3D grid graphs like the one in figure 2.1a. This is a simple consequence of the fact that graph nodes often represent regular image pixels or voxels.

All directed edges in the graph are assigned some weight or capacity. The cost w_{ij} of directed edge $(i \rightarrow j)$ may differ from the cost w_{ji} of the reverse edge $(j \rightarrow i)$. In fact, the ability to assign different edge weights for $(i \rightarrow j)$ and $(j \rightarrow i)$ is important for many applications in vision.

It is common to distinguish two types of edges: n-links and t-links. The n-links connect pairs of neighboring pixels or voxels:

$$\{(i \rightarrow j), (j \rightarrow i) \mid (i, j) \in \mathcal{E}\} \qquad \text{(n-links)}.$$

---

1. We assume throughout the chapter that the set $\mathcal{E}$ does not have parallel edges, and that $(i, j) \in \mathcal{E}$ implies $(j, i) \notin \mathcal{E}$.

Thus, they represent a neighborhood system in the image. In the context of computer vision, the cost of n-links may correspond to penalties for discontinuities between pixels. t-links connect pixels with terminals (labels):

$$\{(s \rightarrow i), (i \rightarrow t) \mid i \in \mathcal{V}\} \qquad \text{(t-links)}.$$

The cost of a t-link connecting a pixel and a terminal may correspond to a penalty for assigning the corresponding label to the pixel.

2.1.2 Min-Cut and Max-Flow Problems

An s-t cut C on a graph with two terminals s, t is a partitioning of the nodes in the graph into two disjoint subsets $\mathcal{S}$ and $\mathcal{T}$ such that the source s is in $\mathcal{S}$ and the sink t is in $\mathcal{T}$. For simplicity, throughout this chapter we refer to s-t cuts as just *cuts*. Figure 2.1b shows an example of a cut. In combinatorial optimization the cost of a cut $C = (\mathcal{S}, \mathcal{T})$ is defined as the sum of the costs of "boundary" edges $(i \rightarrow j)$ where $i \in \mathcal{S}$ and $j \in \mathcal{T}$. Note that the cut cost is "directed" as it sums weights of directed edges specifically from $\mathcal{S}$ to $\mathcal{T}$. The *minimum cut* problem on a graph is to find a cut that has the minimum cost among all cuts.

One of the fundamental results in combinatorial optimization is that the minimum s-t cut problem can be solved by finding a *maximum flow* from the source s to the sink t. Loosely speaking, maximum flow is the maximum "amount of water" that can be sent from the source to the sink by interpreting graph edges as directed "pipes" with capacities equal to edge weights. The theorem of Ford and Fulkerson [146] states that a maximum flow from s to t saturates a set of edges in the graph, dividing the nodes into two disjoint parts $(\mathcal{S}, \mathcal{T})$ corresponding to a minimum cut. Thus, min-cut and max-flow problems are equivalent. In fact, the maximum flow value is equal to the cost of the minimum cut. The close relationship between maximum flow and minimum cut problems is illustrated in figure 2.2 in the context of image segmentation. The max-flow displayed in figure 2.2a saturates the edges in the min-cut boundary in figure 2.2b. It turns out that max-flow and min-cut are dual problems, as explained in the appendix (section 2.5).

We can intuitively show how min-cut (or max-flow) on a graph may help with energy minimization over image labelings. Consider an example in figure 2.1. The graph corresponds to a 3×3 image. Any s-t cut partitions the nodes into disjoint groups each containing exactly one terminal. Therefore, any cut corresponds to some assignment of pixels (nodes) to labels (terminals). If edge weights are appropriately set based on parameters of an energy, a minimum cost cut will correspond to a labeling with the minimum value of this energy.

2.1.3 Standard Algorithms in Combinatorial Optimization

An important fact in combinatorial optimization is that there are polynomial algorithms for min-cut/max-flow problems on directed weighted graphs with two terminals. Most well-known algorithms belong to one of the following groups: Ford–Fulkerson-style

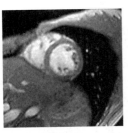 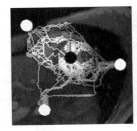 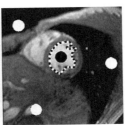

Original image   (a) Maximum flow   (b) Minimum cut

Figure 2.2
Graph cut/flow example in the context of interactive image segmentation (see chapter 7). Object and background seeds (white and black circles in a and b) are "hardwired" to the source s and the sink t, correspondingly, by ∞ cost t-links. The cost of n-links between the pixels (graph nodes) is low in places with high intensity contrast. Thus, cuts along object boundaries in the image are cheaper. Weak edges also work as "bottlenecks" for a flow. In (a) we show a maximum flow from s to t. This flow saturates graph edges corresponding to a minimum cut (black/white contour) shown in (b).

"augmenting paths" [146, 126], the network simplex approach [170], and Goldberg–Tarjan-style "push-relabel" methods [171].

Standard augmenting path-based algorithms [146, 126] work by pushing flow along nonsaturated paths from the source to the sink until the maximum flow in the graph $\mathcal{G} = (\hat{\mathcal{V}}, \hat{\mathcal{E}}, w)$ is reached. A typical augmenting path algorithm stores information about the distribution of the current $s \to t$ flow f among the edges of $\mathcal{G}$, using a *residual graph* $\mathcal{G}_f$. The topology of $\mathcal{G}_f$ is identical to $\mathcal{G}$, but the capacity of an edge in $\mathcal{G}_f$ reflects the residual capacity of the same edge in $\mathcal{G}$, given the amount of flow already in the edge. At the initialization there is no flow from the source to the sink ($f = 0$) and edge capacities in the residual graph $\mathcal{G}_0$ are equal to the original capacities in $\mathcal{G}$. At each new iteration the algorithm finds the shortest $s \to t$ path along nonsaturated edges of the residual graph. If a path is found, then the algorithm *augments* it by pushing the maximum possible flow Δf that saturates at least one of the edges in the path. The residual capacities of edges in the path are reduced by Δf while the residual capacities of the reverse edges are increased by Δf. Each augmentation increases the total flow from the source to the sink $f = f + \Delta f$. The maximum flow is reached when any $s \to t$ path crosses at least one saturated edge in the residual graph $\mathcal{G}_f$.

The Dinic algorithm [126] uses a breadth-first search to find the shortest paths from s to t on the residual graph $\mathcal{G}_f$. After all shortest paths of a fixed length k are saturated, the algorithm starts the breadth-first search for $s \to t$ paths of length $k + 1$ from scratch. Note that the use of shortest paths is an important factor that improves theoretical running time complexities for algorithms based on augmenting paths. The worst case running time complexity for the Dinic algorithm is $O(mn^2)$, where n is the number of nodes and m is the number of edges in the graph. In practice, the blocking flow approach of Dinic is known to outperform max-flow algorithms based on network simplex [170].

Push-relabel algorithms [171] use quite a different approach to the max-flow/min-cut problem. They do not maintain a valid flow during the operation; there are "active" nodes that have a positive "flow excess." Instead, the algorithms maintain a labeling of nodes giving a lower bound estimate on the distance to the sink along nonsaturated edges. The algorithms attempt to "push" excess flows toward nodes with a smaller estimated distance to the sink. Typically, the "push" operation is applied to active nodes with the largest distance (label) or is based on a FIFO selection strategy. The distances (labels) progressively increase as edges are saturated by push operations. Undeliverable flows are eventually drained back to the source. We recommend our favorite textbook on basic graph theory and algorithms [101] for more details on push-relabel and augmenting path methods.

Note that the most interesting applications of graph cut to vision use directed N-D grids with locally connected nodes. It is also typical that a large portion of the nodes is connected to the terminals. Unfortunately, these conditions rule out many specialized min-cut/max-flow algorithms that are designed for some restricted classes of graphs. Examples of interesting but inapplicable methods include randomized techniques for dense undirected graphs [226] and methods for planar graphs assuming a small number of terminal connections [340, 188], among others.

2.1.4 The BK Algorithm

This section describes an algorithm developed as an attempt to improve empirical performance of standard augmenting path techniques on graphs in vision [68]. Normally (see section 2.1.3) augmenting path-based methods start a new breadth-first search for $s \rightarrow t$ paths as soon as all paths of a given length are exhausted. In the context of graphs in computer vision, building a breadth-first search tree typically involves scanning the majority of image pixels. Practically speaking, it could be a very expensive operation if it has to be performed too often. Indeed, real-data experiments in vision confirm that rebuilding a search tree on graphs makes standard augmenting path techniques perform poorly in practice [68]. Several ideas were developed in [68] that improve the empirical performance of augmenting path techniques on sparse grid graphs in computer vision.

The BK (Boykov–Kolmogorov) algorithm [68] belongs to the group of algorithms based on augmenting paths. Similarly to Dinic [126], it builds search trees for detecting augmenting paths. In fact, BK builds two search trees, one from the source and the other from the sink. The other difference is that BK reuses these trees and never starts building them from scratch. The drawback of BK is that the augmenting paths found are not necessarily the shortest augmenting paths; thus the time complexity of the shortest augmenting path is no longer valid. The trivial upper bound on the number of augmentations for the BK algorithm is the cost of the minimum cut $|C|$, which results in the worst case complexity $O(mn^2|C|)$. Theoretically speaking, this is worse than the complexities of the standard algorithms discussed in section 2.1.3. However, experimental comparison conducted in

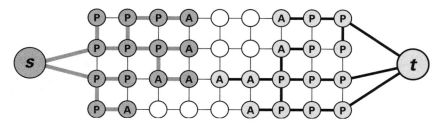

Figure 2.3
Example of search trees S (nodes with dense dots) and T (nodes with sparse dots) at the end of the growth stage when a path (gray(yellow) line) from the source s to the sink t is found. Active and passive nodes are labeled A and P, correspondingly. Free nodes are white.

[68, 11] shows that on many typical problem instances in vision (particularly for 2D cases) BK can significantly outperform standard max-flow algorithms.

Figure 2.3 illustrates BK's basic ideas. The algorithm maintains two non-overlapping search trees S and T with roots at the source s and the sink t, correspondingly. In tree S all edges from each parent node to its children are non-saturated, while in tree T edges from children to their parents are nonsaturated. The nodes that are not in S or T are "free." We have

$$S \subset V, \quad s \in S, \quad T \subset V, \quad t \in T, \quad S \cap T = \emptyset.$$

The nodes in the search trees S and T can be either "active" or "passive". The active nodes represent the outer border in each tree and the passive nodes are internal. The point is that active nodes allow trees to "grow" by acquiring new children (along nonsaturated edges) from a set of free nodes. The passive nodes cannot grow because they are completely blocked by other nodes from the same tree. It is also important that active nodes may come in contact with the nodes from the other tree. An augmenting path is found as soon as an active node in one of the trees detects a neighboring node that belongs to the other tree.

The algorithm iteratively repeats the following three stages:

• Growth stage: search trees S and T grow until they touch, giving an $s \to t$ path.

• Augmentation stage: the found path is augmented and search tree(s) break into forest(s).

• adoption stage: trees S and T are restored.

At the growth stage the search trees expand. The active nodes explore adjacent nonsaturated edges and acquire new children from a set of free nodes. The newly acquired nodes become active members of the corresponding search trees. As soon as all neighbors of a given active node are explored, the active node becomes passive. The growth stage terminates if an active node encounters a neighboring node that belongs to the opposite tree. In this case BK detects a path from the source to the sink, as shown in figure 2.3.

The augmentation stage augments the path found at the growth stage. Since we push through the largest flow possible, some edge(s) in the path become(s) saturated. Thus, some of the nodes in the trees S and T may become "orphans," that is, the edges linking them to their parents are no longer valid (they are saturated). In fact, the augmentation phase may split the search trees S and T into forests. The source s and the sink t are still roots of two of the trees and orphans form roots of all other trees.

The goal of the adoption stage is to restore the single-tree structure of sets S and T with roots in the source and the sink. At this stage we try to find a new valid parent for each orphan. A new parent should belong to the same set, S or T, as the orphan. A parent should also be connected through a nonsaturated edge. If there is no qualifying parent, we remove the orphan from S or T and make it a free node. The algorithm also declares all its former children as orphans. The stage terminates when no orphans are left and, thus, the search tree structures of S and T are restored. Since some orphan nodes may become free, the adoption stage results in contraction of sets S and T.

After the adoption stage is completed, the algorithm returns to the growth stage. The algorithm terminates when the search trees S and T cannot grow (no active nodes) and the trees are separated by saturated edges. This implies that a maximum flow is achieved. The corresponding minimum cut $C = \{S, T\}$ is defined as follows: nodes in the source search trees S form subset $\mathcal{S}$ and nodes in the sink tree T form subset $\mathcal{T}$. More details on implementing BK can be found in [68]. The code for the BK algorithm can be downloaded for research purposes from the authors' Web pages.

2.1.5 Further Comments on Time and Memory Efficiency

The ability to compute globally optimal solutions for many large problems in computer vision is one of the main advantages of graph cut methods. Max-flow/min-cut algorithms outlined in the previous sections normally take only a few seconds to solve problems on graphs corresponding to typical 2D images [68, 11]. However, these algorithms may take several minutes to solve bigger 3D problems such as segmentation of medical volumetric data or multiview volumetric reconstruction.

Efficiency of max-flow/min-cut algorithms for graphs in computer vision is actively studied, and one should be aware that significant improvements are possible in specific situations. For example, one can use flow recycling [244] or cut recycling [221] techniques in dynamic applications (e.g., in video) where max-flow has to be computed for similar graphs corresponding to different time frames. Such methods are shown to work well when graphs and solutions change very little from one instance to the next. Methods for GPU-based acceleration of the push-relabel approach were also proposed [69]. Given fast advancements of the GPU technology, such methods may become very effective for grid graphs corresponding to 2D images.

Limited memory resources could be a serious problem for large N-D problems, as standard max-flow/min-cut algorithms practically do not work as soon as the whole graph does not fit into available RAM. This issue was addressed in [120], where a scalable version of the push-relabel method was developed specifically for large regular N-D graphs (grids or complexes).

Note that the speed and memory efficiency of different max-flow/min-cut algorithms can be tested on problems in computer vision using a database of graphs (in the standard DIMACS format) that recently become available.[2] The posted graphs are regular grids or complexes corresponding to specific examples in segmentation, stereo, multiview reconstruction, and other applications.

2.2 Max-flow Algorithm as an Energy Minimization tool

Section 2.1 described the min-cut/max-flow problem and several max-flow algorithms. As already mentioned, they have a close relationship with the problem of minimizing pseudo-Boolean functions of the form (2.1). To see this, consider an undirected graph $(\mathcal{V}, \mathcal{E})$ and the corresponding directed weighted graph $(\hat{\mathcal{V}}, \hat{\mathcal{E}}, w)$ defined in section 2.1.1. Any s-t cut $(\mathcal{S}, \mathcal{T})$ can be viewed as a binary labeling $\mathbf{x}$ of the set of nodes $\mathcal{V}$ defined as follows: $x_i = 0$ if $i \in \mathcal{S}$, and $x_i = 1$ if $i \in \mathcal{T}$ for node $i \in \mathcal{V}$. The energy of labeling $\mathbf{x}$ (i.e., the cost of the corresponding cut $(\mathcal{S}, \mathcal{T})$) equals

$$E(\mathbf{x}) = \sum_{i \in \mathcal{V}} (w_{si} x_i + w_{it} \overline{x}_i) + \sum_{(i,j) \in \mathcal{E}} (w_{ij} \overline{x}_i x_j + w_{ji} x_i \overline{x}_j). \qquad (2.4)$$

There is a 1:1 correspondence between binary labelings and cuts; therefore, computing a minimum cut in $(\hat{\mathcal{V}}, \hat{\mathcal{E}}, w)$ will yield a global minimum of function (2.4). Note that standard max-flow/min-cut algorithms reviewed in sections 2.1.3 and 2.1.4 work only for graphs with nonnegative weights $w \geq 0$. Thus, equation (2.4) implies that such algorithms can minimize quadratic pseudo-Boolean functions (2.1) with coefficients $(\{\theta_{i;a}\}, \{\theta_{ij;ab}\})$ satisfying the following conditions:

$$\theta_{i;0} \geq \qquad\qquad 0 \quad \theta_{i;1} \geq 0 \qquad\qquad\qquad\qquad (2.5a)$$

$$\theta_{ij;00} = 0 \quad \theta_{ij;01} \geq 0 \quad \theta_{ij;10} \geq 0 \quad \theta_{ij;11} = 0 \qquad\qquad (2.5b)$$

for all nodes $i \in \mathcal{V}$ and edges $(i, j) \in \mathcal{E}$.

Can we use a max-flow algorithm for a more general class of quadratic pseudo-Boolean functions? In the next section we define operations on coefficients θ that do not change the energy $E(\mathbf{x})$; such operations are called *reparameterizations*. We will then explore which functions can be reparameterized to satisfy (2.5), arriving at the class of *submodular*

---

2. http://vision.csd.uwo.ca/viki/Max-flow_problem_instances_in_vision. Special thanks to Andrew Delong for preparing most of the data sets and for setting up the site. The idea of such a database was proposed by Andrew Goldberg.

functions. In section 2.2.2 we will see that any submodular QPB (quadratic pseudo-Boolean) function can be transformed to (2.5), and thus can be minimized in polynomial time via a max-flow algorithm.

Unfortunately, this transformation does not work for nonsubmodular functions, which should not be surprising, given that minimizing such functions is an NP-hard problem (it includes, e.g., the MAXCUT problem, which is NP-hard [156]). Still, the max-flow algorithm can be quite useful for certain nonsubmodular functions, (e.g., it can identify a *part* of an optimal labeling). We will review some known results in section 2.3.

2.2.1 Reparameterization and Normal Form

Recall that energy (2.1) depends on vector θ, which is a concatenation of all coefficients θ_{const}, $\theta_{i;a}$, and $\theta_{ij;ab}$. To emphasize this dependence, we will often write the energy defined by θ as $E(\mathbf{x} \mid \theta)$ instead of $E(\mathbf{x})$.

Given some node $i \in \mathcal{V}$ and some real number $\delta \in \mathbb{R}$, consider an operation transforming vector θ as follows:

$$\theta_{i;0} := \theta_{i;0} - \delta \qquad \theta_{i;1} := \theta_{i;1} - \delta \qquad \theta_{\text{const}} := \theta_{\text{const}} + \delta \tag{2.6}$$

where ":=" denotes the assignment operator as used in programming languages. It is easy to see that this transformation does not change the function $E(\mathbf{x} \mid \theta)$ and the cost of any labeling $\mathbf{x}$ stays the same. This follows from the fact that $x_i + \overline{x}_i = 1$. This motivates the following definition:

Definition 2.1 *Vector θ' is called a* reparameterization *of vector θ if they define the same energy function, that is, $E(\mathbf{x} \mid \theta') = E(\mathbf{x} \mid \theta)$ for any labeling $\mathbf{x}$. In this case we may also write $\theta' \sim \theta$.*

Consider an edge $(i, j) \in \mathcal{E}$. Identities $\overline{x}_j = \overline{x}_j(x_i + \overline{x}_i)$ and $x_j = x_j(x_i + \overline{x}_i)$ yield two more reparameterization operations:

$$\theta_{ij;00} := \theta_{ij;00} - \delta \qquad \theta_{ij;10} := \theta_{ij;10} - \delta \qquad \theta_{j;0} := \theta_{j;0} + \delta \tag{2.7a}$$

$$\theta_{ij;01} := \theta_{ij;01} - \delta \qquad \theta_{ij;11} := \theta_{ij;11} - \delta \qquad \theta_{j;1} := \theta_{j;1} + \delta. \tag{2.7b}$$

Similarly, identities $\overline{x}_i = \overline{x}_i(x_j + \overline{x}_j)$ and $x_i = x_i(x_j + \overline{x}_j)$ give

$$\theta_{ij;00} := \theta_{ij;00} - \delta \qquad \theta_{ij;01} := \theta_{ij;01} - \delta \qquad \theta_{i;0} := \theta_{i;0} + \delta \tag{2.7c}$$

$$\theta_{ij;10} := \theta_{ij;10} - \delta \qquad \theta_{ij;11} := \theta_{ij;11} - \delta \qquad \theta_{i;1} := \theta_{i;1} + \delta. \tag{2.7d}$$

Operation 2.7a is illustrated in figure 2.4b. It can be shown that any possible reparameterization can be obtained as a combination of operations (2.6 and 2.7), assuming that graph $(\mathcal{V}, \mathcal{E})$ is connected (e.g., [520]).

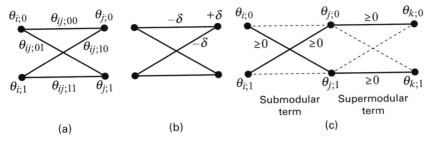

Figure 2.4
(a) Convention for displaying parameters $\theta_{i;a}$, $\theta_{ij;ab}$, $\theta_{j;b}$. (b) Example of a reparameterization operation (equation 2.7a). (c) Normal form. Dotted lines denote links with zero cost. The first term is submodular, the second is supermodular. Unary parameters must satisfy $\min\{\theta_{i;0}, \theta_{i;1}\} = \min\{\theta_{j;0}, \theta_{j;1}\} = \min\{\theta_{k;0}, \theta_{k;1}\} = 0$.

Definition 2.2 *Vector θ is in a* normal *form if each node $i \in \mathcal{V}$ satisfies*

$$\min\{\theta_{i;0}, \theta_{i;1}\} = 0 \tag{2.8}$$

and each edge $(i, j) \in \mathcal{E}$ satisfies either (2.9a) or (2.9b) below:

$$\theta_{ij;00} = 0, \quad \theta_{ij;01} \geq 0, \quad \theta_{ij;10} \geq 0, \quad \theta_{ij;11} = 0 \tag{2.9a}$$

$$\theta_{ij;00} \geq 0, \quad \theta_{ij;01} = 0, \quad \theta_{ij;10} = 0, \quad \theta_{ij;11} \geq 0. \tag{2.9b}$$

Figure 2.4c illustrates conditions (2.9a) and (2.9b) on edges (i, j) and (j, k), correspondingly. Note that (2.9a) agrees with (2.5b).

It is not difficult to verify that any quadratic pseudo-Boolean function $E(\mathbf{x} \mid \theta)$ can be reparameterized to a normal form in linear time. For example, this can be done by the following simple algorithm:

1. For each edge $(i, j) \in \mathcal{E}$ do the following:
- Make $\theta_{ij;ab}$ nonnegative: compute $\delta = \min_{a,b \in \{0,1\}} \theta_{ij;ab}$ and set

$$\theta_{ij;ab} := \theta_{ij;ab} - \delta \quad \forall\, a, b \in \{0, 1\}, \qquad \theta_{\text{const}} := \theta_{\text{const}} + \delta.$$

- For each label $b \in \{0, 1\}$ compute $\delta = \min\{\theta_{ij;0b}, \theta_{ij;1b}\}$ and set

$$\theta_{ij;0b} := \theta_{ij;0b} - \delta, \quad \theta_{ij;1b} := \theta_{ij;1b} - \delta, \qquad \theta_{j;b} := \theta_{j;b} + \delta.$$

- For each label $a \in \{0, 1\}$ compute $\delta = \min\{\theta_{ij;a0}, \theta_{ij;a1}\}$ and set

$$\theta_{ij;a0} := \theta_{ij;a0} - \delta, \quad \theta_{ij;a1} := \theta_{ij;a1} - \delta, \qquad \theta_{i;a} := \theta_{i;a} + \delta.$$

2. For each node i compute $\delta = \min\{\theta_{i;0}, \theta_{i;1}\}$ and set

$$\theta_{i;0} := \theta_{i;0} - \delta, \quad \theta_{i;1} := \theta_{i;1} - \delta, \qquad \theta_{\text{const}} := \theta_{\text{const}} + \delta.$$

The first step of this algorithm performs a fixed number of operations for each edge, and the second step performs a fixed number of operations for each node, giving linear overall complexity $O(|\mathcal{V}| + |\mathcal{E}|)$.

In general, the normal form is not unique for vector θ. For example, in the appendix it is shown that each augmentation of a standard max-flow algorithm can be interpreted as a reparameterization of energy $E(\mathbf{x} \mid \theta)$ from one normal form to another. The set of all reparameterizations of θ in a normal form will be denoted by $\Omega(\theta)$:

$$\Omega(\theta) = \{\theta' \sim \theta \mid \theta' \text{ is in normal form}\}.$$

2.2.2 Submodularity

It is easy to check that reparameterization operations (2.7) for edge (i, j) preserve the quantity

$$\Delta_{ij} = (\theta_{ij;00} + \theta_{ij;11}) - (\theta_{ij;01} + \theta_{ij;10}). \tag{2.10}$$

Thus, Δ_{ij} is an invariant that can be used to classify each edge (i, j).

Definition 2.3

(a) Edge (i, j) is called submodular *with respect to given energy function $E(\mathbf{x} \mid \theta)$ if $\Delta_{ij} \leq 0$. It is called* supermodular *if $\Delta_{ij} \geq 0$.*

(b) A quadratic pseudo-Boolean function $E(\mathbf{x} \mid \theta)$ is called submodular *if all its edges (i, j) are submodular, that is, they satisfy*

$$\theta_{ij;00} + \theta_{ij;11} \leq \theta_{ij;01} + \theta_{ij;10}. \tag{2.11}$$

We have already seen a definition of submodularity for general pseudo-Boolean functions in chapter 1 (1.59). It is not difficult to show that for *quadratic* pseudo-Boolean functions the two definitions are equivalent. We leave this proof as an exercise.

Equation 2.11 encodes some notion of smoothness. It says that the combined cost of homogeneous labelings $(0, 0)$ and $(1, 1)$ is smaller than the combined cost of discontinuous labelings $(0, 1)$ and $(1, 0)$. The smoothness assumption is natural in vision problems where nearby points are likely to have similar labels (object category, disparity, etc.).

Note that for energy $E(\mathbf{x} \mid \theta)$ in a normal form, condition (2.9a) describes *submodular* edges and condition (2.9b) describes *supermodular* edges (see also fig.2.4(c)).

Now we can return to the question of what energy functions $E(\mathbf{x} \mid \theta)$ can be reparameterized to the form of equations (2.5). Any energy can be transformed to a normal form by a simple reparameterization algorithm described in section 2.2.1. Condition (2.8) will satisfy (2.5a). Since submodularity is preserved under reparameterization, all submodular edges will satisfy (2.9a) and, thus, (2.5b). This proves the following.

Theorem 2.1 *Global minima* $\hat{x} = \arg\min_x E(\mathbf{x} \mid \theta)$ *of any submodular quadratic pseudo-Boolean function can be obtained in polynomial time, using the following steps:*

1. Reparameterize θ to a normal form as described in section 2.2.1.

2. Construct the directed weighted graph $\hat{\mathcal{G}} = (\hat{\mathcal{V}}, \hat{\mathcal{E}}, w)$ as described in section 2.1.1 with the following nonnegative arc capacities:

$$w_{si} = \theta_{i;1}, \quad w_{it} = \theta_{i;0}, \quad w_{ij} = \theta_{ij;01}, \quad w_{ji} = \theta_{ji;10}.$$

3. Compute a minimum s-t cut in $\hat{\mathcal{G}}$ and the corresponding labeling $\mathbf{x}$.

Note that supermodularity is also preserved under reparameterization. After conversion to a normal form any (strictly) supermodular edge will satisfy (2.9b), which is inconsistent with (2.5b). Therefore, nonsubmodular functions with one or more supermodular edges cannot be converted to (2.5) and, in general, they cannot be minimized by standard max-flow algorithms. Optimization of nonsubmodular functions is known to be an NP-hard problem. However, section 2.3 describes one approach that may work for some cases of non-submodular functions.

2.3 Minimizing Nonsubmodular Functions

Let us now consider the case when not all edges for function $E(\mathbf{x})$ satisfy the submodularity condition (2.11). Minimizing such a function is an NP-hard problem, so there is little hope that there exists a polynomial time algorithm for solving arbitrary instances. It does not mean, however, that all instances that occur in practice are equally hard. This section describes a *linear programming relaxation* approach that can solve many of the instances that occur in computer vision applications, as can be seen in several other chapters of the book.

Relaxation is a general technique applicable to many optimization problems. It can be described as follows. Suppose that we want to minimize function $E(\mathbf{x})$ over a set $X \subset \mathbb{Z}^n$ containing a finite number of integer-valued points. First, we extend function E to a larger domain $\hat{X}$, $X \subset \hat{X}$ so that $\hat{X}$ is a convex subset of $\mathbb{R}^n$. Assuming that E is a convex function over $\hat{X}$, one can usually compute a global minimizer $\hat{\mathbf{x}}$ of function E over $\hat{X}$, using one of many efficient methods for convex optimization problems. (More information on relaxation techniques can be found in chapter 16.)

For some "easy" instances it may happen that a minimizer $\hat{\mathbf{x}}$ is integer-valued and lies in the original domain X; then we know that we have solved the original problem. In general, however, the vector $\hat{\mathbf{x}}$ may have fractional components. In that case there are several possibilities. We may try to round $\hat{\mathbf{x}}$ to an integer-valued solution so that the objective function E does not increase too much. (This scheme is used for a large number of approximation algorithms in combinatorial optimization.) Another option is to use the minimum value

$\min_{\mathbf{x} \in \hat{X}} E(\mathbf{x})$ as a lower bound on the original optimization problem in a branch-and-bound framework.

This section reviews the LP relaxation of energy (2.1) introduced earlier, in section 1.9 of chapter 1:

$$\text{Minimize} \quad \theta_{\text{const}} + \sum_{\substack{i \in \mathcal{V}, \\ a \in \{0,1\}}} \theta_{i;a} y_{i;a} + \sum_{\substack{(i,j) \in \mathcal{E}, \\ a,b \in \{0,1\}}} \theta_{ij;ab} y_{ij;ab} \tag{2.12a}$$

$$\text{s.t.} \quad y_{ij;0b} + y_{ij;1b} = y_{j;b} \quad \forall (i,j) \in \mathcal{E}, b \in \{0,1\}, \tag{2.12b}$$

$$y_{ij;a0} + y_{ij;a1} = y_{i;a} \quad \forall (i,j) \in \mathcal{E}, a \in \{0,1\}, \tag{2.12c}$$

$$y_{i;0} + y_{i;1} = 1 \quad \forall i \in \mathcal{V}, \tag{2.12d}$$

$$y_{i;a}, y_{ij;ab} \in [0,1] \quad \forall i \in \mathcal{V}, (i,j) \in \mathcal{E}, a, b \in \{0,1\}. \tag{2.12e}$$

Note that forcing variables $y_{i;a}$, $y_{ij;ab}$ to be integral would make (2.12) equivalent to the minimization problem (2.1); $y_{i;a}$ and $y_{ij;ab}$ would be the indicator variables of events $x_i = a$ and $(x_i, x_j) = (a, b)$, respectively. Thus, (2.12) is indeed a relaxation of (2.1). It is known as the *roof duality relaxation* [179, 61].

Equation (2.12) is a linear program. (Interestingly, it can be shown to be the LP dual of problem (DUAL) formulated in the appendix to this chapter. Thus, there is a strong duality between (2.17) and LP relaxation (2.12), but there may be a "duality gap" between (2.17) and the original integer problem (2.1) in a general nonsubmodular case.) It can be shown [179] that the extreme points of this LP are *half-integral*. That is, an optimal solution $\hat{\mathbf{y}}$ may have components $\hat{y}_{i;a}$, $\hat{y}_{ij;ab}$ belonging to $\left\{0, 1, \frac{1}{2}\right\}$. Two important questions arise:

• Does $\hat{\mathbf{y}}$ give any information about minimizers of function (2.1)? This is discussed in section 2.3.1.

• How can $\hat{\mathbf{y}}$ be computed? Since (2.12) is a linear program, one could use a number of generic LP solvers. However, there exist specialized combinatorial algorithms for solving (2.12). The method in [62] based on the max-flow algorithm is perhaps the most efficient; it is reviewed in section 2.3.2. We will refer to it as the *BHS algorithm*.

2.3.1 Properties of Roof Duality Relaxation

Let $\hat{\mathbf{y}}$ be a half-integral optimal solution of (2.12). It is convenient to define a *partial* labeling $\mathbf{x}$ as follows: $x_i = \hat{y}_{i;1}$ if $\hat{y}_{i;1} \in \{0, 1\}$ and $x_i = \varnothing$ if $\hat{y}_{i;1} = \frac{1}{2}$. In the former case we say node i is *labeled*; otherwise it is *unlabeled*.

An important property of roof duality relaxation is that $\mathbf{x}$ gives a *part* of an optimal solution. In other words, function E has a global minimum $\mathbf{x}^*$ such that $x_i^* = x_i$ for all labeled nodes i. This property is known as *persistency* or *partial optimality* [179, 61, 261].

Clearly, the usefulness of roof duality relaxation depends on how many nodes are labeled and this depends heavily on the application. If the number of nonsubmodular terms is small and they are relatively weak compared with unary terms, then we can expect most nodes to be labeled. In other situations all nodes can remain unlabeled. Refer to [403] and chapter 18 for some computational experiments in computer vision.

An important question is what to do with remaining unlabeled nodes. If the number of such nodes is small or the remaining graph has low tree width, then one could use a junction tree algorithm to compute a global minimum. Another option is to use the *PROBE* technique [63]. The idea is to fix unlabeled nodes to a particular value (0 or 1) and apply roof duality relaxation to the modified problem. After this operation more nodes may become labeled, giving further information about minimizers of function E. This information is used to simplify function E, and the process is repeated until we cannot infer any new constraints on minimizers of E. For certain functions the PROBE procedure labels many more nodes compared with the basic roof duality approach [63, 403].[3]

In computer vision applications QPB functions are often used inside iterative move-making algorithms, such as expansion moves (chapter 3) or fusion moves (chapter 18). In that case the roof duality approach can be used as follows. Suppose that the current configuration is represented by a binary labeling $\mathbf{z}^\circ$, and solving the LP relaxation gives partial labeling $\mathbf{x}$. Let us replace $\mathbf{z}^\circ$ with the following labeling $\mathbf{z}$: if node i is labeled, then $z_i = x_i$, otherwise $z_i = z_i^\circ$. In such an iterative optimization the energy can never increase. This follows from the *autarky* property that says $E(\mathbf{z}) \leq E(\mathbf{z}^\circ)$ [179, 61].

2.3.2 Solving Roof Duality Relaxation via Max-flow: The BHS Algorithm

The LP relaxation (2.12) can be solved in many different ways, including generic LP solvers. We review the method in [62], which is perhaps the most efficient, and we call this the BHS algroithm.[4] On the high level, it can be described as follows. The original energy (2.1) is relaxed to a symmetric submodular function using binary indicator variables $x_{i;1}$ and $x_{i;0}$, introduced for each variable x_i and its negation $\overline{x}_i = 1 - x_i$, respectively. This submodular formulation can be solved by max-flow algorithms. The corresponding result can also be shown to solve LP (2.12).

Below we provide more details. The first step is to reparameterize the energy $E(\mathbf{x} \mid \theta)$ into a normal form, as described in section 2.2.1. Then, submodular edges will have the form (2.9a) and supermodular edges will have the form (2.9b). The second step is to construct

---

3. The code can be found online on V. Kolmogorov's Web page. This includes the BHS algorithm, the PROBE procedure, and the heuristic IMPROVE technique (see [403]).

4. BHS is an abbreviation of the inventors' names. Sometimes it has also been called the QPBO algorithm in the computer vision literature, as in [403]. This is, however, misleading; the optimization problem is already called QPBO (chapter 1).

a new energy function $\widetilde{E}(\{x_{i;1}\}, \{x_{i;0}\})$ by transforming terms of the original function (2.1) as follows:

$$\theta_{i;0}\overline{x}_i \qquad \mapsto \qquad \frac{\theta_{i;0}}{2}[\overline{x}_{i;1} + x_{i;0}] \tag{2.13a}$$

$$\theta_{i;1}x_i \qquad \mapsto \qquad \frac{\theta_{i;1}}{2}[x_{i;1} + \overline{x}_{i;0}] \tag{2.13b}$$

$$\theta_{ij;01}\overline{x}_i x_j \qquad \mapsto \qquad \frac{\theta_{ij;01}}{2}[\overline{x}_{i;1}x_{j;1} + x_{i;0}\overline{x}_{j;0}] \tag{2.13c}$$

$$\theta_{ij;10}x_i\overline{x}_j \qquad \mapsto \qquad \frac{\theta_{ij;10}}{2}[x_{i;1}\overline{x}_{j;1} + \overline{x}_{i;0}x_{j;0}] \tag{2.13d}$$

$$\theta_{ij;00}\overline{x}_i\overline{x}_j \qquad \mapsto \qquad \frac{\theta_{ij;00}}{2}[x_{i;0}\overline{x}_{j;1} + \overline{x}_{i;1}x_{j;0}] \tag{2.13e}$$

$$\theta_{ij;11}x_i x_j \qquad \mapsto \qquad \frac{\theta_{ij;11}}{2}[x_{i;1}\overline{x}_{j;0} + \overline{x}_{i;0}x_{j;1}]. \tag{2.13f}$$

The constant term θ_{const} remains unmodified.

The constructed function $\widetilde{E}$ has several important properties. First, it is equivalent to the original function if we impose the constraint $x_{i;0} = 1 - x_{i;1}$ for all nodes i:

$$\widetilde{E}(\mathbf{x}, \overline{\mathbf{x}}) = E(\mathbf{x}) \qquad \forall \mathbf{x}. \tag{2.14}$$

Second, function $\widetilde{E}$ is submodular. (Note that all pairwise terms are of the form $c \cdot x_{i;a}\overline{x}_{j;b}$ where $c \geq 0$ and $x_{i;a}$, $x_{j;b}$ are binary variables.) This means that we can minimize this function by computing a maximum flow in an appropriately constructed graph (see section 2.2). This graph will have twice as many nodes and edges compared with the graph needed for minimizing submodular functions $E(\mathbf{x})$.

After computing a global minimum $(\{x_{i;1}\}, \{x_{i;0}\})$ of function $\widetilde{E}$ we can easily obtain a solution $\hat{y}$ of the relaxation (2.12). The unary components for node $i \in V$ are given by

$$\hat{y}_{i;1} = \frac{1}{2}[x_{i;1} + \overline{x}_{i;0}] \tag{2.15a}$$

$$\hat{y}_{i;0} = \frac{1}{2}[x_{i;0} + \overline{x}_{i;1}]. \tag{2.15b}$$

Clearly, we have $\hat{y}_{i;1} + \hat{y}_{i;0} = 1$ and $\hat{y}_{i;1}, \hat{y}_{i;0} \in \{0, 1, \frac{1}{2}\}$. It also is not difficult to derive pairwise components $\hat{y}_{ij;ab}$: we just need to minimize (2.12) over $\{\hat{y}_{ij;ab}\}$ with fixed unary components $\{\hat{y}_{i;a}\}$. We omit the formulas because they are rarely used in practice.

A complete proof that the algorithm above indeed solves problem (2.12) is a bit involved, and we do not give it here. The original proof can be found in [61]. Below we provide a sketch of an alternative proof that follows the general approach in [195]. The idea is to establish some correspondence between LP relaxation (2.12) of the original nonsubmodular energy E and the same type of relaxation for submodular energy $\widetilde{E}$. To be concise, we will refer to these two relaxation problems as LP and $\widetilde{LP}$. Assuming that $\mathcal{F}(LP)$ and $\mathcal{F}(\widetilde{LP})$ are the sets of feasible solutions of the two problems, it is possible to define linear mappings $\varphi : \mathcal{F}(LP) \to \mathcal{F}(\widetilde{LP})$ and $\psi : \mathcal{F}(\widetilde{LP}) \to \mathcal{F}(LP)$, which preserve the cost of the solutions. This implies that LP and $\widetilde{LP}$ have the same minimum value, and any solution of one problem yields an optimal solution for the other one. Relaxation $\widetilde{LP}$ corresponds to a submodular energy, and therefore it can be solved via a max-flow algorithm. Applying mapping ψ to the optimal solution of $\widetilde{LP}$ yields formulas (2.15).

2.4 Conclusions

This chapter described standard optimization techniques for binary pairwise models. A large number of problems in the following chapters are represented using such quadratic pseudo-Boolean functions. Equation (2.1) is a different representation of energy convenient for binary variables x. This representation is common in combinatorial optimization literature, where optimization of pseudo-Boolean functions has been actively studied for more than forty years.

This chapter studied an important class of pseudo-Boolean functions whose minimization can be reduced to min-cut/max-flow problems on graphs. Such functions are characterized by a submodularity condition. We also reviewed several classical polynomial complexity algorithms (augmenting paths [146, 126] and push-relabel [171]) for solving min-cut/max-flow problems. Efficient versions of such algorithms were also developed specifically for sparse grids common in computer vision [68, 120]. This chapter reviewed the BK algorithm [68] that is widely used in imaging.

Section 2.3 concluded this chapter by describing more general graph cut techniques that can be applied to nonsubmodular binary models. Such general quadratic pseudo-Boolean optimization (QPBO) methods are based on roof duality relaxation of the integer programming problem. They are not guaranteed to find the global minima solution, but they can find partial solutions.

2.5 Appendix

2.5.1 Max-flow as a Reparameterization

We showed how to minimize any submodular QPB function using a max-flow algorithm. At this point the reader may ask why we solve a *maximization* problem (computing a flow of maximum value) for *minimizing* a function. As was mentioned in section 2.2, the maximization and minimization problems are dual to one another. In this section we will illustrate this duality using the notion of reparameterization.

First, let us formulate the dual problem in the context of energy minimization. Without loss of generality, we will assume that energy $E(\mathbf{x} \mid \theta)$ was already converted to a normal form (2.8 and 2.9), as described in section 2.2.1. It is easy to see that for any vector θ with nonnegative components ($\{\theta_{i;a}\}$, $\{\theta_{ij;ab}\}$) the constant term θ_{const} is a lower bound on the function $E(\mathbf{x} \mid \theta)$ defined by (2.1), that is,

$$\theta_{\text{const}} \leq \min_{\mathbf{x}} E(\mathbf{x} \mid \theta). \tag{2.16}$$

In order to obtain the *tightest* possible bound, one can solve the following maximization problem:

(DUAL) Given θ, find its reparameterization θ^* with nonnegative components ($\{\theta^*_{i;a}\}$, $\{\theta^*_{ij;ab}\}$) such that the lower bound θ^*_{const} is maximized.

It is easy to check that the solution to (DUAL) can be found among normal form reparameterizations of θ, that is, (DUAL) is equivalent to

$$\max_{\theta' \in \Omega(\theta)} \theta'_{\text{const}}. \tag{2.17}$$

It is not difficult to show that problems (DUAL) and (2.17) correspond to some linear programs.[5] Also note that inequality (2.16) and problems (DUAL) and (2.17) make sense for both submodular and nonsubmodular functions. In any case, θ_{const} is a lower bound on $\min_{\mathbf{x}} E(\mathbf{x} \mid \theta)$ as long as vector θ is nonnegative (e.g., in normal form).

When the energy function $E(\mathbf{x} \mid \theta)$ is submodular, (2.17) is the exact maximization problem solved by max-flow algorithms on graph $\hat{\mathcal{G}}$ described in theorem 2.1. For example, consider an augmenting path-style algorithm from section 2.1.3. Pushing flow through an arc changes residual capacities of this arc and its reverse arc, thus changing vector θ.[6] If we send δ units of flow from the source to the sink via arcs $(s \to i_1)$, $(i_1 \to i_2)$, ..., $(i_{k-1} \to i_k)$, $(i_k \to t)$, then the corresponding transformation of vector θ is

$$
\begin{aligned}
&\theta_{i_1;1} := \theta_{i_1;1} - \delta \\
&\theta_{i_1 i_2;01} := \theta_{i_1 i_2;01} - \delta \qquad \theta_{i_1 i_2;10} := \theta_{i_1 i_2;10} + \delta \\
&\qquad \vdots \qquad\qquad\qquad\qquad \vdots \\
&\theta_{i_{k-1} i_k;01} := \theta_{i_{k-1} i_k;01} - \delta \quad \theta_{i_{k-1} i_k;10} := \theta_{i_{k-1} i_k;10} + \delta \\
&\quad \theta_{i_k;0} := \theta_{i_k;0} - \delta \\
&\theta_{\text{const}} := \theta_{\text{const}} + \delta.
\end{aligned} \tag{2.18}
$$

5. The definition of reparameterization involves an exponential number of linear constraints. But the fact that any reparameterization $\theta' \sim \theta$ can be expressed via operations (2.6 and 2.7) allows polynomial size LP formulations for (DUAL) and (2.17).

6. Recall that the reduction given in theorem 2.1 associates each arc of graph $\hat{\mathcal{G}}$ with one component of vector θ. Thus, we can define a 1:1 mapping between residual capacities of graph $\hat{\mathcal{G}}$ and components of vector θ.

It can be checked that this transformation of θ is indeed a reparameterization obtained by combining operations (2.6 and 2.7) for the sequence of edges above. Furthermore, it keeps vector θ in a normal form and increases the lower bound by δ. Thus, each augmentation greedily improves the objective function of the maximization problem (2.17). This relationship between reparameterization and augmenting path flows has been used to design dynamic algorithms for energy minimization [66, 221, 244].

Upon termination the max-flow algorithm yields a minimum s-t cut $(\mathcal{S}, \mathcal{T})$ corresponding to some labeling $\hat{\mathbf{x}}$ and a maximum flow corresponding to some reparameterization $\hat{\theta}$. Using the property that all arcs from $\mathcal{S}$ to $\mathcal{T}$ have zero residual capacity, one can check that $\hat{\theta}_{i;\hat{x}_i} = 0$ for all nodes i and $\hat{\theta}_{ij;\hat{x}_i\hat{x}_j} = 0$ for all edges (i, j). Therefore, from equation (2.1') we get

$$E(\hat{\mathbf{x}} \mid \hat{\theta}) = \hat{\theta}_{\text{const}} + \sum_{i \in \mathcal{V}} \hat{\theta}_{i;\hat{x}_i} + \sum_{(i,j) \in \mathcal{E}} \hat{\theta}_{ij;\hat{x}_i\hat{x}_j} = \hat{\theta}_{\text{const}}, \tag{2.19}$$

that is, lower bound $\hat{\theta}_{\text{const}}$ in (2.16) equals the cost of labeling $\hat{\mathbf{x}}$. This confirms the optimality of $\hat{\mathbf{x}}$ and $\hat{\theta}$. Moreover, (2.19) implies that for submodular energies $E(\mathbf{x} \mid \theta)$ there is no *duality gap*, that is,

$$\max_{\theta' \in \Omega(\theta)} \theta'_{\text{const}} = \min_{\mathbf{x}} E(\mathbf{x} \mid \theta), \tag{2.20}$$

which is also known as a *strong duality* relationship.

Note that inequality (2.16) holds for arbitrary quadratic pseudo-Boolean functions $E(\mathbf{x} \mid \theta)$ in a normal form including any combination of submodular and supermodular terms. Presence of supermodular terms, however, may result in the optimal lower bound in the problem (DUAL) being smaller than the minimum of $E(\mathbf{x} \mid \theta)$. In other words, we may have a *weak duality* relationship $\max_{\theta' \in \Omega(\theta)} \theta'_{\text{const}} < \min_{\mathbf{x}} E(\mathbf{x} \mid \theta)$, instead of the *strong duality* (2.20). In the next chapter we will study some optimization algorithms for general non-submodular quadratic pseudo-Boolean functions that may include supermodular terms.

3 Optimizing Multilabel MRFs Using Move-Making Algorithms

Yuri Boykov, Olga Veksler, and Ramin Zabih

Chapter 2 addresses minimization of energies with binary variables, that is, pseudo-Boolean optimization. Many problems encountered in vision, however, require multilabel variables. Unfortunately, most of these are NP-hard to minimize, making it necessary to resort to approximations. One approach to approximate optimization is the *move-making* algorithms. Interestingly, this approach reduces to solving a certain sequence of pseudo-Boolean problems, that is, the problems discussed in chapter 2). At each iteration a move-making algorithm makes a proposal (move) for a site i either to keep its old label or to switch to a new label. This process can be encoded as binary optimization. For example, $x_i = 0$ means that a site i keeps its old label, and $x_i = 1$ means that site i switches to the proposed label. The goal is then to find the optimal (i.e., giving the largest energy decrease) subset of sites to switch to the proposed labels. Depending on the nature of the new proposal (move), such binary optimization can be submodular, and therefore solvable exactly with graph cuts (see chapter 2). The algorithm considers a new move at each iteration until there is no available move that decreases the energy. This chapter explains in detail two widely used move-making algorithms: expansion and swap. The classes of energy functions under which expansion and swap moves are submodular are characterized. The effectiveness of the approach is tested for the applications of image restoration and stereo correspondence. In particular for stereo, the expansion algorithm has advanced the state of the art by bringing to the forefront the advantages of the global optimization methods versus local methods, which were commonly used at the time. (See a detailed comparison of optimization methods in chapter 11). In the last decade, the swap and expansion algorithms have been widely used in numerous practical applications in vision.

3.1 Introduction

The energy function for many commonly used Markov random fields can be written as

$$E(\mathbf{x}) = \sum_{i \in \mathcal{V}} \Phi_i(x_i) + \sum_{(i,j) \in \mathcal{E}} \Psi_{ij}(x_i, x_j), \tag{3.1}$$

where, as in chapter 1, $\mathcal{V}$ and $\mathcal{E}$ are the set of vertices and edges corresponding to the MRF, x_i is the label of vertex (or site) i, and $\Phi_i(x_i)$ are the unary terms and $\Psi_{ij}(x_i, x_j)$ are the binary terms. Chapter 2 addresses optimization of the energy in (3.1) when the label set $\mathcal{L}$ has size 2 (i.e., pseudo-Boolean optimization). This chapter addresses the general multilabel case.

The choice of Φ_i does not affect optimization of the energy in (3.1). The choice of Ψ_{ij}, however, decides the difficulty of optimizing this energy. Some choices lead to tractable polynomially solvable problems [421, 116] (see also chapter 4), and others to NP-hard problems [72]. Unfortunately, many useful Ψ_{ij}, and in particular many discontinuity-preserving [54] Ψ_{ij}, lead to NP-hard energies, and therefore approximation techniques are needed. This chapter describes two popular optimization algorithms, the expansion and the swap, which are based on the common idea of *move making*. These algorithms were originally developed in [70, 71, 72].

The idea of move-making algorithms is to permit, for a given labeling x^c, switching to another labeling x^n only if this switch belongs to a certain set of allowed *moves*. Ideally, the set of allowed moves is designed in such a way that an optimal move, that is, the move resulting in the largest energy decrease, can be found efficiently. A move-making algorithm starts from an initial labeling and proceeds by making a series of allowed moves that lead to solutions having lower (or equal) energy. The algorithm converges when no lower energy solution can be found.

There are two algorithms that approximately minimize the energy $E(\mathbf{x})$ under two fairly general classes of binary terms Ψ_{ij}. In particular, the swap algorithm can be used whenever the following condition is satisfied:

$$\Psi_{ij}(\alpha, \alpha) + \Psi_{ij}(\beta, \beta) \leq \Psi_{ij}(\alpha, \beta) + \Psi_{ij}(\beta, \alpha) \quad \forall \alpha, \beta \in \mathcal{L}. \tag{3.2}$$

The condition for the expansion algorithm is more restrictive:

$$\Psi_{ij}(\alpha, \alpha) + \Psi_{ij}(\beta, \gamma) \leq \Psi_{ij}(\beta, \alpha) + \Psi_{ij}(\alpha, \gamma) \quad \forall \alpha, \beta, \gamma \in \mathcal{L}. \tag{3.3}$$

It is important to note that move-making algorithms, in particular expansion and swap algorithms, can still be used even if the move is not the optimal one and the conditions above do not hold. Chapter 18 discusses such move-making methods in detail, and shows that many applications do successfully use nonoptimal moves (e.g., [7, 404]).

In order to connect (3.3) and (3.2) to familiar concepts, recall the definitions from metric spaces. Ψ_{ij} is a metric if $\forall \alpha, \beta, \gamma \in \mathcal{L}$:

$$\Psi_{ij}(\alpha, \beta) \geq 0, \tag{3.4}$$

$$\Psi_{ij}(\alpha, \beta) = 0 \Leftrightarrow \alpha = \beta, \tag{3.5}$$

$$\Psi_{ij}(\alpha, \beta) = \Psi_{ij}(\beta, \alpha), \tag{3.6}$$

$$\Psi_{ij}(\alpha, \beta) \leq \Psi_{ij}(\alpha, \gamma) + \Psi_{ij}(\gamma, \beta). \tag{3.7}$$

There are useful generalizations of a metric, such as a *quasi-metric*, for which the symmetry (i.e., (3.6)) is dropped, and a *semi-metric*, for which the triangular inequality (i.e., (3.7)) is dropped. Clearly, (3.2) is satisfied when Ψ_{ij} is a metric, quasi-metric, or semi-metric; (3.3) is satisfied when Ψ_{ij} is a metric or a quasi-metric.

Note that both semi-metrics and metrics include important cases of discontinuity-preserving Ψ_{ij}. Informally, a discontinuity-preserving binary term Ψ_{ij} should be bounded from above. This avoids overpenalizing sharp jumps between the labels of neighboring sites; see [523, 308] and the experimental results in section 3.5. Examples of discontinuity-preserving binary terms for a one-dimensional label set $\mathcal{L}$ include the truncated quadratic $\Psi_{ij}(\alpha, \beta) = \min(K, |\alpha - \beta|^2)$ (a semi-metric) and the truncated absolute distance $\Psi_{ij}(\alpha, \beta) = \min(K, |\alpha - \beta|)$ (a metric), where K is some constant. If $\mathcal{L}$ is multidimensional, one can replace $|\cdot|$ by any norm (e.g., $||\cdot||_{L_2}$). These models encourage labelings consisting of several regions where sites in the same region have similar labels, and therefore one informally calls them piecewise smooth models.

Another important discontinuity-preserving function is given by the Potts model $\Psi_{ij}(\alpha, \beta) = K_{ij} \cdot T(\alpha \neq \beta)$ (a metric), where $T(\cdot)$ is 1 if its argument is true, and otherwise 0. This model encourages labelings consisting of several regions where sites in the same region have equal labels, and therefore one informally calls it a piecewise constant model.

Both expansion and swap algorithms find a local minimum of the energy in (3.1) with respect to an exponentially large set of moves (see section 3.2.1). Unlike the ordinary local minima, there are optimality guarantees. In particular, the local minimum found by the expansion algorithm is guaranteed to be within a multiplicative factor from the global minimum. This factor is as low as 2 for the Potts model.

In this chapter the effectiveness of expansion and swap algorithms is demonstrated on the energies arising for the problems of image restoration and stereo correspondence. In particular for stereo, the expansion algorithm advanced the state of the art. It significantly surpassed the accuracy of the local correlation-based methods that were common at the time [419]. Almost all of the top-performing stereo correspondence methods nowadays are based on energy minimization.[1]

3.2 Overview of the Swap and Expansion Algorithms

This section is an overview of the swap and expansion algorithms. Section 3.2.1 discusses local optimization in a discrete setting. Section 3.2.2 defines expansion and swap moves. Section 3.2.3 describes the algorithms and lists their basic properties.

---

1. See http://vision.middlebury.edu/stereo/eval/.

3.2.1 Local Minima in Discrete Optimization

Due to the inefficiency of computing the global minimum, many authors have opted for a local minimum. In general, a labeling $\hat{\mathbf{x}}$ is a local minimum of the energy E if

$$E(\hat{\mathbf{x}}) \leq E(\mathbf{x}') \quad \text{for any } \mathbf{x}' \text{ "near to" } \hat{\mathbf{x}}. \tag{3.8}$$

In discrete labeling, the labelings near $\hat{\mathbf{x}}$ are those that lie within a single *move* of $\hat{\mathbf{x}}$. Many local optimization techniques use the so-called *standard* moves, where only one site can change its label at a time (see figure 3.2(b)). For standard moves, (3.8) can be read as follows: if you are at a local minimum with respect to standard moves, then you cannot decrease the energy by changing a single site's label. In fact, this is a very weak condition. As a result, optimization schemes using standard moves frequently generate low-quality solutions. For instance, consider the local minimum with respect to standard moves in figure 3.1(c). Some example methods using standard moves are Iterated Conditional Modes (ICM) [38] and simulated annealing [161] (see chapter 1).

Not surprisingly, in general a local minimum can be arbitrarily far from the optimum. It thus may not convey any of the global image properties that were encoded in the energy function. In such cases it is difficult to determine the cause of an algorithm's failures. When an algorithm gives unsatisfactory results, it may be due either to a poor choice of the energy function or to the fact that the answer is far from the global minimum. There is no obvious way to tell which of these is the problem.[2] Another common issue is that local minimization techniques are naturally sensitive to the initial estimate.

The NP-hardness result [72] of optimizing energy in (3.1) effectively forces computing a local minimum. However, the methods described in this chapter generate a local minimum with respect to very large moves. This approach overcomes many of the problems associated with local minima. The algorithms introduced in this section generate a labeling that is a local minimum of the energy in (3.1) for two types of large moves: expansion and swap. In contrast to the standard moves described above, the swap and expansion moves allow a large number of sites to change their labels simultaneously. This makes the set of labelings within a single move of a locally optimal $\mathbf{x}$ exponentially large, and the condition in (3.8) very demanding. For example, expansion moves are so strong that one is able to prove that any labeling locally optimal with respect to these moves is within a known factor of the global minimum.[3] Figure 3.1 compares local minima for standard moves (c) and for expansion moves (d) obtained from the same initial solution (b). The experiments (see section 3.5)

---

2. In special cases where the global minimum can be rapidly computed, it is possible to separate these issues. For example, [176] points out that the global minimum of a special case of the Ising energy function is not necessarily the desired solution for image restoration; [49, 176] analyze the performance of simulated annealing in cases with a known global minimum.

3. In practice most often the actual solution is much closer to the global minimum than the theoretical bound (see chapter 11).

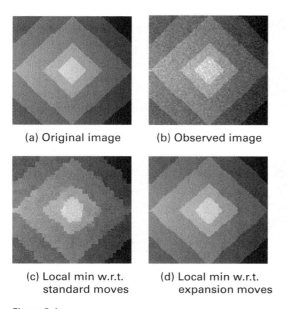

(a) Original image　　　(b) Observed image

(c) Local min w.r.t.　　(d) Local min w.r.t.
　　standard moves　　　　expansion moves

Figure 3.1
Comparison of local minima with respect to standard and large moves in image restoration. The energy (4.1) is used with the quadratic Φ_i penalizing deviations from the observed intensities. (b) Ψ_{ij} is a truncated L_2 metric. Both local minima (c) and (d) were obtained using labeling (b) as an initial solution.

show that for many problems the solutions do not change significantly by varying the initial labelings. In most cases, starting from a constant labeling gives good results.

3.2.2 Definitions of Swap and Expansion Moves

For every pair of labels $\alpha, \beta \in \mathcal{L}$, the swap algorithm has one possible move type, an α-β *swap*. Given $\alpha, \beta \in \mathcal{L}$, a move from a labeling $\mathbf{x}$ to another labeling $\mathbf{x}'$ is called an α-β *swap* if $x_i \neq x_i'$ implies that $x_i, x_i' \in \{\alpha, \beta\}$. This means that the only difference between $\mathbf{x}$ and $\mathbf{x}'$ is that some sites that were labeled α in $\mathbf{x}$ are now labeled β in $\mathbf{x}'$, and some sites that were labeled β in $\mathbf{x}$ are now labeled α in $\mathbf{x}'$.

For each $\alpha \in \mathcal{L}$, the expansion algorithm has one possible move type, an α-expansion. Given a label α, a move from a labeling $\mathbf{x}$ to another labeling $\mathbf{x}'$ is called an α-*expansion* if $x_i \neq x_i'$ implies $x_i' = \alpha$. In other words, an α-expansion move allows any set of sites to change their labels to α. An example of an α-expansion is shown in figure 3.2d.

Recall that ICM and annealing use *standard* moves allowing only one site to change its intensity. An example of a standard move is given in figure 3.2b. Note that a move that assigns a given label α to a single site is both an α-β swap (for β equal to the site's old label) and an α-expansion. As a consequence, a standard move is a special case of both an α-β swap and an α-expansion.

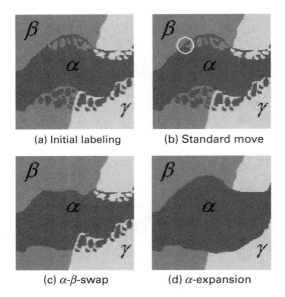

(a) Initial labeling   (b) Standard move

(c) α-β-swap   (d) α-expansion

Figure 3.2
Examples of standard and large moves from a given labeling (a). The number of labels is $|\mathcal{L}| = 3$. A standard
move (b) changes a label of a single site (in the circled area). Strong moves (c and d) allow a large number of sites
to change their labels simultaneously.

3.2.3 Algorithms and Properties

The swap and expansion algorithms find a local minimum when swap or expansion moves
are allowed, respectively. Finding such a local minimum is not a trivial task. Given a labeling
x, there is an exponential number of swap and expansion moves. Therefore, even checking
for a local minimum requires exponential time if performed naïvely. In contrast, checking for
a local minimum when only the standard moves are allowed is linear. A large move space
allows extensive changes to the current solution. This makes the algorithm less prone to
getting stuck in local minima and also results in a faster rate of convergence.

Thus the key step is a method to find the optimal α-β swap or α-expansion from a given
labeling **x**. This step is developed in section 3.3. Once these are available, it is easy to design
variants of the "fastest descent" technique that can efficiently find the corresponding local
minima. The algorithms are summarized in figure 3.3.

The two algorithms are quite similar in their structure. A single execution of steps 3.1
and 3.2 is called an *iteration*, and an execution of steps 2–4 is a *cycle*. In each cycle the
algorithm performs an iteration for every label (expansion algorithm) or for every pair of
labels (swap algorithm), in a certain order that can be fixed or random. A cycle is successful
if a strictly better labeling is found at any iteration. The algorithms stop after the first
unsuccessful cycle since no further improvement is possible. A cycle in the swap algorithm
takes $|\mathcal{L}|^2$ iterations, and a cycle in the expansion algorithm takes $|\mathcal{L}|$ iterations.

```
1. Start with an arbitrary labeling x
2. Set success := 0
3. For each pair of labels {α, β} ⊂ L
     3.1. Find x̂ = arg min E(x') among x' within one α-β swap of x
     3.2. If E(x̂) < E(x), set x := x̂ and success := 1
4. If success = 1 goto 2
5. Return x
```

```
1. Start with an arbitrary labeling x
2. Set success := 0
3. For each label α ∈ L
     3.1. Find x̂ = arg min E(x') among x' within one α-expansion of x
     3.2. If E(x̂) < E(x), set x := x̂ and success := 1
4. If success = 1 goto 2
5. Return x
```

Figure 3.3
The swap algorithm (top) and expansion algorithm (bottom).

These algorithms are guaranteed to terminate in a finite number of cycles. Under a very reasonable assumption that Φ_i and Ψ_{ij} in (3.1) are constants independent of the size of the vertex set $\mathcal{V}$, one can easily prove termination in $O(|\mathcal{V}|)$ cycles [494]. However, in the experiments reported in section 3.5, the algorithms stop after a few cycles, and most of the improvements occur during the first cycle.

Pseudo-Boolean optimization (see chapter 2) based on a graph cut is used to efficiently find $\hat{\mathbf{x}}$ for the key part of each algorithm in step 3.1. At each iteration the corresponding graph has $O(|\mathcal{V}|)$ vertices. The exact number of vertices, the topology of the graph, and its edge weights vary from iteration to iteration. The optimization details of step 3.1 for the expansion and swap algorithms are in section 3.3.

3.3 Finding the Optimal Swap and Expansion Moves

For a given labeling, the number of expansion and swap moves is exponential. The key idea of finding the optimal swap and expansion moves efficiently is to convert the problem of finding an optimal move to binary energy optimization. In [72] the authors formulate the problem as that of finding a minimum cut on a certain graph, describe the corresponding graph construction, and prove that it is correct. Because of the work on pseudo-Boolean optimization [61, 266] (also see chapter 2) here, one just needs to formulate the pseudo-Boolean energy function corresponding to the swap and expansion moves and prove that it is submodular. Once this is shown, the submodular pseudo-Boolean energies can be efficiently minimized, for example, by finding a minimum cut on a certain graph (see chapter 2).

The moves of the expansion and swap algorithms can be encoded as a vector of binary variables $\mathbf{t} = \{t_i, \forall i \in \mathcal{V}\}$. The *transformation* function $T(\mathbf{x}^c, \mathbf{t})$ of a move algorithm takes the current labeling $\mathbf{x}^c$ and a move $\mathbf{t}$ and returns the new labeling $\mathbf{x}^n$ that has been induced by the move.

Recall that an $\alpha\beta$-swap allows a random variable whose current label is α or β to switch it to α or β. The transformation function $T_{\alpha\beta}()$ for an $\alpha\beta$-swap transforms the current label x_i^c of a random variable X_i as

$$x_i^n = T_{\alpha\beta}(x_i^c, t_i) = \begin{cases} x_i^c & \text{if} \quad x_i^c \neq \alpha \text{ and } x_i^c \neq \beta, \\ \alpha & \text{if} \quad x_i^c = \alpha \text{ or } \beta \text{ and } t_i = 0, \\ \beta & \text{if} \quad x_i^c = \alpha \text{ or } \beta \text{ and } t_i = 1. \end{cases} \tag{3.9}$$

Recall that an α-expansion allows a random variable either to retain its current label or switch to α. The transformation function $T_{\alpha}()$ for an α-expansion transforms the current label x_i^c of a random variable X_i as

$$x_i^n = T_{\alpha}(x_i^c, t_i) = \begin{cases} \alpha & \text{if} \quad t_i = 0 \\ x_i^c & \text{if} \quad t_i = 1. \end{cases} \tag{3.10}$$

The energy of a move $\mathbf{t}$ is the energy of the labeling $\mathbf{x}^n$ that the move $\mathbf{t}$ induces, that is, $E_m(\mathbf{t}) = E(T(\mathbf{x}^c, \mathbf{t}))$. The move energy is a pseudo-Boolean function ($E_m : \{0, 1\}^n \to \mathbb{R}$) and will be denoted by $E_m(\mathbf{t})$. At step 3.1 (see figure 3.3) of the expansion and swap move algorithms, the *optimal* move $\mathbf{t}^*$ (the move decreasing the energy of the labeling by the greatest amount) is computed. This is done by minimizing the move energy, that is, $\mathbf{t}^* = \arg\min_{\mathbf{t}} E(T(\mathbf{x}^c, \mathbf{t}))$.

The pseudo-Boolean energy corresponding to a swap move is

$$\begin{aligned} E(T_{\alpha\beta}(\mathbf{x}^c, \mathbf{t})) = {}& \sum_{i \in \mathcal{V}} \Phi_i \left(T_{\alpha\beta}(x_i^c, t_i) \right) \\ & + \sum_{(i,j) \in \mathcal{E}} \Psi_{ij} \left(T_{\alpha\beta}(x_i^c, t_i), T_{\alpha\beta}(x_j^c, t_j) \right), \end{aligned} \tag{3.11}$$

where $\mathbf{x}^c$ is fixed and $\mathbf{t}$ is the unknown variable. The submodularity condition from chapter 2 and the definition in (3.9) imply that the energy function in (3.11) is submodular, and therefore can be optimized with a graph cut if

$$\Psi_{ij}(\alpha, \alpha) + \Psi_{ij}(\beta, \beta) \leq \Psi_{ij}(\beta, \alpha) + \Psi_{ij}(\alpha, \beta), \tag{3.12}$$

as in (3.2).

The pseudo-Boolean energy corresponding to an expansion move is

$$\begin{aligned} E(T_{\alpha}(\mathbf{x}^c, \mathbf{t})) = {}& \sum_{i \in \mathcal{V}} \Phi_i \left(T_{\alpha}(x_i^c, t_i) \right) \\ & + \sum_{(i,j) \in \mathcal{E}} \Psi_{ij} \left(T_{\alpha}(x_i^c, t_i), T_{\alpha}(x_j^c, t_j) \right). \end{aligned} \tag{3.13}$$

The submodularity condition from chapter 2 and the definition in (3.10) imply that the energy function in (3.13) is submodular, and therefore can be optimized with a graph cut if

$$\Psi_{ij}(\alpha, \alpha) + \Psi_{ij}(x_i^c, x_j^c) \leq \Psi_{ij}(x_i^c, \alpha) + \Psi_{ij}(\alpha, x_j^c), \tag{3.14}$$

as in (3.3), assuming that x_i^c can take any value in $\mathcal{L}$.

3.4 Optimality Properties

This section addresses the optimality properties of the expansion algorithm. The bounds obtained in this section are usually much larger than those observed in practice (see chapter 11). Nevertheless, they are of theoretical interest.

3.4.1 The Expansion Algorithm

Assuming a metric Ψ_{ij}, a local minimum when expansion moves are allowed is within a known factor of the global minimum. This factor, which can be as small as 2, will depend on Ψ_{ij}. Specifically, let

$$c = \max_{i,j \in \mathcal{E}} \left(\frac{\max_{\alpha \neq \beta \in \mathcal{L}} \Psi_{ij}(\alpha, \beta)}{\min_{\alpha \neq \beta \in \mathcal{L}} \Psi_{ij}(\alpha, \beta)} \right)$$

be the ratio of the largest nonzero value of Ψ_{ij} to the smallest nonzero value of Ψ_{ij}. Note that c is well defined since $\Psi_{ij}(\alpha, \beta) \neq 0$ for $\alpha \neq \beta$ because it is assumed that Ψ_{ij} is a metric.

Theorem 3.1   *Let $\hat{\mathbf{x}}$ be a local minimum when expansion moves are allowed and $\mathbf{x}^*$ be the globally optimal solution. Then $E(\hat{\mathbf{x}}) \leq 2cE(\mathbf{x}^*)$.*

For the proof of the theorem, see [72]. Even though in practice the results are very close to the global minima, artificial examples can be constructed that come as close as one wishes to the bound in the theorem above (see figure 3.4). Note that [236] develops an algorithm for minimizing E that also has the bound of 2 for the Potts Ψ_{ij}. For a general metric Ψ_{ij}, it has a bound of $O(\log k \log \log k)$ where k is the number of labels. However, the algorithm uses linear programming, which is impractical for a large number of variables.

3.4.2 Approximating a Semi-metric

A local minimum when swap moves are allowed can be arbitrarily far from the global minimum. This is illustrated in figure 3.5. In fact, one can use the expansion algorithm to get an answer within a factor of $2c$ from the optimum of energy (3.1) even when Ψ_{ij} is a semi-metric. Here c is the same as in theorem 3.1. This c is still well defined for a semi-metric. Suppose that Ψ_{ij} is a semi-metric. Let r be any real number in the interval $[m, M]$ where

$$m = \min_{\alpha \neq \beta \in \mathcal{L}} \Psi_{ij}(i, j) \quad \text{and} \quad M = \max_{\alpha \neq \beta \in \mathcal{L}} \Psi_{ij}(i, j).$$

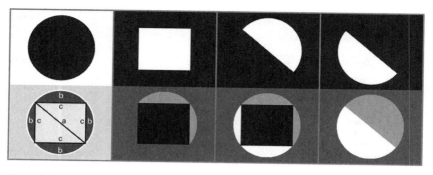

Figure 3.4
Example of an expansion algorithm getting stuck in a local minimum far from the global optimum. Here $\mathcal{L} =$ $\{0, 1, 2, 3\}$. The top row shows the data terms for these labels in consecutive order. White means zero cost and black means an infinitely high data cost. The Potts model is used, with K_{ij} illustrated in the left image of the bottom row. All the costs are infinite except those along the arcs and segments outlined in black and white. The accumulated cost of cutting along these arcs and segments is shown; for example, cutting along the top part of the rectangle costs c in total, and cutting along the diagonal of the rectangle costs a in total. Here $b = \epsilon$ and $2c = a - \epsilon$. The expansion algorithm is initialized with all pixels labeled 0. Expansion proceeds on labels 1 and 2, the results of which are shown in the second picture, bottom row. Expansion on label 3 results in the solution shown in the third picture, bottom row, at which point the algorithm converges to a local minimum with cost $C_{sub} = 4b + 4c$. The optimum is shown in the last picture, bottom row, and its cost is $C_{opt} = 4b + a$. The ratio $\frac{C_{sub}}{C_{opt}} \to 2$ as $\epsilon \to 0$.

	1	2	3
a	0	K	K
b	K	0	K
c	2	2	0

1	2	3
a	b	c

(a) Local min

1	2	3
c	c	c

(b) Global min

(c) Values of Φ_i

Figure 3.5
The image consists of three sites $\mathcal{V} = \{1, 2, 3\}$. There are two pairs of neighbors $\mathcal{E} = \{\{1, 2\}, \{2, 3\}\}$. The set of labels is $\mathcal{L} = \{a, b, c\}$. Φ_i is shown in (c). $\Psi_{ij}(a, b) = \Psi_{ij}(b, c) = \frac{K}{2}$ and $\Psi_{ij}(a, c) = K$, where K is a suitably large value. It is easy to see that the configuration in (a) is a local minimum with the energy of K, while the optimal configuration (b) has energy 4.

Define a new energy based on the Potts model:

$$E_P(\mathbf{x}) = \sum_{i \in \mathcal{V}} \Phi_i(x_i) + \sum_{(i,j) \in \mathcal{E}} r \cdot T(x_i \neq x_j).$$

Theorem 3.2 *If $\hat{\mathbf{x}}$ is a local minimum of E_P under the expansion moves and $\mathbf{x}^*$ is the global minimum of $E(\mathbf{x})$, then $E(\hat{\mathbf{x}}) \leq 2cE(\mathbf{x}^*)$.*

For the proof of the theorem, see [72]. Thus, to find a solution within a fixed factor of the global minimum for a semi-metric Ψ_{ij}, one can take a local minimum $\hat{\mathbf{x}}$ under the expansion moves for E_P as defined above. Note that such an $\hat{\mathbf{x}}$ is not a local minimum of $E(\mathbf{x})$ under expansion moves. In practice, however, the local minimum under swap moves gives empirically better results than using $\hat{\mathbf{x}}$. In fact, the estimate $\hat{\mathbf{x}}$ can be used as a good starting point for the swap algorithm. In this case the swap algorithm will also generate a local minimum whose energy is within a known factor of the global minimum.

3.5 Experimental Results

This section presents experimental results on image restoration and stereo correspondence. For extensive experimental evaluation of the swap and expansion algorithms as energy optimization techniques, see chapter 11. The minimum cut is computed using the max-flow algorithm in [68].

3.5.1 Image Restoration

Image restoration is a classical problem for evaluation of an energy optimization method. The task is to estimate the original image from a noisy one. The labels are all possible intensities. The restored intensity should be close to the observed one, and intensities are expected to vary smoothly everywhere except at object boundaries. Here the unary term is $\Phi_i(x_i) = \min(|x_i - I_i|^2, const)$, where $I_i \in [0, 255]$ is the intensity observed at pixel i. The parameter $const$ is set to 400, and it is used to make the data penalty more robust against outliers.

Figure 3.6 shows an image consisting of several regions with constant intensities after it was corrupted by $N(0, 100)$ noise. Figure 3.6b shows image restoration results for the truncated absolute difference model $\Psi_{ij}(x_i, x_j) = 80 \cdot \min(3, |x_i - x_j|)$, which is discontinuity-preserving. Since it is a metric, the expansion algorithm is used. For comparison, figure 3.6c shows the result for the absolute difference model $\Psi_{ij}(x_i, x_j) = 15 \cdot |x_i - x_j|$, which is not discontinuity-preserving. For the absolute difference model one can find the exact solution using the method in chapter 4. For both models the parameters that minimize the average absolute error from the original image are chosen. The average errors were 0.34 for the truncated model and 1.8 for the absolute difference model, and the running times were 2.4

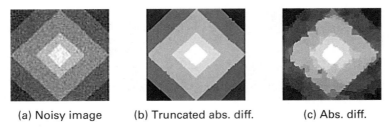

(a) Noisy image   (b) Truncated abs. diff.   (c) Abs. diff.

Figure 3.6
Image restoration. The results in (b and c) are histograms equalized to reveal oversmoothing in (c), which does not happen in (b).

and 5.6 seconds, respectively. The image size is 100×100. This example illustrates a well-known fact [54] about the importance of using discontinuity-preserving Ψ_{ij}. The results in figure 3.6b and c were histogram equalized to reveal oversmoothing in (c), which does not happen in (b). Similar oversmoothing occurs for stereo correspondence (see [494, 42]).

3.5.2 Stereo Correspondence
In stereo correspondence two images are taken at the same time from different viewpoints. For most pixels in the first image there is a corresponding pixel in the second image that is a projection along the line of sight of the same real-world scene element. The difference in the coordinates of the corresponding points is called the disparity, which one can assume to be one-dimensional because of image rectification [182]. The labels are the set of discretized disparities, and the task is to estimate the disparity label for each pixel in the first image.[4] Note that here $\mathcal{V}$ contains the pixels of the first image.

The disparity varies smoothly everywhere except at object boundaries, and corresponding points are expected to have similar intensities. Therefore one could set $\Phi_i(l) = (I_i - I'_{i+l})^2$, where I and I' are the first and second images, respectively, and $i + l$ is pixel i shifted by disparity l in I'. Instead, the sampling-insensitive $\Phi_i(l)$ from [44] is used, which is a better model and is just slightly more complex.

Figure 3.7 shows results from a real stereo pair with known ground truth, provided by Dr. Y. Ohta and Dr. Y. Nakamura from the University of Tsukuba (see also [419]). The left image is in figure 3.7a, and the ground truth is in 3.7b. The label set is $\{0, 1, \ldots, 14\}$, and $\Psi_{ij}(x_i, x_j) = K_{ij} \cdot T(x_i \neq x_j)$. K_{ij} is inversely proportional to the gradient strength between pixels i and j. Specifically, $K_{ij} = 40$ if $|I_p - I_q| \leq 5$ and $K_{i,j} = 20$ otherwise.

The results in figure 3.7c and d are clearly superior compared with annealing and normalized correlation in figure 3.7e and f. Note that results such as in figure 3.7e and f used to be close to the state of the art before the expansion and swap algorithms were developed.

---

4. For a symmetric approach to stereo based on expansion moves, see [264].

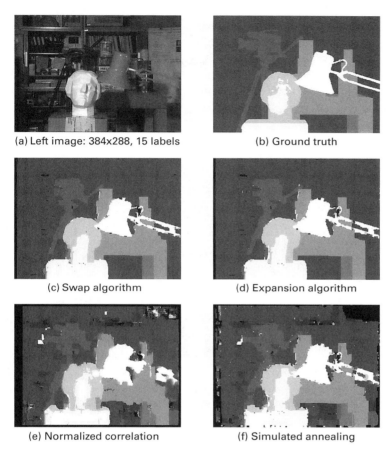

(a) Left image: 384x288, 15 labels   (b) Ground truth

(c) Swap algorithm   (d) Expansion algorithm

(e) Normalized correlation   (f) Simulated annealing

Figure 3.7
Real imagery with ground truth.

For normalized correlation, parameters that give the best statistics were chosen. To give it a good starting point, simulated annealing was initialized with the correlation results. In contrast, swap and expansion algorithms are not sensitive to the initialization. Averaging over 100 random initializations, the results differed by less than 1 percent of pixels.

Figure 3.8 summarizes the errors, running times, and energies. Expansion and swap algorithms are clearly superior to the other two methods. Compared with one another, they perform similarly. The observed difference in errors is less than 1%. At each cycle the label order is chosen randomly. Another run of the algorithm might give slightly different results, and on average about 1% of pixels change their labels between runs. The expansion algorithm converges 1.4 times faster than the swap algorithm, on average.

algorithm	all err.	err. > ± 1	time	energy
exp. (1iter.)	7.9	2.7	0.98	254700
exp. (conv.)	7.2	2.1	6.9	253700
swap (conv.)	7.0	2.0	11.1	251990
sim. anneal.	20.3	5.0	600	442000
norm. corr.	24.7	10.0	0.89	N/A

Figure 3.8
Comparison of Accuracy (in %), Running Time (in sec), and Energy

3.6 Conclusion

Since their invention, swap and and expansion algorithms have proved useful in a wide variety of applications. Compared with the expansion algorithm, the swap algorithm, can be applied to a wider set of energy functions, since (3.2) is less restrictive. However, the expansion algorithm usually performs better in practice [464] (see also chapter 11), in terms of the running time and of accuracy, and therefore it is more popular. Both algorithms have been used for such diverse applications as image restoration [70], stereo correspondence [70, 45], motion segmentation [45, 521, 532, 366], texture synthesis [287], motion magnification [317], object recognition and segmentation [525, 198] (see also chapter 25), digital photomontage [7], digital tapestry [404], image generation [349], computational photography [304], image completion [183], and digital panoramas [6].

4 Optimizing Multilabel MRFs with Convex and Truncated Convex Priors

Hiroshi Ishikawa and Olga Veksler

Usually, submodular pseudo-Boolean energies as discussed in chapters 1 and 2 arise from optimizing binary (i.e., two-label) MRFs. Interestingly, it is possible to encode a multilabel MRF with a pseudo-Boolean energy. The resulting energy is submodular and, therefore, can be optimized exactly when $\Psi_{ij}(x_i, x_j)$ terms are convex. This chapter addresses that case. Though convex $\Psi_{ij}(x_i, x_j)$ are useful for problems with a small label set $\mathcal{L}$, they are less suitable as the label set grows larger, due to the nondiscontinuity-preserving nature of convex $\Psi_{ij}(x_i, x_j)$. To ensure discontinuity preservation, MRFs with truncated convex $\Psi_{ij}(x_i, x_j)$ are commonly used in computer vision. Interestingly, the construction presented in this chapter for MRFs with convex $\Psi_{ij}(x_i, x_j)$ is also useful for approximately optimizing MRFs with truncated convex $\Psi_{ij}(x_i, x_j)$. To demonstrate the effectiveness of the proposed methods, experimental evaluations of image restoration, image inpainting, and stereo correspondence are presented.

4.1 Introduction

It is rarely possible to solve exactly a large combinatorial optimization problem. Yet, there are exceptional circumstances where one can use a known method to find a global optimum. For instance, when the state of the problem is described as a string of linearly ordered local states, as in HMM, dynamic programming can be used (see chapter 1). Another case that can be solved exactly is a certain binary MRF (see chapter 2). The present chapter points out yet another such instance and describes a method that can be used: a method to solve a first-order MRF with $\Psi_{ij}(x_i, x_j)$ that is convex in terms of a linearly ordered label set. This method was originally presented in [211].

As in chapter 1, the following energy function is minimized:

$$E(\mathbf{x}) = \sum_{i \in \mathcal{V}} \Phi_i(x_i) + \sum_{(i,j) \in \mathcal{E}} \Psi_{ij}(x_i, x_j), \tag{4.1}$$

where $\mathcal{V}$ and $\mathcal{E}$ are the set of sites and edges for the MRF, x_i is the label of site i, and $\Phi_i(x_i)$ are the unary terms and $\Psi_{ij}(x_i, x_j)$ are the binary terms.

Chapter 3 addresses approximation algorithms for a relatively general multilabel case. The present chapter first addresses the case of the convex term Ψ_{ij}, which can be solved exactly. Two common examples are the absolute linear $\Psi_{ij}(x_i, x_j) = w_{ij} \cdot |x_i - x_j|$ and the quadratic $\Psi_{ij}(x_i, x_j) = w_{ij} \cdot (x_i - x_j)^2$. These are convex functions of the absolute difference $|x_i - x_j|$ of the labels. As in chapter 3, there are no restrictions on the unary terms $\Phi_i(x_i)$.

A function $f(x)$ is said to be convex if

$$f(tx + (1-t)y) \leq tf(x) + (1-t)f(y) \quad (0 \leq \forall t \leq 1). \tag{4.2}$$

Consider figure 4.1a. It is easy to see that for singly connected graphs, Ψ_{ij}, which is a strictly convex function of $|x_i - x_j|$, encourages smaller changes of labels at more edges. To encourage fewer but larger changes, a truncated concave Ψ_{ij} (see chapter 3) can be used. In between, the absolute linear potential is neutral with respect to this choice.

For general graphs, the biases observed in a singly connected case are still present, though they are less straightforward due to the constraints from more general graph topology. For example, consider a 2D labeling in figure 4.1b. Assume that the absolute linear Ψ_{ij} is used. A site that is outlined with a thick line strongly prefers the label printed inside it (notice that these labels are the same for all three labelings). A site that is outlined with a thin line considers all labels equally likely. The three labelings in figure 4.1b are ordered by their total cost (from smaller to larger) under the absolute linear Ψ_{ij}. Notice that the absolute linear Ψ_{ij} is not neutral now with respect to whether it prefers a few large changes or many small ones. The left (most preferred) labeling has fewer but larger jumps compared with the middle labeling, which has more but smaller jumps. The rightmost labeling has fewer jumps than the middle but a higher cost.

Assume now the unary terms Φ_i are such that the labeling on the right is preferred. Depending on the relative weight of the unary and binary terms, the middle labeling may be

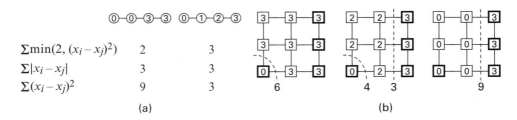

	⓪–⓪–③–③	⓪–①–②–③
$\sum \min(2, (x_i - x_j)^2)$	2	3
$\sum |x_i - x_j|$	3	3
$\sum (x_i - x_j)^2$	9	3

(a)   (b)

Figure 4.1
(a) At the top are two configurations, each with four nodes. Below is the sum of truncated convex, linear, and convex potentials. The truncated convex potential favors the left configuration; the convex potential, the right one. The linear potential gives the same energy for both. (b) 2D example with nine nodes; the cut is shown as a dashed line. Assume that the linear Ψ_{ij} is used and the data term fixes the labels at thick squares. This Ψ_{ij} favors the labeling on the left the most, then the middle one, and disfavors the right one. When the data term indicates the labeling on the right but the result is the middle, it is "oversmoothing." When the middle labeling is indicated by the data term but the left one is the result, it is "undersmoothing."

the optimum one, since it has a lower cost under binary terms. In this case oversmoothing will occur. Similarly, if the unary terms indicate the labeling in the middle but the binary terms Ψ_{ij} have more weight, the labeling on the left may be the optimum one, resulting in the "undersmoothed" result.

Recall that labels correspond to some property to be estimated at each site. In vision, while undersmoothing can be an issue, for most problems oversmoothing is more likely to occur, since the property to be estimated changes sharply at the boundaries of objects. Thus, to counter this bias, a potential that actively encourages concentration of changes is usually preferred. Such a Ψ_{ij} limits the growth of the value as a function of label difference. In particular, convex or linear functions can be truncated to give $\Psi_{ij}(x_i, x_j) = w_{ij} \cdot \min\{T, |x_i - x_j|\}$ and $\Psi_{ij}(x_i, x_j) = w_{ij} \cdot \min\{T, (x_i - x_j)^2\}$. These energies are commonly used in vision; for example, the energy evaluation study in chapter 11 includes them. In general, any convex binary potential can be truncated for the sake of robustness in the presence of discontinuities.

Unfortunately, the energy in (4.1) is NP-hard to optimize with truncated convex Ψ_{ij} [72]. The swap and expansion algorithms from chapter 3 can be used for optimization, but according to the energy evaluation study in chapter 11, they do not perform very well for the truncated quadratic.

Interestingly, the exact method for convex Ψ_{ij} that is developed here can also be used as a base for a move-making algorithm (see chapter 3) for approximate optimization of truncated convex Ψ_{ij}. These moves were originally developed in [495], and they are called *range moves*. Range moves are able to give a pixel a choice of several labels, and significantly outperform the swap and expansion algorithms for the truncated convex Ψ_{ij}.

4.2 Optimizing for Convex $\Psi_{ij}(i, j)$

The rest of the chapter assumes that the labels can be represented as consecutive integers in the range $\{0, 1, \ldots k\}$. Integer labels rule out direct use of the methods in this chapter for problems such as motion estimation, since in motion, labels are 2D. However, there are componentwise optimization approaches to motion, that is, fixing one component of a motion vector and letting the other one vary [406].

This chapter also assumes that $\Psi_{ij}(l_1, l_2)$ is a function of the label difference $|l_1 - l_2|$. First a definition of a convex function in a discrete setting is given. A binary term $\Psi_{ij}(l_1, l_2) = w_{ij} \cdot g(l_1 - l_2)$ is said to be convex if and only if for any integer y, $g(y+1) - 2g(y) + g(y-1) \geq 0$. It is assumed that $g(y)$ is symmetric,[1] otherwise it can be replaced with $g(y) + g(-y)/2$ without changing the optimal labeling. Convex Ψ_{ij} include the absolute and squared difference functions as a special case. Note that [421] extends the notion of convexity to a more general one.

---

1. A function is symmetric if $g(y) = g(-y)$.

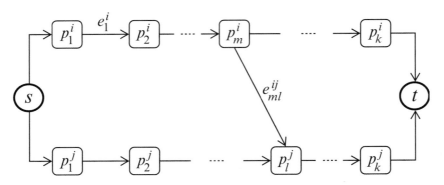

Figure 4.2
Part of the graph construction for sites $i, j \in \mathcal{E}$.

This chapter follows a simplified version of the original approach described in [211], which is based on computing a minimum cut in a certain graph.

We are now ready to describe the graph construction. Before proceeding further, the reader who is unfamiliar with graph cut is encouraged to read chapter 2. Part of the construction is illustrated in figure 4.2. There are two special nodes in the graph, the source s and the sink t. For each $x_i \in \mathcal{V}$, a set of nodes $p_0^i, p_1^i, \ldots, p_{k+1}^i$ is created. Node p_0^i is identified with the source s, and p_{k+1}^i is identified with the sink t. Node p_m^i is connected to node p_{m+1}^i with a directed edge e_m^i for $m = 0, 1, \ldots, k$. In addition, for $m = 0, 1, \ldots, k$, node p_{m+1}^i is connected to p_m^i with a directed edge of infinite weight. This ensures that for each i, only one of the edges e_m^i, $m = 0, 1, \ldots$ will be in the minimum cut. If an edge e_m^i is cut, then variable x_i is assigned label m. Thus a cut C of finite cost corresponds to a unique labeling $\mathbf{x}^C$.

Furthermore, for any $(i, j) \in \mathcal{E}$, an edge e_{ml}^{ij} that connects p_m^i to p_l^j is created for $m = 0, \ldots, k+1$ and $l = 0, \ldots, k+1$. For reasons explained later, edge weights are set to

$$w(e_{ml}^{ij}) = \frac{w_{ij}}{2}[g(m - l + 1) - 2g(m - l) + g(m - l - 1)]. \tag{4.3}$$

The weight in (4.3) is nonnegative because $g(y)$ is convex. This is crucial, since min-cut algorithms require nonnegative edge weights.

Let C be a finite cost cut. Let $(i, j) \in \mathcal{E}$. If edges e_m^i and e_l^j are in C, then all the edges in the set S_{ij}^{ml}, defined below, also have to be in C.

$$S_{ij}^{ml} = \{e_{qr}^{ij} | 0 \le q \le m, l+1 \le r \le k+1\} \cup \{e_{qr}^{ij} | m+1 \le q \le k+1, 0 \le r \le l\}.$$

When summing over S_{ij}^{ml}, most weights cancel out, and one gets

$$\sum_{e \in S_{ij}^{ml}} w(e) = w_{ij}[g(m - l) + g(k + 2) + h(m) + h(l)],$$

where $h(m) = -\frac{1}{2}[g(k+1-m) + g(m+1)]$. Recall that the cut C corresponds to a labeling $\mathbf{x}^C$. Except for some extra terms, the sum above is almost exactly $\Psi_{ij}(m, l) = \Psi_{ij}(x_i^C, x_j^C) = w_{ij} \cdot g(m-l)$. The term $g(k+2)$ can be ignored since it is a constant and does not change the minimum cut, just its cost. Terms $h(m)$ and $h(l)$ can be subtracted from the costs of edges e_m^i and e_l^j. Therefore one sets

$$w(e_m^i) = \Phi_i(m) - \sum_{j \in \mathcal{E}_i} w_{ij} \cdot h(m),$$

where $\mathcal{E}_i$ is the set of neighbors of site i. Under this assignment of edge weights, the cost of any finite cut C is exactly $E(\mathbf{x}^C)$ plus a constant. Therefore the minimum cut gives the optimal labeling.

For the absolute linear function Ψ_{ij} this construction leads to a graph with $O(|\mathcal{V}| \cdot |\mathcal{L}|)$. ($|S|$ is the size of set S) vertices and edges, assuming a 4-connected grid. This is because edges e_{ml}^{ij} have zero weight unless $m = l$. For more general Ψ_{ij}, for example, the squared difference, the number of vertices is still $O(|\mathcal{V}| \cdot |\mathcal{L}|)$, but the number of edges is $O(|\mathcal{V}| \cdot |\mathcal{L}|^2)$.

Note that [262] develops an algorithm for minimizing energy with convex Ψ_{ij} that is more memory- and time-efficient. However, it can be used only when the Φ_i's are convex.

4.3 Optimizing for Truncated Convex $\Psi_{ij}(x_i, x_j)$

This section describes *range moves*, an approximation approach for the case when Ψ_{ij} is a truncated convex function. It is assumed, again, that $\Psi_{ij}(x_i, x_j)$ depends only on the label difference $x_i - x_j$. A binary term Ψ_{ij} is defined to be truncated convex if there exists a symmetric function $g(y)$ such that $g(y+1) - 2g(y) + g(y-1) \geq 0$ and

$$\Psi_{ij}(l_1, l_2) = w_{ij} \cdot \min\{g(l_1 - l_2), T\}. \tag{4.4}$$

In this section it is assumed that Ψ_{ij} in (4.1) is defined by (4.4).

As mentioned in section 4.1, swap and expansion moves do not perform as well with truncated convex Ψ_{ij} as with the Potts model. The reason is that these moves are essentially binary, giving each site a choice of two labels to switch to. For the Potts model the optimal labeling is expected to be piecewise constant. Thus there are large groups of sites that prefer the same label, and binary moves perform well. For the truncated convex model, there may be no large group of sites that prefer the same label, since the optimal labeling is expected to be piecewise smooth. For example, in figure 4.3 there is no large group of sites that prefer exactly the same label. There are large groups of sites that prefer similar labels, though; one of them is outlined in dark gray (red) in figure 4.3. Thus, to get a better approximation, moves that allow each site a choice of several labels are needed. There is a theorem in [495] that supports this intuition.

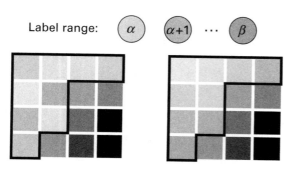

Figure 4.3
Illustrating range moves. Left: initial labeling. Right: range move from labeling on the left. Allowed range of labels $\{\alpha, \alpha+1, \ldots \beta\}$ is on top. Sites participating in the move are outlined in dark gray (red).

4.3.1 α-β Range Moves

Recall that the label set is $\mathcal{L} = \{0, 1, \ldots, k\}$. Let $\mathcal{L}_{\alpha\beta} = \{\alpha, \alpha+1, \ldots, \beta\}$, where $\alpha < \beta \in \mathcal{L}$. Given a labeling $\mathbf{x}$, $\mathbf{x}'$ is an α-β *range* move from $\mathbf{x}$ if $x_i \neq x_i' \Rightarrow \{x_i, x_i'\} \subset \mathcal{L}_{\alpha\beta}$. The set of all α-β range moves from $\mathbf{x}$ is denoted as $M^{\alpha\beta}(\mathbf{x}) = \{\mathbf{x}'|x_i' \neq x_i \Rightarrow x_i', x_i \in \mathcal{L}_{\alpha\beta}\}$.

One can view α-β range moves as a generalization of α-β swap moves. An α-β swap move reassigns labels α, β among sites that are currently labeled α and β. An α-β range move reassigns the labels in the range $\{\alpha, \alpha+1, .., \beta\}$ among the sites that currently have labels in the range $\{\alpha, \alpha+1, .., \beta\}$. An illustration of an α-β range move is in figure 4.3.

Of course, if one knew how to find the best α-β range move for $\alpha = 0$ and $\beta = k$, one would find a global optimum, which is impossible because the problem is, in general, NP-hard. However, it is possible to find the best α-β range move if $|\alpha - \beta| \leq T$.

4.3.2 α-β Range Moves for $|\alpha - \beta| \leq T$

For simplicity, it is assumed here that $|\alpha - \beta| = T$. Extending to the case $|\alpha - \beta| < T$ is trivial. Suppose that a labeling $\mathbf{x}$ is given, and one wishes to find the optimal α-β range move, where $|\alpha - \beta| = T$. The graph construction is similar to that in section 4.2. Let $\mathcal{T} = \{i | \alpha \leq x_i \leq \beta\}$. Notice that the truncated convex terms Ψ_{ij} become convex when $i, j \in \mathcal{T}$, since for any $i, j \in \mathcal{T}$, $\Psi_{ij}(x_i, x_j) = w_{ij}g(x_i - x_j) \leq w_{ij} \cdot T$.

Label set $\mathcal{L}_{\alpha\beta}$ is identified with label set $\{0, 1, \ldots, T\}$ and the construction in section 4.2 is employed, but only on the sites in the subset $\mathcal{T}$ and with a correction for the boundary of $\mathcal{T}$.

Essentially, the problem is that the construction in section 4.2 does not consider the effect of terms Ψ_{ij} on the boundary of $\mathcal{T}$, that is, those Ψ_{ij} for which $|\{p, q\} \cap \mathcal{T}| = 1$. This boundary problem is easy to fix. For each site $i \in \mathcal{T}$, if there is a neighboring site $j \notin \mathcal{T}$, an additional cost $\Psi_{ij}(m, x_j)$ is added to the weight of edge e_m^i, for all $m = 0, 1, \ldots, k$. Recall that the label set $\{\alpha, \alpha+1, \ldots \beta\}$ is identified with the label set $\{0, 1, \ldots, T\}$. Therefore $\Psi_{ij}(m, x_j) = \Psi_{ij}(m+\alpha, x_j)$. This additional weight to edges e_m^i makes sure that the terms

Ψ_{ij} on the boundary of $\mathcal{T}$ are accounted for. This corrected construction will find an optimal α-β range move (see [495] for a precise proof).

Just as with an α-β swap, the algorithm starts at some labeling $\mathbf{x}$. Then it iterates over a set of label ranges $\{\alpha, .., \beta\}$ with $|\alpha - \beta| = T$, finding the best α-β range move $\mathbf{x}'$ and switching the current labeling to $\mathbf{x}'$.

4.3.3 α-β Generalized Range Moves

It is possible to slightly generalize the construction in the previous section as follows. As previously, let $|\alpha - \beta| = T$ (the case of $|\alpha - \beta| < T$ is basically identical) and, as before, let $\mathcal{T} = \{i | \alpha \leq x_i \leq \beta\}$. Let

$$\mathcal{L}_{\alpha\beta t} = \{\alpha - t, \alpha - t + 1, \ldots, \beta + t - 1, \beta + t\} \cap \mathcal{L},$$

that is, $\mathcal{L}_{\alpha\beta t}$ extends the range of $\mathcal{L}_{\alpha\beta}$ by t in each direction, making sure that the resulting range is still a valid range of labels in $\mathcal{L}$. Let

$$M^{\alpha\beta t}(\mathbf{x}) = \{\mathbf{x}' | x_i' \neq x_i \Rightarrow x_i \in \mathcal{L}_{\alpha\beta}, x_i' \in \mathcal{L}_{\alpha\beta t}\}.$$

That is, $M^{\alpha\beta t}(\mathbf{x})$ is a set of moves that change pixel labels from $\mathcal{L}_{\alpha\beta}$ to labels in $\mathcal{L}_{\alpha\beta t}$. Notice that $M^{\alpha\beta}(\mathbf{x}) \subset M^{\alpha\beta t}(\mathbf{x})$. It is actually not possible to find the optimal move in $M^{\alpha\beta t}(\mathbf{x})$, but one can find $\hat{\mathbf{x}} \in M^{\alpha\beta t}(\mathbf{x})$ s.t. $E(\hat{\mathbf{x}}) \leq E(\mathbf{x}^*)$, where $\mathbf{x}^*$ is the optimal move in $M^{\alpha\beta}(\mathbf{x})$. Thus labeling $\hat{\mathbf{x}}$ is not worse, and can be significantly better, than the optimal move $\mathbf{x}^*$ in $M^{\alpha\beta}(\mathbf{x})$.

Almost the same construction as in section 4.3.2 is used. A graph for pixels in $\mathcal{T} = \{i | \alpha \leq x_i \leq \beta\}$ is constructed. However, the label range is now $\mathcal{L}_{\alpha\beta t}$ and, as before, it is identified with label set $\{0, 1, \ldots, |\mathcal{L}_{\alpha\beta t}| - 1\}$. The rest is identical to that in section 4.3.2.

Suppose $\hat{\mathbf{x}}$ is the optimum labeling found by the construction above. This construction may overestimate, but not underestimate, the actual energy of $\hat{\mathbf{x}}$. Also, its (possibly over-estimated) energy is not higher than the energy of $\mathbf{x}^*$, the optimal range move in $M^{\alpha\beta}(\mathbf{x})$, since $M^{\alpha\beta}(\mathbf{x}) \subset M^{\alpha\beta t}(\mathbf{x})$. Thus $E(\hat{\mathbf{x}}) \leq E(\mathbf{x}^*)$. See [495] for a precise proof.

In practice it is enough to set t to a small constant, because the larger the value of t, the more the graph construction overestimates the energy, and it is less likely that the labels at the ends of the range will be assigned. Using small t saves computational time, especially for the truncated quadratic model, since the size of the graph is quadratic in the number of labels.

4.4 Experimental Results

The generalized range moves (section 4.3.3) were used for all the experiments presented in this section, with $t = 3$. For max-flow computation, the algorithm in [68] was used. The performance is evaluated on image restoration, image inpainting, and stereo correspondence.

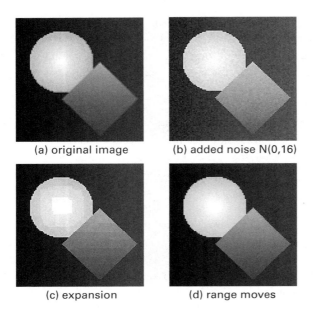

| (a) original image | (b) added noise N(0,16) |

| (c) expansion | (d) range moves |

Figure 4.4
Comparison of optimization algorithms applied to image restoration. Note the stripey artifacts in (c) that are absent in (d).

4.4.1 Image Restoration

In image restoration the task is to reconstruct the original image from a noisy one. $\mathcal{V}$ is the set of all pixels and $\mathcal{L} = \{0, 1, \ldots, 255\}$. The unary and binary terms were $\Phi_i(x_i) = (I_i - x_i)^2$, where I_i is the intensity of pixel i in the observed image, and $\Psi_{ij}(x_i, x_j) = 8 \cdot \min\{(x_i - x_j)^2, 50\}$, respectively.

Figure 4.4a shows an artificial image with smoothly varying intensities inside the circle, square, and background. Figure 4.4b shows the image in (a) corrupted by $N(0, 16)$ noise. Figures 4.4c and Figures 4.4d show the result of the expansion and range moves algorithms, respectively. The results of the swap algorithm are visually similar to those of the expansion algorithm and are omitted here. The energies of the ground truth, expansion algorithm, and range moves are, respectively: 4.1×10^5, 4.5×10^5, and 3.8×10^5. Notice that the range moves algorithm not only produces an answer with a significantly lower energy, but also gives the answer that looks smoother. The expansion algorithm tends to assign the same label to a subset of pixels that is too large, and the resulting answer looks piecewise constant as opposed to piecewise smooth. This is because the expansion moves algorithm seek to change a large subset of pixels to the *same* label, as opposed to the range moves algorithm, which can change a subset of pixels to a smooth range of labels. Range moves results are also much closer to the ground truth. The absolute average error (compared with the ground truth in figure 4.4a) for range moves is 0.82, for the swap algorithm it is 1.35,

	Tsukuba	Venus	Teddy	Cones
Range moves	1758	2671	6058	7648
Swap	1805	2702	6099	7706
Expansion	1765	2690	6124	7742

Figure 4.5
Energies on the Middlebury database. All numbers were divided by 10^3

and for the expansion algorithm it is 1.38. Range moves take about twice as long to run as the expansion algorithm on this example. Running times were approximately 80 and 40 seconds, respectively.

4.4.2 Image Inpainting

Image inpainting is similar to image restoration, except that some pixels have been occluded and therefore have no preference for any label; that is, for an occluded pixel i, $\Phi_i(l) = 0$ for all $l \in \mathcal{L}$. Here, an example from chapter 11 was used. The energy terms are $\Psi_{ij}(x_i, x_j) = 25 \cdot \min\{(x_i - x_j)^2, 200\}$. The expansion algorithm gives a labeling with energy 1.61×10^7, the labeling from the swap algorithm has energy 1.64×10^7, and for range moves, the energy is 1.53×10^7, which is significantly lower. The energies that swap and expansion algorithms have in this implementation are slightly different from those in chapter 11, probably because the iteration over labels is performed in random order, and different runs of the swap and expansion algorithms will give slightly different results. The TRW-S algorithm gives better results than range moves (see chapter 11). The optimal energy with TRW-S is 1.5100×10^7. It is worth noting that for stereo, graph cut performs better than TRW-S when longer-range interactions are present see [260].

4.4.3 Stereo Correspondence

This section presents results on stereo correspondence for the Middlebury database images [419].[2] Here $\mathcal{V}$ is the set of all pixels in the left image and $\mathcal{L}$ is the set of all possible disparities. The disparities are discretized at subpixel precision, in quarter of a pixel steps. That is, if $|x_i - x_j| = 1$, then the disparities of pixels i and j differ by 0.25 pixel. Let d_l stand for the actual disparity corresponding to the integer label l—for example, label 2 corresponds to disparity 0.5. The data costs are $\Phi_i(l) = |I_L(i) - [I_R(i - \overline{d_l}) \cdot (d_l - \underline{d_l}) + I_R(p - \underline{d_l})(\overline{d_l} - d_l)]|$, where $\underline{x}$ stands for rounding down, $\overline{x}$ stands for rounding up, and $i - d$ stands for the pixel that has the coordinates of pixel i shifted to the left by d. The truncated quadratic $\Psi_{ij}(x_i, x_j) = 10 \cdot \min\{(x_i - x_j)^2, 16\}$ is used.

Figure 4.5 compares the energies obtained with range moves to those obtained with the swap and expansion algorithms. The accuracy of the labelings is summarized in figure 4.6.

2. The images were obtained from www.middlebury.edu/stereo.

	Tsukuba	Venus	Teddy	Cones
Range moves	6.7	3.25	15.1	6.79
Swap	7.47	4.04	15.8	7.64
Expansion	7.14	4.19	16.0	7.81

Figure 4.6
Accuracy on the Middlebury database

(a) expansion algorithm   (b) range moves

Figure 4.7
Zooming in on the details of expansion and large moves—see text.

Each number in figure 4.6 gives the percentage of pixels away from ground truth by more than 0.5 pixel. *Tsukuba, Venus, Teddy,* and *Cones* are four different scenes in the Middlebury database. The range moves algorithm performs better not only in terms of energy but also in terms of ground truth. The accuracy improvement is slight but consistent across all scenes.

Figure 4.7 shows zoomed detail for the *Cones* sequence. Range moves produce smoother results compared with the expansion algorithm.

4.5 Further Developments

Since the original work [211] on optimization with convex Ψ_{ij}, many extensions have been developed. In [421, 116] the notion of convexity is extended to a more general one of submodularity with respect to the order of labels. In particular, Ψ_{ij} does not have to be symmetric, which is useful for some applications [322]. In [420] it is shown that if there exists an ordering for a set of labels that makes a given energy submodular, it can be found in a polynomial time. The idea of encoding multiple labels by binary ones also has been examined further. In [384] the space of possible encodings of multilabel variables by two or more binary variables is examined in general, including the higher-order cases (i.e., when terms that depend on more than two pixels are allowed in the energy).

Other extensions improve the time and memory requirements. In [262] it is shown how to reduce memory, which in practice also leads to a reduction in running time. The approach is based on computing several minimum cuts on smaller graphs. The limitation is that the Φ_i terms are also required to being convex. In [85, 117] similar ideas on improving computational time are presented. Again, Φ_i is restricted to being convex. The approach in [82] improves the time and memory requirement without restriction to convex Φ_i. However, there are no optimality guarantees. The approach is similar in spirit to the range moves, without requiring the label range to be consecutive. In [373, 547] a spatially continuous formulation of the energy function in section 4.2 is proposed. Its benefits are reduction of metrication errors and improved time and memory efficiency.

The underlying idea of the range move algorithm is to design multilabel moves (as opposed to binary moves) in order to improve optimization. There are several related works that explore this idea. In [277] it is shown how to modify the range moves algorithm to achieve a multiplicative bound for approximation. The algorithm can be considered a generalization of the expansion algorithm, that is, expansion on a range of labels as opposed to expansion on a single label (as in the original expansion algorithm). In [496] various generalizations of the range move algorithm are considered, including moves that can be considered as generalizations of the expansion algorithm. The authors of [322] develop multilabel moves for a very specific energy function with strong ordering constraints on labels. In [173] approximation algorithms are developed that are based on multilabel moves for general binary terms Ψ_{ij}, not just truncated convex ones.

5 Loopy Belief Propagation, Mean Field Theory, and Bethe Approximations

Alan Yuille

This chapter describes methods for estimating the marginals and maximum a posteriori (MAP) estimates of *probability distributions defined over graphs* by approximate methods including mean field theory (MFT), variational methods, and belief propagation. These methods typically formulate this problem in terms of minimizing a *free energy function* of *pseudo marginals*. They differ by the design of the free energy and the choice of algorithm to minimize it. These algorithms can often be interpreted in terms of *message passing*. In many cases the free energy has a *dual formulation* and the algorithms are defined over the *dual variables* (e.g., the messages in belief propagation). The quality of performance depends on the types of free energies used—specifically, how well they approximate the *log partition function* of the probability distribution—and whether there are suitable algorithms for finding their minima. Section 5.1 introduces two types of Markov field models that are often used in computer vision. I proceed to define MFT/variational methods in section 5.2; their free energies are lower bounds of the log partition function, and describe how inference can be done by expectation maximization, steepest descent, or discrete iterative algorithms. Section 5.3 describes message-passing algorithms, such as belief propagation and its generalizations, which can be related to free energy functions (and dual variables). Finally, in section 5.4 I describe how these methods relate to Markov Chain Monte Carlo (MCMC) approaches, which gives a different way to think of these methods and can lead to novel algorithms.

5.1 Two Models

Two important probabilistic vision models are presented that will be used to motivate the algorithms described in the rest of the section.

The first type of model is formulated as a standard Markov Random Field (MRF) with input $\mathbf{z}$ and output $\mathbf{x}$. We will describe two vision applications for this model. The first application is image labeling where $\mathbf{z} = \{z_i : i \in \mathcal{D}\}$ specifies the intensity values $z_i \in \{0, 255\}$ on the image lattice $\mathcal{D}$, and $\mathbf{x} = \{x_i : i \in \mathcal{D}\}$ is a set of image labels $x_i \in \mathcal{L}$; see figure 5.1. The nature of the labels will depend on the problem. For edge detection, $|\mathcal{L}| = 2$

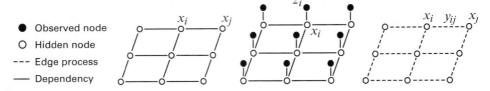

Figure 5.1
Graphs for different MRFs. Conventions (far left), basic MRF graph (middle left), MRF graph with inputs z_i (middle right), and graph with line processes y_{ij} (far right).

and the labels l_1, l_2 will correspond to "edge" and "non-edge." For labeling the MSRC data set [437], $|\mathcal{L}| = 23$ and the labels $l_1, \ldots, l_{23}$ include "sky," "grass," and so on. A second application is binocular stereo (see figure 5.2, where the input is the input images to the left and right cameras, $\mathbf{z} = (\mathbf{z}^L, \mathbf{z}^R)$, and the output is a set of disparities $\mathbf{x}$ that specify the relative displacements between corresponding pixels in the two images and hence determine the depth (see figure 5.2 and also chapter 23).

We can model these two applications by a posterior probability distribution $P(\mathbf{x} \mid \mathbf{z})$, a conditional random field [288]. This distribution is defined on a graph $\mathcal{G} = (\mathcal{V}, \mathcal{E})$ where the set of nodes $\mathcal{V}$ is the set of image pixels $\mathcal{D}$ and the edges $\mathcal{E}$ are between neighboring pixels (see figure 5.1). The $\mathbf{x} = \{x_i : i \in \mathcal{V}\}$ are random variables specified at each node of the graph. $P(\mathbf{x} \mid \mathbf{z})$ is a Gibbs distribution specified by an energy function $E(\mathbf{x}, \mathbf{z})$ that contains unary potentials $U(\mathbf{x}, \mathbf{z}) = \sum_{i \in \mathcal{V}} \phi(x_i, \mathbf{z})$ and pairwise potentials $V(\mathbf{x}, \mathbf{x}) = \sum_{ij \in \mathcal{E}} \psi_{ij}(x_i, x_j)$. The unary potentials $\phi(x_i, \mathbf{z})$ depend only on the label/disparity at node/pixel i, and the dependence on the input $\mathbf{z}$ will depend on the application: (1) for the labeling application $\phi(x_i, \mathbf{z}) = g(\mathbf{z})_i$, where $g(.)$ is a nonlinear filter that can be obtained by an algorithm like AdaBoost [500] and evaluated in a local image window surrounding pixel i; (2) for binocular stereo we can set $\phi(x_i, \mathbf{z}^L, \mathbf{z}^R) = |f(\mathbf{z}^L)_i - f(\mathbf{z}^R)_{i+x_i}|$, where $f(.)$ is a vector-value filter and $|\cdots|$ is the L1 norm, so that $\phi(.)$ takes small values at the disparities x_i for which the filter responses are similar on the two images. The pairwise potentials impose prior assumptions about the local context of the labels and disparities. These models typically assume that neighboring pixels will tend to have similar labels/disparities (see figure 5.2).

In summary, the first type of model is specified by a distribution $P(\mathbf{x} \mid \mathbf{z})$ defined over discrete-valued random variables $\mathbf{x} = \{x_i : i \in \mathcal{V}\}$ defined on a graph $\mathcal{G} = (\mathcal{V}, \mathcal{E})$:

$$P(\mathbf{x} \mid \mathbf{z}) = \frac{1}{Z(\mathbf{z})} \exp \left\{ -\sum_{i \in \mathcal{V}} \phi_i(x_i, \mathbf{z}) - \sum_{ij \in \mathcal{E}} \psi_{ij}(x_i, x_j) \right\}. \qquad (5.1)$$

The goal will be to estimate properties of the distribution such as the MAP estimator and the marginals (which relate to each other, as discussed in subsection 5.2.4):

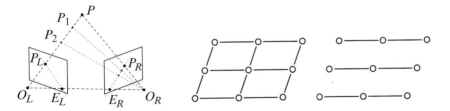

Figure 5.2
Stereo. The geometry of stereo (left). A point P in 3D space is projected onto points P_L, P_R in the left and right images. The projection is specified by the focal points O_L, O_R and the directions of gaze of the cameras (the camera geometry). The geometry of stereo enforces that points in the plane specified by P, O_L, O_R must be projected onto corresponding lines E_L, E_R in the two images (the epipolar line constraint). If we can find the correspondence between the points on epipolar lines, then we can use trigonometry to estimate their depth, which is (roughly) inversely proportional to the disparity, which is the relative displacement of the two images. Finding the correspondence is usually ill-posed and requires making assumptions about the spatial smoothness of the disparity (and hence of the depth). Current models impose weak smoothness priors on the disparity (center). Earlier models assumed that the disparity was independent across epipolar lines that lead to similar graphic models (right) where inference could be done by dynamic programming.

$$\mathbf{x}^* = \arg \max_{\mathbf{x}} P(\mathbf{x} \mid \mathbf{z}), \text{ the MAP estimate,}$$

$$p_i(x_i) = \sum_{\mathbf{x}/i} P(\mathbf{x} \mid \mathbf{z}), \ \forall i \in \mathcal{V} \text{ the marginals.}$$

(5.2)

The *second type of model* has applications to image segmentation, image denoising, and depth smoothing. Called the weak membrane model, it was proposed independently by Geman and Geman [161] and Blake and Zisserman [54]. This model has additional "hidden variables" $\mathbf{y}$, which are used to explicitly label discontinuities. It is also a generative model that specifies a likelihood function and a prior probability (in contrast to conditional random fields, which specify only the posterior distribution). This type of model can be extended by using more sophisticated hidden variables to perform tasks such as long-range motion correspondence [544], object alignment [96], and the detection of particle tracks in high-energy physics experiments [355].

The input to the weak membrane model is the set of intensity (or depth) values $\mathbf{z} = \{z_i : i \in \mathcal{D}\}$, and the output is $\mathbf{x} = \{x_i : i \in \mathcal{D}\}$ defined on a corresponding output lattice. (Formally we should specify two different lattices, say $\mathcal{D}_1$ and $\mathcal{D}_2$, but this makes the notation too cumbersome.) We define a set of edges $\mathcal{E}$ that connect neighboring pixels on the output lattice and define the set of line processes $\mathbf{y} = \{y_j : j \in \mathcal{D}_e\}$ with $y_{ij} \in \{0, 1\}$ over these edges (see figure 5.1. The weak membrane is a generative model, so it is specified by two probability distributions: (1) the likelihood function $P(\mathbf{z} \mid \mathbf{x})$, which specifies how the observed image $\mathbf{z}$ is a corrupted version of the image $\mathbf{x}$, and (2) the prior distribution $P(\mathbf{x}, \mathbf{y})$, which imposes a *weak membrane* by requiring that neighboring pixels take similar values except at places where the line process is activated.

The simplest version of the weak membrane model is specified by the distributions

$$P(\mathbf{z} \mid \mathbf{x}) = \prod_{i \in \mathcal{D}} \sqrt{\frac{\tau}{\pi}} \exp\{-\tau (z_i - x_i)^2\}, \quad P(\mathbf{x}, \mathbf{y}) \propto \exp\{-E(\mathbf{x}, \mathbf{y})\},$$

$$(5.3)$$

$$\text{with } E(\mathbf{x}, \mathbf{y}) = A \sum_{(i,j) \in \mathcal{E}} (x_i - x_j)^2 (1 - y_{ij}) + B \sum_{(i,j) \in \mathcal{E}} y_{ij}.$$

In this model the intensity variables x_i, z_i are continuous-valued and the line processor variables $y_{ij} \in \{0, 1\}$, where $y_{ij} = 1$ means that there is an (image) edge at $ij \in \mathcal{E}_x$. The likelihood function $P(\mathbf{z} \mid \mathbf{x})$ assumes independent zero-mean Gaussian noise (for other noise models, such as shot noise, see Geiger and Yuille [159] and Black and Rangarajan [47]). The prior $P(\mathbf{x}, \mathbf{y})$ encourages neighboring pixels i, j to have similar intensity values $x_i \approx x_j$ except if there is an edge $y_{ij} = 1$. This prior imposes piecewise smoothness, or weak smoothness, which is justified by statistical studies of intensities and depth measurements (see Zhu and Mumford [550], Roth and Black [397]). More advanced variants of this model will introduce higher-order coupling terms of the form $y_{ij} y_{kl}$ into the energy $E(\mathbf{x}, \mathbf{y})$ to encourage edges to group into longer segments that may form closed boundaries. The weak membrane model leads to a particularly hard inference problem since it requires estimating continuous and discrete variables, $\mathbf{x}$ and $\mathbf{y}$, from $P(\mathbf{x}, \mathbf{y} \mid \mathbf{z}) \propto P(\mathbf{z} \mid \mathbf{x}) P(\mathbf{x}, \mathbf{y})$.

5.2 Mean Field Theory and Variational Methods

Mean Field Theory (MFT), also known as a variational method, offers a strategy to design inference algorithms for MRF models. The approach has several advantages: (1) It takes optimization problems defined over discrete variables and converts them into problems defined in terms of continuous variables. This enables us to compute gradients of the energy and to use optimization techniques that depend on them, such as steepest descent. In particular, we can take hybrid problems defined in terms of both discrete and continuous variables, such the weak membrane, and convert them into continuous optimization problems. (2) We can use deterministic annealing methods to develop continuation methods in which we define a one-parameter family of optimization problems indexed by a temperature parameter T. We can solve the problems for large values of T (for which the optimization is simple) and track the solutions to low values of T (where the optimization is hard; see section 5.2.4). (3) We can show that MFT gives a fast deterministic approximation to Markov Chain Monte Carlo (MCMC) stochastic sampling methods, as described in section 5.4, and hence can be more efficient than stochastic sampling. (4) MFT methods can give bounds for quantities, such as the partition function $\log Z$, that are useful for model selection problems, as described in [46].

5.2.1 Mean Field Free Energies

The basic idea of MFT is to approximate a distribution $P(\mathbf{x} \mid \mathbf{z})$ by a simpler distribution $B^*(\mathbf{x} \mid \mathbf{z})$ that is chosen so that it is easy to estimate the MAP estimate of $P(.)$, and any other estimator, from the approximate distribution $B^*(.)$. This requires specifying a class of approximating distributions $\{B(.)\}$, a measure of similarity between distributions $B(.)$ and $P(.)$, and an algorithm for finding the $B^*(.)$ that minimizes the similarity measure.

In MFT the class of approximating distributions is chosen to be factorizable so that $B(\mathbf{x}) = \prod_{i \in \mathcal{V}} b_i(x_i)$, where $\mathbf{b} = \{b_i(x_i)\}$ are *pseudo marginals* that obey $b_i(x_i) \geq 0$, $\forall i, x_i$ and $\sum_{x_i} b_i(x_i) = 1$, $\forall i$. This means that the MAP estimate of $\mathbf{x} = (x_1, \ldots, x_N)$ can be approximated by $\overline{x}_i = \arg\max_{x_i} b^*(x_i)$ once we have determined $B^*(\mathbf{x})$. But note that MFT can be extended to structured mean field theory, which allows more structure to the $\{B(.)\}$ (see [46]). The similarity measure is specified by the Kullback-Leibler divergence $KL(B, P) = \sum_{\mathbf{x}} B(\mathbf{x}) \log \frac{B(\mathbf{x})}{P(\mathbf{x})}$, which has the properties that $KL(B, P) \geq 0$ with equality only if $B(.) = P(.)$. It can be shown (see section 5.2.2), that this is equivalent to a mean field free energy $\mathcal{F} = \sum_{\mathbf{x}} B(\mathbf{x}) E(\mathbf{x}) - \sum_{\mathbf{x}} B(\mathbf{x}) \log B(\mathbf{x})$.

For the first type of model we define the mean field free energy $\mathcal{F}_{\text{MFT}}(\mathbf{b})$ by

$$
\begin{aligned}
\mathcal{F}_{\text{MFT}}(\mathbf{b}) = &\sum_{ij \in \mathcal{E}} \sum_{x_i, x_j} b_i(x_i) b_j(x_j) \psi_{ij}(x_i, x_j) \\
&+ \sum_{i \in \mathcal{V}} \sum_{x_i} b_i(x_i) \phi_i(x_i, \mathbf{z}) + \sum_{i \in \mathcal{V}} \sum_{x_i} b_i(x_i) \log b_i(x_i).
\end{aligned}
\tag{5.4}
$$

The first two terms are the expectation of the energy $E(\mathbf{x}, \mathbf{z})$ with respect to the distribution $\mathbf{b}(\mathbf{x})$, and the third term is the negative entropy of $\mathbf{b}(\mathbf{x})$. If the labels can take only two values (i.e., $x_i \in \{0, 1\}$), then the entropy can be written as $\sum_{i \in \mathcal{V}} \{b_i \log b_i + (1 - b_i) \log(1 - b_i)\}$ where $b_i = b_i(x_i = 1)$. If the labels take a set of values $l = 1, \ldots, N$, then we can express the entropy as $\sum_{i \in \mathcal{V}} \sum_{l=1}^{M} b_{il} \log b_{il}$ where $b_{il} = b_i(x_i = l)$, and hence the $\{b_{il}\}$ satisfy the constraint $\sum_{l=1}^{M} b_{il} = 1$, $\forall i$.

For the second (weak membrane) model we use pseudo marginals $\mathbf{b}(\mathbf{y})$ only for the line processes $\mathbf{y}$. This leads to a free energy $\mathcal{F}_{\text{MFT}}(\mathbf{b}, \mathbf{x})$ specified by

$$
\begin{aligned}
\mathcal{F}_{\text{MFT}}(\mathbf{b}, \mathbf{x}) = &\tau \sum_{i \in \mathcal{V}} (x_i - z_i)^2 + A \sum_{ij \in \mathcal{E}} (1 - b_{ij})(x_i - x_j)^2 \\
&+ B \sum_{ij \in \mathcal{E}} b_{ij} + \sum_{ij \in \mathcal{E}} \{b_{ij} \log b_{ij} + (1 - b_{ij}) \log(1 - b_{ij})\},
\end{aligned}
\tag{5.5}
$$

where $b_{ij} = b_{ij}(y_{ij} = 1)$ (the derivation uses the fact that $\sum_{y_{ij}=0}^{1} b_{ij}(y_{ij}) y_{ij} = b_{ij}$). As described below, this free energy is exact and involves no approximations.

5.2.2 Mean Field Free Energy and Variational Bounds

I now describe in more detail the justifications for the mean field free energies. For the first type of models the simplest derivations are based on the Kullback–Leibler divergence, which was introduced into the machine learning literature by Saul and Jordan [414]. (Note that the mean field free energies can also be derived by related statistical physics techniques [365], and there were early applications to neural networks [201], vision [239], and machine learning [369].)

Substituting $P(\mathbf{x}) = \frac{1}{Z} \exp\{-E(\mathbf{x})\}$ and $B(\mathbf{x}) = \prod_{i \in \mathcal{V}} b_i(x_i)$ into the Kullback–Leibler divergence $KL(B, P)$ gives

$$KL(B, P) = \sum_{\mathbf{x}} B(\mathbf{x}) E(\mathbf{x}) + \sum_{\mathbf{x}} B(\mathbf{x}) \log B(\mathbf{x}) + \log Z = \mathcal{F}_{\mathrm{MFT}}(B) + \log Z. \qquad (5.6)$$

Hence minimizing $\mathcal{F}_{\mathrm{MFT}}(B)$ with respect to B gives (1) the best factorized approximation to $P(\mathbf{x})$ and (2) a lower bound to the partition function $\log Z \geq \min_B \mathcal{F}_{\mathrm{MFT}}(B)$, which can be useful to assess model evidence [46].

For the weak membrane model the free energy follows from Neal and Hinton's variational formulation of the Expectation Maximization (EM) algorithm [348]. The goal of EM is to estimate $\mathbf{x}$ from $P(\mathbf{x} \,|\, \mathbf{z}) = \sum_{\mathbf{y}} P(\mathbf{x}, \mathbf{y} \,|\, \mathbf{z})$ after treating the $\mathbf{y}$ as nuisance variables that should be summed out [46]. This can be expressed [348] in terms of minimizing the free energy function:

$$\mathcal{F}_{\mathrm{EM}}(B, \mathbf{x}) = -\sum_{\mathbf{y}} B(\mathbf{y}) \log P(\mathbf{x}, \mathbf{y} \,|\, \mathbf{z}) + \sum_{\mathbf{y}} B(\mathbf{y}) \log B(\mathbf{y}). \qquad (5.7)$$

The equivalence of minimizing $\mathcal{F}_{\mathrm{EM}}[B, \mathbf{x}]$ and estimating $\mathbf{x}^* = \arg \max_{\mathbf{x}} P(\mathbf{x} \,|\, \mathbf{z})$ can be verified by reexpressing

$$\mathcal{F}_{\mathrm{EM}}[B, \mathbf{x}] = -\log P(\mathbf{x} \,|\, \mathbf{z}) + \sum_{\mathbf{y}} B(\mathbf{y}) \log \frac{B(\mathbf{y})}{P(\mathbf{y} \,|\, \mathbf{x}, \mathbf{z})}, \qquad (5.8)$$

from which it follows that the global minimum occurs at $\mathbf{x}^* = \arg \min_{\mathbf{x}} \{-\log P(\mathbf{x} \,|\, \mathbf{z})\}$ and $B(\mathbf{y}) = P(\mathbf{y} \,|\, \mathbf{x}^*, \mathbf{z})$ (because the second term in (5.8) is the Kullback–Leibler divergence, which is minimized by setting $B(\mathbf{y}) = P(\mathbf{y} \,|\, \mathbf{x}, \mathbf{z})$).

The EM algorithm minimizes $\mathcal{F}_{\mathrm{EM}}[B, \mathbf{x}]$ with respect to B and $\mathbf{x}$ alternatively, which gives the E-step and the M-step, respectively. For the basic weak membrane model, both steps of the algorithm can be performed simply. The E-step requires minimizing a quadratic function, which can be performed by linear algebra, and the M-step can be computed analytically:

$$\text{Minimize wrt } \mathbf{x} \left\{ \sum_i \tau (x_i - z_i)^2 + A \sum_{(i,j) \in E} b_{ij} (x_i - x_j)^2, \right. \qquad (5.9)$$

$$B(\mathbf{y}) = \prod_{(i,j)\in E} b_{ij}(y_{ij}) \quad b_{ij} = \frac{1}{1 + \exp\{-A(x_i - x_j)^2 + B\}}. \tag{5.10}$$

The EM algorithm is only guaranteed to converge to a local minimum of the free energy, so good choices of initial conditions are needed. A natural initialization for the weak membrane model is to set $\mathbf{x} = \mathbf{z}$, perform the E-step, then the M-step, and so on. Observe that the M-step corresponds to performing a weighted smoothing of the data $\mathbf{z}$ where the smoothing weights are determined by the current probabilities $B(\mathbf{y})$ for the edges. The E-step estimates the probabilities $B(\mathbf{y})$ for the edges, given the current estimates for the $\mathbf{x}$.

Notice that the EM free energy does not enforce any constraints on the form of the distribution B, yet the algorithm results in a factorized distribution (see 5.10). This results naturally because the variables that are being summed out—the $\mathbf{y}$ variables—are conditionally independent (i.e., there are no terms in the energy $E(\mathbf{x}, \mathbf{z})$ that couple y_{ij} with its neighbors). In addition we can compute

$$P(\mathbf{x} \mid \mathbf{z}) = \sum_{\mathbf{y}} P(\mathbf{x}, \mathbf{y} \mid \mathbf{z}) \tag{5.11}$$

analytically to obtain

$$P(\mathbf{x} \mid \mathbf{z}) = \frac{1}{Z} \exp\left\{ -\tau \sum_{i \in mD} (x_i - z_i)^2 - \sum_{ij \in mE} g(x_i - x_j) \right\}, \tag{5.12}$$

where

$$g(x_i - x_j) = -\log\{\exp\{-A(x_i - x_j)^2\} + \exp\{B\}\}. \tag{5.13}$$

The function $g(x_i - x_j)$ penalizes $x_i - x_j$ quadratically for small $x_i - x_j$ but tends to a finite value asymptotically for large $|x_i - x_j|$.

Suppose, however, that we consider a modified weak membrane model that includes interactions between the line processes—terms in the energy such as $C \sum_{(ij)\times(kl)\in\mathcal{E}_y} y_{ij} y_{kl}$ that encourage lines to be continuous. It is now impossible either to (a) solve for $B(\mathbf{y})$ in closed form for the E-step of EM or (b) to compute $P(\mathbf{x} \mid \mathbf{y})$ analytically. Instead, we use the mean field approximation by requiring that B is factorizable—$B(\mathbf{y}) = \prod_{ij\in\mathcal{E}} b_{ij}(y_{ij})$. This gives a free energy:

$$\mathcal{F}_{\mathrm{MFT}}(\mathbf{b}, \mathbf{x}) = \tau \sum_{i \in \mathcal{V}} (x_i - z_i)^2 + A \sum_{ij \in \mathcal{E}} (1 - b_{ij})(x_i - x_j)^2 + B \sum_{ij \in \mathcal{E}} b_{ij}$$

$$+ C \sum_{(ij)\times(kl)\in\mathcal{E}_y} b_{ij} b_{kl} + \sum_{ij \in \mathcal{E}} \{b_{ij} \log b_{ij} + (1 - b_{ij}) \log(1 - b_{ij}). \tag{5.14}$$

5.2.3 Minimizing the Free Energy by Steepest Descent and Its Variants

The mean field free energies are functions of continuous variables (since discrete variables have been replaced by continuous probability distributions) that enable us to compute gradients of the free energy. This allows us to use steepest descent algorithms and their many variants. Suppose we take the MFT free energy from (5.4), restrict $x_i \in \{0, 1\}$, set $b_i = b_i(x_i = 1)$; then the basic steepest descent can be written as

$$
\frac{db_i}{dt} = -\frac{\partial \mathcal{F}_{\text{MFT}}}{\partial b_i},
$$

$$
= 2 \sum_j \sum_{x_j} \psi_{ij}(x_i, x_j) b_j + \phi_i(x_i) - \{b_i \log b_i + (1 - b_i) \log(1 - b_i)\}.
$$

(5.15)

The MFT free energy decreases monotonically because

$$
\frac{d\mathcal{F}_{\text{MFT}}}{dt} = \sum_i \frac{\partial \mathcal{F}_{\text{MFT}}}{\partial b_i} \frac{db_i}{dt} = -\sum_i \left\{ \frac{\partial \mathcal{F}_{\text{MFT}}}{\partial b_i} \right\}^2.
$$

(Note that the energy decreases very slowly for small gradients because the square of a small number is very small.) The negative entropy term $\{b_i \log b_i + (1 - b_i) \log(1 - b_i)\}$ is guaranteed to keep the values of b_i within the range $[0, 1]$ (since the gradient of the negative entropy equals $\log b_1/(1 - b_i)$, which becomes infinitely large as $b_i \mapsto 0$ and $b_i \mapsto 1$).

In practice, we must replace (5.15) with a discrete approximation of the form

$$
b_i^{t+1} = b_i^t - \Delta \frac{\partial \mathcal{F}_{\text{MFT}}}{\partial b_i},
$$

where b_i^t is the state at time t. But the choice of the step size Δ is critical. If it is too large, the algorithm will fail to converge, and if it is too small, the algorithm will converge very slowly. (Refer to Press et al. [378] for a detailed discussion of variants of steepest descent and their numerical stability and convergence properties.) A simple variant that has often been used for mean field theory applications to vision [239, 542] is to multiply the free energy gradient $\partial \mathcal{F}_{\text{MFT}}/\partial b_i$ in (5.15) by a positive function (ensuring that the free energy decreases monotonically). A typical choice of function is $b_i(1 - b_i)$, which, interestingly, gives dynamics that are identical to models of artificial neural networks [201].

There is a related class of *discrete iterative algorithms* that can be expressed in the form $b^{t+1} = f(b^t)$ for some function $f(.)$. They have two advantages over steepest descent algorithms: (1) they are guaranteed to decrease the free energy monotonically (i.e., $\mathcal{F}_{MFT}(b^{t+1}) \leq \mathcal{F}_{MFT}(b^t)$), and (2) they are nonlocal, so that b^{t+1} may be distant from b^t, which can enable them to escape some of the local minima that can trap steepest descent. Algorithms of this type can be derived by closely using principles such as variational bounding [408, 220], majorization [119], and CCCP [546]. It can be shown that many existing discrete iterative algorithms (e.g., EM, generalized iterative scaling, Sinhkorn's algorithm) can be derived using the CCCP principle [546]. For a recent discussion and entry point into this literature, see [447].

5.2.4 Temperature and Deterministic Annealing

So far we have concentrated on using MFT to estimate the marginal distributions. I now describe how MFT can attempt to estimate the most probable states of the probability distribution $\mathbf{x}^* = \arg\max_{\mathbf{x}} P(\mathbf{x})$. The strategy is to introduce a temperature parameter T and a family of probability distributions related to $P(\mathbf{x})$. (This strategy is also used in chapter 6.)

More precisely, we define a one-parameter family of distributions $\propto \{P(\mathbf{x})\}^{1/T}$ where T is a temperature parameter (the constant of proportionality is the normalization constant; see figure 5.3). This is equivalent to specifying Gibbs distributions $P(\mathbf{x}; T) = 1/Z(T)$ $\exp\{-E(\mathbf{x})/T\}$, where the default distribution $P(\mathbf{x})$ occurs at $T = 1$. The key observation is that as $T \mapsto 0$, the distribution strongly peaks about the state $\mathbf{x}^* = \arg\min_{\mathbf{x}} E(\mathbf{x})$ with lowest energy (or states if there are two or more global minima). Conversely, at $T \mapsto \infty$ all states will become equally likely and $P(\mathbf{x}; T)$ will tend to the uniform distribution.

Introducing this temperature parameter modifies the free energies by multiplying the entropy term by T. For example, we modify (5.4) to be

$$\mathcal{F}_{\mathrm{MFT}}() = \sum_{ij \in \mathcal{E}} \sum_{x_i, x_j} b_i(x_i) b_j(x_j) \psi_{ij}(x_i, x_j)$$

$$+ \sum_{i \in \mathcal{V}} \sum_{x_i} b_i(x_i) \phi_i(x_i, \mathbf{z}) + T \sum_{i \in \mathcal{V}} \sum_{x_i} b_i(x_i) \log b_i(x_i). \tag{5.16}$$

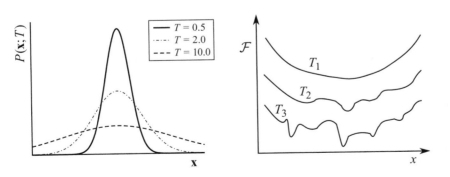

Figure 5.3
The probability distribution $P(\mathbf{x}; T)$ peak sharply as $T \mapsto 0$ and tends to a uniform distribution for large T (left). The mean field free energy $\mathcal{F}$ is convex for large T and becomes less smooth as T decreases (right). This motivates simulated annealing and deterministic annealing, which are related to graduated nonconvexity. For some models there are phase transitions where the minima of the free energy change drastically at a critical temperature T_c.

Observe that for large T, the convex entropy term will dominate the free energy, causing it to become convex. But for small T the remaining terms dominate. In general, we expect that the landscape of the free energy will become smoothed as T increases, and in some cases it is possible to compute a temperature T_c above which the free energy has an obvious solution [131]. This motivates a continuation approach known as *deterministic annealing*, which involves minimizing the free energy at high temperatures, and using this to provide initial conditions for minimizing the free energies at lower temperatures. In practice, the best results often require introducing temperature dependence into the parameters [131]. At sufficiently low temperatures the global minima of the free energy can approach the MAP estimates, but technical conditions need to be enforced (see [545]).

Deterministic annealing was motivated by *simulated annealing*[234] and performs stochastic sampling (see section 5.4) from the distribution $P(\mathbf{x}; T)$, gradually reducing T so that eventually the samples come from $P(\mathbf{x} : T = 0)$ and, hence, correspond to the global minimum $\mathbf{x} = \arg\min_{\mathbf{x}} E(\mathbf{x})$. This approach is guaranteed to converge [161], but the theoretically guaranteed rate of convergence is impractically slow and so, in practice, rates are chosen heuristically. Deterministic annealing is also related to the continuation techniques described by Blake and Zisserman [54] to obtain solutions to the weak membrane model.

5.3 Belief Propagation and Bethe Free Energy

I now present a different approach to estimating (approximate) marginals and MAPs of an MRF. This is called belief propagation (BP). It was originally proposed as a method for doing inference on trees (e.g., graphs without closed loops) [367], for which it is guaranteed to converge to the correct solution (and is related to dynamic programming). But empirical studies showed that belief propagation will often yield good approximate results on graphs that do have closed loops [337].

To illustrate the advantages of belief propagation, consider the binocular stereo problem that can be addressed by using the first type of model. For binocular stereo there is the epipolar line constraint, which means that, provided we know the camera geometry, we can reduce the problem to one-dimensional matching (see figure 5.2). We impose weak smoothness in this dimension only, and then use dynamic programming to solve the problem [158]. But a better approach is to impose weak smoothness in both directions, which can be solved (approximately) using belief propagation [457] (see figure 5.2).

Surprisingly, the fixed points of belief propagation algorithms correspond to the extrema of the Bethe free energy [540]. This free energy (see (5.22)), appears to be better than the mean field theory free energy because it includes pairwise pseudo marginal distributions and reduces to the MFT free energy if those distributions are replaced by the product of unary marginals. But, except for graphs without closed loops (or with a single closed loop), there are no theoretical results showing that the Bethe free energy yields a better approximation

Figure 5.4
Message passing (left) is guaranteed to converge to the correct solution on graphs without closed loops (center) but gives only approximations on graphs with a limited number of closed loops (right).

than mean field theory (see figure 5.4). There is also no guarantee that BP will converge for general graphs, and it can oscillate widely.

5.3.1 Message Passing

BP is defined in terms of messages $m_{ij}(x_j)$ from i to j, and is specified by the sum product update rule:

$$m_{ij}^{t+1}(x_j) = \sum_{x_i} \exp\{-\psi_{ij}(x_i, x_j) - \phi_i(x_i)\} \prod_{k \neq j} m_{ki}^t(x_i). \tag{5.17}$$

The unary and binary pseudo marginals are related to the messages by

$$b_i^t(x_i) \propto \exp\{-\phi_i(x_i)\} \prod_k m_{kj}^t(x_j), \tag{5.18}$$

$$b_{kj}^t(x_k, x_j) \propto \exp\{-\psi_{kj}(x_k, x_j) - \phi_k(x_k) - \phi_j(x_j)\} \prod_{\tau \neq j} m_{\tau k}^t(x_k) \prod_{l \neq k} m_{lj}^t(x_j). \tag{5.19}$$

The update rule for BP is not guaranteed to converge to a fixed point for general graphs and can sometimes oscillate wildly. It can be partially stabilized by adding a damping term to (5.17), for example, by multiplying the right-hand side by $(1 - \epsilon)$ and adding a term $\epsilon m_{ij}^t(x_j)$.

To understand the convergence of BP, observe that the pseudo marginals b satisfy the *admissibility constraint*:

$$\frac{\prod_{ij} b_{ij}(x_i, x_j)}{\prod_i b_i(x_i)^{n_i - 1}} \propto \exp\left\{ -\sum_{ij} \psi_{ij}(x_i, x_j) - \sum_i \phi(x_i) \right\} \propto P(\mathbf{x}), \tag{5.20}$$

where n_i is the number of edges that connect to node i. This means that the algorithm reparameterizes the distribution from an initial specification in terms of the ϕ, ψ to one in terms of the pseudo marginals b. For a tree this reparameterization is exact (i.e., the pseudo marginals become the true marginals of the distribution—we can, e.g., represent a one-dimensional distribution by $P(\mathbf{x}) = \frac{1}{Z}\{-\sum_{i=1}^{N-1}\psi(x_i, x_{i+1}) - \sum_{i=1}^{N}\phi_i(x_i)\}$ or by $\prod_{i=1}^{N-1} p(x_i, x_{i+1})/\prod_{i=2}^{N-1} p(x_i)$.

It follows from the message updating equations (5.17, 5.19) that at convergence, the bs satisfy the *consistency constraints*:

$$\sum_{x_j} b_{ij}(x_i, x_j) = b_i(x_i), \quad \sum_{x_i} b_{ij}(x_i, x_j) = b_j(x_j). \tag{5.21}$$

This follows from the fixed point conditions on the messages, $m_{kj}(x_j) = \sum_{x_k} \exp\{-\phi_k(x_k)\}\exp\{-\psi_{jk}(x_j, x_k)\}\prod_{l\neq j} m_{lk}(x_k) \ \forall k, j, x_j$.

In general, the admissibility and consistency constraints characterize the fixed points of belief propagation. This has an elegant interpretation within the framework of information geometry [206].

5.3.2 The Bethe Free Energy

The Bethe free energy [128] differs from the MFT free energy by including pairwise pseudo marginals $b_{ij}(x_i, x_j)$:

$$\mathcal{F}[b; \lambda] = \sum_{ij} \sum_{x_i, x_j} b_{ij}(x_i, x_j)\psi_{ij}(x_i, x_j) + \sum_{i} \sum_{x_i} b_i(x_i)\phi_i(x_i)$$
$$+ \sum_{ij} \sum_{x_i, x_j} b_{ij}(x_i, x_j)\log b_{ij}(x_i, x_j) - \sum_{i}(n_i - 1)\sum_{x_i} b_i(x_i)\log b_i(x_i). \tag{5.22}$$

But we must also impose consistency and normalization constraints by Lagrange multipliers $\{\lambda_{ij}(x_j)\}$ and $\{\gamma_i\}$, giving the additional terms

$$\sum_{i,j} \sum_{x_j} \lambda_{ij}(x_j)\left\{\sum_{x_i} b_{ij}(x_i, x_j) - b_j(x_j)\right\}$$
$$+ \sum_{i,j} \sum_{x_i} \lambda_{ji}(x_i)\left\{\sum_{x_j} b_{ij}(x_i, x_j) - b_i(x_i)\right\} + \sum_{i} \gamma_i\left\{\sum_{x_i} b_i(x_i) - 1\right\}. \tag{5.23}$$

It is straightforward to verify that the extrema of the Bethe free energy also obey the admissibility and consistency constraints. Hence the fixed points of belief propagation correspond to extrema of the Bethe free energy.

If the goal of belief propagation is to minimize the Bethe free energy, then why not use direct methods such as steepest descent or discrete iterative algorithms instead? One disadvantage is that these methods require working with pseudo marginals that have higher dimensions than the messages (contrast $b_{ij}(x_i, x_j)$ with $m_{ij}(x_j)$). Discrete iterative algorithms (DIA) have been proposed [543, 191] that are more stable than belief propagation and can reach lower values of the Bethe free energy. But these DIA must have an inner loop to deal with the consistency constraints, and hence take longer to converge than belief propagation. The difference between these direct algorithms and belief propagation can also be given an elegant geometric interpretation in terms of information geometry [206].

5.3.3 Where Do the Messages Come From? The Dual Formulation

Where do the messages in belief propagation come from? At first glance, they do not appear directly in the Bethe free energy. But observe that the consistency constraints are imposed by Lagrange multipliers $\lambda_{ij}(x_j)$ that have the same dimensions as the messages.

We can think of the Bethe free energy as specifying a *primal problem* defined over *primal variables* b and *dual variables* λ. The goal is to minimize $\mathcal{F}[b; \lambda]$ with respect to the primal variables and maximize it with respect to the dual variables. There is a corresponding *dual problem* that can be obtained by minimizing $\mathcal{F}[b; \lambda]$ with respect to b to get solutions $b(\lambda)$ and substituting them back to obtain $\hat{\mathcal{F}}_d[\lambda] = \mathcal{F}[b(\lambda); \lambda]$. Extrema of the dual problem correspond to extrema of the primal problem (and vice versa).

It is straightforward to show that minimizing $\mathcal{F}$ with respect to the bs gives the equations

$$b_i^t(x_i) \propto \exp\left\{-1/(n_i - 1)\left\{\gamma_i - \sum_j \lambda_{ji}(x_i) - \phi_i(x_i)\right\}\right\}, \tag{5.24}$$

$$b_{ij}^t(x_i, x_j) \propto \exp\left\{-\psi_{ij}(x_i, x_j) - \lambda_{ij}^t(x_j) - \lambda_{ji}^t(x_i)\right\}. \tag{5.25}$$

Observe the similarity between these equations and those specified by belief propagation (see (5.17)). They become identical if we identify the messages with a function of the λs:

$$\lambda_{ji}(x_i) = -\sum_{k \in N(i)/j} \log m_{ki}(x_i). \tag{5.26}$$

There are, however, two limitations of the Bethe free energy. First, it does not provide a bound of the partition function (unlike MFT), and so it is not possible to use bounding arguments to claim that Bethe is "better" than MFT (i.e., it is not guaranteed to give a tighter bound). Second, Bethe is nonconvex (except on trees), which has unfortunate consequences for the dual problem—the maximum of the dual is not guaranteed to correspond to the minimum of the primal. Both problems can be avoided by an alternative approach, described in chapter 6, which gives convex upper bounds on the partition function and specifies convergent (single-loop) algorithms.

5.4 Stochastic Inference

Stochastic sampling methods—Markov Chain Monte Marlo (MCMC)—also can be applied to obtain samples from an MRF that can be used to estimate states. For example, Geman and

Geman [161] used simulated annealing—MCMC with changing temperature—to perform inference on the weak membrane model. As I describe, stochastic sampling is closely related to MFT and BP. Indeed, both can be derived as deterministic approximations to MCMC.

5.4.1 MCMC

MCMC is a stochastic method for obtaining samples from a probability distribution $P(\mathbf{x})$. It requires choosing a transition kernel $K(\mathbf{x} \mid \mathbf{x}')$ that obeys the fixed point condition $P(\mathbf{x}) = \sum_{\mathbf{x}'} K(\mathbf{x} \mid \mathbf{x}') P(\mathbf{x}')$. In practice the kernel is usually chosen to satisfy the stronger *detailed balance* condition $P(\mathbf{x}) K(\mathbf{x}' \mid \mathbf{x}) = K(\mathbf{x} \mid \mathbf{x}') P(\mathbf{x}')$ (the fixed point condition is recovered by taking $\sum_{\mathbf{x}'}$). In addition the kernel must satisfy conditions $K(\mathbf{x} \mid \mathbf{x}') \geq 0$ and $\sum_{\mathbf{x}} K(\mathbf{x} \mid \mathbf{x}') = 1 \ \forall \mathbf{x}'$, and for any pair of states $\mathbf{x}, \mathbf{x}'$ it must be possible to find a trajectory $\{\mathbf{x}_i : i = 0, \ldots, N\}$ such that $\mathbf{x} = \mathbf{x}_0$, $\mathbf{x}' = \mathbf{x}_N$, and $K(\mathbf{x}_{i+1} \mid \mathbf{x}_i) > 0$ (i.e., there is a nonzero probability of moving between any two states by a finite number of transitions).

This defines a random sequence $\mathbf{x}_0, \mathbf{x}_1, \ldots, \mathbf{x}_n$ where $\mathbf{x}_0$ is specified and $\mathbf{x}_{i+1}$ is sampled from $K(\mathbf{x}_{i+1} \mid \mathbf{x}_i)$. It can be shown that $\mathbf{x}_n$ will tend to a sample from $P(\mathbf{x})$ as $n \mapsto \infty$, independent of the initial state $\mathbf{x}_0$, and the convergence is exponential, at a rate depending on the magnitude of the second largest eigenvalue of $K(. \mid .)$. Unfortunately, this eigenvalue can almost never be calculated, and in practice, tests must be used to determine if the MCMC has converged to a sample from $P(\mathbf{x})$ (see [315]).

I now introduce the two most popular types of transition kernels $K(\mathbf{x} \mid \mathbf{x}')$, the Gibbs sampler and the Metropolis-Hastings sampler. Both satisfy the detailed balance condition and are straightforward to sample from (i.e., they do not depend on quantities that are hard to compute, such as the normalization constant Z of $P(\mathbf{x})$). To specify these kernels compactly, I use the notation that r denotes a set of graph nodes with state $\mathbf{x}_r$, and $/r$ denotes the remaining graph nodes with state $\mathbf{x}_{/r}$. For example, for the image labeling problem with MRF given by (5.1), r can label a point i on the image lattice, $\mathbf{x}_r$ would be the label x_i of that lattice point, and $\mathbf{x}_{/r}$ would be the labels of all the other pixels $-\mathbf{x}_{/r} = \{x_j : j \in \mathcal{V} \ j \neq i\}$. But it is important to realize that these kernels can be extended to cases where r represents a set of points on the image lattice, for example, two neighboring points i, j where $ij \in \mathcal{E}$ and $\mathbf{x}_r$ is x_i, x_j.

The Gibbs sampler is one of the most popular MCMCs, partly because it is so simple. It has transition kernel $K(\mathbf{x} \mid \mathbf{x}') = \sum_r \rho(r) K_r(\mathbf{x} \mid \mathbf{x}')$, where $\rho(r)$ is a distribution on the lattice sites $r \in \mathcal{V}$. The default choice for $\rho(.)$ is the uniform distribution, but other choices may be better, depending on the specific application. The $K_r(\mathbf{x} \mid \mathbf{x}')$ are specified by

$$K_r(\mathbf{x} \mid \mathbf{x}') = P(\mathbf{x}_r \mid \mathbf{x}'_{N(r)}) \delta_{\mathbf{x}_{/r}, \mathbf{x}'_{/r}}, \tag{5.27}$$

where $\delta_{a,b}$ is the delta function (i.e., $\delta_{a,b} = 1$ for $a = b$ and $= 0$ otherwise). $P(\mathbf{x}_r \mid \mathbf{x}'_{N(r)})$ is the conditional distribution that, as illustrated below, takes a simple form for MRFs that makes it easy to sample from. Each $K_r(. \mid .)$ satisfies the detailed balance condition, and hence so does $K(.\,|\,.)$ by linearity. Note that we require $\rho(r) > 0$ for all r; otherwise we will not be able to move between any pair of states $\mathbf{x}$, $\mathbf{x}'$ in a finite number of moves.

The Gibbs sampler proceeds by first picking (a) lattice site(s) at random from $\rho(.)$ and then sampling the state $\mathbf{x}_r$ of the site from the conditional distribution $P(\mathbf{x}_r\,|\,\mathbf{x}'_{N(r)})$. The conditional distribution will take a simple form for MRFs, and so sampling from it is usually straightforward. For example, consider the binary-valued case with $x_i \in \{0, 1\}$ and with potentials $\psi_{ij}(x_i, x_j) = \psi_{ij}x_ix_j$ and $\phi_i(x_i) = \phi_ix_i$. The Gibbs sampler samples x_i^{t+1} from the distribution

$$P(x_i\,|\,x_{/i}) = \frac{1}{1 + \exp\left\{x_i\left(\sum_j \psi_{ij}x_j + \phi_i\right)\right\}}. \tag{5.28}$$

In fact, updates for Gibbs sampling are similar to the updates for MFT. A classic result, described in [13], shows that MFT can be obtained by taking the expectation of the update for the Gibbs sampler. Surprisingly, belief propagation can also be derived as the expectation of a more sophisticated variant of the Gibbs sampler that updates pairs of states simultaneously—where r denotes neighboring lattice sites i, j (for details, see [392]).

The Metropolis–Hastings sampler is the most general transition kernel that satisfies the detailed balance conditions. It has the form

$$K(\mathbf{x}\,|\,\mathbf{x}') = q(\mathbf{x}\,|\,\mathbf{x}')\min\left\{1, \frac{p(\mathbf{x})q(\mathbf{x}'\,|\,\mathbf{x})}{p(\mathbf{x}')q(\mathbf{x}\,|\,\mathbf{x}')}\right\}, \text{ for } \mathbf{x} \neq \mathbf{x}'. \tag{5.29}$$

Here $q(\mathbf{x}\,|\,\mathbf{x}')$ is a proposal probability (that depends on the application and usually takes a simple form). The sampler proceeds by selecting a possible transition $\mathbf{x}' \mapsto \mathbf{x}$ from the proposal probability $q(\mathbf{x}\,|\,\mathbf{x}')$ and accepting this transition with probability $\min\left\{1, \frac{p(\mathbf{x})q(\mathbf{x}'\,|\,\mathbf{x})}{p(\mathbf{x}')q(\mathbf{x}\,|\,\mathbf{x}')}\right\}$. A key advantage of this approach is that it only involves evaluating the ratios of the probabilities $P(\mathbf{x})$ and $P(\mathbf{x}')$, which are typically simple quantities to compute (see the examples below).

In many cases the proposal probability $q(.\,|\,.)$ is selected to be a uniform distribution over a set of possible states. For example, for the first type of model we let the proposal probability choose at random a site i at a new state value x_i' (from uniform distributions) that proposes a new state $\mathbf{x}'$. We always accept this proposal if $E(\mathbf{x}') \leq E(\mathbf{x})$, and we accept it with probability $\exp\{E(\mathbf{x}) - E(\mathbf{x}')\}$ if $E(\mathbf{x}') > E(\mathbf{x})$. Hence each iteration of the algorithm usually decreases the energy, but there is also the possibility of going uphill in energy space, which means it can escape the local minima that can trap steepest descent methods. But it must be realized that an MCMC algorithm converges to samples from the distribution $P(\mathbf{x})$ and not to a fixed state, unless we perform annealing by sampling from the distribution $\frac{1}{Z[T]}P(\mathbf{x})^{1/T}$ and letting T tend to zero. As discussed in section 5.2.4, annealing rates must be determined by trial and error because the theoretical bounds are too slow.

In general, MCMC can be slow unless problem-specific knowledge is used. Gibbs sampling is popular because it is very simple and easy to program but can exploit only a limited amount of knowledge about the application being addressed. Most practical applications use Metropolis–Hastings with proposal probabilities that exploit knowledge of the problem. In computer vision, data-driven Markov chain Monte Carlo (DDMCMC) [486, 485] shows how effective proposal probabilities can be, but this requires sophisticated proposal probabilities and is beyond the scope of this chapter. For a detailed introduction to MCMC methods, see [315].

5.5 Discussion

This chapter described mean field theory and belief propagation techniques for performing inference of marginals on MRF models. It discussed how these methods could be formulated in terms of minimizing free energies, such as mean field free energies and the Bethe free energies. (See [540] for extensions to the Kikuchi free energy, and chapter 6 for discussion of convex free energies). It described a range of algorithms that can be used to perform minimization. This includes steepest descent, discrete iterative algorithms, and message passing. It showed how belief propagation can be described as dynamics in the dual space of the primal problem specified by the Bethe free energy. It introduced a temperature parameter that enables inference methods to obtain MAP estimates and also motivates continuation methods, such as deterministic annealing. It briefly described stochastic MCMC methods, such as Gibbs and Metropolis–Hastings sampling, and showed that mean field algorithms and belief propagation can both be thought of as deterministic approximations to Gibbs sampling.

There have been many extensions to the basic methods described in this chapter. (Refer to [46] for an entry into the literature on structured mean field methods, expectation maximization, and the trade-offs between these approaches). Other recent variants of mean field theory methods are described in [392]. Recently CCCP algorithms have been shown to be useful for learning latent structural SVMs with latent variables [541]. Work by Felzenszwalb and Huttenlocher [141] shows how belief propagation methods can be made extremely fast by taking advantage of properties of the potentials and the multiscale properties of many vision problems. Researchers in the UAI community have discovered ways to derive generalizations of BP starting from the perspective of efficient exact inference [91]. Convex free energies introduced by Wainwright et al. [506] have nicer theoretical properties than the Bethe free energy and have led to alternatives to BP, such as TRW and provably convergent algorithms (see chapter 6). Stochastic sampling techniques such as MCMC remain a very active area of research. (See [315] for an advanced introduction to techniques such as particle filtering that have had important applications to tracking [209]). The relationship between sampling techniques and deterministic methods is an interesting area of research, and there are successful algorithms that combine both aspects. For example, there are recent non-parametric approaches that combine particle filters with belief propagation to do inference on graphical models where the variables are continuous-valued [453, 208]. It is unclear, however, whether the deterministic methods described in this chapter can be extended to perform the types of inference that advanced techniques like data-driven MCMC can perform [486, 485].

Acknowledgments

I would like to thank George Papandreou , Xingyao Ye, and Xuming He for giving detailed feedback on this chapter. George also kindly drew the figures. This work was partially supported by the NSF with grant number 0613563.

6 Linear Programming and Variants of Belief Propagation

Yair Weiss, Chen Yanover, and Talya Meltzer

6.1 Introduction

The basic problem of energy minimization in an MRF comes up in many application domains ranging from statistical physics [22] to error-correcting codes [137] and protein folding [537]. *Linear programming (LP) relaxations* are a standard method for approximating combinatorial optimization problems in computer science [34] and have been used for energy minimization problems for some time [23, 137, 233]. They have an advantage over other energy minimization schemes in that they come with an optimality guarantee: if the LP relaxation is "tight" (i.e., the solution to the linear program is integer), then it is guaranteed to give the global optimum of the energy.

Despite this advantage there have been very few applications of LP relaxations for solving MRF problems in vision. This can be traced to the computational complexity of LP solvers—the number of constraints and equations in LP relaxation of vision problems is simply too large. Instead, the typical algorithms used in MRF minimization for vision problems are based on either message passing (in particular belief propagation (BP) and the tree reweighted version of belief propagation (TRW)) or graph cut (or variants of it).

Since 2005, however, an intriguing connection has emerged among message passing algorithms, graph cut algorithms, and LP relaxation. In this chapter we give a short, introductory treatment of this intriguing connection (focusing on message passing algorithms). Specifically, we show that BP and its variants can be used to solve LP relaxations that arise from vision problems, sometimes far more efficiently than using off-the-shelf LP software packages. Furthermore, we show that BP and its variants can give additional information that allows one to provably find the global minimum even when the LP relaxation is not tight.

6.1.1 Energy Minimization and Its Linear Programming Relaxation

The energy minimization problem and its LP relaxation were described in chapter 1, and we briefly define them again here in a slightly different notation (that will make the connection to BP more transparent).

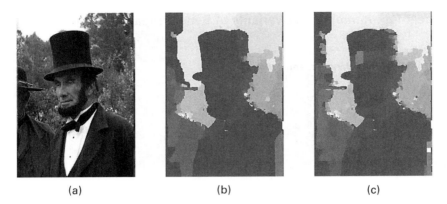

(a)   (b)   (c)

Figure 6.1
(a) A single frame from a stereo pair. Finding the disparity is often done by minimizing an energy function. (b) The results of graph cut using a Potts model energy function. (c) The results of ordinary BP, using the same energy function.

For simplicity, we discuss only MRFs with pairwise cliques in this chapter, but all statements can be generalized to higher-order cliques [519].

We work with MRFs of the form

$$P(x) = \frac{1}{Z} \prod_i \exp(-\Phi_i(x_i)) \prod_{<i,j>} \exp(-\Psi_{ij}(x_i, x_j)), \tag{6.1}$$

where $<i, j>$ denotes the set of pairwise cliques that was denoted in earlier chapters, $(i, j) \in \mathcal{E}$.

We wish to find the most probable configuration x^* that maximizes $P(x)$ or, equivalently, the one that minimizes the energy:

$$x^* = \arg\min \sum_i \Phi_i(x_i) + \sum_{ij} \Psi_{ij}(x_i, x_j). \tag{6.2}$$

For concreteness, let's focus on the stereo vision problem (figure 6.1). Here x_i will denote the disparity at a pixel i and $\Phi_i(x_i)$ will be the local data term in the energy function and $\Psi_{ij}(x_i, x_j)$ is the pairwise smoothness term in the energy function. As shown in [71], for many widely used smoothness terms (e.g., the Potts model) exact minimization is NP-hard. Figure 6.1b,c show the results of graph cut and ordinary belief propgation on the Potts model energy function. In this display the lighter a pixel is, the farther it is calculated to be from the camera. Note that both graph cut and BP calculate the depth of the hat and shirt to have "holes"—there are pixels inside the hat and the shirt whose disparities are calculated to be larger than the rest of the hat. Are these mistakes due to the energy function or the approximate minimization?

We can convert the minimization into an integer program by introducing binary indicator variables $q_i(x_i)$ for each pixel and $q_{ij}(x_i, x_j)$ for any pair of connected pixels. We can then rewrite the minimization problem as

$$\{q_{ij}^*, q_i^*\} = \arg\min \sum_i \sum_{x_i} q_i(x_i)\Phi_i(x_i) + \sum_{<i,j>} \sum_{x_i, x_j} \Psi_{ij}(x_i, x_j)q_{ij}(x_i, x_j). \tag{6.3}$$

The minimization is done subject to the following constraints:

$$q_{ij}(x_i, x_j) \in \{0, 1\}$$

$$\sum_{x_i, x_j} q_{ij}(x_i, x_j) = 1$$

$$\sum_{x_i} q_{ij}(x_i, x_j) = q_j(x_j),$$

where the last equation enforces the consistency of the pairwise indicator variables with the singleton indicator variable.

This integer program is completely equivalent to the original MAP problem, and hence is computationally intractable. We can obtain the linear programming relaxation by allowing the indicator variables to take on noninteger values. This leads to the following problem:

The LP Relaxation of Pairwise Energy Minimization   Minimize:

$$J(\{q\}) = \sum_{<i,j>} \sum_{x_i, x_j} q_{ij}(x_i, x_j)\Psi_{ij}(x_i, x_j) + \sum_i \sum_{x_i} q_i(x_i)\Psi_i(x_i) \tag{6.4}$$

subject to

$$q_{ij}(x_i, x_j) \in [0, 1] \tag{6.5}$$

$$\sum_{x_i, x_j} q_{ij}(x_i, x_j) = 1 \tag{6.6}$$

$$\sum_{x_i} q_{ij}(x_i, x_j) = q_j(x_j). \tag{6.7}$$

This is now a linear program (the cost and the constraints are linear). It can therefore be solved in polynomial time and we have the following guarantee:

Observation   If the solutions $\{q_{ij}(x_i, x_j), q_i(x_i)\}$ to the MAP LP relaxation are all *integer*, that is $q_{ij}(x_i, x_j), q_i(x_i) \in \{0, 1\}$, then $x_i^* = \arg\max_{x_i} q_i(x_i)$ is the MAP solution.

6.1.2 The Need for Special-Purpose LP Solvers

Having converted the energy minimization problem to a linear program (LP), it may seem that all we need to do is use off-the-shelf LP solvers and apply them to computer vision problems. However, by relaxing the problem we have increased its size tremendously—there are many more variables in the LP than there are nodes in the original graph.

Formally, denote by k_i the number of possible states of node i. The number of variables and constraints in the LP relaxation is given by

$$N_{variables} = \sum_i k_i + \sum_{<i,j>} k_i k_j$$

$$N_{constraints} = \sum_{<i,j>} (k_i + k_j + 1).$$

The additional $\sum_{<i,j>} 2k_i k_j$ bound constraints, derived from (6.5), are usually not considered part of the constraint matrix.

Figure 6.2 shows the number of variables and constraints as a function of image size for a stereo problem with thirty disparities. If the image is a modest 200×200 pixels and each disparity can take on thirty discrete values, then the LP relaxation will have over seventy-two million variables and four million constraints. The vertical line shows the largest size image that could be solved using a commercial powerful LP solver (CPLEX 9.0) on a desktop machine with 4GB of memory in [535]. Obviously, we need a solver that can somehow take advantage of the problem structure in order to deal with such a large-scale problem.

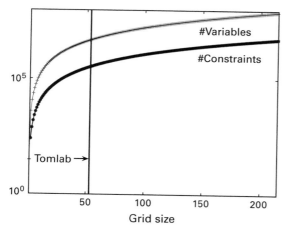

Figure 6.2
The number of variables and constraints in a stereo problem with thirty disparities as a function of image size. Even modestly sized images have millions of variables and constraints. The largest image that could be solved with commercial LP software on a machine with 4GB of memory in [535] is approximately 50×50.

6.2   Ordinary Sum-Product Belief Propagation and Linear Programming

The sum-product belief propagation (BP) algorithm was introduced by Pearl [367] as a method for performing exact probabilistic calculations on singly connected MRFs. The algorithm receives as input a graph G and the functions $F_{ij}(x_i, x_j) = \exp(-\Psi(x_i, x_j))$, $F_i(x_i) = \exp(-\Psi_i(x_i))$. At each iteration a node x_i sends a message $m_{ij}(x_j)$ to x_j, its neighbor in the graph. The messages are updated as follows:

$$m_{ij}(x_j) \leftarrow \alpha_{ij} \sum_{x_i} F_{ij}(x_i, x_j) F_i(x_i) \prod_{k \in N_i \backslash j} m_{ki}(x_i) \tag{6.8}$$

where $N_i \backslash j$ refers to all neighbors of node x_i except x_j. The constant α_{ij} is a normalization constant typically chosen so that the messages sum to 1 (the normalization has no influence on the final beliefs). Given the messages, each node can form an estimate of its local "belief" defined as

$$b_i(x_i) \propto F_i(x_i) \prod_{j \in N_i} m_{ji}(x_i), \tag{6.9}$$

and every pair of nodes can calculate its "pairwise belief":

$$b_{ij}(x_i, x_j) \propto F_i(x_i) F_j(x_j) F_{ij}(x_i, x_j) \prod_{k \in N_i \backslash j} m_{ki}(x_i) \prod_{k \in N_j \backslash i} m_{kj}(x_j). \tag{6.10}$$

Pearl [367] showed that when the MRF graph is singly connected, the algorithm will converge and these pairwise beliefs and singleton beliefs will exactly equal the correct marginals of the MRF (i.e., $b_i(x_i) = P(x_i)$, $b_{ij}(x_i, x_j) = P(x_i, x_j)$). But when there are cycles in the graph, neither convergence nor correctness of the beliefs is guaranteed. Somewhat surprisingly, however, for any graph (with or without cycles) there is a simple relationship between the BP beliefs and the LP relaxation.

In order to show this relationship, we need to define the BP algorithm at temperature T. This is exactly the same algorithm defined in (6.8), and the only difference is the definition of the local functions $F_{ij}(x_i, x_j)$, $F_i(x_i)$. The new definition depends both on the energy function parameters $\Psi_{ij}(x_i, x_j)$, $\Phi_i(x_i)$ and on a new parameter T that we call temperature.

$$F_{ij}(x_i, x_j) = \exp -\frac{1}{T} \Psi_{ij}(x_i, x_j) \tag{6.11}$$

$$F_i(x_i) = \exp -\frac{1}{T} \Phi_i(x_i). \tag{6.12}$$

Observation   For any MRF as $T \to 0$ there exists a fixed point of ordinary BP at temperature T whose beliefs approach the LP solution.

This observation follows directly from the connection between BP and the Bethe free energy [539]. As explained in chapter 5, there is a 1:1 correspondence between the fixed points of BP at temperature T and stationary points of the following problem.

The Bethe Free Energy Minimization Problem Minimize   Minimize

$$G(\{b\}; T) = \sum_{<i,j>} \sum_{x_i, x_j} b_{ij}(x_i, x_j) \Psi_{ij}(x_i, x_j) + \sum_i \sum_{x_i} b_i(x_i) \Phi_i(x_i)$$

$$- T \left(\sum_{ij} H(b_{ij}) + \sum_i (1 - \deg_i) H(b_i) \right), \tag{6.13}$$

subject to

$$b_{ij}(x_i, x_j) \in [0, 1] \tag{6.14}$$

$$\sum_{x_i, x_j} b_{ij}(x_i, x_j) = 1 \tag{6.15}$$

$$\sum_{x_i} b_{ij}(x_i, x_j) = b_j(x_j) \tag{6.16}$$

where $H(b_i)$ is the Shannon entropy of the belief $H(b_i) = - \sum_{x_i} b_i(x_i) \ln b_i(x_i)$ and $\deg_i$ is the degree of node i in the graph.

Comparing the Bethe free energy minimization problem and the LP relaxation problem, we see that the constraints are the same, and the first term in the objective is also the same. The only difference is the existence of additional entropy terms in the Bethe free energy. But these terms are multiplied by T, so that as $T \to 0$ the two problems coincide (recall that the Shannon entropy is bounded).

Figure 6.3 illustrates the convergence of the Bethe free energy to the LP relaxation. We consider a graphical model corresponding to a toroidal grid. The nodes are binary, and all the pairwise potentials are of the form

$$F = \begin{pmatrix} 3 & 1 \\ 1 & 2 \end{pmatrix}.$$

These potentials correspond to an Ising model with a uniform external field—nodes prefer to be similar to their neighbors and there is a preference for one state over the other. In order to visualize the approximate free energies, we consider beliefs that are symmetric and identical for all pairs of nodes:

$$b_{ij} = \begin{pmatrix} x & y \\ y & 1 - (x + 2y) \end{pmatrix}.$$

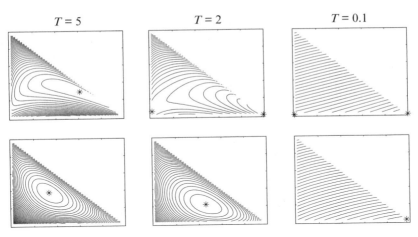

Figure 6.3
Contour plots of the Bethe free energy (top) and a convex free energy (bottom) for a 2D Ising model with uniform external field at different temperatures. The stars indicate local stationary points. Both free energies approach the LP as temperature is decreased, but for the Bethe free energy a local minimum is present even for arbitrarily low temperatures.

Note that the MAP (and the optimum of the LP) occur at $x = 1$, $y = 0$, in which case all nodes are in their preferred state. Figure 6.3 shows the Bethe free energy (top) for this problem at different temperatures. At high temperature the minimization problems are quite different, but as temperature is decreased, the Bethe free energy is dominated by the linear term and becomes equivalent to the LP relaxation.

Note, however, that the convergence of the Bethe free energy problem to the LP relaxation does not guarantee that any BP fixed point will solve the LP relaxation as the temperature approaches zero. It only guarantees that there exists a good fixed point; there may be other fixed points as well. The stars in figure 6.3 indicate the local stationary points of the Bethe free energy. A bad local minimum exists for low temperatures at $x = 0$, $y = 0$. This corresponds to a solution where all nodes have the same state but it is not the preferred state.

6.2.1 Convex BP and the LP Relaxation

In order to avoid local minima, we need a version of the Bethe free energy that has a unique stationary point. The question of when the Bethe free energy has a unique stationary point is surprisingly delicate (see, e.g., [190, 391, 412, 475]) and can depend nontrivially on the graph and the energy function. Perhaps the simplest condition that guarantees a unique stationary point is *convexity*. As illustrated in figure 6.4a, a 1D function is convex if its second derivative is always positive, and this guarantees that it has a unique stationary point. Convexity is a sufficient but not necessary condition for uniqueness of stationary points. Figure 6.4b shows a 1D function that has a unique stationary point but is not

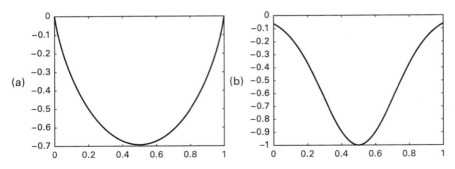

Figure 6.4
Two 1D functions defined on the range $[0, 1]$. The function in (a) is the negative Shannon entropy and is convex. The function in (b) (an inverted Gaussian) has a unique stationary point but is not convex. In order to guarantee uniqueness of BP fixed points, we seek free energies that are convex.

convex. Nevertheless, the easiest way to guarantee uniqueness of BP fixed points is to require convexity of the free energy.

In dimensions larger than 1, the definition of convexity simply requires positivity of the Hessian. This means that the convexity of the free energy does *not* depend on the terms in the energy function $\Psi_{ij}(x_i, x_j)$, $\Phi_i(x_i)$. These terms only change the linear term in the free energy and do not influence the Hessian. Thus the free energy will be convex if the sum of entropy terms is convex. This sum of entropies $H_\beta = \sum_{ij} H(b_{ij}) + \sum_i (1 - \deg_i) H(b_i)$ is called the Bethe entropy approximation. The negative Bethe entropy can be shown to be convex when the graph is a tree or has a single cycle. However, when the graph has multiple cycles, as in the toroidal grid discussed earlier, the Bethe negative entropy is not convex and hence BP can have many fixed points.

We can avoid this problem by "convexifying" the Bethe entropy. We consider a family of entropy approximations of the form

$$\tilde{H} = \sum_{ij} c_{ij} H(b_{ij}) + \sum_i c_i H(b_i). \tag{6.17}$$

Heskes [190] has shown that a sufficient condition for such an approximate entropy to be convex is that it can be rewritten as a *positive* combination of three types of terms: (1) pairwise entropies (e.g., $H(b_{ij})$), (2) singleton entropies (e.g., $H(b_i)$), and (3) conditional entropies (e.g., $H(b_{ij}) - H(b_i)$). Thus the Bethe entropy for a chain of three nodes will be convex because it can be written $H_\beta = H_{12} + H_{23} - H_2$, which is a positive combination of a pairwise entropy H_{12} and a conditional entropy $H_{23} - H_2$. However, for the toroidal grid discussed above, the Bethe entropy cannot be written in such a fashion. To see this, note that a 3×3 toroidal grid has nine nodes with degree 4 and eighteen edges. This means that the Bethe entropy will have twenty-seven negative entropy terms (i.e., nine times we will subtract $3H_i$). However, the maximum number of negative terms we can create with conditional entropies is eighteen (the number of edges), so we have more negative terms than we can create with conditional entropies. In contrast, the entropy approximation $\sum_{<i,j>}(H_{ij} - H_i)$ is convex, since it is the sum of eighteen conditional entropies.

Given an approximate entropy that satisfies the convexity conditions, we can replace the Bethe entropy with this new convex entropy and obtain a convex free energy. But how can we minimize it? It turns out that a slight modification of the BP update rules gives a new algorithm whose fixed points are stationary points of any approximate free energy. The algorithm defines an extra scalar variable for each node i: $\rho_i = \frac{1}{c_i + \sum_{j \in Ni} c_{ij}}$, and for each edge: ij $\rho_{ij} = \rho_j c_{ij}$ (note that ρ_{ij} may differ from ρ_{ji}). Using these extra scalars, the update equations are

$$m_{ij}(x_j) \leftarrow \sum_{x_i} F_{ij}^{\frac{1}{c_{ij}}}(x_i, x_j) F_i^{\rho_i}(x_i) \cdot \prod_{k \in N_i \setminus j} m_{ki}^{\rho_{ki}}(x_i) m_{ji}(x_i)^{\rho_{ji}-1} \tag{6.18}$$

$$b_i(x_i) = F_i^{\rho_i}(x_i) \prod_{j \in N(i)} m_{ji}^{\rho_{ji}}(x_i) \tag{6.19}$$

$$b_{ij}(x_i, x_j) = F_{ij}(x_i, x_j)^{\frac{1}{c_{ij}}} F_i^{\rho_i}(x_i) F_j^{\rho_j}(x_j)$$
$$\times \prod_{k \in N_i \setminus j} m_{ki}^{\rho_{ki}}(x_i) m_{ji}(x_i)^{\rho_{ji}-1} \prod_{k \in N_j \setminus i} m_{kj}^{\rho_{kj}}(x_j) m_{ij}(x_j)^{\rho_{ij}-1}. \tag{6.20}$$

Note that this algorithm is very similar to ordinary BP, so it requires very little modification of an existing implementation of BP. In particular, we can use algorithms for efficient calculations of BP messages for certain energy functions (e.g., [141]). Note that for the Bethe free energy, $c_{ij} = 1$ and $c_i = 1 - \deg_i$ (and thus ρ_i, $\rho_{ij} = 1$), so the above update equation reduces to ordinary BP. However, by choosing c_{ij}, c_i so that the approximate free energy is convex, we can guarantee that this modified algorithm will have a single, unique fixed point at any temperature.

Returning to the toroidal grid we discussed earlier, figure 6.3 (bottom row) shows the convexified free energy (with an entropy approximation of the form $18H_{12} - 18H_1$) for this problem for different temperatures. As was the case for the Bethe free energy, at high temperature the minimization problems are quite different, but as temperature is decreased, the free energy is dominated by the linear term and becomes equivalent to the LP relaxation. However, unlike the Bethe free energy, the convex free energy always has a unique minimum (indicated by the star), so the fixed point of the generalized BP algorithm is guaranteed to give the LP solution.

An important special case of a convex free energy is the class of tree reweighted (TRW) free energies. In these free energies the entropy is approximated as a linear combination of entropies over trees $\tilde{H} = \sum_\tau \rho_\tau H_\tau$. For this free energy the generalized BP algorithm reduces to the TRW algorithm (since $\rho_i = 1$ and $\rho_{ij} = \rho_{ji}$ in this case).

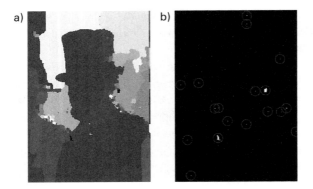

Figure 6.5
(a) The solution to the LP obtained by running convex BP. Using convex BP, we can solve the LP relaxation for full-sized images. Pixels for which the LP solution is fractional are shown in black. (b) A binary image indicating in white the pixels for which the LP solution is fractional.

To summarize, by choosing a convex free energy and running the generalized BP algorithm at low temperature, we can approximate the LP solution. Returning to the stereo problem depicted in figure 6.1, even though standard LP solvers fail on such a large problem, convex BP solved it in less than two hours. The results are shown in figure 6.5a,b. Figure 6.5a displays the disparity encoded by the LP solution. If the LP solution was indeed integer, we display the disparity for which the LP solution was nonzero. If the LP solution was fractional, that pixel is shown in black. In figure 6.5b we show a binary mask indicating which pixels had noninteger values in the LP solution. The existence of such pixels means that the LP relaxation is not tight.

6.3 Convex Max-Product BP

Although we have shown that one can use sum-product convex BP to solve the linear program, one needs to be able to run the sum-product algorithm at sufficiently low temperatures. There are two problems with this approach. First, running the algorithm at low temperatures requires defining $F_{ij} = \exp(-\Psi_{ij}(x_i, x_j)/T)$, $F_i(x_i) = \exp(-\Phi_i(x_i)/T)$ for low T. Note that as $T \to 0$ we are dividing by a number that approaches zero, and this can cause numerical problems. In the appendix to this chapter, we discuss how to implement the algorithm in log space (i.e., by working with the logarithms of the potentials and messages). This can greatly increase the numerical precision at low temperatures.

A second problem, however, is that it is not obvious how to choose the temperature so that it is "sufficiently low." As evident in the discussion in the previous section, we need the temperature to be low enough so that the entropy contribution is negligible relative to the the average energy. Thus the requirement of the temperature being sufficiently low is problem dependent—as we change terms in the energy function, the scale of the average energy may change as well, requiring a different temperature.

In order to avoid choosing a sufficiently low temperature, we can work with the "zero temperature limit" of the convex BP algorithm. This algorithm, called the max-product convex BP algorithm, is exactly the same as (6.18) but with the "sum" operator replaced with a "max." It is easy to show that as the temperature T approaches zero, the update equations of the sum-product algorithm at temperature T approach those of the max-product algorithm at $T = 1$—formally, if a set of messages forms a fixed point of sum-product at temperature T. As $T \to 0$, these same messages, raised to the $1/T$ power, will form a fixed point of the max-product algorithm. This proof follows from the fact that the ℓ_p norm approaches the max norm as $p \to \infty$ [519, 184].

Despite this direct connection to the sum-product algorithm, the max-product algorithm is more difficult to analyze. In particular, even for a convex free energy approximation, the max-product algorithm may have multiple fixed points even though the sum-product algorithm has a unique fixed point. Thus one cannot guarantee that any fixed point of convex max-product BP will solve the linear programming relaxation.

An important distinction in analyzing the fixed points of max-product BP is the notion of "ties." We say that a belief at a node has a tie if it does not have a unique maximizing value. Thus a belief of the form $(0.7, 0.2, 0.1)$ has no ties and the belief $(0.4, 0.4, 0.2)$ has a tie. Max-product fixed points without ties can easily be shown to correspond to a limit of the sum-product algorithm at zero temperature. This leads to the following result.

Claim If max-product convex BP converges to a fixed point without ties, then the assignment $x_i^* = \arg\max_{x_i} b_i(x_i)$ is the global minimum of the energy function.

This result is analogous to the claim on the LP relaxation. Only if the LP relaxation ends up being integral can we say that it corresponds to the global minimum of the energy. Unfortunately, in many vision problems neither is the LP all integer nor are the max-product beliefs all tied. A typical example is shown in figure 6.6a, where we have indicated in black the pixels for which ties exist (these same pixels are, not coincidentally, the pixels where the LP solution is nonintegral). In all the nontied pixels we have shown the disparity that maximizes the beliefs at the fixed point. It can be seen that a small number of pixels are black (see also the mask of black pixels in figure 6.6b) so that we cannot guarantee optimality of the solution. Yet the disparities at the nontied pixels seem reasonable. Under what conditions can we trust the values in the nontied pixels?

In recent years a number of results have been obtained that allow us still to prove partial optimality of an assignment obtained by maximizing the belief at a nontied node after running max-product convex BP. Partial optimality means that we can fix the values at the nontied nodes and optimize only over the remaining, tied, nodes. Under certain conditions this procedure can still be guaranteed to find the global optimum.

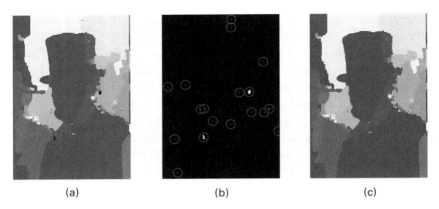

(a)   (b)   (c)

Figure 6.6
(a) Results of using convex max-product BP on the stereo problem shown in figure 6.1a. Pixels for which there are ties in the belief are shown in black. (b) A binary image indicating which pixels had ties. Note that these are exactly the same pixels for which the LP solution had noninteger values (see figure 6.5). (c) The *global* optimum found by resolving the tied pixels and verifying that the conditions for optimality hold. Note that this solution is not much better than the local optima found before (figure 6.1). Both the hat and the shirt of the foreground person are calculated to have "holes."

We list here some results on partial optimality and refer the reader to [519, 535] for more exact definitions and proofs.

• When each node has only two possible states, partial optimality holds.

• Consider the subgraph formed by looking only at the tied nodes. If this graph is a tree, then partial optimality holds.

• Consider the subgraph formed by looking only at the tied nodes. Define its boundary as those nodes in the subgraph that are connected to other nodes. If the beliefs at the boundary nodes are uniform, then partial optimality holds.

• Consider the subgraph formed by looking only at the tied nodes. Define a new energy function on this subgraph and find the assignment in the tied nodes that minimizes this energy function. If that assignment does not contradict the beliefs at the boundary of the subgraph, then partial optimality holds.

Note that verifying that partial optimality holds may require additional computation after running max-product convex BP. Yet in many vision problems we have found that this verification can be done efficiently, and this allows us to provably find the global optimum of the energy function. Code implementing these verification steps is available at http://www.cs .huji.ac.il/talyam/stereo.html. Figure 6.6c shows the *global* optimum of the energy function for the image shown in figure 6.1. Although this is the global optimum for the energy function, it still suffers from mistakes. In particular, the calculated depth for the hat and the shirt still has holes. This indicates that a crucial part of stereo research is choosing a good energy function to minimize.

6.4 Discussion

Despite the NP-hardness of energy minimization in many computer vision problems, it is actually possible to find the global optimum of the energy in many instances. Theoretically, this could be done by relaxing the problem into a linear program. However, the large number of variables and constraints makes this linear program unsuitable for standard LP solvers. In this chapter we have reviewed how variants of belief propagation can be used to solve the LP relaxation. Furthermore, we have shown how the max-product convex BP algorithm can be used to find the global optimum even if the LP relaxation is not tight.

Though we have focused on the connection between BP and the LP relaxation, it can also be shown that the alpha expansion graph cut algorithm is also intimately connected to the same LP relaxation. In particular, Komodakis and Tzritas [269] have shown that the alpha expansion algorithm can be seen as an iterative "primal integer-dual" algorithm for solving the LP relaxation (see chapter 17). Thus the graph cut algorithm and BP, which are often seen as competing algorithms, are actually closely related. One important conclusion from this relationship is that both algorithms are not expected to work well when the LP relaxation is loose. Indeed, despite the success recounted here in finding global optima for some energy functions in stereo vision, for other energy functions the number of "tied" pixels is far too large for the methods described here to be successful. Understanding the conditions under which energy minimization problems in computer vision have a tight LP relaxation is a promising direction for future research.

6.5 Appendix: Implementation Details

6.5.1 Implementation in Log Space

To be able to run the algorithm with a low temperature T, we use the log-space. That is, we work directly with the costs/energies Φ_i, Ψ_{ij} instead of the potentials F_i, F_{ij}, and a set of messages $n_{ji}(x_i) = -T \log m_{ji}(x_i)$.

Yet when running sum-product, we need to sum over terms that are the exponents of the log-terms calculated, and then take the log again. Thus rewriting the generalized BP updates in log-space gives

$$n_{ji}(x_i) = -T \log \sum_{x_j} \exp \left(-\left(\Phi_j(x_j) + \frac{\Psi_{ij}(x_i, x_j)}{\rho_{ij}} \right. \right.$$

$$\left. \left. + \sum_{k \in Nj \backslash i} \rho_{jk} n_{kj}(x_j) - (1 - \rho_{ij}) n_{ij}(x_j) \right) / T \right). \tag{6.21}$$

For efficiency and numerical stability we use the equality

$$\log(\exp(x) + \exp(y)) = x + \log(1 + \exp(y - x)) \tag{6.22}$$

for $x \geq y$. In particular, when x is much greater than y, we can ignore the second term and avoid exponentiating or taking the logarithm during the message update.

6.5.2   Efficient Message Computation for Potts Model

Calculating the vector $m_{ji}(x_i)$ is actually performing a matrix-vector multiplication:

$$m_{ji} = A_{ij} \cdot y_j \tag{6.23}$$

where A_{ij} is a matrix and y_j is a vector. In the case of the generalized BP update, the matrix and vector are given by $A_{ij}(x_i, x_j) = F_{ij}^{1/\rho_{ij}}(x_i, x_j)$ and $y_j(x_j) = F_j(x_j) \prod_{k \in Nj \setminus i} m_{kj}^{\rho_{jk}}(x_j) \cdot m_{ij}^{\rho_{ij}-1}(x_j)$, respectively.

We consider the case where the pairwise potentials are of the Potts model, and thus $A_{ij} = (a_{ij} - b_{ij}) \cdot I + b_{ij}$. We then obtain

$$A_{ij}y_j = (a_{ij} - b_{ij})y_j + b_{ij} \sum_{x_j} y_j(x_j). \tag{6.24}$$

Note that this way, we could compute the outgoing messages vector m_{ji} in $O(|X_j| + |X_i|)$ complexity: one loop of $O(|X_j|)$ for computing the sum $S_j = \sum_{x_j} y_j(x_j)$, and another loop of $O(|X_i|)$ for computing the value

$$m_{ji}(x_i) = (a_{ij} - b_{ij})y_j(x_i) + b_{ij}S_j \tag{6.25}$$

for each assignment x_i.

Acknowledgments

This work was supported by the Israeli Science Foundation. We thank Danny Rosenberg for his help in generating the figures.

II Applications of MRFs, including Segmentation

Part II of the book shows that relatively simple, pairwise MRF models, as introduced in chapter 1, paired with powerful inference engines (as introduced in part I of the book), are capable of producing impressive results for a large number of applications. These solutions sometimes even represent the state of the art in the field and are part of commercial products.

The first two chapters utilize a binary (two-label) MRF where each pixel is probabilistically dependent only on a few, here four or eight, neighboring pixels. The application is the separation of foreground and background in still images, given additional hints from the user. Chapter 7 introduces in detail the most simple realization of such an MRF model, and then builds a more complex, higher-order MRF model. Chapter 8 revisits the low-connected, pairwise MRF model of chapter 7 and casts it as a continuous-valued MRF. In this way a continuum of models, including well-known models such as random walker and shortest path, can be expressed in a unified framework. This makes it possible to study different trade-offs of these models, such as sensitivity to metrication artifacts. Chapter 9 increases the level of difficulty by performing foreground and background separation in a monocular video stream in real time. The main visual cue is that the object and the background move differently. This is achieved by introducing for each pixel a second-order Hidden Markov model with respect to time (as explained in chapter 1), which is then paired with standard 2D MRFs for each frame. Chapter 10 considers the important applications of superresolution (up-scaling an image) and texture synthesis (creating a large image from a small exemplar. The basic idea is to assemble a new image, from a large collection of exemplar patches, in such a way that the synthesized image is spatially coherent. This problem is expressed in the form of a 4-connected, pairwise MRF and is used as the basic building block in several state-of-the-art approaches in this domain. Chapter 11 considers pairwise, multi-abeled MRF models for stereo vision, panoramic stitching, image segmentation, inpainting, and denoising. Its focus is on the comparison of existing inference techniques, introduced in part I of the book, with respect to these applications.

There are many other application scenarios that are not covered in the book but have been realized with low-connected, pairwise MRF or CRF models. Examples in low-level vision are registration, matching and optical flow (examples in [482] and chapter 18), 3D reconstruction (examples in chapter 12), photo and video summarization or collages (e.g, [399]), image manipulation [368], and image and video retargeting [17]). MRFs also play an essential role in large vision-based systems and for high-level vision tasks, such as object recognition, which is the subject of part V.

7 Interactive Foreground Extraction: Using Graph Cut

Carsten Rother, Vladimir Kolmogorov, Yuri Boykov, and Andrew Blake

Interactive image segmentation has received considerable attention in the computer vision community in the last decade. Today this topic is mature, and commercial products exist that feature advanced research solutions. This means that today interactive image segmentation is probably one of the most widespread computer vision technologies. In this chapter we review one class of interactive segmentation techniques that use discrete optimization and a regional selection interface. We begin the chapter by explaining the seminal work of Boykov and Jolly [66]. After that, the GrabCut technique [401] is introduced, which extends [66] by additionaly estimating the appearance model. The joint estimation of segmentation and appearance model parameters can significantly simplify accurate object extraction. GrabCut is the underlying algorithm for the Background Removal tool in Microsoft Office 2010 products. In the third section of the chapter many interesting features and details are explained that are part of the product. In this process several recent research articles are reviewed. Finally, the Background Removal tool, as well as [66, 401], are evaluated in different ways on publicly available databases. This includes static and dynamic user inputs. (An extended version of this chapter is available at [402].[1]

7.1 Introduction

This chapter addresses the problem of extracting an object in an image, given additional hints from the user. This is different from the long-standing research topic of automatically partitioning an image into the objects present in the scene (e.g., [434]). First, user interaction

---

1. A historical note. The Background Removal tool was fully developed at the end of 2004 by Carsten Rother and Vladimir Kolmogorov. It was part of an external release of Microsoft Expression Acrylic Graphics Designer (technology preview) in June 2005 (called "smart select"). This included engineering solutions to many practically interesting problems (see section 7.4) that were not addressed in [401]. For some problems our solutions are in fact very similar to recent work [323, 321]. Some of these practical problems motivated our recent articles on the following topics: initialization and optimality [499], connectivity [497], bounding-box prior [298], and segmentation-based matting [390]. To fine-tune the Background Removal tool we employed the robot user (see section 7.5.2), which was also used in [178] and motivated our very recent work on learning interactive segmentation systems [350].

is needed to specify the object of interest. Second, quite often the user wants to select only part of an object (e.g., head of a person, or an arbitrary region of interest). The intrinsically interactive nature of this problem makes it both very attractive and challenging. Hence, it has been a fruitful research topic for more than two decades, with some work concentrating more on theoretical aspects, such as model and optimization, and other work more on user aspects.

The question of what is the best interactive segmentation system today is hard to answer. Many factors have to be considered: (1) What is the user group (e.g., novice or advanced users)? (2) What is the user interface? (3) How should the user involvement (such as total interaction time or number of user hints) be measured?

Approaches for interactive image segmentation have influenced many related tasks. One example is the problem of joint object recognition and segmentation, as in the TextonBoost framework [437] or the OBJCut system [281]. Another example is the Web-based retrieval system for classical vases [286], which automatically runs segmentation technology in the background.

Note that the focus of this chapter is on the binary segmentation problem. Each pixel belongs to either foreground or background. This is a simplified view of the problem, since some pixels, especially those close to the object boundary, are semitransparent—a mix of foreground and background colors. A brief discussion of this issue in the context of a practical segmentation system is given in [402].

The chapter is organized as follows. After a brief literature review in section 7.1.1, three systems are presented, in order of increased model complexity: the Boykov and Jolly approach (section 7.2), the GrabCut system (section 7.3), and the commercial Background Removal tool (section 7.4). In section 7.5 the methods are compared with other state-of-the-art techniques in two experiments.

7.1.1 Interactive Image Segmentation: A Brief Review

In the following we categorize different approaches to interactive image segmentation by their methodology and user interfaces. Our brief review is not meant to be comprehensive.

Magic Wand   This is probably the simplest technique. Given a user-specified "seed" point (or region), a set of pixels is computed that is connected to the seed point, where all pixels in the set deviate from the color of the seed point only within a given tolerance. Figure 7.1a shows the result using Magic Wand in Adobe Photoshop 7 [3]. Because the distributions in color space of foreground and background pixels have a considerable overlap, a satisfactory segmentation cannot be achieved.

Intelligent Scissors   This approach (a.k.a. Live Wire or Magnetic Lasso) [343] allows a user to choose a "minimum cost contour" by roughly tracing the object's boundary with the mouse. As the mouse moves, the minimum cost path from the cursor position back to the

Figure 7.1
Foreground extraction with four different systems: (a) Magic Wand, (b) Intelligent Scissors, (c) graph cut [66], and (d) GrabCut [401], with segmentation result in the bottom row and user interaction in the top row (image colors were changed for better visualization; see original color image in figure 1.7(a) in chapter 1). While the results b–d are all visually acceptable, GrabCut needs fewest user interactions (two clicks). Note that result (d) is the final result of GrabCut, including semitransparency using border matting.

last "seed" point is shown. If the computed path deviates from the desired one, additional user-specified seed points are necessary. In figure 7.1b the Magnetic Lasso of Photoshop 7 was used in which a large number of seed points (here nineteen) were needed, since both foreground and background are highly textured. One problem is that this technique is not effective for objects with a long boundary (e.g., a tree with many branches).

Segmentation in the Discrete Domain   Boykov and Jolly were the first to formulate a simple generative MRF model in discrete domain for the task of binary image segmentation [66]. This basic model can be used for interactive segmentation. Given some user constraints in the form of foreground and background brushes (i.e., regional constraints), the optimal solution is computed very efficiently with graph cut (see an example in figure 7.1c. The main benefits of this approach are global optimality, practical efficiency, numerical robustness, ability to fuse a wide range of visual cues and constraints, unrestricted topological properties of segments, and applicability to N-D problems. For these reasons this approach inspired many other methods for various applications in computer vision (see, e.g., chapter 9, on bilayer segmentation in video). It also inspired the GrabCut system [401, 52], which is the main focus of this chapter. GrabCut solves a more challenging problem, namely, the joint optimization of segmentation and estimation of global properties of the segments. The benefit is a simpler user interface in the form of a bounding box (see the example in figure 1.7d). Note that such joint optimization has been done in other contexts. An example is depth estimation in stereo images [45] where the optimal partitioning of the stereo images and the global properties (affine warping) of each segment are optimized jointly.

Since the work of Boykov and Jolly, many articles on interactive segmentation using graph cut and a brush interface have been published; a few are [312, 175, 129, 499, 19, 440, 321, 350, 178], which we will discuss in more detail later. We would like to refer to chapter 8, where the discrete labeling problem is relaxed to a continuous one, which gives a common framework for explaining and comparing three popular approaches: random walker [175], graph cut [66], and geodesic distance [19]. Another interesting set of discrete functionals is based on ratio (e.g., area over boundary length; see [105, 217, 257]).

Segmentation in the Continuous Domain   There are very close connections between the spatially discrete MRFs, as mentioned above, and variational formulations in the continuous domain. The first continuous formulations were expressed in terms of snakes [227] and geodesic active contours [84], related to the well-known Mumford-Shah functional [344]. The goal is to find a segmentation that minimizes a boundary (surface) under some metric, typically an image-based Riemannian metric. Traditionally, techniques such as level sets were used; however, they are only guaranteed to find a local optimum. Recently many of these functionals were reformulated using convex relaxation (i.e., the solution lives in the [0, 1] domain), which allows achievement of global optimality and bounds in some practical cases (see chapter 12). An example of interactive segmentation with a brush interface is [489], where the optimal solution of a weighted TV norm is computed efficiently. Instead of using convex relaxation techniques, the continuous problem can be approximated on a discrete grid and solved globally optimally, using graph cut. This can be done for a large set of useful metrics (see [67]). Theoretically, the discrete approach is inferior because the connectivity of the graph has to be large in order to avoid metrication artifacts. In practice, however, artifacts are rarely visible when using a *geodesic* distance (see, e.g., figure 7.1d) with an underlying 8-connected graph. In section 7.3.1 we will show another relationship between the continuous Chan–Vese functional [88] and the discrete GrabCut functional.

Paint Selection   Conceptually the brush interface and the so-called paint selection interface [321] are very similar. The key difference is that a new segmentation is visualized after each mouse movement (i.e., instant feedback while drawing a stroke). Section 7.4 gives a more detailed comparison with the Background Removal tool.

7.2   Basic Graph Cut Model for Image Segmentation

Boykov and Jolly [66] addressed the problem of interactive image segmentation based on initial trimap $T = \{T_F, T_B, T_U\}$. The trimap partitions the image into three sets: T_F and T_B comprise pixels selected by the user as either foreground or background, respectively, and T_U is the remaining set of unknown pixels. The image is an array $\mathbf{z} = (z_1, \ldots, z_n, \ldots, z_N)$

of intensities (gray, color, or any other n-dimensional values), indexed by integer n. The unknown segmentation of the image is expressed as an array of "opacity" variables $\mathbf{x} = (x_1, \ldots, x_N)$ at each pixel. In general, $0 \leq x_n \leq 1$ (e.g., in α-matting), but [66] uses discrete-valued (hard) segmentation variables $x_n \in \{0, 1\}$, with 0 for background and 1 for foreground. The parameter ω describes the distributions for foreground and background intensities. The basic approach in [66] assumes that such distributions (intensity models or histograms $\omega = \{h_B(z_i), h_F(z_i)\}$ for foreground and background) are either known a priori or are assembled directly from labeled pixels in the respective trimap regions T_B, T_F. Histograms are normalized to sum to 1 over the range of intensities, (i.e. $\int_z h_F(z) = 1$. This means that the histograms represent the observation likelihood, that is, $P(z_i|x_i = 0) = h_B(z_i)$ and $P(z_i|x_i = 1) = h_F(z_i)$.

The segmentation task addressed in [66] is to infer the unknown opacity variables $\mathbf{x}$ from the given model ω and image data $\mathbf{z}$. For this, an energy function E is defined so that its minimum should correspond to a good segmentation, in the sense that it is guided by both the given foreground and background intensity histograms and that the opacity is "coherent," reflecting a tendency to solidity of objects. This is captured by a Gibbs energy of the form

$$E(\mathbf{x}, \omega, \mathbf{z}) = U(\mathbf{x}, \omega, \mathbf{z}) + V(\mathbf{x}, \mathbf{z}). \tag{7.1}$$

The data term U evaluates the fit of the segmentation $\mathbf{x}$ to the data $\mathbf{z}$, given the model ω, and is defined for all pixels in T_U as

$$U(\mathbf{x}, \omega, \mathbf{z}) = \sum_{n \in T_U} - \log h_B(z_i)[x_n = 0] - \log h_F(z_i)[x_n = 1] + \sum_{n \in T_F \cup T_B} H(x_n, n) \tag{7.2}$$

where $[\phi]$ denotes the indicator function taking values 0, 1 for a predicate ϕ, and the term $H(x_n, n)$ constrains certain variables to belong to foreground or background, respectively, that is, $H(x_n, n) = \gamma([x_n = 0][n \in T_F] + [x_n = 1][n \in T_B])$, where γ is a large enough constant. The smoothness term can be written as

$$V(\mathbf{x}, \mathbf{z}) = \sum_{(m,n) \in \mathcal{N}} \mathrm{dis}(m, n)^{-1} \, (\lambda_1 + \lambda_2 \exp\{-\beta||z_m - z_n||^2\}) \, [x_n \neq x_m], \tag{7.3}$$

where $\mathcal{N}$ is the set of pairs of neighboring pixels and $\mathrm{dis}(\cdot)$ is the Euclidean distance of neighboring pixels. This energy encourages coherence in regions of similar intensity level. In practice, good results are obtained by defining pixels to be neighbors if they are adjacent either horizontally/vertically or diagonally (8-way connectivity). Factor $dis(\cdot)$ and larger neighborhoods help the smoothness term $V(\mathbf{x}, \mathbf{z})$ to better approximate a geometric length of the segmentation boundary according to some continuous metric (see [67]). This reduces geometric artifacts. When the constant λ_2 is set to 0, the smoothness term is simply the well-known Ising prior, encouraging smoothness everywhere. Practically, however, as shown in [66], it is far more effective to set $\lambda_2 > 0$, as this relaxes the tendency to smoothness in regions of high contrast. The constant β is chosen to be $\beta = (2\langle (z_m - z_n)^2 \rangle)^{-1}$, where $\langle \cdot \rangle$ denotes expectation over an image sample. This choice of β ensures that the exponential term in (7.3) switches appropriately between high and low contrast (see [53]). The constants λ_1 and λ_2 should be learned from a large corpus of training data. Various learning approaches have been suggested in the past, ranging from simple cross validation [53] over max-margin learning [466] and, very recently, parameter estimation in an interactive setting [350]. In most of our experiments the values were fixed to the reasonable choice of $\lambda_1 = 5$ and $\lambda_2 = 50$.

Now that energy (7.1) is fully defined, the Boykov-Jolly [66] model for binary segmentation can be formulated as an estimation of a global minimum

$$\hat{\mathbf{x}} = \arg\min_{\mathbf{x}} \ E(\mathbf{x}, \omega, \mathbf{z}). \tag{7.4}$$

Exact global minima can be found using a standard minimum-cut/maximum-flow algorithm [68] (see chapter 2). Since the desired results are often not achieved with the initial trimap, additional user interactions are necessary. The maximum-flow computation for these additional interactions can be made very efficient by reusing flow from the previous computation (see details in [66]).

7.3 GrabCut+: Image Segmentation Using Iterative Graph Cut

The following description of GrabCut contains additional details, and a few minor modifications, compared with the original version [401, 52]; hence the name GrabCut+ is used.

The algorithm described in section 7.2 often gives good results in practice, as shown in figure 7.1c; however, it relies on the user to define the color distributions for foreground and background. One problem is that it does not exploit the information given by the unlabeled data to help learn the unknown parameter ω. In the following we describe one approach that makes use of the unlabeled data. The simple idea is to find the optimal settings for the model parameter ω and segmentation $\mathbf{x}$ jointly. This is done as before, by minimizing the functional in (7.1) subject to the given user constraints. Note that by optimizing ω we implicitly assume that both foreground and background are represented well by compact distributions. The implications of this assumption are discussed later in detail. By exploiting the unlabeled data we are able to achieve good results with fewer user inputs compared with the approach in section 7.2. In particular we show that it is sometimes sufficient simply to specify the object with a bounding box, so that the set T_F is empty (see the example in figure 7.1d). Unfortunately, optimizing this energy with respect to both unknowns, ω and $\mathbf{x}$, is a very challenging problem. In fact it is NP-hard [499], as discussed later. Hence, in this section and the following one, questions concerning different optimization procedures, optimality, and initialization are addressed.

7.3.1 The GrabCut Model

The first modification of the basic segmentation model, as described in section 7.2, is done by switching from an explicit representation of intensity distributions via histograms to a parametric representation via Gaussian Mixture Models (GMMs) [401, 53, 409]. This more compact form of representation is particularly helpful in the case of RGB colors (n-dimensional intensities).

Foreground and background are modeled separately with each K full-covariance Gaussian (here $K = 7$). In order to deal with the GMM tractably, in the optimization framework an additional vector $\mathbf{k} = \{k_1, \ldots, k_n, \ldots, k_N\}$ is introduced with $k_n \in \{1, \ldots K\}$, assigning each pixel a unique GMM component, one component from either the foreground or the background model, according to $x_n = 1$ or 0.[2] This means that the unknown parameter ω comprises the variables

$$\omega = \{\mathbf{k}, \pi_F(k), \mu_F(k), \Sigma_F(k), \pi_B(k), \mu_B(k), \Sigma_B(k), \ k = 1 \ldots K\},$$

with π as mixture-weighting coefficients that sum to 1, and $\mu(k)$, $\Sigma(k)$ as mean and covariance matrix for each Gaussian k.[3] It is important to note that fitting a GMM model is, strictly speaking, an ill-posed problem since an infinite likelihood (energy of minus infinity) can be obtained when the variance is 0 (see [46], section 9.2.1). Hence, the covariance matrix is restricted to have a minimum variance of $1/255^2$.

Using the same energy (7.1), the GrabCut model is defined as the joint optimization (estimation) for segmentation x and parameters ω:

$$\hat{\mathbf{x}} = \arg \min_{\mathbf{x}} \ \min_{\omega} E(\mathbf{x}, \omega, \mathbf{z}). \tag{7.5}$$

The key difference between the Boykov–Jolly model (7.4) and the GrabCut model (7.5) is that in (7.5) the minimization is also done with respect to ω. It is worth noting that the GrabCut model and the functional of Chan-Vese [88, 299] in the continuous domain, related to the Mumford-Shah functional [344], share some properties. In both models the key problem is the joint optimization of segmentation and global properties of the segmented regions.

7.3.2 The Optimization Procedure

The pseudo code for GrabCut+ is given in figure 7.2. The user starts by defining the initial trimap, using either a bounding box or a lasso interface. This means that T_B is outside the marked region, T_U is inside the marked region, and T_F is an empty set. As suggested

---

2. Using "soft assignments" of probabilities for each component to a given pixel would give a significant additional computational expense for a negligible practical benefit.

3. An efficient variant for using GMMs in a segmentation framework has been suggested in [437]. A different GMM model with $2K$ Gaussian is fitted first to the whole image. This gives a fixed assignment vector $\mathbf{k}$, which is not updated during the optimization of ω and $\mathbf{x}$.

Algorithm 1 : GrabCut+

Require: T_B using bounding box or lasso user interface. Set $T_F = \emptyset, T_U = \bar{T}_B$
  1: Initialize $x_n = 0$ for $n \in T_B$ and $x_n = 1$ for $n \in T_U$
  2: Estimate initial ω using EM (with smart initialization for **k**)
  3: **for** $sweep = 1 - 5$ **do**
  4:     Update **x** given current ω using graph cut
  5:     Update ω given current **x** using EM
  6: **end for**
User Edit: Update user trimap $T = \{T_F, T_B, T_U\}$ and go to step 3

Figure 7.2
The pseudo code for GrabCut+ with bounding box or lasso input.

in [401], results improve if T_B comprises only pixels that are inside a strip around the outside of the marked region.[4] The intuition is that the relevant background training data are often close to the object. In fact, pixels outside this strip are ignored throughout the whole optimization procedure. The trimap T uniquely defines the segmentation x, which is used to initialize the unknown color model ω. Though this initialization step was not discussed in [401], it is quite important. One choice is a random initialization for **k**, but the following "smart initialization" works better. Consider the set of background pixels, $x_n = 0$. The first principal axis is computed from image data z_n of this set. Then the data are projected onto this axis and sorted accordingly. Finally, the sorted set is divided into K groups that for each pixel n define the assignment variable k_n. Given **k**, a standard EM-style procedure for GMM fitting can be invoked. This means that in the M step the Gaussians (i.e., π, μ, Σ), are fitted in a standard way; see [401] for details. In the E step **k** is optimized by enumerating all components $k \in K$ and choosing the one with lowest energy. In practice these two steps are executed four times. The foreground pixels are processed similarly.

The main procedure alternates the following two steps: (1) Given ω, the segmentation **x** is inferred with graph cut as in section 7.2, (2) Given the segmentation **x**, the unknown model ω is inferred using the above EM-style procedure for GMM fitting. In each step the total energy E is guaranteed not to increase. The method can be run until a local minimum is found, but in practice we simply stop it after five iterations. Figure 7.3 shows the power of running the iterative GrabCut+ procedure. Finally, the user can update the trimap and the main procedure is run again. As in the previous section, reusing of flow gives a speedup.

Note that a small modification of this procedure lets us apply GrabCut+ for a standard brush interface [66], as done in the experiments. For that, step 1 in figure 7.2 is initialized as $x_n = 0$ for $n \in T_B$, as $x_n = 1$ for $n \in T_F$, and as $x_n =$ "?" for $n \in T_U$, where the label "?"

---

4. The width of the strip is chosen as a small fraction of the bounding box dimensions. In the experiments, section 7.5.1, the width is set to ten pixels, as in [298].

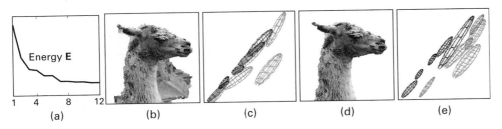

Figure 7.3
(a) The energy of the GrabCut+ model decreases over twelve iterations. (b) Initial result after first iteration of the GrabCut+ algorithm, where initialization is as in figure 7.1d. (c) The GMMs, here $K = 5$, for foreground (bright/blue) and background (dark/red) overlap considerably (visualized RG-slice). (d) and (e) The final result for segmentation and GMMs.

means unlabeled and those pixels are ignored in step 2 of the algorithm. Other interesting user inputs, such as no user intervention (as in [286]), are discussed in [402].

7.3.3 Properties of the GrabCut Model

In the GrabCut model there is the freedom to choose appropriate foreground and background color distributions ω. It is straightforward to see that distributions that are more compact and model the data well give a lower energy.[5] This means that it is implicitly assumed that both foreground and background segments are more likely to be represented by a compact distribution in color space.

One important question is whether the GrabCut model has an implicit bias toward certain segmentations. This was analyzed in Vicente et al. [499] by disregarding the smoothing term V in (7.3). They first showed that by using a histogram representation in RGB space, it is possible to write the term "$\min_\omega E(\mathbf{x}, \omega, \mathbf{z})$" in (7.5) explicitly in the form of a new energy $E'(\mathbf{x}, \mathbf{z})$ with higher-order cliques on $\mathbf{x}$. This higher-order energy E' has two types of terms: (1) a convex function over $\sum_n x_n$, and (2) a concave function, for each histogram bin k, over $\sum_n x_n [n \in Bin(k)]$, that is, all pixels that are assigned to bin k. The convex function (first type) has lowest energy if exactly half of the pixels in the image are assigned to foreground and half to background, respectively. Hence, this is a bias toward balanced segmentations. The concave function (second type) has lowest energy if all pixels that are assigned to the same bin have the same label, either 0 or 1. Note that these two types of terms often counterbalance each other in practice, so that the optimal segmentation is not a degenerate solution—not all undefined pixels are either all foreground or all background. In an extreme case the bias toward balanced segmentation is more prominent. This is when all pixels are assigned to unique histogram bins. Then all concave terms are constants, so that the energy consists of the convex part only. At the other extreme, however, when all

---

5. For example, assume all foreground pixels have the same color; then the lowest unary term is achieved by modeling the foreground distribution with one (or many identical) Gaussian, with minimum variance.

pixels are assigned to the same histogram bin, the bias disappears, since then concave and convex terms cancel each other out. An interesting observation was made in [499] that results improve considerably when choosing the weight of this bias individually for each image.

Unfortunately, optimizing the higher-order energy E' with respect to $\mathbf{x}$ is an NP-hard problem [499]. An optimization procedure for E' was suggested in [499], based on dual decomposition ([35] and in chapter 22, which also provides a lower bound for the energy. This procedure achieved global optimality in 61% of test cases for the GrabCut database of forty-nine images [203] and a bounding-box input. However, for the remaining 39% of test cases, the dual decomposition approach performed rather poorly. Many of those test cases were "camouflage images," where foreground and background colors overlap considerably, (example in [499], figure 2). In comparison, the iterative GrabCut+ procedure (figure 7.2) performs quite well for all types of images and, hence, achieves a lower total error rate (8.1%) than the dual decomposition approach (10.5%); more details are in [402, 499].

7.4   Background Removal: Image Segmentation in MS Office 2010

Designing a product based on GrabCut+ (section 7.3) meant that many interesting practical and theoretical issues had to be addressed. This section discusses some of the topics on which the Background Removal tool and the GrabCut+ tool differ. In [402] further details are given, including a discussion on how to deal with large images and semitransparency. We begin by revisiting the optimization procedure and then examine additional model constraints.

7.4.1   Initialization and the Bounding-Box Prior

It turns out that choosing the initial segmentation $\mathbf{x}$, based on the user trimap T (i.e., step 1 in figure 7.2), is crucial for performance. In the following, three initialization schemes are compared for the bounding-box input. All approaches have in common that $x_n = 0$ for $n \in T_B$, though, they differ in the treatment of pixels in T_U. The first approach, called *Init-FullBox*, is described in section 7.3.2, and sets $x_n = 1$ for all $n \in T_U$. The second method, called *InitThirds*, was suggested in [298]. First, a background color model is trained from pixels in T_B. Then the probabilities of all pixels in T_U are evaluated under the background GMM. One third of the pixels with lowest probability are set to foreground, and one third with highest probability are set to background.[6] The remaining pixels are set to "?," and are ignored in step 2 of figure 7.2. The last approach, called *InitParametric*, is implemented in the Background Removal tool and is similar to the InitThirds procedure but in addition considers the smoothing term V of the energy. For this a new parametric energy is introduced, $E''(\mathbf{x}, \omega, \mathbf{z}) = E(\mathbf{x}, \omega, \mathbf{z}) + \sum_n \lambda x_n$, with E as defined in section 7.3.1. Here ω is chosen

---

6. The choice of using a third as the threshold is arbitrary and should be learned from data.

such that the background GMM is trained from pixels in T_B, and the distribution for the foreground is constant and uniform. The global optimum of E'' for all continuous values of λ can be computed efficiently using parametric max-flow [257].[7] From the set of all solutions for E'', one solution $\mathbf{x}$ is selected using the following heuristic. The segmentation with smallest foreground area is selected that also meets the criterion that the maximum distance of the largest connected component to any four sides of the box is smaller than a fixed threshold (e.g., 25% of a side of the bounding box).[8] The inspiration for the Init-Parametric initialization procedure is the following. First, the user is more likely to select a bounding box that is tight around the object. We refer to this idea as the *bounding box prior*; it motivated the work in [298]. Second, as in InitThirds, the foreground segmentation is often "far away" in feature space from the given background distribution. However, in contrast to InitThirds the foreground segmentation is spatially coherent with this procedure.

An experiment gives an indication of the quality of results that can be achieved with these three methods. For this test the GrabCut data set (fity images) is used together with the bounding boxes from [298] (see online [203]).[9] It has to be stressed that the following error rates must be taken with care, since the data set is rather small,[10] and parameters were not trained.[11] The exact settings for GrabCut+ are as defined in section 7.3: $\lambda_1 = 5$, $\lambda_2 = 50$, $K = 7$. Results are as follows. Initializing GrabCut+ with InitFullBox gave an error rate of 9.0%.[12] It seems that the initialization of InitThirds is clearly a better choice, since the error rate dropped from 9.0% to 5.0%, which is the same conclusion as in [298]. Running the Background Removal tool, which uses InitParametric, gave a slightly higher error rate of 5.95%.

Note that this experiment did not enforce the very sensible bounding box prior, which ensures that the final segmentation is close to the user-selected bounding box. Indeed, by enforcing this prior the error rate can be reduced to 3.7%. The algorithm to achieve this is described in [298] and runs graph cut iteratively while forcing certain pixels to belong to the foreground. We refer the interested reader to [298] for several alternative procedures for

---

7. Since we were not aware of parametric maxflow in 2004, a simple iterative procedure is utilized that reuses flow.

8. This is the same criterion as the weak tightness condition defined in [298].

9. Note, the bounding boxes from [298] deviate slightly from the original set of bounding boxes. The bounding boxes that are different touch the image boundary, while the object does not. This modification simplifies the segmentation task and also removes the problem that in one image the original bounding box was of the same size as the image itself.

10. A larger, (e.g., 1000+), data set with high-quality ground truth is needed in the future. Note that for product testing, a medium-sized data set was created that includes images that are not photographs (e.g., graphics and hand-drawn sketches).

11. As discussed in detail later, image segmentation is an interactive process; hence parameters have to be trained anyway with the user in the loop (as in section 7.5.2).

12. One small modification did reduce the error rate to 7.1 percent. This was done by choosing a random initialization for $\mathbf{k}$ in step 2 in figure 7.2. It shows that initialization is very important and can affect the final result considerably, and that the data set may be too small.

enforcing the bounding box prior. An interesting direction of future work could be to use InitThirds as the initialization procedure and to exploit the parametric max-flow approach of InitParametric to enforce the bounding box prior.

7.4.2 Modeling User Intention

The ultimate goal of a segmentation system is that a user achieves the desired result in as short a time as possible. For this goal the energy defined in section 7.3.1 might not be the optimal model. One problem with the above model is that it is agnostic to the *sequence* of user interactions. By exploiting this sequence the intention of the user can be modeled in a better way. Two simple ideas, which are realized in the Background Removal tool, will be discussed.[13] Other ideas for modeling the user's intention are presented in recent works [509, 321] that investigate alternative models and different user interfaces.

The first idea is to avoid the so-called fluctuation effect [321]. Consider a current imperfect segmentation where the user has placed the (latest) foreground brushstroke. Two effects are undesirable: (1) pixels change label from foreground to background and (2) pixels that are spatially far away change label from background to foreground, since the user may not notice it. We enforce the sensible constraint that the change in the segmentation must be, in this case, from background to foreground and also 4-connected to the latest foreground brushstroke. Achieving connectivity is in general an NP-hard problem (see chapter 22 and [497]); hence we solve it with a simple postprocessing step.[14] The same procedure is applied for a background brushstroke. With this connectivity prior, parameters in the GrabCut+ model may be chosen quite differently (see [350]).[15] Also, many systems that do not use an explicit unary term, such as [19] and random walker [175], are guaranteed to satisfy this connectivity property.[16]

The second idea achieves the desired property that the latest brushstroke always has a noticeable effect on the current segmentation, which is related to the progressive labeling concept in [321]. Consider the case where the current segmentation has a dominant color of red in the background and a small region of the true foreground that is also red but is currently incorrectly labeled. A foreground brushstroke in this small region may fail to

13. These ideas were realized in Microsoft Expression Acrylic Graphics Designer (technology preview). Unfortunately, due to constraints in the Microsoft Office product, it was not possible to realize them exactly as described below. The difference is that in the MS Office version all user foreground and background brushstrokes are treated as one (latest) foreground or background brushstroke, respectively.

14. Note that other automatic techniques can be used in the future, such as [390], based on [497], or the the geodesic star convexity prior of [178].

15. The reason is that one of the main effects of the Ising prior in an MRF (weight λ_1 in (7.3)) is to smooth out wrongly labeled isolated regions. By enforcing connectivity these isolated regions are not permitted in the solution space; hence a different weight for the Ising prior might perform better.

16. In this context we also postprocess the initial segmentation, which is the result of a bounding box (or lasso) input, such that only one 4-connected foreground component is present. No constraint on the background label is enforced, since many objects do have holes.

select the whole region, since the unary terms in the region strongly favor the background label, that is, red being background. The underlying problem is that the general global color model as defined in section 7.3.1 is not always appropriate for modeling objects. A practical solution to overcome this problem is simply to give pixels that are in the latest foreground brushstroke a much higher weight (e.g., 80%), and all other foreground pixels a lower weight (e.g., 20%). The same procedure is applied for a (latest) background brushstroke.[17] This aggressive color modeling procedure works only in conjunction with the above idea of connectivity with the latest brushstroke.

7.5 Evaluation and Future Work

As mentioned in section 7.1, the question of what is the best interactive segmentation system today is hard to answer. To cast some light on this question, two experiments were performed: first, with a static user input and second, with a so-called "robot user" that simulates a simple novice user. The robot user is used to train and compare different systems in a truly interactive setting.

7.5.1 Static User Input

A plausible type of user interaction, for objects with boundaries that are not excessively long, is that the user draws with a "fat pen" around the boundary of the object, which produces a relatively tight trimap. Obviously a method should exploit the fact that the true boundary is more likely to be in the middle of the user-drawn band. As above, the GrabCut database (fifty images) is used; it provides such a trimap, derived by simply eroding the ground truth segmentation (see the example in figure 1.7(b) in chapter 1, and online in [203]). Several articles have reported error statistics for this data set, using the percentage of misclassified pixels within the unknown trimap region T_U.[18] As above, the following error rates have to be taken with care, since the database is small and the methods were not properly trained. Also, all parameter settings for GrabCut+ (and variants of it) are as described above.

Applying simple graph cut without any global color modeling (i.e., energy in (7.1) without unary term U) gives an error rate of 9.0%. As discussed in detail in chapter 8, one bias of graph cut is the so-called "shrinking bias": segmentations with a short boundary are preferred. In contrast, random walker [175] has less of a shrinking bias and instead has a "proximity bias" toward segmentations that are equally far from the given foreground and background trimap, respectively. Obviously, this is a better bias for this data set; hence

17. An improvement could be to model, in the case of a foreground brushstroke, the background color model in a different way, such that it is more representative for this segmentation task.

18. A small fraction of pixels in the ground truth are unlabeled, due to transparency effects. These pixels are not counted when computing the error rate.

the error rate for random walker is just 5.4% (see [129]).[19] In [440] (see also chapter 8) a continuum of solutions is presented that vary with respect to the proximity bias. As to be expected, the setting $p = \infty$ in [440], which exploits the proximity bias most, is the best. On this note, a simple baseline method that ignores the image data achieves quite a low error rate of 4.5%. The baseline method simply classifies each pixel according to the Euclidean distance to the foreground and background regions, respectively.[20] It is worth noting that there is a method that beats the baseline: that is, random walker with an "adaptive thresholding," which better exploits the proximity bias (see [129]).

Finally, the effect of adding global color models is investigated. The error rate of graph cut decreases from 9.0% to 6.6% when using the GrabCut+ algorithm in figure 7.2 with one sweep (step 3). Multiple iterations of GrabCut+ reduce the error rate further to 5.6%, and the Background Removal tool achieves basically the same error rate, 5.8%.[21] To conclude, global color models do considerably help graph cut-based techniques, and they may also help the best performing methods for this data set (see [129]), as also conjectured in [129].

7.5.2 Dynamic User Input

The setup is described in detail in Gulshan et. al. [178], so only some aspects are mentioned here. To measure the amount of user interaction in an interactive system, we invented the so-called "robot user" [350]. It can be used for both learning and evaluating segmentation systems (see [350]). Given a new image, it starts with an initial set of brushstrokes[22] and computes a segmentation. It then places a circular brushstroke in the largest connected component of the segmentation *error* area, at a point farthest from the boundary of the component. The process is repeated up to twenty times, generating a sequence of twenty simulated user strokes that is different for each algorithm. Figure 7.4b shows an example (see also video in [203]). From the sequence of interactions, one number for the amount of user interaction is derived that measures, in rough words, the average number of brushstrokes necessary to achieve a good-quality result (details in [178]). A small user study confirmed that the interaction effort of the robot user indeed correlates reasonably well with the true effort of a *novice user* (see [350]).

The data set for this experiment consists of 151 images with ground truth segmentations, and is a mix of existing data sets including GrabCut and VOC'09 (see [203]). The free

---

19. In [129] some variations of the random walker formulation are given, but however, produce quantitatively the same results.

20. The baseline method does not treat thin structures well; hence a skeletonization approach might perform even better.

21. Note that by additionally exploiting the idea that the relevant training data for the background GMM are more likely in a strip around the unknown region (as provided with the data set), the error rate of GrabCut+ drops from 5.6% to 5.3%.

22. They were chosen manually with one stroke for foreground and three strokes for background.

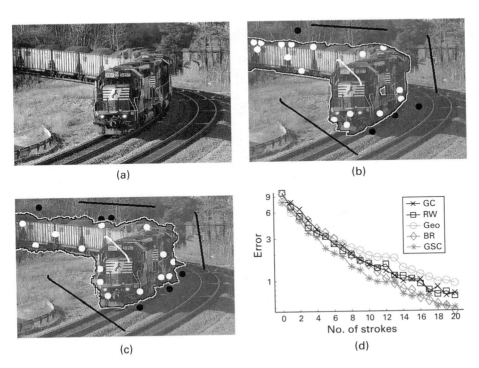

Figure 7.4
(a) Input image (original in color). (b) Result of the robot user employing the BR system, with 0.85% of misclassified pixels (image colors adapted for better visualization). The segmentation is outlined with a black-white line, and the robot user inputs are white and black circles for the foreground and background, respectively (long strokes are initial manual user strokes). (c) Result from Geo system, which is considerably worse (error 1.61%). (d) Performance of five systems utilizing the robot user (error in log-scale).

parameters for all systems were trained using cross validation, 75–76 split repeated ten times.

Table 7.1 presents the results for five different methods, and figure 7.4d depicts the average error rate for the sequence of robot user interactions. The Geo method of [19], based on geodesic distance, performed worst. This is not surprising, since the method does not regularize the boundary and is sensitive to the exact locations of brushstrokes (see chapter 8). Figure 7.4c gives an example. Graph cut GC (section 7.2) performed considerably better.[23] The main difference in graph cut compared with the following three systems is that it does not impose any "shape" prior. Random walker (RW) [175], for instance, guarantees a connectivity of the segmentation with respect to brushstrokes (e.g., a pixel with label 0 is 4/8-connected to a background brushstrokes). Hence, even without global color models,

---

23. Here the implementation of [203] was used. It includes an important additional trick that mixes the GMMs with a uniform distribution.

Table 7.1
Comparison of five different systems in terms of the average number of brush strokes needed by the robot user to achieve good results

Method	Geo [20]	GC (sec. 7.2)	RW [176]	BR (sec. 7.3)	GSC [179]
Effort	15.14	12.35	12.31	10.82	9.63

random walker performs as well as graph cut. The Background Removal tool (BR) is the second-best-performing system (example in figure 7.4b). It exploits the same connectivity property as random walker, but additionally utilizes global color models. Finally, the best-performing method, GSC [178], imposes a strong geodesic star convexity prior on top of the simple graph cut system (GC). This convexity prior is even more restrictive than a connectivity prior (see [178], figure 14), which seems to be an advantage in practice.[24]

7.5.3 Future Work
Many ideas for future work were mentioned above. Certainly, the model for Background Removal can be improved further by using stronger shape priors, (e.g., [178]), improved local MRF modeling (e.g., flux [390]), or better global color models (e.g., [178]). Apart from improving the model, we believe that further improvements may be achieved by focusing more on user aspects.

Acknowledgments

Many people helped with discussions, experiments and great new ideas on the topic of interactive image segmentation. We would like gratefully thank Toby Sharp, Varun Gulshan, Victor Lempitsky, Pushmeet Kohli, Sara Vicente, Antonio Criminisi, Christoph Rhemann, Dheeraj Singaraju, Hannes Nickisch, and Patrick Perez.

24. This is supported by testing against another variant of GC, which performed slightly worse (effort 10.66). It removes all foreground islands that are not connected to a foreground brushstroke in a postprocessing step.

8 Continuous-Valued MRF for Image Segmentation

Dheeraj Singaraju, Leo Grady, Ali Kemal Sinop, and René Vidal

Research on image segmentation has focused on algorithms that *automatically* determine how to group pixels into different regions on the basis of homogeneity of intensity, color, texture, or other features [434, 100, 138, 533]. However, since images generally contain several objects that are surrounded by clutter, it is often not possible to define a unique segmentation. In many such cases, different users may be interested in obtaining different segmentations of an image. Hence, recent research in segmentation has focused on *interactive* methods that allow different users to interact with the system and to segment different objects of interest from the same image.

One genre of interactive segmentation algorithms offers the user a *scribble interface* to label two disjoint sets of pixels as belonging to the object of interest and to the background. The algorithms' goal is then to output a label for each unmarked pixel into one of these two categories. The labeling is typically obtained by minimizing an energy function defined on a weighted combinatorial graph. In general, this can be done using several methods, such as graph cut [66, 72], random walker [175], shortest path [18, 113], region growing [2], fuzzy connectivity [487], seeded watershed [24], and many more examples given in chapter 7. This genre has become very popular, notably due to the availability of numerical solvers that efficiently produce the global optimizer of the defined energy function.

This chapter discusses a generalized graph-theoretic algorithm that estimates the segmentation via a continuous-valued optimization as opposed to the traditional view of segmentation as a discrete-valued optimization, as in chapter 7. The algorithm proceeds by associating a continuous-valued variable with each node in the graph. An energy function is then defined by considering the p-norm of the difference between these variables at neighboring nodes. The minimizer of this energy function is thresholded to produce a binary segmentation.

This formulation includes algorithms such as graph cut [66], random walker [175], and shortest path [18] as special cases for specific values of the p-norm (i.e., $p = 1, 2$, and ∞, respectively). Due to the choices of the p-norm, these algorithms have their characteristic disadvantages. Three such concerns that will be discussed in detail later are *metrication artifacts* (blockiness of the segmentation due to the underlying grid structure), *proximity bias* (bleeding of the segmentation due to sensitivity to the location of user interaction), and *shrinking bias* (shortcutting of the segmentation boundary due to bias toward shorter boundaries).

The use of an intermediate *p*-norm for segmentation might compensate for these drawbacks. However, the optimization of intermediate *p*-norms has been somewhat neglected, due to the focus on fast dedicated solvers for the cases of $p = 1$, $p = 2$, and $p = \infty$ (e.g., max-flow for $p = 1$, linear system solver for $p = 2$, and Dijkstra's shortest path algorithm for $p = \infty$). The lack of a general solver precludes the ability to merge these algorithms or employ the generalized algorithm with an intermediate *p*-value. For this purpose, the present chapter discusses the use of *iterative reweighted least squares* (IRLS) techniques to find the segmentation for any arbitrary *p*-norm ($1 < p < 3$) by solving a series of ℓ_2 optimizations. The use of IRLS hence allows one to find segmentation algorithms that are proper hybrids of existing segmentation algorithms such as graph cut, random walker, and shortest path.

8.1 A Generalized Image Segmentation Algorithm

A given image is represented by a weighted graph $\mathcal{G} = (\mathcal{V}, \mathcal{E})$. The nodes $\mathcal{V}$ represent the pixels in the image and the edges $\mathcal{E}$ represent the choice of neighborhood structure. The weight of an edge, $e_{ij} \in \mathcal{E}$, is denoted by w_{ij}, and the weights are assumed here to be symmetric and nonnegative (i.e., $w_{ij} = w_{ji} \geq 0$).

Since this chapter assumes a scribble interface, it is assumed that some pixels in the image have been labeled as foreground and some others have been labeled as background. Let $\mathcal{M} \subset \mathcal{V}$ contain the locations of the nodes marked by the user and let $\mathcal{U} \subset \mathcal{V}$ contain the locations of the unmarked nodes. The set $\mathcal{M}$ is further divided into the sets $\mathcal{F} \subset \mathcal{M}$ and $\mathcal{B} \subset \mathcal{M}$ that contain the locations of the nodes labeled as the foreground object and the background, respectively. By construction, $\mathcal{M} \cap \mathcal{U} = \emptyset$, $\mathcal{M} \cup \mathcal{U} = \mathcal{V}$, $\mathcal{F} \cap \mathcal{B} = \emptyset$, and $\mathcal{F} \cup \mathcal{B} = \mathcal{M}$.

A Bernoulli random variable $y_i \in \{0, 1\}$ is defined for each node $i \in \mathcal{V}$, to indicate its binary segmentation as object ($y_i = 1$) or background ($y_i = 0$). A continuous-valued random variable x_i is introduced at each node to define the *success probability* for the distribution of the random variable y_i, that is, $p(y_i = 1 \mid x_i)$. For example, [143] uses logistic regression on a real-valued variable x_i to define the success probability as $p(y_i = 1 \mid x_i) = \frac{e^{x_i}}{1+e^{x_i}}$. In this chapter the success probability of y_i at node i is defined as

$$p(y_i = 1 \mid x_i) = \max\{\min\{x_i, 1\}, 0\} = \begin{cases} 1 & \text{if } x_i > 1, \\ x_i & \text{if } 0 \leq x_i \leq 1 \text{ and} \\ 0 & \text{if } x_i < 0. \end{cases} \tag{8.1}$$

For notational convenience, define vectors $\mathbf{x} \in \mathbb{R}^{|\mathcal{V}|}$ and $\mathbf{y} \in \mathbb{R}^{|\mathcal{V}|}$, whose *i*th entries are given by x_i and y_i, respectively. Now the goal is to infer the hidden variables, $\mathbf{x}$ and $\mathbf{y}$, from the observed quantity (i.e., the image I). These hidden parameters can be estimated in a Bayesian framework by considering the following posterior probability model:

$$p(\mathbf{x}, \mathbf{y} \mid I) \propto p(\mathbf{x})p(\mathbf{y} \mid \mathbf{x})p(I \mid \mathbf{y}) = p(\mathbf{x}) \prod_{i \in \mathcal{V}} p(y_i \mid x_i) \prod_{i \in \mathcal{V}} p(I_i \mid y_i). \tag{8.2}$$

The term $p(\mathbf{x})$ is the prior term that encodes constraints on how the parameters of the Bernoulli variables vary spatially. Unlike most of the discussions in this book, in this chapter the smoothness constraints are enforced on the hidden variables $\mathbf{x}$ rather than on the segmentation $\mathbf{y}$ itself. The spatial smoothness prior is explicitly parameterized as

$$p(\mathbf{x}) \propto \exp\left(-\lambda \sum_{e_{ij} \in \mathcal{E}} (w_{ij}|x_i - x_j|)^p\right), \tag{8.3}$$

where $\lambda > 0$ and the weights w_{ij} are positive (i.e., $\forall e_{ij} \in \mathcal{E}$, $w_{ij} > 0$). Different choices for the p-norms result in different priors on $\mathbf{x}$. For example, $p = 1$ gives a Laplacian prior and $p = 2$ gives a Gaussian prior. The term $p(y_i \mid x_i)$ at each node is given completely by (8.1), where $p(y_i = 0 \mid x_i)$ is defined as $1 - p(y_i = 1 \mid x_i)$. The term $p(I_i \mid y_i)$ is the standard likelihood term as used in the rest of this book.

One of the drawbacks of the model discussed so far is that the edge weights for the pairwise terms, $\{w_{ij}\}$, do not depend on the image. Specifically, the edge weights are used as the parameters of the spatial prior model $p(\mathbf{x})$ and hence cannot depend on the image. However, as discussed in other chapters, in practice it is preferable to use contrast-sensitive edge weights, such as $w_{ij} = e^{-(I_i - I_j)^2}$, to align the segmentation boundary with the edges in the image. However, modifying the probabilistic model to accommodate contrast-sensitive weights is not straightforward. In the case of discrete MRFs, a modification of the likelihood term was proposed by Blake et al. [53], that better accommodates contrast-sensitive weights. However, it is unclear how such results would be applicable to the formulation of this chapter, which considers both continuous and discrete variables.

To this effect, this chapter follows an alternative formulation, which directly models the posterior, rather than attempting to decompose it in a likelihood and a prior term. Specifically, the posterior distribution of the hidden variables x and y is modeled as

$$p(\mathbf{x}, \mathbf{y}|I) \propto p(\mathbf{y}|\mathbf{x}, I)p(\mathbf{x}|I) = p(\mathbf{y}|\mathbf{x})p(\mathbf{x}|I)$$

$$= \prod_{i \in \mathcal{V}} (x_i^{y_i}(1 - x_i)^{1-y_i}) \prod_{i \in \mathcal{V}} \left(x_i^{-H(x_i - 0.5)}(1 - x_i)^{-(1 - H(x_i - 0.5))}\right)$$

$$\times \exp\left(-\lambda \sum_{e_{ij} \in \mathcal{E}} (w_{ij}|x_i - x_j|)^p\right) \exp\left(-\sum_{i \in \mathcal{V}} w_{i0}^p|x_i - 0|^p - \sum_{i \in \mathcal{V}} w_{i1}^p|x_i - 1|^p\right), \tag{8.4}$$

where $H(\cdot)$ is the Heaviside function and $\forall i \in \mathcal{V}$, $w_{i0} \geq 0$ and $w_{i1} \geq 0$. The reduction of the term $p(\mathbf{y}|\mathbf{x}, I)$ to $p(\mathbf{y}|\mathbf{x})$ in the first line comes from the assumption that y is conditionally independent of I, given x. The terms introduced in the bottom row of (8.4) act as the unary terms and the weights w_{i0} and w_{i1} bias the parameters x_i towards 0 and 1. Firstly, these unary terms serve the purpose of encoding the user's interaction. If a node $i \in \mathcal{M}$ is labelled as object or backgraound, the algorithm sets the corresponding unary terms as $(w_{i0}, w_{i1}) = (0, \infty)$ or $(w_{i0}, w_{i1}) = (\infty, 0)$, respectively. It can be verified that this is equivalent to hardcoding the value of x_i at the marked nodes $i \in \mathcal{M}$ as $\forall i \in \mathcal{F}$, $x_i = 1$ and $\forall i \in \mathcal{B}$, $x_i = 0$. The unary terms may also be used to encode the extent to which the appearance (color, texture, etc.) of a node i obeys an appearance model for the object or the backgraound.

Given the expression (8.4), the goal is now to estimate the hidden variables $\mathbf{x}$ and $\mathbf{y}$ as $\operatorname*{argmax}_{\mathbf{x},\mathbf{y}} p(\mathbf{x}, \mathbf{y}|I)$. It can be verified that estimating $\hat{\mathbf{y}} = \operatorname*{argmax}_{\mathbf{y}} p(\mathbf{x}, \mathbf{y}|I)$ gives for each node $i \in \mathcal{V}$, $y_i = 1$ if $x_i \geq 0.5$ and $y = 0$ otherwise. It can also be verified that estimating the optimal value of $\hat{\mathbf{x}}$ as $\operatorname*{argmax}_{\mathbf{x}} p(\mathbf{x}, \hat{\mathbf{y}}|I)$, is equivalent to estimating $\hat{\mathbf{x}}$ as the minimizer of the energy function $E(\mathbf{x})$, where $E(\mathbf{x})$ is defined as

$$E(\mathbf{x}) = \sum_{i \in \mathcal{V}} w_{i0}^{p}|x_i - 0|^p + \sum_{i \in \mathcal{V}} w_{i1}^{p}|x_i - 1|^p + \lambda \sum_{e_{ij} \in \mathcal{E}}(w_{ij}|x_i - x_j|)^p, \tag{8.5}$$

where $\lambda > 0$ is the same parameter as in (8.4), that accounts for the trade-off between the unary terms and the pairwise terms.

For notational convenience, one can introduce two auxiliary nodes for the foreground and the background: f and b, respectively. The parameters x_i at these nodes are hardcoded as $x_f = 1$ and $x_b = 0$. The unary terms can then be rewritten as $w_{i0}^{p}|x_i - 0|^p = w_{i0}^{p}|x_i - x_b|^p$ and $w_{i1}^{p}|x_i - 1|^p = w_{i1}^{p}|x_i - x_f|^p$. Hence, without loss of generality, $E(\mathbf{x})$ can be rewritten in terms of pairwise interactions only, as

$$E(\mathbf{x}) = \sum_{e_{ij} \in \mathcal{E}}(w_{ij}|x_i - x_j|)^p, \tag{8.6}$$

where, with abuse of notation, the set $\mathcal{E}$ is modified to include the original set of edges $\mathcal{E}$ defined in (8.5), as well as the additional edges introduced by representing the unary terms as pairwise interactions.

Now, note that $E(\mathbf{x})$ is parameterized by a finite-valued p-norm, $p < \infty$. The limiting case $p = \infty$ is admitted by generalizing $E(\mathbf{x})$ as

$$E_p(\mathbf{x}) = \left[\sum_{e_{ij} \in \mathcal{E}}(w_{ij}|x_i - x_j|)^p \right]^{\frac{1}{p}}. \tag{8.7}$$

Due to the monotonicity of the $(\cdot)^{\frac{1}{p}}$ operator, (8.6) and (8.7) have the same optimum for a finite $0 < p < \infty$. As shown later, the generalization to $p = \infty$ allows the shortest path segmentation algorithm to be admitted as a special case of the generalized algorithm for $p = \infty$.

Therefore, the problem of computing the segmentation is recast as the problem of computing the optimal $\hat{\mathbf{x}}$ that minimizes $E_p(\mathbf{x})$, subject to the constraints enforced by the user's interaction, as

$$\hat{\mathbf{x}} = \arg\min_{\mathbf{x}} E_p(\mathbf{x}) \text{ s.t. } x_i = 1, \text{ if } i \in \mathcal{F} \text{ and } x_i = 0, \text{ if } i \in \mathcal{B}. \tag{8.8}$$

It is shown later that the solution to (8.8) naturally satisfies the constraint that $\forall i \in \mathcal{U}, 0 \leq x_i \leq 1$. We can redefine $\mathbf{y}$ to be the *hard* segmentation produced from the real-valued $\mathbf{x}$ by thresholding at $x = 0.5$. This is equivalent to obtaining the segmentation of node i as $\hat{y}_i = \arg\max_{y_i} p(y_i \mid \hat{x}_i)$. This segmentation procedure is summarized in algorithm 8.1. This generalized segmentation algorithm is referred to as the **p-brush** algorithm, due to the dependence of the solution on the *p*-norm. It will be shown later that the graph cut, random walker, and shortest path segmentation algorithms can be viewed as special instances of this *p*-brush algorithm when $p = 1, 2$, and ∞, respectively.

Algorithm 8.1 (*p-Brush: A Generalized Image Segmentation Algorithm*)

Given:

- Two sets of pixels marked for the foreground object ($\mathcal{F} \in \mathcal{V}$) and the background ($\mathcal{B} \in \mathcal{V}$).

- A norm $p \geq 1$ for the energy function $E_p = \left[\sum_{e_{ij} \in \mathcal{E}} (w_{ij} |x_i - x_j|)^p \right]^{\frac{1}{p}}$ that includes unary terms as well as the spatial prior.

Compute: $\hat{\mathbf{x}} = \arg\min_{\mathbf{x}} E_p(\mathbf{x})$, s.t. $x_i = 1$ if $i \in \mathcal{F}$ and $x_i = 0$ if $i \in \mathcal{B}$.

Output: Segmentation $\mathbf{y}$ defined as $\hat{y}_i = 1$ if $\hat{x}_i \geq \frac{1}{2}$ and $\hat{y}_i = 0$ if $\hat{x}_i < \frac{1}{2}$.

8.2 Solutions to the *p*-Brush Problem

This section initially discusses some interesting properties of the solutions of the *p*-brush algorithm. The remaining discussion focuses on efficient solvers for particular values of the *p*-norm.

An important property of $E_p(\mathbf{x})$ is its convexity for all values of $p \geq 1$. Therefore, any solution of (8.8) must be a global minimizer of $E_p(\mathbf{x})$. In what follows, a global minimizer of $E_p(\mathbf{x})$ is denoted as $\hat{\mathbf{x}}_p$ and its ith entry is denoted as $\hat{x}_{p,i}$. It was shown in [440] that these minimizers have interesting properties.

Extremum Value Property   The value of $\hat{x}_{p,i}$ at every node $i \in \mathcal{V}$ is bounded by the values of $\hat{x}_{p,j}$ at the marked nodes $j \in \mathcal{M}$. Formally, this can be written as $\forall i \in \mathcal{V}$, $\min_{j \in \mathcal{M}} \hat{x}_{p,j} \leq \hat{x}_{p,i} \leq \max_{j \in \mathcal{M}} \hat{x}_{p,j}$.

Now recall that by construction, the entries of $\hat{\mathbf{x}}_p$ are fixed at the marked nodes as $\forall i \in \mathcal{F}$, $\hat{x}_{p,i} = 1$, and $\forall i \in \mathcal{B}$, $\hat{x}_{p,i} = 0$. Hence, the extremum value property can be used to conclude that the value of $\hat{x}_{p,i}$ at each unmarked node $i \in \mathcal{U}$ lies in $[0, 1]$. As a result, the set of solutions for the entries of $\hat{\mathbf{x}}_p$ at the unmarked nodes $\mathcal{U}$ is $[0, 1]^{|\mathcal{U}|}$, which is a compact and convex set. This result, coupled with the fact that the energy function $E_p(\mathbf{x})$ is convex in $\mathbf{x}$, implies that any descent algorithm can be used to calculate the global minimizer of $E_p(\mathbf{x})$.

Right Continuity in the p-Norm   This property characterizes the continuity of the solutions of the p-brush algorithm as a function of the p-norm. In particular it can be shown that if $\hat{\mathbf{x}}_{p+\epsilon}$ is a minimizer of $E_{p+\epsilon}(\mathbf{x})$, where $\epsilon \geq 0$, then $\hat{\mathbf{x}}_{p+\epsilon}$ is right continuous in p, that is, $\lim_{\epsilon \to 0^+} \hat{\mathbf{x}}_{p+\epsilon} = \hat{\mathbf{x}}_p$. The significance of this property will be illustrated later while discussing the IRLS algorithm for estimating the solutions of the p-brush algorithm for the range $1 < p < 3$.

8.2.1 Special Cases of the p-Brush Algorithm

Before studying the case for a general p, it is of interest to study the instances of the p-brush algorithm resulting from the choices of $p = 1, 2$, and ∞ since they correspond to existing segmentation algorithms.

The $p = 1$ Case: Graph Cut   After substituting $p = 1$ in the p-brush algorithm, the second step of the algorithm requires the solution to the problem

$$\min_{\mathbf{x}} \sum_{e_{ij} \in \mathcal{E}} w_{ij}|x_i - x_j|, \text{ s.t. } x_i = 1 \text{ if } i \in \mathcal{F}, \text{ and } x_i = 0 \text{ if } i \in \mathcal{B}. \tag{8.9}$$

It is known that the problem in (8.9) admits a purely binary solution, $x_i \in \{0, 1\}$, due to the totally unimodular property of the min-cut problem [363]. This is precisely the solution that is produced by the graph cut algorithm using the min-cut/max-flow solver [66]. Notice that (8.9) provides a continuous-valued interpretation of the graph cut algorithm as opposed to the traditional discrete-valued interpretation.

Although (8.9) admits a purely binary solution, the solution may not be unique and there may be continuous-valued nonbinary solutions to (8.9). A result in [85] can be used to obtain a purely binary-valued minimizer from any continuous-valued minimizer. Specifically, a binary-valued minimizer ($\hat{\mathbf{x}}_1^B \in \{0, 1\}^{|\mathcal{V}|}$) can be produced from a continuous-valued minimizer ($\hat{\mathbf{x}}_1^C \in [0, 1]^{|\mathcal{V}|}$) of (8.9) by thresholding its entries at any value $\nu \in (0, 1)$, that is, $\forall i \in \mathcal{V}$: $\hat{x}_{1,i}^B = 1$ if $\hat{x}_{1,i}^C \geq \nu$, and $\hat{x}_{1,i}^B = 0$ otherwise. It was shown in [85] that both solutions, $\hat{\mathbf{x}}_1^B$ and $\hat{\mathbf{x}}_1^C$, are minimizers of (8.9). Hence, thresholding any solution to (8.9) at $\nu = 0.5$ produces a valid minimum cut. It is interesting that although this model deals with continuous-valued solutions as opposed to discrete MRF models (e.g., chapter 7), the thresholded solution is indeed equivalent to the solution of the discrete model.

The $p = 2$ Case: Random Walker For the case $p = 2$, the second step of the p-brush algorithm requires the solution to the problem

$$\min_{\mathbf{x}} \sum_{e_{ij} \in \mathcal{E}} w_{ij}^2 \left(x_i - x_j \right)^2 , \ \text{s.t.} \ x_i = 1 \ \text{if} \ i \in \mathcal{F}, \ \text{and} \ x_i = 0 \ \text{if} \ i \in \mathcal{B}. \tag{8.10}$$

This is exactly the optimization problem solved by the random walker algorithm in [175] (for the case of two labels). A random walk is defined on the graph such that the probability that a random walker at node $i \in \mathcal{V}$ moves to a neighboring node $j \in \mathcal{N}_i$ is given as $w_{ij} / \sum_{k \in \mathcal{N}_i} w_{ik}$. The random walk is terminated when the random walker reaches any of the marked nodes. [175] showed that the solution of (8.10), $\hat{\mathbf{x}}_2$, satisfies the property that $\hat{x}_{2,i}$ corresponds to the probability that a random walker starting from node $i \in \mathcal{V}$ will reach a node labeled as foreground before a node labeled as background. These probabilities are thresholded at $x = 0.5$ to obtain the segmentation. Hence, the random walker algorithm with two labels gives the same solution as the p-brush algorithm when $p = 2$.

The $p = \infty$ Case: Shortest Path When $p \to \infty$, the limit of $E_p(\mathbf{x})$ is given as

$$\lim_{p \to \infty} E_p(\mathbf{x}) = \underbrace{\max_{e_{ij} \in \mathcal{E}} w_{ij} |x_i - x_j|}_{\rho(\mathbf{x})} \underbrace{\lim_{p \to \infty} \sqrt[p]{\sum_{e_{ij} \in \mathcal{E}} \left(\frac{w_{ij} |x_i - x_j|}{\rho(\mathbf{x})} \right)^p}}_{1} = \rho(\mathbf{x}), \tag{8.11}$$

where $\rho(\mathbf{x})$ is defined as $\rho(\mathbf{x}) = \max_{e_{ij} \in \mathcal{E}} w_{ij} |x_i - x_j|$. Now the optimization problem in (8.11) can be rewritten as

$$\min_{\mathbf{x}} \left[\max_{e_{ij} \in \mathcal{E}} (w_{ij} |x_i - x_j|) \right], \text{s.t.} \ x_i = 1 \ \text{if} \ i \in \mathcal{F}, \ \text{and} \ x_i = 0 \ \text{if} \ i \in \mathcal{B}. \tag{8.12}$$

This optimization problem may be viewed as a combinatorial formulation of the minimal Lipschitz extension problem [15]. It has been shown that the solution to (8.12) is not unique in general [15]. Theorem 8.1 provides one possible interesting construction to minimize $E_\infty(\mathbf{x})$.

Theorem 8.1 **Infinity-Norm Optimization** *Define the distance between neighboring nodes i and j as $d_{ij} = \frac{1}{w_{ij}}$. Denote the shortest path lengths from node $i \in \mathcal{V}$ to a node marked foreground and background as d_i^F and d_i^B, respectively. The vector, $\hat{\mathbf{x}}_\infty$, defined as $\forall i \in \mathcal{U} : \hat{x}_{\infty,i} = d_i^B / d_i^B + d_i^F$, is a solution to (8.12).*

Proof   Given in the appendix to this chapter.   ∎

Note that a node $i \in \mathcal{V}$ is assigned to the foreground if $\hat{x}_{\infty,i} > 0.5$ (i.e., $d_i^F < d_i^B$). This implies that the segmentation given by the shortest path algorithm [18] is a valid solution to the p-brush algorithm for the case $p = \infty$. Hence $\hat{\mathbf{x}}_\infty$ may be computed efficiently using Dijkstra's shortest path algorithm. However, as mentioned earlier, this is not the only solution to (8.12). One could introduce other constructions and additional regularizers, as in [441], to obtain a unique solution.

8.2.2 Segmentation with an Arbitrary p-Norm

In the special cases discussed so far, a specific solver is used for each case due to the properties of the employed p-norm. For any arbitrary finite $p \in (1, 3)$, algorithm 8.2 can be used to estimate $\hat{\mathbf{x}}_p$, employing iterative reweighted least squares (IRLS). Each iteration of the algorithm has two steps. The first step, *reweighting*, involves the update of the weights based on the current estimate of $\mathbf{x}$ (see (8.13)). The second step, *least squares estimation*, involves updating the value of $\mathbf{x}$ by solving a least squares problem with the updated weights (see (8.14)). IRLS can also be thought of as an iterative random walker algorithm with the weights being updated at each iteration. The rationale behind the algorithm is as follows. For $p > 1$, the function $(E_p(\mathbf{x}))^p$ is differentiable. In this case, algorithm 8.2 is equivalent to performing a Newton descent of $(E_p(\mathbf{x}))^p$ with step size $(p - 1)$ [440]. This is because, when $\forall e_{ij} \in \mathcal{E}, x_i^{(n)} \neq x_j^{(n)}$, the matrix $W^{(n)}$, whose (i, j) entry is given by $w_{ij}^{(n)}$, is exactly the Hessian (say $H_p(\mathbf{x})$) of $(E_p(\mathbf{x}))^p$ evaluated at $\mathbf{x} = \mathbf{x}^{(n)}$. If $x_i = x_j$ for some $e_{ij} \in \mathcal{E}$, then

---

Algorithm 8.2 *(Estimation of $\hat{\mathbf{x}}_p$ for Any $1 < p < 3$, Using IRLS)*

---

1. Set $n = 0$ and choose a value $\alpha > 0$ and a stopping criterion $\delta > 0$.

2. Initialize the membership vector $\mathbf{x}^{(0)}$ as $\forall i \in \mathcal{F} : x_i^{(0)} = 1, \forall i \in \mathcal{B} : x_i^{(0)} = 0$, and $\forall i \in \mathcal{U} : x_i^{(0)} = 0.5$.

3. For each edge $\mathbf{e}_{ij} \in \mathcal{E}$, define the edge weight as $w_{ij}^{(n)}$:

$$w_{ij}^{(n)} = \begin{cases} w_{ij}^p |x_i^{(n)} - x_j^{(n)}|^{p-2} & \text{if } x_i \neq x_j \\ \alpha^{p-2} & \text{if } x_i = x_j. \end{cases} \tag{8.13}$$

4. Calculate $\mathbf{x}^{(n+1)}$ as the solution of

$$\arg \min_{\mathbf{x}} \sum_{e_{ij} \in E} w_{ij}^{(n)} \left(x_i - x_j\right)^2, \qquad \text{s.t. } x_i = 0/1 \text{ if } i \in \mathcal{F}/\mathcal{B}. \tag{8.14}$$

5. If $|\mathbf{x}_U^{(n+1)} - \mathbf{x}_U^{(n)}| > \delta$, update $n = n + 1$ and go to step 3.

$H_p(\mathbf{x})$ does not exist for $1 < p < 2$. This is resolved by approximating $H_p(\mathbf{x})$, using the weights defined in (8.13). It can be verified that IRLS still produces a descent direction for updating $\mathbf{x}^{(n)}$ at each step.

For $p = 1$, $E_1(\mathbf{x})$ is not differentiable. However, recall from the properties of $\hat{\mathbf{x}}_p$ discussed earlier in this section that the minimizers of $E_p(\mathbf{x})$ are right continuous with respect to the p-norm. Therefore, the minimizer of $(E_{1+\epsilon}(\mathbf{x}))^{1+\epsilon}$ can be calculated using IRLS and used as an approximation of $\hat{\mathbf{x}}_1$ with a desired accuracy by choosing ϵ to be sufficiently small. In general, IRLS is provably convergent only for $1 < p < 3$ [359]. However, solutions for $p \geq 3$ can be obtained by using Newton descent with an adaptive step size rather than $p - 1$.

8.3 Experiments

This section evaluates the performance of the p-brush algorithm on synthetic medical as well as natural images. The experiments aim to highlight common problems in the segmentation results and to analyze how they might depend on the choice of the p-norm. The results first present the image to be segmented and then show the segmentation results obtained for various values of p. The segmentation boundary is superimposed on the image either as a dashed line or as a bold line to ensure visibility. The user interaction for the object and background is superimposed in different shades of gray to distinguish them.

A practical segmentation system has many components that can significantly affect its performance, such as unary terms and neighborhood. Most existing algorithms rely on good unary terms that, on their own, produce near-perfect segmentations. When the unary terms are uninformative, the segmentation relies primarily on the spatial prior. Therefore, unary terms are ignored in the following evaluation to isolate and analyze the effect of the p-norm on the spatial regularization of the segmentation boundary. It should, however, be noted that unary terms have been employed in existing literature for $p = 1$ [67], $p = 2$ [174], and $p = \infty$ [18]. Though it is not within the goals of this chapter, it is of future interest to analyze how the unary terms behave for general values of p. Along the same lines, a simple 4-connected lattice is used to define the neighborhood in order to inspect metrication artifacts that might otherwise be eliminated by considering higher connected neighborhoods. The contrast-sensitive weight for an edge $e_{ij} \in \mathcal{E}$ is defined as $w_{ij} = e^{-\beta \| I_i - I_j \|}$, where $\beta > 0$ and I_i is the gray scale intensity or RGB color of pixel i.

8.3.1 Metrication Artifacts

The artifacts correspond to blocky segmentations that follow the topology of the neighborhood structure. They occur in the case of $p = 1$ and $p = \infty$, due to the neighborhood structure [67]. In contrast, the case $p = 2$ corresponds to a finite differences discretization of a continuous (inhomogeneous) Laplace equation. Chapter 12 shows that discretization of continuous formulations can reduce metrication errors. Hence, it may be conjectured that metrication artifacts are reduced in the case $p = 2$.

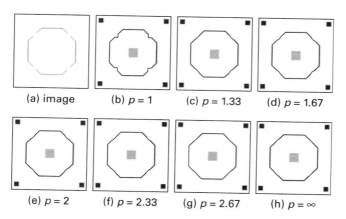

Figure 8.1
Analysis of metrication artifacts in the segmentation of the synthetic image shown in (a). Light and dark marks (squares in this example) indicate user labelings of foreground and background, respectively. The segmentations obtained for various p-norms are shown in (b)–(h). Blocky artifacts are present for $p = 1$ but not for higher values of p.

To understand this better, consider the experiments in figure 8.1, where the goal is to segment the octagon in figure 8.1a. Graph cut ($p = 1$) produces a squared-off effect at the portion where the octagon's boundary has been erased. This is the metrication artifact. The artifacts are absent as p increases from 1 to 2.67. Although they are avoided for $p = \infty$ in this synthetic example, they are exhibited for $p = \infty$ in the examples on real images. Figure 8.2 shows metrication artifacts in the segmentation of an aneurysm in an MR image. The metrication artifacts are clearly visible for $p = 1$. They seem to reduce as p increases, but not as drastically as in the previous example. Specifically, for $p = 1.25$, the segmentation boundary to the left of the aneurysm is less blocky compared with the result for $p = 1$. However, the boundary is still blocky at the top and bottom of the aneurysm. These artifacts reduce as p increases from 1 to 2.75, but they reappear for $p = \infty$. The same trend can be seen in the results in figure 8.5.

In general, the metrication artifacts may be reduced by choosing a higher connected neighborhood [67]. For example, a 8-neighborhood instead of a 4-neighborhood would have given the desired result for $p = 1$ in the example in figure 8.1. However, increasing the connectivity is equivalent to increasing the number of edges in the graph, and hence comes at the expense of higher memory usage and higher computation.

8.3.2 Proximity Bias

This bias corresponds to the sensitivity of the segmentation to the location of the user's interaction. The proximity bias is best understood in $p = \infty$, since the segmentation of an unmarked pixel depends on its distance from the marked pixels. It was shown in [175]

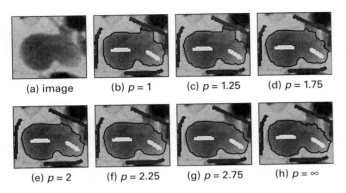

(a) image   (b) $p = 1$ (c) $p = 1.25$ (d) $p = 1.75$

(e) $p = 2$ (f) $p = 2.25$ (g) $p = 2.75$ (h) $p = \infty$

Figure 8.2
Analysis of metrication artifacts in the segmentation of the medical image shown in (a). The segmentations obtained for various p-norms are shown in (b)–(h). The artifacts reduce as p increases from 1 to 2.75, but are present for $p = \infty$.

that for $p = 2$, the segmentation of an unmarked pixel depends on the distances of all the parallel paths from that pixel to the marked pixels, thus reducing dependence on a single path. No such interpretation is known for $p = 1$.

To understand this, consider the experiments in figure 8.3, where the goal is to segment the image into equal halves along the vertical dark line. The user's scribbles are not symmetric with respect to the line. If the scribbles were symmetric, the segmentation computed for the various p-norms would be as desired. In this case the desired segmentation is obtained for $p = 1$ and $p = 1.33$. As p increases, the segmentation begins to *leak* through the portions where the dark line has been erased. This is the proximity bias.

This bias is further explored in the results in figure 8.4. In contrast to the user interaction in figure 8.2, the one for the aneurysm has been erased toward the bottom right. This is done to analyze the effect on the segmentation boundary near the weak edge at the bottom right of the aneurysm. It can be seen that for $p = 1$ and $p = 1.1$, the segmentation boundary is correctly aligned with the aneurysm. However, as p increases, the segmentation begins to leak and the boundary is incorrectly aligned with the aneurysm's interior.

In general, the proximity bias can be reduced by further user interaction to correct any errors. However, this might require greater levels of interaction from the user, which can prove to be a burden for real-time applications. Moreover, additional user interaction might not be possible in unsupervised applications, where the user interaction is automatically generated by the algorithm, based on appearance models learned a priori for the object and background.

8.3.3 Shrinking Bias
The shrinking bias corresponds to the bias toward segmentation boundaries with shorter length. This can be understood better for $p = 1$ (i.e., graph cut), because it has been shown

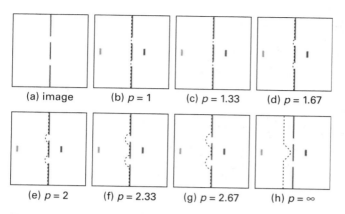

Figure 8.3
Analysis of proximity bias in the segmentation of the synthetic image shown in (a). The segmentations obtained for various p-norms are shown in (b)–(h). The desired segmentation is produced for $p = 1$ and $p = 1.33$. As p increases, the segmentation boundary leaks through the erased portions of the vertical line and gradually moves toward the distance based segmentation produced when $p = \infty$.

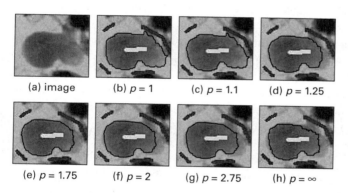

Figure 8.4
Analysis of proximity bias in the segmentation of the image shown in (a). The segmentation boundary does not leak for $p = 1$ and $p = 1.1$. However, as p increases, the proximity bias increases and the segmentation boundary leaks.

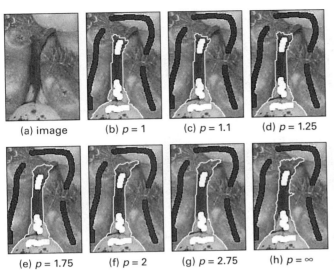

(a) image   (b) $p = 1$ (c) $p = 1.1$ (d) $p = 1.25$

(e) $p = 1.75$ (f) $p = 2$ (g) $p = 2.75$ (h) $p = \infty$

Figure 8.5
Analysis of shrinking bias in the segmentation of a banana in the natural image shown in (a). The segmentations obtained for various p-norms are shown in (b)–(h). The tip of the banana is cut off for $p = 1, 1.1, 1.25,$ and $1.75,$ with the portion being cut off gradually reducing. As p increases, the shrinking bias seems to reduce and the segmentation boundary aligns with the banana. Also, the metrication artifacts along the right boundary decrease as p increases.

that the smoothness prior, that is, $p(\mathbf{x})$ in (8.3), can be viewed as a penalty on the length of the segmentation boundary [67]. For higher values of p, there is no such known relationship between the boundary length and the prior. Due to this bias, the segmentation boundary might collapse, thereby resulting in a *shortcutting* of the segmentation boundary.

In order to appreciate this, consider the results in figure 8.5, where the goal is to segment the top portion of a banana. The top of the banana is cut off for $p = 1, 1.1, 1.25,$ and $1.75,$ with the portion being cut off gradually reducing. Also, the segmentation boundary toward the central left portion of the banana incorrectly aligns with the edges inside the banana. As p increases, the segmentation begins to align correctly with the boundary of the banana. The shrinking bias reduces as p increases.

This trend can also be seen in figure 8.6, where the goal is to segment the ultrasound image shown in figure 8.6a along the interface of the dark and bright portions of the image. The shortcutting effect (i.e., the shrinking bias) reduces as p increases.

In general, such errors caused by shortcutting of the segmentation boundary can be resolved by further user interaction. However, as mentioned earlier, higher levels of user interaction are not preferable for real-time segmentation or unsupervised segmentation.

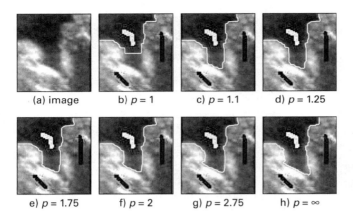

(a) image   b) $p = 1$ c) $p = 1.1$ d) $p = 1.25$

e) $p = 1.75$ f) $p = 2$ g) $p = 2.75$ h) $p = \infty$

Figure 8.6
Analysis of shrinking bias in the segmentation of the medical image shown in (a). The goal is to segment the interface between the bright and the dark regions. The segmentations obtained for various p-norms are shown in (b)–(h). As p increases, the shrinking bias seems to reduce.

8.4 Conclusion

The p-brush segmentation algorithm provides a generalized framework that includes existing algorithms such as graph cut, random walker, and shortest path as special cases for particular values of $p = 1, 2,$ and ∞, respectively. Due to the nature of their cost functions, these algorithms have specific efficient solvers and characteristic drawbacks.

The experiments suggest that there is a correlation between the discussed biases and the p-norm. Specifically, the proximity bias increases and the shrinking bias decreases as p increases. Metrication artifacts are observed for $p = 1$ and $p = \infty$, but not for $p = 2$. Since $\hat{\mathbf{x}}_p$ is continuous in p, it is conjectured that these artifacts reduce as p increases from 1 to 2, but reappear for p beyond some $\tilde{p} > 2$. Due to the interplay of these issues, it cannot be determined beforehand which p-norm would be the best for a general segmentation system. However, if the system is to be used for a specific segmentation goal, an optimal value for p may be learned through a user study or by training on representative exemplar images. IRLS may be used to obtain the segmentation for several values of p with the aim of obtaining a trade-off among the properties of these three special cases. However, IRLS may be potentially slower than the efficient solvers for the cases of $p = 1, 2,$ and ∞.

8.5 Appendix: Proof of Infinity Norm Optimization Theorem

In order to verify that $\hat{\mathbf{x}}_\infty$ defined in the hypothesis is indeed a solution of (8.12), it must satisfy the following two conditions.

1. $\hat{\mathbf{x}}_{\infty,i} = 1$ or $\hat{\mathbf{x}}_{\infty,i} = 0$ if the pixel i is labeled as foreground ($i \in \mathcal{F}$) or as background ($i \in \mathcal{B}$), respectively.

This condition can be verified very easily. Note that $d_i^F = 0$ and $d_i^B > 0$ for all the pixels i labeled as belonging to the foreground. This implies that $\forall i \in \mathcal{F} : \hat{\mathbf{x}}_{\infty,i} = \frac{d_i^B}{d_i^B + 0} = 1$. Since $d_i^B = 0$ and $d_i^F > 0$ for all the pixels i labeled as belonging to the background, this implies that $\forall i \in \mathcal{B} : \hat{\mathbf{x}}_{\infty,i} = \frac{0}{0 + d_i^F} = 0$.

2. If $\mathbf{x}_\infty^*$ is a solution to (8.12), then $\rho(\hat{\mathbf{x}}_\infty) = \rho(\mathbf{x}_\infty^*)$.

In order to verify this, it shall be proved that $\rho(\hat{\mathbf{x}}_\infty) \leq \rho(\mathbf{x}_\infty^*)$. The definition of $\mathbf{x}_\infty^*$ being a solution to (8.12) would imply that $\rho(\hat{\mathbf{x}}_\infty) = \rho(\mathbf{x}_\infty^*)$, and the proof would be complete. Since $\rho(\hat{\mathbf{x}}_\infty)$ is defined as $\max_{\mathbf{e}_{ij} \in \mathcal{E}} (w_{ij}|\hat{\mathbf{x}}_{\infty,i} - \hat{\mathbf{x}}_{\infty,j}|)$, it is sufficient to show that $\forall \mathbf{e}_{ij} \in \mathcal{E} :$ $w_{ij}|\hat{\mathbf{x}}_{\infty,i} - \hat{\mathbf{x}}_{\infty,j}| \leq \rho(\mathbf{x}_\infty^*)$ to prove that $\rho(\hat{\mathbf{x}}_\infty) \leq \rho(\mathbf{x}_\infty^*)$.

Now, for any edge $\mathbf{e}_{ij} \in \mathcal{E}$, one can conclude from the triangle inequality that $|d_i^B - d_j^B| \leq w_{ij}^{-1}$ and $|d_i^F - d_j^F| \leq w_{ij}^{-1}$. This can be used to derive the following inequalities.

$w_{ij}|\hat{\mathbf{x}}_{\infty,i} - \hat{\mathbf{x}}_{\infty,j}|$

$$= w_{ij} \frac{|d_i^B(d_j^F - d_i^F) + d_i^F(d_i^B - d_j^B)|}{(d_j^B + d_j^F)(d_i^F + d_i^B)} \quad \text{(rearranging the terms)}$$

$$\leq w_{ij} \frac{d_i^B|d_j^F - d_i^F| + d_i^F|d_i^B - d_j^B|}{(d_j^B + d_j^F)(d_i^F + d_i^B)} \quad \text{(using triangle inequality)} \tag{8.15}$$

$$\leq \frac{d_i^B + d_i^F}{(d_j^B + d_j^F)(d_i^F + d_i^B)} \quad \left(\text{since } |d_i^B - d_j^B| \leq w_{ij}^{-1} \text{ and } |d_i^F - d_j^F| \leq w_{ij}^{-1}\right)$$

$$= \frac{1}{d_j^B + d_j^F}.$$

In order to complete the proof, a result from [441] will be used to show that $\forall k \in \mathcal{V}$, $\frac{1}{d_k^B + d_k^F} \leq \rho(\mathbf{x}_\infty^*)$. Specifically, let $\pi : u \rightsquigarrow v$ denote a path π in $\mathcal{G}$ from node $u \in \mathcal{V}$ to $v \in \mathcal{V}$. It was shown in [441] that

$$\rho(\mathbf{x}_\infty^*) \geq \left(\sum_{e_{ij} \in \pi} w_{ij}^{-1}\right)^{-1}, \forall \pi : f \rightsquigarrow b, \text{ where } f \in \mathcal{F} \text{ and } b \in \mathcal{B}. \tag{8.16}$$

Now, consider any node $k \in \mathcal{V}$ and denote the marked nodes labeled as foreground and background that are closest to this node k as $f_k \in \mathcal{F}$ and $b_k \in \mathcal{B}$, respectively. Denote the shortest path from f_k to k as $\pi_{f_k,k} : f_k \rightsquigarrow k$ and the shortest path from k to b_k as $\pi_{k,b_k} : k \rightsquigarrow b_k$. Now, consider the path $\pi_{f_k,b_k} : f_k \rightsquigarrow b_k$ from f_k to b_k that is obtained by traversing from f_k to k along $\pi_{f_k,k}$ and then from k to b_k along π_{k,b_k}. By using (8.16), it can be seen that $\rho(\mathbf{x}_\infty^*) \geq \left(\sum_{e_{ij} \in \pi_{f_k, b_k}} w_{ij}^{-1}\right)^{-1} = (d_k^F + d_k^B)^{-1}$. Since this holds true for every node $k \in \mathcal{V}$, it can be seen that

$$\forall k \in \mathcal{V}, \frac{1}{d_k^B + d_k^F} \leq \rho(\mathbf{x}_\infty^*). \tag{8.17}$$

Hence it can be concluded from (8.15) and (8.17) that $\forall \mathbf{e}_{ij} \in \mathcal{E} : w_{ij} |\hat{\mathbf{x}}_{\infty,i} - \hat{\mathbf{x}}_{\infty,j}| \leq \rho(\mathbf{x}_\infty^*)$. The proof is complete with this result.

Acknowledgments

The authors Dheeraj Singaraju and Rene Vidal would like to thank the Office of Naval Research, USA for supporting this work through the grant ONR YIP N00014-09-1-0839. The authors would also like to thank Donald Geman for his helpful discussions about the probability model for the p-brush algorithm.

9 Bilayer Segmentation of Video

Antonio Criminisi, Geoffrey Cross, Andrew Blake, and Vladimir Kolmogorov

This chapter presents another application of Markov random fields: accurately extracting a foreground layer from video in real time. A prime application is live background substitution in teleconferencing. This demands layer separation to near computer graphics quality, including transparency determination as in video-matting [95, 94], but with computational efficiency sufficient to attain live streaming speed.[1]

9.1 Introduction

Layer extraction from images or sequences has long been an active area of research [31, 219, 278, 480, 510, 521, 531]. The challenge addressed here is to segment the foreground layer *efficiently*, without restrictions on appearance, motion, camera viewpoint, or shape, yet with sufficient *accuracy* for use in background substitution and other synthesis applications. Frequently, motion-based segmentation has been achieved by estimating optical flow (i.e., pixel velocities) and then grouping pixels into regions according to predefined motion models [510]. Spatial priors can also be imposed by means of graph cut [66, 266, 278, 521, 531]. However, the grouping principle generally requires some assumption about the nature of the underlying motion (translational, affine, etc.), which is restrictive. Furthermore, regularization to constrain ill-posed optical flow solutions tends to introduce undesirable inaccuracies along layer boundaries. Last, accurate estimation of optical flow is computationally expensive, requiring an extensive search in the neighborhood of each point. In our approach, explicit estimation of pixel velocities is altogether avoided. Instead, an efficient discriminative model, to separate motion from stasis by using spatiotemporal derivatives, is learned from labeled data.

Recently, interactive segmentation techniques exploiting color/contrast cues have been demonstrated to be very effective for static images [66, 401] (see also chapter 7). Segmentation based on color/contrast alone is nonetheless beyond the capability of fully automatic methods. This suggests a robust approach that fuses a variety of cues—for example, stereo,

---

1. This chapter is based on [112].

color, contrast, and spatial priors [258] are known to be effective and comfortably computable in real time. This chapter shows that comparable segmentation accuracy can be achieved monocularly, avoiding the need for stereo cameras with their inconvenient necessity for calibration. Efficiency with motion in place of stereo is actually enhanced, in that stereo match likelihoods no longer need to be evaluated, and the other significant computational costs remain approximately the same. Additionally, temporal consistency is imposed for increased segmentation accuracy, and temporal transition probabilities are modeled with reduction of flicker artifacts and explicit detection of temporal occlusions.

Notation and Image Observables   Given an input sequence of images, a frame is represented as an array $\mathbf{z} = (z_1, z_2, \ldots, z_n, \ldots, z_N)$ of pixels in YUV color space, indexed by the single index n. The frame at time t is denoted $\mathbf{z}^t$. Temporal derivatives are denoted

$$\dot{\mathbf{z}} = (\dot{z}_1, \dot{z}_2, \ldots, \dot{z}_n, \ldots, \dot{z}_N), \tag{9.1}$$

and, at each time t, are computed as $\dot{z}_n^t = |G(z_n^t) - G(z_n^{t-1})|$ with $G(.)$ a Gaussian kernel at the scale of σ_t pixels. Then, spatial gradients

$$\mathbf{g} = (g_1, g_2, \ldots, g_n, \ldots, g_N) \text{ where } g_n = |\nabla z_n| \tag{9.2}$$

also are computed by convolving the images with first-order derivatives of Gaussian kernels with standard deviation σ_s. Here we use $\sigma_s = \sigma_t = 0.8$, approximating a Nyquist sampling filter. Spatiotemporal derivatives are computed on the Y color space channel only. Motion observables are denoted $\mathbf{m} = (\mathbf{g}, \dot{\mathbf{z}})$ and are used as the raw image features for discrimination between motion and stasis.

Segmentation is expressed as an array of opacity values $\boldsymbol{\alpha} = (\alpha_1, \alpha_2, \ldots, \alpha_n, \ldots, \alpha_N)$. We focus on binary segmentation (i.e., $\alpha \in \{F, B\}$), with F and B denoting foreground and background, respectively. Fractional opacities are discussed briefly in section 9.3.

9.2 Probabilistic Segmentation Model

This section describes the probabilistic model for foreground/background segmentation in an energy minimization framework. This extends previous energy models for segmentation [66, 258, 401] by the addition of a second-order, temporal Markov chain prior and an observation likelihood for image motion. The posterior model is a conditional random field (CRF) [288] with a factorization that contains some recognizably generative structure, and this is used to determine the precise algebraic forms of the factors. Various parameters are then set discriminatively [284]. The CRF is denoted as

$$p(\boldsymbol{\alpha}^1, \ldots, \boldsymbol{\alpha}^t \mid \mathbf{z}^1, \ldots, \mathbf{z}^t, \mathbf{m}^1, \ldots, \mathbf{m}^t) \propto \exp - \left\{ \sum_{t'=1}^{t} E^{t'} \right\} \tag{9.3}$$

where $E^t = E(\boldsymbol{\alpha}^t, \boldsymbol{\alpha}^{t-1}, \boldsymbol{\alpha}^{t-2}, \mathbf{z}^t, \mathbf{m}^t)$. $\tag{9.4}$

Note the second-order temporal dependence in the Markov model (to be discussed more fully later). The aim is to estimate $\boldsymbol{\alpha}^1, \ldots, \boldsymbol{\alpha}^t$, given the image and motion data, and in principle this would be done by joint maximization of the posterior or, equivalently, minimization of energy:

$$(\hat{\boldsymbol{\alpha}}^1, \ldots, \hat{\boldsymbol{\alpha}}^t) = \arg\min \sum_{t'=1}^{t} E^{t'}. \tag{9.5}$$

However, such batch computation is of no interest for real-time applications because of the causality constraint—each $\hat{\boldsymbol{\alpha}}^{t'}$ must be delivered on the evidence from its past, without using any evidence from the future. Therefore estimation will be done by separate minimization of each term E^t (details are given later).

9.2.1 Conditional Random Field Energy Terms

The energy E^t associated with time t is a sum of terms in which likelihood and prior are not entirely separated, and so does not represent a pure generative model, although some of the terms have clearly generative interpretations. The energy decomposes as a sum of four terms:

$$E(\boldsymbol{\alpha}^t, \boldsymbol{\alpha}^{t-1}, \boldsymbol{\alpha}^{t-2}, \mathbf{z}^t, \mathbf{m}^t) = V^{\mathrm{T}}(\boldsymbol{\alpha}^t, \boldsymbol{\alpha}^{t-1}, \boldsymbol{\alpha}^{t-2}) + V^{\mathrm{S}}(\boldsymbol{\alpha}^t, \mathbf{z}^t)$$
$$+ U^{\mathrm{C}}(\boldsymbol{\alpha}^t, \mathbf{z}) + U^{\mathrm{M}}(\boldsymbol{\alpha}^t, \boldsymbol{\alpha}^{t-1}, \mathbf{m}^t), \tag{9.6}$$

in which the first two terms are "priorlike" and the second two are observation likelihoods. Briefly, the roles of the four terms are the following:

- **Temporal prior** term $V^{\mathrm{T}}(\ldots)$ is a second-order Markov chain that imposes a tendency to temporal continuity of segmentation labels.

- **Spatial prior** term $V^{\mathrm{S}}(\ldots)$ is an Ising term that imposes a tendency to spatial continuity of labels, and is inhibited by high contrast.

- **Color likelihood** term $U^{\mathrm{C}}(\ldots)$ evaluates the evidence for pixel labels based on color distributions in foreground and background.

- **Motion likelihood** term $U^{\mathrm{M}}(\ldots)$ evaluates the evidence for pixel labels based on the expectation of stasis in the background and frequently occurring motion in the foreground. Motion $\mathbf{m}^t$ is explained in terms of the labeling at both the current frame $\boldsymbol{\alpha}^t$ and the previous one $\boldsymbol{\alpha}^{t-1}$.

This energy resembles a spatiotemporal hidden Markov model (HMM), and this is illustrated graphically in figure 9.1. Details of the prior and likelihood factors are given in the remainder of this section.

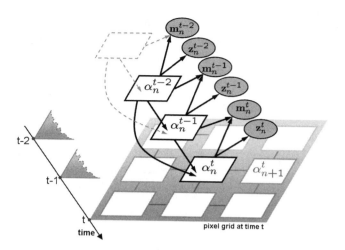

Figure 9.1
Spatiotemporal hidden Markov model. This graphical model illustrates the color and motion likelihoods together with the spatial and temporal priors. The same temporal chain is repeated at each pixel position. Spatial dependencies are illustrated for a 4-neighborhood system.

9.2.2 Temporal Prior Term

Figure 9.2 illustrates the four kinds of temporal transitions a pixel can undergo in a bilayer scene, based on a two-frame analysis. For instance, a foreground pixel may remain in the foreground (pixels labeled FF in figure 9.2c) or move to the background (pixels labeled FB), and so on. The critical point here is that a first-order Markov chain is inadequate to convey the nature of temporal coherence in this problem; a second-order Markov chain is required. For example, a pixel that was in the background at time $t-2$ and is in the foreground at time $t-1$ is far more likely to remain in the foreground at time t than to go back to the background. Note that BF and FB transitions correspond to temporal occlusion and disocclusion events, and that a pixel cannot change layer without going through an occlusion event.

These intuitions are captured probabilistically and incorporated into our energy minimization framework by means of a second-order Markov chain, as illustrated in the graphical model of figure 9.1. The temporal transition priors are learned from labeled data and then stored in a table, as in figure 9.3. Despite there being eight (2^3) possible transitions, due to probabilistic normalization ($p(\alpha^t = \text{B}|\alpha^{t-1}, \alpha^{t-2}) = 1 - p(\alpha^t = \text{F}|\alpha^{t-1}, \alpha^{t-2})$) the temporal prior table has only four degrees of freedom, represented by the four parameters $\beta_{\text{FF}}, \beta_{\text{FB}}, \beta_{\text{BF}}, \beta_{\text{BB}}$. This leads to the following joint temporal prior term:

$$V^{\text{T}}(\boldsymbol{\alpha}^t, \boldsymbol{\alpha}^{t-1}, \boldsymbol{\alpha}^{t-2}) = \eta \sum_{n}^{N} \left[-\log p\left(\alpha_n^t \mid \alpha_n^{t-1}, \alpha_n^{t-2}\right) \right] \tag{9.7}$$

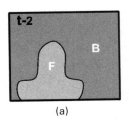 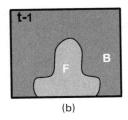 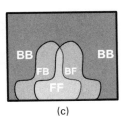

Figure 9.2
Temporal transitions at a pixel. (a,b) An object moves toward the right from frame $t-2$ to frame $t-1$. (c) Between the two frames pixels may remain in their own foreground or background layer (denoted F and B, respectively) or change layer, thus defining four kinds of temporal transitions: B $\to$ B, F $\to$ B, F $\to$ F, B $\to$ F. Those transitions influence the label that a pixel is going to assume at frame t.

α^{t-1}	α^{t-2}	$p(\alpha^t = F | \alpha^{t-1}, \alpha^{t-2})$
F	F	β_{FF}
F	B	β_{FB}
B	F	β_{BF}
B	B	β_{BB}

Figure 9.3
Learned priors for temporal transitions. The background probabilities are the complement of the foreground ones. See text for details.

in which $\eta < 1$ is a discount factor to allow for multiple counting across nonindependent pixels. The optimal value of η (as well as of the other CRF parameters) is trained discriminatively from ground truth.

9.2.3 Ising Spatial Energy
There is a natural tendency for segmentation boundaries to align with contours of high image contrast. Similarly to [66, 401] and chapter 7, this is represented by an energy term of the form

$$V^S(\boldsymbol{\alpha}, \mathbf{z}) = \gamma \sum_{(m,n)\in\mathbf{C}} [\alpha_m \neq \alpha_n] \left(\frac{\epsilon + e^{-\mu\|z_m - z_n\|^2}}{1 + \epsilon} \right) \tag{9.8}$$

where (m, n) index neighboring pixel pairs. $\mathbf{C}$ is the set of pairs of neighboring pixels. The contrast parameter μ is chosen to be $\mu = \left(2\langle\|z_m - z_n\|^2\rangle\right)^{-1}$, where $\langle \cdot \rangle$ denotes expectation over all pairs of neighbors in an image sample. The energy term $V(\boldsymbol{\alpha}, \mathbf{z})$ represents a combination of an Ising prior for labeling coherence with a contrast likelihood that acts to partially discount the coherence terms. The constant γ is a strength parameter for the coherence prior and also for the contrast likelihood. The constant ϵ is a "dilution" constant for contrast; previously [66] set to $\epsilon = 0$ for pure color segmentation. However, multiple cue experiments with color and stereo [258] have suggested $\epsilon = 1$ as a more appropriate value.

9.2.4 Likelihood for Color

The term $U^C(.)$ in (21.5) is the log of the color likelihood. In [258, 401] color likelihoods were modeled in terms of Gaussian mixture models (GMM) in RGB, where foreground and background mixtures were learned via expectation maximization (EM). However, we have found that issues with the initialization of EM and with local minima affect the discrimination power of the final likelihood ratio. Instead, here we model the foreground and background color likelihoods nonparametrically, as histograms in the YUV color space. The color term $U^C(.)$ is defined as

$$U^C(\boldsymbol{\alpha}, \mathbf{z}) = -\rho \sum_n^N \log p(z_n \mid \alpha_n). \tag{9.9}$$

Probabilistic normalization requires that $\sum_z p(z \mid \alpha = \text{F})$, and similarly for the background likelihood. This nonparametric representation negates the need for having to set the number of GMM components, as well as having to wait for EM convergence.

The foreground color likelihood model is learned adaptively over successive frames similarly to [258], based on data from the segmented foreground in the previous frame. The likelihoods are then stored in 3D lookup tables constructed from the raw color histograms with a modest degree of smoothing to avoid overfitting. The background color distribution is constructed from an initial extended observation of the background, rather as in [405, 450], to build in variability of appearance. The distribution is then static over time. It is also shared by the entire background, to give additional robustness against camera shake, and studies suggest that the loss of precision in segmentation, compared with pixelwise color models (such as those used in [458]), should not be very great [258]. The distribution is represented as a smoothed histogram, rather than as a GMM, to avoid initialization problems.

9.2.5 Likelihood for Motion

The treatment of motion could have been addressed via an intermediate computation of optical flow. However, reliable computation of flow is expensive and beset with difficulties concerning the aperture problem and regularization. Those difficulties can be finessed in the segmentation application by bypassing flow and directly modeling the characteristics of the feature normally used to compute flow: the spatial and temporal derivatives $\mathbf{m} = (\mathbf{g}, \dot{\mathbf{z}})$. The motion likelihood therefore captures the characteristics of those features under foreground and background conditions, respectively.

However, the nature of our generative model suggests an approach to motion likelihood modeling that should capture even richer information about segmentation. Referring back to figure 9.2, the immediate history of the segmentation of a pixel falls into one of four

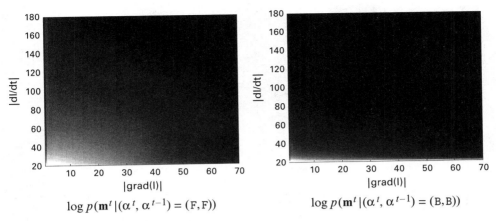

Figure 9.4
Learned motion likelihoods. Two of the four learned likelihoods of motion data, conditioned on the segmentation in the two previous frames. Bright indicates high density, and dark, low density. The distributions are modeled as normalized histograms.

classes: FF, BB, FB, BF. We model the observed image motion features $\mathbf{m}_n^t = (g_n^t, \dot{z}_n^t)$, at time t and for pixel n, as conditioned on those combinations of the segmentation labels α_n^{t-1} and α_n^t. This is a natural model because the temporal derivative $\dot{z}_n^t$ is computed from frames $t-1$ and t, so clearly it should depend on segmentations of those frames. The joint distributions learned for each of the four label combinations are shown in figure 9.4. Empirically, the BB distribution reflects the relative constancy of the background state—temporal derivatives are small in magnitude. The FF distribution reflects larger temporal change and, as expected, that is somewhat correlated with spatial gradient magnitude. Transitional FB and BF distributions show the largest temporal changes because the temporal samples at time $t-1$ and t straddle an object boundary. The distributions for BF and FB are distinct in shape from those for BB and FF [112], and this is one indication that the second-order model does indeed capture additional motion information, compared with a first-order model. (The first-order model would be conditioned on just F and B, for which the likelihoods are essentially identical to those for FF and BB.)

The four motion likelihoods are learned from some labeled ground truth data and then stored (smoothed) as 2D histograms to use in likelihood evaluation. The likelihoods are evaluated as part of the total energy, in the term

$$U^{\mathrm{M}}(\boldsymbol{\alpha}^t, \boldsymbol{\alpha}^{t-1}, \mathbf{m}^t) = -\sum_n \log p(\mathbf{m}_n^t \mid \alpha_n^t, \alpha_n^{t-1}). \tag{9.10}$$

Illustrating the Motion Likelihoods   Figure 9.5 shows the results of a likelihood ratio test using the likelihood ratio R of the FF model versus the BB model, applied to *two* frames of the VK test sequence. Motion and nonmotion events are accurately separated in textured

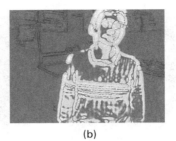

(a)   (b)

Figure 9.5
Testing the motion classifier. (a) A frame from the VK test sequence. (b) The corresponding motion likelihood map as output of a likelihood ratio test. Bright pixels indicate motion (likelihood ratio $R > 1$) and dark ones, stasis ($R < 1$). Thanks to our joint motion likelihood, strong stationary edges are assigned a lower (more negative, darker) value of R than stationary textureless areas.

areas. In fact, moving edges are clearly marked with bright pixels ($R > 1$) and stationary edges are marked with dark pixels ($R < 1$). However, textureless regions remain ambiguous and are automatically assigned a likelihood ratio close to unity (mid-gray in the figure). This suggests that motion alone is not sufficient for an accurate segmentation. Fusing motion and color with CRF spatial and Markov chain temporal priors as in (21.5) is expected to help fill the remaining gaps. In stereo, as opposed to motion segmentation [258], it is known that good segmentation can be achieved even without the temporal model. However, as we show later, the gaps in the motion likelihood also demand the temporal model for satisfactory filling in.

9.2.6   Inference by Energy Minimization

At the beginning of this section the principal aim of estimation was stated to be the maximization of the joint posterior (9.5). However, it was also plain that the constraints of causality in real-time systems do not allow that. Under causality, having estimated $\hat{\boldsymbol{\alpha}}^1, \ldots, \hat{\boldsymbol{\alpha}}^{t-1}$, one way to estimate $\hat{\boldsymbol{\alpha}}^t$ would be

$$\hat{\boldsymbol{\alpha}}^t = \arg\min \quad E(\boldsymbol{\alpha}^t, \hat{\boldsymbol{\alpha}}^{t-1}, \hat{\boldsymbol{\alpha}}^{t-2}, \mathbf{z}^t, \mathbf{m}^t). \tag{9.11}$$

Freezing all estimators before generating t is an extreme approach, and better results are obtained by acknowledging the variability in at least the immediately previous time step. Therefore, the energy in (9.11) is replaced by the expected energy:

$$\mathcal{E}_{\boldsymbol{\alpha}^{t-1} \mid \hat{\boldsymbol{\alpha}}^{t-1}} E(\boldsymbol{\alpha}^t, \boldsymbol{\alpha}^{t-1}, \hat{\boldsymbol{\alpha}}^{t-2}, \mathbf{z}^t, \mathbf{m}^t), \tag{9.12}$$

where $\mathcal{E}$ indicates expectation and the conditional density for time $t - 1$ is modeled as

$$p(\boldsymbol{\alpha}^{t-1} \mid \hat{\boldsymbol{\alpha}}^{t-1}) = \prod_n p(\alpha_n^{t-1} \mid \hat{\alpha}_n^{t-1}), \quad \text{and} \tag{9.13}$$

$$p(\alpha^{t-1} \mid \hat{\alpha}^{t-1}) = \nu + (1 - \nu)\delta(\alpha^{t-1}, \hat{\alpha}^{t-1}), \tag{9.14}$$

(a) input sequence   (b) automatic background substitution in three frames

Figure 9.6
An example of automatic bilayer segmentation in monocular image sequences. The foreground person is accurately extracted from the sequence and then composited free of aliasing upon a different background—a useful tool in videoconferencing applications. The sequences and ground truth data used throughout this chapter are available from http://research.microsoft.com/projects/i2i.

and v (with $v \in [0, 1]$) is the degree to which the binary segmentation at time $t - 1$ is "softened" to give a segmentation distribution. In practice, allowing $v > 0$ (typically $v = 0.1$) prevents the segmentation from becoming erroneously "stuck" in either foreground or background states.

This factorization of the segmentation distribution across pixels makes the expectation computation (9.12) entirely tractable. The alternative of fully representing uncertainty in segmentation is computationally too costly. Finally, the segmentation $\hat{\alpha}^t$ is computed by binary graph cut [66].

9.3   Experimental Results

This section validates the proposed segmentation algorithm through comparison both with stereo-based segmentation and with hand-labeled ground truth.[2]

Bilayer Segmentation and Background Substitution
In figure 9.6 foreground and background of a video sequence have been separated automatically. After an initial period when the subject is almost stationary, the segmentation converges to a good solution. Real-time "border matting" [401] has been used to compute fractional opacities along the boundary, and this is used for anti-aliased compositing onto a new background. Segmentation and background substitution for another test sequence is demonstrated in figure 9.7. Notice that good segmentation is achieved even in frames containing rapid motion, as in figures 9.1b and 9.7d. In figure 9.7 fusion of color with motion enables correct filling of large, textureless foreground (the black jumper).

Detecting Temporal Occlusions
Figure 9.8 shows examples of temporal occlusion detection for the JM sequence, made possible by the spatiotemporal priors. Pixels transitioning from foreground to background are marked with a checkerboard pattern.

---

2. Ground truth sequences available at http://research.microsoft.com/projects/i2i

(a)   (b)   (c)   (d)

Figure 9.7
Bilayer segmentation and background substitution. (a) A frame from the MS test sequence; (b–d) foreground extraction and anti-aliased background substitution, over several frames. (d) The algorithm is capable of handling complex motions.

Figure 9.8
Segmentation and occlusion detection. Two frames from the JM test sequence. Pixels undergoing an F → B transition are marked with a checkerboard pattern.

Quantitative Evaluation and Comparisons

Following [258], error rates are measured as a percentage of misclassified pixels, with respect to ground truth segmentation.[3] Figure 9.9 presents the results for four of the six Microsoft test sequences. The error rates obtained monocularly (blue) are compared with those obtained by layered graph cut (LGC) stereo segmentation [258]. While monocular segmentation cannot be expected to perform better than stereo, its accuracy is comparable with that of LGC segmentation. Figure 9.9 provides an objective measure of visual accuracy, while videos (on our Web site) offer a subjective impression that is hard to capture numerically. Despite some flicker artifacts, the quality of monocular segmentation is generally convincing.

Finally, the contribution of the temporal model is evaluated. Figure 9.10 compares error rates for the following three cases: (1) no temporal modeling, (2) first-order HMM, (3) second-order HMM (including both the second-order temporal prior and the two-frame motion likelihood). Error is computed for the AC test sequence with model parameters fully optimized for best performance. Color information is omitted to avoid confounding factors in the comparison. From figure 9.10 it is clear that the second-order HMM model achieves

---

3. The published ground truth based on motion rather than that based on depth.

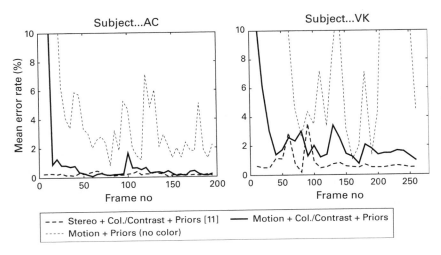

Figure 9.9
Accuracy of segmentation. Error rates for the AC and VK sequences, respectively. The thick dashed curve indicates the error rates obtained by LGC stereo segmentation [258]. The solid curve indicates errors obtained by the proposed monocular algorithm. In both sequences an initial period of stasis prevents correct segmentation, but after a few frames the errors drop to a value close to that of LGC stereo. After the model is burned in, it can tolerate periods of stasis. Omitting the color component of the model increases the error (thin dotted line).

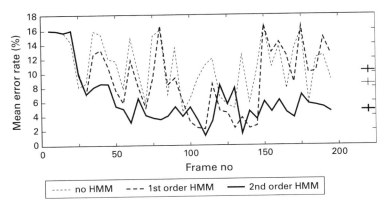

Figure 9.10
The advantage of the second-order temporal model. Error plots for different orders of temporal HMM, for the AC test sequence. Crosses indicate error averaged over all frames. Averages were computed from frame 10 onward to exclude the burn-in period. The second-order model achieves the lowest error.

the lowest error, followed by the first-order model, with highest error occurring when the temporal model is entirely absent.

Robustness to Photometric Variations

Accurate segmentation of *all* six test sequences in the Microsoft repository has proved difficult in view of particularly large photometric variability in some sequences. The variations have been found to be due mostly to camera AGC (automatic gain control). We found that the IJ and IU sequences exhibit illumination variation about an order of magnitude higher than in the remaining four sequences [112]. While stereo-based segmentation is relatively immune to such problems [258], monocular algorithms are more prone to be disturbed. However, such large levels of photometric variation are easily avoided in practice by switching off the AGC facility. More examples, results, and comparisons are reported in [112].

9.4 Conclusions

This chapter has presented an algorithm for the accurate segmentation of videos by probabilistic fusion of motion, color, and contrast cues together with spatial and temporal priors. The model forms a conditional random field, and its parameters are trained discriminatively. The motion component of the model avoids the computation of optical flow, and instead uses a novel and effective likelihood model based on spatiotemporal derivatives and conditioned on frame pairs. Spatiotemporal coherence is exploited via a contrast-sensitive Ising energy combined with a second-order temporal Markov chain.

In terms of efficiency our algorithm compares favorably with respect to existing real-time stereo techniques [258] and achieves comparable levels of accuracy. Computationally intensive evaluation of stereo match scores is replaced by efficient motion likelihood and color model evaluation, using efficient lookup table.

Quantitative evaluation has confirmed the validity of the proposed approach and has highlighted advantages and limitations with respect to stereo-based segmentation. Finally, combining the proposed motion likelihoods and second-order temporal model with stereo matching information may well, in the future, lead to greater levels of accuracy and robustness than either motion or stereo alone.

Acknowledgments

The authors acknowledge helpful discussions with C. Rother, M. Cohen, C. Zhang and R. Zabih.

10   MRFs for Superresolution and Texture Synthesis

William T. Freeman and Ce Liu

Suppose we want to digitally enlarge a photograph. The input is a single low-resolution image, and the desired output is an estimate of the high-resolution version of that image. This problem can be phrased as one of "image interpolation": interpolating the pixel values between observed samples. Image interpolation is sometimes called superresolution, since it estimates data at a resolution beyond that of the image samples. In contrast with multi-image superresolution methods, where a high-resolution image is inferred from a video sequence, here high-resolution images are estimated from a single low-resolution example [150].

There are many analytic methods for image interpolation, including pixel replication, linear and cubic spline interpolation [378], and sharpened Gaussian interpolation [426]. When interpolating in resolution by a large factor, such as four or more in each dimension, these analytic methods typically suffer from a blurred appearance. Following a simple rule, they tend to make conservative, smooth guesses for image appearance.

This problem can be addressed with two techniques. The first is to use an example-based representation to handle the many expected special cases. Second, a graphical model framework can be used to reason about global structure. The superresolution problem has a structure similar to other low-level vision tasks: accumulate local evidence (which may be ambiguous) and propagate it across space. An MRF is an appropriate structure for this: local evidence terms can be modeled by unary potentials $\psi_i(x_i)$ at a node i with states x_i. Spatial propagation occurs through pairwise potentials $\phi_{ij}(x_i, x_j)$ between nodes i and j, or through higher-order potentials. The joint probability then has the factorized form

$$P(\mathbf{x}) = \frac{1}{Z} \prod_i \psi_i(x_i) \prod_{(i,j)\in\mathcal{E}} \phi_{ij}(x_i, x_j), \tag{10.1}$$

where $\mathcal{E}$ is the set of edges in the MRF denoted by the neighboring nodes i and j, and Z is a normalization constant such that the probabilities sum to 1 [309]. The local statistical relationships allow information to propagate long distances over an image.

10.1 Image Prefiltering

The superresolution algorithm first specifies the desired model of subsampling and image degradation that needs to be undone. For the examples in this chapter the degradation is assumed to be low-pass filtering, followed with subsampling by a factor of 4 in each dimension, to obtain the observed low-resolution image. The low-pass filter is a 7×7 pixel Gaussian filter, normalized to have unit sum, of standard deviation 1 pixel. Starting from a high-resolution image, it is blurred and subsampled to generate the corresponding low-resolution image. This model is applied to a set of training images, in order to generate some number of paired examples of high-resolution and low-resolution image patch pairs.

It is convenient to handle the high- and low-resolution images at the same sampling rate—the same number of pixels. After creating the low-resolution image, we perform an initial interpolation up to the sampling rate of the full-resolution image. Usually this is done with cubic spline interpolation, to create the "up-sampled low-resolution image."

We want to exploit whatever invariances we can, to let the training data generalize beyond the training examples. Two heuristics are used to try to extend the reach of the examples. First, we do not believe that all spatial frequencies of the low resolution image are needed to predict the missing high-frequency image components, and storing a different example patch for each possible value of the low-frequency components of the low-resolution patch is undesirable. Thus a low-pass filter is applied to the up-sampled low-resolution image in order to divide it into two spatial frequency bands. We call the output of the low-pass filter the "low-band," L; the up-sampled low-resolution image minus the low-band image gives the "mid-band," M. The difference between the up-sampled low-resolution image and the original image is the "high-band," H.

A second operation to increase the scope of the examples is contrast normalization. It is assumed that the relationship of the mid-band data to the high-band data is independent of the local contrast level, so the contrast of the mid- and high-band images is normalized in the following way:

$$[\hat{M}, \hat{H}] = \frac{[M, H]}{\text{std}(M) + \delta} \tag{10.2}$$

where $\text{std}(\cdot)$ is the standard deviation operator, and δ is a small value that sets the local contrast level below which we do not adjust the contrast. Typically, $\delta = 0.0001$ for images that range over 0 to 1.

10.2 Representation of the Unknown State

There is a choice about what is estimated at the nodes of the MRF. If the variable to be estimated at each node is a single pixel, then the dimensionality of the unknown state at a node is low, which is good. However, it may not be feasible to draw valid conclusions about

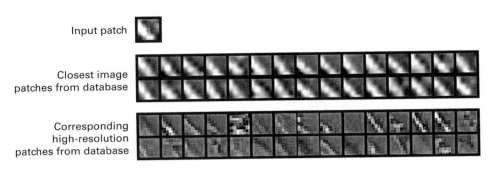

Figure 10.1
Top: input patch (mid-band band-pass filtered, contrast-normalized). We seek the high-resolution patch associated with this. Middle: Nearest neighbors from database to the input patch. These patches match this input patch reasonably well. Bottom: The corresponding high-resolution patches associated with each of the retrieved mid-band band-pass patches. These show more variability than the mid-band patches, indicating that more information than simply the local image matches is needed to select the proper high-resolution image estimate. Since the resolution requirements for the color components are lower than for luminance, we use an example-based approach for the luminance, and interpolate the color information by a conventional cubic spline interpolation.

single pixel states simply by performing computations between pairs of pixels. That may place an undue burden on the MRF inference. That burden can be removed if a large patch of estimated pixels is assigned to one node, but then the state dimensionality at a node may be unmanageably high.

This is addressed by working with entire image patches at each node, to provide sufficient local evidence, but using other means to constrain the state dimensionality at a node. First, restrict the solution patch to be one of some number of exemplars, typically image examples from some training set. In addition, take advantage of local image evidence to further constrain the choice of exemplars to be from some smaller set of candidates from the training set. The result is an unknown state dimension of twenty to forty states per node.

Figure 10.1 illustrates this representation. The top row shows an input patch from the (band-passed, contrast-normalized) low-resolution input image. The next two rows show the thirty nearest-neighbor examples from a database of 658,788 image patches extracted from forty-one images. The low-res patches are of dimension 25×25, and the high-res patches are of dimension 9×9. The bottom two rows of figure 10.2 show the corresponding high-resolution image patches for each of those thirty nearest neighbors. The mid-band images look approximately the same as each other and as the input patch, while the high-resolution patches look considerably different from each other. This tells us that the local information from the patch by itself is not sufficient to determine the missing high-resolution information, and some other source of information must be used to resolve the ambiguity. The state representation is then an index into a collection of exemplars, indicating which of the unknown high-resolution image patches is the correct one, as illustrated in figure 10.2. The resulting MRF is shown in figure 10.3.

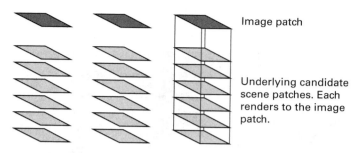

Figure 10.2
The state to be estimated at each node. Using the local evidence, at each node we have a small collection of image candidates, selected from our database. We use the belief propagation to select between the candidates, based on compatibility information.

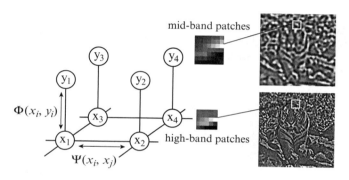

Figure 10.3
Patch-based MRF for low-level vision. The observations y_i are patches from the mid-band image data. The states to be estimated are indices into a data set of high-band patches.

10.3 MRF Parameterization

We can define a local evidence term and pairwise potentials of the Markov random field if we make assumptions about the probability of encountering a training set exemplar in the test image. We assume that any of our image exemplars can appear in the input image with equal probability. We account for differences between the input and training set patches as independent, identically distributed Gaussian noise added to every pixel. Then the local evidence for a node being in sample state x_i depends on the amount of noise needed to translate from the low-resolution patch corresponding to state x_i to the observed mid-band image patch, $\mathbf{p}$. If we denote the band-passed, contrast-normalized mid-band training patch associated with state x_i as $\mathbf{M}(x_i)$, then

$$\psi_i(x_i) = \exp -|\mathbf{p} - \mathbf{M}(x_i)|^2/(2\sigma^2) \tag{10.3}$$

where we write 2D image patches as rasterized vectors.

To construct the compatibility term $\phi_{ij}(x_i, x_j)$, we assume we have overlapping high-band patches that should agree with their neighbors in their regions of overlap. Any disagreements are again attributed to a Gaussian noise process. If we denote the band-passed, contrast-normalized high-band training patch associated with state x_i as $\mathbf{H}(x_i)$, and introduce an operator O_{ij} that extracts as a rasterized vector the pixels of the overlap region between patches i and j (with the ordering compatible for neighboring patches), then we have

$$\phi_{ij}(x_i, x_j) = \exp -|O_{ij}(H(x_i)) - O_{ji}(H(x_j))|^2/(2\sigma^2). \tag{10.4}$$

In the examples below, we used a mid-band and high-band patch size of 9×9 pixels, and a patch overlap region of size 3 pixels.

10.4 Loopy Belief Propagation

We have set up the Markov random field such that each possible selection of states at each node corresponds to a high-resolution image interpretation of the input low-resolution image. The MRF probability, dervied from all the local evidence and pairwise potentials in the MRF, assigns a probability to each possible selection of states according to (10.1). Each configuration of states specifies an estimated high-band image, and we seek the high-band image that is most favored by the MRF we have specified. This is the task of finding a point estimate from a posterior probability distribution.

In Bayesian decision theory [32] the optimal point estimate depends on the loss function used—the penalty for guessing wrong. With a penalty proportional to the square of the error, the best estimate (MMSE) is the mean of the posterior. However, if all deviations from the true value are equally penalized, then the best estimate is the maximum of the posterior. Using belief propagation [367], both estimates can be calculated exactly for an MRF that is a tree. The use of BP on a graph with loops or cycles in this way has been described fully in chapters 1 and 5. As described earlier, the BP update and marginal probability equations are applied, and give an approximation to the marginals. The message updates are run until convergence or for a fixed number of iterations (here, we used thirty iterations). Fixed points of these iterative update rules correspond to stationary points of a well-known approximation used in statistical physics, the Bethe approximation [538]. Good empirical results have been obtained with that approximation [153, 150], and we use it here.

To approximate the MMSE estimate, take the mean (weighted by the marginals from (5.18)) of the candidate patches at a node. It is also possible to approximate the MAP estimate by replacing the summation operator of (5.17) with "max," then selecting the patch maximizing the resulting "max-marginal" given in (5.18). These solutions are often sharper, but with more artifacts, than the MMSE estimate.

To piece together the final image, undo the contrast normalization of each patch, average neighboring patches in regions where they overlap, add in the low- and mid-band images and the analytically interpolated chrominance information. Figure 10.4 summarizes the steps in

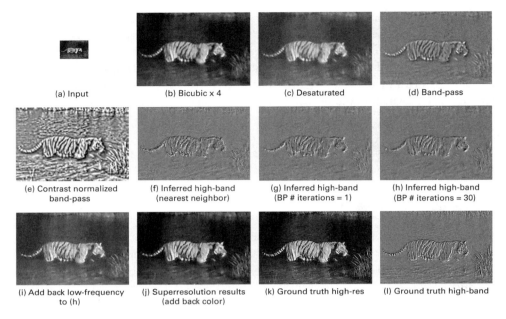

| (a) Input | (b) Bicubic x 4 | (c) Desaturated | (d) Band-pass |

| (e) Contrast normalized band-pass | (f) Inferred high-band (nearest neighbor) | (g) Inferred high-band (BP # iterations = 1) | (h) Inferred high-band (BP # iterations = 30) |

| (i) Add back low-frequency to (h) | (j) Superresolution results (add back color) | (k) Ground truth high-res | (l) Ground truth high-band |

Figure 10.4
Images showing example-based superresolution processing. (a) input image of resolution 120×80. (b) Cubic spline interpolation up to a factor of 4 higher resolution in each dimension. (c) Extract the luminance component for example-based processing (and use cubic spline interpolation for the chrominance components). (d) High-pass filtering of this image gives the mid-band output, shown here. (e) Display of the contrast-normalized mid-band. The contrast normalization extends the utility of the training database samples beyond the contrast value of each particular training example. (f) The high frequencies corresponding to the nearest neighbor of each local low-frequency patch. (g) After one iteration of belief propagation, much of the choppy, high-frequency details of (f) are removed. (h) Converged high-resolution estimates. (i) Image (c) added to image (h)—the estimated high frequencies added back to the mid- and low-frequencies. (j) Color components added back in. (k) Comparison with ground truth. (l) True high-frequency components.

the algorithm, and figure 10.5 shows other results. The perceived sharpness is significantly improved, and the belief propagation iterations significantly reduce the artifacts that would result from estimating the high-resolution image based on local image information alone. (Figure 10.6 provides enlargements of cropped regions from figures 10.4 and 10.5) The code used to generate the images in this section is available online.[1]

10.5   Texture Synthesis

This same example-based MRF machinery can be applied to other low-level vision tasks [150]. Another application involving image patches in Markov random fields is texture synthesis. Here, the input is a small sample of a texture to be synthesized. The output is a

---

1. Download at http://people.csail.mit.edu/billf/.

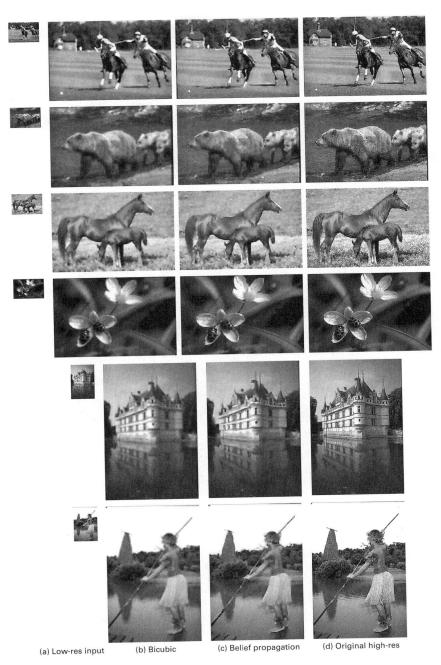

(a) Low-res input   (b) Bicubic   (c) Belief propagation   (d) Original high-res

Figure 10.5
Other example-based superresolution outputs. (a) Input low-resolution images. (b) Bicubic interpolation (×4 resolution increase). (c) Belief propagation output. (d) The true high-resolution images.

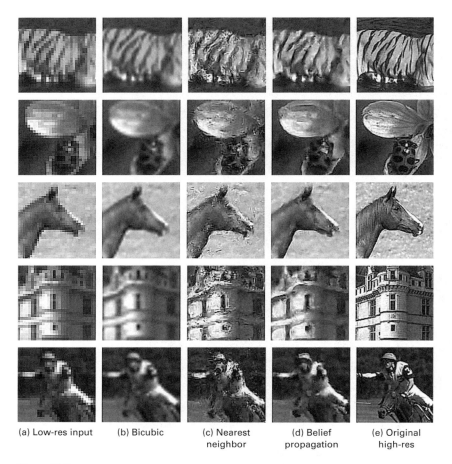

(a) Low-res input   (b) Bicubic   (c) Nearest   (d) Belief   (e) Original
                                     neighbor   propagation   high-res

Figure 10.6
The close-ups of figures 10.4 and 10.5. (a) Input low-res images. (b) Bicubic interpolation (×4 resolution increase). (c) Nearest neighbor output. (d) Belief propagation output. (c) The true high-resolution images.

larger portion of that texture, having the same appearance but not made by simply repeating the input texture.

Nonparametric texture methods have revolutionized texture synthesis. Notable examples include Heeger and Bergen [187], De Bonet [59], and Efros and Leung [133]. However, these methods can be slow. To speed them up and address some image quality issues, Efros and Freeman [132] developed a nonparametric patch-based method; a related method was developed independently by Liang et al. [313]. This is another example of the patch-based, nonparametric Markov random field machinery described above for the superresolution problem.

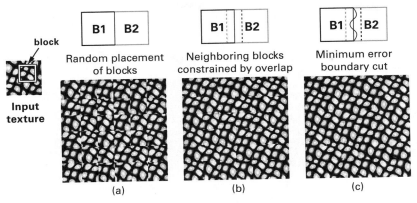

Figure 10.7
Patch samples of an input texture can be composited to form a larger texture in a number of different ways. (a) A random placement of texture samples gives strong patch boundary artifacts. (b) Selecting only patches that match well with neighbors in an overlap region leaves some boundary artifacts in the composite image. (c) Selecting the best seam through the boundary region of neighboring patches removes most artifacts. Figure reprinted from [132].

For texture synthesis the idea is to draw patch samples from random positions within the source texture, then piece them together seamlessly. Figure 10.7, from [132], tells the story. In (a), random samples are drawn from the source texture and placed in the synthesized texture. With random selection the boundaries between adjacent texture blocks are quite visible. (b) shows texture synthesis with overlapping patches selected from the input texture to match the left and top borders of the texture region that has been synthesized so far. The border artifacts are greatly suppressed, yet some are still visible. (c) shows the result of adding an additional step to the processing of (b): select an optimal ragged boundary using "image quilting" (described below).

There is an MRF implied by the model above, with the same ψ_{ij} compatibility term between neighboring patches as for the superresolution problem. For this texture synthesis problem there is no local evidence term.[2] This makes it nearly impossible to solve the problem using belief propagation, since there is no small list of candidate patches available at each node. The state dimension cannot be reduced to a manageable level.

As an alternative, a greedy algorithm, described in detail in [132], approximates the optimal assignment of training patch to MRF node. The image is processed in a raster scan fashion, top-to-bottom in rows, left-to-right within each row. Except at the image boundaries, there are two borders with patches filled in for any patch we seek to select. To add a patch, randomly select a patch from the source texture from the top five matches to the top and left boundary values. This algorithm can be thought of as a particularly simple, approximate method to find the patch assignments that maximize the MRF of (10.1), where

---

2. A related problem, texture transfer [132], includes local evidence constraints.

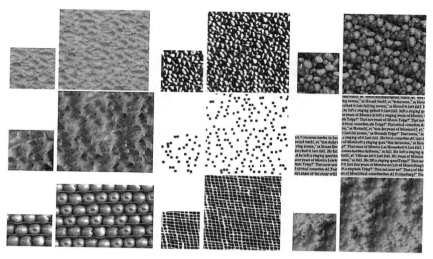

Figure 10.8
A collection of source (small image) and corresponding synthesized textures made using the patch-based image-quilting method. Figure reprinted from [132].

the pairwise compatibilities $\phi_{ij}(x_i, x_j)$ are as for superresolution, but there are no local evidence terms $\phi_i(x_i)$. Figure 10.8 shows nine examples of textures synthesized from input examples (shown in the smaller images to the left of each synthesis example). The examples exhibit the perceptual appearance of the smaller patches but are synthesized in a realistic nonrepeating pattern.

10.5.1 Image Quilting by Dynamic Programming

To return to the goal of finding the optimal ragged boundary between two patches, we seek the optimal tear to minimize the visibility of artifacts caused by differences between the neighboring patches. The algorithm for finding the optimal tear in a vertical region has an obvious extension to a horizontal tear. Let the difference between two adjacent patches in the region of overlap be $d(i, j)$, where i and j are horizontal and vertical pixel coordinates, respectively. For each row, seek the column $q(j)$ of an optimal path of tearing between the two patches. This optimal path should follow a contour of small difference values between the two patches. Now minimize

$$\hat{q} = \arg \min_{q(j)} \sum_{j}^{K} d(q(j), j)^2 \tag{10.5}$$

under the constraint that the tear forms a continuous line, $|q(j) - q(j-1)| \leq 1$.

This optimal path problem has a well-known solution through dynamic programming [36], which has been exploited in various vision and graphics applications [430, 132]. It is equivalent to finding the maximum posterior probability through max-product belief propagation. Here is a summary of the algorithm:

```
Initialization:
p(i,1)) = d(i, 1)

for j = 2:N
  p(i,j) = p(i, j-1) + min_k d(k,j)
end
```

where the values considered for the minimization over k are i, and $i \pm 1$. Using an auxiliary set of pointers indicating the optimal value of the $\min_k$ operation at each iteration, the path $q(i)$ can be found from the values of $p(i, j)$. This method has also been used to hide image seams in "seam carving" [17].

10.6 Some Related Applications

Markov random fields have been used extensively in image processing and computer vision. Geman and Geman brought Markov random fields to the attention of the vision community and showed how to use MRFs as image priors in restoration applications [161]. Poggio et al. used MRFs in a framework unifying different computer vision modules [374].

The example-based approach has been built on by others. This method has been used in combination with a resolution enhancement model specific to faces [20] to achieve excellent results in hallucinating details of faces [316]. Huang and Ma have proposed finding a linear combination of the candidate patches to fit the input data, then applying the same regression to the output patches, simulating a better fit to the input [533]. (A related approach was used in [151].)

Optimal seams for image transitions were found in a 2D framework, using graph cut, by Kwatra et al. [287]. Example-based image priors were used for image-based rendering in the work of Fitzgibbon et al. [145]. Fattal used edge models for image up-sampling [135]. Glasner et al. also used an example-based approach for superresolution, relying on self-similarity within a single image [167].

Acknowledgments

William T. Freeman thanks the co-authors of the original research papers which are described in this chapter: Egon Pasztor, Alexi Efros, and Owen Carmichael. He acknowledges support from Royal Dutch/Shell Group, NGA NEGI-1582-04-0004, MURI Grant N00014-06-1-0734 and gifts from Microsoft, Adobe, and Texas Instruments.

11 A Comparative Study of Energy Minimization Methods for MRFs

Richard Szeliski, Ramin Zabih, Daniel Scharstein, Olga Veksler, Vladimir Kolmogorov, Aseem Agarwala, Marshall F. Tappen, and Carsten Rother

Many of the previous chapters have addressed the task of expressing computer vision problems, such as depth or texture computation, as discrete labeling problems in the form of a Markov Random Field. The goal of finding the best solution to the problem at hand then refers to the task of optimizing an energy function over a discrete domain with discrete binary or multilabel variables. Many different optimization, or inference, techniques have been discussed in previous chapters (see part I of the book). The focus of this chapter is to analyze the trade-offs among different energy minimization algorithms for different application scenarios. Three promising recent optimization techniques are investigated—graph cut, LBP, and tree-reweighted message passing (TRW)—in addition to the well-known older iterated conditional modes (ICM) algorithm. The main part of this chapter investigates applications where the MRF has a 4-connected grid graph structure and multilabeled variables. The applications are stereo without occlusion, image stitching, interactive segmentation, and denoising. The study is based on [464], for which benchmarks, code, images, and results are available online at http://vision.middlebury.edu/MRF. The main conclusion of the study is that some existing techniques, in particular graph cut and TRW, work very well for many applications. At the end of this chapter a different study is briefly discussed that considerers the application scenario of stereo with occlusions. Here, the conclusion is different, since the resulting highly connected MRF with multilabeled variables is hard to optimize, and only graph cut-based techniques work well.

11.1 Introduction

Over the last few years energy minimization approaches have had a renaissance, primarily due to powerful new optimization algorithms such as graph cut [72, 266] and loopy belief propagation (LBP) [540]. The results, especially in stereo, have been dramatic; according to the widely used Middlebury stereo benchmarks [419], almost all the top-performing stereo methods rely on graph cut or LBP. Moreover, these methods give substantially more accurate results than were previously possible. Simultaneously, the range of applications of pixel-labeling problems has also expanded dramatically (see this part II and part V);

examples are image restoration [38], texture modeling [162], image labeling [93], stereo matching [26, 72], interactive photo segmentation [66, 401], and the automatic placement of seams in digital photomontages [7].

Relatively little attention has been paid, however, to the relative performances of various optimization algorithms. Among the few exceptions are [68, 468, 260, 403]. In [68] the efficiency of several different max-flow algorithms for graph cut is compared, and [468] compares graph cut with LBP for stereo on a 4-connected grid graph. The main part of this chapter also considers problems on 2D grid graphs, since they occur in many real-world applications. In [260] a model with a more complex graph topology is considered: the problem of stereo with occlusion, which can be expressed as a highly connected graph. The main conclusions of this study will be summarized here. The study in [403] considers applications with a rather different type of Markov random field. In contrast to stereo, where pairwise terms of neighboring nodes encode a smoothness prior, that is, prefer to have the same labels, several problems in computer vision are of a different nature.

In domains such as new view synthesis, superresolution, or image deconvolution, pairwise terms are often of a repulsive nature, that is, neighboring nodes prefer to have different labels. The study in [403] considered a range of such problems, with the limitation of allowing only binary labels. These problems are in general NP-hard, which means that graph cut-based techniques are not directly applicable and more recent methods, such as the graph cut-based BHS algorithm (referred to as QPBO in [403]), have to be used instead (see details in chapter 2). Probably the most interesting insight of the study in [403] is that the relative performance of different techniques depends heavily on the connectivity of the graph. For low-connectivity graphs, advanced methods such as BP and the BHS algorithm perform very well. However, for highly connected graphs, where each node is connected to fifteen (up to eighty) other nodes, older techniques such as simulated annealing perform extremely well, even outperforming all other techniques for one example. This is in sharp contrast to the study presented in this chapter and also motivates a future large-scale comparison of arbitrary, multilabeled MRFs.

The chapter is organized as follows. Section 11.2 defines the energy function and evaluation methodology. In section 11.3 different optimization techniques are discussed. Section 11.4 presents the benchmark problems. Section 11.5 provides the experimental comparisons of different energy minimization methods. Section 11.6 introduces the more advanced model of stereo with occlusion and an experimental comparison between two models, stereo with and without occlusion, is given.

11.2   Problem Formulation and Experimental Infrastructure

11.2.1   Energy Model

We define a pixel-labeling problem as assigning to every pixel i a label that we write as l_i. The collection of all pixel label assignments is denoted by l, the number of pixels is N, and the number of labels is K. Using the same notation as in earlier chapters, the energy function E, which can also be viewed as the log-likelihood of the posterior distribution of a Markov random field [161, 308], is composed of a data energy U and a smoothness energy V (i.e., $E = U + \lambda V$). The data energy is the sum of a set of per-pixel data costs $\Phi_i(l_i)$, that is, $U = \sum_i \Phi_i(l_i)$, which typically comes from the (negative) log-likelihood of the measurement noise.

We assume that pixels form a 2D grid, so that each i can also be written in terms of its coordinates $i = (p, q)$. We use the standard 4-connected neighborhood system, so that the smoothness energy is the sum of spatially varying horizontal and vertical nearest-neighbor smoothness costs. If we let $\mathcal{N}$ denote the set of all such neighboring pixel pairs, the smoothness energy is $V = \sum_{\{i,j\}\in\mathcal{N}} \Psi_{ij}(l_i, l_j)$. Here $\{i, j\}$ stands for an unordered set.

In the MRF framework the smoothness energy typically comes from the negative log of the prior. In this chapter we consider a general form of the smoothness costs, where different pairings of adjacent labels can lead to different costs. This is important in a number of applications, for example, image stitching and texture quilting [7, 132, 287].

A more restricted form of the smoothness energy is

$$V = \sum_{\{i,j\}\in\mathcal{N}} w_{ij} \cdot \Psi(|l_i - l_j|), \tag{11.1}$$

where the smoothness terms are the product of spatially varying, per-pairing weights w_{ij} and a nondecreasing function of the label difference $\Psi(\Delta l) = \Psi(|l_i - l_j|)$. Such energy functions typically arise in stereo matching [72] and image denoising. Though we could represent Ψ using a K-valued lookup table, for simplicity we instead parameterize Ψ using a simple clipped monomial form $\Psi(\Delta l) = \min(|\Delta l|^r, \Psi_{\max})$, with $r \in \{1, 2\}$. If we set $\Psi_{\max} = 1.0$, we get the Potts model, $\Psi(\Delta l) = 1 - \delta(\Delta l)$, which penalizes any pair of different labels uniformly (δ is the unit impulse function).

Depending on the choice of Ψ and the number of labels, a number of important special cases exist with fast and exact algorithms (see chapters 1, 2, 4). In this chapter, however, the class of energy functions is quite broad and, in general, NP-hard to optimize. Also, not all energy minimization methods can handle the entire class. For example, acceleration techniques based on distance transforms [141] can significantly speed up message-passing algorithms such as LBP or TRW, yet these methods are applicable only to certain smoothness costs Ψ. Other algorithms, such as graph cut, have good theoretical guarantees only for certain choices of Ψ (see chapter 3). In this chapter we assume that any algorithm can run on any benchmark problem; this can generally be ensured by reverting to a weaker or slower version of the algorithm, if necessary, for a particular benchmark.

11.2.2 Evaluation Methodology and Software Interface

The algorithms were implemented in C or C++ and all experiments were run on the same machine (Pentium 4; 3.4 GHz, 2GB RAM). A standard software interface (API) was designed that allows a user to specify an energy function E and to easily call a variety of energy minimization methods to minimize E. (For details see [464].)

11.3 Energy Minimization Algorithms

Most optimization methods used in this study are discussed in other chapters. In particular, Iterated Conditional Modes (ICM) [38] is explained in chapter 1. The graph cut-based swap-move and expansion-move algorithms [72] are described in chapter 3. Max-Product Loopy belief propagation (LBP) is explained in chapters 1 and 5, based on [367, 154, 150]. For a detailed explantation of Tree-Reweighted Message Passing (TRW) the reader is referred to [504, 255] and chapters 5 and 6. In the following, some aspects of the exact implementation of each method are outlined (see [464] for a more general description).

11.3.1 Iterated Conditional Mode (ICM)
It is well known that ICM, that is, coordinate descent, is extremely sensitive to the initial estimate, especially in high-dimensional spaces with nonconvex energies (such as arise in vision), due to the huge number of local minima. In this study ICM was initialized in a winner-take-all manner by assigning each pixel the label with the lowest data cost.

11.3.2 Graph Cut-Based Move-Making Methods
For graph-cut-based techniques, it can occur that the energy does not obey the submodularity constraint (see details in chapter 3). In short, for the expansion-move algorithm, the submodularity constraint holds if for all labels α, β, and γ it is

$$\Psi_{ij}(\alpha, \alpha) + \Psi_{ij}(\beta, \gamma) \leq \Psi_{ij}(\alpha, \gamma) + \Psi_{ij}(\beta, \alpha). \tag{11.2}$$

If the constraint is violated, the "truncation" procedure of [404] is performed; however, it is no longer guaranteed that the optimal labeling is found. Note that for the energy functions used in this study, only the expansion-move, and not the swap-move, algorithm sometimes requires truncation. In practice, this technique seems to work well, probably because relatively few terms have to be truncated (see details in section 11.5).

The main computational cost of graph cut lies in computing the minimum cut, which is done via max-flow. The implementation used in this work is described in detail in chapter 2, based on [68]. This algorithm is designed specifically for the graphs that arise in vision applications, and in [68] it is shown to perform particularly well for such graphs.

11.3.3 Max-Product Loopy Belief Propagation (LBP)
Two different variants of LBP were implemented: BP-M, an updated version of the max-product LBP implementation of [468], and BP-S, an LBP implementation derived from the TRW-S implementation described below. The most significant difference between the two implementations is in the schedules for passing messages on grids. In the BP-M

implementation, messages are passed along rows, then along columns. When a row or column is processed, the algorithm starts at the first node and passes messages in one direction—similar to the forward-backward algorithm for Hidden Markov Models. Once the algorithm reaches the end of a row or column, messages are passed backward along the same row or column. In the BP-S implementation, the nodes are processed in scan-line order, with a forward and a backward pass. In the forward pass each node sends messages to its right and bottom neighbors. In the backward pass messages are sent to the left and upper neighbors. Another difference between our LBP implementations is how the labeling is computed. In BP-M each pixel independently chooses the label with the highest belief, while in BP-S the labeling is computed from messages (as described in the next section). Based on some experiments, we do not believe that the performance of BP-S would be improved by adopting the label computing technique of BP-M. Note that BP-S uses integers for messages, to provide additional efficiency. The performance of the two versions differs by a surprisingly large margin (see section 11.5). For both methods the distance transform method described in [141] is used when applicable, that is, when the label set is ordered. This significantly reduces the running time of the algorithm. In the latest benchmark the BP implementation of [141] was included for comparison.

11.3.4 Tree-Reweighted Message Passing (TRW)

Tree-reweighted message passing [504] is a message-passing algorithm similar, on the surface, to LBP. Let $M_{i \to j}^t$ be the message that pixel i sends to its neighbor j at iteration t; this is a vector of size K (the number of labels). The message update rule is

$$M_{i \to j}^t(l_j) = \min_{l_i} \left(c_{ij} \left(\Phi_i(l_i) + \sum_{s \in \mathcal{N}(i)} M_{s \to i}^{t-1}(l_i) \right) - M_{j \to i}^{t-1}(l_i) + \Psi_{ij}(l_i, l_j) \right). \quad (11.3)$$

The coefficients c_{ij} are determined in the following way. First, a set of trees from the neighborhood graph (a 2D grid in our case) is chosen so that each edge is in at least one tree. A probability distribution ρ over the set of trees is then chosen. Finally, c_{ij} is set to ρ_{ij}/ρ_i, that is, the probability that a tree chosen randomly under ρ contains edge (i, j), given that it contains i. Note that if c_{ij} were set to 1, the update rule would be identical to that of standard LBP.

An interesting feature of the TRW algorithm is that it computes a lower bound on the energy. We use this lower bound in our experimental results (section 11.5 below) to assess the quality of the solutions. The best solutions are typically within 1% of the maximum lower bound.

The original TRW algorithm does not necessarily converge and does not, in fact, guarantee that the lower bound always increases with time. In this chapter we use an improved version of TRW due to [255], which is called sequential TRW (TRW-S). In this version the lower bound estimate is guaranteed not to decrease, which results in certain convergence properties. In TRW-S we first select an arbitrary pixel-ordering function $S(i)$. The messages are updated in order of increasing $S(i)$ and at the next iteration in the reverse order. Trees are constrained to be chains that are monotonic with respect to $S(i)$. The algorithm can be implemented using half as much memory as some versions of BP since it needs to store one message per edge.

Given messages M, we compute labeling l as described in [255]: we go through pixels in the order $S(i)$ and choose the label l_i that minimizes

$$\Phi_i(l_i) + \sum_{S(j)<S(i)} \Psi_{ij}(l_i, l_j) + \sum_{S(j)>S(i)} M_{j\rightarrow i}(l_i).$$

Note that this rule is heuristic, and there is no guarantee that the energy might not actually increase with time—it is guaranteed only that the lower bound does not decrease. In practice the energy sometimes starts to oscillate. To deal with this issue, one could keep track of the lowest energy to date and return that state when the algorithm is terminated.

11.4 Benchmark Problems

For the benchmark a representative set of low-level energy minimization problems was created, drawn from a range of different applications. The input images for each benchmark are shown in figure 11.1.

11.4.1 Stereo Matching

For stereo matching, a simple energy function, as in [70, 468], is applied to images from the widely used Middlebury stereo data set [419]. The labels are the disparities, and the data costs are the absolute color differences between corresponding pixels for each disparity. Here, the cost variant by Birchfield and Tomasi [44] is used, for increased robustness to image sampling.

To make the optimization problems more varied, different smoothness costs for the different image pairs were used (see introduction of energy model in 11.2.1). For *Tsukuba* with $K = 16$ labels, a truncated linear cost is used ($r = 1$, $\Psi_{\max} = 2$) with $\lambda = 20$. For *Venus* with $K = 20$ labels, a truncated quadratic cost is used ($r = 2$, $\Psi_{\max} = 7$) with $\lambda = 50$. Since this smoothness term is not a metric, applying the expansion-move algorithm requires truncation. For *Teddy* with $K = 60$ labels, the Potts model ($r = 1$, $\Psi_{\max} = 1$) with $\lambda = 10$ is used. The default local smoothness weight is $w_{ij} = 1$ at all pixels. For *Tsukuba* and *Teddy*, the weights are increased at locations where the intensity gradient ∇_{ij} in the left image is small: $w_{ij} = 2$ if $|\nabla_{ij}| \leq 8$ for *Tsukuba*, and $w_{ij} = 3$ if $|\nabla_{ij}| \leq 10$ for *Teddy*.

11.4.2 Photomontage

The Photomontage system [7] seamlessly stitches together multiple photographs for different photo merging applications. Here, two such applications are considered: panoramic

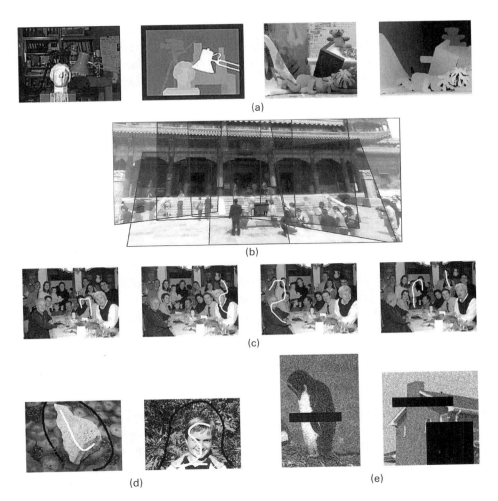

Figure 11.1
Some images used for the benchmark (see [464] for the full set). (a) Stereo matching: *Tsukuba*, and *Teddy*, left images and true disparity. (b) Photomontage *Panorama*. (c) Photomontage *Family*. (d) Binary image segmentation: *Sponge* and *Person*. (e) Denoising and inpainting: *Penguin* and *House*.

stitching and group photo merging. The input is a set of aligned images $S_1, S_2, \ldots, S_K$ of equal dimension; the labels are the image indices, and the final output image is formed by copying colors from the input images according to the computed labeling. If two neighbors i and j are assigned to the same input image, that is, $l_i = l_j$, they should appear natural in the composite, and thus $\Psi_{ij}(l_i, l_j) = 0$. If $l_i \neq l_j$, that is, a seam exists between i and j, and Ψ_{ij} measures how visually noticeable the seam is in the composite. The data term $\Phi_i(l_i)$ is 0 if pixel i is in the field of view of image S_{l_i}, and ∞ otherwise.

The first benchmark, *Panorama*, automatically stitches together the panorama in figure 11.1(b) ([7], figure 8). The smoothness energy, derived from [287], is

$$\Psi_{ij}(l_i, l_j) = |S_{l_i}(i) - S_{l_j}(i)| + |S_{l_i}(j) - S_{l_j}(j)|. \tag{11.4}$$

This energy function is suitable for the expansion-move algorithm without truncation.

The second benchmark, *Family*, stitches together five group photographs and is shown in figure 11.1(c) ([7], figure 1). The best depiction of each person is to be included in a composite. Photomontage itself is interactive, but to make the benchmark repeatable, the user strokes are saved into a data file. For any pixel i underneath a drawn stroke, $\Phi_i(l_i) = 0$ if l_i equals the user-indicated source image, and ∞ otherwise. For pixels i not underneath any strokes, $\Phi_i(l_i) = 0$ for all labels. The smoothness terms are modified from the first benchmark to encourage seams along strong edges. More precisely, the right-hand side of (11.4) is divided by $|\nabla_{ij}S_{l_i}| + |\nabla_{ij}S_{l_j}|$, where $\nabla_{ij}I$ is the gradient between pixels i and j in image I. The expansion-move algorithm is applicable to this energy only after truncating certain terms.

11.4.3   Binary Image Segmentation

Binary MRFs are widely used in medical image segmentation [66], stereo matching using minimal surfaces [80, 443], and video segmentation using stereo disparity cues [259]. For the natural Ising model smoothness cost, the global minimum can be computed rapidly via graph cut [176]; this result has been generalized to other smoothness costs by [266]. Nevertheless, such energy functions still form an interesting benchmark, since there may well be other heuristic algorithms that perform faster while achieving nearly the same level of performance.

Our benchmark consists of three segmentation problems inspired by the interactive segmentation algorithm of [66, 401] (see chapter 7). As above, this application requires user interaction, which is handled by saving the user interactions to a file and using them to derive the data costs.

The data cost is the negative log-likelihood of a pixel belonging to either the foreground or the background, and is modeled as two separate Gaussian mixture models, as in [401]. The smoothness term is a standard Potts model that is contrast-sensitive:

$$w_{ij} = \exp(-\beta \|S(i) - S(j)\|^2) + \lambda_2, \tag{11.5}$$

where $\lambda = 50$, $\lambda_2 = 1/5$, and $S(i)$, $S(j)$ are the RGB colors of two neighboring pixels i, j.[1] The quantity β is set to $(2\langle \|S(i) - S(j)\|^2 \rangle)^{-1}$ where the expectation denotes an average over the image, as motivated in [401]. The purpose of λ_2 is to remove small and isolated areas that have high contrast.

11.4.4 Image Denoising and Inpainting

For the denoising and inpainting benchmark, the *Penguin* image is used ([141], figure 8), along with the *House* image, a standard test image in the denoising literature. Random noise is added to each pixel, and we also obscure a portion of each image (figure 11.1e). The labels are intensities ($K = 256$), and the data cost Φ_i for each pixel is the squared difference between the label and the observed intensity except in the obscured portions, where $\Phi_i(l_i) = 0$ for all intensities. For the *Penguin* image a truncated quadratic smoothness cost is used ($r = 2$, $\Psi_{\max} = 200$) with $\lambda = 25$. For the *House* image a nontruncated quadratic cost is used ($r = 2$, $\Psi_{\max} = \infty$) with $\lambda = 5$. In both cases the expansion-move algorithm requires truncation. Unlike all of the other benchmarks, the *House* example is a convex minimization problem amenable to quadratic solvers, since both data and smoothness costs are quadratics. The implications of this are discussed in the next section.

11.5 Experimental Results

Experimental results from running the different optimization algorithms on these benchmarks are given in figure 11.2 (stereo), figure 11.3 (Photomontage), figure 11.4 (segmentation), and figure 11.5 (denoising and inpainting). (Note that this is a selection and that all plots can be found online and in [464].) In each plot the x-axis shows the running times in seconds on a log-scale, and the y-axis shows the energy. In some of these figures the right figure is a zoomed-in version of the left figure. As mentioned before, instead of showing absolute energy values, the energy is divided by the best lower bound computed by TRW-S.[2] Note that the lower bound increases monotonically [255] and is included in the plots.

Let us first summarize the main insights from these experiments. On all benchmarks the best methods achieve results that are extremely close to the global minimum, with less than 1% error in all cases, and often less than 0.1%. For example, on *Tsukuba*, TRW-S gets to within 0.02% of the of the optimum, and on *Panorama*, expansion-move is within 0.9%. These statistics may actually slightly understate the performance of the methods since they are based on the TRW-S lower bound rather than on the global minimum, which is unknown. This means that most theoretical guarantees on bounds of certain methods are in practice irrelevant, at least for these examples. For instance, expansion-move is in the best cases within a factor of 2 of the global minimum (note that a 1% error corresponds to a factor of 1.01; see chapter 3).

1. Note that in [464] this setting was incorrect, with $\lambda_2 = 10$.
2. It was checked that for all applications the lower bound is positive.

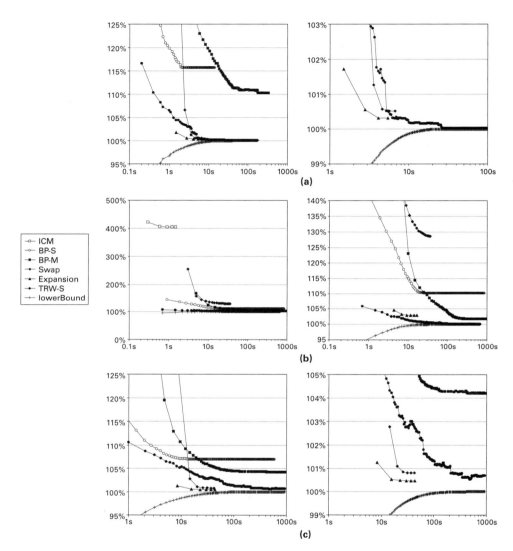

Figure 11.2
Results on the stereo matching benchmarks. (a) *Tsukuba* energy, with truncated linear smoothness cost Ψ. (b) *Venus* energy, with truncated quadratic smoothness cost Ψ. (c) *Teddy* energy, with the Potts model for Ψ. In each row the right figure is a zoomed-in version of the left figure. The legend for all plots is in (b). Some of the plots may not contain the poorer-performing algorithms (e.g., ICM). Further plots are available online. The plots in other figures are generated in the same manner.

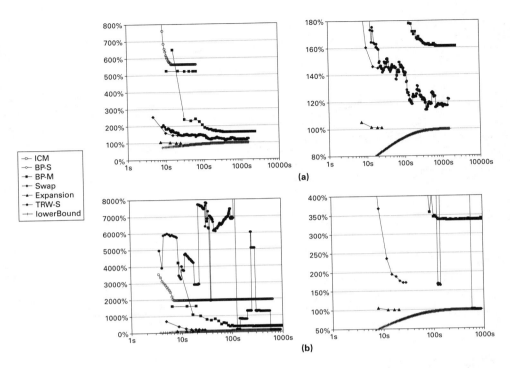

Figure 11.3
Results on the Photomontage benchmark. (a) *Panorama*. (b) *Family*.

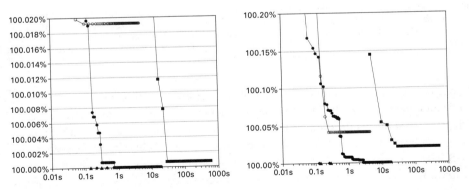

Figure 11.4
Results of binary segmentation benchmarks *Sponge* (left) and *Person* (right). Here the global minimum can be computed rapidly by graph cut or TRW-S. See the legend in figure 11.2b.

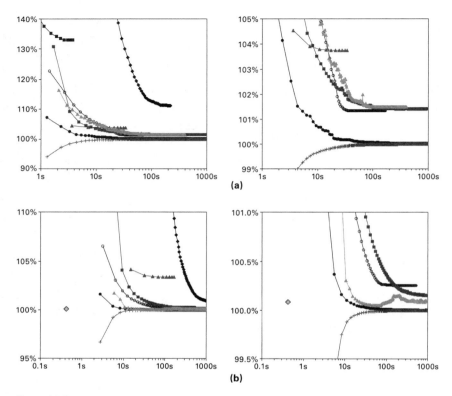

Figure 11.5
Results on the denoising and inpainting benchmarks. (a) *Penguin* energy, with truncated quadratic smoothness cost Ψ. (b) *House* energy, with nontruncated quadratic smoothness cost Ψ. On these benchmarks the LBP implementation of [141] is included, labeled as BP-P (triangle (blue)); otherwise see legend in figure 11.2b. The *House* example is a convex energy minimization problem amenable to quadratic solvers; we include the results of the fast algorithm of [462], labeled as HBF (diamond on the left-hand side).

As one can see, there is a dramatic difference in performance among the various energy minimization methods. On the Photomontage benchmark, expansion-move performs best, which provides some justification for the fact that this algorithm is used by various image-stitching applications [7, 8]. On the stereo benchmark the two best methods seem to be TRW-S and expansion-move. There are also some obvious paired comparisons; for instance, there never seems to be any reason to use swap-move instead of expansion-move. In terms of runtime, expansion-move is clearly the winner among the competitive methods (i.e., all except ICM), but it should be noted that not all methods have been equally optimized for speed. Concerning the two different implementations of BP, BP-M and BP-S, for most examples there is a large gap between their relative performances. BP-S is on average faster but typically converges to a higher energy.

Figure 11.6
Results on *Panorama* benchmark, with swap-move at left and expansion-move at right. The solution of swap-move has higher energy and is also visually inferior (e.g., person in the center is "sliced"). Larger versions of these images are online.

In terms of visual quality of the resulting labelings (note that all results are available online), the ICM results look noticeably worse, but the others are difficult to distinguish on most of the benchmarks. The major exception is the Photomontage benchmarks. Here ICM, BP-S, and swap-move all make some major errors, leaving slices of people floating in the air, while the other methods produce the fewest noticeable seams, as shown in figure 11.6.

The individual plots show some further interesting features.

On the stereo benchmarks (figure 11.2) expansion-move finds near-optimal solutions quickly and is the overall winner for *Teddy*. Though slower, TRW-S does extremely well, eventually beating all other methods on *Tsukuba* and *Venus*. The *Venus* results are particularly interesting: expansion-move does much worse here than on the other stereo images, presumably due to the quadratic smoothness term and the slanted surfaces present in this data set.

The Photomontage benchmarks (figure 11.3), with their label-dependent smoothness costs, seem to present the largest challenge for the energy minimization methods, many of which come nowhere near the best solution. The exception is expansion-move, which finds solutions with less than 1% error on both benchmarks in a few iterations. TRW-S oscillates wildly but eventually beats expansion-move on *Family*, though not on *Panorama*.

On the binary image segmentation benchmarks (figure 11.4), graph cut-based methods are guaranteed to compute the global minimum, as is TRW-S (but not the original TRW [504]). Both LBP implementations come extremely close (under 0.1% error in all cases), but never actually attain the global minimum.

In the final benchmark, denoising and inpainting (figure 11.5), two different cost functions were used: (1) a nonconvex (truncated quadratic) Ψ for the *Penguin* data set, and (2) a convex (quadratic) Ψ for the *House* data set. Since in the latter case both the data and the smoothness energies are quadratic, this is a Gaussian MRF for which a real-valued solution can be found in closed form. On this problem, hierarchically preconditioned conjugate gradient descent [462], labeled HBF in figure 11.5b, outperforms all other algorithms by a large margin, requiring only five iterations and a fraction of a second. However, since the resulting floating-point solution is rounded to integers, the resulting energy is slightly higher than the integer solution found by TRW-S. The graph cut variants are not performing well, perhaps due to the nonmetric smoothness terms, and also because there are no constant-valued regions to propagate over large distances. On these benchmarks, results for the popular LBP (BP-P) implementation of [141] were also included, which performs comparably to the other two BP implementations.

A final issue deserving investigation is the impact of truncation when using the expansion-move algorithm. It turns out that the total number of pairwise terms that require truncation is very low—typically a fraction of 1%. Thus, it is unlikely that truncation strongly affects the performance of the expansion-move algorithm. Furthermore, the BHS algorithm described in chapter 2 could resolve this problem (see an example in [259]).

11.6 Experimental Comparison: Stereo with and Without Occlusion

Let us first briefly explain the model of stereo with occlusion. (A detailed explanation and the corresponding energy can be found in [265].) The model can be seen as an extension of the simple 4-connected stereo model introduced in section 11.4, since the unary matching costs and pairwise smoothing costs are of the same form. The two main differences of the stereo with occlusion model are that (1) the left and right stereo images are labeled simultaneously, and (2) a large number of pairwise terms, are added across the two images. These pairwise terms encode the occlusion property and have costs 0 or ∞. This means that the ∞ cost makes sure that two pixels which are matched are not occluded by any other pixel matches (i.e., 3D voxels). While stereo without occlusion is a simple 4-connected MRF, this model corresponds to a more complex highly connected MRF. In particular, each node has $K + 4$ pairwise terms, where K is the number of disparities.

The study in [260] on stereo with occlusion compared three optimization techniques—TRW-S, BP-S, and alpha-expansion, for six different benchmarks (*Tsukuba, Venus, Teddy, Sawtooth, Map, Cones*). Figure 11.7 shows plots for *Tsukuba* and *Teddy*, with $K = 16$ and $K = 54$ levels of disparities, respectively (see more plots in [260]). In contrast to the 4-connected stereo model, alpha-expansion is in this case the clear winner. On all examples it reaches a slightly lower energy than TRW-S. More important, alpha-expansion converges in about 10–100 sec (depending on the number of disparities), and TRW-S typically needs several hours to reach a solution that is close to the graph cut one. The relative performance between BP-S and TRW-S depends on the number of disparities, with BP-S performing better when the number of disparities is large. The potential reason for graph cut outperforming message-passing techniques is that in each expansion-move, the corresponding binary energy has considerably fewer pairwise terms for each node than the full number of pairwise terms (i.e., $K + 4$).

For comparing stereo with and without occlusion, we used the stereo without occlusion model of [254]. It corresponds to a 4-connected MRF, as in section 11.4, but uses exactly the same matching costs as the above stereo with occlusion model [265]. As a check, the

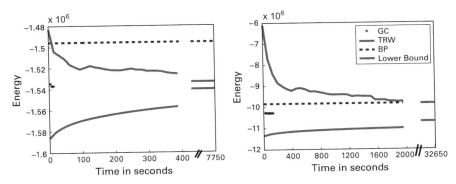

Figure 11.7
Comparison of optimization methods for stereo with occlusion [260], with *Tsukuba* (K=16 disparities) benchmark (left) and *Teddy* (K=54 disparities) benchmark (right). The optimization methods are expansion-move (labeled GC), TRW-S (labeled TRW), and BP-S (labeled BP).

energies of stereo with and without occlusion differ only by a factor of 3 for the *Tsukuba* data set, that is, they are of the same order of magnitude. As in the previous section, we normalize the energies with respect to the optimal bound of the respective TRW-S result (see details in [260]). For the four data sets the normalized energies for stereo without occlusion are *Tsukuba* (100.0037%), *Map* (100.055%), *Sawtooth* (100.096%), and *Venus* (100.014%). The respective normalized energies for stereo with occlusion are *Tsukuba* (103.09%), *Map* (103.28%), *Sawtooth* (101.27%), and *Venus* (102.26%). This means that the difference from 100% is on average two to three orders of magnitude larger for the more complex model. Consequently, we may conclude that stereo with occlusion is much harder to optimize than stereo without occlusion. This is also supported by the fact that Meltzer et al. [338] have shown that for a 4-connected stereo model, it is possible to achieve global optimality for many examples, including *Tsukuba* and *Venus*, using a combination of TRW and the junction tree algorithm. (The global optimum for *Tsukuba*[3] is shown in figure 4 of [338]). The global optimum for a stereo example with a highly connected MRF is so far unknown.

It is quite obvious that properly modeling occlusion leads to a better stereo model, as can be seen from the ranking on the Middlebury stereo benchmark. Figure 11.8 shows the best results of the two models, where a clear difference is visible. Another way of evaluating the quality of a model is to compute the energy of the ground truth labeling. For the stereo without occlusion model (section 11.4), the energy of the ground truth is very high (e.g., 144% for *Venus*), whereas most optimization methods reach an energy close to 100%, (e.g., TRW-S achieves 100.02%. In contrast, for stereo with occlusion [265] the ground truth labeling for *Venus* has a lower energy of 115%, where the best method (expansion-move)

---

3. They may use a slightly different energy function (e.g., matching cost) than in this study.

Figure 11.8
The results of the best optimization methods for stereo without occlusion (left and middle) and with occlusion (right). The result on the right is visually superior because it is smoother and more accurate (see ground truth in figure 11.1a). The result on the left uses the model described in section 11.4; the result in the middle is based on the model in [254]; and the result on the right uses the model of [265]. The results in the middle and right use the identical matching cost function.

reaches an energy of 102.26%. These numbers have to be taken with care, since (1) the models are quite different (e.g., different matching costs), and (2) the lower bound of TRW-S for stereo with occlusion might not be very tight. As expected, if only the labelings of the nonoccluded ground truth pixels are considered, the ground truth energy drops to 113% for the stereo without occlusion model. Further examples can be found in table 1 of [464].

11.7 Conclusions

The strongest impression one gets from the study on 4-connected grid graphs is how much better modern energy minimization methods are than ICM, and how close they come to computing the global minimum. We do not believe that this is purely due to flaws in ICM, but simply reflects the fact that the algorithms used until the late 1990s performed poorly. (As additional evidence, [72] compared the energy produced by graph cut with simulated annealing, and obtained a similarly large improvement.)

Our study has also shown that there is a demand for better MRF models, such as stereo with occlusion handling, as discussed in section 11.6. However, this highly connected MRF model clearly poses a challenge for existing optimization techniques. Toward this end, a recent study [403] has shown that for highly connected and highly nonsubmodular energies, basic techniques such as simulated annealing outperform all existing state-of-the-art techniques. These different studies nicely reflect the current positive trend in this domain of computer vision: (1) faster and better optimization techniques motivate many researchers to use MRF models; and (2) new and sophisticated MRF models motivate many researchers, especially from the optimization community, to develop faster and better optimization techniques. In the future it would be interesting to perform a new benchmark study that includes highly connected MRFs (e.g., [403]) or higher-order MRFs (e.g., [240, 530, 400]), and, using very recent optimization techniques, such as the enhanced BHS algorithm (QPBO-P/I, [403]), the cycle repair technique [267], the range move algorithm [495], or the primal-dual method [269].

III   Further Topics: Inference, Parameter Learning, and Continuous Models

This part of the book is composed of two groups of chapters. The first group deals with MRF models defined using continuous latent variables, and the second group discusses some recently proposed approaches for MAP inference and parameter learning that have become quite popular in the research community.

The preceding parts of the book discussed Markov random fields defined on discrete variables. This is somehow natural, considering that input to vision systems comes as digital images that themselves are discrete. That said, many low- and mid-level vision problems are more naturally thought of as being parameterized by a set of continuous variables, such as problems involving pixel intensities and depth values. Discrete-valued formulations for such problems are possible but require a large number of states, which leads to efficiency issues during inference and parameter learning.

This part of the book deals with MRFs defined on continuous latent variables. More specifically, it will show how vision problems are formulated using models defined on continuous variables, how the parameters of the model are learned, and, finally, how inference is performed in these models. Chapter 12 focuses on recent developments in the theory of variational methods and partial differential equations, which make continuous latent variable models a powerful alternative to discrete formulations for solving a variety of computer vision problems. Chapter 13 provides a brief summary of models based on continuous latent variables and focuses on the development of powerful, efficient learning algorithms for simple models.

Performing inference in models involving continuous latent variables is a hard problem. A common approach for performing inference in such models is to convert the continuous-valued problem into a discrete-valued one in order to use existing algorithms for discrete inference. This conversion is typically achieved by restricting the latent variable to a compact subset of $\mathcal{R}^N$ and then discretizing that subset—in other words, dividing it into partitions of equal volume and assigning a discrete value to each partition.

This uniform discretization process becomes impractical if a very fine discretization is needed or if the latent variable is in a high-dimensional space, because discrete inference methods require both time and space that are at best linear in the number of discrete states.

Chapter 14 describes two techniques that can be used to perform inference on continuous-valued latent variables when straightforward uniform discretization is impractical. Both use algorithms that are closely related to belief propagation (BP).

A number of algorithms for performing MAP inference in MRFs have been discussed in preceding chapters. These minimize the energy function defined over discrete variables. But to make sure these techniques can solve the vision problem successfully, we need to know how to construct the best energy function—or, in other words, how to estimate the parameters of the MRF. Parameter learning, as this problem is referred to in the literature, aims to find parameters that fit the training data and that also generalize to unseen test data. This is a difficult problem that in the past led many researchers to hand-tune model parameters. However, this is feasible only for simple models and may produce suboptimal results. Chapter 15 briefly discusses some popular methods for parameter learning before investigating the large margin learning technique that is becoming increasingly popular for vision problems.

MAP inference in MRFs defined over discrete-valued latent variables can be performed as solving an optimization problem—to be more specific, an integer programming problem, which in itself is NP-hard to solve. The standard approach to solving such problems is to solve a relaxation. Chapters 16 and 17 deal with convex relaxations of the MAP inference problems. Chapter 16 analyzes and compares many popular convex relaxations proposed for the MAP inference problem, and chapter 17 discusses the *primal-dual schema*, a powerful method used for deriving approximation algorithms to hard combinatorial problems based on LP duality theory, and how it applies to MAP inference of discrete MRFs.

Chapter 18 also addresses the inference problem. It describes a recently proposed technique that has become quite popular. It works by generating continuous-valued proposal solutions that are then combined (or fused) to get solutions with even better energy. The fusion step uses algorithms developed for minimizing energy functions of integer variables.

12 Convex Relaxation Techniques for Segmentation, Stereo, and Multiview Reconstruction

Daniel Cremers, Thomas Pock, Kalin Kolev, and Antonin Chambolle

Digital images are discrete, and hence it appears quite intuitive to revert to a spatially discrete representation and Markov random fields for modeling and solving problems in image processing and computer vision. Such discrete graphical representations of the computational domain have become very popular due to a multitude of highly efficient combinatorial algorithms for solving problems such as shortest paths or minimum cuts on graphs that have been emerging since the 1950s.

Nevertheless, the world that is captured in digital images is not spatially discrete, and ideally algorithms to process images should be independent of the choice of the underlying grid on which they are sampled. Unfortunately, for many of the classical graph algorithms this is not the case. For example, when searching for the shortest path from the lower left corner to the upper right corner of a unit square, the classical algorithm of Dijkstra for computing shortest paths will give a distance of 2 when applied to a regular 4-connected grid, although the Euclidean distance is clearly $\sqrt{2}$. The algorithm is not *consistent* in the sense that the numerical error does not go to zero when increasing the resolution of the graph. In fact, this concept of *continuum limit* is rarely considered in graph theoretic approaches.

This chapter focuses on describing recent developments in the theory of variational methods and partial differential equations that make these a powerful alternative to Markov random field approaches for solving a variety of computer vision problems. While Markov random fields are inherently based on discrete graph representations, variational methods are based on a representation of images as continuous-valued functions $I : \Omega \to \mathbb{R}^n$ on spatially continuous domains $\Omega \subset \mathbb{R}^d$. Similarly, solutions to respective vision problems such as image segmentation or stereo and multiview reconstruction can be represented by respective functions on continuous domains.

12.1 Variational Methods, Partial Differential Equations, and Convexity

A solution u to a given computer vision problem is determined by minimizing an appropriate functional $E(u)$. A necessary condition for optimality of E is given by the *Euler–Lagrange equation*, which states that the variation of E with respect to u must vanish.

The last decades have brought a number of breakthroughs in the application of variational methods for computer vision. These include the variational approach of Horn and Schunck [202] for computing optical flow fields from pairs of images, the segmentation methods of Kass et al. [227] and of Mumford and Shah [344] with respective level set formulations of Caselles et al. [84], Kichenassamy et al. [229], and Chan and Vese [88], and level set formulations for 3D reconstruction from multiple views pioneered by Faugeras and Keriven [136].

Unfortunately, none of the above variational methods are based on convex functionals. As a consequence, solutions will merely correspond to *local* minima of the respective functional and typically depend on appropriate initializations. Since there exists no reliable procedure to compute configurations with any kind of optimality guarantee, the practical usefulness of such approaches is limited.

This chapter will provide a variety of recently developed convex relaxation techniques that allow one to cast respective computer vision problems in terms of convex functionals. As a consequence one can compute globally optimal solutions (or solutions with bounded optimality) that are independent of the initialization. Experimental comparison shows that the resulting PDE-based solutions typically require less memory, are substantially faster, and provide more accurate solutions for the underlying vision problem than corresponding state-of-the-art graph-theoretic algorithms.

Central ideas presented in this chapter were developed in various conference and journal papers, in particular [87, 251, 76, 250, 247, 86, 373, 489, 371]. The reader is referred to these works for further details.

12.2 Image Segmentation and Minimal Partitions

12.2.1 Classical Variational Approaches

One of the first areas of application for variational methods was image segmentation, where the goal is to partition the image plane into a set of meaningful regions. Among the most influential variational approaches were those of Kass et al. [227], of Blake and Zisserman [54], and of Mumford and Shah [344]. They are complementary in the sense that the first (often called *edge-based* segmentation method) aims at identifying boundaries in the image that are supported by strong intensity gradients, whereas the latter two approaches (often called *region-based* segmentation methods) aim at identifying regions of smooth (or homogeneous) intensity.

Kass et al. [227] suggested computing a segmentation of an image $I : \Omega \to \mathbb{R}$ on the domain $\Omega \subset \mathbb{R}^2$ in terms of a boundary C by minimizing a functional of the form

$$E(C) = \int_C -|\nabla I(C(s))|^2 + \alpha |C_s(s)|^2 + \beta |C_{ss}(s)|^2 \, ds \qquad (12.1)$$

where the first term favors the boundary to lie in areas of strong intensity gradient, whereas the last two terms (weighted by parameters α and β) impose a certain regularity of the boundary.

Mumford and Shah [344] suggested computing a piecewise smooth approximation u of the intensity function I by minimizing the functional

$$E(U, C) = \int_{\Omega} (u - I)^2 \, dx + \lambda \int_{\Omega - C} |\nabla u|^2 \, dx + \nu |C|. \tag{12.2}$$

While the first term imposes pointwise similarity of the approximation u with the input image I, the second term (weighted by λ) imposes smoothness of u everywhere except at the boundary C, the length of which is penalized with a weight ν. In the limit $\lambda \to \infty$ one obtains a piecewise constant approximation.

One of the central algorithmic challenges addressed in this chapter is how to minimize such types of functionals. Though parametric boundary representations [111] or implicit level set representations [88, 84, 229] typically find only locally optimal solutions with little or no optimality guarantees, recently developed convex relaxation schemes provide solutions that are either optimal or within a bound of the optimum. Some of these developments will be detailed below.

12.2.2 A General Variational Formulation

Let $I : \Omega \to \mathbb{R}$ be a gray value input image on the domain $\Omega \subset \mathbb{R}^d$. Among a variety of variational approaches to image segmentation, let us consider the following rather general model:

$$\min_{\Omega_i} \left\{ \frac{1}{2} \sum_{i=0}^{k} \mathrm{Per}_g (\Omega_i; \Omega) + \sum_{i=0}^{k} \int_{\Omega_i} f_i(x) \, dx \right\}, \tag{12.3}$$

$$\text{such that} \bigcup_{i=0}^{k} \Omega_i = \Omega, \quad \Omega_s \cap \Omega_t = \emptyset \, \forall s \neq t.$$

Minimizing (12.3) partitions the domain $\Omega \subset \mathbb{R}^d$ into $k + 1$ pairwise disjoint sets Ω_i. The first term imposes regularity of solutions. It measures the perimeter of the set Ω_i with respect to a metric defined by the nonnegative function $g(x)$.[1] The second term is the data term that is based on nonnegative weight functions $f_i : \Omega \to \mathbb{R}^+$.

The model defined in (12.3) includes as a special case the piecewise constant Mumford–Shah functional [344] discussed above, which arises when choosing

$$f_i(x) = (I(x) - c_i)^2,$$

---

1. For simplicity we will consider only *isotropic* metrics. The approach is easily generalized to *anisotropic* metrics where boundaries favor certain orientations.

which is the squared difference of the input image I from some mean intensity c_i. More generally, one can choose

$$f_i(x) = -\log P_i(I(x))$$

as the negative log-likelihood for observing a certain intensity or color value [551, 230, 109]. Model (12.3) also includes, as a special case, edge-based segmentation approaches such as the geodesic active contours [84, 229] where a spatially inhomogeneous metric favors boundaries passing through areas of strong gradient by choosing, for example,

$$g(x) = \frac{1}{1 + |\nabla I(x)|}.$$

The discrete analogue of (12.3) is the *Potts model* [377], which is known to be NP-hard. Several algorithms have been proposed to approximately minimize the Potts model. Though the discrete problem can be tackled using iterated binary optimization via α-expansion [72] or roof duality relaxation [179, 403], such algorithms tend to exhibit a grid bias (metrication errors) in representing the continuous perimeters in (12.3). In the continuous domain, popular methods are based on level set methods [88, 84, 229] or parametric boundary representations [111]. The most crucial drawback of these methods is that there is no guarantee of finding globally optimal solutions.

12.2.3 Convex Representation

In the following, the $k+1$ regions Ω_i in (12.3) are represented by a labeling function $u : \Omega \rightarrow \{0, \ldots, k\}$, where $u(x) = l$ if and only if $x \in \Omega_i$. One can equivalently represent this multilabel function by k binary functions $\boldsymbol{\theta}(x) = (\theta_1(x), \ldots, \theta_k(x))$ defined by

$$\theta_i(x) = \begin{cases} 1 & \text{if} \quad u(x) \geq l \\ 0 & \text{otherwise} \end{cases}, \tag{12.4}$$

representing its upper-level sets. In turn, the labeling function u can be recovered from these functions via the relation

$$u(x) = \sum_{i=1}^{k} \theta_i(x). \tag{12.5}$$

Figure 12.1a, b shows examples of partitionings with one or two binary functions θ_i. This representation is well known in the context of functions of discrete variables and was used in [211] for minimizing such functions.

A 1:1 correspondence between multilabel functions $u(x)$ and vectors $\boldsymbol{\theta} = (\theta_1, \ldots, \theta_k)$ of binary functions is guaranteed by constraining $\boldsymbol{\theta}$ to the ordered set

$$\mathcal{B} = \left\{ \boldsymbol{\theta} : \Omega \rightarrow \{0, 1\}^k, 1 \geq \theta_1(x) \geq \cdots \geq \theta_k(x) \geq 0, \forall x \in \Omega \right\}. \tag{12.6}$$

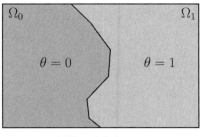
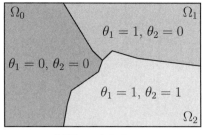

| (a) Two-label case | (b) Three-label case |

Figure 12.1
(a) One binary function θ is used to partition the image domain Ω into two regions. (b) Two binary functions $\theta_1 \geq \theta_2$ are used to partition the image domain Ω into three regions.

How can one rewrite the optimization problem (12.3) in terms of the binary functions θ_i? Let us start with the simple case of two regions ($k = 1$), where the region Ω_1 is defined by a single binary function θ_1. The perimeter of the set Ω_1 is given by the weighted total variation of θ_1:

$$\mathrm{Per}_g(\Omega_1; \Omega) = \int g|D\theta_1| = \sup_{|\xi_1| \leq g} \int \xi_1 D\theta_1 = \sup_{|\xi_1| \leq g} - \int \theta_1 \mathrm{div}\, \xi_1 dx, \qquad (12.7)$$

where $D\theta$ denotes the distributional derivative of θ. For differentiable functions θ it is simply given by $D\theta = \nabla\theta\, dx$. For binary-valued functions $\theta \in BV(\Omega)$ it is a surface measure supported on the boundary of the set $\{\theta = 1\}$. The second equality in (12.7) expresses this boundary length using the dual vector field $\xi_1 : \Omega \to \mathbb{R}^2$. These dual vector fields in fact play the role of the flow in the analogous graph cut approaches, and Fenchel duality leads to a spatially continuous version of the min-cut/max-flow equivalence. We can now use standard LP relaxation and let $\theta_1 \in [0, 1]$; then the *co-area formula* will ensure that the relaxed problem has the same solutions as the initial one.

The extension of this formulation to multiple regions in (12.3) is not straightforward. Simply summing the total variations of each function θ_i—as done in the analogous level set formulation of Chan and Vese [88]—would imply that certain boundaries are counted more than once. For the example shown in Figure 12.1b, the boundary between Ω_0 and Ω_2 would be counted twice.

This "overcounting" of boundaries can be elegantly supressed by appropriate constraints that couple the dual variables $\boldsymbol{\xi} = (\xi_0, \dots, \xi_k)$.

Proposition 12.1 *The optimization problem (12.3) is equivalent to the problem*

$$\min_{\theta \in \mathcal{B}} \max_{\boldsymbol{\xi} \in \mathcal{K}} \left\{ \sum_{i=0}^{k} - \int_\Omega \theta_i \mathrm{div}\, \xi_i\, dx + \int_\Omega (\theta_i(x) - \theta_{i+1}(x))\, f_i(x)\, dx \right\}, \qquad (12.8)$$

with a set $\boldsymbol{\xi} = (\xi_0, \ldots, \xi_k)$ of dual vector fields $\xi_i : \Omega \to \mathbb{R}^2$ constrained to the set

$$\mathcal{K} = \left\{ \boldsymbol{\xi} : \Omega \to \mathbb{R}^{d \times k}, \left| \sum_{i_1 \leq i \leq i_2} \xi_i(x) \right| \leq g(x), \forall x \in \Omega, 1 \leq i_1 \leq i_2 \leq k \right\}. \quad (12.9)$$

Proof For a proof see [86].   ∎

The constraints on the dual variables $\xi_i(x)$ in (12.9) assure that each interface is counted exactly once. For the three-region case shown in figure 12.1b, for example, the above constraint implies that $|\xi_1(x) + \xi_2(x)| \leq 1$. This assures that the transition between Ω_0 and Ω_2 is counted only once. Interestingly, this coupling constraint ties nicely into the subsequent convex optimization technique.

Proposition 12.2 *The set $\mathcal{K}$ defined in (12.9) is convex.*

Proof For any two functions $\boldsymbol{\xi}, \boldsymbol{\xi}' \in \mathcal{K}$ and any $\alpha \in [0, 1]$, $\alpha\boldsymbol{\xi} + (1 - \alpha)\boldsymbol{\xi} \in \mathcal{K}$:

$$\left| \sum_{i_1 \leq i \leq i_2} \alpha\xi_i(x) + (1 - \alpha)\xi_i'(x) \right| \leq \alpha \left| \sum_{i_1 \leq i \leq i_2} \xi_i(x) \right| + (1 - \alpha) \left| \sum_{i_1 \leq i \leq i_2} \xi_i'(x) \right| \leq g(x). \quad (12.10)$$

                                                                                    ∎

12.2.4 Convex Relaxation

Unfortunately, the overall optimization problem (12.8) is nonconvex because the set $\mathcal{B}$ defined in (12.6) is not convex. We therefore propose a convex relaxation that allows the functions θ_i to take on intermediate values between 0 and 1. To this end the set $\mathcal{B}$ in the optimization problem (12.8) is replaced by the convex set

$$\mathcal{R} = \left\{ \boldsymbol{\theta} : \Omega \to [0, 1]^k, 1 \geq \theta_1(x) \geq \cdots \geq \theta_k(x) \geq 0, \forall x \in \Omega \right\}. \quad (12.11)$$

For $k = 1$ this formulation turns out to be equivalent to the two-region problem considered by Chan et al. [87], for which we have the following optimality guarantee.

Proposition 12.3 *Let θ_1 be the optimum of the relaxed (convex) version of (12.8) for $k = 1$ with $\mathcal{B}$ replaced by $\mathcal{R}$. Then thresholding the solution θ_1 at any value $s \in (0, 1)$ will provide a global solution of the original nonconvex labeling problem (12.8).*

Proof For a proof see [87].   ∎

Though this thresholding theorem does not extend to the general problem of more than two regions ($k > 1$), one can prove the following optimality bound.

Proposition 12.4 *Let $\boldsymbol{\theta}^* \in \mathcal{R}$ be the solution of the relaxed version of (12.8) and let $\mathbf{1}_{\{\theta^* \geq s\}} \in \mathcal{B}$ be a thresholded binary version for any $s \in [0, 1]$. Furthermore, let $\boldsymbol{\theta}' \in \mathcal{B}$ be* *the true global minimizer of the binary problem (12.8). Then one can provide the following bound on the energy of the computed solution:*

$$\left| \mathcal{E}\left(\mathbf{1}_{\{\theta^* \geq s\}}\right) - \mathcal{E}(\theta') \right| \leq \left| \mathcal{E}(\theta^*) - \mathcal{E}\left(\mathbf{1}_{\{\theta^* \geq s\}}\right) \right|. \tag{12.12}$$

Proof The bound follows directly, because in terms of their energies the optimal binary solution θ lies between the relaxed solution θ^* and the thresholded solution $\mathbf{1}_{\{\theta^* \geq s\}}$:

$$\mathcal{E}(\theta^*) \leq \mathcal{E}(\theta') \leq \mathcal{E}(\mathbf{1}_{\{\theta^* \geq s\}}). \tag{12.13}$$

∎

In many real-world experiments this bound is actually zero or near zero, such that for these examples the solutions are essentially optimal.

12.2.5 Experimental Segmentation Results
The convex relaxation framework for image segmentation introduced above is closely related to the theory of minimal surfaces. Figure 12.2 presents examples of minimal surface problems where the data term in (12.3) is switched off and the three or four colors are imposed as boundary constraints.

Figure 12.3 shows image segmentations computed with the proposed convex relaxation technique for model (12.3) with four and eight labels, respectively.

12.3 Stereo Reconstruction

Characteristic for the segmentation model in (12.3) is that transitions in the labeling function $u : \Omega \rightarrow \{0, \dots, k\}$ are penalized in a manner that is independent of the size of the transition. In stereo reconstruction, where $u(x)$ denotes the depth at a given image point $x \in \Omega$, one may want a penalty that favors spatially smooth depth fields. Moreover, a data term $f(u, x)$ will favor different depth values for different points—for example, based on the normalized

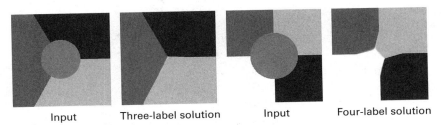

Input   Three-label solution   Input   Four-label solution

Figure 12.2
Three- and four-label solutions for predescribed boundary colors computed for the round area in the center with model (12.3) and no data term. The proposed relaxation scheme allows accurate approximation of triple junctions that are known to be the analytically optimal configurations of the respective minimal partition problems.

 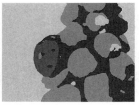 

Input   Four-label segmentation   Eight-label segmentation

Figure 12.3
Image segmentations computed using the convex relaxation of model (12.3) with four and eight labels.

cross correlation of respective patches in either of the two input images. For a simple linear smoothness constraint, the resulting optimization problem is given by

$$\min_{u:\Omega\to\{0,\dots,k\}} \int_\Omega f(u(x),x)dx + \int_\Omega g(x)|Du|dx. \tag{12.14}$$

Due to the data term f, functional (12.14) is not convex. Yet, it turns out that one can replace this nonconvex approach with a corresponding convex one by relying once more on the representation of the multilabel function u in terms of a vector of binary functions θ_i (see (12.4)).

Proposition 12.5   *The minimization problem (12.14) is equivalent to the minimization problem*

$$\min_{\theta\in\mathcal{B}} \left\{ \sum_{i=0}^{k} \int_\Omega g|D\theta_i|dx + \int_\Omega f(i,x)(\theta_i(x) - \theta_{i+1}(x))dx \right\}. \tag{12.15}$$

Proof   A complete proof is in [86, 373].   ∎

Moreover, one can compute optimal solutions to the original problem (12.14) by means of convex relaxation and thresholding.

Proposition 12.6   *The minimization problem (12.15) can be solved globally by relaxation to a convex problem (replacing the domain $\mathcal{B}$ with its convex hull $\mathcal{R}$ defined in (12.11), solving the convex problem and thresholding the solution.*

Proof   A complete proof is in [86, 373].   ∎

The above relaxation approach thus allows one to optimally solve the original nonconvex multilabel problem (12.14) by reducing it to the convex problem (12.15). A formulation with a continuous label space was developed in [373]. It shows that the proposed solution amounts to an anisotropic minimal surface problem. Using appropriate combinations of the convex constraints imposed in approaches (12.8) and (12.15), one can generalize this formulation to truncated linear potentials.

12.3.1   Experimental Stereo Results

The convex relaxation approach introduced above can be seen as the spatially continuous analogue of the discrete algorithm proposed by Ishikawa [211]. Figure 12.4 shows a comparison of stereo reconstructions computed with the proposed approach compared with respective results obtained with Ishikawa's graph cut formulation obtained with 4- and 8-connected neighborhoods. Close-ups show that the proposed spatially continuous solution does not exhibit any grid bias (metrication errors). Experimental comparisons show that in comparison with discrete graph cut methods, the proposed continuous shape optimization techniques typically provide more accurate solutions while requiring substantially less memory and lower computation times. (See [237] for a detailed study).

Due to substantially reduced memory requirements, the algorithm can be applied to higher-resolution image data. Figure 12.5 shows the depth reconstruction computed with

Ishikawa 4-connected   Ishikawa 8-connected   Convex formulation

Figure 12.4
Absence of grid bias /metrication error in stereo reconstructions. In contrast to the spatially discrete approach of Ishikawa [211] (shown here for 4- and 8-connected neighborhoods), the continuous solution based on convex relaxation does not favor solutions aligned to the underlying grid, such as 90 degree or 45 degree angles visible in the close-ups.

Figure 12.5
Depth reconstruction (brightness coded) computed from two aerial images of 1500 × 1400 pixels. The image on the right shows the global minimum of the function (12.14) computed using the convex relaxation.

the convex relaxation technique for a pair of aerial images of resolution 1500×1400 pixels. The brightness-encoded depth values clearly show fine-scale details such as trees, cars, lampposts, and chimneys.

12.4 Multiple View Reconstruction

The reconstruction of three-dimensional shapes from a collection of calibrated images is among the classical challenges in computer vision. Rather than estimating point correspondences among pairs of images and triangulating them, a popular alternative to computing stereo-based reconstructions from multiple views pioneered by Faugeras and Keriven [136] is directly computing a reconstruction as minimal weighted surfaces S in the volume $\Omega \subset \mathbb{R}^3$ by solving the optimization problem

$$\min_{S} \int_{S} \rho(x) dA(x), \tag{12.16}$$

where $\rho : (\Omega \subset \mathbb{R}^3) \to [0, 1]$ is a *photoconsistency measure*. Based on the assumption of a Lambertian surface, $\rho(x)$ takes on small values if the projection of voxel x into pairs of images gives rise to similar color observations (i.e., the voxel is likely to be on the surface), while high values of $\rho(x)$ indicate that the colors observed in pairs of images are very different (i.e., the voxel x is likely not to be on the surface). Thus, minimizing (12.16) gives rise to maximally photoconsistent surfaces.

The functional (12.16) has two important drawbacks. First, it is not convex such that computing good-quality surfaces is not straightforward. Second, the global minimum of (12.16) is evidently the empty set that has zero energy while any other solution clearly has nonnegative energy. In practice this latter drawback can be alleviated either by reverting to local optimization techniques such as the level set method [136] or by constraining the search space to some band around the visual hull [503].

Two alternative methods to remove the above problems are sketched below.

Solution 1: Volumetric Photoconsistencies   One can extend the functional by additional volumetric integrals over the interior int(S) and exterior ext(S) of the surface S:

$$\min_{S} \int_{S} \rho(x) dA(x) + \int_{\text{int}(S)} \rho_{int}(x) dx + \int_{\text{ext}(S)} \rho_{ext}(x) dx, \tag{12.17}$$

with appropriately defined regional photoconsistencies ρ_{int} and ρ_{ext} to model the log likelihood that a voxel is inside or outside the surface. Details on the computation of these functions are in [250].

Figure 12.6
Stereo-based multiview reconstruction via convex relaxation: two of thirty-three input images of resolution 1024×768 and three views of the reconstructed surface at volume resolution $216 \times 288 \times 324$. This solution corresponds to a global minimum of (12.18) obtained by convex relaxation and thresholding.

Representing the surface S by a binary labeling function $\theta : \Omega \rightarrow \{0, 1\}$, where $\theta(x) = 1$ if $x \in \text{int}(S)$ and $\theta(x) = 0$ otherwise, the minimization problem (12.17) is equivalent to

$$\min_{\theta : \Omega \rightarrow \{0,1\}} \int_{\Omega} \rho(x)|D\theta| + \int_{\Omega} \theta(x)(\rho_{int}(x) - \rho_{ext}(x))dx. \qquad (12.18)$$

This turns out to be the two-region case of the model presented in section 12.2.4. It can be solved optimally by minimizing the convex relaxation and thresholding the minimizer.

Figure 12.6 shows reconstructions computed from multiple images of a bunny.

Solution 2: Imposing Silhouette Consistency What makes the empty set not a good reconstruction for a given image set is that its projection into each image does not match the observed silhouettes. Let us assume that we are also given the silhouettes $S_i : \Omega_i \rightarrow \{0, 1\}$ of the observed object in each image $\Omega_i \subset \mathbb{R}^2$ for $i = 1, \ldots, n$, where $S_i(x) = 1$ if x is inside the object's silhouette. In reconstruction problems with known or homogeneous background these are typically rather straightforward to obtain beforehand. The following formulation allows one to combine stereo and silhouette information via convex functionals over convex sets.

A silhouette-consistent optimally photoconsistent reconstruction can then be computed by solving the constrained optimization problem

$$\min_{S} \int_{S} \rho(x)dA(x), \qquad (12.19)$$

s.t. $\pi_i(S) = S_i, \forall i = 1, \ldots, n,$

where π_i denotes the projection into image i.

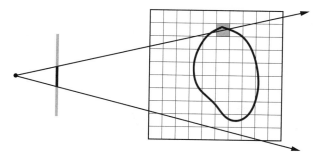

Figure 12.7
Schematic view of the silhouette consistency constraint. For a silhouette-consistent reconstruction at least one voxel along each visual ray from the camera center through silhouette pixels (bold area) must be occupied, whereas all voxels along a ray through a nonsilhouette pixel must be empty.

As above, one can revert to an implicit representation of the surface with an indicator function $\theta : \Omega \to \{0, 1\}$. Problem (12.19) is equivalent to

$$\min_{\theta:\Omega\to\{0,1\}} \int_\Omega \rho(x)|D\theta(x)|$$

(12.20)

$$\text{s.t.} \quad \int_{R_{ij}} \theta(x)dR_{ij} \geq \delta \text{ if } j \in S_i, \quad \int_{R_{ij}} \theta(x)dR_{ij} = 0 \text{ if } j \notin S_i.$$

Here the parameter $\delta > 0$ denotes a material-dependent constant corresponding to the thickness of material below which the object becomes translucent. In numerical implementations one can set $\delta = 1$. Thus the two constraints in (12.20) simply reflect the silhouette-consistency constraint: For any pixel j that is part of the silhouette S_i observed in image i, the visual ray R_{ij} from the camera center through that pixel must cross the object in at least one voxel. On the other hand, for pixels j outside the silhouette S_i, the ray R_{ij} through that pixel may not intersect with the object, that is, the integral of θ along that ray must be zero. See figure 12.7 for a schematic drawing.

Again, one can perform a relaxation of problem (12.20) by allowing θ to take on values intermediate between 0 and 1:

$$\min_{\theta\in D} \int_\Omega \rho(x)\,|D\theta(x)|,$$

(12.21)

with

$$\mathcal{D} := \left\{ \theta : V \to [0, 1] \,\middle|\, \begin{array}{ll} \int_{R_{ij}} \theta(x)dR_{ij} \geq 1 & \text{if } j \in S_i\ \forall i, j \\ \int_{R_{ij}} \theta(x)dR_{ij} = 0 & \text{if } j \notin S_i\ \forall i, j \end{array} \right\}.$$

(12.22)

It turns out that in the implicit representation, the silhouette constraint ties nicely into the convex optimization framework.

Proposition 12.7 *The set $\mathcal{D}$ of all silhouette-consistent functions defined in (12.22) forms a convex set.*

Proof Let $\theta_1, \theta_2 \in \mathcal{D}$ be two elements of $\mathcal{D}$. Then any convex combination $\theta = \alpha\theta_1 + (1 - \alpha)\theta_2$ with $\alpha \in [0, 1]$ is also an element in $\mathcal{D}$. In particular, $\theta(x) \in [0, 1]$ for all x. Moreover,

$$\int_{R_{ij}} \theta \, dR_{ij} = \alpha \int_{R_{ij}} \theta_1 dR_{ij} + (1 - \alpha) \int_{R_{ij}} \theta_2 dR_{ij} \geq 1 \text{ if } j \in S_i, \tag{12.23}$$

and similarly

$$\int_{R_{ij}} \theta \, dR_{ij} = \alpha \int_{R_{ij}} \theta_1 dR_{ij} + (1 - \alpha) \int_{R_{ij}} \theta_2 dR_{ij} = 0 \text{ if } j \notin S_i. \tag{12.24}$$

Thus $\theta \in \mathcal{D}$. ∎

Since we are interested in minimizers of the nonconvex binary labeling problem (12.20), a straightforward methodology is to threshold the solution of the convex problem (12.21) appropriately. Although this will not guarantee finding the global minimum of (12.20), the proposed strategy entails a series of advantages over classical local optimization techniques. Extending the set of admissible functions, computing the global minimum over this domain, and subsequently projecting to the nearest point within the original set will provide a solution that is independent of initialization. Moreover, one can compute an upper bound on the energetic deviation of the computed solution from the global minimum.

Proposition 12.8 *Let θ^* be a minimizer of the relaxed problem (12.21) and let $\hat{\theta}^*$ be a projection onto the binary silhouette-consistent solutions. Then $\hat{\theta}^*$ is of bounded distance (in terms of its energy E) from the true solution θ':*

$$\left| \mathcal{E}(\hat{\theta}^*) - \mathcal{E}(\theta') \right| \leq \left| \mathcal{E}(\theta^*) - \mathcal{E}(\hat{\theta}^*) \right|. \tag{12.25}$$

Proof The proof is analogous to that of proposition 12.4. ∎

The projection $\hat{\theta}^*$ of a minimizer θ^* onto the silhouette-consistent binary functions can be computed by simple thresholding:

$$\hat{\theta}(x) = \begin{cases} 1, & \text{if } \theta^*(x) \geq \mu \\ 0, & \text{otherwise} \end{cases}, \tag{12.26}$$

where

$$\mu = \min\left\{\left(\min_{i\in\{1,...,n\}, j\in S_i}\ \max_{x\in R_{ij}} \theta^*(x)\right), 0.5\right\}. \tag{12.27}$$

This threshold μ provides the closest silhouette-consistent binary function to the solution of the relaxed problem.

Proposition 12.9 *The computed binary solution exactly fulfills all silhouette constraints.*

Proof A proof is in [247].   ∎

12.4.1 Experimental Multiview Results

Figure 12.8 shows an experimental comparison of the two alternative multiview methods for the reconstruction of a metal head. Due to the strong reflections and highlights, the stereo information becomes unreliable and the resulting reconstruction is substantially deteriorated (left). Incorporating the silhouette constraint allows substantial improvement of the reconstruction (right).

The minimal surface formulation suffers from a shrinking bias in the sense that small scale and elongated structures tend to be supressed (as this leads to smaller surface energy). The silhouette constraint, on the other hand, allows preservation of many small scale structures.

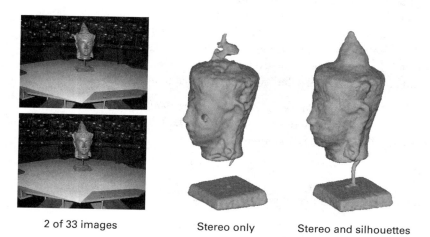

2 of 33 images   Stereo only   Stereo and silhouettes

Figure 12.8
Silhouette and stereo integration. While the purely stereo-based reconstruction method (12.17) (middle) tends to remove thin structures and is heavily affected by specular reflections such as those of metal objects (left), the fusion of stereo and silhouette information using approach (12.20) allows one to compute stereo-based reconstructions that are guaranteed to be silhouette-consistent. As a consequence, concave areas (around the ears), as well as fine geometric details such as the pedestal, are preserved in the reconstruction.

Figure 12.9
Warrior sequence. Two of twenty-four input images of resolution 1600×1600 and multiple views of the reconstructed surface. Note that thin structures such as hammer and sword, as well as concavities—for example, at the chest—are reconstructed accurately.

Figure 12.9 shows reconstructions from twenty-four images of a warrior statue, computed by solving the constrained optimization problem (12.21). The image data are courtesy of Yasutaka Furukawa (see http://www.cs.washington.edu/homes/furukawa/research/mview/index.html). Note that the silhouette constraint allows preservation of fine details such as the hammer and the sword.

12.5 Summary and Conclusion

This chapter provided several convex relaxation techniques for central computer vision problems such as image segmentation, and stereo and multiview reconstruction. Optimal solutions or solutions of bounded optimality are computed in a spatially continuous representation through the minimization of convex functionals and subsequent projection. In contrast to level set approaches, the presented convex relaxation schemes are independent of initialization and provide solutions with known optimality guarantees. In contrast to graph cut-based solutions, the spatially continuous formulation does not suffer from metrication errors (see [237] for a detailed comparison). In addition, physical constraints such as the silhouette consistency of 3D reconstructions often give rise to convex constraints and therefore can be directly imposed in the optimization scheme.

Due to space limitations the numerical solution of the arising convex optimization problems was not discussed in detail. There are many different algorithms, from simple gradient descent to more efficient algorithms based on fixed point iteration and successive over-relaxation [250] or primal-dual algorithms [373, 372]. These algorithms are typically straightforward to parallelize on the pixel or voxel grid. As a consequence, implementations on graphics hardware lead to substantial speedups over CPU implementations.

The concept of convex relaxation has become increasingly popular in computer vision over the last year. In addition to the approaches discussed in this chapter, there are further convex relaxation schemes to find optimal solutions to *anisotropic* minimal surface problems [373, 547, 488, 248] or to *ratio functionals* [249]. Recently, the first algorithm for minimizing convex relaxations of the *piecewise smooth Mumford-Shah functional* was proposed in [372]. All these developments indicate that the spatially continuous representation and PDE-based optimization techniques provide a powerful alternative to graph-theoretic Markov random field approaches.

13 Learning Parameters in Continuous-Valued Markov Random Fields

Marshall F. Tappen

When formulating a Markov random field model to accomplish some task, a key decision must be made at the beginning of the process: Should nodes in the MRF model be discrete-valued or continuous-valued variables? While the advances in inference in discrete-valued models, many of which are described in other chapters, make discrete-valued models attractive for a wide range of problems, continuous-valued models have some unique advantages.

A significant advantage is that a continuous formulation can naturally handle an infinite number of states. Many low-level and midlevel vision problems are more naturally thought of as being parameterized by a set of continuous variables, such as problems involving pixel intensities and depth values. In both cases a discrete-valued formulation for these problems often requires a large number of possible states, which leads to efficiency issues in inference and learning, sometimes making it necessary to implement complex heuristics to dynamically reduce the number of states [307]. Continuous-valued models, on the other hand, are unaffected by these issues.

MAP inference in continuous models is straightforward to implement, using the wide range of continuous optimization algorithms, from basic steepest descent to more advanced quasi-Newton methods. In many cases this reduces the implementation of the MAP inference step only to the implementation of a function that calculates the gradient of the energy function, denoted $E(\mathbf{x})$, with respect to the value of each node in the MRF. The continuous nature of such models also makes it possible to apply basic differentiation techniques to learning parameters in a discriminative fashion. The development of powerful, efficient learning algorithms for continuous models, discussed starting in section 13.4.1, will be the focus of much of this chapter.

13.1 Continuous MRF Models in Computer Vision

Continuous-valued MRFs have most often been used to impose smoothness or continuity constraints [54, 460]. These models also have a strong connection to regularization schemes in ill-posed vision problems [330].

The early use of these models focused particularly on piecewise smooth reconstructions of noisy or scattered data. Work such as Blake and Zisserman's *Visual Reconstruction* [54] demonstrated both how to formulate the models so that discontinuities are preserved and how to optimize the resulting models, using techniques such as graduated non-convexity. Black and Rangajaran also have connected these models to robust statistics [47].

More recent research, such as Roth and Black's Field of Experts model [397], has taken advantage of the ease of implementing inference in continuous-valued MRFs to learn higher-order MRFs. Because inference in these models could be reduced to basic filtering steps [394, 550], these models go beyond the typical pairwise cliques to cliques corresponding to 5×5 patches of pixels.

13.2   Basic Formulation

Following the basic notation in chapter 1, the distribution over vectors $\mathbf{x}$, $p(\mathbf{x})$ will be denoted as a Gibbs distribution:

$$p(\mathbf{x}) = \frac{1}{Z(\omega)} \exp - E(\mathbf{x}, \omega), \qquad (13.1)$$

where $Z(\omega)$ is the partition function, or normalization constant. The term $E(\mathbf{x})$ is an energy function made up of a set of potential functions. There is one potential function, $\Psi(\mathbf{x}_c, \omega)$, per clique c in the graph, such that $E(\mathbf{x}) = \sum_{c \in \mathcal{C}} \Psi_x(\mathbf{x})$. Similar to chapter 1, the parameters of the model are denoted as the vector ω.

13.3   Parameter Estimation in Continuous Models

The basic distribution in (13.1) does not contain the notion of observed and hidden variables. In computer vision applications, MRF models are most often employed when where a set of variables, $\mathbf{x}$, is being estimated from a set of observation variables, $\mathbf{z}$. Approaches for learning the parameter vector ω can be broadly grouped into generative approaches, where ω is found by maximizing the joint distribution $p(\mathbf{x}, \mathbf{z})$ on training examples, and discriminative approaches, where ω is found instead by maxinmizing the conditional distribution $p(\mathbf{x} \mid \mathbf{z})$. Nonprobabilistic classifiers, such as boosting-based classifiers or the support vector machine, also are often referred to as discriminative methods.

Techniques for estimating the parameter vector ω can be broadly grouped into two classes: methods based on maximum likelihood methods and loss-based methods. Methods based on maximum likelihood parameter estimation, which can be used for both generative and discriminative approaches, have been the traditional approach for parameter estimation, but loss-based methods offer unique benefits for continuous models, in terms of both efficiency and flexibility. In maximum likelihood methods the learning is tied to maximizing the distribution defined by the MRF. Thus, the learning criterion and structure of the model are tied together.

The loss-based approach adds flexibility by separating the learning criterion from the structure of the model. In a loss-based approach the parameters are chosen to optimize a loss function that expresses the quality of any particular solution. This loss function is chosen separately from the structure of the model, thus separating the structure of the model from the learning criterion and allowing them both to be tailored to specific requirements of a particular application.

Both methods are reviewed below. Section 13.4 will first review maximum likelihood parameter estimation in MRF. Following this, section 13.4.1 introduces the loss-based approach for parameter estimation.

13.4 Maximum Likelihood Parameter Estimation

Given a set of N training images, $\mathbf{t}_1 \cdots \mathbf{t}_N$, the maximum likelihood (ML) estimate of ω is the parameter vector that maximizes the likelihood function. Denoting the ML estimate as ω^*, this is formally expressed as

$$\omega^* = \arg \max_\omega \prod_{k=1}^N p(\mathbf{t}_k). \tag{13.2}$$

Note that ω contains the parameters of $p(\mathbf{t})$. If observations, $\mathbf{z}_k$, are available, the training criterion becomes

$$\left[\omega^* = \arg \max_\omega \prod_{k=1}^N p(\mathbf{t}_k, \mathbf{z}_k) \right] \text{ or } \left[\omega^* = \arg \max_\omega \prod_{k=1}^N p(\mathbf{t}_k \mid \mathbf{z}_k) \right], \tag{13.3}$$

depending on whether the training is generative or discriminative. For brevity, the observed variables will not be included in the derivations below.

Since the log-function is montonic, the product on the right-hand side can be replaced with a summation of log-terms:

$$\omega^* = \arg \max_\omega \sum_{k=1}^N \log p(\mathbf{t}_k) \tag{13.4}$$

$$= \arg \max_\omega \sum_{k=1}^N -E(\mathbf{t}_k, \omega) - \log Z(\omega). \tag{13.5}$$

This maximization can be accomplished with a number of methods, including gradient-based techniques and iterative scaling [288], though research has indicated that gradient-based quasi-Newton methods, such as BFGS, perform the best [336].

Defining the criterion in (13.5) as $\mathcal{L}(\omega)$, computing the gradient of $\mathcal{L}(\omega)$ reveals the difficulty in maximum likelihood estimation. Focusing on the log of the partition function, $Z(\omega)$, the gradient is

$$\frac{\partial Z}{\partial \omega} = \frac{1}{Z(\omega)} \int_{\mathbf{x}} -\frac{\partial E}{\partial \omega} \exp-(E(\mathbf{x}, \omega)), \tag{13.6}$$

where the differentiation has been interchanged with the integration, as is typical [507]. This derivative can be rewritten as an expectation under the distribution $p(x)$:

$$\begin{aligned}
\frac{\partial Z}{\partial \omega} &= \frac{1}{Z(\omega)} \int_{\mathbf{x}} -\frac{\partial E}{\partial \omega} \exp(-E(\mathbf{x}, \omega)) = \int_{\mathbf{x}} -p(\mathbf{x}) \frac{\partial E}{\partial \omega} \\
&= \left\langle -\frac{\partial E}{\partial \omega} \right\rangle_{\mathbf{x}},
\end{aligned} \tag{13.7}$$

where $\langle \cdot \rangle_{\mathbf{x}}$ denotes the expectation under the distribution $p(\mathbf{x})$.

With this result the gradient of $\mathcal{L}(\omega)$ can easily be computed:

$$\frac{\partial L}{\partial \omega} = \sum_{i=k}^{N} - \left(\frac{\partial E}{\partial \omega} \right)_{\mathbf{t}_k} + \left\langle \frac{\partial E}{\partial \omega} \right\rangle_{\mathbf{x}}, \tag{13.8}$$

where $\left(\frac{\partial E}{\partial \omega} \right)_{\mathbf{t}_k}$ is the gradient evaluated at $\mathbf{t}_k$. As an interesting side note, (13.8) indicates that parameters ω have reached a minimum of $\mathcal{L}(\omega)$ when the average of the gradient over the training samples equals the expected value of the gradient.

The difficulty in maximum likelihood parameter estimation for MRFs lies in the expectation in (13.8). As described in chapter 1, computing this expectation is generally intractable for MRFs with loops. The most notable exception to this is Gaussian models, where the expectations can be computed by first inverting the precision matrix to obtain the covariance matrix, then using that matrix to compute the necessary expectations. The disadvantage of this is that it will be impractical to store this matrix for models with large numbers of nodes, which are common in low-level vision applications such as segmentation and noise removal.

Approximate Solutions for Maximum Likelihood Learning   Though it is often impossible to compute the exact value of the expectations in (13.8), it is possible to compute approximate values of the expectations efficiently.

One of the most popular approaches for computing these expectations is to draw samples from $p(\mathbf{x})$, then use these samples to approximate the expected value of the gradient such as [550]. More recently, methods based on the contrastive divergence techniques proposed by Carriera-Perpignan and Hinton [83] have proven especially successful. Chapter 19, which describes the Field of Experts model, discusses this approach in more detail.

A popular alternative to sampling is to compute approximate distributions over labeling and use these distributions to compute the gradient. In [305] Levin and Weiss use the tree-reweighted belief propagation algorithm, also discussed in chapter 6, to compute these distributions. Standard belief propagation has also been used with some success [501].

A simpler strategy of using the MAP estimate as a substitute for expected values has been proposed in [283, 418].

13.4.1 Loss-Based Parameter Estimation for MRFs

Rather than fitting distributions to training samples, loss-based approaches instead seek to directly optimize the estimate of $\mathbf{x}$ produced by the model. Assuming that the estimate produced by the model will be the MAP solution of the MRF,[1] the loss-based learning formulation can be posed formally as

$$\omega^* = \arg \min_{\omega} L(\mathbf{t}, \mathbf{x}^*)$$
$$\text{where } \mathbf{x}^* = \arg \min_{\mathbf{x}} E(\mathbf{x}, \mathbf{z}, \omega). \tag{13.9}$$

In this formulation $L(\mathbf{t}, \mathbf{x}^*)$ denotes a loss function that measures the similarity between the ground truth training example $\mathbf{t}$ and the estimate, $\mathbf{x}$, obtained from the MRF model. The loss function can be something as simple as $||\mathbf{x} - \mathbf{t}||^2$ or a more complicated function, such as the perceptually accurate SSIM image quality metric [513]. The energy function in (13.9) has also been modified to show explicitly the dependence on the vector of observations $\mathbf{z}_k$ that correspond to each training example. If the task is denoising, then $\mathbf{z}$ would be the noisy image, and $\mathbf{t}$ would hold the noise-free ground truth image.

In this formulation the choice of parameters ω influences the loss function through $\mathbf{x}^*$. As the parameters change, the estimate $\mathbf{x}^*$ also changes. The goal in this formulation is to find the parameters that cause the MAP solution of $p(\mathbf{x})$ to be as close as possible to the ground truth. Similar formulations have been proposed for discrete models [12, 473, 484].

13.4.2 Implementing Parameter Estimation

As with maximum likelihood learning, the general strategy for implementing the minimization is to compute the gradient $\partial L / \partial \omega$ for use with a gradient-based optimization algorithm. Using the chain rule, the gradient can be broken into two parts:

$$\frac{\partial L}{\partial \omega} = \frac{\partial \mathbf{x}^*}{\partial \omega}^T \frac{\partial L}{\partial \mathbf{x}^*}. \tag{13.10}$$

The difficult step in computing the gradient is $\partial \mathbf{x}^* / \partial \omega$, since $\mathbf{x}^*$ relates to ω through an arg min operation. Fortunately, in continuously valued MRF models it is possible to compute this gradient.

13.5 Loss-Based Parameter Estimation for Gaussian MRF Models

This chapter's discussion of loss-based MRF parameter estimation techniques will begin with Gaussian MRF models, where $p(\mathbf{x})$ has a jointly normal distribution, since computing

---

1. In MRF models defined by an energy function, the MAP solution corresponds to the vector $\mathbf{x}$ with the lowest energy.

the gradient of the loss function is particularly straightforward in these models. Building on the ideas in this section, section 13.6 will show how loss-based parameter estimation can be implemented in non-Gaussian models.

For the case of Gaussian models, it will be assumed that the energy function $E(\mathbf{x})$ has the form

$$E(\mathbf{x}) = \mathbf{x}^T A^T A \mathbf{x} + 2\mathbf{x}^T A^T \mathbf{h} + C, \tag{13.11}$$

where C is a constant and $\mathbf{h}$ is a vector of constants.

In this case the MAP estimate from $p(\mathbf{x})$ will be the mean of $(\mathbf{x})$:

$$\mathbf{x}^* = \mu = (A^T A)^{-1} A^T \mathbf{h}. \tag{13.12}$$

To implement the loss-based learning formulation described in the previous section, A and $\mathbf{h}$ will depend on the parameters ω. As described in section 13.4.2, the key step now is to compute the derivative $\partial \mathbf{x}^* / \partial \omega_j$, where ω_j is the jth parameter in ω. This derivative can be shown to be

$$\frac{\partial \mathbf{x}^*}{\partial \omega_j} = (A^T A)^{-1} \left[-\frac{\partial A}{\partial \omega_j} A \mathbf{x}^* + -A \frac{\partial A}{\partial \omega_j} \mathbf{x}^* + \frac{\partial A^T}{\partial \omega_j} \mathbf{h} + A^T \frac{\partial \mathbf{h}}{\partial \omega_j} \right]. \tag{13.13}$$

Of course, the real quantity of interest is the derivative of $L(\mathbf{t}, \mathbf{x}^*)$. Applying the chain rule and factoring, the derivative of $L(\mathbf{t}, \mathbf{x}^*)$ with respect to ω_j becomes

$$\frac{\partial L}{\partial \omega_j} = \left(\frac{\partial L}{\partial \mathbf{x}^*} \right)^T (A^T A)^{-1} \left[-\frac{\partial A}{\partial \omega_j} A \mathbf{x}^* - A \frac{\partial A}{\partial \omega_j} \mathbf{x}^* + \frac{\partial A^T}{\partial \omega_j} \mathbf{h} + A^T \frac{\partial \mathbf{h}}{\partial \omega_j} \right]. \tag{13.14}$$

For computation reasons it is better to precompute the matrix-vector product $(\partial L / \partial \mathbf{x}^*)^T (A^T A)^{-1}$, since the value of that vector does not change as the loss function is being differentiated with respect to different parameters ω_j.

While this matrix-vector product could be computed by first computing the inverse of $A^T A$, in practice it is more efficient to compute that product by computing the solution to the linear system $(A^T A)\mathbf{z} = \partial L / \partial \mathbf{x}^*$, with the resulting vector $\mathbf{z}$ containing the product $(A^T A)^{-1} \partial L / \partial \mathbf{x}^*$.

13.5.1 Example Application: Gaussian Conditional Random Fields for Image Denoising

This approach can be readily applied to the task of denoising images. When comparing image models, denoising is a particularly convenient task because data can be readily created.

Successfully adapting this approach to denoising will require the transition to a conditional random field model [288], where the parameters of the different clique potentials depend on the observed noisy image. Using a CRF is vital to good performance in a Gaussian model because traditional Gaussian MRF models, where the clique potentials are identical at each pixel, are well known for oversmoothing images.

The rest of this section will describe how the loss-based learning method described above can be used to train a Gaussian conditional random field (GCRF) model for denoising images.

13.5.2 GMRF Model for Denoising

For clarity, the explanation of the GCRF model will begin by discussing the basic GMRF model and its limitations. Like the Field of Experts model in chapter 19, this model will be defined by set of 2D convolution filters, $f_1, \ldots, f_{N_f}$, and weights, $w_1, \ldots, w_{N_f}$. The joint distribution of the clean image, $\mathbf{x}$, and the noisy observed image, $\mathbf{z}$, will be defined by the energy function

$$E(\mathbf{x}; \mathbf{z}) = \sum_{j=1}^{N_f} \sum_i v_j(((f_i * \mathbf{x})_i)^2 + \sum_i (x_i - z_i)^2. \tag{13.15}$$

Here, $(f_j * \mathbf{x})_i$ denotes pixel i from the image produced by convolving $\mathbf{x}$ with the filter f_j. The summation $\sum_j$ denotes the sum over all pixels j in the image. The weight from the final term, $\sum_i (x_i - z_i)^2$, has been dropped because only the MAP solution of this model is of interest. Because scaling the entire energy function does not change the MAP solution, it can be assumed that the weight of one component is constant.

Though the weights, $v_1, \ldots, v_{N_f}$, could be found using the loss-based technique described above, the results produced by that model would still perform poorly when compared with MRF models that better match the statistics of natural images, such as the Field of Experts model. If the filters in (13.15) respond strongly to edges, the quadratic penalties will tend to minimize the edge response as much as possible, leading to an image with overly smoothed edges.

One successful solution to this problem is to construct $E(\mathbf{x})$ from a more robust function, such as the Lorentzian [47, 394], which will result in sharp transitions in the estimated image. However, this change makes it impossible to use the differentiation steps just described; section 13.6 will discuss alternative techniques for non-Gaussian models.

Alternatively, the weakness of the GMRF model in handling edges can be alleviated by using the observed image to find edges and deal correctly with those edges. This transforms the GMRF model into a Gaussian conditional random field, or GCRF, where the weight assigned to each term in the CRF is conditioned on the observed image. Formally, this change can be expressed by modifying (13.15):

$$E(\mathbf{x}; \mathbf{z}) = \sum_{j=1}^{N_f} \sum_i v_j(i, \mathbf{z}, \omega_j)(((f_j * \mathbf{x})_i)^2 + \sum_i (x_i - z_i)^2. \tag{13.16}$$

In this GCRF model the weight parameter v_j has been transformed into a function of the observed image $\mathbf{z}$, the pixel location p, and parameters ω_j. In the remainder of this chapter

ω_j will be used to denote a vector of parameters associated with the jth term in this energy function.

The key idea behind this change is to use the weight functions to decrease the amount of smoothing in areas with edges. These weight functions examine the image to determine if it is likely that an edge is present, and adjust the smoothing accordingly.

13.5.3 Designing and Learning Weighting Functions for Denoising

The key to success in the GCRF model from (13.16) is the weight functions. For denoising, good results can be obtained with a relatively basic weighting function. Following [470], the weight at a pixel p can be computed from a vector $\mathbf{r}_i$ comprising the absolute response, at pixel i, of a set of linear filters. The weight function is then

$$v_j(p, \mathbf{z}, \omega_j) = \exp\left(\omega_j^T \mathbf{r}_i\right).$$ (13.17)

As is common, any necessary bias terms can be incorporated into $\mathbf{r}_j$. In this formulation only the parameters of the weighting function are being trained. Other parameters of the system, such as the filters, are predetermined, though it would be possible to use this method to learn them also.

The weights, $\omega_1, \ldots, \omega_{N_f}$, can be optimized using the method described above. In this particular GCRF model the derivation can be expressed compactly, using a set of convolution matrices $F_1, \ldots, F_{N_f}$, such that computing $F_j \mathbf{z}$, where $\mathbf{z}$ is an image that has been reordered into a vector, is the same as convolving the image with the filter f_j. The GCRF energy function can then be rewritten as

$$E(\mathbf{x}; \mathbf{z}) = (\mathbf{x} - \mathbf{z})^T (\mathbf{x} - \mathbf{z}) + \sum_{j=1}^{N_f} \mathbf{x}^T F_j^T W_j F_j \mathbf{x},$$ (13.18)

where W_j is a diagonal matrix with the ith entry along the diagonal defined as $[W_j]_i = v_j(p, \mathbf{z}, \omega_j) = \exp(\omega_j^T \mathbf{r}_j)$.

This can be further simplified by stacking $F_1, \ldots, F_{N_f}$ on top of each other into one block matrix, F, and creating a block-diagonal matrix, W, with $W_1, \ldots, W_{N_f}$ along the diagonal—making the energy function

$$E(\mathbf{x}) = \mathbf{x}^T (F^T W F + I)\mathbf{x} + 2\mathbf{z}^T \mathbf{x} + \mathbf{z}^T \mathbf{z}.$$ (13.19)

The minimum of this energy function, $\mathbf{x}^*$, is then

$$\mathbf{x}^* = (F^T W F + I)^{-1} \mathbf{z}.$$ (13.20)

Calculating the derivatives of the loss with respect to the parameters ω is simplified because only the W_j matrices vary. Following (13.14), the derivative of the loss, with respect to the ith entry in ω_j, denoted as ω_j^i, can be computed as

$$\frac{\partial L}{\partial \omega_j^i} = \left(\frac{\partial L}{\partial \mathbf{x}^*}\right)^T (F^T W F + I)^{-1} F^T \left(\frac{\partial W}{\partial \omega_j^i}\right) F (F^T W F + I)^{-1} \mathbf{z}$$

$$= \left(\frac{\partial L}{\partial \mathbf{x}^*}\right)^T (F^T W F + I)^{-1} F^T \left(\frac{\partial W}{\partial \omega_j^i}\right) F \mathbf{x}^*, \tag{13.21}$$

where ω_j^i denotes the ith entry in the vector ω_j.

Computing the gradient vector with respect to every entry in ω_j can be made easier by introducing a new vector $\mathbf{v}(\omega)$, which holds the values along the diagonal of W. The gradient from (13.21) can be rewritten as

$$\frac{\partial L}{\partial \omega_j^i} = \left(\frac{\partial L}{\partial \mathbf{x}^*}\right)^T (F^T W F + I)^{-1} F^T D_{F\mathbf{x}^*} \frac{\partial \mathbf{v}}{\partial \omega_j^i}, \tag{13.22}$$

where a new matrix $D_{F\mathbf{x}^*}$ has been introduced. Like W, $D_{F\mathbf{x}^*}$ is also a diagonal matrix, but its diagonal is equal to $F\mathbf{x}^*$.

Expressing the gradient in this fashion makes $\partial \mathbf{v}/\partial \omega_j^i$ a vector. Differentiating $\mathbf{v}(\omega)$ with respect to ω_j leads to the matrix $\partial \mathbf{v}/\partial \omega_j$. The gradient vector can now be computed as

$$\frac{\partial L}{\partial \omega_j} = \left(\frac{\partial L}{\partial \mathbf{x}^*}\right)^T (F^T W F + I)^{-1} F^T D_{F\mathbf{x}^*} \frac{\partial \mathbf{v}}{\partial \omega_j}. \tag{13.23}$$

As mentioned earlier, computing the gradient vector with respect to the vectors $\omega_1, \ldots, \omega_{N_f}$ can be implemented efficiently by precomputing the matrix-vector product $(\partial L/\partial \mathbf{x}^*)^T (F^T W F + I)^{-1}$.

Choosing the Filters The weight function associated with each filter is based on the absolute response of the observed image to a set of multiscale oriented edge and bar filters, which are described in more detail in [469].

The same responses are used to compute the weights for all of the filters, $f_1, \ldots, f_{N_f}$. In the experiments the parameter vectors, $\omega_1, \ldots, \omega_{N_f}$, were optimized using the pixelwise squared error, $L(\mathbf{x}^*) = ||\mathbf{x} - \mathbf{t}||^2$, where $\mathbf{t}$ is the ground truth image. The parameters were trained using 182 images taken from the same set of training images used in [394], which come from the Berkeley Segmentation Database [331]. A 91×91 pixel patch was taken from the center of each image.

The actual optimization was implemented using a basic steepest descent algorithm. The main motivation for using this technique was to minimize the amount of line search necessary, since even evaluating the loss function requires the expensive solution of a set of linear equations. Fortunately, this process parallelizes easily and it was possible to optimize the parameters in several hours.

13.5.4 Denoising Performance

Similar to [394], the denoising results are evaluated using the PSNR metric :

$$PSNR(\mathbf{x}) = 20 \log_{10}(255/\sigma_e),\tag{13.24}$$

where σ_e denotes the standard deviation of the pixelwise difference between the estimated image and the ground truth image.

After training the GCRF model, it was used to denoise the sixty-eight test images used in [394], also taken from the Berkeley Segmentation Database. The results produced by the Field of Experts model and the GCRF model are shown in table 13.1, which shows that the GCRF model is able to denoise the images more accurately, despite relying on a Gaussian model. Essentially, the GCRF utilizes the noisy observations to overcome the limitations of the underlying Gaussian model. Figure 13.1 compares of the results produced using these models. In general, the GCRF model better retains details in the image.

As table 13.1 shows, taking advantage of the observed image makes it possible for this Gaussian model to perform comparably with the Field of Experts model. It should be noted that using a simpler set of filters performs only slightly worse. This makes it possible to significantly reduce the amount of time spent computing the responses needed to compute weights.

This GCRF model can also be adapted to perform classification tasks, as described in [471].

Efficient Computation of Denoised Images   One of the largest drawbacks of this model is that computing the MAP solution exactly can be infeasible for large images. Fortunately, good solutions can be quickly generated using an iterative solver, such as the conjugate gradients method. As shown in [469], after 300 iterations the average per-pixel difference between the image produced using the exact solver and that using conjugate gradients was less than 5×10^{-5}. Because the model is based on convolution matrices, all of the matrix-vector products required can be implemented with convolutions.

Table 13.1
Comparison of the average error in denoised estimates produced by the GCRF model described in this chapter and the Field of Experts model from [394]

Model	Average PSNR($\sigma = 15$) (Higher is Better)	Average PSNR ($\sigma = 25$)
Field of experts	30.56	27.75
GCRF	30.69	28.18

The results are averaged over the same 68 test images used in [394]. Results are shown for two different noise levels, $\sigma = 15$ and $\sigma = 25$.

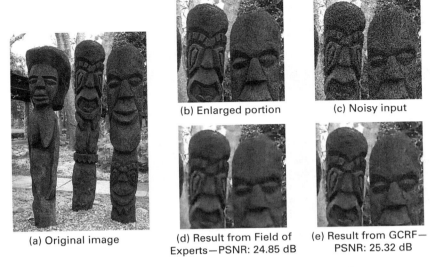

(a) Original image

(b) Enlarged portion

(c) Noisy input

(d) Result from Field of Experts—PSNR: 24.85 dB

(e) Result from GCRF— PSNR: 25.32 dB

Figure 13.1
The images on the right are produced using the GCRF model from the noisy images shown in the figure, which have been corrupted with white Gaussian noise with $\sigma = 15$. The GCRF model is better able to preserve texture in the image.

13.6 Loss-Based Learning Algorithms for Non-Gaussian Models

Loss-based parameter learning is particularly straightforward when applied to Gaussian models because the arg min operation is implemented with a matrix inverse, which can be differentiated analytically. However, as argued in section 13.5.2, Gaussian models have the drawback of oversmoothing images. Though taking advantage of the observed image, as in the GCRF model, can alleviate this issue, the strategy may not always be feasible. For example, in problems with missing data, such as inpainting, no observations are available.

Fortunately, it is possible to apply similar learning strategies to non-Gaussian models, such as the Field of Experts model, that can overcome the limitations of the GCRF model. The overall learning formulation does not need to be modified, but the gradient vector must be calculated in a different fashion. Instead of computing the gradient by differentiating an inverse matrix, it will instead be computed using an implicit differentiation method also employed in hyperparameter learning [127].

This approach relies on the fact that $\mathbf{x}^*$ is a minimum of $E(\mathbf{x})$. Because $\mathbf{x}^* = \arg\min_{\mathbf{x}} E(\mathbf{x})$, the gradient of $E(\mathbf{x})$ evaluated at $\mathbf{x}^*$ will be equal to $\mathbf{0}$. For clarity in the remaining discussion, we will replace $\partial E(\mathbf{x})/\partial \mathbf{x}$ with the function $\mathbf{g}(\mathbf{x}, \mathbf{v}(\omega))$, such that $\mathbf{g}(\mathbf{x}, \mathbf{v}(\omega)) \triangleq \partial E(\mathbf{x})/\partial \mathbf{x}$. An explicit dependence on the function $\mathbf{v}(\omega)$ has been included in $\mathbf{g}(\cdot)$. The function $\mathbf{v}(\omega)$ can be thought of as a function that transforms ω into the weights actually used in the model.

Using this notation, the fact that the gradient will be equal to $\mathbf{0}$ can be expressed formally as

$$\mathbf{g}(\mathbf{x}^*(\omega), \mathbf{v}(\omega)) = \mathbf{0}. \tag{13.25}$$

Both sides of (13.25) can now be differentiated with respect to a parameter ω_j. After applying the chain rule, the derivative of the left side of (13.25) is

$$\frac{\partial \mathbf{g}}{\partial \omega_j} = \frac{\partial \mathbf{g}}{\partial \mathbf{x}^*}\frac{\partial \mathbf{x}^*}{\partial \omega_j} + \frac{\partial \mathbf{g}}{\partial \mathbf{v}}\frac{\partial \mathbf{v}}{\partial \omega_j}. \tag{13.26}$$

Note that if $\mathbf{x}$ and $\mathbf{x}^*$ are $N \times 1$ vectors, then $\partial \mathbf{g}/\partial \mathbf{x}^*$ is an $N \times N$ matrix. As stated in (13.25), this gradient will be equal to the 0 vector at $\mathbf{x}^*$, making it possible to solve for $\partial \mathbf{x}^*/\partial \omega_j$:

$$\frac{\partial \mathbf{x}^*}{\partial \omega_j} = -\left(\frac{\partial \mathbf{g}}{\partial \mathbf{x}^*}\right)^{-1}\frac{\partial \mathbf{g}}{\partial \mathbf{v}}\frac{\partial \mathbf{v}}{\partial \omega_j}. \tag{13.27}$$

Note that because ω_j is a scalar, $\partial \mathbf{g}/\partial \mathbf{v}\partial \mathbf{v}/\partial \omega_j$ is an $N \times 1$ vector.

The matrix $\partial \mathbf{g}/\partial \mathbf{x}^*$ is easily computed by noticing that $\mathbf{g}(\mathbf{x}^*, \mathbf{v}(\omega))$ is the gradient of $E(\cdot)$, with each term from $\mathbf{x}$ replaced with a term from $\mathbf{x}^*$. This makes the $\partial \mathbf{g}/\partial \mathbf{x}^*$ term in the above equations the Hessian matrix of $E(\mathbf{x})$ evaluated at $\mathbf{x}^*$.

Denoting the Hessian of $E(\mathbf{x})$ evaluated at $\mathbf{x}^*$ as $H_E(\mathbf{x}^*)$ and applying the chain rule leads to the derivative of the overall loss function with respect to ω_j:

$$\frac{\partial L(\mathbf{x}^*(\omega), \mathbf{t})}{\partial \omega_j} = -\left(\frac{\partial L(\mathbf{x}^*(\omega), \mathbf{t})}{\partial \mathbf{x}^*}\right)^T H_E(\mathbf{x}^*)^{-1}\frac{\partial \mathbf{g}}{\partial \mathbf{v}}\frac{\partial \mathbf{v}}{\partial \omega_j}. \tag{13.28}$$

As with the GCRF model, the Hessian does not need to be inverted. Instead, only the value

$$\left(\frac{\partial L(\mathbf{x}^*(\omega), \mathbf{t})}{\partial \omega_j}\right)^T H_E(\mathbf{x}^*)^{-1}$$

needs to be computed. This can be accomplished efficiently in a number of ways, including iterative methods such as the conjugate gradients method. Second, by computing $(\partial L(\mathbf{x}^*(\omega), \mathbf{t})/\partial \omega_j^T)H_E(\mathbf{x}^*)^{-1}$ rather than $H_E(\mathbf{x}^*)^{-1}(\partial \mathbf{g}/\partial \mathbf{v})(\partial \mathbf{v}/\partial \omega_j)$, only one call to the solver is necessary to compute the gradient for all parameters in the vector ω.

If the energy function, $E(\mathbf{x})$, is nonconvex, then $\mathbf{x}^*$ may be only a local minimum. In the experiments described in section 13.6.3, this was not a significant issue.

13.6.1 Overall Steps for Computing Gradient

This formulation provides us with a convenient framework to learn the parameter ω using basic optimization routines. The steps are the following:

1. Compute $\mathbf{x}^*(\omega)$ for the current parameter vector ω. In our work this is accomplished using nonlinear conjugate gradient optimization.

2. Compute the Hessian matrix at $\mathbf{x}^*(\omega)$, $H_E(\mathbf{x}^*)$. Also compute the training loss, $L(\mathbf{x}^*(\omega), \mathbf{t})$, and its gradient with respect to $\mathbf{x}^*$.

3. Compute the gradient of the $L(\cdot)$ using (13.28). As described above, performing the computations in the correct order can lead to significant gains in computational efficiency.

13.6.2 Related Work

This approach is most closely related to the variational mode learning approach proposed in [470]. This method works by treating a series of variational optimization steps as a continuous function and differentiating the result with respect to the model parameters. The key advantage of this approach over variational mode learning is that the result of the variational optimization must be recomputed every time the gradient of the loss function is recomputed. In [470] the variational optimization often required twenty–thirty steps. This translates into twenty to thirty calls to the matrix solver each time a gradient must be recomputed. On the other hand, our method requires only one call to the matrix solver to compute a gradient.

It is also possible to use an optimization method that avoids gradients altogether, as in [310]. However, experiments presented in [411] indicate that the method described here outperforms these other approaches on the denoising problem.

13.6.3 Evaluation

This learning approach was evaluated on the denoising problem using the Berkeley Segmentation Database, as described in section 13.5.4. In this comparison each approach was used to train a Field of Experts model for denoising. The form of all of the models was kept the same, and only the parameters, as selected by the different training approaches, changed. As shown in table 13.2, the model trained with this approach, which is referred to as the "implicit differentiation" approach in the table, outperformed the models trained using other methods.

Table 13.2
Comparison of the results of the various methods used to learn the parameters of the Field of Experts denoising model

Training System	Average PSNR
Approximate ML [284, 418]	29.56
SPSA [311]	29.87
Field of Experts	30.55
Implicit differentiation	30.58

The test images were all corrupted with white Gaussian noise of standard deviation $\sigma = 15$.

13.7   Conclusion

This chapter has focused largely on loss-based approaches for learning parameters in MRF and CRF models. The continuous nature of the energy functions makes it possible to rely on differentiation techniques to implement loss-based learning techniques.

At an intuitive level these loss-based learning techniques can be thought of as replacing the integration in maximum likelihood methods with an optimization, leading to efficient learning techniques that are straightforward to implement.

Acknowledgments

The help of Edward H. Adelson, William T. Freeman, Ce Liu, and Kegan G. G. Samuel, who co-authored papers described in this chapter, is greatly appreciated. This research was funded by grants from the National Geo-Spatial Intelligence Agency, through the NURI program, and a grant from Shell Research.

14 Message Passing with Continuous Latent Variables

Michael Isard

The bulk of the methods in this book are concerned with performing inference in Markov random fields in which the latent variables are modeled using discrete-valued quantities. For many computer vision tasks, including stereo reconstruction, motion estimation, image reconstruction, and jointed-object localization, the underlying latent variables are continuous-valued.

In many cases laid out in other chapters, it makes sense to convert the continuous-valued problem into a discrete-valued one in order to make use of existing algorithms for discrete inference. This conversion is typically achieved by restricting the latent variable to a compact subset of $\mathcal{R}^N$ and then discretizing that subset, in other words, dividing it into partitions of equal volume and assigning a discrete value to each partition. This uniform discretization process becomes impractical if a very fine discretization is needed or if the latent variable is in a high-dimensional space, because discrete inference methods require both time and space that are at best linear in the number of discrete states.

Because of the computational cost of fine-scale discretization, conventional discrete-valued MRF techniques are not typically used for tasks such as color superresolution reconstruction in which the hidden pixel values occupy the full three-dimensional color space, or estimation problems where, for example, the task is to jointly infer both the stereo disparity field and the surface pixel intensities or colors of an object, or to jointly infer stereo and motion fields in a multicamera video sequence. Equally, traditional discrete inference methods are not directly applied to complex three-dimensional jointed models—for example, to perform human body tracking—since the state-spaces of the joint angles to be inferred are too large to permit uniform discretization.

This chapter describes two techniques that can be used to perform inference on continuous-valued latent variables when straightforward uniform discretization is impractical. Both use algorithms that are closely related to belief propagation (BP). The first employs a nonuniform discretization, so that regions of the latent space that have low posterior probability are represented more coarsely (using fewer discrete labels) than high-probability regions. The nonuniform discretization is updated as the algorithm progresses, and the algorithm is known as continuously adaptive discretization for message passing

(CAD-MP) [210]. The second technique performs inference directly in the continuous state-space and approximates the resulting messages and beliefs using nonparametric sample sets, and hence is called nonparametric belief propagation [208, 453].

The techniques described in this chapter can be used for computer vision tasks that require high-dimensional MRFs or joined models described above, as suggested by the accompanying tutorial examples.

14.1 Continuously Adaptive Discretization

The CAD-MP algorithm is most simply stated using the factor graph notation for a graphical model [276]. Message passing is a class of algorithms for approximating these distributions, in which messages are iteratively updated between factors and variables. For example, BP is a message-passing algorithm that can be used when the latent variables are all discrete-valued. Unfortunately, exact inference is possible only when the distribution to be inferred can be represented by a tree and the model is either linear Gaussian or fully discrete [104, 114].

In order to perform inference over more general continuous distributions, it is necessary to use approximate inference. In this case, when a given message is to be updated, all other messages in the graph are fixed and treated as though they were exact. The algorithm proceeds by picking, from a family of approximate functions, the message that minimizes a divergence from the local "exact" message.

A general recipe for producing message-passing algorithms, summarized by Minka [342], is as follows: (1) pick a family of approximating distributions; (2) pick a divergence measure to minimize; and (3) construct an optimization algorithm to perform this minimization within the approximating family.

A suitable choice for step (1) is to adopt the family of piecewise-constant probability densities with a bounded number of piecewise-constant regions. This family has also been used successfully in tree-structured inference problems [275]. For step (2) the "inclusive" KL-divergence [342] may be used—this is a standard choice that leads to the well-known belief propagation message update equations in the discrete case. Step (3) can be performed using a greedy optimization called "informed splitting" that is explained in section 14.2.

There are at least two useful interpretations of CAD-MP. In one interpretation, instead of choosing functional approximations from the family of exponential distributions, as is common, distributions are modeled using a family of piecewise-constant functions (or discretizations) described in section 14.2. Looked at this way, the method starts from a continuous model and approximates the underlying continuous beliefs as piecewise-constant. A second interpretation starts with a standard underlying model that is a *uniform* discretization of a continuous state-space, and exploits the structure of the model to summarize (or compress) the messages and beliefs so that only information about the most salient parts of the state-space is stored.

14.2 Discretizing a Factor Graph

Let us consider what it means to *discretize* an inference problem represented by a factor graph with factors f_i and continuous variables x_α taking values in some subset of $\mathbb{R}^N$. A nonuniform discretization of the factor graph can be constructed by partitioning the state-space of each variable x_α into K regions H_α^k for $k = 1, \dots, K$. This discretization induces a discrete approximation f_i' of the factors, which are now regarded as functions of discrete variables x_α' taking integer values in the set $\{1, 2, \dots, K\}$:

$$f_i'(k, l, \dots) = \int_{x_\alpha \in H_\alpha^k, x_\beta \in H_\beta^l, \dots} f_i(x_\alpha, x_\beta, \dots), \tag{14.1}$$

for $k, l, \dots = 1, \dots, K$. A slight variant of BP [540] can then be used to infer the marginals on x_α' according to the update equations for messages m and beliefs b:

$$m_{\alpha,i}(k) = \prod_{f_j' \sim x_\alpha' \backslash f_i'} m_{j,\alpha}(k) \tag{14.2}$$

$$m_{i,\alpha}(k) = \frac{1}{|H_\alpha^k|} \sum_{\mathbf{x}' | x_\alpha' = k} f_i'(\mathbf{x}') \prod_{x_\beta' \sim f_i' \backslash x_\alpha'} m_{\beta,i}(x_\beta') \tag{14.3}$$

$$b_\alpha(k) = |H_\alpha^k| \prod_{f_j' \sim x_\alpha'} m_{i,\alpha}(k), \tag{14.4}$$

where $a \sim b \backslash c$ means "all neighbors a of b except c," $\mathbf{x}'$ is an assignment of values to all variables, and $|H_\alpha^k| = \int_{H_\alpha^k} 1$. Thus, given a factor graph of continuous variables and a particular choice of discretization $\{H_\alpha^k\}$, one gets a piecewise-constant approximation to the marginals by first discretizing the variables according to (14.1), then using BP according to (14.2)–(14.4). The error in the approximation to the true marginals arises from (14.3) when $f_i'(\mathbf{x})$ is not constant over $\mathbf{x}$ in the given partition.

The above procedure assumes a known discretization, that is, assumes that a good choice of H_α^k is known for each factor x_α. In practice it is best to adapt this discretization dynamically, and some criterion is needed to select among all the different possible discretizations of the continuous probability distribution $p(x)$ over some subset U of Euclidean space. A *discretization* of p consists in partitioning U into K disjoint subsets $V_1, \dots, V_K$ and assigning a weight w_k to each V_k, with $\sum_k w_k = 1$. The corresponding discretized probability distribution $q(x)$ assigns density $w_k/|V_k|$ to V_k. A good choice of discretization is one for which the KL divergence $\mathrm{KL}(p||q)$ is as small as possible. The optimal choice of the w_k for any fixed partitioning $V_1, \dots, V_K$ is to take $w_k = \int_{x \in V_k} p(x)$ [275]; we call these the *natural* weights for $p(x)$, given the V_k. There is a simple relationship between the quality of a *naturally weighted* discretization and its entropy $\mathbb{H}(\cdot)$:

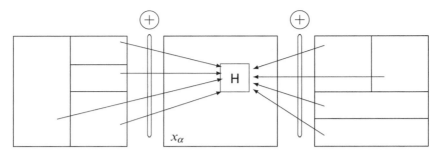

Figure 14.1
Informed belief at a hypercube. Given a discretization of the neighbors of a node x_α in the factor graph, the
"informed belief" $\hat{b}(H)$ can be computed for any hypercube subset H of x_α. The "informed" messages $m_{i,\alpha}(H)$
entering H are sums of terms computed by integrating the model and neighboring messages over the source and
destination hypercubes, as set out in (14.1)–(14.3). See section 14.2 for details.

Theorem 14.1   *Among any collection of naturally weighted discretizations of $p(x)$, the
minimum KL-divergence to $p(x)$ is achieved by a discretization of minimal entropy.*

Proof   For a naturally weighted discretization q, $\mathrm{KL}(p\|q) = -\sum_{k=1}^{K} w_k \log \frac{w_k}{|V_k|} + \int_U p \log p = \mathbb{H}(q) - \mathbb{H}(p)$. $\mathbb{H}(p)$ is constant, so $\mathrm{KL}(p\|q)$ is minimized by minimizing
$\mathbb{H}(q)$.   ∎

Suppose a message-passing algorithm has access to a discretization $\{H_\alpha^k\}$ and has
computed messages and beliefs for every node, using (14.2)–(14.4). For any arbitrary hypercube H at x_α (not necessarily in its current discretization) one can define the *informed belief*,
denoted $\hat{b}(H)$, to be the belief that H would receive if all other nodes and their incoming
messages were left unaltered. To compute the informed belief, one first computes new discrete factor function values involving H, using integrals such as (14.1). These values can be
fed into (14.2) and (14.3) to produce "informed" messages $m_{i,\alpha}(H)$ arriving at x_α from each
neighbor f_i. Finally, the informed messages can be fed into (14.4) to obtain the informed
belief $\hat{b}(H)$. This is shown schematically for the two-dimensional case in figure 14.1.

14.3   The Discretization Algorithm

The core of the CAD-MP algorithm is the procedure for passing a message to a variable x_α.
Given fixed approximations at every other node, any discretization of α induces an approximate belief distribution $q_\alpha(x_\alpha)$. The task of the algorithm is to select the best discretization
and, as theorem 14.1 shows, a good strategy for this selection is to look for a naturally
weighted discretization that minimizes the entropy of q_α. The algorithm to achieve this is
called informed splitting and is described next.

CAD-MP employs an axis-aligned binary split kd-tree [29] to represent the discrete partitioning of a D-dimensional continuous state-space at each variable (the same representation

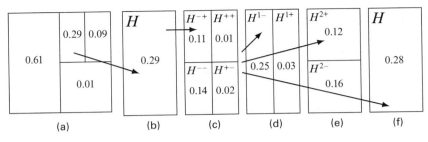

Figure 14.2
Expanding a hypercube in two dimensions. Hypercube H (b), a subset of the full state-space (a), is first expanded into the subcubes $\{H^{--}, H^{+-}, H^{-+}, H^{++}\}$ (c) by splitting along each possible dimension. These subcubes are then recombined to form two possible split candidates $\{H^{1-}, H^{1+}\}$ (d) and $\{H^{2-}, H^{2+}\}$ (e). Informed belief values are computed for the recombined hypercubes, including a new estimate for $\hat{b}(H)$ (f), by summing the beliefs in the finer-scale partitioning. The new estimates are more accurate since the error introduced by the discretization decreases as the partitions become smaller.

was used in [275], where it was called a binary split partitioning). For the purposes of CAD-MP, a kd-tree is a binary tree in which each vertex is assigned a subset—actually a hypercube—of the state-space. The root is assigned the whole space, and any internal vertex splits its hypercube equally between its two children, using an axis-aligned plane. The subsets assigned to all leaves partition the state-space into hypercubes.

The kd-tree is built greedily by recursively splitting leaf vertices: at each step the algorithm must choose a hypercube H_α^k in the current partitioning to split, and a dimension d to split it. According to theorem 14.1, the correct choice of k and d will minimize the entropy of the resulting discretization—provided that this discretization has "natural" weights. In practice, the natural weights are estimated using informed beliefs; the algorithm nevertheless proceeds as though they were exact and chooses the k- and d-values leading to lowest entropy. A subroutine of the algorithm involves "expanding" a hypercube into subcubes, as illustrated in the two-dimensional case in figure 14.2. The expansion procedure generalizes to D dimensions by first expanding to 2^D subcubes and then recombining these into $2D$ candidate splits. Note that for all $d \in \{1, \ldots, D\}$

$$\hat{b}(H) \equiv \hat{b}(H^{d-}) + \hat{b}(H^{d-}). \tag{14.5}$$

Once each hypercube in the current partitioning has been expanded, and thus values for $\hat{b}(H_\alpha^k)$, $\hat{b}(H_\alpha^{k,d-})$, and $\hat{b}(H_\alpha^{k,d+})$ have been computed for all k and d, CAD-MP chooses k and d to minimize the split entropy

$$\gamma_\alpha(k, d) = -\sum_{i \neq k} \hat{b}(H_\alpha^i) \log \frac{\hat{b}(H_\alpha^i)}{|H_\alpha^i|} \tag{14.6}$$

$$- \hat{b}(H_\alpha^{k,d-}) \log \frac{\hat{b}(H_\alpha^{k,d-})}{|H_\alpha^{k,d-}|} - \hat{b}(H_\alpha^{k,d+}) \log \frac{\hat{b}(H_\alpha^{k,d+})}{|H_\alpha^{k,d+}|}.$$

This minimization can be performed without normalizing the $\hat{b}(\cdot)$, as a consequence of (14.5).

The full CAD-MP algorithm using informed splitting can now be described. A variable of the factor graph is repartitioned by producing a new kd-tree whose leaves are the hypercubes in the new partitioning:

1. Initialize the root vertex of the kd-tree with its associated hypercube being the whole state-space, with belief 1. Add this root to a leaf set $\mathcal{L}$ and expand it as shown in figure 14.2.

2. While the number of leaves $|\mathcal{L}|$ is less than the desired number of partitions in the discretized model:

a. Pick the leaf H and split dimension d that minimize the split entropy (14.6).

b. Create two new vertices H^- and H^+ by splitting H along dimension d, and expand these new vertices.

c. Remove H from $\mathcal{L}$, and add H^- and H^+ to $\mathcal{L}$.

All variables in the factor graph are initialized with the trivial discretization (a single partition). Variables can be visited according to any standard message-passing schedule, where a visit consists of repartitioning according to the above algorithm. A simple example of the evolution of the belief at one variable is shown in figure 14.3.

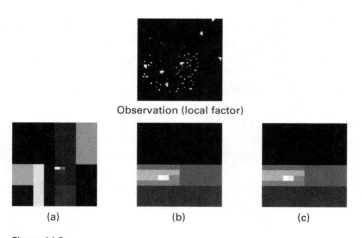

Observation (local factor)

(a)   (b)   (c)

Figure 14.3
Evolution of discretization at a single variable. The top image is the local (single-variable) factor at the first node in a simple chain MRF whose nodes have 2D state-spaces. The bottom three images, from left to right, show the evolution of the informed belief. Initially (a) the partitioning is informed simply by the local factor, but after messages have been passed once along the chain and back (b), the posterior marginal estimate has shifted and the discretization has adapted accordingly. Subsequent iterations over the chain (c) do not substantially alter the estimated marginal belief. For this toy example only sixteen partitions are used, and the normalized log of the belief is displayed to make the structure of the distribution more apparent.

If the variable being repartitioned has T neighbors and is partitioned into K hyper-cubes, then a straightforward implementation of this algorithm requires the computation of $2K \times 2^D \times KT$ message components. Roughly speaking, then, informed splitting pays a factor of 2^{D+1} over BP that must compute K^2T message components. But CAD-MP trades this for an exponential factor in K since it can home in on interesting areas of the state-space using binary search; Thus, if BP requires K partitions for a given level of accuracy, CAD-MP (empirically) achieves the same accuracy with only $O(\log K)$ partitions. In special cases, including some low-level vision applications [140], classical BP can be performed in $O(KT)$ time and space; however, this is still prohibitive for large K.

14.4 CAD-MP Example

In order to investigate the performance of an approximate algorithm, it would be ideal to compare its output with the marginal belief distributions that would be computed by exact inference. Unfortunately, no exact inference algorithm is known for the continuous-valued models of interest in this domain, so instead one can construct a fine-scale uniform discretization $\mathcal{D}_f$ of a model and input data, and compute the marginal belief distributions $p(x_\alpha; \mathcal{D}_f)$ at each variable x_α, using the standard forward-backward BP algorithm. Given a candidate approximation $\mathcal{C}$, one can then compare the marginals $p(x_\alpha; \mathcal{C})$ under that approximation with the fine-scale discretization by computing the KL-divergence $KL(p(x_\alpha; \mathcal{D}_f)||p(x_\alpha; \mathcal{C}))$ at each variable. The comparison can be summarized by computing the mean of this divergence across all variables in the graph, which is denoted $\mu(\mathcal{C})$ below. Though a "fine enough" uniform discretization will tend to the true marginals, it is not clear a priori how fine that is, but one can construct a sequence of coarser uniform discretizations $\mathcal{D}_c^i$ of the same model and data, and compute $\mu(\mathcal{D}_c^i)$ for each of them. If $\mu(\mathcal{D}_c^i)$ is converging rapidly enough to zero, as is the case in the examples below, it is reasonable to assume the fine-scale discretization is a good approximation to the exact marginals.

The example illustrated here uses ten randomly generated input sequences of a one-dimensional target moving through structured clutter of similar-looking distractors. One of the sequences is shown in figure 14.4a, where time goes from bottom to top. The measurement at a time step consists of 240 pixels (piecewise-constant regions of uniform width) generated by simulating a small one-dimensional target in clutter, with additive Gaussian shot noise. There are stationary clutter distractors, as well as periodic "forkings" where a moving clutter distractor emerges from the target and proceeds for a few time steps before disappearing. The factors tying the observations to the hidden states favor pixels with intensities close to that of the target or distractors: the model for generating the data and for inference is that the target intensity is Gaussian distributed with a mean of 128 and a standard deviation of 15. The rendered model is smoothed with Gaussian blur, and shot noise is added to make the inference problem more realistic. The factors tying observations at adjacent time steps imply a simple "constant position" model whereby a target's

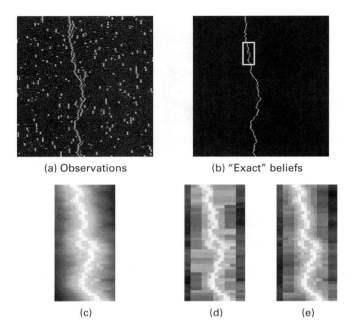

(a) Observations   (b) "Exact" beliefs

(c)   (d)   (e)

Figure 14.4
One of the one-dimensional test sequences. The region of the white rectangle in (b) is expanded in (c)–(e), with beliefs now plotted on log-intensity scale to expand their dynamic range. CAD-MP, using only sixteen partitions per time step, (d) already produces a faithful approximation to the exact belief (c), and increasing to 128 partitions (e) fills in more details.

location is Gaussian distributed around its previous location with a standard deviation of two pixel widths. This simple model could easily be extended to more realistic models used, for instance, in stereo reconstruction and motion estimation.

Each sequence contains 256 time steps, and the "exact" marginals (figure 14.4b) are computed using standard discrete BP with 15,360 states per time step. The modes of the marginals generated by all the experiments are similar to those in figure 14.4b.

Figure 14.5 shows the divergences $\mu(\cdot)$ for uniform discretization at various degrees of coarseness, as well as adaptive discretization using CAD-MP with varying numbers of partitions. Each data point shows the mean divergence $\mu(\cdot)$ for one of the ten simulated one-dimensional data sets. As the number of adaptive partitions increases, the variance of $\mu(\cdot)$ across trials increases, but the divergence stays small. Higher divergences in CAD-MP trials correspond to a misestimation of the tails of the marginal belief at a few time steps. The straight line on the log/log plot for the uniform discretizations provides confidence that the fine-scale discretization is a close approximation to the exact beliefs. The adaptive discretization provides a very faithful approximation to this "exact" distribution with vastly fewer partitions.

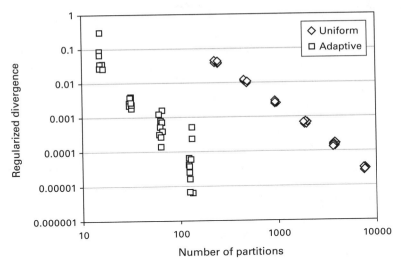

Figure 14.5
Adaptive discretization achieves the same accuracy as uniform discretization and uses many fewer partitions.

14.5 Work Related to CAD-MP

The work most closely related to CAD-MP is the 1997 algorithm of Kozlov and Koller [275] (KK97), which is described in a junction tree setting and computes the marginal posterior of just the root node. CAD-MP computes beliefs everywhere in the graph and so can be used for more general MRFs. Coarse-to-fine techniques can speed up the convergence of loopy BP [140], but this does not address the discrete state-space explosion. One can also prune the state-space based on local evidence [102, 103], which works best when the data function does not have high entropy.

Another interesting approach is to retain the uniform discretization but enforce sparsity on messages to reduce computational cost. This was done in both [362] (in which messages are approximated using a mixture of delta functions, which in practice results in retaining the K largest message components) and [292] (which uses an additional uniform distribution in the approximating distribution to ensure nonzero weights for all states in the discretization).

Expectation propagation [341] is a highly effective algorithm for inference in continuous-valued networks but is not valid for densities that are multimodal mixtures.

14.6 Belief Propagation in Particle Networks

The adaptive discretization approach above makes heavy use of integrals such as (14.1). For some models these integrals are hard to compute or approximate. The remainder of this chapter describes another method for performing inference over continuous models that requires only the evaluation of data functions at discrete locations rather than integrating over volumes of state-space.

The standard discrete BP equations from chapter 1 can be converted to continuous-valued form by substituting continuous random variables for the discrete variables and integrals for summations:

$$p(\{\mathbf{x}_j\}) = \frac{1}{Z} \left(\prod_{(i,j)\in\mathcal{P}} \psi_{ij}(\mathbf{x}_j, \mathbf{x}_i) \right) \left(\prod_i \phi_i(\mathbf{x}_i) \right). \tag{14.7}$$

In the continuous analogues of the message update and belief equations, $m_{ij}(\cdot)$ and $b_i(\cdot)$ are now assumed to be normalizable functions rather than L-element arrays. When additionally every $\psi_{ij}(\mathbf{x}_j, \mathbf{x}_i)$ has the form of a cpd $\psi_{ij}(\mathbf{x}_j, \mathbf{x}_i) \equiv p_{ij}(\mathbf{x}_j|\mathbf{x}_i)$, then

$$m_{ij}(\mathbf{x}_j) \leftarrow \int_{\mathbb{R}^D} \psi_{ij}(\mathbf{x}_j, \mathbf{x}_i)\phi_i(\mathbf{x}_i) \prod_{k\in\mathcal{P}(i)\backslash j} m_{ki}(\mathbf{x}_i)\mathrm{d}\mathbf{x}_i. \tag{14.8}$$

If the structure of the network is such that the marginal distribution at each node is Gaussian, this integral can be performed exactly [341]. As noted above, if any of the m_{ij} or ϕ_i violate this conditional linear Gaussian structure, exact inference is intractable and the m_{ij} must be replaced by an approximation.

A suitable approach for many computer vision models is to replace the integral in (14.8) with a Monte Carlo approximation. The general algorithmic framework for performing this approximation is as follows.

The function

$$p_{ij}^M(\mathbf{x}_i) \equiv \frac{1}{Z_{ij}}\phi_i(\mathbf{x}_i) \prod_{k\in\mathcal{P}(i)\backslash j} m_{ki}(\mathbf{x}_i) \tag{14.9}$$

is denoted the *foundation* of message $m_{ij}(\cdot)$ where Z_{ij} is a constant of proportionality that turns $p_{ij}^M(\cdot)$ into a probability density. A Monte Carlo integration of (14.8) yields $\tilde{m}_{ij}$, an approximation of m_{ij}, by drawing N samples from the foundation $\mathbf{s}_{ij}^n \sim p_{ij}^M(\cdot)$ and setting

$$\tilde{m}_{ij}(\mathbf{x}_j) = \frac{1}{N}\sum_{n=1}^N \psi_{ij}(\mathbf{x}_j, \mathbf{s}_{ij}^n). \tag{14.10}$$

In general it is possible to pick an *importance function* $g_{ij}(\mathbf{x}_i)$ from which to generate samples $\mathbf{s}_{ij}^n \sim g_{ij}(\cdot)$ with (unnormalized) importance weights $\pi_{ij}^n \propto p_{ij}^M(\mathbf{s}_{ij}^n)/g(\mathbf{s}_{ij}^n)$, in which case the $\tilde{m}_{ij}$ is a weighted mixture

$$\tilde{m}_{ij}(\mathbf{x}_j) = \frac{1}{\sum_{k=1}^N \pi_{ij}^k}\sum_{n=1}^N \pi_{ij}^n \psi_{ij}(\mathbf{x}_j, \mathbf{s}_{ij}^n). \tag{14.11}$$

When the marginal distribution over $\mathbf{x}_i$ is required, samples $\mathbf{s}_i^n$ can be drawn from the estimated belief distribution

$$\tilde{b}_i(\mathbf{x}_i) = \frac{1}{Z_i}\phi_i(\mathbf{x}_i) \prod_{j\in\mathcal{P}(i)} \tilde{m}_{ji}(\mathbf{x}_i) \tag{14.12}$$

either directly or by importance sampling as above; these samples can be used to compute expectations over the belief, for example, its mean and higher moments. By fixing a set of samples $\mathbf{s}_i^n$ at each node, a Gibbs sampler can be used to generate samples from the joint distribution over the graph.

14.7 Choice of Importance Function

Some limitations of the approach in section 14.6 can be seen by considering a simple example. Suppose that it is necessary to perform inference on a three-node network $(\mathbf{X}_1, \mathbf{X}_2, \mathbf{X}_3)$ that has the chain structure

$$\mathcal{P}(1) = (2), \quad \mathcal{P}(2) = (1, 3), \quad \mathcal{P}(3) = (2).$$

Two distinct inference chains are being sampled—$\mathbf{X}_1 \to \mathbf{X}_2 \to \mathbf{X}_3$ and $\mathbf{X}_3 \to \mathbf{X}_2 \to \mathbf{X}_1$— but the information is not combined in any of the messages; there is no mixing between the forward and backward directions. This situation also arises whenever the graph has a layered structure with a set of low-level nodes passing information up to higher levels and high-level information propagating back down. Of course the belief does correctly incorporate information from both directions, but the efficiency of a Monte Carlo algorithm is strongly dependent on the sample positions and, where possible, it is desirable to use all the available information when choosing these positions.

One solution is to use importance sampling for some of the particles [252], and a natural choice of function is the current belief estimate $g(\mathbf{x}_i) = \tilde{b}_i(\mathbf{x}_i)$ where the importance weights are $\pi_{ij}^n = 1/\tilde{m}_{ji}(\mathbf{s}_{ij}^n)$. In the context of the simple chain given above, this algorithm amounts to *smoothing* the distribution.

14.8 Nonparametric Belief Propagation

A property of many computer vision models is that the potentials $\psi_{ij}(\mathbf{x}_j, \mathbf{x}_i)$ can be written as a mixture of Gaussians and that the likelihoods $\phi_i(\mathbf{x}_i)$ are complex and difficult to sample from, but can be evaluated up to a multiplicative constant. The following algorithm is specialized to perform belief propagation for this type of model. A more general algorithm, for which these Gaussian restrictions do not apply, can be found in [453].

For notational simplicity the algorithm is described for the case in which each potential is a single Gaussian plus a Gaussian outlier process, though the extension to mixtures of

Gaussians is straightforward. Setting λ^o to be the fixed outlier probability and μ_{ij} and Λ_{ij} to be the parameters of the outlier process,

$$\psi_{ij}(\mathbf{x}_j, \mathbf{x}_i) = (1 - \lambda^o)\mathcal{N}(\mathbf{x}_j; f_{ij}(\mathbf{x}_i), G_{ij}(\mathbf{x}_i)) + \lambda^o\mathcal{N}(\mathbf{x}_j; \mu_{ij}, \Lambda_{ij}) \tag{14.13}$$

where $f_{ij}(\cdot)$ and $G_{ij}(\cdot)$ are deterministic functions, potentially nonlinear, and respectively computing the mean and the covariance matrix of the conditional Gaussian distribution. Each message approximation $\tilde{m}_{ij}$ is now a mixture of N Gaussians:

$$\tilde{m}_{ij}(\mathbf{x}_j) = \frac{(1 - \lambda^o)}{\sum_{k=1}^{N'} \pi_{ij}^k} \sum_{n=1}^{N'} \pi_{ij}^n \mathcal{N}(\mathbf{x}_j; f_{ij}(\mathbf{s}_{ij}^n), G_{ij}(\mathbf{s}_{ij}^n)) + \lambda^o\mathcal{N}(\mathbf{x}_j; \mu_{ij}, \Lambda_{ij}), \tag{14.14}$$

where $N' = N - 1$ is the number of samples drawn during the Monte Carlo integration. The message is summarized by N triplets:

$$\tilde{m}_{ij} = \{(\pi_{ij}^n, \mathbf{s}_{ij}^n, \Lambda_{ij}^n) : 1 \leq n \leq N\}, \tag{14.15}$$

where π_{ij}^N, $\mathbf{s}_{ij}^N$, and Λ_{ij}^N correspond to the outlier process and are fixed throughout the algorithm. A potential that encodes a mixture of J Gaussians with K Gaussian outliers will lead to $N' = (N - K)/J$, which is practical only for fairly small values of J.

As indicated in section 14.7, it makes sense to importance-sample some fraction of the message particles from the approximate belief distribution. In fact, because ϕ_i is assumed to be hard to sample from but easy to evaluate, importance-sampling is used for all the particles but with two distinct importance distributions and corresponding weight functions. A fraction $(1 - \nu)N'$ of the particles, by slight abuse of terminology, are denoted direct samples:

$$\mathbf{s}_{ij}^n \sim \frac{1}{\tilde{Z}_{ij}} \prod_{k \in \mathcal{P}(i) \setminus j} \tilde{m}_{ki}(\mathbf{x}_i), \quad \pi_{ij}^n = \phi_i(\mathbf{s}_{ij}^n) \tag{14.16}$$

and the remaining $\nu N'$ particles are referred to as importance samples:

$$\mathbf{s}_{ij}^n \sim \frac{1}{\tilde{Z}_{ij}} \prod_{k \in \mathcal{P}(i)} \tilde{m}_{ki}(\mathbf{x}_i), \quad \pi_{ij}^n = \phi_i(\mathbf{s}_{ij}^n)/\tilde{m}_{ji}(\mathbf{s}_{ij}^n). \tag{14.17}$$

If the network is a forward chain where $\mathcal{P}(i) \equiv i - 1$ and $\nu = 0$, the algorithm reduces exactly to a standard form of particle filtering [209].

Both (14.16) and (14.17) require sampling from a foundation F that is the product of D mixtures indexed by a label vector $L = (l_1, \ldots, l_D)$:

$$F(\cdot) = \frac{1}{Z} \sum_L \eta_L \mathcal{N}(\cdot; \mu_L, \Lambda_L) \tag{14.18}$$

where from the standard Gaussian product formula

$$\Lambda_L^{-1} = \sum_{d=1}^{D} (\Lambda_d^{l_d})^{-1} \qquad \Lambda_L^{-1} \mu_L = \sum_{d=1}^{D} (\Lambda_d^{l_d})^{-1} \mu_d^{l_d} \tag{14.19}$$

$$\eta_L = \frac{\prod_{d=1}^{D} \pi_d^{l_d} \mathcal{N}(\cdot; \mu_d^{l_d}, \Lambda_d^{l_d})}{\mathcal{N}(\cdot; \mu_L, \Lambda_L)}. \tag{14.20}$$

This product F is a Gaussian mixture with N^D componenents, so direct sampling is effectively infeasible for $D > 3$ for reasonable N.

One solution, proposed by Sudderth et al. [453], is to use a Gibbs sampler that performs approximate sampling from the message product F in $O(KDN)$ operations per sample, where K is the number of iterations of the sampler. A sample is drawn from F by first choosing a label vector L using a Gibbs sampler, and then generating a random sample from the Gaussian F_L. The Gibbs sampler works by sampling l_d with all the other labels in L held fixed for each d in turn. With all of L but l_d fixed, the marginal product-component weights are given by

$$\eta_d^n \propto \frac{\pi_d^n \mathcal{N}(\cdot; \mu_d^n; \Lambda_d^n)}{\mathcal{N}(\cdot; \mu_{L^n}, \Lambda_{L^n})} \tag{14.21}$$

where $L^n = (l_1, \ldots, l_{d-1}, n, l_{d+1}, \ldots, l_D)$. This sampling algorithm is shown in figure 14.6.

The message update algorithm for continuous belief propagation using particle networks is given in figure 14.7.

When N belief samples $\mathbf{s}_i^n$ have been drawn for each node in $\mathcal{X}$, they can be used to sample from the joint distribution over the graph. This can be done by Gibbs sampling from the discrete probability distribution over labels $L' = (l_1, \ldots, l_M)$ where L' indexes a sample $\mathbf{s}_m^{l_m}$ at each of the M nodes. The Gibbs sampler updates in turn each component of this label vector where the marginal probability of choosing label l_d when the other labels are fixed is

$$P(l_d = n) = \phi_d(\mathbf{s}_i^n) \prod_{j \in \mathcal{P}(i)} \psi_{ji}(\mathbf{s}_i^n, \mathbf{s}_j^{l_j}). \tag{14.22}$$

14.9 Nonparametric BP Example

Nonparametric BP is shown here applied to the problem of locating a jointed object in a cluttered scene. This is a greatly simplified version of the task of tracking three-dimensional articulated objects that has been addressed using NBP in the cases of hands [454] and of people [439]. The model consists of nine nodes: a central circle with four jointed arms, each made up of two rectangular links. The circle node $\mathbf{x}_1 = (x_0, y_0, r_0)$ encodes a position and

To generate a sample from the product of D mixtures m_d:

1. Initialize L. For $1 \leq d \leq N+1$:

    a. Choose l_d uniformly from $\{1, \ldots, N+1\}$.

2. Iterate:

    a. Choose d uniformly from $\{1, \ldots, D\}$.

    b. For $1 \leq n \leq N+1$:

        i. Set $L^n = (l_1, \ldots, l_{d-1}, n, l_{d+1}, \ldots, l_D)$.

        ii. Compute Λ_{L^n} and μ_{L^n} from (14.19).

        iii. Compute η_d^n from (14.21).

3. Sample a value $\bar{n}$ where $P(l^d = \bar{n}) \propto \eta_d^{\bar{n}}$.

4. Update $L = (l_1, \ldots, l_{d-1}, \bar{n}, l_{d+1}, \ldots, l_D)$.

Figure 14.6
Gibbs sampling of a product of mixtures.

radius. Each arm node $\mathbf{x}_i = (x_i, y_i, \alpha_i, w_i, h_i)$, $2 \leq i \leq 9$ encodes a position, angle, width, and height and prefers one of the four compass directions (to break symmetry). The arms pivot around their inner joints, so the potential to go from an inner arm, $2 \leq i \leq 5$, to the outer arms, $j = i + 4$, is given by

$$x_j = x_i + h_i \cos(\alpha_i) + \mathcal{N}(\cdot; 0, \sigma_p^2)$$

$$y_j = y_i + h_i \sin(\alpha_i) + \mathcal{N}(\cdot; 0, \sigma_p^2)$$

$$\alpha_j = \alpha_i + \mathcal{N}(\cdot; 0, \sigma_\alpha^2)$$

$$w_j = w_i + \mathcal{N}(\cdot; 0, \sigma_s^2) \quad h_j = h_i + \mathcal{N}(\cdot; 0, \sigma_s^2),$$

and the $\psi_{1i}(\mathbf{x}_i, \mathbf{x}_1)$ from the circle outward are similar. Going from the outer arm to the inner arm, the potential is not Gaussian, but we approximate it with the following:

$$x_i = x_j - h_j \cos(\alpha_i) + \mathcal{N}(\cdot; 0, h_j \sigma_s | \sin((i-2)\pi/2) | \sigma_p^2)$$

$$y_i = y_j - h_j \sin(\alpha_i) + \mathcal{N}(\cdot; 0, h_j \sigma_s | \cos((i-2)\pi/2) | \sigma_p^2)$$

$$\alpha_i = \alpha_j + \mathcal{N}(\cdot; 0, \sigma_\alpha^2)$$

$$w_i = w_j + \mathcal{N}(\cdot; 0, \sigma_s^2) \quad h_i = h_j + \mathcal{N}(\cdot; 0, \sigma_s^2).$$

1. Draw samples from the incoming message product.

   a. For $1 \le n \le (1-\nu)(N-1)$:

      i. Draw $\tilde{\mathbf{s}}_{ij}^n \sim \prod_{k \in \mathcal{P}(i) \setminus j} \tilde{m}_{ki}(\cdot)$.

      ii. Set $\tilde{\pi}_{ij}^n = 1/(N-1)$.

   b. For $(1-\nu)(N-1) < n \le N-1$:

      i. Draw $\tilde{\mathbf{s}}_{ij}^n \sim \prod_{k \in \mathcal{P}(i)} \tilde{m}_{ki}(\cdot)$.

      ii. Set $\gamma_{ij}^n = 1/\tilde{m}_{ji}(\tilde{\mathbf{s}}_{ij}^n)$.

   c. For $(1-\nu)(N-1) < n \le N-1$:

      i. Set $\tilde{\pi}_{ij}^n = \nu \gamma_{ij}^n / \sum_{k=1+(1-\nu)(N-1)}^{N-1} \gamma_{ij}^k$.

2. Apply importance correction from likelihood. For $1 \le n \le N-1$:

   a. Set $\tilde{\pi}_{ij}^n = \tilde{\pi}_{ij}^n \phi_i(\tilde{\mathbf{s}}_{ij}^n)$.

3. Store normalized weights and mixture components. For $1 \le n \le N-1$:

   a. Set $\pi_{ij}^n = (1 - \pi_{ij}^N)\tilde{\pi}_{ij}^n / \sum_{k=1}^{N-1} \tilde{\pi}_{ij}^k$.

   b. Set $\mathbf{s}_{ij}^n = f_{ij}(\tilde{\mathbf{s}}_{ij}^n)$.

   c. Set $\Lambda_{ij}^n = G_{ij}(\tilde{\mathbf{s}}_{ij}^n)$.

Figure 14.7
The message update algorithm.

The $\psi_{i1}(\mathbf{x}_1, \mathbf{x}_i)$ are straightforward:

$$x_1 = x_i + \mathcal{N}(\cdot; 0, \sigma_p^2) \quad y_1 = y_i + \mathcal{N}(\cdot; 0, \sigma_p^2)$$

$$r_1 = 0.5(w_i/\delta_w + h_i/\delta_h) + \mathcal{N}(\cdot; 0, \sigma_s^2).$$

The object has been placed in image clutter in figure 14.8. The clutter is made up of 12 circles and 100 rectangles placed randomly in the image. The messages are initialized with a simulated specialized feature detector: $\mathbf{x}_1$ is sampled from positions near the circles in the image, and the arms are sampled to be near the rectangles, with rectangles closer to the preferred direction of each arm sampled more frequently. Each node contains $N = 75$ particles, so the space is undersampled. After initialization the algorithm is iterated without further recourse to the feature detector information. All of the potentials include a Gaussian outlier covering the whole image, which allows samples to be generated far from the initialization particles. After two or three iterations the belief distribution has converged

Figure 14.8
A jointed object is located in clutter. Two experiments are shown: with and without a simulated occlusion. The top two images show a sample from the joint distribution for each experiment, and the lower images show the full distributions. The second experiment models an occluded object with no circle present in the image where the belief has placed it.

on the object. In this case it might be argued that it would be more straightforward simply to detect the circles and perform an exhaustive search near each. The second example of figure 14.8 demonstrates the power of the probabilistic modeling approach, since now the circle at the center of the object has not been displayed, simulating occlusion. Of course no x_1 initialization samples are generated near the "occluded" circle, but even after one iteration the belief at that node has high weight at the correct location due to the agreement of the nearby arm nodes. After a few iterations the belief has converged on the correct object position despite the lack of the central circle.

14.10 Discussion

This chapter outlines two techniques that can be used for approximate inference in MRFs when it is impractical to perform a uniform discretization of an underlying continuous state-space. Of the two approaches, CAD-BP is more similar to standard discrete message-passing algorithms, and may be applicable to state-spaces of relatively low dimension (say two–six dimensions), where it is practical to efficiently compute or approximate region integrals such as those in (14.1). NBP is closely related to particle filtering and may be suitable for problems with higher-dimensional state-spaces as long as sampling from the model's conditional probability distributions is practical, and the marginal posterior distributions are smooth enough that a sample set representation can efficiently approximate the solution to the desired accuracy.

By broadening the complexity of models over which approximate inference can be performed, both of the methods described in this chapter promise to extend the range of computer vision problems that can be effectively tackled using Markov random field approaches.

Acknowledgments

The development of the Continuously-Adaptive Discretization algorithm was joint work with John MacCormick and Kannan Achan. I would also like to thank Eric Sudderth, Alex Ihler, Bill Freeman and Alan Willsky for fruitful discussions on the topic of non-parametric belief propagation.

15   Learning Large-Margin Random Fields Using Graph Cuts

Martin Szummer, Pushmeet Kohli, and Derek Hoiem

The availability of efficient and provably optimal MAP estimation algorithms, such as graph cuts [266] and its approximate extensions [72], has inspired progress in many areas of computer vision. For example, the efficiency of graph cut-based algorithms enables interactive image and real-time video segmentation tasks [66, 401]. The optimality guarantees of these algorithms allow computing the maximum a posteriori (MAP) solution of the model distribution.

The rise of such optimal inference techniques has created the need for matching learning methods that can estimate the parameters of rich random field models. In the past, model parameters were often hand-tuned, which was feasible only for simple models. The ability to compute the minimum energy solution has revealed that simplistic energy models (e.g., with one unary term and an isotropic smoothing penalty in grid labeling problems) are insufficient to model the complex structures inherent in computer vision problems [25, 463]. Despite this knowledge, overly simplistic hand-tuned random field models continue to be common practice. We believe that this is due largely to absence of tractable machine learning techniques for large MRF and CRF problems. Currently, the most widely used learning approaches include cross validation and simple partition function approximations [283] that have not kept pace with the advances in inference methods.

This chapter discusses efficient and easy-to-implement techniques that are capable of learning dozens of parameters from millions of pixels in minutes. It describes approaches that develop learning methods that leverage new optimal inference techniques such as graph cuts. This leads to algorithms based on energy-based learning [295], the structured support vector machine (SVM-STRUCT) framework of Tsochantaridis et al. [484], and the maximum-margin network learning of Taskar et al. [14, 473].

For a given parameterized energy function, our goal is to learn the parameters so that the training data (the ground truth) has the lowest energy by the largest possible margin or, if that is not possible, that the energy of the ground truth is as close as possible to that of the minimum energy solution. We begin with arbitrary initial parameters and an empty contrastive solution set. Then, iteratively, we find the minimum energy solution for the current parameters, add it to our alternative set, and find the parameters that maximize our objective function, considering only the ground truth and the current alternative set of solutions.

When the energy is a linear function of the parameters (as is typically the case) and can be optimally minimized, we can estimate the parameters accurately in a highly efficient manner, typically requiring a few dozen iterations for problems involving dozens of unary and pairwise random field parameters. We describe several extensions of our technique, evaluating the suitability of alternative objective functions and dealing with cases for which optimal energy minimization is not possible. We validate the algorithm and its extensions on the problems of image segmentation and multiclass geometry labeling.

We present an efficient and practical algorithm to train random field models for images. The main points of this approach include the following:

1. Use of graph cuts to do maximum-margin learning of parameters *exactly* and *efficiently* for submodular MRFs and CRFs. Generalization to new images is ensured via a large-margin regularizer. Approximations such as pseudo likelihood or approximate inference are not required.

2. Learning parameters of nonsubmodular problems using alpha-expansions.

3. Investigation of loss functions for segmentation and geometry labeling.

15.1 Overview of Learning in Random Fields

Many computer vision tasks, such as segmentation and stereo estimation, can be modeled with random fields, which describe a joint probability distribution of all random variables either jointly or conditionally on the input pixels. The presented method is described in the context of conditional random fields (CRFs), which are MRFs conditioned on a set of observations. However, the algorithms also apply to general random fields.

In our notation $\{z^{(n)}\}$ is the input collection of instances $z^{(n)}$, with corresponding labelings $\{x^{(n)}\}$, where n indexes the instances. For example, an instance may be an image with z denoting a vector of pixel values and x, their segmentation labels (foreground or background). A conditional random field then has the form

$$P(x \mid z, w) = \frac{1}{Z(z, w)} e^{-E(x, z; w)}, \tag{15.1}$$

where w are parameters (weights) and Z is a normalizer (the partition function). A typical energy decomposes over nodes $\mathcal{V}$ (e.g., individual pixels) and edges $\mathcal{E}$ (e.g., pairs of adjacent pixels). We consider energies E that are linear in the parameters w and the set of node and edge features Φ and Ψ, such as

$$E(x, z; w) = \sum_{i \in \mathcal{V}} w_1 \Phi_i(x_i, z) + \sum_{(i,j) \in \mathcal{E}} w_2 \Psi_{ij}(x_i, x_j, z), \tag{15.2}$$

which we can abbreviate as $E(x, z; w) = w^T \Psi(z, x)$. Thus, we have a log-linear model in the exponential family.

Applying this model involves (1) learning the parameters w of the model from training data and (2) inferring the most likely labels for the test data, using the learned parameters. Inference in this model amounts to an energy minimization problem, which can frequently be solved via graph cuts.

Parameter learning aims to find parameters that fit the training data and that also generalize to unseen test data. The learning is usually formulated as minimizing a loss function on the training set. The choice of this loss function leads to two families of methods, maximum likelihood learning and energy-based/large-margin learning.

Maximum likelihood learning strives to maximize the likelihood of the training data (the loss function is thus the negative likelihood). To reduce the risk of overfitting, we typically include a prior over the parameters to maximize the a posteriori probability. Unfortunately, exact maximum likelihood learning is intractable for the large grid-structured random fields typical in computer vision. The difficulty is that the likelihood normalizer Z is a sum with exponentially many terms. The likelihood gradients are similarly intractable expectations: in particular they reduce to calculating marginal probabilities $P(x_i)$ and $P(x_i, x_j)$. Exact marginalization for grids whose height and width both exceed 30 is not practical, so approximations must be used.

One could approximate the marginals using sum-product belief propagation [502], but this can yield wildly fluctuating gradients, and belief propagation may oscillate rather than converge. Alternatively, one could attempt a saddle point approximation by including only the MAP configuration in the normalizer Z. A more promising direction is to apply contrastive divergence [193], which approximates the expectation by samples from a short Markov chain. (More details can be found in chapter 19.) Finally, one could modify the likelihood itself, so that its gradients are tractable: this leads to the classic and fairly successful pseudo likelihood approximation [37] (see chapter 1) and mean field approximation. [189] (see chapter 5), as well as to newer methods such as piecewise learning [459]. A comparison of some of these methods is given in [283].

Rather than finding a fixed set of parameters that maximizes likelihood, one can take a fully Bayesian approach to find the posterior distribution over the parameters, which can then be integrated out for predictions. One deterministic approximation for this task is based on power expectation propagation [379, 380]. Standard stochastic sampling methods are not tractable, but a special method exists [346].

Energy-based learning methods [295] offer a pragmatic alternative to likelihood-based methods. Rather than approximating the normalizer Z in the ways described above, energy-based methods eschew the normalizer altogether. Instead, they try to find parameters for which the energy of the training set labeling is at least as low as for all the other labelings. MAP inference would then recover the correct labels of the training examples. Thus, the learning is guided entirely by the decision boundary, unlike the likelihood-based approach, which considers the confidence of its decisions, given by probabilities. Energy-based methods thus provide a direct solution to a specific end-to-end task, and encompass a large set of possible loss functions and approaches including particularly simple ones, but are not composable as part of a larger system where uncertainty may need to be propagated across modules.

Energy-based learning involves shaping the energy landscape such that the minimum energy configurations adhere to the training data. Thus MAP inference is a key subroutine for learning: to infer labels of a test input z, given parameters w, we will find the maximum a posteriori (MAP) labelings $x^* = \arg \max_x P(x \mid z, w)$. The same graph cut methods that have proved so effective for inference in vision MRFs can then be applied during learning as well.

Large-margin learning extends energy-based methods by adding a regularizer that favors solutions with a large separation of positive and negative training examples [484, 473].

This chapter focuses on energy-based and large-margin methods on loopy graphs and grids (images), and in particular uses graph cut inference during learning. There has been a significant amount of earlier work, but it has mostly used other inference methods that are not practical for images: for instance, [99] applied the Viterbi algorithm algorithm on a linear chain, which is an easier problem not applicable to images. LeCun et al. [294], Tsochantaridis et al. [484], and Taskar et al. [473] consider grids or general graphs and rely on MAP inference, but do not use graph cut for learning. Anguelov et al. [14] use a generic CPLEX solver, which can work only on small vision problems (equivalent to 30,000 pixels, unlike 10^7 pixels in our case).

There exist learning methods that do use graph cut, such as Kumar et al. [283]. However, they use the maximum likelihood framework, which is not compatible with MAP inference, requiring a drastic approximation of the partition function by a single MAP configuration. Our choice, the large-margin framework, allows us to solve the problem exactly with high probability.

15.1.1 An Energy-Based Learning Algorithm

In this section we start from a basic energy-based learning objective, and develop it into a learning algorithm. In section 15.2 we refine the loss function to incorporate degrees of labeling error. This makes the method robust to outliers and ensures good generalization to test data. We begin by detailing the model and motivating the loss function.

During training we look for weights w that assign the training labels $x^{(n)}$ an equal or greater probability than any other labeling x of instance n, that is,

$$P(x^{(n)} \mid z^{(n)}, w) \geq P(x \mid z^{(n)}, w) \ \forall x \neq x^{(n)} \forall n. \tag{15.3}$$

If this is successful, the inferred MAP labelings for the training data will equal the training labels (except for possible ties). We can cancel the normalizer Z from both sides of the

---

STRUCTURED PERCEPTRON ALGORITHM

Input:

- Input-labeling pairs $\{(\boldsymbol{z}^{(n)}, \boldsymbol{x}^{(n)})\}$ training set
- Initial parameters: $\boldsymbol{w} = \boldsymbol{w}_0$

Repeat for T epochs, or until $\boldsymbol{w}$ stops changing
Loop over training instances n

1. Find the MAP labeling of instance n
   $\boldsymbol{x}^* \leftarrow \arg \min_{\boldsymbol{x}} E(\boldsymbol{x}, \boldsymbol{z}^{(n)}; \boldsymbol{w})$.

2. If $\boldsymbol{x}^* \neq \boldsymbol{x}^{(n)}$, update the parameters $\boldsymbol{w}$ so that the energy of the ground truth is lowered relative to the current optimum
   $\boldsymbol{w} \leftarrow \boldsymbol{w} + \Psi(\boldsymbol{z}^{(n)}, \boldsymbol{x}^{(n)}) - \Psi(\boldsymbol{z}^{(n)}, \boldsymbol{x}^*)$.

Figure 15.1
Pseudo code for the perceptron random field learning algorithm.

constraints (15.3) and express the constraints in terms of energies:

$$E(\boldsymbol{x}^{(n)}, \boldsymbol{z}^{(n)}; \boldsymbol{w}) \leq E(\boldsymbol{x}, \boldsymbol{z}^{(n)}; \boldsymbol{w}) \; \forall \boldsymbol{x} \neq \boldsymbol{x}^{(n)} \forall n. \tag{15.4}$$

Thus, we desire weights that give the training labels at least as low an energy as any other label configurations on the training data. The simplest learning algorithm for this purpose is the structured perceptron [294, 99], outlined in figure 15.1. This is like a regular perceptron [130], except that the output space is structured according to the random field. Whenever the current parameter settings yield the incorrect labeling, they are updated so that the energy of the correct labeling is lowered and that of the incorrect labeling is raised. Crucially, if the data are separable with a margin, the perceptron will make a small number of mistakes and thus learning will terminate quickly [99].

Each step of this algorithm is a standard task. The MAP labeling in step 1 can be solved exactly via max-product belief propagation for random fields with a chain or tree structure. Unfortunately, images have a grid structure, for which max-product may not converge. In the next section we will formulate the problem so that the energy function is submodular, enabling the use of efficient graph cut inference.

15.1.2 A Large-Margin Learning Objective
The solution found by the structured perceptron is somewhat arbitrary and depends on the order in which the data were presented. In particular, the inequalities in (15.4) may have multiple or no solutions. We resolve this by finding the parameters that satisfy the inequalities with the largest possible energy margin γ, so that the ground truth labeling has the lowest energy relative to other labelings. The margin may be negative if the original inequalities had

no solutions. More important, this large-margin concept is a general approach that serves to regularize the problem and provide generalization to unseen test data. Thus we have

$$\max_{\boldsymbol{w}:\|\boldsymbol{w}\|\leq 1} \gamma \quad \text{subject to}$$

$$E(\boldsymbol{x}, \boldsymbol{z}^{(n)}; \boldsymbol{w}) - E(\boldsymbol{x}^{(n)}, \boldsymbol{z}^{(n)}; \boldsymbol{w}) \geq \gamma \quad \forall \boldsymbol{x} \neq \boldsymbol{x}^{(n)} \ \forall n. \tag{15.5}$$

We have constrained the weight norm $\|\boldsymbol{w}\|$ to at most 1 in order to prevent weights from growing without bounds.

15.1.3 An Efficient Learning Algorithm

Here we describe a simple yet efficient learning algorithm based on the optimization problem (15.5). It is not feasible to solve that program, as it has an exponential number of constraints, one for each possible labeling $\boldsymbol{x}$ of each instance. Instead, we will perform the optimization over a much smaller set of labelings $\{S^{(n)}\}$. We explicitly enforce that the ground truth has lower energy than labelings in this set. We check whether this also holds true for the remaining labelings, by finding a labeling that has the lowest energy via graph cuts, or any other efficient method. If this labeling has lower energy than the ground truth, or does not achieve the margin, we add it to the constraint set. Finally, we update the parameters to satisfy the new constraint, and iterate. If the parameters do not change (for example, if we do not find any example better than the ground truth), we stop. This is detailed in figure 15.2. Step 3 is written as a general optimization for clarity, but is in fact just a quadratic program (given in section 15.2). Thus it is convex and is free from local minima. The overall procedure converges because there are only a finite number of labelings that can be added. Crucially, it converges in a low number of steps in practice, and even in the worst case is proven to require only a polynomial number of steps if a global optimum can be found in step 1 (see [484], theorem 18, and [144]), which is true for the case of submodular energy functions. At convergence all label configurations outside of $S^{(n)}$ will be at least a margin distance away from the ground truth, which is why it is important to study the choice of margin measure in the loss function (see section 15.2).

The constraint $\boldsymbol{w}_2 \geq 0$ in (15.6) is needed in the context of graph cuts to ensure that the problem remains submodular for energies $E(\boldsymbol{y}, \boldsymbol{x}; \boldsymbol{w})$ that would become nonsubmodular for $\boldsymbol{w}_2 < 0$ (we have assumed that all pairwise potentials $\Psi_{ij}(x_i, x_j, \boldsymbol{z})$ are nonnegative and convex); for other exact optimization techniques (e.g., max-product belief propagation on junction trees, or branch-and-bound), this constraint can be lifted.

Generating Multiple Solutions Using Graph Cuts The objectives (programs (15.5)–(15.10)) require us to enforce constraints for all $\boldsymbol{x} \neq \boldsymbol{x}^{(n)}$. In step 1 (figure 15.1 and 15.6) it is possible that graph cuts find a minimum energy labeling $\boldsymbol{x}^*$ equal to the ground truth $\boldsymbol{x}^{(n)}$. This would not provide any constraint on which to enforce the margin. If this occurred for all training instances, the parameters would not change and the algorithm would terminate

---

BASIC LARGE-MARGIN ALGORITHM

Input:
- Input-labeling pairs $\{(z^{(n)}, x^{(n)})\}$ training set
- Empty set of competing low-energy labelings: $S = \emptyset$
- Initial parameters: $w = w_0$

    Repeat until w is unchanged (within a tolerance)

      Loop over training instances n

1. Find the MAP labeling of instance n, using, e.g., graph cuts
$$x^* \leftarrow \operatorname{argmin}_x E(x, z^{(n)}; w)$$

2. If $x^* \neq x^{(n)}$, add x^* to the constraint set
$$S^{(n)} \leftarrow S^{(n)} \cup \{x^*\}$$

3. Update the parameters w to ensure ground truth has the lowest energy
$$\max_{w: \|w\| \leq 1} \gamma \quad \text{such that} \tag{15.6}$$
$$E(x, z^{(n)}; w) - E(x^{(n)}, z^{(n)}; w) \geq \gamma \quad \forall x \in S^{(n)} \, \forall n$$
$$w_2 \geq 0$$

Figure 15.2
Pseudo code for the basic random field learning algorithm.

without enforcing the margin. This problem can be overcome by adding multiple low-energy labelings at every iteration, instead of just one. The global minima of a submodular function can be found using graph cuts. Kohli and Torr [245] showed how exact min-marginal energies can be efficiently computed for submodular functions. We use these min-marginals to compute the N-best solutions for the energy minimization problem. The time to compute these multiple solutions is three–four times more than that for computing the MAP solution.

Nonsubmodular Energy Functions Some problems in computer vision involve nonsubmodular energy functions that are NP-hard and generally cannot be exactly minimized in polynomial time. Examples include multilabel problems such as multiclass geometric labeling [197] and stereo [72]. In these cases approximate inference can be used in step 3 of the cutting plane algorithm in figure 15.2. The choice of the optimization technique affects the convergence and correctness guarantees of this method [144].

The approximate algorithms commonly used in computer vision include (1) message-passing algorithms such as tree-reweighed message passing (TRW), quadratic pseudo-Boolean optimization (the BHS algorithm) [61, 403], and loopy max-product belief propagation, and (2) move-making algorithms such as alpha-expansion [72] and Fast-PD [269]. Algorithms such as TRW and Fast-PD work by formulating the energy minimization problem as an integer programming problem and then solving its linear relaxation. These algorithms, in addition to giving an approximate solution, produce a per-instance lower bound of the energy that can be used to check how close the approximate solution is to the global minima. We could use this information to isolate good solutions and add them to the solution set. If, for a particular set of weights, the lower bound is far from the energy of the resulting solution, we know that this set of parameters is not appropriate, as it results in a difficult inference problem and will not lead to good solutions.

For our experiments with the nonsubmodular geometric labeling problem (section 15.3.2), we chose to use alpha-expansion. We were motivated by the result [269] showing that alpha-expansion yields close to optimal results for the nonsubmodular Potts model (although our model is more complex).

15.1.4 Parameter Learning for Image Segmentation

In figure 15.3 we illustrate our method on a small problem: the binary image segmentation into foreground (cow) and background based on color models estimated from user-given patches and smoothness constraints. In this example the energy has a single node term (negative log-likelihood of the color, given the label) and two interaction terms: a constant penalty and a contrast-based penalty C for neighboring pixels having different labels. Our energy function can be written as

$$E(z^{(n)}, x^{(n)}; w) = w_1 \sum_{i \in V} -\log P(z_i^{(n)} \mid x_i^{(n)}) + w_2 \sum_{(i,j) \in \mathcal{E}} \mathbb{I}_{x_i^{(n)} \neq x_j^{(n)}}$$

$$+ w_3 \sum_{(i,j) \in \mathcal{E}} \mathbb{I}_{x_i^{(n)} \neq x_j^{(n)}} C(z_i^{(n)}, z_j^{(n)}), \tag{15.7}$$

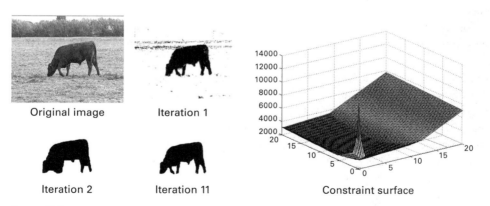

Original image   Iteration 1

Iteration 2   Iteration 11   Constraint surface

Figure 15.3
Parameter learning for image segmentation. The figure illustrates the working of the basic parameter learning algorithm on the image segmentation problem modeled with three parameters (15.7). The segmentations shown in the figure correspond to the results of using the parameter estimates in iterations 1, 2, and 11 of the learning algorithm. These solutions are added to the minimal solution set $S^{(n)}$. The algorithm converges in eleven iterations. For iteration 11 we also show the plot of the 0-1 loss cost function surface on the smoothness w_2 and contrast w_3 parameters of the segmentation energy (15.7), keeping w_1 constant. The optimal values of the weights were $w_2 = 1.96$ and $w_3 = 6.94$.

where $\mathbb{I}$ denotes an indicator function equaling 1 for differing labels. The indicator functions enforce a Potts model penalty on the labeling. The likelihood $P(z_i^{(n)} \mid x_i^{(n)})$ is computed from color models of the foreground and background. These models are built with user-specified cues or seeds. The working of the simple parameter learning algorithm for the image segmentation problem is illustrated in figure 15.3.

15.2 Objectives

In this section we review alternative objectives that are more robust to noisy training data and have refined loss functions. Using the substitution $\|w\| \leftarrow 1/\gamma$, we can write (15.5) as a standard quadratic program (recall that $E(x^{(n)}, z^{(n)}; w)$ is linear in w ((15.2)):

$$\min_w \frac{1}{2} \|w\|^2 \quad \text{s.t.}$$

(15.8)

$$E(x, z^{(n)}; w) - E(x^{(n)}, z^{(n)}; w) \geq 1 \quad \forall x \neq x^{(n)} \, \forall n.$$

To add robustness for noisy training data, we relax the margin constraints by adding slack variables ξ_n. Thus, the individual margins may be smaller, but that is discouraged through a slack penalty in the objective, regulated by the slack penalty parameter C.

$$\min_{w, \xi} \frac{1}{2} \|w\|^2 + \frac{C}{N} \sum_n \xi_n \quad \text{s.t.}$$

(15.9)

$$E(x, z^{(n)}; w) - E(x^{(n)}, z^{(n)}; w) \geq 1 - \xi_n \, \forall x \neq x^{(n)} \, \forall n$$

$$\xi_n \geq 0 \qquad \forall n.$$

These are all standard large-margin formulations. In the context of optimization over joint labelings x, we now review two refinements to the standard margin and also introduce a new refinement.

15.2.1 Rescaled Margin

The energy constraints above enforce the same unit margin for all labelings x competing with the training data labeling $x^{(n)}$, regardless of how similar x and $x^{(n)}$ are (as long as they are not exactly identical). However, for vision problems it is sensible to adapt the margin according to how much competing labelings differ from the ground truth labeling. The idea is to enforce a relatively larger margin for labelings that are far from the ground truth. The desired difference between the ground truth $x^{(n)}$ and a labeling x will be quantified via a loss function $\Delta(x^{(n)}, x)$. For example, an appropriate loss may be the Hamming loss $\Delta(x^{(n)}, x) = \sum_i \delta(x_i^{(n)}, x_i)$. For a 0-1 loss function $\Delta(x^{(n)}, x) = \delta(x^{(n)}, x)$ we reduce to the previous formulation.

MARGIN RESCALED ALGORITHM

Input: as in figure 15.2
Repeat until w is unchanged (within a tolerance)
  Loop over training instances n

1. Run graph cuts to find the MAP labeling of instance n
$$x^* \leftarrow \arg\min_x E(x, z^{(n)}; w) - \Delta(x^{(n)}, x)$$

2. If $x^* \neq x^{(n)}$, add x^* to the constraint set
$$S^{(n)} \leftarrow S^{(n)} \cup \{x^*\}$$

3. Update the parameters w to ensure ground truth has the lowest energy

$$\min_{w,\xi} \frac{1}{2}\|w\|^2 + \frac{C}{N}\sum_n \xi_n \quad \text{s.t.} \quad \forall x \in S^{(n)} \ \forall n \qquad (15.11)$$

$$E(x, z^{(n)}; w) - E(x^{(n)}, z^{(n)}; w) \geq \Delta(x^{(n)}, x) - \xi_n$$

$$\xi_n \geq 0$$

$$w_2 \geq 0$$

Figure 15.4
Pseudo code for the margin rescaled learning algorithm.

Taskar et al. [472] proposed to rescale the margin to enforce the constraint

$$E(x, z^{(n)}; w) - E(x^{(n)}, z^{(n)}; w) \geq \Delta(x^{(n)}, x) - \xi_n \qquad (15.10)$$

for all $x \neq x^{(n)}$ and all n.

To construct a learning algorithm that takes loss into account, we again iteratively collect a set of competing labelings. Now, however, we must find examples that violate these new constraints, which requires us to look beyond minimum energy labelings with respect to E.

Importantly, the margin rescaled formulation still allows graph cuts to find the minimum energy solutions under Hamming loss, or any loss that decomposes in the same way as the energy. The Hamming loss decomposes across nodes, which allows us to absorb the loss into the node energies and define a refined energy function $E'(x, z; w) = E(x, z; w) - \Delta(x^{(n)}, x)$. We then arrive at the algorithm in figure 15.4. Note that the loss Δ is incorporated only during parameter learning. When inferring labels of test data, energy minima of E are found as before.

15.2.2 Rescaled Slack

Tsochantaridis et al. [484] proposed an alternative way to incorporate a loss into the margin constraints. They rescale the slack variables by the loss, requiring that $\forall x \neq x^{(n)}$:

$$E(x, z^{(n)}; w) - E(x^{(n)}, z^{(n)}; w) \geq 1 - \frac{\xi_n}{\Delta(x^{(n)}, x)}. \qquad (15.12)$$

This formulation has the advantage that the loss Δ and slack penalty C share the same scale. In particular, it enforces the same default margin of 1 for all examples. In contrast, the margin rescaled formulation requires large margins of labelings differing significantly from the ground truth, which could cause the algorithm to focus on assigning high energies to poor labelings rather than assigning low energies to labelings close to ground truth. Unfortunately, graph cut optimization cannot directly find labelings that violate the constraints (15.12). Instead, we use graph cuts to find a minimum energy solution and check whether it violates the constraints (alternatively see [413]).

15.2.3 Minimum Energy Loss

While the rescaled margin and rescaled slack methods are a large improvement over the 0-1 loss, they may still minimize training error poorly because they focus on the constraints that require the largest slack rather than on the minimum energy solutions for a particular set of parameters. For instance, in the case of Taskar et al., even if the ground truth is the minimum energy solution, if any high loss solution does not have a sufficiently high margin, the algorithm will change the parameters. The modification of Tsochantaridis et al. is better, since the same margin is required of all examples, but often the cost function still will concern itself with solutions that are not minimum energy solutions (and thus would not be returned during inference). We therefore provide a new cost function that minimizes the training error more directly:

$$\min_{\boldsymbol{w},\xi} \frac{1}{2}\|\boldsymbol{w}\|^2 + \frac{C}{N}\sum_n \xi_n + \frac{C_2}{N}\sum_n \Delta(\boldsymbol{x}^{(n)}, \hat{\boldsymbol{x}}^{(n)}), \tag{15.13}$$

subject to margin constraints as before in (15.10) or (15.12), and where $\hat{\boldsymbol{x}}^{(n)} = \arg\min_{\boldsymbol{x}\in S^{(n)}\cup\{\boldsymbol{x}^{(n)}\}} E(\boldsymbol{x}, \boldsymbol{z}^{(n)}; \boldsymbol{w})$.

The last term is novel and penalizes the minimum energy solution found so far directly by its loss, unless the ground truth has the lowest energy (if the ground truth achieves the minimum, it is chosen so that the loss is 0). As before, the middle term penalizes insufficient margin of any labelings found so far, using the margin-based or slack-based rescaling loss.

To optimize this objective, we iteratively find the minimum energy solution for given parameters via graph cuts, and then find new parameters by gradient descent with line search, as implemented by Matlab's `fmincon` optimizer.

15.3 Experiments

The goals of these experiments are to demonstrate the efficacy of the large margin learning method for computer vision problems and to study the behavior of different loss functions in this framework. To do this, we perform experiments on two tasks: segmentation and geometry labeling. For these tasks there are too many parameters to tune by hand. Our results demonstrate that our method is highly efficient and that training with our new loss-augmented cost functions improves test accuracy considerably.

15.3.1 Refining Segmentations

While completely automatic segmentation is extremely difficult, refining a coarse user-provided segmentation with a nearly pixel-perfect segmentation is achievable and quite useful. For instance, in a photo editing program, a person could draw a polygon around the object, and the computer would attempt to produce a pixel-accurate segmentation. We evaluate our algorithm on this task, with runtime and accuracy comparisons to other methods. See figure 15.5 for some qualitative examples.

The input to our algorithm is an image and a 4-, 6-, or 12-point polygon that approximates the foreground region. We train on fifty segments from fifty separate images in the Berkeley Segmentation Dataset and test on fifty segments from a different set of fifty images. We define three unary potentials: a foreground prior, signed distance from the nearest polygon boundary, and a color histogram term. On an 8-connected graph, we define three associative pairwise terms that penalize connected pixels having different labels: constant, intensity contrast-based, and color contrast-based (Euclidean distances, of A and B channels in Lab space). We learn separate parameters for horizontal, vertical, and diagonal edges to give a total of three unary and nine pairwise parameters. To evaluate, we define segmentation accuracy as the intersection-to-union ratio of the ground truth and resulting foreground regions, and report the average test accuracy.

Comparison of Cost Functions   In table 15.1 we report accuracy when training based on the cost functions described in section 15.2, using 12-point input polygons. The baseline case is to return the input polygon as the final foreground region (80.9 percent accuracy; note that this is based on a rough human segmentation and does not correspond to a learned model). As expected, the cost function based on 0–1 loss performs poorly (80.7 percent), while the margin rescaling and slack rescaling methods offer some improvement (83.0 percent and 82.3 percent, respectively). During training, we define loss as pixel error for the margin rescaling method to ensure that we can reach the global minimum cost with our graph cut method. We cannot make the same guarantee when using the slack rescaling method, regardless of the label loss function used, so we define loss as the intersection: union ratio, as is used to report test error. More general (but slower) minimization methods may be able to apply the slack rescaling method more effectively (e.g., [413]). Training with our new loss-augmented cost functions provides significant further improvement to test accuracies of 85.7 percent and 84.8 percent, when using margin rescaling and slack rescaling, respectively. For comparison we also trained a model using maximum likelihood including the three unary potentials only; this gave 79.7 percent accuracy (exact ML training including the pairwise terms is intractable). Note that these improvements of 4–5 percent over the baseline do not fully convey the large qualitative improvement that can be seen in figure 15.5.

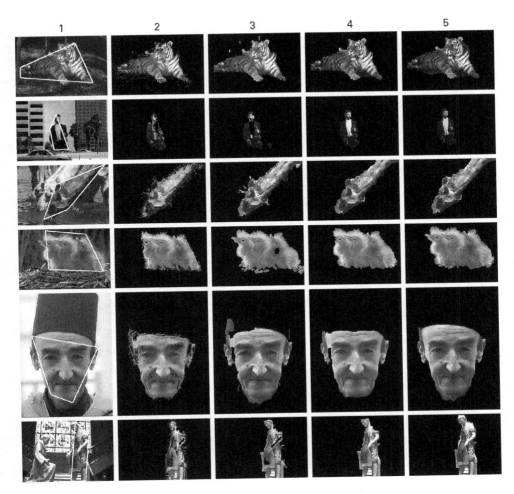

Figure 15.5
Parameter learning for image segmentation. Given the input image and a 4-corner polygon denoting the approximate foreground region (column 1), the goal is to produce a refined pixel-perfect segmentation. Shown are the segmentation results from exact maximum likelihood learning using unary features (column 2), and after learning CRF parameters with our algorithm using rescaled margin (column 3), rescaled margin with augmented loss (column 4), and rescaled slack with augmented loss (column 5).

Table 15.1
Number of training iterations and test accuracy for each cost function using our graph cuts learning method to learn parameters for segmentation

Cost Function	Iterations	Accuracy
Maximum likelihood, unary only	N/A	79.7%
0-1 Loss	13	80.7%
Rescaled margin	43	83.0%
Rescaled slack	13	82.3%
Rescaled margin + loss	45	85.7%
Rescaled slack + loss	90	84.8%

The training data consisted of rough 12-point polygon segmentations. The method is highly efficient under all cost functions (an iteration of processing fifty images of size 320×240 takes about 45 seconds). Our new loss-augmented functions provide the best test accuracy.

Table 15.2
As table 15.1, but with coarser 6-point polygon training data

Cost Function	Iterations	Accuracy
Maximum likelihood, unary only	N/A	64.3%
Rescaled margin	11	74.5%
Rescaled slack	13	70.7%
Rescaled margin + loss	184	76.1%
Rescaled slack + loss	118	76.2%

We also trained on coarser polygon inputs. This task is more challenging and accuracy decreases, as seen in table 15.2 for 6-point polygons. For figure 15.5 even coarser 4-point polygons were used.

Intuitively, for a learning problem involving many parameters, a large set of minimum energy solutions will be needed to constrain the feasible parameter space of our convex program. Some experiments required up to 184 iterations, as our parameter learning algorithm adds only one solution to the solution set in each iteration.

15.3.2 Geometry Labeling

With this experiment we seek to determine whether our algorithm remains tractable on a large-scale vision problem with several dozen parameters. Our task is to label each pixel in the image as "ground," "vertical," or "sky," using the geometric context data set provided by Hoiem et al. [197].

To do this, we define eight unary parameters to model the priors, general appearance, and image-specific appearance. The appearance terms are modeled as the logistic outputs of boosted decision tree classifiers trained separately on four sets of features described by Hoiem et al.: color, texture, position and shape, and perspective. For each image we also

Figure 15.6
Results of geometry ("ground," "vertical," or "sky") estimation based on our CRF learning method. Input images (top row), results based on unary energies alone (middle), and the learned CRF (bottom).

estimate the color of each class within that image, based on an initial estimate of the geometry likelihoods. Our pairwise interaction terms model texture and color gradients between neighboring pixels and the relative positions. In total there are seventy-two interaction terms (four directions, including diagonal, nine pairwise labelings, and two types of gradients). We could learn, for example, that "sky" is unlikely to appear directly beneath vertical regions (although it can happen with overhanging objects) or that certain types of gradients are indicative of a boundary for particular geometric classes.

What we are chiefly interested in here, however, is whether our learning algorithm can do anything useful on this large-scale, multiclass learning problem. To handle multiple classes, we replace our regular graph cut inference step with alpha-expansion graph cuts. Our results, shown in figure 15.6 and table 15.3, reveal that we are able to learn parameters that significantly outperform the unary classifier. Despite the large number of parameters, the learning required only about fifty iterations for each objective, indicating that our method is suitable for large parameter problems.

15.4 Discussion and Conclusion

We have reviewed learning in random fields and have introduced the two main frameworks of maximum likelihood learning and energy-based/large-margin learning. Each framework has its own advantages, but experimental comparisons between them are

Table 15.3

Accuracy on the geometry labeling problem

Cost Function	Accuracy
Unary energies only	84.6%
Rescaled margin	87.7%
Rescaled slack + loss	86.8%
Rescaled margin + loss	87.0%

currently scant [484]. However, we believe that the energy-based framework is a natural fit for MAP inference methods such as graph cuts. The combination of the two gives us exact learning of submodular random fields that is also fast and practical.

Nevertheless, the general learning problem in random fields is far from solved. For nonsubmodular random fields there is no guarantee of finding, a lowest energy labeling, which means that the learning algorithm could progress slowly or not at all. Even though we could successfully learn the nonsubmodular geometry labeling, it remains to be seen how effective the method is in these cases.

There are broader classes of random fields that we have not considered: random fields with latent variables, such as hidden random fields [465], and Boltzmann machines. Since the latent variables represent uncertainty, one should marginalize them out. Unfortunately, marginalization is not possible via graph cuts. Instead, some works have replaced the marginalization by a maximization [139, 541], which would make graph cuts applicable (if submodularity constraints were added). However, this could be a poor approximation to the model. Likelihood-based approaches are probably a better fit for latent variable models, but are challenging because the likelihoods are nonconvex.

Yet another model class includes continuous random fields, where the nodes of the random field take on real rather than discrete values. Large-margin methods have been successfully applied to this case in [55], using exact branch-and-bound inference.

We believe there are ripe opportunities for future work in many of these areas.

Acknowledgments

With kind permission of Springer Science and Business Media we are re-using material from the article "Learning CRFs using Graph Cuts" by Martin Szummer, Pushmeet Kohli and Derek Hoiem, appearing in the proceedings of D. Forsyth, P. Torr, and A. Zisserman (Eds.): European Conference on Computer Vision 2008, Part II, Springer Lecture Notes on Computer Science vol 5303, pp. 582–595, 2008. (c) Springer-Verlag Berlin Heidelberg 2008 ISBN: 978-3-540-88685-3.

16 Analyzing Convex Relaxations for MAP Estimation

M. Pawan Kumar, Vladimir Kolmogorov, and Philip H. S. Torr

When faced with a difficult-to-solve problem, it is standard practice in the optimization community to resort to convex relaxations, that is, to approximate the original problem using an easier (convex) problem. The widespread use of convex relaxations can be attributed to two factors: (1) recent advances in convex optimization imply that the relaxation can be solved efficiently; and (2) the relaxed problem readily lends itself to theoretical analysis that often reveals interesting properties.

In this chapter we will focus on theoretical analysis for MAP estimation of discrete MRFs, with the aim of highlighting the importance of designing *tight* relaxations. In more detail we will provide a reformulation of the MAP estimation problem in terms of a linear integer program, that is, an optimization problem with a linear objective function defined over variables that are constrained to take integral values. Although this reformulation leads to a nonconvex problem that is NP-hard (which is expected, since MAP estimation itself is NP-hard), it allows us to design convex relaxations by replacing integer variables with real-valued ones and enforcing valid convex constraints on them.

There are numerous convex relaxations that can be specified for any integer programming problem. Thus, when solving an MAP estimation problem, a practitioner faces the daunting task of choosing one relaxation from the several that have been reported in the literature. The naïve approach of trying out all possible relaxations to identify the best among them is practically infeasible. Furthermore, such an approach is unlikely to provide any insights into designing new, better relaxations.

We argue that the right relaxation to employ is the one whose constraints provide the smallest *feasible region* (where a feasible region is the set of points that satisfy the constraints). Such constraints would specify the best approximation to the convex hull of the original integer variables. It is worth noting that, for the general MAP estimation problem, we will not be able to specify all the constraints required to exactly characterize the convex hull.[1] In other words, regardless of how tight the relaxation is, we cannot be guaranteed

---

1. Recall that the objective function is linear. So if we were able to specify a feasible region that was the convex hull of integer variables, we would have at least one integer optimal solution. This would imply that the general MAP estimation problem can be solved efficiently—something that is so far not known to be true.

that it will result in integer solutions instead of fractional ones. Thus, in order to obtain the final MAP assignment, we would have to *round* the fractional solutions to integers.

The following question now arises: If the solutions have to be rounded, is the relaxation with the smallest feasible region guaranteed to provide the best final solution? Unfortunately, the answer to this question is no, since this would depend on the rounding scheme. However, comparing feasible regions is still a reasonable way of choosing relaxations for the following reasons:

• In many cases the expected energy of the final solution can be bounded to lie within a constant factor of the optimal value of the relaxation. Thus, the tighter the relaxation, the better the bound.

• Although one can construct examples where a tighter relaxation provides worse solutions, in practice (for real-data problems) the standard rounding schemes do not exhibit this contradictory behavior.

• Finally, from a practical viewpoint, a study of relaxations that explicitly considers a particular rounding scheme suffers from the disadvatage of focusing on a very narrow domain while also requiring a far more complex theoretical analysis.

To reiterate the above-mentioned thesis, we should compare the feasible regions of the different relaxations and choose the one that provides the tightest approximation to the original problem. Although such an approach may sound even more difficult than the naïve way of blind testing, the mathematical framework of convex relaxations makes the task easy. In order to illustrate this, we review three standard convex relaxation approaches that have been proposed in the literature:

• The linear programming (LP) relaxation first proposed by Schlesinger for the satisfiability problem [422], and later developed independently for the general case in [90, 273, 504]. We denote this relaxation by LP-S, where S stands for Schlesinger.

• The quadratic programming (QP) relaxation proposed by Ravikumar and Lafferty [388], which we denote by QP-RL, where RL stands for Ravikumar and Lafferty.

• The second-order cone programming (SOCP) relaxation, first proposed by Muramatsu and Suzuki for the maximum cut problem [345], and later extended for general MAP estimation of discrete MRFs in [282]. We denote this relaxation by SOCP-MS, where MS stands for Muramatsu and Suzuki.

Note that it is well-known that any LP can be expressed as a QP and any QP can be expressed as an SOCP. Yet, despite the expressive power of QP and SOCP, we show that the relaxations of [345, 388] are *dominated* by (that is, provide a weaker approximation than) the LP relaxation. Furthermore, we show that this result can be generalized to a large class of QP and SOCP relaxations.

Before proceeding with the analysis, we describe some basic concepts in mathematical optimization that will be used throughout the chapter.

16.1 Preliminaries

Optimization Problem An optimization problem has the following form:

$$\mathbf{y}^* = \arg\min_{\mathbf{y}} g(\mathbf{y}),$$

$$\text{s.t.} \quad h_i(\mathbf{y}) \le 0, i = 1, \dots, C. \tag{16.1}$$

Here $\mathbf{y}$ is called the *variable*, $g(\cdot)$ is the *objective function*, and $h_i(\cdot), i = 1, \dots, C$, which restrict the values that $\mathbf{y}$ can take, are called the *constraints*. The set of all $\mathbf{y}$ that satisfy all the constraints of the optimization problem is called the *feasible region*. The value $\mathbf{y}^*$ is called an *optimal solution*, and $g(\mathbf{y}^*)$ is called the *optimal value*. Note that, in general, there may be more than one optimal solution. However, as indicated in the above problem, our task is to find one optimal solution.

Integer Program Integer programs (IP) are the class of optimization problems where the elements of the variable $\mathbf{y}$ are constrained to take integer values. In other words, the feasible region of an IP consists of points $\mathbf{y} \in \mathbb{Z}^n$ (where $\mathbb{Z}$ is the set of integers and n is the dimensionality of $\mathbf{y}$). The class of problems defined by IP is generally NP-hard to solve. In contrast, the following four types of problems have convex objective functions and convex feasible regions. This allows us to solve them efficiently [64].

Linear Program A linear program (LP) is an optimization problem with a linear objective function and linear constraints. Formally, an LP is specified as follows:

$$\mathbf{y}^* = \arg\min_{\mathbf{y}} \mathbf{c}^\top \mathbf{y}$$

$$\text{s.t.} \quad \mathbf{A}\mathbf{y} \le \mathbf{b}. \tag{16.2}$$

The vector $\mathbf{c}$ defines the objective function, and the matrix $\mathbf{A}$ and vector $\mathbf{b}$ specify the constraints.

Convex Quadratic Program A convex quadratic program (QP) is an optimization problem with a convex quadratic objective function and linear constraints, that is,

$$\mathbf{y}^* = \arg\min_{\mathbf{y}} ||\mathbf{A}\mathbf{y} + \mathbf{b}||^2 + \mathbf{c}^\top \mathbf{y}$$

$$\text{s.t.} \quad \mathbf{A}'\mathbf{y} \le \mathbf{b}'. \tag{16.3}$$

Second-Order Cone Program A second-order cone program (SOCP) is an optimization problem with a linear objective function and convex quadratic constraints, that is,

$$\mathbf{y}^* = \arg\min_{\mathbf{y}} \mathbf{c}^\top \mathbf{y},$$

$$\text{s.t.} \quad \|\mathbf{A}_i \mathbf{y} + \mathbf{b}_i\|^2 \le \mathbf{c}_i^\top \mathbf{y} + d_i, i = 1, \dots, C. \tag{16.4}$$

Convex quadratic constraints are also known as second-order cone (SOC) constraints, Lorentz cone constraints, or (because of their shape) ice cream cone constraints [64].

Semidefinite Program A semidefinite program (SDP) is an optimization problem with a linear objective function and linear constraints defined over a variable matrix $\mathbf{Y}$ that is restricted to be positive semidefinite[2] (denoted by $\mathbf{Y} \succeq 0$). Formally, an SDP is written as

$$\mathbf{Y}^* = \arg\min_{\mathbf{Y}} \mathbf{C} \bullet \mathbf{Y},$$

$$\text{s.t.} \quad \mathbf{Y} \succeq 0,$$

$$\mathbf{A}_i \bullet \mathbf{Y} \le b_i, i = 1, \dots, C. \tag{16.5}$$

Here the operator ($\bullet$) denotes the Frobenius inner product, that is, $\mathbf{A} \bullet \mathbf{B} = \sum_i \sum_j A_{ij} B_{ij}$.

Relaxation A relaxation of an optimization problem A is another optimization problem B such that (1) the feasible region of B is a superset of the feasible region of A, and (2) if $\mathbf{y}$ belongs to the feasible region of A and B, then the value of the objective function of B is less than or equal to the value of the objective function of A at $\mathbf{y}$.

In the next section we formulate MAP estimation as an IP and describe its various convex relaxations. All the relaxations discussed here are special cases of relaxations (as defined above), in that their value is exactly equal to the value of the integer program for feasible integer solutions. The subsequent sections identify the best relaxation among them.

16.2 MAP Estimation and Its Convex Relaxations

16.2.1 Integer Programming Formulation

We define a binary variable vector $\mathbf{y}$ of length NK where N is the number of random variables and K is the number of possible labels. We denote the element of $\mathbf{y}$ at index $i \cdot K + a$ as $y_{i;a}$ where $i \in \mathcal{V}$ and $l_a \in \mathcal{L}$. The vector $\mathbf{y}$ specifies a labeling $\mathbf{x}$ such that

$$y_{i;a} = \begin{cases} 1 & \text{if } x_i = l_a, \\ 0 & \text{otherwise.} \end{cases}$$

---

2. An $n \times n$ matrix $\mathbf{Y}$ is said to be positive semidefinite if all its n eigenvalues are nonnegative. Equivalently, $\mathbf{Y}$ is positive semidefinite if $\mathbf{c}^\top \mathbf{Y} \mathbf{c} \ge 0$, for all $\mathbf{c} \in \mathbb{R}^n$. It is worth noting that any positive semidefinite matrix $\mathbf{Y}$ can be written as $\mathbf{Y} = \mathbf{U}\mathbf{U}^\top$ for an appropriate matrix $\mathbf{U}$.

Let $\mathbf{Y} = \mathbf{y}\mathbf{y}^\top$. We refer to the $(i \cdot K + a, j \cdot K + b)$th element of the matrix $\mathbf{Y}$ as $y_{ij;ab}$ where $i, j \in \mathcal{V}$ and $l_a, l_b \in \mathcal{L}$. Using the above definitions, we see that the MAP estimation problem is equivalent to the following IP:

$$\mathbf{y}^* = \arg \min_{\mathbf{y}} \sum_{i,l_a} \Phi_i(l_a) y_{i;a} + \sum_{(i,j) \in \mathcal{E}, l_a, l_b} \Psi_{ij}(l_a, l_b) y_{ij;ab}$$

$$\text{s.t.} \quad \mathbf{y} \in \{0, 1\}^{NK}, \mathbf{Y} = \mathbf{y}\mathbf{y}^\top, \tag{16.6}$$

$$\sum_{l_a \in \mathcal{L}} y_{i;a} = 1. \tag{16.7}$$

Constraint (16.6) specifies that the variables $\mathbf{y}$ and $\mathbf{Y}$ are binary such that $y_{ij;ab} = y_{i;a} y_{j;b}$. We will refer to them as the *integer constraints*. Constraint (16.7), which specifies that each variable should be assigned only one label, is known as the *uniqueness constraint*. Since the above IP is equivalent to MAP estimation, it follows that in general it is NP-hard to solve.

16.2.2 Linear Programming Relaxation
The LP relaxation, proposed in [422] for a special case (where the pairwise potentials specify a hard constraint, that is, they are either 0 or ∞), and independently in [90, 273, 504] for the general case, is given as follows:

$$\mathbf{y}^* = \arg \min_{\mathbf{y}} \sum_{i,l_a} \Phi_i(l_a) y_{i;a} + \sum_{(i,j) \in \mathcal{E}, l_a, l_b} \Psi_{ij}(l_a, l_b) y_{ij;ab}$$

$$\text{s.t.} \quad y_{i;a} \geq 0, y_{ij;ab} = y_{ji;ba} \geq 0, \sum_{l_a \in \mathcal{L}} y_{i;a} = 1, \tag{16.8}$$

$$\sum_{l_b \in \mathcal{L}} y_{ij;ab} = y_{i;a}. \tag{16.9}$$

In the above relaxation, which we call LP-S, only those elements $y_{ij;ab}$ of $\mathbf{Y}$ for which $(i, j) \in \mathcal{E}$ are used. Unlike the IP, the feasible region of the above problem is relaxed such that the variables $y_{i;a}$ and $y_{ij;ab}$ lie in the interval $[0, 1]$. Further, the constraint $\mathbf{Y} = \mathbf{y}\mathbf{y}^\top$ is replaced by (16.9), which is called the *marginalization constraint* [504]. One marginalization constraint is specified for each $(i, j) \in \mathcal{E}$ and $l_a \in \mathcal{L}$. Note that the above convex constraints are not exhaustive. In other words, it is possible to specify other convex constraints for the problem of MAP estimation, such as those used by the relaxations below.

16.2.3 Quadratic Programming Relaxation
We now describe the QP relaxation proposed in [388], which we call QP-RL. To this end it would be convenient to reformulate the objective function of the IP, using a vector of

unary potentials of length NK (denoted by $\hat{\Phi}$) and a matrix of pairwise potentials of size $NK \times NK$ (denoted by $\hat{\Psi}$). The elements of the unary potential vector and the pairwise potential matrix are defined as

$$\hat{\Phi}_{i;a} = \Phi_i(l_a) - \sum_{k \in \mathcal{V}} \sum_{l_c \in \mathcal{L}} |\Psi_{ik}(l_a, l_c)|,$$

$$\hat{\Psi}_{ij;ab} = \begin{cases} \sum_{k \in \mathcal{V}} \sum_{l_c \in \mathcal{L}} |\Psi_{ik}(l_a, l_c)|, & \text{if } i = j, a = b, \\ \Psi_{ij}(l_a, l_b) & \text{otherwise,} \end{cases} \qquad (16.10)$$

where $i, j \in \mathcal{V}$ and $l_a, l_b \in \mathcal{L}$. In other words, the potentials are modified by defining a pairwise potential $\hat{\Psi}_{ii;aa}$ and subtracting the value of that potential from the corresponding unary potential $\Phi_{i;a}$. The advantage of this reformulation is that the matrix $\hat{\Psi}$ is guaranteed to be positive semidefinite. This can be seen by observing that for any vector $\mathbf{y} \in \mathbb{R}^{NK}$ the following holds true:

$$\mathbf{y}^\top \hat{\Psi} \mathbf{y} = \sum_{(i,j) \in \mathcal{E}} \sum_{l_a, l_b \in \mathcal{L}} (|\Psi_{ij}(l_a, l_b)| y_{i;a}^2 + |\Psi_{ij}(l_a, l_b)| y_{j;b}^2$$

$$+ 2\Psi_{ij}(l_a, l_b) y_{i;a} y_{j;b})$$

$$= \sum_{(i,j) \in \mathcal{E}} \sum_{l_a, l_b \in \mathcal{L}} \left(|\Psi_{ij}(l_a, l_b)| \left(y_{i;a} + \frac{\Psi_{ij}(l_a, l_b)}{|\Psi_{ij}(l_a, l_b)|} y_{j;b} \right)^2 \right) \qquad (16.11)$$

$$\geq 0.$$

Using the fact that for $y_{i;a} \in \{0, 1\}$, $y_{i;a}^2 = y_{i;a}$, it can be shown that the following is equivalent to the MAP estimation problem [388]:

$$\mathbf{y}^* = \arg \min_{\mathbf{y}} \mathbf{y}^\top \hat{\Phi} + \mathbf{y}^\top \hat{\Psi} \mathbf{y},$$

$$\text{s.t.} \quad \sum_{l_a \in \mathcal{L}} y_{i;a} = 1, \forall i \in \mathcal{V}, \qquad (16.12)$$

$$\mathbf{y} \in \{0, 1\}^{NK}. \qquad (16.13)$$

By relaxing the feasible region of the above problem to $\mathbf{y} \in [0, 1]^{NK}$, the resulting QP can be solved in polynomial time since $\hat{\Psi} \succeq 0$ (thereby ensuring that the above relaxation is convex).

16.2.4 Semidefinite Programming Relaxation

In order to describe the SDP relaxation of MAP estimation, it would be useful to reformulate the IP using binary variables $y'_{i;a} = 2y_{i;a} - 1$ and $y'_{ij;ab} = 4y_{ij;ab} - y'_{i;a} - y'_{j;b} - 1$ that take values $\{-1, 1\}$. Clearly, the above IP is equivalent to the previous one:

$$\min_{\mathbf{y}'} \left(\sum_{i,a} \Phi_i(l_a) \left(\frac{1 + y'_{i;a}}{2} \right) + \sum_{(i,j) \in \mathcal{E}, l_a, l_b} \Psi_{ij}(l_a, l_b) \left(\frac{1 + y'_{i;a} + y'_{j;b} + y'_{ij;ab}}{4} \right) \right)$$

$$\mathbf{y}' \in \{-1, 1\}^{NK}, \mathbf{Y}' = \mathbf{y}'\mathbf{y}'^{\top}, \sum_{l_a \in \mathcal{L}} y'_{i;a} = 2 - K. \tag{16.14}$$

The SDP relaxation replaces the nonconvex constraint $\mathbf{Y}' = \mathbf{y}'\mathbf{y}'^{\top}$ with the convex semidefinite constraint $\mathbf{Y}' - \mathbf{y}'\mathbf{y}'^{\top} \succeq 0$ [169]. Further, it relaxes the integer constraints by allowing the variables to lie in the interval $[-1, 1]$. Finally, using the fact that in the IP $y'_{ij;ab} = y'_{i;a}y'_{j;b}$, it ensures that $1 + y'_{i;a} + y'_{j;b} + y'_{ij;ab} \geq 0$, $y'_{ij;ab} = y'_{ji;ba}$, and $y'_{ii;aa} = 1$. The SDP relaxation is a well-studied approach that provides accurate solutions for the MAP estimation problem (e.g., see [479, 505]). However, due to its computational inefficiency, it is not practically useful for large-scale problems with $NK > 1000$.

16.2.5 Second-Order Cone Programming Relaxation

We now describe the SOCP relaxation that was proposed in [345] for the special case where $K = 2$ and later was extended for a general label set [282]. This relaxation, which we call SOCP-MS, is based on the technique of [231]. For completeness we first describe the general technique of [231] and later show how SOCP-MS can be derived using it.

SOCP Relaxations   In [231] the authors observed that the SDP constraint $\mathbf{Y}' - \mathbf{y}'\mathbf{y}'^{\top} \succeq 0$ can be further relaxed to SOC constraints. Their technique uses the fact that the Frobenius inner product of two semidefinite matrices is nonnegative. For example, consider the inner product of a fixed matrix $\mathbf{S} = \mathbf{U}\mathbf{U}^{\top} \succeq 0$ with $\mathbf{Y}' - \mathbf{y}'\mathbf{y}'^{\top}$ (which, by the SDP constraint, is also positive semidefinite). The nonnegativity of this inner product can be expressed as an SOC constraint as follows:

$$\mathbf{S} \bullet (\mathbf{Y}' - \mathbf{y}'\mathbf{y}'^{\top}) \geq 0 \Rightarrow \|(\mathbf{U})^{\top}\mathbf{y}'\|^2 \leq \mathbf{S} \bullet \mathbf{Y}'. \tag{16.15}$$

Hence, by using a set of matrices $\mathcal{S} = \{\mathbf{S}^c | \mathbf{S}^c = \mathbf{U}^c(\mathbf{U}^c)^{\top} \succeq 0, c = 1, 2, \ldots, C\}$, the SDP constraint can be further relaxed to C SOC constraints, that is, $\|(\mathbf{U}^c)^{\top}\mathbf{y}'\|^2 \leq \mathbf{S}^c \bullet \mathbf{Y}', c = 1, \ldots, C$. It can be shown that for the above set of SOC constraints to be equivalent to the SDP constraint, $C = \infty$. However, in practice we can specify only a finite set of SOC constraints. Each of these constraints may involve some or all variables $y'_{i;a}$ and $y'_{ij;ab}$. For example, if $S^c_{ij;ab} = 0$, then the cth SOC constraint will not involve $y'_{ij;ab}$ (since its coefficient will be 0).

The SOCP-MS Relaxation   Consider a pair of neighboring variables $(i, j) \in \mathcal{E}$, and a pair of labels l_a and l_b. These two pairs define the following variables: $y'_{i;a}, y'_{j;b}, y'_{ii;aa} = y'_{jj;bb} = 1$, and $y'_{ij;ab} = y'_{ji;ba}$ (since $\mathbf{Y}'$ is symmetric). For each such pair of variables and labels, the

SOCP-MS relaxation specifies the following two SOC constraints [282, 345]:

$$(y'_{i;a} + y'_{j;b})^2 \le 2 + 2y'_{ij;ab}, \quad (y'_{i;a} - y'_{j;b})^2 \le 2 - 2y'_{ij;ab}. \tag{16.16}$$

It can be verified that the above constraints correspond to the following semidefinite matrices $\mathbf{S}^1$ and $\mathbf{S}^2$, respectively:

$$S^1_{i'j';a'b'} = \begin{cases} 1 & \text{if } i' = i, j' = i, a' = a, b' = a, \\ 1 & \text{if } i' = j, j' = j, a' = b, b' = b, \\ 1 & \text{if } i' = i, j' = j, a' = a, b' = b, \\ 1 & \text{if } i' = j, j' = i, a' = b, b' = a, \\ 0 & \text{otherwise.} \end{cases}$$

$$S^2_{i'j';a'b'} = \begin{cases} 1 & \text{if } i' = i, j' = i, a' = a, b' = a, \\ 1 & \text{if } i' = j, j' = j, a' = b, b' = b, \\ -1 & \text{if } i' = i, j' = j, a' = a, b' = b, \\ -1 & \text{if } i' = j, j' = i, a' = b, b' = a, \\ 0 & \text{otherwise.} \end{cases} \tag{16.17}$$

Hence, the SOCP-MS formulation is given by

$$\mathbf{y}'^* = \arg\min_{\mathbf{y}'} \left(\sum_{i,a} \Phi_i(l_a) \left(\frac{1 + y'_{i;a}}{2} \right) + \sum_{(i,j) \in \mathcal{E}, l_a, l_b} \Psi_{ij}(l_a, l_b) \left(\frac{1 + y'_{i;a} + y'_{j;b} + y'_{ij;ab}}{4} \right) \right)$$

$$\text{s.t.} \quad y'_{i;a} \in [-1, 1], y'_{ij;ab} \in [-1, 1], \tag{16.18}$$

$$y'_{ij;ab} = y'_{ji;ba}, \sum_{l_a \in \mathbf{l}} y'_{i;a} = 2 - K, \tag{16.19}$$

$$(y'_{i;a} - y'_{j;b})^2 \le 2 - 2y'_{ij;ab}, \tag{16.20}$$

$$(y'_{i;a} + y'_{j;b})^2 \le 2 + 2y'_{ij;ab}. \tag{16.21}$$

We refer the reader to [282, 345] for details. The SOCP-MS relaxation yields the supremum and the infimum for the elements of the matrix $\mathbf{Y}'$, using constraints (16.20) and (16.21), respectively. That is,

$$\frac{(y'_{i;a} + y'_{j;b})^2}{2} - 1 \le y'_{ij;ab} \le 1 - \frac{(y'_{i;a} - y'_{j;b})^2}{2}. \tag{16.22}$$

These constraints are specified for all $(i, j) \in \mathcal{E}$ and $l_a, l_b \in \mathcal{L}$. When the objective function of SOCP-MS is minimized, one of the two inequalities will be satisfied as an equality. This can be proved by assuming that the value for the vector $\mathbf{y}'$ has been fixed. Hence, the elements of the matrix $\mathbf{Y}'$ should take values such that it minimizes the objective function subject to the constraints (16.20) and (16.21). Clearly, the objective function would be minimized when $y'_{ij;ab}$ equals either its supremum or its infimum value, depending on the sign of the corresponding pairwise potential $\Psi_{ij}(l_a, l_b)$, that is,

$$y'_{ij;ab} = \begin{cases} \frac{(y'_{i;a}+y'_{j;b})^2}{2} - 1 & \text{if } \Psi_{ij}(l_a, l_b) > 0, \\ 1 - \frac{(y'_{i;a}-y'_{j;b})^2}{2} & \text{otherwise.} \end{cases} \qquad (16.23)$$

16.3 Comparing the Relaxations

16.3.1 A Criterion for Comparison

In order to compare the relaxations described above, we require the following definitions. We say that a relaxation R_1 *dominates* [90] a relaxation R_2 (alternatively, R_2 is dominated by R_1) if and only if the optimal value of R_1 is greater than or equal to the optimal value of R_2 for all MAP estimation problems. We note here that the concept of domination was used previously in [90] (to compare LP-S with the linear programming relaxation of [236]).

Relaxations R_1 and R_2 are said to be *equivalent* if R_1 dominates R_2 and R_2 dominates R_1, that is, their optimal values are equal to one another for all MAP estimation problems. A relaxation R_1 is said to *strictly dominate* relaxation R_2 if R_1 dominates R_2 but R_2 does not dominate R_1. In other words, R_1 dominates R_2 and there exists at least one MAP estimation problem for which the optimal value of R_1 is strictly greater than the optimal value of R_2. Note that, by definition, the optimal value of any relaxation will always be less than or equal to the energy of the MAP labeling. Hence, the optimal value of a strictly dominating relaxation R_1 is closer to the optimal value of the MAP estimation IP compared with that of relaxation R_2. In other words, R_1 provides a tighter lower bound than R_2 and, in that sense, is a better relaxation than R_2.

It is worth noting that the concept of domination (or strict domination) applies to the optimal (possibly fractional) solutions of the relaxations. In practice, the optimal solution is *rounded* to a feasible integer solution in order to obtain a labeling of the MRF. For example, the simplest rounding scheme would be to treat the fractional value $y_{i;a}$ as the probability of assigning the random variable $i \in \mathcal{V}$ the label $l_a \in \mathcal{L}$, and to sample labelings from this distribution. In such a scenario it is possible that the dominating relaxation R_1 may provide a labeling with higher energy than R_2. The natural question that arises is "Why not compare the final solutions directly?" Unfortunately, although this would be the ideal comparison criterion, there exist too many rounding schemes in the literature to make such an approach practical and feasible. Having said that, the concept of domination as described above provides a nice balance between computability and usefulness. In fact, one could argue that if a dominating relaxation provides worse final integer solutions, then the deficiency of the method may be rooted in the rounding technique used.

Using domination as the criterion for comparison, we now analyze the convex relaxations described in the previous section. Note that we provide only a sketch of the proofs here. We refer the reader to [280] for the details.

16.3.2 LP-S Versus SOCP-MS

We now provide a comparison of the LP-S and SOCP-MS relaxations. To this end it will be helpful to formulate the constraints of both the relaxations, using the same variables. Hence, we rewrite the LP-S constraints as

$$y'_{i;a} \in [-1, 1], \; y'_{ij;ab} \in [-1, 1], \tag{16.24}$$

$$\sum_{l_a \in \mathcal{L}} y'_{i;a} = 2 - K, \tag{16.25}$$

$$\sum_{l_b \in \mathcal{L}} y'_{ij;ab} = (2 - K)y'_{i;a}, \tag{16.26}$$

$$y'_{ij;ab} = y'_{ji;ba}, \tag{16.27}$$

$$1 + y'_{i;a} + y'_{j;b} + y'_{ij;ab} \geq 0. \tag{16.28}$$

Recall that the SOCP-MS constraints are given by

$$y'_{i;a} \in [-1, 1], \; y'_{ij;ab} \in [-1, 1], \tag{16.29}$$

$$\sum_{l_a \in \mathcal{L}} y'_{i;a} = 2 - K, \tag{16.30}$$

$$(y'_{i;a} - y'_{j;b})^2 \leq 2 - 2y'_{ij;ab}, \tag{16.31}$$

$$(y'_{i;a} + y'_{j;b})^2 \leq 2 + 2y'_{ij;ab}, \tag{16.32}$$

$$y'_{ij;ab} = y'_{ji;ba}. \tag{16.33}$$

We show that the feasible region of LP-S is a strict subset of the feasible region of SOCP-MS. This would allow us to prove the following.

Theorem 16.1 LP-S strictly dominates SOCP-MS.

Sketch of the Proof   The LP-S and the SOCP-MS relaxations differ only in the way they relax the nonconvex constraint $\mathbf{Y}' = \mathbf{y}'\mathbf{y}'^\top$. While LP-S relaxes $\mathbf{Y}' = \mathbf{y}'\mathbf{y}'^\top$ using the marginalization constraint (16.26), SOCP-MS relaxes it to constraints (16.31) and (16.32). The SOCP-MS constraints provide the supremum and infimum of $y'_{ij;ab}$ as

$$\frac{(y'_{i;a} + y'_{j;b})^2}{2} - 1 \leq y'_{ij;ab} \leq 1 - \frac{(y'_{i;a} - y'_{j;b})^2}{2}. \tag{16.34}$$

In order to prove this theorem, we use the following lemmas.

Lemma 16.1 If $y'_{i;a}$, $y'_{j;b}$, and $y'_{ij;ab}$ satisfy the LP-S constraints, that is, constraints (16.24)–(16.28), then $|y'_{i;a} - y'_{j;b}| \leq 1 - y'_{ij;ab}$. The above result holds true for all $(i, j) \in \mathcal{E}$ and $l_a, l_b \in \mathcal{L}$.

Lemma 16.2 If $y'_{i;a}$, $y'_{j;b}$, and $y'_{ij;ab}$ satisfy the LP-S constraints, then $|y'_{i;a} + y'_{j;b}| \leq 1 + y'_{ij;ab}$. This holds true for all $(i, j) \in \mathcal{E}$ and $l_a, l_b \in \mathcal{L}$.

Squaring both sides of the above inequalities, we can show that LP-S provides a smaller supremum and a larger infimum of the elements of the matrix $\mathbf{Y}'$ than the SOCP-MS relaxation. Thus, the feasible region of LP-S is a strict subset of the feasible region of SOCP-MS.

One can also construct potentials for which the set of all optimal solutions of SOCP-MS do not lie in the feasible region of LP-S. For example, see figure 16.1. Together with the two lemmas, this implies that LP-S strictly dominates SOCP-MS. ∎

Note that the above theorem does not apply to the variation of SOCP-MS described in [282, 345] that includes *triangular inequalities* [92]. However, since triangular inequalities are linear constraints, LP-S can be extended to include them. The resulting LP relaxation would strictly dominate the SOCP-MS relaxation with triangular inequalities.

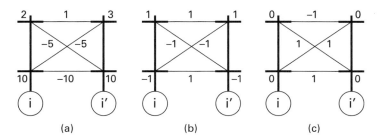

(a)　　　　　　　　(b)　　　　　　　　(c)

Figure 16.1
(a) An example MRF defined using two neighboring random variables. Note that the observed nodes are not shown for the sake of clarity of the image. Each random variable can take one of two labels, represented by the branches (i.e., the horizontal lines) of the trellises (i.e., the vertical lines) on top of the variables. The value of the unary potential $\Phi_i(l_a)$ is shown next to the ath branch of the trellis on top of i. For example, $\Phi_i(l_1) = 10$ (shown next to the lower branch of the trellis on top of i and $\Phi_j(l_2) = 3$ (shown next to the upper branch of the trellis on top of j. The pairwise potential $\Psi_{ij}(l_a, l_b)$ is shown next to the connection between the ath and bth branches of the trellises on top of i and i, respectively. For example, $\Psi_{ij}(l_1, l_1) = -10$ (shown next to the bottommost connection between the two trellises) and $\Psi_{ij}(l_1, l_2) = -5$ (shown next to the diagonal connection between the two trellises). (b) The optimal solution obtained using the LP-S relaxation. The value of $y'_{i;a}$ is shown next to the ath branch of the trellis on top of i. Similarly, the value of $y'_{ij;ab}$ is shown next to the connection between the ath and bth branches of the trellises on top of i and j respectively. Note that the value of the objective function for the optimal solution is 6. (c) A feasible solution of the SOCP-MS relaxation that does not belong to the feasible region of LP-S and has an objective function value of 2.5. It follows that the optimal solution of SOCP-MS would lie outside the feasible region of LP-S and have a value of at most 2.5. Together with lemmas 16.1 and 16.2, this proves that LP-S strictly dominates SOCP-MS.

16.3.3 QP-RL Versus SOCP-MS

We now prove that QP-RL and SOCP-MS are equivalent (i.e., their optimal values are equal for MAP estimation problems defined over all MRFs). To aid the comparison, we rewrite QP-RL using the variables $\mathbf{y}'$ as

$$\min_{\mathbf{y}'} \left(\frac{1+\mathbf{y}'}{2}\right)^{\top} \hat{\Phi} + \left(\frac{1+\mathbf{y}'}{2}\right)^{\top} \hat{\Psi} \left(\frac{1+\mathbf{y}'}{2}\right),$$

$$\sum_{l_a \in \mathcal{L}} y'_{i;a} = 2 - K, \forall i \in \mathcal{V}, \tag{16.35}$$

$$\mathbf{y} \in [-1, 1]^{NK}, \tag{16.36}$$

where $\mathbf{1}$ is a vector of dimension $NK \times 1$ whose elements are all equal to 1. We consider a vector $\mathbf{y}'$ that lies in the feasible regions of the QP-RL and SOCP-MS relaxations, that is, $\mathbf{y}' \in [-1, 1]^{NK}$. For this vector we show that the values of the objective functions of the QP-RL and SOCP-MS relaxations are equal. This would imply that if $\mathbf{y}'^*$ is an optimal solution of QP-RL for some MRF, then there exists an optimal solution $(\mathbf{y}'^*, \mathbf{Y}'^*)$ of the SOCP-MS relaxation. Further, if e^Q and e^S are the optimal values of the objective functions obtained using the QP-RL and SOCP-MS relaxations, then $e^Q = e^S$.

Theorem 16.2   QP-RL and SOCP-MS are equivalent.

Sketch of the Proof   Recall that in the QP-RL relaxation

$$\hat{\Phi}_{i;a} = \Phi_i(l_a) - \sum_{k \in \mathcal{V}} \sum_{l_c \in \mathcal{L}} |\Psi_{ik}(a, c)|, \tag{16.37}$$

$$\hat{\Psi}_{ij;ab} = \begin{cases} \sum_{k \in \mathcal{V}} \sum_{l_c \in \mathcal{L}} |\Psi_{ik}(a, c)| & \text{if } i = j, a = b, \\ \Psi_{ij}(l_a, l_b) & \text{otherwise.} \end{cases} \tag{16.38}$$

Here the terms $\Phi_i(l_a)$ and $\Psi_{ij}(a, m)$ are the (original) unary potentials and pairwise potentials for the given MRF. Consider a feasible solution $\mathbf{y}'$ of the QP-RL and the SOCP-MS relaxations. Further, let $\mathbf{y}'$ be the solution obtained when minimizing the objective function of the SOCP-MS relaxation while keeping $\mathbf{y}'$ fixed. In order to prove the theorem, we compare the coefficients of $\Phi_i(l_a)$ and $\Psi_{ij}(l_a, l_b)$ for all $i \in \mathcal{V}$, $(i, j) \in \mathcal{E}$. It can be verified that the coefficients are the same for both QP-RL and SOCP-MS [280]. This proves the theorem. ∎

Theorems 16.1 and 16.2 prove that the LP-S relaxation strictly dominates the QP-RL and SOCP-MS relaxations.

16.3.4 SOCP Relaxations over Trees and Cycles

We now generalize the above results to a large class of SOCP (and equivalent QP) relaxations. Recall that SOCP relaxations further relax the SDP constraint to the following SOC constraints:

$$\|(\mathbf{U}^c)^\top \mathbf{y}'\|^2 \leq \mathbf{S}^c \bullet \mathbf{Y}', c = 1, \ldots, C. \tag{16.39}$$

Consider one such SOC constraint defined by the semidefinite matrix $\mathbf{S}^c = \mathbf{U}^c (\mathbf{U}^c)^\top$. Using this constraint, we define a graph $\mathcal{G}^c = (\mathcal{V}^c, \mathcal{E}^c)$ as follows:

- The set $\mathcal{E}^c$ is defined such that $(i, j) \in \mathcal{E}^c$ if and only if it satisfies the following conditions:

$$(i, j) \in \mathcal{E}, \exists l_a, l_b \in \mathcal{L} \text{ such that } S^c_{ij;ab} \neq 0. \tag{16.40}$$

In other words, $\mathcal{E}^c$ is the subset of the edges in the graphical model of the MRF such that $\mathbf{S}^c$ specifies constraints for the random variables corresponding to those edges.

- The set $\mathcal{V}^c$ is defined as $i \in \mathcal{V}^c$ if and only if there exists a $j \in \mathcal{V}$ such that $(i, j) \in \mathcal{E}^c$. In other words, $\mathcal{V}^c$ is the subset of hidden nodes in the graphical model of the MRF such that $\mathbf{S}^c$ specifies constraints for the random variables corresponding to those hidden nodes.

We say that the constraint specified by $\mathbf{S}^c$ is *defined over* the graph $\mathcal{G}^c$. Note that, according to the above definitions, the constraints used in SOCP-MS are defined over graphs that consist of a single edge, that is, $\mathcal{V}^c = \{i, j\}$ and $\mathcal{E}^c = \{(i, j)\}$. Hence, the following theorem provides a generalization of theorem 16.1.

Theorem 16.3 Any SOCP relaxation whose constraints are defined over arbitrarily large trees is dominated by LP-S.

We can go a step further and characterize those SOCP relaxations that define constraints over arbitrarily large cycles and are dominated by LP-S. For example, consider the case where the pairwise potentials are of the form $\Psi_{ij}(l_a, l_b) = w_{ij} d(l_a, l_b)$, where w_{ij} is the weight of the edge (i, j) and $d(\cdot, \cdot)$ is a nonnegative distance function. Then the following theorem holds true.

Theorem 16.4 An SOCP relaxation whose constraints are defined over nonoverlapping graphs $\mathcal{G}^c$ that form arbitrarily large, even cycles with all positive or all negative weights is dominated by LP-S. The result also holds if $\mathcal{G}^c$ form arbitrarily large odd cycles with only one positive or only one negative weight.

The proofs of theorems 16.3 and 16.4 are given in [280].

16.4 Discussion

We reviewed three standard relaxations for MAP estimation of discrete MRFs: LP-S, QP-RL, and SOCP-MS. We showed that despite the flexibility in the form of the objective function and constraints afforded by QP and SOCP, both QP-RL and SOCP-MS are dominated by LP-S. In fact, the domination by LP-S can be extended to a large class of QP and SOCP relaxations.

It is worth noting that although LP-S is provably tighter than several relaxations, it is by no means the tightest possible relaxation. In fact, recent work has focused on obtaining tighter relaxations by adding more constraints to LP-S, such as cycle inequalities, clique web inequalities, and positive semidefinite inequalities [125]. Among them the most popular and best-studied class of constraints is cycle inequalities. These constraints are defined over subgraphs of $\mathcal{G}$ that form a cycle. Although there exist exponentially many cycle inequalities (in terms of the number of random variables) for a given MAP estimation problem, it has been shown that they yield to a polynomial time separation algorithm [444]. In other words, given a fractional labeling specified by $(\mathbf{y}, \mathbf{Y})$, we can find a cycle inequality that it violates in polynomial time. This allows us to design efficient cutting plane algorithms where we initially enforce only the LP-S constraints and keep adding a violated cycle inequality after each iteration until we obtain a good approximation to MAP labeling. We refer the interested reader to [444] for more details.

Another way to strengthen the LP-S relaxation is to add constraints defined over a clique containing a small number of nodes (3,4,...). This is sometimes known as a *cluster-based* LP relaxation. Such an approach has been successfully used, for example, in some bio-informatics problems [445].

We hope that this chapter has helped illustrate the amenability of convex relaxations to theoretical analysis. Such an analysis often makes it possible to choose the *right* approach for the problem at hand. Though several other properties of convex relaxations for MAP estimation have been reported in the literature (for example, its integrality gap [90] for special cases), there still remain some open questions. One such question concerns the worst case multiplicative bounds obtained by LP-S (or any convex relaxation in general). It has recently been shown that all the known multiplicative bounds of LP-S for $N \geq K$ can be obtained via some recently proposed move-making algorithms that employ only the efficient minimum cut procedure [277, 279]. However, it is not clear whether this result can be generalized to all MAP estimation problems (for example, when $N < K$ or when the pairwise potentials do not form a semi-metric distance).

Acknowledgments

M. Pawan Kumar was funded by DARPA and the Boeing company. Vladimir Kolmogorov thanks EPSRC for support. Philip Torr is in receipt of a Royal Society Wolfson Research Merit Award, and would like to acknowledge support from Royal Society and Wolfson foundation.

17   MAP Inference by Fast Primal-Dual Linear Programming

Nikos Komodakis

The *primal-dual schema* is a powerful method used for deriving approximation algorithms to hard combinatorial problems based on LP duality theory. This chapter describes the basic principles upon which this technique relies, and explains how it applies to MAP inference of discrete MRFs. The theoretical and practical properties of the resulting optimization framework are then analyzed. It is thus shown that the corresponding algorithms yield approximately optimal solutions to a wide class of MRFs encountered in computer vision and are, at the same time, extremely efficient as well as much faster compared with earlier art. Furthermore, it is explained how state-of-the-art MRF optimization methods such as the α-expansion algorithm are derived merely as special cases of the presented primal-dual framework.

17.1 Introduction

Discrete MRF optimization is ubiquitous in computer vision, and has been used with great success in a wide variety of problems such as optical flow estimation, image segmentation, stereo matching, and image restoration (denoising), to mention only a few. As explained in previous chapters, in all these cases one seeks to minimize an energy $E(\mathbf{x}) = \sum_{p \in \mathcal{V}} \Phi(x_p) + \sum_{pq \in \mathcal{E}} \Psi(x_p, x_q)$, where each x_p takes values in a discrete label set $\mathcal{L}$. In this energy, unary MRF potentials $\Phi(x_p)$ encode the data likelihood, whereas pairwise potentials $\Psi(x_p, x_q)$ act as regularizers and thus play a very important role in obtaining high quality results. In most cases the latter potentials usually take the following form:

$$\Psi(x_p, x_q) = w_{pq} d(x_p, x_q), \tag{17.1}$$

where w_{pq} is a per-edge weight representing the strength of relationship between adjacent objects p and q, while $d(x_p, x_q)$ is a distance function measuring the dissimilarity between labels. This distance $d(\cdot, \cdot)$ is assumed here to be a semi-metric,[1] that is, it satisfies $d(a, b) = 0 \Leftrightarrow a = b, d(a, b) \geq 0$ (in contrast, a metric also has to satisfy the triangle inequality). The

---

1. The described algorithms actually apply to more general distances.

intuition behind definition (17.1) is that tightly related objects should have similar labels assigned to them. For instance, in the case of stereo matching (where a per-pixel disparity x_p between two images $I_{\text{left}}, I_{\text{right}}$ is sought), the MRF potentials can be set as follows. The unary potentials can be defined as the intensity/color difference between corresponding pixels, that is, $\Phi(x_p) = \|I_{\text{left}}(p) - I_{\text{right}}(p + x_p)\|^2$. The weights w_{pq} (where p, q are adjacent pixels in a 4-connected image grid) may be defined based on the fact that disparity discontinuities very often coincide with edges in the image domain. Therefore, w_{pq} can be made small across such edges, for instance, by allowing them to vary as a decreasing function of $|I_{\text{left}}(p) - I_{\text{left}}(q)|$. As for the choice of the distance function $d(\cdot, \cdot)$, this plays an important role. The most obvious option is to set it equal to the labels' squared Euclidean distance, that is, $d(x_p, x_q) = \|x_p - x_q\|^2$. However, this overpenalizes sharp disparity jumps and thus results in oversmoothing. To fix this, it is much better to use a discontinuity-preserving distance function such as $d(x_p, x_q) = \min(\|x_p - x_q\|^2, K)$, where K is a constant representing the maximum possible penalty imposed by $d(\cdot, \cdot)$.

As has become obvious from the very simple example above, optimization algorithms for MRFs must be able to handle energies that are as general as possible, since this allows a better modeling of the problem at hand. Of course, the difficulty of MAP inference varies greatly for different energy types, for instance, for different pairwise potentials (see figure 17.1). Besides the above requirement, however, it is also of utmost importance for the inference algorithms to be extremely efficient, since most computer vision problems nowadays are of a very large scale.

To address these challenges, a general algorithmic framework for MRF energy minimization is described in this chapter [269, 271]. Its theoretical setting rests on the duality theory of linear programming and, in particular, on the so-called primal-dual schema. This powerful technique relies on recovering pairs of solutions both for the original primal problem (in this case the MAP inference task) and a dual one, in such a way that the gap between them

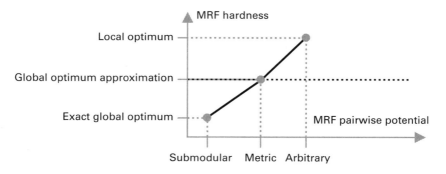

Figure 17.1
The difficulty of MRF optimization depends crucially on the type of pairwise potentials. Ideally, MAP inference algorithms should remain below the horizontal dashed line, i.e., they should provide approximately optimal solutions.

is minimized. By using this technique, the derived algorithms can guarantee approximately optimal solutions for a wide class of MRFs encountered in practical computer vision problems. The guarantees come in the form of worst case suboptimality bounds, as well as very tight per-instance approximation factors that are updated online. Besides their high accuracy, these algorithms do not make compromises regarding their computational efficiency. Due to exploiting both primal and dual information, they thus offer a substantial speedup over existing methods for both static and dynamic MRFs (i.e., MRFs whose potentials vary smoothly over time), where one naturally expects that successive primal-dual solutions remain close to one another. The latter type of MRFs is frequently used in computed vision (e.g., in applications dealing with video data).

Before proceeding, it should be noted that apart from the semi-metric property of the distance $d(\cdot, \cdot)$, no other assumption is made for the MRF potentials throughout this chapter.

17.2 The Primal-Dual Schema

The primal-dual schema is a well-known technique in combinatorial optimization, which is based on LP duality theory. Interestingly, it started as an exact method for solving linear programs, where its first use probably goes back to Edmond's famous blossom algorithm for matching. It can thus be used for deriving exact polynomial-time algorithms to many other cornerstone problems in combinatorial optimization, including max-flow, shortest path, minimum branching, and minimum spanning tree [363] (for instance, max-flow techniques based on augmenting paths are essentially applications of this schema to the min-cut/max-flow problem pair). Later, however, it was realized that it can also be a very powerful tool for deriving approximation algorithms to NP-hard combinatorial problems. Thus, it has been applied for this purpose to many problems including set cover, Steiner network, scheduling, Steiner tree, feedback vertex set, and facility location, to mention only a few [493, 194]. The interested reader is referred to the book by Vazirani [493], which provides an excellent introduction to this topic. The primal-dual schema was introduced into vision by Komodakis et al. [269, 271], who applied it to the problem of discrete MRF optimization. Also, in a more recent work [262] Kolmogorov and Shioura proposed a primal-dual method that optimizes exactly a class of MRFs with convex potentials, which are encountered in certain vision applications.

In order to understand how the prima-dual schema works in general, one needs to consider the following pair of primal and dual LPs:

$$\text{PRIMAL: } \min \mathbf{c}^T \mathbf{x} \qquad\qquad \text{DUAL: } \max \mathbf{b}^T \mathbf{y}$$
$$\text{s.t.} \quad \mathbf{A}\mathbf{x} = \mathbf{b}, \mathbf{x} \geq 0 \qquad\qquad \text{s.t.} \quad \mathbf{A}^T \mathbf{y} \leq \mathbf{c}$$

Here $\mathbf{A} = [a_{ij}]$ represents a matrix of size $m \times n$, and $\mathbf{b}, \mathbf{c}$ are column vectors of size m and n, respectively. One seeks an optimal solution to the primal program under the additional constraint that it is integral. The latter requirement makes the problem NP-hard and, as a result, only an approximate solution can be found. To this end a primal-dual f-approximation algorithm makes use of the following principle:

Theorem 17.1 (Primal-dual principle) *If* $\mathbf{x}$ *and* $\mathbf{y}$ *are integral-primal and dual feasible solutions satisfying*

$$\mathbf{c}^T \mathbf{x} \le f \cdot \mathbf{b}^T \mathbf{y}, \tag{17.2}$$

then $\mathbf{x}$ *is an* f-approximation to the optimal integral solution $\mathbf{x}^*$, that is, it holds $\mathbf{c}^T \mathbf{x}^* \le \mathbf{c}^T \mathbf{x} \le f \cdot \mathbf{c}^T \mathbf{x}^*$.

The proof of the above principle is rather simple and is illustrated graphically in figure 17.2a. Namely, by weak duality it is well known that the cost $\mathbf{c}^T \mathbf{x}^*$ of the optimal integral solution $\mathbf{x}^*$ lies between the dual cost $\mathbf{b}^T \mathbf{y}$ and the primal cost $\mathbf{c}^T \mathbf{x}$, that is, it holds $\mathbf{b}^T \mathbf{y} \le \mathbf{c}^T \mathbf{x}^* \le \mathbf{c}^T \mathbf{x}$. Therefore, if the primal and dual costs $\mathbf{b}^T \mathbf{y}$, $\mathbf{c}^T \mathbf{x}$ are close to each other (e.g., if their ratio $r_1 = \mathbf{c}^T \mathbf{x} / \mathbf{b}^T \mathbf{y}$ is less than or equal to f, as in (17.2)), then the same will necessarily hold for the costs $\mathbf{c}^T \mathbf{x}^*$ and $\mathbf{c}^T \mathbf{x}$ (i.e., the ratio $r_0 = \mathbf{c}^T \mathbf{x} / \mathbf{c}^T \mathbf{x}^*$ will also be less than f), which is exactly what is meant by the statement that $\mathbf{x}$ is an f-approximation to $\mathbf{x}^*$.

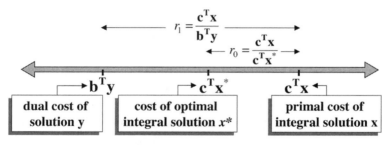

(a) The primal-dual principle

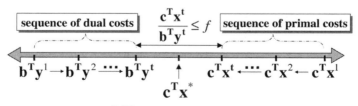

(b) The primal-dual schema

Figure 17.2
(a) By weak duality, for any pair $(\mathbf{x}, \mathbf{y})$ of integral-primal and dual feasible solutions, the optimal cost $\mathbf{c}^T \mathbf{x}^*$ lies between the costs $\mathbf{b}^T \mathbf{y}$, $\mathbf{c}^T \mathbf{x}$. Therefore, if $\mathbf{b}^T \mathbf{y}$ and $\mathbf{c}^T \mathbf{x}$ are close enough (e.g., their ratio r_1 is $\le f$), so are $\mathbf{c}^T \mathbf{x}^*$ and $\mathbf{c}^T \mathbf{x}$ (e.g., their ratio r_0 is $\le f$ as well), thus meaning that $\mathbf{x}$ is an f-approximation to $\mathbf{x}^*$. (b) According to the primal-dual schema, integral-primal and dual feasible solutions make local improvements to each other until the final costs $\mathbf{b}^T \mathbf{y}^t$, $\mathbf{c}^T \mathbf{x}^t$ are close enough (e.g., their ratio is $\le f$). One can then apply the primal-dual principle (as in (a) above) to conclude that $\mathbf{x}^t$ is an f-approximation to $\mathbf{x}^*$.

Put otherwise, the above principle uses the fact that the dual linear program yields (by weak duality) a lower bound to the primal linear program, which in turn provides a lower bound to the primal integer program (i.e., to MRF optimization).

The above principle lies at the heart of any primal-dual technique. In fact, the various primal-dual methods differ mostly in the way that they manage to estimate a pair $(\mathbf{x}, \mathbf{y})$ satisfying the fundamental inequality (17.2). One very common way to do that, but not the only one, is by relying on the the so-called primal complementary slackness conditions associated with any optimal solution $(\mathbf{x}, \mathbf{y})$ of the pair of primal-dual linear programs above. These conditions require that if $x_j > 0$, then it should hold $\mathbf{a}^T_{.j} \cdot \mathbf{y} = c_j$, where $\mathbf{a}^T_{.j}$ denotes the jth column of $\mathbf{A}$. Such a condition can hold only if there is no duality gap, which is exactly what happens for primal-dual linear programs but is not, in general, possible when an integrality requirement is imposed on $\mathbf{x}$. Therefore, in the latter case, to derive an approximate solution, one has to relax the complementary slackness conditions by a factor f [493].

Theorem 17.2 (Relaxed Complementary Slackness)   *If the pair* $(\mathbf{x}, \mathbf{y})$ *of integral-primal and dual feasible solutions satisfies the following relaxed primal complementary slackness conditions*

$$\forall\, x_j > 0 \Rightarrow \mathbf{a}^T_{.j} \cdot \mathbf{y} \geq c_j/f_j, \qquad\qquad (17.3)$$

then $(\mathbf{x}, \mathbf{y})$ *satisfies the aforementioned primal-dual principle with* $f = \max_j f_j$, *and therefore* $\mathbf{x}$ *is an* f-*approximate solution.*

The proof of the above theorem follows directly from combining (17.3) with the primal-dual feasibility conditions $\mathbf{Ax} = \mathbf{b}$, $\mathbf{x} \geq \mathbf{0}$, and $\mathbf{A}^T\mathbf{y} \leq \mathbf{c}$. Therefore, based on theorem, a primal-dual f-approximation algorithm can make use of the following iterative schema:

Theorem 17.3 (Primal-dual schema)   *Keep generating pairs of integral primal-dual solutions* $\{(\mathbf{x}^k, \mathbf{y}^k)\}^t_{k=1}$ *until the elements* $\mathbf{x}^t$, $\mathbf{y}^t$ *of the last pair are both feasible and satisfy the relaxed primal complementary slackness conditions.*

This schema is illustrated graphically in figure 17.2b. What happens is that at each iteration, the current primal-dual pair $(\mathbf{x}^k, \mathbf{y}^k)$ is perturbed so that the primal and dual costs $\mathbf{c}^T\mathbf{x}^k$ and $\mathbf{b}^T\mathbf{y}^k$ are brought closer together. This is typically achieved by an alternating update between primal and dual variables based on the relaxed complementary slackness conditions. A new primal-dual pair, say $(\mathbf{x}^{k+1}, \mathbf{y}^{k+1})$, is thus generated, and this procedure is repeated until the costs of the final primal-dual pair come close enough. The remarkable thing about this scheme is that the two processes, the primal and the dual, make local improvements to one another, yet manage to achieve an approximately globally optimal result at the end. It is also worth mentioning that one can derive different approximation algorithms merely by choosing different relaxations of the complementary slackness conditions (i.e., by choosing different f_j), which is exactly what will be attempted next for the case of MRF optimization.

17.3 The Primal-Dual Schema for MRFs

Based on the above discussion, to apply the primal-dual schema to MRF optimization, one must complete three tasks: express the MRF problem as a linear integer program, form the dual LP, and finally choose the relaxed complementary slackness conditions. Regarding the first of these tasks, the following integer LP from chapter 1 can be used [90]:

$$\min \sum_{p \in V} \left(\sum_{a \in \mathcal{L}} \Phi_p(a) x_p(a) \right) + \sum_{(p,q) \in \mathcal{E}} \left(w_{pq} \sum_{a,b \in \mathcal{L}} d(a,b) x_{pq}(a,b) \right) \tag{17.4}$$

$$\text{s.t.} \sum_a x_p(a) = 1 \qquad\qquad \forall p \in V \tag{17.5}$$

$$\sum_a x_{pq}(a,b) = x_q(b) \qquad \forall b \in L, \ (p,q) \in E \tag{17.6}$$

$$x_p(\cdot), \ x_{pq}(\cdot,\cdot) \in \{0,1\}. \tag{17.7}$$

The above binary variables $\{x_p(\cdot)\}$ (resp. $\{x_{pq}(\cdot,\cdot)\}$) are indicators for the labels assigned to each node p (resp. pair of nodes p, q), (that is, it holds $x_p(a) = 1 \Leftrightarrow p$ takes label a, and $x_{pq}(a,b) = 1 \Leftrightarrow p, q$ take labels a, b). Constraints (17.5) simply encode the fact that each node can be assigned only one label, and constraints (17.6) enforce consistency between unary variables $\{x_p(\cdot)\}, \{x_q(\cdot)\}$ and pairwise variables $\{x_{pq}(\cdot,\cdot)\}$ by ensuring that $x_{pq}(a,b) = 1$ holds whenever $x_p(a) = x_q(b) = 1$ holds.

If integrality constraints (17.7) are then relaxed to $x_p(\cdot), x_p(\cdot,\cdot) \geq 0$, the resulting LP has a dual linear program[2] of the following form:

$$\max_{\mathbf{h},\mathbf{y}} \sum_p \min_{a \in \mathcal{L}} h_p(a) \tag{17.8}$$

$$\text{s.t.} y_{pq}(a) + y_{qp}(b) \leq w_{pq} d(a,b), \quad \forall (p,q) \in \mathcal{E}, \ (a,b) \in \mathcal{L} \times \mathcal{L} \tag{17.9}$$

$$h_p(a) \equiv \Phi_p(a) + \sum_{q:qp \in \mathcal{E}} y_{pq}(a), \ \forall p \in V, a \in \mathcal{L}. \tag{17.10}$$

The dual variables of this LP, that is, $y_{pq}(\cdot)$ and $h_p(\cdot)$, are called *balance* and *height* variables, respectively. The latter are auxiliary variables, since by their definition (17.10) they are fully specified in terms of the former variables. As can be seen, there exist two balance variables $y_{pq}(a), y_{qp}(a)$ per edge (p, q) and label a, as well as one height variable $h_p(a)$ per node p and label a. Variables $y_{pq}(a), y_{qp}(a)$ will also be called *conjugate* and, due to (17.9) and the fact that it is assumed $d(a,a) = 0$, these must be opposite one another for the dual solution to be feasible, that is, it always holds $y_{qp}(\cdot) = -y_{pq}(\cdot)$.

---

2. To recognize that the dual (17.8) is an LP, one needs to introduce auxiliary variables $\{z_p\}_{p \in V}$ that satisfy the linear constraints $z_p \leq h_p(\cdot)$, i.e, $z_p = \min_a h_p(a)$.

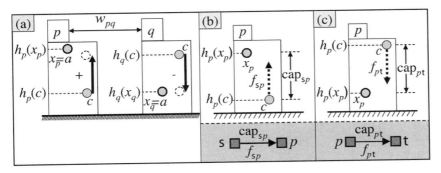

Figure 17.3
(a) Dual variables' visualization for a simple MRF with two nodes $\{p, q\}$ and two labels $\mathcal{L} = \{a, c\}$. A copy of labels $\{a, c\}$ exists for every node, and all these labels are represented by balls floating at certain heights. The role of the *height variables* $h_p(\cdot)$ is to specify these heights exactly. Furthermore, balls are not static, but may move (i.e., change their heights) in pairs by updating *conjugate balance variables*. For instance, here ball c at p is pulled up by δ (due to increasing $y_{pq}(c)$ by δ), so ball c at q moves down by δ (due to decreasing $y_{qp}(c)$ by δ). Active labels are drawn with a thicker circle. (b) During a c-iteration, if label c at p is below x_p, then (due to (17.13) or (17.17)) label c should be raised so as to reach x_p. Since, in this case, flow f_{sp} represents the total raise of c (see (17.20)), node p is connected to source node s with an edge that has capacity $\text{cap}_{sp} = h_p(x_p) - h_p(c)$. (c) Similarly, if label c at p is above x_p, then label c should not be allowed to go below x_p. Since, in this case, flow f_{pt} represents the total decrease in the height of c (see (17.20)), node p is connected to sink node t with an edge that has capacity $\text{cap}_{pt} = h_p(c) - h_p(x_p)$, which thus ensures that label c remains at a greater height than x_p.

A useful physical interpretation of all the above dual variables, which will help to explain the resulting primal-dual approximation algorithms later on, is the following: for each node p, a separate copy of all labels in $\mathcal{L}$ is considered (see figure 17.3a). It is then assumed that all these labels represent balls that float at certain heights relative to a reference plane. The role of the height variables is then to determine the balls' heights. For instance, the height of label a at vertex p is given by the dual variable $h_p(a)$, and so expressions like "label a at p is below/above label b" mean $h_p(a) \lessgtr h_p(b)$. Furthermore, balls are not static, but may move in pairs via updating pairs of conjugate balance variables. For instance, in figure 17.3a label c at p is raised by δ (due to adding δ to $y_{pq}(c)$), so label c at q has to move down by δ due to subtracting δ from $y_{qp}(c)$ so that conjugate variables $y_{pq}(c)$, $y_{qp}(c)$ remain opposite one another. Therefore, the role of balance variables is to raise or lower labels. In particular, due to (17.10) the height of label a at p may change only if at least one of the balance variables $\{y_{pq}(a)\}_{q:qp \in \mathcal{E}}$ changes. The value of balance variable $y_{pq}(a)$ thus represents the partial raise of label a at p due to edge pq, while the total raise of a at p equals the sum of all partial raises due to edges in $\mathcal{G}$ incident to p.

As a last step toward applying the primal-dual schema, one needs to derive the relaxed complementary slackness conditions, which relate the primal and the dual variables. Since only $\{0, 1\}$ primal solutions will be considered, that is, $x_p(\cdot), x_{pq}(\cdot, \cdot) \in \{0, 1\}$, a primal solution $\mathbf{x}$ can be fully described by a set of labels $\{x_p\}_{p \in \mathcal{V}}$, where x_p denotes the label of node p.[3] Under this notation the relaxed complementary slackness conditions reduce to the following form,[4] where f_1, f_2 are adjustable parameters that determine the approximation factor:

$$\min_a h_p(a) \geq \Phi_p(x_p)/f_1 + \sum_{q:qp\in\mathcal{E}} y_{pq}(x_p), \tag{17.11}$$

$$y_{pq}(x_p) + y_{qp}(x_q) \geq w_{pq}d(x_p, x_q)/f_2. \tag{17.12}$$

Based on the above general complementary slackness conditions, two different primal-dual MRF optimization strategies, called class I and class II, will be described next. They rely on different choices for the parameters f_1, f_2, and, according to theorem 17.2, they both lead to an approximation factor $f_{app} = 2\frac{d_{max}}{d_{min}}$ (where $d_{max} = \max_{a\neq b} d(a, b)$, $d_{min} = \min_{a\neq b} d(a, b)$). This is due to the fact that in both cases the parameters f_1, f_2 are chosen such that they satisfy $\max(f_1, f_2) = f_{app}$.

17.3.1 Class I Primal-Dual Methods

The class I algorithm uses the following relaxation parameters: $f_1 = 1$, $f_2 = f_{app}$. In this case the relaxed conditions (17.11) and (17.12) reduce to

$$h_p(x_p) = \min_a h_p(a), \tag{17.13}$$

$$y_{pq}(x_p) + y_{qp}(x_q) \geq w_{pq}d(x_p, x_q)/f_{app}. \tag{17.14}$$

In addition, a class I primal-dual method always ensures feasibility of dual solution $\mathbf{y}$ via imposing the following constraint:

$$y_{pq}(\cdot) \leq w_{pq}d_{min}/2. \tag{17.15}$$

In this case constraints (17.9) are satisfied due to the fact that $y_{pq}(a) + y_{qp}(b) \leq 2w_{pq}d_{min}/2 = w_{pq}d_{min} \leq w_{pq}d(a, b)$, and so $\mathbf{y}$ is indeed dual feasible.

Therefore, according to theorem 17.2, it suffices that the class I method finds a primal-dual pair $\mathbf{x}, \mathbf{y}$ that satisfies all of the conditions (17.13)–(17.15). To this end it uses the following strategy: it maintains solutions $\mathbf{x}, \mathbf{y}$ that satisfy conditions (17.14) and (17.15), and iteratively drives $\mathbf{x}, \mathbf{y}$ toward fulfilling (17.13) as well. For this purpose it also helps to maintain the following invariant, which states that *active balance variables*, that is, variables of the form $y_{pq}(x_p)$, are nonnegative:

$$\forall p \in \mathcal{V}, \quad y_{pq}(x_p) \geq 0. \tag{17.16}$$

---

3. In this case it holds $x_p(a) = 1 \Leftrightarrow x_p = a$, and $x_{pq}(a, b) = 1 \Leftrightarrow x_p = a, x_q = b$. Hence, knowing $\{x_p\}$ completely determines $\{x_p(\cdot), x_{pq}(\cdot, \cdot)\}$, and vice versa.

4. (17.11) and (17.12) are the primal complementary slackness conditions with respect to variables $x_p(\cdot)$ and $x_{pq}(\cdot, \cdot)$, respectively.

As is typical with all methods based on the primal-dual schema (see section 17.2), the above strategy is carried out via alternating updates of primal and dual variables. Before examining these updates at a high level, let us first reinterpret conditions (17.13)–(17.15) based on the physical interpretation of the dual variables mentioned in section 17.3:

- (17.13) requires that at each node p, its active label x_p is at the lowest height.
- (17.14) requires that the active labels of any two adjacent nodes are raised at least proportionally to their distance.
- (17.15) imposes an upper bound on how much a label can be raised.

Based on all the above, the update of the primal and dual variables can proceed as follows:

Dual Variables Update Given the current active labels (i.e., the current primal), the balance variables are updated so that for any node p, nonactive labels below x_p increase their heights in order either to reach active label x_p or to attain the maximum raise allowed by (17.15). One thus aims to get closer to fulfilling (17.13). Notice that conditions (17.14) and (17.15) remain true (assuming they were true before the update), because no active labels were moved to spoil (17.14) and no labels went beyond their maximum raise to spoil (17.15).

Primal Variables Update Given the new heights (i.e., the new dual), there might still be vertices violating (17.13), that is, their active labels are not at the lowest height. For each such vertex p, a nonactive label below x_p that has already reached its maximum raise allowed by (17.15) is selected. That label, say c, is then made the new active label of p, that is, one sets $x_p = c$, so that (17.13) is brought closer to being fulfilled. Notice, again, that conditions (17.14) and (17.15) remain true, since if the new active label $x_p = c$ has already reached its maximum raise at p, it then holds

$$y_{pq}(x_p) = \frac{w_{pq}d_{\min}}{2} \geq \frac{w_{pq}d_{\min}}{2}\frac{d(x_p, x_q)}{d_{\max}} = \frac{w_{pq}d(x_p, x_q)}{f_{\mathrm{app}}},$$

which proves that (17.14) is valid, given that $y_{qp}(x_q) \geq 0$ due to (17.16).

By repeating the above primal and dual updates, it can be shown that (17.13) will finally be fulfilled, because one keeps assigning lower active labels to nodes. The algorithm can then terminate, since conditions (17.14) and (17.15) are already maintained throughout.

17.3.2 Class II Primal-Dual Methods

Algorithms in this class are parameterized by $\mu \in \left[\frac{1}{f_{\mathrm{app}}}1\right]$. For any such μ, the corresponding class II method chooses the following relaxation factors: $f_1 = \mu f_{\mathrm{app}}$, $f_2 = f_{\mathrm{app}}$.[5] An important difference between a class I and a class II algorithm is that the former always

---

5. The requirement $\mu \geq \frac{1}{f_{\mathrm{app}}}$ comes from the fact that it cannot hold $f_1 < 1$.

maintains a feasible dual solution via imposing constraints (17.15), whereas the latter may allow a dual solution to become infeasible by imposing a looser set of constraints (see constraints (17.19) below).

To compensate for this fact, however, a class II algorithm requires that the final infeasible primal-dual pair $(\mathbf{x}, \mathbf{y})$ satisfies the following relaxed complementary slackness conditions, which are tighter because they result from using the relaxation parameters $f_1 = 1$, $f_2 = \frac{1}{\mu}$:

$$h_p(x_p) = \min_a h_p(a), \tag{17.17}$$

$$y_{pq}(x_p) + y_{qp}(x_q) = \mu w_{pq} d(x_p, x_q). \tag{17.18}$$

In addition, a class II algorithm ensures that the dual solution $\mathbf{y}$, although probably infeasible, is still not too far from feasibility. This is achieved via imposing the following constraints on $\mathbf{y}$:

$$y_{pq}(a) + y_{qp}(b) \le 2\mu w_{pq} d_{max} \quad \forall a, b \in L, \ \forall (p, q) \in E. \tag{17.19}$$

Practically, this almost-feasibility of $\mathbf{y}$ means that if this solution is divided by a suitable factor, it becomes feasible again.[6] Not only that, but it turns out that the resulting primal-dual pair also satisfies all wanted complementary slackness conditions.

Indeed, first of all, if a $\mathbf{y}$ satisfying (17.19) is divided by μf_{app}, then the resulting solution $\mathbf{y}^{fit} = \mathbf{y}/\mu f_{app}$ satisfies dual constraints (17.9) and is thus feasible, as the following quick derivation shows:

$$y_{pq}^{fit}(a) + y_{qp}^{fit}(b) = \frac{y_{pq}(a) + y_{qp}(b)}{\mu f_{app}} \overset{(17.19)}{\le} \frac{2\mu w_{pq} d_{max}}{\mu f_{app}} = w_{pq} d_{min} \le w_{pq} d_{ab}.$$

Furthermore, if the infeasible pair $(\mathbf{x}, \mathbf{y})$ satisfies constraints (17.17) and (17.18), that is, the relaxed complementary slackness conditions with $f_1 = 1$, $f_2 = \frac{1}{\mu}$, then it is easy to show that the feasible pair $(\mathbf{x}, \mathbf{y}^{fit})$ satisfies the same conditions with $f_1 = \mu f_{app}$, $f_2 = f_{app}$, thus leading to an f_{app}-approximate solution according to theorem 17.2, as intended.

Therefore, the goal of a class II algorithm is to fulfill conditions (17.17)–(17.19). To this end it uses a strategy similar to a class I method: it maintains $\mathbf{x}, \mathbf{y}$ that satisfy (17.18) and (17.19), and iteratively drives these solutions toward fulfilling (17.17) via alternating primal-dual updates.

17.4   Fast Primal-Dual Schema for MRFs via Max-Flow

It turns out that each iteration of the aforementioned primal-dual schemes (i.e., each alternating update of the primal and dual variables) can be implemented very efficiently via solving

---

6. This method, turning an infeasible dual solution into a feasible one by scaling, is also known as *"dual fitting"* [493] in the linear programming literature.

1:   $\mathbf{x} \mathbf{y}] \leftarrow$ INIT_DUALS_PRIMALS$()$; $\mathbf{x}_{\text{old}} \leftarrow \mathbf{x}$
2:   **for** each label c in $\mathcal{L}$ **do**
3:       $\mathbf{y} \leftarrow$ PREEDIT_DUALS$(c, \mathbf{x}, \mathbf{y})$;
4:       $[\mathbf{x}', \mathbf{y}'] \leftarrow$ UPDATE_DUALS_PRIMALS$(c, \mathbf{x}, \mathbf{y})$;
5:       $\mathbf{y}' \leftarrow$ POSTEDIT_DUALS$(c, \mathbf{x}', \mathbf{y}')$;
6:       $\mathbf{x} \leftarrow \mathbf{x}'$; $\mathbf{y} \leftarrow \mathbf{y}'$;
7:   **end for**
8:   **if** $\mathbf{x} \neq \mathbf{x}_{\text{old}}$ **then**
9:       $\mathbf{x}_{\text{old}} \leftarrow \mathbf{x}$; **go to** 2;
10: **end if**

Figure 17.4
The basic structure of FastPD.

a max-flow problem. This problem is constructed based on the current pair $(\mathbf{x}^k, \mathbf{y}^k)$, and its solution (i.e., the flows) directly determines how to construct the next pair $(\mathbf{x}^{k+1}, \mathbf{y}^{k+1})$. Such an implementation of a primal-dual method is called FastPD [271], short for Fast Primal-Dual.

The basic structure of FastPD is shown in figure 17.4. The initial primal-dual solutions are generated inside INIT_DUALS_PRIMALS. During each iteration of the algorithm (lines 3–6 in figure 17.4), a label $c \in \mathcal{L}$ is selected and a new primal-dual pair of solutions $(\mathbf{x}', \mathbf{y}')$ is generated by updating the current pair $(\mathbf{x}, \mathbf{y})$. The main part of this update takes place inside subroutine UPDATE_DUALS_PRIMALS, where the max-flow problem is solved (routines PREEDIT_DUALS and POSTEDIT_DUALS apply minor corrections to the dual variables before and after the main update, respectively). This is called a c-iteration, since among all balance variables of $\mathbf{y}$ (i.e., $y_{pq}(.)$), only the balance variables of c-labels (i.e., $y_{pq}(c)$) are modified, resulting in a new set of balance variables $\{y'_{pq}(c)\}_{pq \in \mathcal{E}}$ (and hence also a new set of height variables $\{h'_p(c)\}_{p \in \mathcal{V}}$) for the next iteration. $|\mathcal{L}|$ such iterations (one c-iteration per label $c \in \mathcal{L}$) make up an outer iteration (lines 2–7 in figure 17.4), and the algorithm terminates if no change in the primal variables exists in the current outer iteration.

The max-flow problem solved during UPDATE_DUALS_PRIMALS$(c, \mathbf{x}, \mathbf{y})$ (for updating $(\mathbf{x}, \mathbf{y})$ into $(\mathbf{x}', \mathbf{y}')$) is with respect to a directed graph $\mathcal{G}^c = (\mathcal{V}^c, \mathcal{E}^c, \mathcal{C}^c)$. The values of the capacities $\mathcal{C}^c$ are defined based on the current pair $\mathbf{x}, \mathbf{y}$, while the nodes $\mathcal{V}^c$ consist of all MRF nodes in $\mathcal{V}$ (the *internal* nodes) plus two *external* nodes, the source s and the sink t. Furthermore, nodes $\mathcal{V}^c$ are connected by two types of edges: *interior* and *exterior*. More specifically, there are two directed interior edges pq, qp for each undirected edge $(p, q) \in \mathcal{E}$ of the original MRF graph, while each internal node p is connected (through an exterior edge) to exactly one of the external nodes s, t. By pushing flow through the interior and exterior edges, one essentially simulates changes in the balance and height variables, respectively (i.e., in variables $\{y_{pq}(c)\}_{pq}, \{h_p(c)\}_p$), thus forming the next dual variables

$\{y'_{pq}(c)\}_{pq}, \{h'_p(c)\}_p$. For example, the flow through the exterior edge connected to p (i.e., flow f_{sp} or f_{pt}) is used for updating the height variable $h_p(c)$ as follows:

$$h'_p(c) = h_p(c) + \begin{cases} f_{sp}, & \text{if } h_p(c) \le h_p(x_p) \\ -f_{pt}, & \text{if } h_p(c) > h_p(x_p). \end{cases} \qquad (17.20)$$

This is also illustrated graphically in figure 17.3b,c, where the rationale of how to set the corresponding exterior capacity cap_{sp} or cap_{pt} is also explained. Similarly, the flows f_{pq}, f_{qp} of the interior edges pq, qp are used for updating the balance variables $y_{pq}(c)$, $y_{qp}(c)$ as follows:

$$y'_{pq}(c) = y_{pq}(c) + f_{pq} - f_{qp}. \qquad (17.21)$$

For a full description and analysis of FastPD, the interested reader is referred to [271]. An implementation of this algorithm is available at http://www.csd.uoc.gr/~ komod/FastPD.

17.5 Optimality Properties of Primal-Dual Algorithms

As explained in sections 17.3.1 and 17.3.2, the final primal-dual solutions of class I and class II methods satisfy the primal complementary slackness conditions relaxed by a factor f_{app}. Therefore, according to theorem 17.2, the following statement holds:

Theorem 17.4 *The last primal solution estimated by FastPD is an f_{app}-approximate solution.*

Furthermore, it holds that class I and class II (for $\mu < 1$) algorithms are nongreedy algorithms, meaning that neither the primal nor the dual objective function necessarily decreases (increases) per iteration. Instead, it can be shown that it is the quantity $\text{APF} = \sum_p h_p(x_p)$, that is, the sum of the heights of active labels, that constantly decreases. Nevertheless, the above algorithms ensure that APF is always kept close to the primal function, and as a result the decrease in APF is finally reflected to the values of the primal function as well, which is the MRF energy $E(\mathbf{x})$. However, a notable thing happens in a class II algorithm with $\mu = 1$ and the distance $d(\cdot, \cdot)$ a metric. In that case it can be shown that APF actually coincides with the primal function, that is, $\text{APF} = E(\mathbf{x})$. Furthermore, FastPD computes (during a c-iteration) a solution $\mathbf{x}'$ that minimizes APF with respect to any other c-expansion of current solution $\mathbf{x}$. As a result, the following theorem holds true, showing that the α-expansion algorithm [72] is included as a special case of this framework:

Theorem 17.5 *If $d(\cdot, \cdot)$ is a metric and $\mu = 1$, then FastPD computes (during a c-iteration) the best c-expansion move.*

Theorem 17.4 above essentially provides worst case (i.e., theoretical) suboptimality bounds. However, FastPD, being a primal-dual method, can also tell, for free, how well

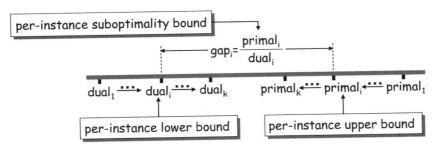

Figure 17.5
During FastPD the ratios of the computed primal and dual costs provide per-instance approximation factors, which become tighter over time.

it performs for any particular problem it is tested on. And it can do that at no extra cost by providing per-instance approximation factors based on the ratio of the computed primal and dual costs (see figure 17.5). Obviously, these factors are continuously refined as the algorithm runs, and actually prove to be much tighter in practice than their theoretical counterparts. For instance, figure 17.6 shows how these ratios vary per iteration for two standard benchmark problems from the Middlebury Dataset, a stereo matching example (*Tsukuba*) and a denoising example (*Penguin*). They finally drop very close to 1, meaning that an almost optimal solution is estimated at the end (despite the problems being NP-hard).

17.6 Computational Efficiency of Primal-Dual Algorithms

17.6.1 Single MRFs

Besides maintaining strong optimality properties, another very important advantage of primal-dual algorithms over other graph cut-based methods, such as α-expansion, is that they prove to be much more efficient in practice. In fact, the computational efficiency of all such methods is largely determined from the time taken by each max-flow problem, which in turn depends on the number of augmenting paths that need to be computed per max-flow. Fortunately for FastPD, this number decreases dramatically over time. This is illustrated in figure 17.7a for the case of the *Penguin* image-denoising problem, where a plot of the corresponding number of augmenting paths per outer iteration (i.e., per group of $|\mathcal{L}|$ iterations) is shown. Whereas this number remains very high (i.e., almost $2 \cdot 10^6$) throughout α-expansion, it drops toward zero very quickly in the case of FastPD. For instance, only 4905 and 7 augmenting paths had to be found during the eighth and the last outer iteration, respectively. In fact, this behavior is typical of FastPD, where, after only a few iterations, a very small number of augmenting paths needs to be computed per max-flow, which of course boosts the algorithm's performance.

This property can be explained by the fact that FastPD makes full use of both primal and dual information throughout its execution. What essentially happens is illustrated in

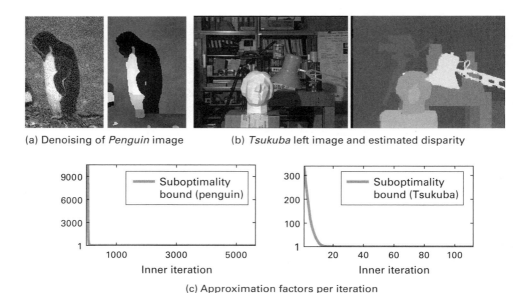

(a) Denoising of *Penguin* image   (b) *Tsukuba* left image and estimated disparity

(c) Approximation factors per iteration

Figure 17.6
FastPD results on image denoising and stereo matching along with corresponding approximation factors per iteration. These factors drop very close to 1, meaning that the generated solutions are almost optimal.

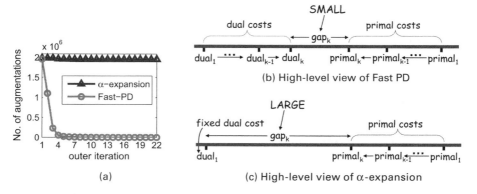

(a)

(b) High-level view of Fast PD

(c) High-level view of α-expansion

Figure 17.7
(a) Number of augmenting paths per outer iteration for the *Penguin* example. Notice the dramatic decrease over time in the case of FastPD. (b) FastPD generates pairs of primal-dual solutions iteratively, with the goal of reducing the gap between the primal and dual costs. Since this gap provides a rough approximation to the number of augmenting paths (see theorem 17.4), the latter is forced to reduce over time. (c) On the contrary, α-expansion works only in the primal domain (i.e., it is as if a fixed dual cost is used at the start of each iteration), and thus the primal-dual gap never becomes small enough. Therefore, no significant reduction in the number of augmenting paths takes place over time.

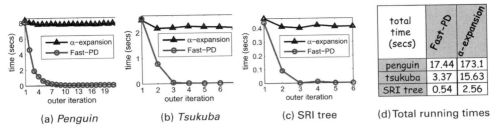

Figure 17.8
(a), (b), and (c) show the running times per outer iteration for three standard benchmark vision problems. (d) lists the corresponding total running times (all experiments were measured on a 1.6GHz CPU).

figure 17.7b. Intuitively, FastPD ultimately wants to close the gap between the primal cost and the dual cost (recall theorem 17.1), and for this it iteratively generates primal-dual pairs, with the goal of continuously decreasing the size of this gap. However, the gap's size can be thought of as a rough approximation to the number of augmenting paths per iteration (see theorem 17.6 below). Therefore, as FastPD keeps reducing this gap throughout its execution, the number of augmenting paths is forced to decrease over time as well, which in turn results in a significant improvement in the efficiency of the max-flow algorithm (recall that a path augmenting algorithm for max-flow essentially proceeds by continuing to find augmenting paths).

On the contrary, a method like α-expansion, which works only in the primal domain, ignores dual solutions completely. It is, roughly speaking, as if α-expansion is resetting the dual solution to zero at the start of each iteration, thus effectively forgetting that solution thereafter (see figure 17.7c). For this reason it fails to substantially reduce the primal-dual gap and thus also fails to achieve a reduction in path augmentations over time, that is, across iterations. This of course results in more time being needed per iteration.

The above-mentioned relationship between primal-dual gap and number of augmenting paths is formally described in the next theorem.

Theorem 17.6 ([271])   For FastPD the primal-dual gap at the current iteration forms an upper bound for the number of augmenting paths at each iteration thereafter.

As a result, the time per iteration of FastPD decreases dramatically over time. This has been verified experimentally with virtually all problems FastPD has been applied to (for a few example applications see [168, 39, 446]). Figure 17.8 shows total running times, as well as running times per outer iteration, for some standard benchmark vision problems. Notice how much faster an outer iteration of FastPD becomes over time. For instance, for the "SRI tree" stereo matching example in figure 17.8, the last outer iteration of FastPD took less than 1 msec (only four augmenting paths had to be computed), and thus it was more than 400 times faster than the corresponding iteration of α-expansion. Similarly, for the *Tsukuba* example in figure 17.8, the last iteration of FastPD was more than 2000 times faster than α-expansion.

17.6.2 Dynamic MRFs

Besides single MRFs, FastPD can easily be adapted to boost the efficiency of dynamic MRFs [246], that is, MRFs varying over time, which are frequently used in computer vision (e.g., in applications dealing with video data). This shows the generality and power of that method. In fact, FastPD fits perfectly to this task. The implicit assumption here is that the change between successive MRFs is small, so by initializing the current MRF with the final primal solution of the previous MRF, one expects to speed up inference. A significant advantage of FastPD in this regard, however, is that it can exploit not only the previous primal solution (say $\bar{\mathbf{x}}$), but also the previous dual solution (say $\bar{\mathbf{y}}$). As a result it can use both $\bar{\mathbf{x}}$, $\bar{\mathbf{y}}$ to initialize the starting primal-dual solutions (say $\mathbf{x}$, $\mathbf{y}$) of the current MRF. The new INIT_DUALS_PRIMALS routine needed for this purpose is shown in figure 17.9, and is actually the only change needed for applying FastPD to dynamic MRFs.

Figure 17.10b shows the running times per frame for a dynamic MRF example used for disparity estimation for the "SRI tree" sequence. As expected, the speedup provided by FastPD is even greater in this case. For instance, the algorithm required, on average, only 0.22 sec per frame (i.e., it ran almost in real time at five frames/sec), and was thus ten times faster than α-expansion. Figure 17.10c shows that a substantial reduction in the number of augmenting paths per frame has been achieved as well.

What essentially happens in dynamic MRFs is illustrated in figure 17.11a. FastPD has already reduced the primal-dual gap of the previous MRF, that is, the gap between costs primal$_{\bar{\mathbf{x}}}$ and dual$_{\bar{\mathbf{y}}}$. However, due to the different singleton or pairwise potentials at the current time, these costs must be perturbed to generate the new initial costs primal$_{\mathbf{x}}$, dual$_{\mathbf{y}}$. Nevertheless, since only slight perturbations take place, the new initial primal-dual gap between primal$_{\mathbf{x}}$, dual$_{\mathbf{y}}$ will remain close to the small previous gap between primal$_{\bar{\mathbf{x}}}$, dual$_{\bar{\mathbf{y}}}$. As a result the initial primal-dual gap of the current MRF will be small from the outset, and thus few augmenting paths will have to be found, which in turn boosts the algorithm's performance. This is in contrast to what happens in a primal-based algorithm, where the previous primal-dual gap (and hence also the current one) remain large (see figure 17.11b).

Put otherwise, FastPD boosts performance, that is, reduces the number of augmenting paths, across two different axes. The first axis lies along different iterations of the same MRF (see vertical arrows in figure 17.11c), whereas the second axis extends across time,

$$
\boxed{
\begin{aligned}
&[\mathbf{x}, \mathbf{y}] \leftarrow \text{INIT\_DUALS\_PRIMALS}(\bar{\mathbf{x}}, \bar{\mathbf{y}}): \\
&\quad \mathbf{x} \leftarrow \bar{\mathbf{x}}; \ \mathbf{y} \leftarrow \bar{\mathbf{y}}; \\
&\quad \forall pq, y_{pq}(x_p) += w_{pq} d(x_p, x_q) - \bar{w}_{pq} \bar{d}(x_p, x_q); \\
&\quad \forall p, \ h_p(\cdot) += \Phi_p(\cdot) - \bar{\Phi}_p(\cdot);
\end{aligned}
}
$$

Figure 17.9
The new INIT_DUALS_PRIMALS routine for dynamic MRFs.

(a) Left image and estimated disparity for one
frame from the "SRI tree" sequence

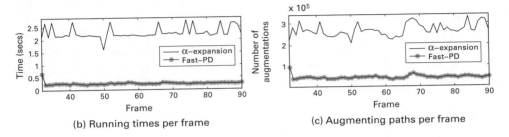

(b) Running times per frame

(c) Augmenting paths per frame

Figure 17.10
Statistics for the "SRI tree" sequence.

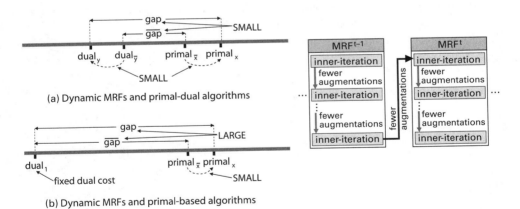

(a) Dynamic MRFs and primal-dual algorithms

(b) Dynamic MRFs and primal-based algorithms

Figure 17.11
Computational efficiency of MAP inference algorithms for dynamic MRFs (see text for explanation).

that is, across different MRFs (see arrow in figure 17.11c connecting the last iteration of MRF^{t-1} to the first iteration of MRF^{t}).

17.7 Conclusions

Due to the diversity, complexity, and large-scale nature of MRFs encountered in computer vision problems nowadays, it is imperative that corresponding MAP estimation algorithms possess very high efficiency, have wide applicability, and also be very effective. The primal-dual methods described in this chapter fulfill these requirements to a great extent, as they manage to deliver approximately optimal solutions for a wide class of MRFs encountered in computer vision, at a very low computational cost. As explained, their theoretical setting rests on the primal-dual schema, which is a powerful technique for deriving approximation algorithms using LP duality theory. Hopefully, due to the generality of this schema, many new applications of it to other problems in computer vision will appear in the future.

Acknowledgments

I thank Andrew Blake, Pushmeet Kohli, and Carsten Rother for encouraging me to write this chapter. I am also grateful to my colleagues Nikos Paragios and Georgios Tziritas for fruitful discussions and suggestions. This work was partially supported from the French ANR-Blanc grant SURF(2005–2008) and Platon (2006–2007).

18 Fusion-Move Optimization for MRFs with an Extensive Label Space

Victor Lempitsky, Carsten Rother, Stefan Roth, and Andrew Blake

The efficient optimization of Markov random fields is in general a very challenging task, as discussed in many of the other chapters in this book (e.g., 11, 3, and 4). One popular class of optimization methods is based on the move-making paradigm, which is introduced in chapter 3. That chapter describes the expansion-move and swap-move algorithms. In the present chapter another move-making algorithm is described, the fusion move. The expansion-move and swap-move algorithms are particular instances of the fusion-move technique. The main benefit of this algorithm is its generality and, hence, its applicability to many different application scenarios, even outside the traditional scope of move-making methods. In particular it is demonstrated that fusion move can be utilized to parallelize the expansion-move algorithm, and can also be applied to MRFs where the underlying label space is continuous, such as those used for optical flow. One practical challenge during the application of the fusion-move algorithm is that it comprises a set of binary optimization problems that in general are NP-hard to optimize. We will discuss how to deal with this issue and analyze the practical relevance of this problem.[1]

18.1 Introduction

This chapter focuses on minimizing energies from pairwise MRFs with either multiple (> 2) discrete or continuous labels. The majority of optimization problems for such MRFs are NP-hard, and thus various approximate algorithms (such as loopy belief propagation [538] in the case of discrete labels, and gradient descent in the case of continuous labels) have been suggested. Graph cut has also been applied to discrete multilabel MRFs either by writing the problem as a large binary-label MRF [211, 421, 243] (see chapter 4) or by applying graph cut iteratively to binary-labeled subproblems (i.e., move-making algorithms; see [3, 72, 71, 269, 495]). While these approaches yield competitive results when compared

---

1. This chapter is based on [300, 297, 299, 398].

with other approximate optimization techniques, their computational demands grow fast with the number of labels.

Unfortunately, many practical applications often have an extensive number of labels (e.g., stereo with up to 160 different depth labels, or even a continuous label space, e.g., optical flow). How to perform efficient and high quality optimization for such applications is the topic of this chapter. The approach that is taken is rather different from traditional ones: we exploit the fact that a variety of approximate solutions to a particular MRF optimization problem can be produced by using various approximate (or local) optimization algorithms, different initializations, parameter settings, or other factors. The question then arises whether different suboptimal solutions can be combined in a principled manner in order to produce a new, better labeling with lower energy.

Given a pair of suboptimal labelings (or *proposals*), it is shown that combining them into a better solution can be expressed as a binary-labeled MRF minimization problem. This auxiliary binary-labeled MRF can be optimized efficiently using graph cut-based techniques, which yields a new combined (*fused*) labeling with decreased (or equal) energy. This operation is called *fusion move* and, after introducing it, several different optimization schemes based on fusion moves are presented. In general, fusion moves allow application of graph cut to a wider class of MRFs, including those with continuous labels. Moreover, in the case of discrete labels, fusion moves can be used to accelerate graph cut minimization drastically.

The approach builds upon two important components from the recent literature. First, the graph cut-based BHS algorithm that can optimize non-submodular binary-labeled MRFs, which are subproblems of this approach. Second, the idea of graph cut-based move-making methods is borrowed from [72, 71] and extended here in order to perform fusions of proposals that themselves are computed by some domain-specific method. It is shown that incorporating this domain-specific knowledge may lead to a considerable gain in both efficiency and quality of results. The versatility and applicability of fusion moves are demonstrated with two different *hybrid* optimization schemes, where fusion moves are used to combine proposal solutions coming from very different processes. First, it is demonstrated how to efficiently parallelize previous graph cut-based algorithms for discrete-label MRFs—the well-known alpha-expansion [72] algorithm—with little parallelization overhead. In this case the proposal labelings that are to be fused are generated by the alpha-expansion algorithm itself. Second, a continuous-valued MRF for optical flow is estimated, and here proposals obtained with classical continuous algorithms are used that in the end yield optical flow fields with state-of-the-art accuracy, and that by far exceed that of the original proposals.

The rest of the chapter is organized as follows. In section 18.2 the fusion-move algorithm is introduced. The relationship to other fusionlike approaches is given in section 18.3, and applications of fusion move are described in section 18.4. Finally, section 18.5 presents some thoughts on proposal generation mechanisms.

18.2   Overview of the Fusion-Move Algorithm

As in other chapters (e.g., 1 and 3) energies associated with pairwise MRFs are considered that take the form

$$E(\mathbf{x}) = \sum_{i \in \mathcal{V}} \Phi_i(x_i) + \sum_{i,j \in \mathcal{N}} \Psi_{ij}(x_i, x_j), \quad \mathbf{x} \in \mathbf{L}^{\mathcal{V}}, \tag{18.1}$$

where $\mathcal{V}$ is a set of nodes and $\mathcal{N}$ is a set of undirected edges connecting pairs of nodes (in computer vision problems $\mathcal{V}$ often corresponds to the pixels in the image, and $\mathcal{N}$ contains pairs of adjacent pixels in 4- or 8-connected neighborhoods). The *labeling* $\mathbf{x}$ assigns a label x_p from some label space $\mathbf{L}$ to every node $p \in \mathcal{V}$. The family of real-valued functions $\Phi_i : \mathbf{L} \to \mathbf{R}$ and $\Psi_{ij} : \mathbf{L}^2 \to \mathbf{R}$, called *unary* and *pairwise potentials*, respectively, define the energy of each labeling. The optimization problem then is to find the labeling with the smallest energy. Since for the majority of interesting combinations of $\mathbf{L}$, Φ_i, and Ψ_{ij} this minimization problem is NP-complete, approximate optimization approaches are considered instead.

18.2.1   Combinatorial Optimization for Binary-Labeled MRFs

Before explaining the fusion-move algorithm, the optimization of binary MRFs is briefly reviewed (see chapter 2 for details). The minimization of (21.5) in the binary-label case ($\mathbf{L} = \{0, 1\}$) is known as *quadratic pseudo-Boolean optimization* (QPBO) and is a well-studied problem in the optimization literature. If the energy is *submodular*, this means all of the pairwise potentials V_{pq} obey $V_{pq}(0, 0) + V_{pq}(1, 1) \le V_{pq}(0, 1) + V_{pq}(1, 0)$, and then the globally optimal labeling $\hat{\mathbf{x}}$ can be found exactly [179, 176, 266]. One popular technique, called graph cut, solves a minimum cut computation in a specially constructed graph [179]. However, it has been realized relatively recently that nonsubmodular QPBO problems can still be reduced to minimum cut computations [62, 61, 261], which is referred to as the BHS algorithm.[2] (See chapter 2 for details.) In the general nonsubmodular case the globally optimal labeling $\hat{\mathbf{x}}$ can be found only partially, however. This means that after the minimum cut computation, each node can be assigned the label 0, 1, or "?" (nodes with labels 0 and 1 are referred to as *labeled*, and the nodes with label "?" are called *unlabeled*). It is then known that a globally optimal labeling coincides with $\hat{\mathbf{x}}$ for all labeled nodes (*partial optimality*). Furthermore, it is known that taking an arbitrary labeling $\mathbf{x}'$ and replacing its labels with those of $\mathbf{x}$ for all nodes that have been labeled in $\hat{\mathbf{x}}$ is guaranteed not to increase the energy of $\mathbf{x}'$ (*persistence* property). In many practical scenarios the number of unlabeled nodes may be negligible; in many other cases some or all such nodes can be further labeled in a globally optimal fashion using certain search heuristics [63, 403, 530].

---

2. The BHS algorithm is often referred to in the computer vision literature (e.g., [261, 403, 530]), as the QPBO algorithm.

18.2.2 The Fusion Move

We now consider a more general case, where the MRF energy (21.5) is defined on a nonbinary label space $\mathbf{L}$ (e.g., $\mathbf{L} = \{0, 1, \ldots, N\}$ or $\mathbf{L} = \mathbf{R}^2$). While the exact minimization of (21.5) is intractable for the absolute majority of cases (see, e.g., chapters 1, 3, and 4), its approximate minimization is still of great use for a broad variety of computational problems. The fusion move introduced here deals with the problem of optimally combining two (suboptimal) proposal labelings. As we shall see later, this methodology can be applied to the approximate minimization of (18.1) in a variety of ways. The most common use is in the context of an iterative move-making algorithm, as introduced in chapter 3. This means that a current (suboptimal) solution is combined with a new proposal labeling, which gives an updated solution. The set of proposal labelings will be called *proposals*.

Given two labelings $\mathbf{x}^0 \in \mathbf{L}^{\mathcal{V}}$ and $\mathbf{x}^1 \in \mathbf{L}^{\mathcal{V}}$, the goal is to combine $\mathbf{x}^0$ and $\mathbf{x}^1$ in a good way. Here the term "combination" refers to a new labeling in which the label of each node is taken from either $\mathbf{x}^0$ or $\mathbf{x}^1$. More formally, a combination $\mathbf{x}^c$ is defined by an auxiliary binary vector $\mathbf{y} \in \{0, 1\}^{\mathcal{V}}$, such that

$$\mathbf{x}^c(\mathbf{y}) = \mathbf{x}^0 \bullet (1 - \mathbf{y}) + \mathbf{x}^1 \bullet \mathbf{y}, \tag{18.2}$$

where $\bullet$ denotes the Hadamard (nodewise or elementwise) product, that is, $x_p^c(\mathbf{y}) = x_p^0$ if $y_p = 0$ and $x_p^c(\mathbf{y}) = x_p^1$ if $y_p = 1$.

Then the energy (18.1) of any such combination, if defined as the energy of the auxiliary vector;

$$E^f(\mathbf{y}) = E(\mathbf{x}^c(\mathbf{y})) = \sum_{p \in \mathcal{V}} U_p^f(y_p) + \sum_{p,q \in \mathcal{N}} V_{pq}^f(y_p, y_q), \tag{18.3}$$

where new auxiliary unary and pairwise potentials are defined as

$$U_p^f(a) = U_i(x_i^a), \quad V_{ij}^f(a, b) = V_{ij}(x_i^a, x_j^b). \tag{18.4}$$

Minimizing equation (18.3) as a function of the binary labeling $\mathbf{y}$, using the BHS algorithm (i.e., nonsubmodular graph cut) yields the labeling $\hat{\mathbf{y}}$. If all nodes of $\mathbf{y}$ are labeled, then this labeling corresponds to the global optimum of (18.3), and therefore the resulting labeling $\mathbf{x}^c(\hat{\mathbf{y}})$ corresponds to the globally optimal combination of $\mathbf{x}^0$ and $\mathbf{x}^1$ in the sense of the original problem (18.1). Such a combination is called a *fusion* of $\mathbf{x}^0$ and $\mathbf{x}^1$, and the process of its computation is the *fusion move*. In the following, the fusion move is denoted with the symbol "$\odot$" (e.g., $\mathbf{x}^c(\hat{\mathbf{y}}) = \mathbf{x}^0 \odot \mathbf{x}^1$).

18.2.3 Dealing with Nonsubmodularity

In some cases solving (18.3) using minimum cut may yield only a partial optimal labeling $\hat{\mathbf{y}}$ that contains some unlabeled nodes. In practice, however, for a variety of problems very few of the nodes are unlabeled when computing the fusion move. Some examples are given in section 18.4, and in the four very different applications discussed in [300] the maximum number of unlabeled nodes is always below 0.1 percent. After giving an informal intuition on why the number of unlabeled nodes is low in practice, a theoretically sound way is introduced that deals with unlabeled nodes.

The number of unlabeled nodes in the partially global optimal labeling for a pairwise MRF with binary labels is closely related to the number of nonsubmodular pairwise terms, which are violating the constraint $V_{pq}(0, 0) + V_{pq}(1, 1) \leq V_{pq}(0, 1) + V_{pq}(1, 0)$ (see [263]). In the fusion-move case this constraint means that taking the labels of two adjacent nodes from the same proposal should on average have smaller pairwise cost than taking them from different proposals. But this is exactly what typically happens in the optimization schemes, because the two proposals are obtained through different, uncommunicating processes. Thus for each pair of nodes, the pairwise cost within each proposal labeling is small (since the proposal labelings are somehow "optimized"), while taking their labels from different proposals may generate a "seam" and, hence, incur a high pairwise cost. Therefore, the number of strongly nonsubmodular terms tends to be small and thus almost all nodes become labeled. A similar observation with respect to the number of nonsubmodular terms during image stitching was made in [261].

The following is a very simple way to deal with unlabeled nodes that was presented in [403]. Assume without loss of generality that $E(\mathbf{x}^0) \leq E(\mathbf{x}^1)$; then all unlabeled nodes in $\hat{\mathbf{y}}$ are labeled with 0. This auxiliary labeling is denoted as $\tilde{\mathbf{y}}$. Thus, $\tilde{y}_p = \hat{y}_p$ if $\hat{y}_p \neq$ "?", and $\tilde{y}_p = 0$ otherwise. The final output of the fusion move is the labeling $\mathbf{x}^c(\tilde{\mathbf{y}})$. In other words, all nodes p for which $\hat{y}_p =$ "?" receive their labels from $\mathbf{x}^0$ in the fused solution. According to the persistence property of the BHS algorithm [61, 261], the energy of the auxiliary labeling $E^f(\tilde{\mathbf{y}})$ is not greater than the energy of the auxiliary labeling $E^f(\mathbf{0})$, which implies

$$E(\mathbf{x}^c(\tilde{\mathbf{y}})) \leq E(\mathbf{x}^0) \leq E(\mathbf{x}^1), \tag{18.5}$$

that is, *the fusion move is guaranteed not to increase the energy (18.1) compared with the smallest of the energies of* $\mathbf{x}^0$ *and* $\mathbf{x}^1$. While this simple strategy for labeling the unlabeled nodes in the auxiliary labeling is sufficient for obtaining nearly global optimal fusions of proposals for many applications [300], fusion moves in harder optimization problems may require more sophisticated search strategies for the unlabeled nodes [63, 403, 530].

18.3 Relationship to Other Fusionlike Approaches

In the following we will outline many different optimization techniques that are in some way related to fusion move.

Chapter 3 introduced two specific move-making methods for multilabeled MRFs, the expansion-move and swap-move approaches. In the following we show that these two algorithms, as well as the jump-move [71] approach, are particular cases of the fusion move.

Expansion move [70, 72, 71]   Given a current labeling $\mathbf{x}^0$ and a label $\alpha \in \mathbf{L}$, each node p can either retain its original label x_p^0 or take the label α during the move. A repeated application of expansion moves where α iterates over the set of labels $\mathbf{L}$ is the alpha-expansion algorithm, which is perhaps the most popular graph cut-based optimization algorithm for multilabel MRFs in vision. Each expansion move can be regarded as a fusion move, where the proposals are $\mathbf{x}^0$ and the constant labeling is $\mathbf{x}^1$, such that for each node p, $x_p^1 = \alpha$.

Swap move [70, 72, 71]   Given a current labeling $\mathbf{x}^0$ and a pair of labels $\alpha \in \mathbf{L}$ and $\beta \in \mathbf{L}$, each node p with $x_p^0 \in \{\alpha, \beta\}$ can either retain its original label or change it from α to β (or vice versa). Nodes with labels that are different from α and β remain unchanged. The swap move can be regarded as a fusion move where the proposals are the current labeling $\mathbf{x}^0$ and the labeling $\mathbf{x}^1$, such that $x_p^1 = \beta$ if $x_p^0 = \alpha$, $x_p^1 = \alpha$ if $x_p^0 = \beta$, and $x_p^1 = x_p^0$ otherwise.

Jump move [71]   The jump move is defined for an ordered discrete label space $\mathbf{L} = \{0, 1, \ldots N\}$. Given a current labeling $\mathbf{x}^0$ and a number $k \in \{-N, -N+1, \ldots, N-1, N\}$, during the move each node p can either retain its original label x_p^0 or change it from x_p^0 to $x_p^0 + k$, provided the latter falls into the range of valid labels $\mathbf{L}$. The jump move can be regarded as a fusion move where the proposals are the current labeling $\mathbf{x}^0$ and the labeling $\mathbf{x}_1$, such that $x_p^1 = x_p^0 + k$ if $x_p^0 + k \in \mathbf{L}$, and $x_p^1 = x_p^0$ otherwise.

More recently the use of graph cut-based moves has been investigated in the context of texture synthesis and image mosaicing [287, 404] as well as object detection and segmentation [525] (see chapter 25). The types of moves proposed there are similar to the expansion move and can also be regarded as a particular instance of the fusion move. Loosely speaking, these approaches create one fixed proposal solution with spatially varying labels and with a larger extent than the given image. Then they introduce an new auxiliary label α that corresponds to the $2d$-shift of the proposal solution with respect to the original image. Iterative alpha-expansion over this auxiliary label is then performed to optimize the energy. Note that the key difference from standard alpha-expansion is that during an expansion each proposal has a spatially varying label (i.e., not constant).

We should emphasize here that all these works [70, 72, 71, 287, 404, 525] have considered the submodularity of the binary-label problem as being necessary for a successful graph cut minimization. For instance, in [404] various so-called truncation schemas that ensure submodularity are discussed. As mentioned earlier, this restriction can be lifted with the application of nonsubmodular graph cut (i.e., the BHS algorithm [61, 261]). Therefore, all the above-mentioned moves can be applied to more general energies than was originally suggested by the authors.

Independent of our work on fusion moves, another group of researchers [529, 530] simultaneously investigated the use of fusionlike graph cut moves for image-based rendering and stereo. The proposals considered there are fronto-parallel planes, or piecewise-planar proposals and smoothed versions of the current proposal in [530]. The latter work [530] also goes beyond pairwise MRFs and considers MRFs with triple cliques for modeling curvature.

Each triple-clique auxiliary MRF with binary labels is then reduced to a pairwise MRF, using the construction developed in [41, 266].

Recently a new variant of the fusion-move algorithm was suggested in [213], termed the gradient-descent fusion move. Instead of creating proposals in an independent manner, as shown here, a generic way of creating proposals is presented. Assuming a derivative of the energy can be computed analytically, then new proposals in the direction of the steepest descent are suggested. In contrast to standard gradient descent, large steps can be taken that are also guaranteed not to increase the energy.

18.4 Applications

As mentioned above, the fusion-move framework has been applied to many different application scenarios: stereo [297, 530, 57], texture synthesis [287, 404], image denoising [213], cartographic label placement [300]. To illustrate the generality of fusion moves, two very different applications are presented here. The first one shows how to run alpha-expansion efficiently on multiple cores. Here the different proposals are created by a standard method, such as alpha-expansion. The second application considers optical flow estimation where the main challenge is that the label space is infinite (continuous $\mathbf{R}^2$ domain). Obviously, applying other move-making methods, such as alpha-expansion, to such a scenario is very challenging, since the optimal set of αs has to be determined first.

18.4.1 Parallelizing Alpha-Expansion Using Fusion Moves

The first example of fusion move considers the problem of parallelizing MRF optimization for multiple CPU cores. More specifically, the optimization scheme shows how to parallelize alpha-expansion. Though relatively little attention is being paid to this problem, the advances of multicore CPU architectures make this a current issue.

To begin, the case of two threads running on two CPU cores is considered. The label set $\mathbf{L}$ is then split into two equal subsets $\mathbf{L}^1$ and $\mathbf{L}^2$ ($\mathbf{L} = \mathbf{L}^1 \sqcup \mathbf{L}^2$, $\left| |\mathbf{L}^1| - |\mathbf{L}^2| \right| \leq 1$). In the experiments the exact way of splitting the label set into two halves did not affect computational performance much; an even-odd split was found to be slightly more efficient than a lower-upper split for ordered label sets.

As a reminder, during alpha-expansion the optimization proceeds by sweeping through the label space. During each sweep the algorithm visits each label $\alpha \in \mathbf{L}$ once and performs an expansion move for this label from the *current solution* $\mathbf{x}_{cur}$: $\alpha \in \mathbf{L}$, $\mathbf{x}_{cur} = \mathbf{x}_{cur} \odot \alpha$. The final labeling will typically differ slightly, depending on the order in which the labels are visited. In all experiments a randomized label order was used, as this typically results in lower energy labelings.

Similar to alpha-expansion, the *parallelized alpha-expansion* also proceeds by sweeps. Unlike alpha-expansion, though, each of the threads maintains its own current solution $\mathbf{x}_{cur}^i$ throughout the process. During a sweep each of the threads visits its own set of labels

---

Algorithm 18.1 Parallelized alpha-expansion

Require: MRF optimization problem with label space $\mathbf{L}$
 1: Split $\mathbf{L}$ into $\mathbf{L}^1$ and $\mathbf{L}^2$
 2: Initialize $\mathbf{x}_{cur}^1$ and $\mathbf{x}_{cur}^2$ to any labelings
 3: **for** several sweeps **do**
 4:     **for** $i = 1, 2$ **in parallel do**
 5:         **for** $\alpha \in \mathbf{L}^i$ **do**
 6:             $\mathbf{x}_{cur}^i \leftarrow \mathbf{x}_{cur}^i \odot \alpha$
 7:         **end for**
 8:     **end for**
 9:     wait for all threads
10:     $\mathbf{x}_{cur}^1 \leftarrow \mathbf{x}_{cur}^1 \odot \mathbf{x}_{cur}^2$
11:     $\mathbf{x}_{cur}^2 \leftarrow \mathbf{x}_{cur}^1$
12: **end for**
13: **return** $\mathbf{x}_{cur}^1$

Figure 18.1
The pseudo code for the parallelized alpha-expansion algorithm for the case of two CPUs.

($\mathbf{L}^1$ or $\mathbf{L}^2$) and performs expansion moves for each of the visited labels, starting from its own current solution.

Both threads perform their own sweep in parallel, running on two separate CPU cores. When both threads have completed their sweeps, the fusion move comes into action; the current solution for the first thread is fused with the current solution for the second thread: $\mathbf{x}^{12} = \mathbf{x}_{cur}^1 \odot \mathbf{x}_{cur}^2$. The current solutions from both threads are then updated with the fused version. After that a new sweep may be performed. The pseudo code for the algorithm is given in figure 18.1.

An example of the fusion move in the context of this application is shown in figure 18.2, using a standard MRF for narrow baseline stereo [70], where the labels correspond to disparities, unary potentials encode matching costs, and pairwise potentials (here, 4-connected Potts) ensure smoothness of the labeling. The fusion move after the first sweep is shown; for the sake of demonstration clarity, the labels (disparities) were split into upper and lower halves.

Parallelizing to multiple threads is similar to the two-thread case and is discussed in detail in [300]. Two cores can give a speedup of 1.6 times, and four cores can achieve an up to 2.5 times speedup.

18.4.2   FusionFlow for Optical Flow Estimation

This application considers the estimation of optical flow and is a shortened version of [299, 398]. Given a pair of frames I^0 and I^1, the goal is to find a 2D *flow vector* $x_p \in \mathbf{R}^2$ for each pixel p in the first image I^0, so that pixel locations p in I^0 and $p + x_p$ in I^1 show corresponding features.

(a) Current solution — 1st core
$E = 472 \cdot 10^4$

(b) Current solution — 2nd core
$E = 325 \cdot 10^4$

c) Auxiliary binary variables
(all nodes labeled)

(d) Fused solution
$E = 183 \cdot 10^4$

Figure 18.2
Using fusion move to parallelize alpha-expansion on two CPU cores. The first core sweeps through label disparities 0 to 7, and the second core sweeps through label disparities 8 to 15. Images (a) and (b) show the current solutions on the first and the second cores after one sweep. These solutions are fused and yield a disparity map potentially containing all disparities and having much lower energy, as shown in (d). The auxiliary binary variables for this fusion move are shown in (c) (0 = black, 1 = white; note that in this case there were no unlabeled nodes). Each of the cores starts the next sweep with the fused solution as initialization.

Apart from the different label space, the optical flow problem is actually quite similar to stereo matching, where graph cut optimization has been applied with great success. Here, optical flow estimation is expressed via a spatially discrete, continuous-valued MRF. The corresponding energy takes the form (18.1), but with the crucial difference from the previous case that the values (labels) at each pixel are continuous and, moreover, two-dimensional (i.e., $\mathbf{L} = \mathbf{R}^2$). As in stereo the unary potentials are used to encode the observation model while the pairwise potentials are used to impose smoothness of the flow field. More specifically, the data term $U_p(x_p)$ encodes the match between the RGB value at pixel p of the first image and pixel $p + x_p$ of the second image. To be more robust to illumination changes and shadows, the input images I^0 and I^1 are first high-pass filtered[3]

---

3. Note that while high-pass filtering improves performance in areas of large-scale brightness changes, it may deteriorate performance in other (e.g., noisy) areas. However, in practice it was found that the advantages outweigh the problems, and the results improved substantially.

by subtracting Gaussian-smoothed versions $G * I^i$. Hence the aim is to match $I^1 - G * I^1$ with $I^0 - G * I^0$. Color and brightness changes are penalized using the Geman–McClure robust penalty $\rho_U(d) = d^2/d^2 + \mu^2$ to account for occlusions and specularities (d here is the Euclidean RGB distance between the corresponding pixels; the constant was set manually to $\mu = 16$). The pairwise term $V_{pq}(x_p, x_q)$ penalizes the difference between horizontal and vertical components of the flow between neighboring pixels p and q, using the nonconvex robust penalty $\rho_V(d) = \log(1 + 1/2\nu^2 d^2)$, which is derived as the log of the Student-t distribution and motivated by the studies of the natural statistics of optical flow [395]. Here, d is the difference between either horizontal or vertical components of the flow vectors at the two adjacent pixels; the parameter ν was set to 0.2.

The proposed MRF energy is more difficult to optimize than the energies used in recent popular optical flow methods based on continuous optimization, such as [364], since both data and spatial terms in the formulation are robust, and thus non-convex. Also, the data term works with the high-frequency content of images, which only adds to its nonlinearity. Therefore, traditional continuous optimization schemes based on coarse-to-fine estimation and gradient descent often end up in poor local minima.

On the other hand, the proposed energy is also harder to optimize than many energies used in stereo matching, since the value at each pixel spans a potentially unbounded 2D domain rather than a bounded 1D domain, making it infeasible for purely discrete techniques to sample it densely enough. The FusionFlow approach addresses this using a new, powerful *discrete-continuous* optimization scheme based on fusion moves that combines the merits of discrete- and continuous-valued optimization approaches.

The minimization proceeds in two stages. During the first stage a number of proposals are generated and combined using fusion moves.[4] It is important to note that the proposal solutions need not be of high quality across the whole image in order to be "useful." Instead, each solution may contribute to a particular region of the final solution only as long as it contains a reasonable flow estimate for that region, no matter how poor it is in other parts. This suggests the use of different flow computation methods with different strengths and weaknesses for computing the proposals. Therefore, the proposals were computed with the two classic flow estimation algorithms, the Lucas-Kanade [326] (LK) and the Horn-Schunck [202] (HS) methods. Indeed, Lucas-Kanade solutions often yield good results in textured regions but are virtually useless in textureless regions, while the Horn-Schunck method often gives good estimates in regions with smooth motion even when lacking image texture, but severely oversmoothes motion discontinuities (see figure 18.3a,b).

To obtain a rich and varying set of proposal solutions, the LK and HS methods were run with various parameter settings and also on images with different resolutions. Finally, various shifted copies of these solutions were created. In total about 200 proposals were derived (see details of proposal generation in [300, 299, 398]).

---

4. Interestingly, it was demonstrated very recently in [483] that the fusion of flow fields may also be accomplished using continuous optimization, with the possibility of introducing higher-order smoothness terms.

(a) Solution HK, E = 7264

(b) Solution LK, E = 44859

(c) Fused solution, E = 6022

(d) Final solution, E = 2041

Figure 18.3
Optical flow estimation using fusion move. A sample fusion during the first iterations of the algorithm. (a) Result using Horn-Schunck with random parameters. (b) Result from Lucas-Kanade with random settings. (c) Fused solution with much lower energy and 99.998 percent labeled nodes. (d) The final result of the complete algorithm (including continuous optimization), which is close to ground truth (see figure 18.4).

The fusion of the proposals is accomplished in a sequential manner, where the initial labeling corresponds to one of the proposals, randomly chosen. After that, the remaining LK and HS proposals are visited in random order, and each of them is fused with the current solution. An example of such a fusion (during the first iteration of the process) for a sample problem is shown in figure 18.3a–c.

After all LK and HS solutions are visited once, new proposals based on the current solution are added. In particular, the motion vectors of the obtained fused solution are collected into sixty-four clusters using the k-means algorithm. The centers of the clusters $c_i \in \mathbf{R}^2$ are used to produce constant proposal flow fields $x_p^i = c_i$. Note that more sophisticated proposals that are dependent on the current solution may also be computed (see, e.g., [43]); our constant solutions are just one step in this direction. The constant proposals are then added to the pool of LK and HS proposals and the fusion process continues until each proposal is visited two more times. At this point the procedure typically converges, that is, the obtained fused solution can no longer be changed by fusion with any of the proposals. The number of unlabeled nodes during each fusion was always negligible (never exceeding 0.1 percent of the nodes).

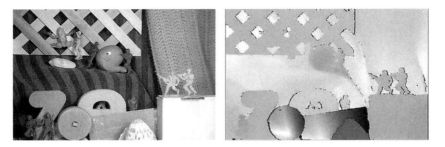

Figure 18.4
The *Army* sequence from [21]. (Left) one of two input images. (Right) the ground truth flow (black = unknown, hue = motion direction, saturation = motion magnitude).

Algorithm 18.2 FusionFlow

Require: Optical flow MRF problem E
  1: Generate a set X of proposal solutions
  2: Initialize $\mathbf{x}^{cur}$ to a random solution from X
  3: **for** $sweep = 1, 2, 3$ **do**
  4:   **for** $\mathbf{x} \in X$ **do**
  5:     $\mathbf{x}^{cur} \leftarrow \mathbf{x}^{cur} \odot \mathbf{x}$
  6:   **end for**
  7:   **if** $sweep = 1$ **then**
  8:     Cluster the set of 2D vectors $\{x_p^{cur}\}$
  9:     Add constant solutions for cluster centers to X
 10:   **end if**
 11: **end for**
 12: **for** several iterations **do**
 13:   $\mathbf{x}^{cur} \leftarrow \mathbf{x}^{cur} + \delta(\mathbf{x}^{cur})$ continuous optimization
 14: **end for**
 15: **return** $\mathbf{x}^{cur}$

Figure 18.5
The pseudo code for the FusionFlow algorithm.

After the fusion of solutions is accomplished, a low-energy solution that is much closer to ground truth and has much smaller energy than any of the proposals is obtained.

During a second stage of the optimization, a continuous optimization step is performed that helps "clean up" areas where the proposal solutions were not diverse enough, which, for example, may happen in relatively smooth areas (visually the difference is typically very small; see example in [300], figure 6). This is done using a standard conjugate gradient method [385]. The pseudo code for the FusionFlow algorithm is given in figure 18.5. A final result is shown in figure 18.3d.

For this application many more interesting experiments were carried out in [299, 398, 300] that are briefly mentioned now. Since the discrete optimization step avoids many of the poor local optima that are problematic for purely continuous optimization methods, the combination of discrete and continuous optimization leads to local minima with a substantially lower energy in most of the experiments. The interested reader is referred to [299, 300], where a detailed comparison of two baseline methods is done: (a) continuous optimization (conjugate gradients applied in a coarse-to-fine manner), and (b) discrete alpha-expansion optimization (1000 uniformly spread labels). Furthermore, it is shown in [398] that spatially varying proposals (as in figure 18.3a,b) work considerably better than constant-label proposals, which were derived from SIFT feature matching. Also in [398] the question of quality of the result versus number of proposals is discussed. To this end it is shown that a fusion with the ground truth result does not lower the energy very much. This may suggest that the optimization reaches a very good local minimum, and that further accuracy may be obtained only by considering a more involved model. Another study, conducted in [300], revealed that results are drastically worse when using ICM during fusion instead of the BHS algorithm. In particular, on the same sequence of fusion moves, thirteen fusions with the BHS algorithm performed as well as 800 fusions with ICM.

18.5 Discussion

This chapter introduced the concept of fusion move, a general and versatile optimization technique that is especially well suited for MRFs with an extensive or continuous label space. It was shown that fusion move can be used to gain efficiency and also accuracy of the solution. A particularly interesting aspect is that in contrast to, for instance, alpha-expansion, domain-specific knowledge can be exploited during proposal generation. The proposals can be created with very different techniques, such as BP [300] or a fast divide-and-conquer algorithm [297].

For a new application, an interesting question is whether there is a generic recipe for generating proposals. Qualitatively, there are two aspects of the proposal set that are relevant to the success of the fusion approach: *quality* of individual proposals and *diversity* among different proposals. The quality of individual proposals ensures that the convergence to a good solution is faster. The quality of individual proposals also serves as a safety net, since the energy of the fused result cannot be higher than the energy of the best solution. The diversity between the proposals determines how much can be added by the fusion move on top of the best solution. Note that this *quality-diversity* issue is a direct analogy with the ensemble classifier creation methods in machine learning, such as bagging.

To illustrate this concept, consider the alpha-expansion algorithm, which works with different constant proposals. Such solutions are quite diverse, but they are not of high quality in terms of energy. As a result, alpha-expansion typically produces a low-energy solution that is much better than any of the proposals but requires an excessive number of proposals (hence is relatively slow). Furthermore, it was shown in this chapter that extending the diversity of proposals beyond constant labelings allows one to obtain even lower energy solutions than those obtained with alpha-expansion.

In the future, we believe, further progress can be achieved by investigating the proposal generation process in more detail, in order to optimize the trade-off between computation time for a proposal versus usefulness of the proposal, that is, how much IT can lower the current energy. One example in this direction is the gradient descent fusion-move technique of [213], and we expect more work to appear on this topic in the future.

IV   Higher-Order MRFs and Global Constraints

Markov random fields (MRF) express the energy of a labeling (a particular assignment of values to the random variables) as a sum of potential functions, each of which depends on a subset of random variables. Typically, the arity of the potential (or its order) is restricted to one (unary potential) or two (pairwise potential), which corresponds to a pairwise energy function. Such an energy function can be efficiently minimized using one of many accurate algorithms that have been proposed in the literature.

Despite substantial work from several communities, solutions to computer vision problems based on pairwise energy functions have met with limited success so far. This observation has led researchers to question the richness of these classical energy functions, which in turn has motivated the development of more sophisticated models. Along these lines many have turned to the use of higher-order potentials that give rise to more expressive MRFs, thereby allowing us to capture statistics of natural images more closely.

This part of the book deals with higher-order models and their applications. Chapters 19 and 20 concern new higher-order models for image labeling problems such as image denoising and object segmentation. Although higher-order MRFs have more expressive power, they make the inference and learning problems much harder. Chapters 20 and 21 propose techniques for finding the MAP solution in higher-order MRFs characterized by certain families of higher-order potentials.

The solutions of certain vision problems are known to satisfy certain properties. For instance, while segmenting an object in 2D or 3D, we might know that all its parts are connected. Standard pairwise MRFs are not able to guarantee that their solutions satisfy such constraints. To overcome this problem, a global potential function is needed that assigns all invalid solutions a zero probability or an infinite energy. Chapter 22 shows how inference can perform in MRFs with such complex constraint enforcing potentials.

19 Field of Experts

Stefan Roth and Michael J. Black

Prior models of image or scene structure are useful for dealing with "noise" and ambiguity that occur in many machine vision problems such as stereo, optical flow, denoising, super-resolution, and surface reconstruction. This chapter describes a method for learning priors represented as high-order Markov random fields defined over large neighborhood systems using ideas from sparse image patch representations. The resulting *Field of Experts* (FoE) models the prior probability of an image, or other low-level representation, in terms of a random field with overlapping cliques whose potentials are represented as a Product of Experts [192]. This model applies to a wide range of low-level representations, such as natural images [397], optical flow [395], image segmentations [451], and others. For simplicity of exposition the chapter focuses on applications to modeling natural images and demonstrates the power of the FoE model with two applications: image denoising and image inpainting [33]. (See figure 19.1 for examples.)

19.1 Introduction

Modeling image priors is challenging due to the high dimensionality of images, their non-Gaussian statistics, and the need to model dependencies of the image structure over extended neighborhoods [204, 375, 448]. There have been many attempts to overcome these difficulties by modeling the statistics of small image patches [357, 476]. These models do not easily generalize to priors for entire images, however, thus limiting their impact for machine vision applications. Markov random fields, on the other hand, can be used to model the statistics of entire images [38, 161]. They have been widely adopted, as evidenced by this book, but still often exhibit serious limitations. In particular, MRF priors have typically exploited handcrafted clique potentials and small, frequently pairwise, neighborhood systems. These choices limit expressiveness, as such models do not capture the statistics of natural images (see, figure 19.2). A notable exception to this is the FRAME model of Zhu et al. [549], which learns clique potentials for larger neighborhoods from training data by modeling the responses of multiple linear filters chosen from a predefined set.

The Field of Experts model presented in this chapter attempts to address these issues and provides a framework for learning expressive, yet generic, prior models for low-level vision

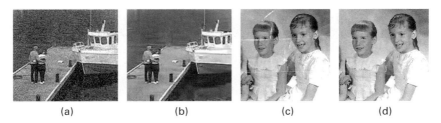

Figure 19.1
Image restoration using a Field of Experts. (a) Image from the Corel database with additive Gaussian noise ($\sigma = 15$, PSNR = 24.63dB, cropped for display). (b) Image denoised using a Field of Experts (PSNR = 30.72dB). (c) Original photograph with scratches. (d) Image inpainting using the FoE model.

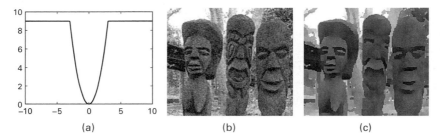

Figure 19.2
Typical pairwise MRF potentials and results. (a) Example of a common robust potential function (negative log-probability): truncated quadratic. (b) Image with Gaussian noise added. (c) Typical result of denoising using an ad hoc pairwise MRF (obtained using the method of [141]). Note the piecewise smooth nature of the restoration and that it lacks the textural detail of natural scenes.

problems. Fields of Experts extend MRFs beyond the pairwise case (as well as FRAME) by modeling the local field potentials as products of nonlinear functions of linear filter responses, where the filters themselves are learned from example data. The FoE model exploits ideas from the Product of Experts (PoE) framework [192], a generic method for learning high-dimensional probability distributions that has been used to model image patch statistics [476] as a product of heavy-tailed functions of linear filter responses. In the FoE model this idea is extended to model potential functions defined over large cliques. The parameters (including the linear filters) of an FoE model of natural images are learned from training data using contrastive divergence [193] and a database of natural images [331]. Fields of Experts provide a principled way to learn high-order MRFs from examples, and the improved modeling power makes them practical for complex vision problems. A diffusion-like scheme is used for approximate Bayesian inference and demonstrates the power of the model for image denoising and image inpainting.

19.1.1 Related Work

Though MRF models are extremely popular for modeling prior knowledge, especially in low-level vision, they nonetheless produce disappointing results in some applications (see figure 19.2). The are two main reasons: (1) the model structure is typically pairwise, which severely restricts the image structures that can be represented; (2) the clique potentials are frequently hand-defined and penalize simple first-order spatial derivatives, thus creating only an ad hoc model of image or scene structure that does not well represent the statistical properties of natural images and scenes. One common property of such models is that the global optimum of the posterior is often much more probable (has lower energy) than the true solution [338]. This suggests that inference methods are not the main limitation of MRF models; rather, the approximate nature of the model itself is.

High-Order Markov Random Fields There have been a number of attempts to go beyond simple pairwise models [160, 550, 549]. The basic insight behind such high-order models is that the generality of MRFs allows for richer models through the use of larger maximal cliques. Geman and Reynolds [160], for example, formulate MRF potentials using polynomials corresponding to image derivatives of varying orders. While such models are capable of representing richer structural properties beyond the piecewise spatial smoothness of pairwise models, the clique potentials remain handcrafted.

Learning MRF Models Handcrafted models not only fail to capture the statistics of complex scenes, but extending them to large numbers of parameters is infeasible. As discussed in chapter 15, while there exist several approaches for learning the parameters of MRFs, such as maximum likelihood (ML) [163], pseudo likelihood [38], or iterative scaling [370], they have not been widely used for learning MRF models in low-level vision. More efficient learning criteria, such as contrastive divergence (CD) [193], an efficient approximation to maximum likelihood, or score matching [205], have recently been applied to MRF learning [274, 285, 397]. The FRAME model of Zhu et al. [549] represents the potential functions of a high-order MRF model using nonlinear functions of linear filter responses. Though the filters are fixed, they are chosen during learning from a larger set of filters, and a flexible nonparametric function of the responses is learned from training data. Unlike FRAME, the FoE approach learns the filters themselves as well as the parameters of parametric potential functions. The learned filters turn out not only to be quite different from standard filters, but also to achieve better performance on a variety of tasks.

Inference To apply high-order MRFs to actual problems in low-level vision, solutions are computed using tools from probabilistic inference, typically maximum a posteriori (MAP) estimation. Since exact inference is usually infeasible, approximate inference methods have to be used (see chapter 1). But while popular methods such as graph cuts or belief propagation can be used in principle, the larger size of the cliques makes them largely infeasible in practice. Only relatively small 2×2 cliques can currently be handled [212, 291, 376]. Because of that, the differentiability of the model is exploited here to enable very simple approximate inference schemes using the conjugate gradient method.

Products of Experts   The FoE uses a Product of Experts (PoE) [192] to model the MRF clique potentials. PoEs model high-dimensional probability distributions by taking the product of several expert distributions, $f_k(\cdot; \cdot)$, where each expert works on a low-dimensional subspace that is relatively easy to model. In the case of modeling images, the experts are typically defined on linear one-dimensional subspaces, $\mathbf{J}_k$, that correspond to linear filters:

$$P(\mathbf{x} \mid \omega) = \frac{1}{Z(\omega)} \prod_{k=1}^{n} f_k(\mathbf{J}_k^{\mathsf{T}} \mathbf{x}; \, \alpha_k), \tag{19.1}$$

where the α_k are expert parameters, $\omega = \{\mathbf{J}_k, \alpha_k \mid k = 1, \dots, n\}$ are the parameters of the model, and $Z(\omega)$ is the partition function. Note that $\mathbf{x}$ here denotes a small image patch and not the full image. Based on the observation that responses of linear filters applied to natural images typically exhibit highly kurtotic marginal distributions, Teh et al. [476] propose the use of Student-t experts. One important property of this model is that all parameters can be learned from training data, that is, both the α_k and the image filters $\mathbf{J}_k$ (for example, using contrastive divergence [476]). Moreover, the number of experts, n, is not necessarily equal to the number of dimensions, which makes PoEs more flexible than typical ICA approaches. Though PoEs have been used to model image patches [476], this does not yield a prior for whole images, making patch-based models difficult to apply to typical low-level vision problems.

19.2 Fields of Experts

To overcome the limitations of pairwise MRFs and patch-based models, this chapter considers high-order Markov random fields for entire images $\mathbf{x} \in \mathbb{R}^N$, using a neighborhood system that connects all nodes in an $m \times m$ square region (cf. [160, 549]). This is done for all *overlapping* $m \times m$ regions of $\mathbf{x}$, which now denotes an entire image rather than a small image patch. Every such neighborhood $c \in \mathcal{C}$ defines a maximal clique $\mathbf{x}_c$ in the graph. Hence, the prior factorizes as

$$P(\mathbf{x} \mid \omega) = \frac{1}{Z(\omega, \mathcal{C})} \prod_{c \in \mathcal{C}} F_c(\mathbf{x}_c; \, \omega), \tag{19.2}$$

where F_c is the factor for clique c, ω are the parameters, and $Z(\omega, \mathcal{C})$ is the partition function. Without loss of generality it is usually assumed that the maximal cliques in the MRF are square pixel patches of a fixed size. Other, nonsquare neighborhoods [160] can be used (see [397]).

The MRF potentials are represented as a Product of Experts [192] with the same basic form as in (19.1). This means that the potentials are defined with a set of expert functions that model filter responses from a bank of linear filters. This global prior for low-level vision is a Markov random field of "experts" or, more concisely, a *Field of Experts*. More formally, (19.1) is used to define the potential (or factor)

$$F_c(\mathbf{x}_c; \omega) = F_{\text{PoE}}(\mathbf{x}_c; \omega) = \prod_{k=1}^{n} f_k(\mathbf{J}_k^{\mathsf{T}} \mathbf{x}_c; \alpha_k). \tag{19.3}$$

Each $\mathbf{J}_k$ is a linear filter that defines the direction (in the vector space of the pixel values in $\mathbf{x}_c$) that the corresponding expert $f_k(\cdot; \cdot)$ is modeling, and α_k is its corresponding (set of) expert parameter(s). $\omega = \{\mathbf{J}_k, \alpha_k \,|\, k = 1, \ldots, n\}$ is the set of all model parameters. The number of experts and associated filters, n, is not prescribed in a particular way; it can be chosen based on criteria such as the quality of the model and computational expense. Since each factor can be unnormalized, the normalization component of (19.1) is neglected for simplicity. Note that the image $\mathbf{x}$ is assumed to be a continuous-valued random vector; discrete-valued spatial data can be dealt with in similar ways [451].

Overall, the Field of Experts model is thus defined as

$$P(\mathbf{x} \,|\, \omega) = P_{\text{FoE}}(\mathbf{x} \,|\, \omega) = \frac{1}{Z(\omega, \mathcal{C})} \prod_{c \in \mathcal{C}} \prod_{k=1}^{n} f_k(\mathbf{J}_k^{\mathsf{T}} \mathbf{x}_c; \alpha_k). \tag{19.4}$$

It is very important to note here that this definition does not imply that a *trained* PoE model with fixed parameters ω is used directly to model the potential function. This would be incorrect, because Products of Experts are trained on independent patches. In contrast, in an FoE the pixel regions $\mathbf{x}_c$ that correspond to the maximal cliques are overlapping and thus are not independent. Instead, an *untrained* PoE model is used to define the potentials, and the parameters ω are learned in the context of the full MRF model. What distinguishes this model from that of Teh et al. [476] is that it explicitly models the overlap of image patches and the resulting statistical dependence; the filters $\mathbf{J}_k$, as well as the expert parameters α_k, must account for this dependence (to the extent they can). It is also important to note that the FoE parameters ω are shared among all maximal cliques and their associated factors. This keeps the number of parameters moderate, because it depends only on the size of the maximal cliques and the number of experts, but not on the size of the image itself. The model applies to images of an arbitrary size and is translation invariant because of the homogeneity of the potential functions. This means that the FoE can be thought of as a translation invariant PoE model.

Following their use in the PoE framework for modeling image patches [476], heavy-tailed Student t-distributions are used as expert functions:

$$f_k(\mathbf{J}_k^{\mathsf{T}} \mathbf{x}_c; \alpha_k) = \left(1 + \frac{1}{2}(\mathbf{J}_k^{\mathsf{T}} \mathbf{x}_c)^2\right)^{-\alpha_k}. \tag{19.5}$$

This choice is motivated by the fact that zero-mean filter responses for natural images and other scene properties have heavy-tailed marginal distributions [448]. Note also that this function is differentiable with respect to the parameters, which will become important for learning and optimization. Other possible experts include the Charbonnier penalty function [89, 397] and Gaussian scale mixtures [327, 396, 518]. To simplify the notation, log-experts are defined as $\Psi_k(\cdot, \alpha_k) = \log f_k(\cdot; \alpha_k)$.

Similar to the PoE (at least in its overcomplete form) [476] and to most Markov random field models (chapter 1), computing the partition function $Z(\omega, \mathcal{C})$ of the FoE is generally intractable. Nevertheless, most inference algorithms, such as the ones discussed in section 19.2.2, do not require this normalization term to be known. During learning, on the other hand, the normalization term does have to be taken into account.

Comparing the FoE with the FRAME model [549], one should note that while the models look similar (both are high-order MRF models with "experts" modeling linear filter responses), there are important differences. While the FRAME model learns the potential functions from data, the candidate set of filters used to define the potentials is chosen by hand. With the FoE it is possible to learn the filters alongside the other parameters; to enable that, the FoE's expert functions are parametric and differentiable, but less flexible. Beyond FRAME, it is also interesting to note the similarities to convolutional neural networks [351]. A crucial difference is that convolutional networks are typically trained discriminatively in the context of a specific application, whereas the probabilistic nature of the FoE allows it to model a generic prior that can be directly used in different applications.

19.2.1 Contrastive Divergence Learning

Let $\omega = \{\omega_1, \ldots, \omega_n\}$ be the set of all expert parameters where ω_l may be an expert parameter α_k or an element of a filter $\mathbf{J}_k$. The parameters are learned by (approximately) maximizing the likelihood of a set of D training images $X = \{\mathbf{x}^{(1)}, \ldots, \mathbf{x}^{(D)}\}$. Since there is no closed form solution for the ML parameters, a gradient ascent on the log-likelihood is performed. Taking the partial derivative of the log-likelihood with respect to a parameter ω_l leads to the parameter update

$$\delta\omega_l = \eta \left[\left\langle \frac{\partial E_{\text{FoE}}}{\partial \omega_l} \right\rangle_P - \left\langle \frac{\partial E_{\text{FoE}}}{\partial \omega_l} \right\rangle_X \right], \tag{19.6}$$

where η is a user-defined learning rate, $\langle \cdot \rangle_X$ denotes the average over the training data X, and $\langle \cdot \rangle_P$ is the expected value with respect to the model distribution $P(\mathbf{x} \mid \omega)$. Moreover, this relies on the fact that the MRF can be rewritten in Gibbs form as $P_{\text{FoE}}(\mathbf{x} \mid \omega) = (1/Z(\omega, \mathcal{C})) \exp\{-E_{\text{FoE}}(\mathbf{x}, \omega)\}$.

While the average over the training data is easy to compute, there is no general closed form solution for the expectation over the model distribution. However, it can be approximated

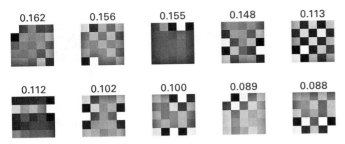

Figure 19.3
Subset of the 5×5 filters obtained by training the *Field of Experts* model with Student-t experts on a generic image database. Each filter is shown with the corresponding α_k, which effectively weigh the filter responses in the energy.

by repeatedly drawing samples from $P(\mathbf{x} \mid \omega)$ using Markov chain Monte Carlo (MCMC) sampling; a hybrid Monte Carlo (HMC) sampler [347] is used here.

Instead of running the Markov chain until convergence, FoE training uses *contrastive divergence* [193]. Hence the sampler is initialized at the data points and is run for only a small, fixed number of steps. If the data distribution is denoted as P^0 and the distribution after j MCMC iterations as P^j, the parameter update is written as

$$\delta\omega_l = \eta \left[\left\langle \frac{\partial E_{\mathrm{FoE}}}{\partial \omega_l} \right\rangle_{P^j} - \left\langle \frac{\partial E_{\mathrm{FoE}}}{\partial \omega_l} \right\rangle_{P^0} \right]. \tag{19.7}$$

The intuition here is that running the MCMC sampler for just a few iterations, starting from the data distribution, will draw the samples closer to the target distribution, which is enough to estimate the parameter updates. Contrastive divergence learning is typically a good approximation to a maximum likelihood estimation of the parameters [193]. Details of the learning method are found in [397].

Figure 19.3 shows some of the filters learned by training an FoE model with 5×5 pixel cliques, 24 filters, and Student-t experts. The training data contained 20,000 image regions (15×15) randomly cropped from a database of natural images [331] and converted to gray scale. The learned filters respond to various edge and texture features at multiple orientations and scales, and, as demonstrated below, capture important structural properties of images. They lack the clearly interpretable structure of the filters learned using models of image patches, such as standard PoEs. These high-frequency filters may, however, be important for distinguishing between natural and unnatural scenes [518].

19.2.2 Inference
Currently, maximum a posteriori (MAP) inference with high-order Markov random fields like the FoE is computationally challenging. For practical inference even with 5×5 cliques,

very simple gradient-based optimization techniques are used for approximate MAP inference. Following Zhu and Mumford [550], the gradient of the log-density w. r. t. the image can be written using simple convolutions:

$$\nabla_{\mathbf{x}} \log P_{\mathrm{FoE}}(\mathbf{x} \mid \omega) = \sum_{k=1}^{n} \mathbf{J}_{-}^{(k)} * \mathbf{\Psi}'(\mathbf{J}^{(k)} * \mathbf{x}, \alpha_k). \tag{19.8}$$

Here $\mathbf{J}^{(k)}$ is a convolution filter corresponding to $\mathbf{J}_k$, $\mathbf{J}_{-}^{(k)}$ is a convolution filter that has been obtained by mirroring $\mathbf{J}^{(k)}$ around its center, and $\mathbf{\Psi}'$ is the derivative of the log-expert w. r. t. the filter responses (evaluated for all cliques simultaneously; see [393] for details). In contrast to FRAME [549], the parametric experts of the FoE allow this derivative to be computed without making approximations. Because the overall expression is based on convolutions, it is very simple and efficient to implement. Moreover, these gradient-based techniques have interesting connections to nonlinear diffusion and related PDE methods [515].

19.3 Example Applications

To illustrate the capabilities of the Field of Experts model as a prior model of images, it is applied to two problems here: image denoising and image inpainting. Both of these image restoration tasks can be formulated as problems of Bayesian inference in which the goal is to find the clean, true image $\mathbf{x}$, given a corrupted, observed image $\mathbf{z}$, by maximizing the posterior probability $P(\mathbf{x} \mid \mathbf{z}) \propto P(\mathbf{z} \mid \mathbf{x}) \cdot P(\mathbf{x})$. The FoE provides the probabilistic prior model, $P(\mathbf{x})$, of the spatial properties of images. To implement denoising and inpainting, the likelihood terms, $P(\mathbf{z} \mid \mathbf{x})$, and inference methods have to be defined.

19.3.1 Image Denoising

In denoising, one commonly assumes that the image is corrupted with homogeneous, pixelwise independent Gaussian noise with known variance. Accordingly, the likelihood is written as

$$P(\mathbf{z} \mid \mathbf{x}) \propto \prod_{i=1}^{N} \exp\left(-\frac{1}{2\sigma^2}(z_i - x_i)^2\right), \tag{19.9}$$

where i ranges over the pixels in the image.

Inference uses a simple (suboptimal) gradient-based local optimization of the logarithm of the posterior probability. The gradient of the log-posterior is written as

$$\nabla_{\mathbf{x}} \log P(\mathbf{x} \mid \mathbf{z}) = \lambda \cdot \left[\sum_{k=1}^{n} \mathbf{J}_{-}^{(k)} * \mathbf{\Psi}'(\mathbf{J}^{(k)} * \mathbf{x}, \alpha_k)\right] + \frac{1}{\sigma^2}(\mathbf{z} - \mathbf{x}), \tag{19.10}$$

where the optional weight λ can be used to adjust the strength of the prior compared with the likelihood. Rather than standard gradient ascent, a conjugate gradient method is used here.

This formulation has clear similarities to standard nonlinear diffusion, but differs in that the FoE prior uses many more filters, captures information in larger neighborhoods, and is learned from examples.

19.3.2 Image Inpainting

In image inpainting [33] the goal is to remove certain parts of an image, for example, scratches on a photograph or unwanted occluding objects, and replace these with image structure that appears natural within the context of the image. Typically the user supplies a mask, $\mathcal{M}$, of pixels that are to be filled in by the algorithm. To define an appropriate likelihood, the masked pixels are assumed to be able to take on any gray value with equal probability; the likelihood is simply uniform there. Pixels that are not masked should not be modified at all. The likelihood for image inpainting is thus written as

$$P(\mathbf{z} \mid \mathbf{x}) = \prod_{i=1}^{N} p(z_i \mid x_i) \propto \prod_{i=1}^{N} \begin{cases} 1, & i \in \mathcal{M} \\ \delta(z_i - x_i), & i \notin \mathcal{M} \end{cases}. \tag{19.11}$$

To perform inpainting, a simple gradient ascent procedure is used that, due to (19.11), leaves the unmasked pixels untouched while modifying the masked pixels based only on the FoE prior. By defining a mask matrix $\mathbf{M}$ that sets the gradient to zero for all pixels outside the masked region $\mathcal{M}$, the gradient ascent is written as

$$\mathbf{x}^{(t+1)} = \mathbf{x}^{(t)} + \eta \mathbf{M} \left[\sum_{k=1}^{n} \mathbf{J}_k^- * \mathbf{\Psi}'(\mathbf{J}_k * \mathbf{x}^{(t)}, \alpha_k) \right]. \tag{19.12}$$

Here η is the step size of the gradient ascent procedure. In contrast to other algorithms, no explicit use of the local image gradient direction is made; local structure information comes only from the responses of the learned filter bank. The filter bank and the α_k are the same as for denoising. Also note that this is a generic prior that is not learned based on the statistics of the image to be inpainted (cf. [306]).

19.4 Experimental Evaluation

The experiments use an FoE model with 5×5 cliques, 24 filters, and Student-t experts to denoise and inpaint corrupted images. The evaluation below measures restored image quality in terms of peak signal-to-noise ratio (PSNR) in decibels (dB); $\text{PSNR} = 20 \log_{10} 255/\sigma_e$, where σ_e is the standard deviation of the pixelwise image error. The conclusions also hold when using a structural similarity index [513] to measure perceptual image quality, (see [395] for details).

(a)   (b)   (c)   (d)   (e)

Figure 19.4
Denoising with a Field of Experts. Full image (top) and detail (bottom). (a) Original noiseless image. (b) Image with additive Gaussian noise ($\sigma = 25$); PSNR $= 20.29$dB. (c) Denoised image using a Field of Experts; PSNR $= 28.72$dB. (d) Denoised image using the approach of Portilla et al. [375]; PSNR $= 28.90$dB. (e) Denoised image using nonlocal means [79]; PSNR $= 28.21$dB.

19.4.1 Denoising Experiments

The denoising performance was evaluated on a test set consisting of 68 images from the Berkeley Segmentation Dataset [331] that were not used for training. For various noise levels the images were denoised using the FoE model, the method of Portilla et al. [375], the nonlocal means method [79], a learned pairwise MRF model [396], simple Wiener filtering (using MATLAB's `wiener2` with a 5×5 window), and a standard nonlinear diffusion scheme [515] with a data term. Figure 19.4 compares denoising performance of several methods on one of the test images. Figure 19.5 shows denoising results on another test image, as well as a comparison with the learned pairwise MRF with fixed derivative filters and Student-t experts [396].

Visually and quantitatively the FoE model substantially outperformed the learned pairwise MRF model, Wiener filtering, and nonlinear diffusion on the test set with varying noise levels (see [395, 396] for experimental details). The FoE method approached, but did not beat, the performance of the specialized wavelet denoising method [375]. Note that [375] uses the statistics of the image to be denoised, whereas the FoE is a generic prior trained on images other than the one to be denoised. This allows the FoE model to be used unchanged in many other applications.

19.4.2 Inpainting Experiments

To demonstrate the generality of FoE models, the model from above is applied to the task of image inpainting. Figure 19.6 shows an example result of applying the simple inpainting

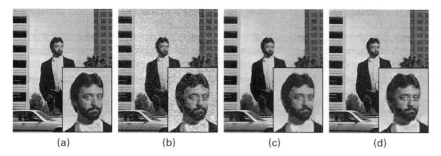

(a)   (b)   (c)   (d)

Figure 19.5
High-order versus pairwise MRF. (a) Original noiseless image (with detail region of face). (b) Image with additive Gaussian noise ($\sigma = 20$); PSNR = 22.49dB. (c) Denoised image using a learned pairwise MRF [396]; PSNR = 27.60dB. (d) Denoised image using a Field of Experts; PSNR = 29.20dB.

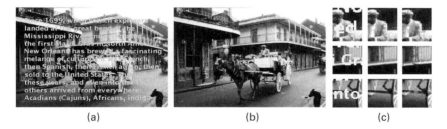

(a)   (b)   (c)

Figure 19.6
Inpainting with a Field of Experts. (a) Original image overlaid with text to be removed. (b) Inpainting result from (c) Close-up comparison between a (left), b (middle), and the results of Bertalmío et al. [33] (right).

scheme described above. The color image was converted to the YCbCr color model, and the algorithm was independently applied to all three channels. Despite training the prior on only on gray scale images, this produced good results. The inpainted result is very similar to the original and is qualitatively superior to that of Bertalmío et al. [33], improving the PSNR by about 1.5dB. The advantage of the FoE prior can be seen in the continuity of edges, which are better restored when compared with [33]. Figure 19.6 also shows a few detail regions comparing the FoE (center) with [33] (right). For example, the axle and the wheels of the carriage have been restored well. Similar qualitative differences can be seen in many parts of the restored image.

Figure 19.7 shows representative image inpainting results for test images that were corrupted using synthetic masks (white pixels). An application of this inpainting algorithm to scratch removal in a photograph is shown in figure 19.1. For further inpainting results, the reader is referred to the detailed study by Gisy [166].

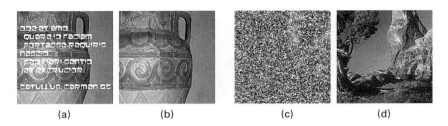

(a)   (b)   (c)   (d)

Figure 19.7
Other image inpainting results. The white areas in (a) and (c) are filled in by the algorithm. (b) and (d) show corresponding restored images obtained using a 5×5 FoE model with 24 filters.

19.5 Extensions and Other Applications

Besides denoising and inpainting, FoE models of natural images have been applied to the problem of image-based rendering [526], where they outperform example-based priors. In contrast to the independent modeling of color channels above, McAuley et al. [335] describe an extension to RGB images in which the cliques and filters are extended to the third dimension (corresponding to the color channels). Lyu and Simoncelli [327] show that Fields of Experts can also be used for modeling wavelet coefficients, and demonstrate excellent denoising results.

Other learning algorithms for FoEs have been studied as well. Köster et al. [274] train FoEs using score matching [205], thus avoiding expensive MCMC sampling, but do not show application results. Weiss and Freeman [518] develop an efficient EM algorithm for learning the filters of FoEs with Gaussian scale mixture potentials. Moreover, they derive likelihood bounds and show that the kinds of high-frequency filters found by training Fields of Experts (figure 19.3) have a provably higher likelihood than more traditional "smooth" filters such as those used in the FRAME model [550] (e. g., derivative filters, Gabors, etc.).

Besides modeling natural images, Fields of Experts have been successfully applied to other domains. Image motion has, for example, been modeled using FoEs in both supervised [395] and unsupervised fashion [339], enabling optical flow estimation, motion denoising, and other applications. A hierarchical extension [352] related to deep belief networks has been used to extract features for object recognition (e. g., the detection of pedestrians). Moreover, Stewart et al. [451] proposed a discrete-valued conditional variant, called CFoE, for image labeling. Consistent with the results shown here, CFoEs substantially outperform pairwise random field models for image labeling.

19.6 Discussion

Despite significantly increasing the modeling power compared with pairwise MRFs, Fields of Experts have several limitations that should be addressed in the future. The present framework models images only at their original spatial scale (resolution) and does not model consistency of filter response statistics across scales. Wavelet-based approaches (e. g., [375]) make use of multiple spatial scales and model dependencies across scales, which may explain their better denoising performance.

While with the FoE one can observe improved denoising performance compared with standard MRF approaches, there is still more to be done with regard to modeling natural image statistics. As noted by Roth [393], images sampled from the learned model do not look "natural"; moreover, the marginal distributions of the learned model (obtained from sampled images) are not a good match to natural image marginals. Multiscale (or longer-range) representations and better learning algorithms may help in capturing more properties of natural scenes. Moreover, while Gaussian scale mixtures have been used as experts [396, 518], even more flexible nonparametric experts, such as in the FRAME model, may be considered as well.

Another limitation is that the clique sizes and shapes have been chosen a priori here, but may instead be selected automatically. Furthermore, the experiments here have assumed that the model is homogeneous. Certain applications may benefit from spatially varying statistics, which motivates further research on inhomogeneous models.

Chapter 24 discusses how Markov random fields can benefit significantly from steering the filters to the local predominant image orientation. So far, this has been done only for simple derivative filters; learning steerable filters in an FoE-like framework seems like a promising avenue for future work. The presented FoE framework has focused solely on modeling the prior distribution of natural images or other low-level representations, and has been combined with simple hand-designed likelihood models. For certain applications it would be beneficial to learn these likelihood models, or a model of the application-specific posterior directly.

With any high-order MRF model like the FoE, inference becomes difficult. While gradient-based optimization methods may be viable for some applications, they are likely to be inferior to graph cuts or belief propagation. Large clique sizes make it difficult to apply these methods to the FoE, and so far only small cliques [212, 376] or restricted kinds of models [240] can be handled. Further investigation of advanced inference techniques for high-order MRF models is thus needed.

19.7 Summary and Conclusions

While Markov random fields are popular in machine vision for their formal properties, their ability to model complex natural scenes has been limited. To make it practical to model expressive image priors, a high-order Markov random field model was formulated based on extended cliques that capture local image statistics beyond simple pairwise neighborhoods. The potentials for these extended cliques were modeled based on the Product of Experts paradigm. The resulting Field of Experts is based on a rich set of learned filters, and is trained on a generic image database using contrastive divergence. In contrast to previous approaches that use a predetermined set of filters, all parameters of the model, including the filters, are learned from data. The resulting probabilistic model can be used in any Bayesian approach requiring a spatial image prior. The usefulness of the FoE was demonstrated with applications to denoising and inpainting with competitive results.

By making MRF models more powerful, many problems in machine vision can be revisited with an expectation of improved results. Beyond image restoration, image-based rendering [526], and optical flow estimation [395], one can expect that applications such as dense stereo estimation, object boundary detection, and others will benefit as well. The methods may also be extended to nonimage-based graphs such as surface meshes or MRF models of object parts.

Acknowledgments

This work was supported by Intel Research, NSF ITR grant 0113679, NSF IIS-0534858, NSF IIS-0535075 and by NIH-NINDS R01 NS 50967-01 as part of the NSF/NIH Collaborative Research in Computational Neuroscience Program. Portions of this work were performed by the authors at Intel Research. We thank Stuart Andrews, Pietro Berkes, Alessandro Duci, Yoram Gat, Stuart Geman, Horst Haussecker, Thomas Hofmann, John Hughes, Dan Huttenlocher, Xi-angyang Lan, Siwei Lyu, Oscar Nestares, Hanno Scharr, Eero Simoncelli, Yair Weiss, Max Welling, and Frank Wood for helpful discussions. We also thank Guillermo Sapiro and Marcelo Bertalmio for making their inpainting examples available for comparison and Javier Portilla for making his denoising software available.

20 Enforcing Label Consistency Using Higher-Order Potentials

Pushmeet Kohli, Lubor Ladicky, and Philip H. S. Torr

This chapter discusses a higher-order conditional random field model that uses potentials defined on sets of pixels (image segments) generated using unsupervised segmentation algorithms. These potentials enforce label consistency in image regions and can be seen as a generalization of the commonly used pairwise contrast sensitive smoothness potentials. The optimal *swap* and *expansion* moves for energy functions composed of these potentials can be computed by solving an st-mincut problem. This enables the use of powerful graph cut-based move-making algorithms for performing inference in the framework. The model is evaluated on the problem of multiclass object segmentation. Experiments on challenging data sets show that integration of higher-order potentials quantitatively and qualitatively improves results, leading to much better definition of object boundaries.

20.1 Introduction

In recent years an increasingly popular way to solve various image labeling problems such as object segmentation, stereo, and single view reconstruction has been to formulate them using image segments (so-called superpixels) obtained from unsupervised segmentation algorithms [185, 196, 383]. These methods are inspired by the observation that pixels constituting a particular segment often have the same label; for instance, they may belong to the same object or have the same surface orientation. This approach has the benefit that higher-order features based on all the pixels constituting the segment can be computed and used for classification. Further, it is also much faster, as inference now needs to be performed over only a small number of superpixels rather than all the pixels in the image.

Methods based on grouping segments make the assumption that segments are consistent with object boundaries in the image [185], that is, segments do not contain multiple objects. As observed in [197] and [407], this is not always the case, and segments obtained using unsupervised segmentation methods are often wrong. To overcome these problems [197, 407], use multiple segmentations of the image (instead of only one) in the hope that although most segmentations are bad, some are correct and thus will prove useful for their task. They merge these multiple superpixels, using heuristic algorithms that lack any optimality

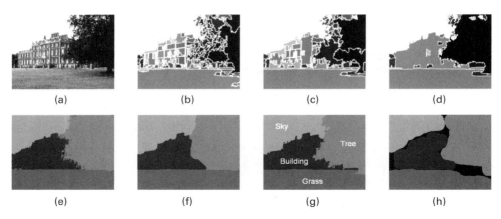

Figure 20.1
Incorporating higher-order potentials for object segmentation. (a) An image from the MSRC-23 data set. (b), (c), and (d) Unsupervised image segmentation results generated by using different parameter values in the mean-shift segmentation algorithm [100]. (e) The object segmentation obtained using the unary likelihood potentials from Textonboost [437]. (f) The result of performing inference in the pairwise CRF defined in section 20.2. (g) The segmentation result obtained by augmenting the pairwise CRF with higher-order potentials defined on the segments shown in (b), (c), and (d). (h) The rough hand-labeled segmentations provided in the MSRC data set. It can be clearly seen that the use of higher-order potentials results in a significant improvement in the segmentation result. For instance, the branches of the tree are much better segmented.

guarantees and thus may produce bad results. The algorithm described in this chapter can compute the solution of the labeling problem (using features based on image segments) in a principled manner. The approach couples potential functions defined on sets of pixels with conventional unary and pairwise cues, using higher-order CRFs. The performance of the method is tested on the problem of object segmentation and recognition. Experiments show that the results of the higher-order model are significantly better than the ones obtained using pairwise CRF models (see figure 20.1).

20.1.1   Object Segmentation and Recognition
Combined object segmentation and recognition is one of the most challenging and funda-mental problems in computer vision. The last few years have seen the emergence of object segmentation algorithms that integrate *object specific* top-down information with *image-based* low-level features [60, 242, 278, 305]. These methods have produced excellent results on challenging data sets. However, they typically deal with only one object at a time in the image independently and do not provide a framework for understanding the whole image. Further, their models become prohibitively large as the number of classes increases. This prevents their application to scenarios where segmentation and recognition of many object classes is desired.

Shotton et al. [437] proposed a method (*Textonboost*) to overcome this problem. In contrast to using explicit models to encode object shape, they used a boosted combination of *texton* features that jointly modeled shape and texture. They combined the result of textons with color and location based likelihood terms in a conditional random field (CRF). Using techniques described in chapter 7, Shotton et al. [437] were able to obtain good segmentation and recognition results; however, the problem of accurate extraction of object boundaries is very hard, and their results on some challenging instances were not perfect. This chapter shows that incorporation of higher-order potentials defined on superpixels helps to improve object segmentation results. In particular, it leads to segmentations with better definition of object boundaries, as shown in figure 20.1.

20.1.2 Higher-Order CRFs

Higher-order random fields are not new to computer vision. They have long been used to model image textures [291, 361, 394]. The initial work in this regard has been quite promising, and higher-order CRFs have been shown to improve results for problems such as image denoising and restoration [394] and texture segmentation [240]. However, their use has been quite limited due to lack of efficient algorithms for performing inference in these models. Kohli et al. [240] showed how certain higher-order clique potentials can be minimized using move-making algorithms for approximate energy minimization such as α-expansion and $\alpha\beta$-swap [72]. They introduced a class of higher-order potentials called the P^n Potts model and showed how the optimal *expansion* and *swap* moves for energy functions containing these potentials can be computed in polynomial time by solving an st-mincut problem. The complexity of their algorithm increased linearly with the size of the clique, and thus it was able to handle cliques composed of thousands of latent variables.

  The higher-order energy functions considered in this chapter are a generalization of the P^n Potts class. It will be shown how energy functions composed of these *robust* potentials can be minimized using move-making algorithms such as α-expansion and $\alpha\beta$-swap [241].

20.2 Pairwise CRFs for Object Segmentation

Consider a discrete random field $\mathbf{X}$ defined over a lattice $\mathcal{V} = \{1, 2, \ldots, N\}$ with a neighborhood system $\mathcal{E}$. Each random variable $X_i \in \mathbf{X}$ is associated with a lattice point $i \in \mathcal{V}$ and takes a value from the label set $\mathcal{L} = \{l_1, l_2, \ldots, l_k\}$. The neighborhood system $\mathcal{E}$ is the set of edges connecting variables in the random field. A clique c is a set of random variables $\mathbf{X}_c$ that are conditionally dependent on each other. Any possible assignment of labels to the random variables will be called a *labeling* (denoted by $\mathbf{x}$) that takes values from the set $\mathbf{L} = \mathcal{L}^N$.

  CRF models commonly used for object segmentation are characterized by energy functions defined on unary and pairwise cliques:

$$E(\mathbf{x}) = \sum_{i \in \mathcal{V}} \psi_i(x_i) + \sum_{(i,j) \in \mathcal{E}} \psi_{ij}(x_i, x_j). \tag{20.1}$$

Here $\mathcal{V}$ corresponds to the set of all image pixels, and $\mathcal{E}$ is the set of all edges connecting the pixels $i, j \in \mathcal{V}$. The edge set is commonly chosen to be either a 4- or an 8-neighborhood. The labels constituting the label set $\mathcal{L}$ represent the different objects. The random variable x_i denotes the labeling of pixel i of the image. Every possible assignment of the random variables $\mathbf{x}$ (or configuration of the CRF) defines a segmentation.

The unary potential ψ_i of the CRF is defined as the negative log of the likelihood of a label being assigned to pixel i. It can be computed from the color of the pixel and the appearance model for each object. However, color alone is not a very discriminative feature and fails to produce accurate segmentations. This problem can be overcome by using sophisticated potential functions based on color, texture, location, and shape priors, as shown in [242, 278, 437]. The unary potential we used can be written as

$$\psi_i(x_i) = \theta_T \psi_T(x_i) + \theta_{col} \psi_{col}(x_i) + \theta_l \psi_l(x_i) \tag{20.2}$$

where θ_T, θ_{col}, and θ_l are parameters weighting the potentials obtained from Texton-Boost(ψ_T) [437], color (ψ_{col}), and location (ψ_l), respectively.

The pairwise terms ψ_{ij} of the CRF take the form of a contrast sensitive Potts model:

$$\psi(x_i, x_j) = \begin{cases} 0 & \text{if } x_i = x_j, \\ g(i, j) & \text{otherwise,} \end{cases} \tag{20.3}$$

where the function $g(i, j)$ is an edge feature based on the difference in colors of neighboring pixels [66]. It is typically defined as

$$g(i, j) = \theta_p + \theta_v \exp(-\theta_\beta \|I_i - I_j\|^2), \tag{20.4}$$

where I_i and I_j are the color vectors of pixel i and j, respectively. θ_p, θ_v, and θ_β are model parameters whose values are learned using training data. The reader is referred to chapter 7 for more details.

Inferring the Most Probable Segmentation   The object segmentation problem can be solved by finding the least energy configuration of the CRF defined above. The pairwise potentials of the energy (20.3) are of the form of a Potts model. This allows the energy to be minimized using the α-expansion algorithm [72]. The resulting segmentation can be seen in figure 20.1. Other energy minimization algorithms, such as sequential tree-reweighted message passing (TRW-S) [255, 504], can also be used. However, the α-expansion algorithm is preferred because it is faster and gives a solution with lower energy compared to TRW-S.

20.2.1 Need for Higher-Order CRFs

The use of the Potts model [72] potentials in the CRF model makes it favor smooth object boundaries. Although this improves results in most cases, it also introduces an undesirable side effect. Smoothness potentials make the model incapable of extracting the fine contours of certain object classes, such as trees and bushes. As seen in the results, segmentations obtained using pairwise CRFs tend to be oversmooth and quite often do not match the actual object contour. It will be shown later in the chapter that these results can be significantly improved by using higher-order potentials derived from multiple segmentations obtained from an unsupervised image segmentation method.

20.3 Incorporating Higher-Order Potentials

Methods based on grouping regions for segmentation generally make the assumption that all pixels constituting a particular segment (set of pixels obtained from unsupervised segmentation) belong to the same object [185]. This is not always the case, and image segments quite often contain pixels belonging to multiple object classes. For instance, in the segmentations shown in figure 20.2 the bottom image segment contains some "building" pixels in addition to all the "grass" pixels.

Unlike other object segmentation algorithms that use the label consistency in segments as a hard constraint, the higher-order method uses it as a *soft constraint*. This is done by using higher-order potentials defined on the image segments generated using unsupervised segmentation algorithms. Specifically, the pairwise CRF model explained in the previous section is extended by incorporating higher-order potentials defined on sets or regions of pixels. The Gibbs energy of this higher-order CRF can now be written as

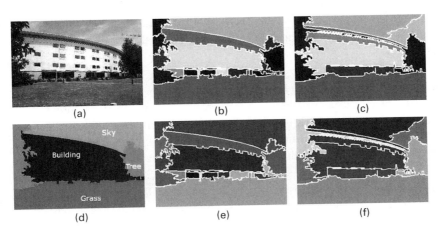

Figure 20.2
Quality sensitive region consistency prior. (a) An image from the MSRC data set. (b) and (c) Two different segmentations of the image obtained using different parameter values for the mean-shift algorithm. (d) A hand-labelled object segmentation of the image. (e) and (f) The value of the variance based quality function $G(c)$ (see equation 20.8) computed over the segments of the two segmentations. Segments with high quality values are darker. It can be clearly seen that segments which contain multiple object classes have been assigned low quality. For instance, the top segment of the left tree in segmentation (c) includes a part of the building and thus is brighter in the image (f), indicating low quality. Potentials defined on such segments will have a lower labeling inconsistency cost and less influence in the CRF.

$$E(\mathbf{x}) = \sum_{i \in \mathcal{V}} \psi_i(x_i) + \sum_{(i,j) \in \mathcal{E}} \psi_{ij}(x_i, x_j) + \sum_{c \in \mathcal{S}} \psi_c(\mathbf{x}_c), \tag{20.5}$$

where $\mathcal{S}$ refers to a set of image segments (or superpixels), and ψ_c are higher-order potentials defined on them. In the experiments the set $\mathcal{S}$ consisted of all segments of multiple segmentations of an image obtained using an unsupervised image segmentation algorithm such as mean-shift [100] (see the end of section 20.3 for more details). The higher-order potentials are described in detail below.

20.3.1 Region-Based Consistency Potential

The *region consistency potential* is similar to the smoothness prior present in pairwise CRFs [66]. It favors all pixels belonging to a segment taking the same label and, as will be shown later, is particularly useful in obtaining object segmentations with fine boundaries. It takes the form of a $\mathcal{P}^n$ Potts model [240]:

$$\psi_c^p(\mathbf{x}_c) = \begin{cases} 0 & \text{if } x_i = l_k, \forall i \in c, \\ \theta_p^h |c|^{\theta_\alpha} & \text{otherwise,} \end{cases} \tag{20.6}$$

where $|c|$ is the cardinality of the pixel set c, which in this case is the number of pixels constituting superpixel c. The expression $\theta_p^h |c|^{\theta_\alpha}$ gives the label inconsistency cost, that is, the cost added to the energy of a labeling in which different labels have been assigned to the pixels constituting the segment. The parameters θ_p^h and θ_α are learned from the training data by cross validation, as described in section 20.7. Note that this potential takes multiple variables as argument and thus cannot be expressed in the conventional pairwise CRF model.

20.3.2 Quality Sensitive Consistency Potential

Not all segments obtained using unsupervised segmentation are equally good; for instance, some segments may contain multiple object classes. A region consistency potential defined over such a segment will encourage an incorrect labeling of the image. This is because the potential (20.6) does not take the quality or *goodness* of the segment into account. It assigns the same penalty for breaking "good" segments that it assigns for "bad" ones. This problem of the consistency potential can be overcome by defining a quality sensitive higher-order potential (see figure 20.2). This new potential works by modulating the label inconsistency cost with a function of the quality of the segment (which is denoted by $G(c)$). Any method for estimating the segment quality can be used in the framework being discussed. A good example is the method of [389], which uses interregion and intraregion similarity to measure the quality or goodness of a segment. Formally, the potential function is written as

$$\psi_c^v(\mathbf{x}_c) = \begin{cases} 0 & \text{if } x_i = l_k, \forall i \in c, \\ |c|^{\theta_\alpha} (\theta_p^h + \theta_v^h G(c)) & \text{otherwise.} \end{cases} \tag{20.7}$$

In the evaluation the variance of the response of a unary feature evaluated on all constituent pixels of a segment is used to measure the quality of a segment, that is,

$$G(c) = \exp\left(-\theta_\beta^h \frac{\|\sum_{i \in c}(f(i) - \mu)^2\|}{|c|}\right), \tag{20.8}$$

where $\mu = \sum_{i \in c} f(i)/|c|$ and $f()$ is a function evaluated on all constituent pixels of the superpixel c. Restricting attention only to pairwise cliques (i.e., $|c| = 2$), the variance sensitive potential becomes

$$\psi_c^v(x_i, x_j) = \begin{cases} 0 & \text{if } x_i = x_j, \\ |c|^{\theta_\alpha}\left(\theta_p^h + \theta_v^h \exp\left(-\theta_\beta^h \frac{\|f(i) - f(j)\|^2}{4}\right)\right) & \text{otherwise.} \end{cases} \tag{20.9}$$

This is the same as the pairwise potential (20.3) commonly used in pairwise CRFs for image labeling problems [66, 401]. Thus, the variance sensitive potential can be seen as a higher-order generalization of the contrast-preserving potential. The variance function response over two segmentations of an image is shown in figure 20.2.

20.3.3 Making the Potentials Robust

The P^n Potts model rigidly enforces label consistency. For instance, if all but one of the pixels in a superpixel take the same label, then the same penalty is incurred as if they all took different labels. Due to this strict penalty, the potential might not be able to deal with inaccurate superpixels or resolve conflicts between overlapping regions of pixels. This phenomenon is illustrated in figure 20.4, in which a part of the bird is merged with the "sky" superpixel, resulting in an inaccurate segmentation. Intuitively, this problem can be resolved using the *Robust* higher-order potentials defined as

$$\psi_c^v(\mathbf{x}_c) = \begin{cases} N_i(\mathbf{x}_c)\frac{1}{Q}\gamma_{\max} & \text{if } N_i(\mathbf{x}_c) \leq Q \\ \gamma_{\max} & \text{otherwise,} \end{cases} \tag{20.10}$$

where $N_i(\mathbf{x}_c)$ denotes the number of variables in the clique c not taking the dominant label, that is, $N_i(\mathbf{x}_c) = \min_k(|c| - n_k(\mathbf{x}_c))$, $\gamma_{\max} = |c|^{\theta_\alpha}(\theta_p^h + \theta_v^h G(c))$, and Q is the truncation parameter that controls the rigidity of the higher-order clique potential. Section 20.4 shows how energy functions composed of such potentials can be minimized using move-making algorithms such as α-expansion and $\alpha\beta$-swap.

Unlike the standard P^n Potts model, this potential function gives rise to a cost that is a linear truncated function of the number of inconsistent variables (see figure 20.3). This enables the robust potential to allow some variables in the clique to take different labels. In figure 20.4 the robust P^n potentials allow some pixels of the "sky" segment to take the label "bird," thus producing a much better segmentation. Experiment results are shown for multiple values of the truncation parameter Q.

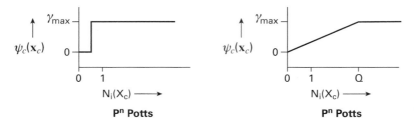

Figure 20.3
Behavior of the rigid P^n Potts potential and the Robust P^n model potential. The figure shows how the cost enforced by the two higher-order potentials' changes with the number of variables in the clique not taking the dominant label, that is, $N_i(\mathbf{x}_c) = min_k(|c| - n_k(\mathbf{x}_c))$.

Figure 20.4
Segmentation using Robust P^n potentials (20.10). (a) Original image. (b) Labeling obtained using the Textonboost classifier [437]. (c) and (d) Segmentations obtained by [100]. (e) Result obtained using pairwise CRF of [437]. (f) Result obtained using P^n Potts potentials defined on segments shown in (c) and (d) that encourage all pixels in a superpixel to take the same label, thus causing certain pixels belonging to the "bird" to erroneously take the label "sky." This problem can be overcome by using Robust P^n potentials defined in (20.10) that allow some variables in the segment to take different labels. (g) and (h) Results obtained by using the Robust potentials with truncation parameter Q equal to $0.1|c|$ and $0.2|c|$, respectively. Here $|c|$ is the size of the clique. (i) Hand-labeled segmentation.

20.3.4 Generating Multiple Segmentations

The framework described above is quite flexible and can handle multiple overlapping or nonoverlapping segments. The set S of segments used for defining the higher-order energy function (20.5) is generated by varying the parameters of the mean-shift segmentation algorithm [100]. The computer vision literature contains many other algorithms for sampling the likely segmentations of an image [486] or for generating multiscale segmentations [432] that can be used as well.

20.4 Inference in Higher-Order CRFs

Efficient graph cut-based expansion and swap-move algorithms have been successfully used to minimize energy functions composed of pairwise potential functions. It has been shown that they can also be applied to a large and useful class of higher-order energy functions [241]. To compute the optimal swap and expansion moves for energy functions composed of higher-order potentials such as the Robust P^n model, higher-order move functions will need to be minimized.

The problem of transforming a general submodular higher-order function to a second-order one has been well studied. Kolmogorov and Zabih [266] showed that all submodular functions of order 3 can be transformed to order 2, and thus can be solved using graph cuts. Freedman and Drineas [147] showed how certain submodular higher-order functions can be transformed to submodular second-order functions. Ishikawa [212] and Rother et al. [400] extended this result by showing how a general higher-order pseudo-Boolean function can be converted to a quadratic one. However, their methods, such as [147], in the worst case needed to add an exponential number of auxiliary binary variables to make the energy function second-order. Due to the special form of the Robust P^n model (20.7), the method described in the chapter needs to add only two binary variables per higher-order potential to transform the move energy to a submodular quadratic function. This allows for the efficient computation of the optimal moves. The complexity of the algorithm for computing the optimal move increases linearly with the size of the clique. This enables us to handle potential functions defined over very large cliques.

The important observation that inspired this method is the fact that higher-order pseudo-Boolean functions of the form

$$f(\mathbf{t}_c) = \min\left(\theta_0 + \sum_{i \in c} w_i^0(1 - t_i), \theta_1 + \sum_{i \in c} w_i^1 t_i, \theta_{\max}\right) \tag{20.11}$$

can be transformed to submodular quadratic pseudo-Boolean functions, and hence can be minimized using graph cuts. Here, $t_i \in \{0, 1\}$ are binary random variables, c is a clique of random variables, $\mathbf{t}_c \in \{0, 1\}^{|c|}$ denotes the labeling of the variables involved in the clique, and $w_i^0 \geq 0$, $w_i^1 \geq 0$, $\theta_0, \theta_1, \theta_{\max}$ are parameters of the potential satisfying the constraints $\theta_{\max} \geq \theta_0, \theta_1$, and

$$\left(\theta_{\max} \geq \theta_0 + \sum_{i \in c} w_i^0(1 - t_i)\right) \vee \left(\theta_{\max} \geq \theta_1 + \sum_{i \in c} w_i^1 t_i\right), \quad \forall \mathbf{t} \in \{0, 1\}^{|c|}$$

where $\vee$ is a Boolean OR operator. The transformation to a quadratic pseudo-Boolean function requires the addition of only two binary auxiliary variables, making it computationally efficient.

Theorem 20.1 *The higher-order pseudo-Boolean function*

$$f(\mathbf{t}_c) = \min\left(\theta_0 + \sum_{i \in c} w_i^0(1 - t_i), \theta_1 + \sum_{i \in c} w_i^1 t_i, \theta_{\max}\right) \qquad (20.12)$$

can be transformed to the submodular QPBF

$$f(\mathbf{t}_c) = \min_{m_0, m_1}\left(r_0(1 - m_0) + m_0 \sum_{i \in c} w_i^0(1 - t_i) + r_1 m_1 + (1 - m_1)\sum_{i \in c} w_i^1 t_i - K\right)$$

by the addition of binary auxiliary variables m_0 and m_1. Here, $r_0 = \theta_{\max} - \theta_0$, $r_1 = \theta_{\max} - \theta_1$, and $K = \theta_{\max} - \theta_0 - \theta_1$.

Proof Proof in [241]. ∎

Multiple higher-order potentials of the form (20.12) can be summed together to obtain higher-order potentials of the more general form

$$f(\mathbf{t}_c) = F_c\left(\sum_{i \in c} t_i\right) \qquad (20.13)$$

where $F_c : \mathbb{R} \to \mathbb{R}$ is any concave function.

20.5 Robust Higher-Order Potentials

The P^n Potts model was defined in [240] as

$$\psi_c(\mathbf{x}_c) = \begin{cases} \gamma_k & \text{if } x_i = l_k, \forall i \in c, \\ \gamma_{\max} & \text{otherwise,} \end{cases} \qquad (20.14)$$

where $\gamma_{\max} \geq \gamma_k$, $\forall l_k \in \mathcal{L}$. This potential is a higher-order generalization of the widely used Potts model potential that is defined over cliques of size 2 as $\psi_{ij}(a, b) = \gamma_k$ if $a = b = l_k$, and $\gamma_{\max}$ otherwise.

The family of higher-order potentials considered in this chapter is a generalization of the P^n Potts model. It contains the P^n Potts model as well as its *robust* variants, and can be used for modeling many computer vision problems. The optimal swap and expansion move energy functions for any Robust P^n model potential can be transformed into second-order submodular functions by the addition of at most two binary auxiliary variables. This transformation enables us to find the optimal swap and expansion moves in polynomial time since all second-order submodular functions of binary variables can be minimized exactly in polynomial time by solving an st-mincut problem [61, 266].

The Robust P^n model potentials take the form

$$\psi_c(\mathbf{x}_c) = \min \left\{ \min_{k \in \mathcal{L}}((|c| - n_k(\mathbf{x}_c))\theta_k + \gamma_k), \gamma_{\max} \right\} \tag{20.15}$$

where $|c|$ is the number of variables in clique c, $n_k(\mathbf{x}_c)$ denotes the number of variables in clique c that take the label k in labeling $\mathbf{x}_c$, and $\gamma_k, \theta_k, \gamma_{\max}$ are potential function parameters that satisfy the constraints

$$\theta_k = \frac{\gamma_{\max} - \gamma_k}{Q} \quad \text{and} \quad \gamma_k \leq \gamma_{\max}, \forall k \in \mathcal{L}. \tag{20.16}$$

Q is called the truncation parameter of the potential and satisfies the constraint $2Q < |c|$. It can be seen that the Robust P^n model (20.15) becomes a P^n Potts model (20.14) when the truncation (Q) is 1.

Example Consider the set of variables $\mathbf{X} = \{X_1, X_2, \ldots, X_7\}$ where each $X_i, i \in \{1, 2, \ldots, 7\}$ takes a value from the label set $\mathcal{L} = \{a, b, c\}$. The P^n Potts model assigns the cost $\gamma_{\max}$ to all labelings of the random variables except those where all variables X_i take the same label. Thus, the configuration $\mathbf{x} = (a, a, b, a, c, a, a)$ will be assigned cost $\gamma_{\max}$ even though there are only two variables (specifically, X_3 and X_5) that are assigned labels (b and c) different from the dominant label a. In contrast, the Robust P^n model with truncation 3 (i.e., $Q = 3$) assigns the cost $\gamma_a + \frac{(\gamma_{\max} - \gamma_a)}{3} \times 2$ to the same configuration.

20.5.1 Approximating Concave Consistency Potentials

Let us now consider the Robust P^n model where the constants γ_k have the same value for all labels $k \in \mathcal{L}$. In this case the higher-order potential can be seen as encouraging all the variables in the clique c to take the same label. In other words, the potential tries to reduce the number of variables in the clique not taking the dominant label, that is, $N_i(\mathbf{x}_c) = \min_k(|c| - n_k(\mathbf{x}_c))$. In the following text these label assignments to variables will be called *inconsistent*.

Unlike the P^n Potts model, which enforces label consistency very rigidly, the Robust P^n Potts model gives rise to a cost that is a linear truncated function of the number of inconsistent variables (see figure 20.3). This enables the robust potential to allow some variables in the clique to take different labels. Multiple Robust P^n model potentials can be combined to approximate any nondecreasing concave consistency potential up to an arbitrary accuracy. This potential takes the form

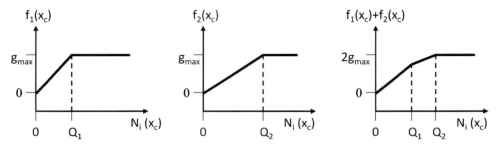

Figure 20.5
Approximating concave consistency potentials. The figure shows the result of combining two Robust higher-order potentials (a) and (b). The resulting potential function is shown in (c).

$$\psi_c(\mathbf{x}_c) = \min \left\{ \min_{k \in \mathcal{L}} \mathcal{F}_c((|c| - n_k(\mathbf{x}_c))), \gamma_{\max} \right\} \qquad (20.17)$$

where $\mathcal{F}_c$ is a nondecreasing concave function, that is, for all (a, b) and λ where $0 \le \lambda \le 1$: $\lambda \mathcal{F}_c(a) + (1 - \lambda)\mathcal{F}_c(b) \le \mathcal{F}_c(\lambda a + (1 - \lambda)b)$. This is illustrated in figure 20.5.

20.5.2 Generalized Form of Robust Higher-Order Potentials
We now provide a characterization of a larger class of functions for which at most two auxiliary variables are sufficient to transform the higher-order swap and expansion move energy functions to second-order functions. The potentials belonging to this new family have the form

$$\psi_c(\mathbf{x}_c) = \min \left\{ \min_{k \in \mathcal{L}}((P - f_k(\mathbf{x}_c))\theta_k + \gamma_k), \gamma_{\max} \right\} \qquad (20.18)$$

where the parameter P and functions $f_k(\mathbf{x}_c)$ are defined as

$$P = \sum_{i \in c} w_i^k, \quad \forall k \in \mathcal{L}, \qquad (20.19)$$

$$f_k(\mathbf{x}_c) = \sum_{i \in c} w_i^k \delta_k(x_i), \qquad (20.20)$$

$$\text{where} \quad \delta_k(x_i) = \begin{cases} 1 & \text{if } x_i = k, \\ 0 & \text{otherwise}, \end{cases} \qquad (20.21)$$

and weights $w_i^k \ge 0$, $i \in c, k \in \mathcal{L}$ encode the relative importance of different variables in preserving consistency of the labeling of the clique. The parameters $\gamma_k, \theta_k, \gamma_{\max}$ of the potential function satisfy the constraints

$$\theta_k = \frac{\gamma_{\max} - \gamma_k}{Q_k} \quad \text{and} \quad \gamma_k \le \gamma_{\max}, \forall k \in \mathcal{L}. \qquad (20.22)$$

$Q_k, k \in \mathcal{L}$ are the truncation parameters of the potential functions and satisfy the constraints $Q_a + Q_b < P, \forall a \neq b \in \mathcal{L}$.

If we assume that $w_i^k = w_i \geq 0$ and $Q_k = Q$ for all $k \in \mathcal{L}$, the potential family (20.18) can be seen as a weighted version of the Robust P^n model. The weights can be used to specify the relative importance of different variables. This can be used to change the Robust region consistency potential (20.10) in order to reduce the inconsistency cost for pixels on the segment boundary by reducing their weights. We will show that for the case of symmetric weights (i.e. $w_i^k = w_i$), the higher-order swap and expansion move energy functions for the potentials (20.18) can be transformed to a submodular second-order binary energy. Higher-order potentials with asymmetric weights can be transformed to quadratic functions in a similar manner. However, we will restrict our attention to potentials with symmetric weights for a cleaner exposition.

20.6 Transforming Higher-Order Move Energies

This section explains how the optimal swap and expansion moves for energy functions containing potential functions of the form (20.15) can be computed using graph cuts. In what follows, it will be shown that any swap move energy for higher-order potentials of the form (20.15) can be converted to a submodular pairwise function if $w_i^k = w_i$ for all $k \in \mathcal{L}$. The new transformation requires the addition of only two binary auxiliary variables. To proceed further, we will need to define the function $W(s), s \subseteq c$: $W(s) = \sum_{i \in s} w_i$. It can be seen from constraint (20.19) that $W(c) = P$. The method for computing the optimal expansion moves is similar and is explained in detail in [241].

20.6.1 Swap Moves

Recall from the definition of the swap move transformation function that only variables that are currently assigned labels α or β can take part in a $\alpha\beta$-swap move. These variables will be called *active*, and the vector of their indices, denoted by c_a. $\mathbf{t}_{c_a}$, will be used to denote the corresponding vector of move variables. Similarly, variables in the clique that do not take part in the swap move are called *passive*, and the set of their indices is denoted by c_p. Let functions $f_k^m(\mathbf{t}_{c_a}), k \in \{0, 1\}$ be defined as $f_k^m(\mathbf{t}_{c_a}) = \sum_{i \in c_a} w_i \delta_k(t_i)$.

The move energy of a $\alpha\beta$-swap move from the current labeling $\mathbf{x}_c^p$ is equal to the energy of the new labeling $\mathbf{x}_c^n$ induced by the move and is given as

$$\psi_c^m(\mathbf{t}_{c_a}) = \psi_c(\mathbf{x}_c^n). \tag{20.23}$$

New labeling $\mathbf{x}_c^n$ is obtained by combining the old labels of the passive variables $\mathbf{X}_{c_p}$ with the new labels of the active variables $\mathbf{X}_{c_a}$ as

$$\mathbf{x}_c^n = \mathbf{x}_{c_p}^p \cup T_{\alpha\beta}(\mathbf{x}_{c_a}^p, \mathbf{t}_{c_a}). \tag{20.24}$$

By substituting the value of $\mathbf{x}_c^n$ from (20.24) into (20.23), and using the definition of the higher-order potential functions (20.15), we get

$$\psi_c^m(\mathbf{t}_{c_a}) = \psi_c(\mathbf{x}_{c_p}^p \cup T_{\alpha\beta}(\mathbf{x}_{c_a}^p, \mathbf{t}_{c_a})) = \min\left\{\min_{k \in \mathcal{L}}(z_k\theta_k + \gamma_k), \gamma_{\max}\right\} \qquad (20.25)$$

where $z_k = P - f_k(\mathbf{x}_{c_p}^p \cup T_{\alpha\beta}(\mathbf{x}_{c_a}^p, \mathbf{t}_{c_a}))$. It can easily be observed that if conditions

$$W(c_a) < P - Q_\alpha \quad \text{and} \quad W(c_a) < P - Q_\beta \qquad (20.26)$$

are satisfied, then the expression $(P - f_k(\mathbf{x}_{c_p}^p \cup T_{\alpha\beta}(\mathbf{x}_{c_a}^p, \mathbf{t}_{c_a})))\theta_k + \gamma_k$ is greater than $\gamma_{\max}$ for both $k = \alpha$ and $k = \beta$. Thus, in this case the move energy $\psi_c^m(\mathbf{t}_{c_a})$ is independent of $\mathbf{t}_{c_a}$ and is equal to the constant

$$\eta = \min\left\{\min_{k \in \mathcal{L}\backslash\{\alpha,\beta\}}((P - f_k(\mathbf{x}_c^p))\theta_k + \gamma_k), \gamma_{\max}\right\}, \qquad (20.27)$$

which can be ignored while computing the swap moves. However, if constraints (20.26) are not satisfied, the move energy becomes $\psi_c^m(\mathbf{x}_{c_a}^p, \mathbf{t}_{c_a}) =$

$$\min\{(W(c_a) - f_0^m(\mathbf{t}_{c_a}))\theta_\alpha + \lambda_\alpha, (W(c_a) - f_1^m(\mathbf{t}_{c_a}))\theta_\beta + \lambda_\beta, \lambda_{\max}\} \qquad (20.28)$$

where $\lambda_\alpha = \gamma_\alpha + R_{\alpha\beta}\theta_\alpha$, $\lambda_\beta = \gamma_\beta + R_{\alpha\beta}\theta_\beta$, $\lambda_{\max} = \gamma_{\max}$, and $R_{\alpha\beta} = W(c - c_a)$.

The higher-order move energy (20.28) has the same form as the function defined in (20.12), and can be transformed to a pairwise function by introducing binary metavariables m_0 and m_1 as

$$\psi_c^m(\mathbf{t}_c) = \min_{m_0, m_1}\left(r_0(1 - m_0) + \theta_\beta m_0 \sum_{i \in c_a} w_i(1 - t_i) + r_1 m_1 + \theta_\alpha(1 - m_1) \sum_{i \in c_a} w_i t_i - \delta\right),$$
$$\qquad (20.29)$$

where $r_0 = \lambda_\alpha + \delta$, $r_1 = \lambda_\beta + \delta$, and $\delta = \lambda_{\max} - \lambda_\alpha - \lambda_\beta$.

The properties $\gamma_{\max} \geq \gamma_k, \forall k \in \mathcal{L}$, and $w_i \geq 0$ of the clique potential (20.15) imply that all coefficients of the energy function (20.29) are nonnegative. The function is thus *submodular* and can be minimized by solving an st-mincut problem [61].

20.7 Experiments

The accuracy of the higher-order model is compared with that of a pairwise CRF that uses unary potentials obtained from TextonBoost [437]. This pairwise CRF model is augmented by adding higher-order potentials defined on segments obtained from mean-shift [100]. The results are not compared with those obtained using the full TextonBoost model, which learns an image-specific appearance model (as explained in chapter 7). Such a comparison would

   (a) Original   (b) Pairwise CRF   (c) Robust Pn model   (d) Ground truth

Figure 20.6
Qualitative results of the method. (a) Original images. (b) Segmentation result obtained using the pairwise CRF (explained in section 20.2). (c) Results obtained by incorporating the Robust P^n higher-order potential (20.10) defined on segments. (d) Hand-labeled result used as ground truth.

be interesting, as we believe there are interesting connections between the two approaches. These have been partially discussed in chapter 7 and by Vicente et al. [499].

The algorithms were tested on the MSRC-23 [437] and Sowerby-7 [185] data sets. In the experiments 50% of the images in the data set were used for training, and the rest were used for testing.

Experimental results show that integration of higher-order P^n Potts model potentials quantitatively and qualitatively improves segmentation results. The use of the robust potentials leads to further improvements (see figures 20.4 and 20.6). Inference on both the pairwise and higher-order CRF models was performed using the graph cut-based expansion move algorithm. The optimal expansion moves for the energy functions containing the Robust P^n potential (20.10) were computed using the method described in the previous section.

20.7.1 Effect of Multiple Segmentations

The use of multiple segmentations allows us to obtain accurate segmentations of objects with thin structures. For instance, consider the image shown in figure 20.7a. The higher-order

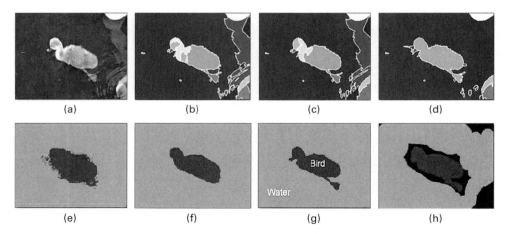

Figure 20.7
Segmenting objects with thin structures using multiple segmentations. (a) MSRC-21 image. (b), (c), and (d) Multiple segmentations obtained by varying parameters of the mean-shift algorithm [100]. (e) Labeling from TextonBoost unary potentials. (f) Result of the pairwise CRF (see section 20.2). (g) Results obtained by incorporating the Robust P^n higher-order potential (20.10) defined on the segments. (h) Hand-labeled ground truth.

method produces an accurate segmentation (figure 20.7g) of the bird that, unlike the solution of the pairwise CRF (figure 20.7f), contains the bird's leg. This result does not require that many super-pixels contain both a part of the bird's leg and a part of the bird's body. In fact, as shown in figure 20.7b and c, many superpixels contain only the leg and many others contain only (a part of) the bird without the leg. As explained below, the method being described can work even if only one superpixel contains both the bird's body and its leg.

The reader should observe that solution of the higher-order CRF (figure 20.7 g) is roughly *consistent* with all superpixels present in the multiple segmentations (figures 20.7b, c, and d). The solution is thus assigned a low cost by the higher-order label consistency potentials. Now let's consider the solution of the pairwise CRF (figure 20.7f). This labeling is consistent with superpixels in two segmentations (figures 20.7b and c), but is inconsistent with regard to the segmentation shown in figure 20.7d. It assigns "bird" and "water" labels to pixels constituting the superpixel that contained the bird, and is thus assigned a high cost by the higher-order label consistency potentials.

20.7.2 Evaluating Accuracy
The hand-labeled ground truth images that come with the MSRC-23 data set are quite rough. In fact, qualitatively they always looked worse than the results obtained from the higher-order method. The hand-labeled images suffer from another drawback. A significant number of pixels in these images have not been assigned any label. In order to get a good

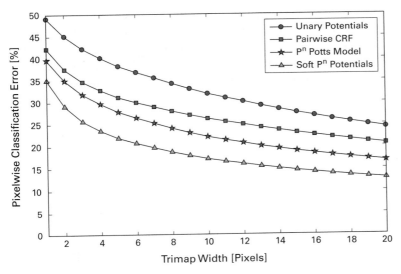

Figure 20.8
Pixelwise classification error in results. The graph shows how the overall pixelwise classification error varies as the width of the evaluation region is increased.

estimate of the algorithm's accuracy, fine segmentations of 27 images were generated that preserved the fine object boundaries.

Typically the performance of a segmentation algorithm is measured by counting the total number of mislabeled pixels in the image. This measure is not appropriate for measuring the segmentation accuracy if the user is interested in obtaining accurate segmentations as alpha mattes with fine object boundaries. Since only a small fraction of image pixels lie on the boundary of an object, a large improvement in the quality of the segmentation will result in only a small increase in the percentage of pixelwise accuracy. The quality of a segmentation is thus evaluated by counting the number of pixels misclassified in the region surrounding the actual object boundary and not over the entire image. The error was computed for different widths of the evaluation region. The accuracy of different segmentation methods is plotted in the graph in figure 20.8.

20.8 Conclusions

This chapter discussed a framework for labeling problems that is capable of utilizing features based on sets of pixels in a principled manner. The framework used a novel family of higher-order potentials, called the robust P^n model, that can be minimized using the graph cut-based expansion and swap move algorithms. Experiments showed that incorporation of P^n Potts and Robust P^n model types of potential functions (defined on segments) in the conditional random field model for object segmentation improved results. The discussed method is generic and can be used to solve many other labeling problems. It can also incorporate more sophisticated higher-order potentials based on the shape and appearance of image segments. Higher-order potentials such as the ones discussed in this chapter have been used to build a framework that allows simultaneous inference of the object appearance and segmentation [499].

21 Exact Optimization for Markov Random Fields with Nonlocal Parameters

Victor Lempitsky, Andrew Blake, and Carsten Rother

Efficient global optimization techniques such as graph cut exist for energies corresponding to binary image segmentation from low-level cues. However, introducing a high-level prior, such as a shape prior or a color distribution prior, into the segmentation process typically results in an energy that is much harder to optimize. This chapter describes a global optimization framework for a wide class of such energies. The framework is built upon two powerful techniques: graph cut and branch-and-bound. These techniques are unified through the derivation of lower bounds on the energies.

21.1 Introduction

Markov random fields (MRFs) are an efficient tool for a variety of computer vision problems. This is in part because efficient MAP inference based on such methods as graph cuts and message passing are available. In many cases these methods permit fast, sometimes global, energy optimization. As a result, difficult vision problems can be solved efficiently, robustly, and independently of initialization. Yet, while such graphical structures can represent energies based on localized low-level cues, they are much less suitable for representing *nonlocal* cues and priors.

For example, the binary image segmentation based on low-level cues such as local intensities and edge contrast is often posed as a binary MRF optimization. The graph cut algorithm can then compute a global optimum of the associated binary submodular MRF energy exactly and efficiently [66]. Consider, however, the situation where the shape of the foreground segment is known a priori to be similar to a particular template (segmentation with shape priors). Graph methods can incorporate such a prior for a single predefined and prelocated shape template [148, 278]. However, once the pose of the template is allowed to change, the relative position of each graph edge with respect to the template becomes unknown, and the *nonlocal* property of shape similarity becomes hard to express with local MRF potentials.

An easy way to circumvent the aforementioned difficulties is to alternate the MRF optimization with the reestimation of nonlocal parameters[1] (such as the template pose). A number of approaches, such as [74, 401], follow this path (also see chapter 7). Despite the use of the global graph cut optimization inside the loop, local search over the prior parameters turns these approaches into local optimization techniques akin to variational segmentation [108, 303, 512]. As a result these approaches may get stuck in local optima, which in many cases correspond to poor solutions.

This chapter introduces the framework for computing the *globally* optimal configuration for a class of MRF energies with the potentials depending on nonlocal parameters, where the optimization is performed *jointly* over the node labels and these nonlocal parameters. The main idea behind our approach is to use the efficient MRF optimization algorithms to search over the combinatorially large set of node labelings, and branch-and-bound search is used to determine the optimal value of nonlocal parameters. These two search processes are integrated in a principled manner, since the MRF optimization is placed *inside* the branch-and-bound framework, so that optimization algorithms are used to compute the lower bounds during the search. Although the worst case complexity of our method is large (essentially the same as the exhaustive search over the space of nonlocal parameters), we demonstrate a range of scenarios where our framework can obtain a significant speedup over the naïve exhaustive search approaches and runs at a speed that makes it practically applicable.

Our first application scenario is concerned with the binary segmentation problems. Here, we use the minimum cut-based optimization to compute the lower bounds inside the branch-and-bound (hence the name of the algorithm, *branch-and-mincut*). In this way we can compute globally optimal segmentation under powerful shape priors where the template shape is allowed to deform and to appear in various poses. Furthermore, global optima may be computed for the functionals concerned with fitting parametric intensity distributions to the segments, such as the Chan–Vese [88] functional. The branch-and-mincut algorithm was introduced in our paper [301].

Our second application is concerned with the part-based object detection within the pictorial structures framework [140]. The underlying MRF in this case is not binary submodular, but multilabel and tree-structured. We then demonstrate how our approach can efficiently and robustly fit the pictorial structures under significant geometric variations of the object in the image.

21.2 Related Work

Our approach is related to a large number of previous works spanning different communities and different applications fields, so only a fraction of related literature may be mentioned

---

1. We use the term "nonlocal parameter" roughly in the same sense that the terms "global latent variable," "factor variable," and others are used in other chapters.

here. First of all, our work builds upon the existence of efficient and exact MRF optimization (MAP inference) algorithms, such as message passing in tree MRFs and graph cuts in submodular binary MRFs (see chapters 1 and 2).

Second, our method is similar to other approaches that put combinatorial optimization algorithms inside branch-and-bound search. Thus, [228] combined dynamic programming and branch-and-bound to accomplish shape matching against a library of shapes, and very recently [452] proposed to combine network flow-based matching and branch-and-bound to do image registration. Our framework may also be related to branch-and-bound search methods in structure-from-motion [4] and object detection [289]. Also, the way our framework handles shape priors is related to previous approaches, such as [157], that used tree search over shape hierarchies.

There is a large body of work that deals with the applications we consider in this chapter. For instance, there is a strong interest in segmentation under shape priors (e.g., [512, 108, 110]). In particular, [108] considers the segmentation based on the optimization of kernel density-based energy estimation, which is similar to our approach. And [110] (which appeared simultaneously with [301]) considers the use of (geometric) branch-and-bound to search over the linear combination of shapes.

The problem of fitting pictorial structures to images [140] also has attracted significant interest. Most recent papers on this topic focus on going beyond tree structures and introducing long-range constraints (e.g., [290, 218]), and our framework gives a new way to accomplish that.

21.3 Optimization Framework

21.3.1 The Energy and the Lower Bound

In this section we introduce the general form of the energies that our approach can optimize. We then discuss how our method handles these energies. In general, our method starts by considering a standard pairwise MRF energy:

$$E(\mathbf{x}) = C(\omega) + \sum_{p \in V} U^p(x_p) + \sum_{p,q \in E} V^{pq}(x_p, x_q). \tag{21.1}$$

Here, V is the set of nodes, $\mathbf{x} = \{x_p \in X \mid p \in V\}$ is the labeling of MRF nodes, X denotes the alphabet of labels, E denotes the set of node pairs (edges) in the MRF structure, and C, U^p, V^{pq} correspond to the constant, unary, and pairwise terms in the MRF energy, respectively. As discussed above, pairwise MRFs are a powerful tool for processing and integrating low-level information, yet have a limited power when high-level knowledge is considered. Therefore, in this chapter we consider the augmentation of the MRF (21.1) with an extra node called a *nonlocal parameter*. During the augmentation each term is made dependent on this nonlocal parameter. In terms of the graphical factor model, such

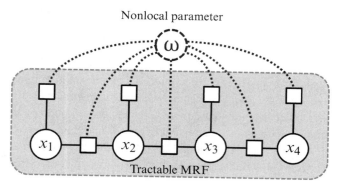

Figure 21.1
Adding a nonlocal parameter (dashed line) to a tractable MRF (solid line) leads to a more expressive model, yet results in a harder MAP inference problem, which we consider in this chapter.

augmentation corresponds to adding an extra node and connecting this node to every factor of the original MRF (as shown in figure 21.1).

As a result the energy of the MRF can be written as

$$E(\mathbf{x}, \omega) = C(\omega) + \sum_{p \in V} U^p(x_p, \omega) + \sum_{p,q \in E} V^{pq}(x_p, x_q, \omega). \tag{21.2}$$

Here, ω denotes the nonlocal parameter, and we use Ω_0 to denote its domain.

The goal of the chapter is to introduce and discuss a general framework for the optimization (MAP inference) of (21.2) under the assumption that the efficient optimization for the original MRF (21.1) is possible. This is achieved within the branch-and-bound framework. That framework is based on the simple lower bound over a set $\Omega \subset \Omega_0$ of nonlocal parameters and all possible X, derived as follows:

$$\min_{\mathbf{x} \in X^V, \omega \in \Omega} E(\mathbf{x}, \omega) = \min_{\mathbf{x} \in X^V} \min_{\omega \in \Omega} \left[C(\omega) + \sum_{p \in V} U^p(x_p, \omega) + \sum_{p,q \in E} V^{pq}(x_p, x_q, \omega) \right]$$

$$\geq \min_{\mathbf{x} \in X^V} \left[\min_{\omega \in \Omega} C(\omega) + \sum_{p \in V} \min_{\omega \in \Omega} U^p(x_p, \omega) + \sum_{p,q \in E} \min_{\omega \in \Omega} V^{pq}(x_p, x_q, \omega) \right]$$

$$= \min_{\mathbf{x} \in X^V} \left[C_\Omega(\omega) + \sum_{p \in V} U_\Omega^p(x_p) + \sum_{p,q \in E} V_\Omega^{pq}(x_p, x_q) \right] = L(\Omega). \tag{21.3}$$

Here, C_Ω, U_Ω^p, and V_Ω^{pq} denote the minima of $C(\omega)$, $U^p(\omega)$, and $V^{pq}(\omega)$ over $\omega \in \Omega$, referred to below as *aggregated potentials*, and the inequality within 21.3 is a Jensen inequality for the min operation.

The proposed lower bound possesses three properties crucial to the branch-and-bound framework:

Monotonicity   For the nested domains of nonlocal parameters $\Omega_1 \subset \Omega_2$, the inequality $L(\Omega_1) \geq L(\Omega_2)$ holds.

Computability   The key property of the derived lower bound is the ease of its evaluation. Indeed, provided that the aggregated potentials are computed, the evaluation of the bound amounts to the minimization of the original MRF energy of the form (21.1). In the cases where the original energy (21.1) permits exact optimization, the bound can be computed exactly. In many other cases the algorithms exist that allow computation of the lower bound of the MRF energy (21.1). Such algorithms can then be used to lower bound the bound (21.3) itself, thus providing the lower bound to the augmented energy (21.2). In the remainder of the chapter, we focus on the cases where the exact optimization of (21.1) and the exact evaluation of the bound (21.3) are possible.

Tightness   For a singleton Ω the bound is trivially *tight*: $L(\{\omega\}) = \min_{\mathbf{x} \in 2^V} E(\mathbf{x}, \omega)$. When the exact optimization for the original MRF and the bound is possible, the value $L(\{\omega\})$ and the corresponding optimal $\mathbf{x}$ can be computed.

21.3.2 Branch-and-Bound Optimization

Finding the global minimum of the augmented energy (21.2) is, in general, very difficult. Indeed, since the potentials can depend arbitrarily on the nonlocal parameter spanning a set Ω_0, in the worst case any optimization has to search exhaustively over Ω. In practice, however, any optimization problem of this kind has some specifically structured space Ω_0. This structure can be exploited efficiently by the branch-and-bound search detailed below.

We assume that the domain Ω_0 is discrete or can be densely discretized, and that it can be hierarchically clustered. The binary tree of its subregions $T_\Omega = \{\Omega = \Omega_0, \Omega_1, \ldots \Omega_N\}$ can then be constructed (binarity of the tree is not essential). Each nonleaf node corresponding to the subregion Ω_k then has two children corresponding to the subregions $\Omega_{ch1(k)}$ and $\Omega_{ch2(k)}$ such that $\Omega_{ch1(k)} \subset \Omega_k$, $\Omega_{ch2(k)} \subset \Omega_k$. Here, $ch1(\cdot)$ and $ch2(\cdot)$ map the index of the node to the indices of its children. Also, leaf nodes of the tree are in 1:1 correspondence with the singleton subsets $\Omega_l = \{\omega_l\}$.

Given such a tree, the global minimum of (21.2) can be efficiently found using the *best-first* branch-and-bound search [97]. This algorithm propagates a *front* of nodes in the top-down direction (figure 21.2). During the search the front contains a set of tree nodes such that each top-down path from the root to a leaf contains exactly one active vertex. In the beginning the front contains the tree root Ω_0. At each step the active node with the smallest lower bound (21.3) is removed from the active front, and two of its children are added to the active front (by the monotonicity property they have higher or equal lower bounds). Thus, an active front moves toward the leaves, making local steps that increase the lowest lower bound of all active nodes. Note that at each moment this lowest lower

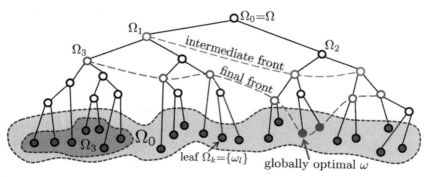

Figure 21.2
Best-first branch-and-bound optimization on the tree of nested regions finds the globally optimal ω by the top-down propagation of the *active front* (see text for details). At the moment when the lowest lower bound of the front is observed at leaf node, the process terminates with the global minimum found without traversing the whole tree.

bound of the front constitutes a lower bound on the global optimum of (21.2) over the whole domain.

At some moment of time the active node with the smallest lower bound turns out to be a leaf $\{\omega'\}$. Let $\mathbf{x}'$ be the optimal labeling for ω'. Then $E(\mathbf{x}', \omega') = L(\omega')$ (tightness property) is by assumption the lowest bound of the front, and hence a lower bound on the global optimum over the whole domain. Consequently, $(\mathbf{x}', \omega')$ is a global minimum of (21.2), and the search terminates without traversing the whole tree. In our experiments the number of the traversed nodes was typically small (one to three orders of magnitude smaller than the size of the full tree). Therefore, the algorithm performed global optimization much faster than exhaustive search over Ω_0.

In addition to the best-first branch-and-bound search we also tried the *depth-first* branch-and-bound [97]. When problem-specific heuristics are available that give good initial solutions, this variant may lead to moderate (up to a factor of 2) time savings. Nevertheless, we stick with the best-first branch-and-bound for the final experiments because of its generality (no need for initialization heuristics).

We now turn to applications and discuss how the augmented MRF energy model (21.2) can be formulated and optimized using our framework in the context of the particular computer vision applications.

21.4 Binary Image Segmentation

The first application we consider is the binary image segmentation problem, where MRF nodes typically correspond to image pixels, the edges of the MRF connect the adjacent pixels, and the labels in the MRF are binary, so that 0 and 1 denote the background and the foreground segments, respectively. Since it is typical to use symmetric pairwise terms that penalize different labels, the MRF energy for the segmentation problem can be rewritten as

$$E(\mathbf{x}) = C + \sum_{p \in V} F^p \cdot x_p + \sum_{p \in V} B^p \cdot (1 - x_p) + \sum_{p,q \in E} P^{pq} \cdot |x_p - x_q|. \tag{21.4}$$

Here, C is the constant potential, which does not depend directly on the segmentation $\mathbf{x}$; $F^p = U^p(1)$ and $B^p = U^p(0)$ are the unary potentials defining the cost for assigning the pixel p to the foreground and to the background, respectively; $P^{pq}(\omega) = V^{pq}(0, 1) = V^{pq}(1, 0)$ is the pairwise potential defining the cost of assigning adjacent pixels p and q to different segments. In our experiments the pairwise potentials were taken to be nonnegative to ensure the tractability of $E(\mathbf{x}, \omega)$ as the function of $\mathbf{x}$ for graph cut optimization [266].

Introducing the dependence on ω, the energy (21.4) can be rewritten as

$$E(\mathbf{x}, \omega) = C + \sum_{p \in V} F^p(\omega) \cdot x_p + \sum_{p \in V} B^p(\omega) \cdot (1 - x_p) + \sum_{p,q \in E} P^{pq}(\omega) \cdot |x_p - x_q|. \tag{21.5}$$

The lower bound (21.3) for (21.5) has the form

$$L(\Omega) = \min_{\mathbf{x} \in \{0,1\}^V} \left[C_\Omega + \sum_{p \in V} F^p_\Omega \cdot x_p + \sum_{p \in V} B^p_\Omega \cdot (1 - x_p) + \sum_{p,q \in E} P^{pq}_\Omega \cdot |x_p - x_q| \right] \tag{21.6}$$

where C_Ω, F^p_Ω, B^p_Ω, and P^{pq}_Ω denote the minima of $C(\omega)$, $F^p(\omega)$, $B^p(\omega)$, and $P^{pq}(\omega)$, respectively, over $\omega \in \Omega$. Both the original segmentation MRF energy (21.4) and the bound (21.6) can be minimized (evaluated) exactly and efficiently using graph cut.

Crucially, in the particular case of the graph cut optimizable bounds considered in this section, the general branch-and-bound scheme described above benefits from the coherence between the graph cut problems solved subsequently. Indeed, the popular algorithm [68] applied to such problems permits the "reuse" of the maximum flow as well as auxiliary structures, such as shortest path trees, leading to significant acceleration [66, 244]. In our experiments we observed that this trick gives an order of magnitude speedup for the evaluation of lower bounds. Thus, for the energy class (21.5) our framework (called in this case "branch-and-mincut" [301]) is particularly efficient. Below, we review some of the results from [301], demonstrating which problems it has a potential to solve.

21.4.1 Segmentation with Shape Priors

We start with the segmentation with shape priors. The success of such segmentation crucially depends on the way shape prior is defined. Earlier works often defined this prior as a Gaussian distribution of some geometrical shape statistics (e.g., control point positions or level set functions) [512, 303]. In reality, however, pose variance and deformations specific to the object of interest lead to highly non-Gaussian, multimodal prior distributions. For better modeling of prior distributions, [108] suggested the use of nonparametric kernel densities. Our approach to shape modeling is similar in spirit, as it also uses an exemplar-based prior. Arguably, it is more direct, since it involves the distances between the binary segmentations themselves, rather than their level set functions. Our approach to shape modeling is also closely related to [157], which used shape hierarchies to detect or track objects in image edge maps.

We assume that the prior is defined by the set of exemplar binary segmentations $\{\mathbf{y}^\omega \mid \omega \in \Omega_0\}$, where Ω_0 is a discrete set indexing the exemplar segmentations. Then the following term introduces a joint prior over the segmentation and the nonlocal parameter into the segmentation process:

$$E_{\text{prior}}(\mathbf{x}, \omega) = \rho(\mathbf{x}, \mathbf{y}^\omega) = \sum_{p \in V} (1 - y_p^\omega) \cdot x_p + \sum_{p \in V} y_p^\omega \cdot (1 - x_p), \tag{21.7}$$

where ρ denotes the Hamming distance between segmentations. This term clearly has the form (21.2), and therefore its combinations with other terms of this form can be optimized within our framework. Being optimized over the domain $\{0, 1\}^V \otimes \Omega_0$, this term would encourage the segmentation $\mathbf{x}$ to be close in the Hamming distance to some of the exemplar shapes. Note that the Hamming distance in the continuous limit may be interpreted as the $L1$-distance between shape masks. It is relatively straightforward to modify the term (21.7) to replace the Hamming distance with discrete approximations of other distances ($L2$, truncated $L1$ or $L2$, data-driven Mahalonobis distance, etc.).

The full segmentation energy may then be defined by adding a standard contrast-sensitive edge term [66]:

$$E_{\text{shape}}(\mathbf{x}, \omega) = E_{\text{prior}}(\mathbf{x}, \omega) + \sum_{p,q \in E} \lambda \frac{e^{-\frac{\|K_p - K_q\|}{\sigma}}}{|p - q|} \cdot |x_p - x_q|, \tag{21.8}$$

where $\|K_p - K_q\|$ denotes the SAD (L1) distance between RGB colors of the pixels p and q in the image (λ and σ were fixed throughout the experiments described in this section), $|p - q|$ denotes the distance between the centers of the pixels p and q (being either 1 or $\sqrt{2}$ for the 8-connected grid). The functional (21.8) thus incorporates the shape prior with edge contrast cues.

In practice the set Ω_0 could be huge (e.g., tens of millions of exemplars). Therefore, representation and hierarchical clustering of the exemplar segmentations y^ω, $\omega \in \Omega_0$ may be challenging. In addition, the aggregated potentials for each node of the tree should be precomputed and stored in memory. Fortunately, this is achievable in many cases where the translation invariance is exploited. In more detail the set Ω_0 is factorized into the Cartesian product of two sets $\Omega_0 = \Delta_0 \otimes \Theta_0$. The factor set Δ_0 indexes the set of all exemplar segmentations y_δ centered at the origin (this set would typically correspond to the variations in scale, orientation, and nonrigid deformations). The factor set Θ_0 then corresponds to the shift transformations and ensures the translation invariance of the prior. Any exemplar segmentation y_ω, $\omega = \delta \otimes \theta$ is then defined as some exemplar segmentation y_δ centered at the origin and then shifted by the shift θ.

Being much smaller than Ω_0, both factor sets can be clustered in hierarchy trees. For the factor set Δ_0 we used agglomerative clustering (a complete linkage algorithm that uses the Hamming distance between the exemplar segmentations). The factor set Θ_0 uses the natural hierarchical clustering of the quad-tree. Then the tree over Ω_0 is defined as a "product" of the two factor trees (we omit the details of the particular implementation). The aggregated potentials F_Ω and B_Ω for tree nodes are precomputed in a bottom-up pass and stored in memory. The redundancy arising from translation invariance is used to keep the required amount of memory reasonable.

Note the three properties of our approach to segmentation with shape priors. First, since any shapes can be included in Ω_0, general 3D pose transformations and deformations can be handled. Second, the segmentations may have general varying topology not restricted to segments with single-connected boundaries. Third, our framework is general enough to introduce other terms in the segmentation process (e.g., regional terms used in a standard graph cut segmentation [66]). For instance, the response of the appearance-based class object detector may be incorporated into the functional via the constant term $C(\omega)$. These properties of our approach are demonstrated within the following two experiments.

Experiment 1: Single Object + 3D Pose Changes In our first experiment we constructed a shape prior for a single object (a coffee cup) undergoing 3D pose changes that are modeled using 30 million exemplar shapes (the set Δ_0 contained about 1900 shapes).

The results of the global optimization of the functional (21.8) for the frames from the two sequences containing clutter and camouflage are shown in figure 21.3. On average we observed that segmenting a 312×272 image took about 30 seconds on an Intel-2.40 GHz CPU and less than 1 Gb of RAM. The proportion of the nodes of the tree traversed by the active front was on average about 1:5000. Thus, branch-and-bound tree search used in our framework improved very considerably over exhaustive search, which would have had to traverse all leaves (1:2 of the tree).

As a baseline algorithm we considered the segmentation with a "standard" graph cut functional, replacing a nonlocal shape prior term with a local intensity-based term $\sum_{p \in V} (I - I_p) \cdot x_p$, adjusting the constant I for each frame so that it gives the best results. However, since the intensity distributions of the cup and the backgrounds overlapped significantly, the segmentations were grossly erroneous (figure 21.3, right column).

Experiment 2: Object Class + Translation Invariance In the second experiment we performed the segmentation with shape priors on the UIUC car data set (the version without scale variations), containing 170 images with cars in uncontrolled environments (city streets). The shape prior was built by manually segmenting 60 translation-normalized

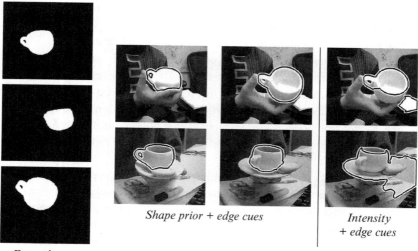

Shape prior + edge cues   Intensity
                                + edge cues

Exemplars y_ω

Figure 21.3
Using the shape prior constructed from the set of exemplars (left column), our approach can accomplish segmentation of an object undergoing general 3D pose changes within two differently illuminated sequences (two middle columns). Note the varying topology of the segmentations. For comparison, we give the results of a standard graph cut segmentation (right column); even with parameters tuned specifically to the test images, separation is entirely inaccurate.

training images and then adding translations (dependent on the extent of each test image). While the test image sizes varyied from 110×75 to 360×176, the size of Ω_0 varied from 18,666 to 2,132,865.

We computed the globally optimal segmentations under the constructed prior, using the energy (21.8). Using the bounding boxes of the cars provided with the data set, we found that in 6.5% of the images the global minima corresponded to clutter rather than cars. To provide a baseline for localization accuracy based on edge cues and a set of shape templates, we considered chamfer matching (as, e.g., in [157]). For the comparison we used the same set of templates that were matched against truncated canny-based chamfer distance (with optimally tuned truncation and canny sensitivity parameters). In this way the optimal localization failed (i.e., corresponded to clutter rather than a car) in 12.4% of the images.

Adding a simplistic appearance-based object detector via the term $C(\omega)$ reduced the number of images, where the global minimum did not correspond to a car, to 1.2%. Adding the appearance-based term improved the robustness of the segmentation, as the global optima corresponded to clutter in only 1.2% of the images. The global minima found for some of the images are shown in figure 21.4. Note that for our appearance-based detector

Figure 21.4
Results of the global optimization of (21.8) plus the detector score on some of the 170 UIUC car images, including one of the two cases where localization failed (bottom left). In the bottom right image, the global minimum of (21.8) (middle shape) and the result of our appearance-based car detector (box) gave erroneous localization, while the global minimum of their combination (right shape) represented an accurate segmentation.

on its own, the most probable bounding box corresponded to clutter on as many as 14.7% of the images.

In terms of the performance, on average, for the functional including the detector term, the segmentation took 1.8 seconds and the proportion of the tree traversed by the active front was 1:441. Without the detector term the segmentation took 6.6 seconds and the proportion of the tree traversed by the active front was 1:131. This difference in performance is natural to branch-and-bound methods: the more difficult and ambiguous the optimization problem, the larger the portion of the tree that has to be investigated.

21.4.2 Segmentation with Intensity Priors

Our framework can also be used to impose nonlocal priors on the intensity or color distributions of the foreground and the background segments. One example of such segmentation is the grayscale image segmentation based on the global optimization of the Chan-Vese functional that we describe below. The second example, concerned with color image segmentation and the GrabCut functional [401], is discussed in [301].

In [88] Chan and Vese proposed the following popular functional for the variational image segmentation problem:

$$E(S, c^f, c^b) = \mu \int_{\partial S} dl + \nu \int_S dp + \lambda_1 \int_S \left(I(p) - c^f\right)^2 dp + \lambda_2 \int_{\bar{S}} \left(I(p) - c^b\right)^2 dp,$$
$$(21.9)$$

where S denotes the foreground segment and $I(p)$ is a gray scale image. The first two terms measure the length of the boundary and the area, and the third and fourth terms are the integrals over the foreground and background of the difference between image intensity and the two intensity values c^f and c^b, which correspond to the average intensities of the respective regions. Traditionally, this functional is optimized using level set framework [360] converging to one of its local minima.

Below, we show that the discretized version of this functional can be optimized globally within our framework. Indeed, the discrete version of (21.9) can be written as (using notation as before)

$$E(\mathbf{x}, (c^f, c^b)) = \sum_{p,q \in E} \frac{\mu}{|p-q|} \cdot |x_p - x_q| + \sum_{p \in V} \left(v + \lambda_1 (I(p) - c^f)^2 \right) \cdot x_p$$
$$+ \sum_{p \in V} \lambda_2 \left(I(p) - c^b \right)^2 \cdot (1 - x_p). \tag{21.10}$$

Here, the first term approximates the first term of (21.9) (the accuracy of the approximation depends on the size of the pixel neighborhood [67]), and the last two terms express the last three terms of (21.9) in a discrete setting.

The functional (21.10) clearly has the form of (21.5) with nonlocal parameter $\omega = \{c^f, c^b\}$. Discretizing intensities c^f and c^b into 255 levels and building a quad-tree over their joint domain, we can apply our framework to find the global minima of (21.9). Examples of globally optimal segmentations, together with the traversed tree proportion and the runtimes (on PIV-2.40 GHz CPU) are shown in figure 21.5.

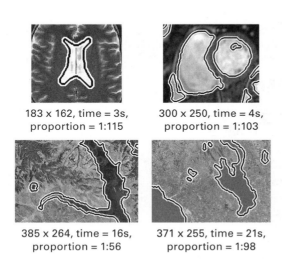

183 x 162, time = 3s,
proportion = 1:115

300 x 250, time = 4s,
proportion = 1:103

385 x 264, time = 16s,
proportion = 1:56

371 x 255, time = 21s,
proportion = 1:98

Figure 21.5
The global minima of the Chan-Vese functional for medical and aerial images. These global minima were found using our framework in the specified amount of time; a specified proportion of the tree was traversed.

21.5 Part-Based Object Detection

While the branch-and-mincut framework demonstrates the efficiency of our approach for binary MRFs, the method can be applied to multilabel MRFs as well. In this section we consider MRFs with large label alphabet that correspond to fitting *pictorial structures* [140] to images containing deformable objects of a certain class (e.g., faces; see figure 21.6, left). Such fitting is defined by the 2D location of landmark points $x_1, \ldots x_N$ that correspond, for instance, to the facial features. The positioning of the landmark points is governed by the following MRF energy [140]:

$$E(\mathbf{x}) = \sum_{p=1..N} U^p \left(x_p \mid I(x_p) \right) + \sum_{p,q \in E} V^{pq} \left(x_q - x_p \mid d^{pq}, \Sigma_{pq} \right), \tag{21.11}$$

where $U^p(x_p \mid I(x_p))$ is the unary potential defined by how well the image neighborhood of x_p (denoted $I(x_p)$) matches the appearance model for the pth landmark, and the pairwise potential V^{pq} measures the squared Mahalanobis deviation between the observed displacement vector $x_q - x_p$ and the canonical displacement d^{pq}:

$$V^{pq}(x_q - x_p \mid d^{pq}, \Sigma_{pq}) = (x_q - x_p - d^{pq})^T \Sigma_{pq}^{-1} (x_q - x_p - d^{pq}). \tag{21.12}$$

The pictorial structure fitting algorithm suggested in [140] benefits from the fast optimization algorithm for the MRF energy (21.11), based on passing messages using generalized distance transforms. Similarly to other message-passing algorithms, it is exact when the graph in the pictorial structure is a tree.

The main limitation of the representation power of the pictorial structure model is that the probabilistic distributions on the offsets are independent between edges. Thus, it cannot

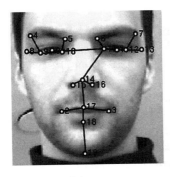
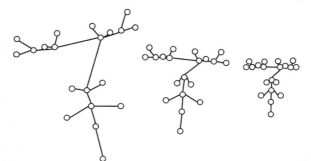

Pictorial structure   Some configurations in our set Ω

Figure 21.6
Left: The pictorial structure that we used in our experiments. Right: Pictorial structures with the offsets equal to their values $\{d^{pq}(\omega)\}$ for 3 out of 10,000 configurations in our set. Note the variability in pose and articulation that is hard to capture with a single offset configuration.

model significant pose changes of the model, such as scalings and both in-plane and out-of-plane rotations, other than by means of increasing covariances Σ_{pq}, thus loosening the structure links between the nodes.

In practice this means that rather than fitting a single pictorial structure to the image, it is common to fit several pictorial structures corresponding to different scales of the template and then picking a fitting with the smallest energy [140]. This allows much tighter distribution on offsets in the model. One can go further and fit a multitude of pictorial structures, corresponding to different scales but also rotations and articulations, so that each pose is parameterized by the parameter ω.

This search over different poses can then be accomplished via the minimization of the energy of the class (21.2), which can be written as

$$E(\mathbf{x}, \omega) = \sum_{p=1..N} U^p(x_p \mid I(x_p)) + \sum_{p,q \in E} V^{pq}(x_q - x_p \mid d^{pq}(\omega), \Sigma_{pq}). \tag{21.13}$$

Here, d^{pq} corresponds to the canonical offset between x_p and x_q for the particular pose ω. Further dependencies on ω may be introduced in (21.15); however, we model the appearance and the covariance of the offsets as being independent from the pose. This is done both for computational reasons and because there are not likely to be enough training data to train the appearance models and covariance matrices separately for each of the multitude of poses that we are going to consider. Note that the covariances Σ^{pq} in the case of the pose-dependent energy (21.15) are much smaller than in (21.11). In practice, as the variation of the offsets for a fixed pose is small, we model its covariance simply using a unit matrix with a small factor $\Sigma^{pq} = \sigma^2 \mathbf{I}$.

The lower bound (21.3) for the energy (21.15) is

$$L(\Omega) = \sum_{p=1..N} U^p(x_p \mid I(x_p)) + \sum_{p,q \in E} \min_{d^{pq}(\omega) \mid \omega \in \Omega} V^{pq}(x_q - x_p \mid d^{pq}(\omega), \Sigma_{pq}). \tag{21.14}$$

For a tree-structured case this lower bound can be computed using message passing in the same way as in the original pictorial structure (21.11). The only difference is that in addition to the generalized distance transform, passing a message in this case involves taking pointwise minima of $|\Omega|$ message maps (all being shifted copies of the same message map corresponding to the sum of incoming message maps with the unary term). The complexity of bound computation thus grows linearly with the size of $|\Omega|$, and our branch-and-bound search is unlikely to bring any time improvement over exhaustive search. A simple way to speed up the computation considerably is to loosen the bound by replacing the minima over a set of displacements with the minima over their bounding box:

$$L'(\Omega) = \min_{\mathbf{x} \in X^V} \sum_{p=1..N} U^p(x_p \mid I(x_p)) + \sum_{p,q \in E} \min_{d \in B^{pq}(\Omega)} V^{pq}(x_q - x_p \mid d, \Sigma_{pq}). \tag{21.15}$$

Here, $B^{pq}(\Omega)$ denotes the bounding box of the offsets $\{d^{pq}(\omega) \mid \omega \in \Omega\}$. The modified lower bound $L'(\Omega)$ obeys $L'(\Omega) \leq L(\Omega) \leq \min_{\mathbf{x} \in X^V \; \omega \in \Omega} E(\mathbf{x}, \omega)$, and hence can be used in the branch-and-bound search. The advantage gained by loosening the bound is that passing a message now involves a single minimum transform with the box-shaped kernel $B^{pq}(\Omega)$. Such a transform can then be computed efficiently (i.e., independent of the size of the box and in constant number operations per pixel in the map) using the van Herk/Gil and Werman algorithm [491, 164]. Thus, the messages can now be passed at a price that is independent of $|\Omega|$ and the branch-and-bound search is accelerated considerably.

The Experiment We conducted a series of experiments on the BioID data set[2] of 1521 photographs of faces of different individuals in varying poses (roughly en face), with varying expressions and illuminations, and shot against cluttered backgrounds. The images have been augmented by the FGNet group with the annotation of 22 facial landmarks, which we used to train and evaluate the pictorial structure fitting. We used the first 800 photographs to train the appearance potentials U^p (a random forest classifier based on box features was trained for each landmark, and U^p was assigned the score of this classifier thereafter). We also defined a pictorial structure by connecting the adjacent facial landmarks into a tree-shaped graph (figure 21.6, left), obtaining a set of 21 edges E along which the similarity to the canonical distances was enforced. The face *configuration* was then defined by 21 2D displacements $\{d^{pq} \mid (p, q) \in E\}$, which define the location of the 22 landmarks up to translation.

By applying rectification, clustering, scaling, and rotations to the set of configurations on the 800 training images, we created a set Ω_0 of 10,000 configurations (see figure 21.6, right) over which the optimization in (21.15) was performed (jointly with $\mathbf{x}$).

This final set of 10,000 configurations was clustered agglomeratively into a hierarchical tree, and the bounding boxes B^{pq} were precomputed for each $(p, q) \in E$ and each nonleaf node Ω in the tree. We then ran the branch-and-bound fitting on the remaining test samples for a fixed σ_0^2 by minimizing the energy (21.15), using our method. We observed that on average the algorithm visited 870 nodes in the search tree (the full tree contained 20,000–1 nodes), which corresponds to the proportion 1:13.5. This figure may go up significantly as long as more deformable objects require more diverse configuration sets. Another acceleration technique that so far has not been elaborated and implemented in our method is the use of the results of the message passing for the parental node in the search tree to prune the search space for $\mathbf{x}$ for the children nodes. This can be done within the depth-first branch-and-bound framework without giving up the global optimality. We expect such pruning to bring the computation times down significantly from the current average of 3 minutes (at PIV-2.40 GHz CPU) per image. The mean error of the landmark positioning by our method was 2.8 pixels.

---

2. http://www.bioid.com/downloads/facedb/index.php.

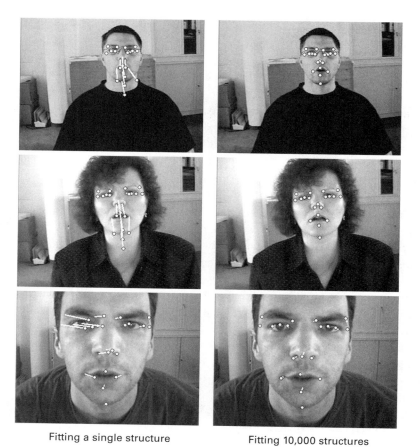

Fitting a single structure   Fitting 10,000 structures

Figure 21.7
While fitting a single pictorial structure by optimizing the energy (21.11) may not handle significant geometric variability, fitting a large number of models using branch-and-bound optimization of the energy (21.15) gives more accurate fittings (see text for details). The dots correspond to the locations of the landmarks. The lines demonstrate the offsets with respect to the ground truth annotations. The images are taken from the BioID data set.

For the purpose of the baseline we also ran the original algorithm of Felzenszwalb and Huttenlocher, [139], fitting the pictorial structure by minimizing the functional (21.11) with the canonical configuration $\{d^{pq}\}_0$ and using three different σ^2 that corresponded to σ_0^2, $10\sigma_0^2$, and $100\sigma_0^2$. Thus we tried progressively looser pictorial structures, the latter typically placing x_p independently according to the appearance cues. The mean errors were 9.66 pixels, 4.2 pixels, and 13.2 pixels, respectively. The comparative results of pictorial structure fittings corresponding to the global optima or our functional (21.15) and the original functional (21.11) with the best of the three covariances (i.e., $10\sigma_0^2$) are given in figure 21.7.

21.6 Discussion

In this chapter we demonstrated how efficient MAP inference may be performed in MRFs augmented with nonlocal parameters. This is accomplished by incorporating efficient MRF energy optimization algorithms inside the branch-and-bound framework.

Augmenting MRFs with nonlocal parameters leads to expressive graphical models that can handle many difficult problems in computer vision. On the one hand, these models benefit from the MRF's efficiency in incorporating and propagating low-level local cues. On the other hand, they have a capability to incorporate high-level knowledge that can be defined both in some parametric form and nonparametrically, using a set of exemplars. In the latter case our method approaches and generalizes the nearest neighbor-based techniques.

22 Graph Cut-Based Image Segmentation with Connectivity Priors

Sara Vicente, Vladimir Kolmogorov, and Carsten Rother

This chapter addresses the same problem as chapters 7 and 8, namely, segmenting an object in an image with interactive help from the user. However, in contrast to those chapters, an additional global (image-wide) constraint is imposed that forces different types of connectivity priors on the segmentation. Although this problem is in general NP-hard, this chapter presents algorithmic solutions to tackle the problem, which leads to an improved interactive segmentation system.[1]

22.1 Introduction

Interactive image segmentation has attracted significant attention in recent years [217, 66, 401, 175, 441, 425] (chapters 7 and 8). The ultimate goal is to extract an object with as few user interactions as possible. It is widely accepted that some prior on segmentations is needed to achieve this goal. Different priors have a preference toward different types of shapes, as is discussed next.

Graph Cut A very popular approach, which is also used in this chapter, is based on graph cut [176, 66, 401]. It minimizes an energy function consisting of a data term (computed using color likelihoods of foreground and background) and a spatial coherence term. The latter is the length of the boundary modulated with the contrast in the image, therefore minimizing the energy with which this term has a bias toward shorter boundaries. (This behavior is sometimes referred to as the "shrinking bias"; see also chapter 8.) In particular, it is hard for the graph cut approach to segment thin, elongated structures. Consider figure 22.1. First the user constrains some pixels to be foreground and background, using brushes (a). The segmentation by graph cut (b) cuts off some of the legs of the insect. If the influence of the coherence term is reduced, then the legs are segmented, but the overall quality of the the segmentation is decreased (c). This shows the trade-off between data terms and regularization, and it indicates that some form of coherence is crucial.

---

1. This chapter is based primarily on [497].

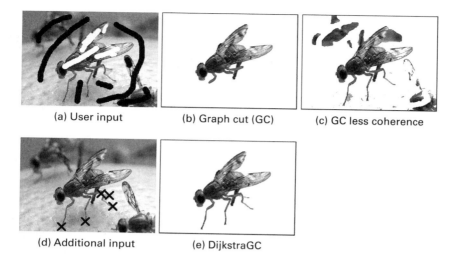

(a) User input   (b) Graph cut (GC)   (c) GC less coherence

(d) Additional input   (e) DijkstraGC

Figure 22.1
Image segmentation with graph cut and DijsktraGC. Results of graph cut with standard (b) and reduced coherence (c) based on input (a). New DijkstraGC method (e) with additional user input (d).

Alternative Segmentation Models   One approach to overcome the shrinking bias is to add the flux of some vector field to the model [217, 492, 232, 256]. It has been shown to be effective for segmenting thin objects such as blood vessels in gray scale images [492]. The vector field was taken as the image gradient, which corresponds to the assumption that the object is bright and the background is dark. However, extending this approach to arbitrary color images, which is the scenario considered in this chapter, may be challenging and has not been addressed so far. The difficulty here is in choosing the vector at each point and the sign of this vector. An imperfect vector field might lower the segmentation quality. The issue of choosing the sign can be overcome in the level set framework [232], but at the expense of losing global optimality.

One possible method to integrate flux into segmentation is to optimize the ratio of flux over boundary length [217, 257]. Thus, the method looks for the boundary with the highest average contrast. Arguably, this model has no bias toward any particular shape [217, 257]. However, the issue of choosing a good vector field for color images remains.

Other interesting approaches include the method that imposes a prior on the curvature of the boundary [425] and the random walker algorithm [175]; results [441] indicate that this method is slightly more robust toward the shrinking bias (see detailed discussion in chapter 8).

Our Approach   This chapter discusses a different way to solve the task of segmenting challenging objects with very thin, elongated parts. The coherence prior is built into the model in the form of an *explicit connectivity prior*. Assume that the user has already segmented a part of the object using graph cut [401], as in figure 22.1(b). In the proposed interactive framework the user has to click only those pixels that must be connected to the main object. As figure 22.1(d) shows, a few clicks are sufficient to obtain a satisfying result (e). This is a new and very powerful user interface for segmenting challenging objects.

Several versions of the connectivity constraint are considered. Unfortunately, the corresponding optimization problems are all NP-hard. To enable the interface shown in figure 22.1, a heuristic algorithm named *DijkstraGC* is proposed. On an abstract level it merges the Dijkstra algorithm and graph cut. Note that Dijkstra-like methods have already been used for extracting thin objects such as blood vessels [123], although without an explicit segmentation. (A fast marching technique was used by Deschamps et al. [123] that can be viewed as a continuous analogue of the Dijkstra algorithm for discrete graphs.) The key feature of the method proposed that distinguishes it from [123] is the addition of the graph cut component. This allows the explicit use of the MAP-MRF formulation that has proved to be very successful [66, 401].

On some practical examples DijkstraGC is able to find the global minimum. In order to verify this, a second (slow) technique based on *dual decomposition* is used that provides a lower bound on the optimal cost.

Related Work Connectivity is automatically enforced in the classical "snakes" approach [227], since the segmentation is represented by a simple closed contour. Han et al. [181] proposed a topology-preserving level set method that allows specification of more general topologies. A disadvantage of both techniques is that the objective is optimized via gradient descent, which can easily get stuck in a local minimum.

Zeng et al. [548] followed a similar approach with a discrete graph-based formulation. After posing the problem the authors proved an NP-hardness result and proposed to modify the maxflow algorithm [68] so that the topology of the segmentation is preserved. However, it was not possible to compare with this approach for the task of segmenting thin objects.[2] (Note, that results in [548] are shown for very different types of objects.)

After the publication of [497], Nowozin and Lampert [353] proposed an LP relaxation approach for the problem of MRF-based segmentation under connectivity constraints, that is, the connectivity constraint C0 as defined below. One difference of this work is that their method has to operate on superpixels instead of individual pixels, due to the large complexity of the optimization problem. Interestingly, working on superpixels could potentially be an advantage, since degenerate solutions that are one pixel wide (details later) are prohibited. A direct comparison between the two approaches would be interesting.

---

2. The source code (ver. 0.9) was downloaded, but its applications to the examples presented were unsuccessful; sometimes user-provided hard constraints were not satisfied, or the segmented thin structure was clearly incorrect. Reimplementing the algorithm in [548] did not look straightforward; many details were missing.

A fast solution for the same problem of segmentation with the general connectivity constraint (C0) was presented in [390]. It exploits the solution of [497] by "automating the user interactions," using heuristics, and speeding up DijkstraGC by using the concept of min-marginal.

Lempitsky et al. [298] combined the connectivity constraint C0 with a so-called bounding box prior. This considerably improved the quality of results for an interactive segmentation system where the user manually specifies a bounding box for the object.

Chapter 7 discusses other forms of connectivity constraints that are practically interesting, such as connectivity with respect to foreground brushstrokes.

22.2 Problem Formulation

The energy function used is of the form that is standard for graph cut-based image segmentation approaches [66, 401] (chapters 1, 2, and 7):

$$E(\mathbf{x}) = \sum_{p \in \mathcal{V}} E_p(x_p) + \sum_{(p,q) \in \mathcal{E}} E_{pq}(x_p, x_q). \qquad (22.1)$$

Here $(\mathcal{V}, \mathcal{E})$ is an undirected graph whose nodes correspond to pixels. $x_p \in \{0, 1\}$ is the segmentation label of pixel p, where 0 and 1 correspond to the background and the foreground, respectively. The pairwise terms E_{pq} are considered submodular.

As stated in the introduction, the goal is to minimize function $E(\mathbf{x})$ under certain connectivity constraints on the segmentation $\mathbf{x}$. Three possible constraints are formulated below. In all of them it is assumed that an undirected graph $(\mathcal{V}, \mathcal{F})$ defining the "connectivity" relations between nodes in $\mathcal{V}$ is given. This graph can be different from the graph $(\mathcal{V}, \mathcal{E})$ that defines the structure of function $E(\mathbf{x})$ in (22.1). In the experiments $(\mathcal{V}, \mathcal{E})$ is an 8-connected 2D grid graph and $(\mathcal{V}, \mathcal{F})$ is a 4-connected one.

Perhaps the most natural connectivity constraint is the following:

C0   *The set* [**x**] *corresponding to segmentation* **x** *must form a single connected component in the graph* $(\mathcal{V}, \mathcal{F})$.

([**x**] denotes the set of nodes with label 1 that is, [**x**] $= \{p \in \mathcal{V} \mid x_p = 1\}$.) This constraint seems to be very useful for solving problems discussed in the introduction. However, minimizing function (22.1) under the constraint **C0** appears to be a very challenging task. This problem can be shown to be NP-hard even if function (22.1) has only unary terms (see below).

The focus of this chapter will be on constraints **C1** and **C2**. It is assumed that the user specified two nodes $s, t \in \mathcal{V}$. Constraint **C1** is then formulated as follows:

C1   *Nodes* s, t *must be connected in the segmentation set* [**x**], *that is, there must exist a path in the graph* $(\mathcal{V}, \mathcal{F})$ *from* s *to* t *such that all nodes* p *in the path belong to the segmentation:* $x_p = 1$.

C1 is very useful for interactive image segmentation. It suggests a natural user interface (figure 22.1). In this interface node s is assumed to lie in the largest connected component of the current segmentation. By clicking at pixel t the user will get a segmentation that connects t to the main object. Multiple clicks are handled in an incremental fashion.

Unfortunately, minimizing (22.1) under **C1** is an NP-hard problem as well (see below). However, it appears that it is easier to design good heuristic algorithms for **C1** than for **C0**. In particular, if function $E(\mathbf{x})$ has only unary terms, then the problem with **C1** can be reduced to a shortest path computation with a single source and a single sink, and thus can be solved in polynomial time (see section 22.3).

Enforcing constraint **C1** may result in a segmentation that has a width of one pixel in certain places, which may be undesirable (see figure 22.6). One way to fix this problem is to allow the user to specify a parameter δ that controls the minimum width of the segmentation.[3]

Formally, assume that for each node $p \in \mathcal{V}$ there is a subset $\mathcal{Q}_p \subseteq \mathcal{V}$. (This subset would depend on δ; for example, for a grid graph, $\mathcal{Q}_p$ could be the set of all pixels q such that the distance from p to q does not exceed δ.) Using these subsets, the following connectivity constraint is defined:

C2   *There must exist a path in the graph $(\mathcal{V}, \mathcal{F})$ from s to t such that for all nodes p in the path, the subset $\mathcal{Q}_p$ belongs to $[\mathbf{x}]$, that is, $x_q = 1$ for $q \in \mathcal{Q}_p$.*

Clearly, **C1** is a special case of **C2** if $\mathcal{Q}_p = \{p\}$ for all nodes p.

Throughout the chapter, **P0**, **P1**, and **P2** denote the problems of minimizing function (22.1) under constraints **C0**, **C1**, and **C2**, respectively. The theorem below shows the difficulty of the problems; the proof is given in [498].

Theorem 22.1   *Problems **P0**, **P1**, and **P2** are NP-hard. **P0** and **P2** remain NP-hard even if the set $\mathcal{E}$ is empty, that is, function (22.1) does not have pairwise terms.*

Note that it was shown in [548] that the following problem is NP-hard: minimize function (22.1) on a planar 2D grid so that the foreground is 4-connected and the background is 8-connected. It is straightforward to modify the argument in [548] to show that the problem is NP-hard if only the 4-connectedness of the foreground is imposed (in other words, **P0** is NP-hard even for planar 2D grids).

To conclude this section, some simple facts about the relationship of problems **P0–P2** and the problem of minimizing function $E(\mathbf{x})$ without any constraints are presented.

Theorem 22.2   *Suppose that $\mathbf{x}$ is a global minimum of function (22.1) without any constraints.*

*(a) There exists an optimal solution $\mathbf{x}^*$ of **P2** that includes $\mathbf{x}$, that is, $[\mathbf{x}] \subseteq [\mathbf{x}^*]$. The same holds for **P1** since it is a special case.*

---

3. In [178] a different solution is presented to overcome this problem; see figure 14 in [178]. By imposing a "geodesic star-convexity prior," one-pixel-wide solutions are sometimes not allowed in the solution space.

(b) Suppose that $\mathcal{E} \subseteq \mathcal{F}$. Let $C_1, \ldots, C_k \subseteq V$ be the connected components of the set $[\mathbf{x}]$ in the graph $(V, \mathcal{F})$. Then there exists an optimal solution $\mathbf{x}^*$ of **P0** *such that each component C_i is either entirely included in $[\mathbf{x}^*]$ or entirely excluded. In other words, if C_i and $[\mathbf{x}^*]$ intersect, then $C_i \subseteq [\mathbf{x}^*]$.*

A proof is given in [498]. The theorem suggests that as a first step the max-flow algorithm could be run to minimize function (22.1) without any constraints, and then connected components of the obtained set $[\mathbf{x}]$ could be contracted to single nodes. However, it leaves open the most challenging question: what to do if a minimum of function (22.1) does not satisfy the desired connectivity constraint.

22.3　Algorithms

The main algorithmic contribution of this chapter is a heuristic method for problem **P2** (and thus for **P1**, since the latter is a special case). This method, named *DijkstraGC*, is presented in section 22.3.1. Then in section 22.3.2 it is proposed as an alternative method for a special case of problem **P1** based on the idea of *problem decomposition*. The main feature of the second technique is that it provides a lower bound on the optimal value of **P1**. It will be used for assessing the performance of DijkstraGC: in the experimental section it will allow verification that for some instances it gives an optimal solution.

22.3.1　DijkstraGC: Merging Dijkstra and Graph Cuts

The idea of the first method is motivated by the Dijkstra algorithm [10]. Recall that the latter technique computes shortest distances $d(p)$ in a directed graph with nonnegative weights from a specified source node s to all other nodes p.

Similar to the Dijkstra method, DijkstraGC computes solutions to problem **P2** for a fixed node s and all nodes $p \in V$ (only now these solutions will not necessarily be global minima). The distance $d(p)$ will now indicate the cost of the computed solution for the pair of nodes $\{s, p\}$.

The algorithm is shown in figure 22.2. During the algorithm the current solution $\mathbf{x}^p$ for node p with $d(p) < +\infty$ can be obtained as follows: using *PARENT* pointers, get path $\mathcal{P}$ and corresponding set $\bar{\mathcal{P}} = \cup_{r \in \mathcal{P}} \mathcal{Q}_r$, then compute a minimum of function (22.1) under the constraint $\bar{\mathcal{P}} \subseteq [\mathbf{x}]$. Clearly, the obtained solution $\mathbf{x}^p$ satisfies the hard constraint **C2** for the pair of nodes $\{s, p\}$.

The set S contains "permanently labeled" nodes: once a node p has been added to S, its cost $d(p)$ and the corresponding solution will not change.

Some of the invariants that are maintained during DijkstraGC are listed below (they follow directly from the description):

---

initialize: $S = \varnothing$, $PARENT(p) = NULL$ for all nodes p,
$\qquad d(s) = \min\{E(\mathbf{x}) \mid Q_s \subseteq [\mathbf{x}]\}$,
$\qquad d(p) = +\infty$ for $p \in V - \{s\}$
while $t \notin S$ and $V - S$ contains nodes p with $d(p) < +\infty$

- find node $p \in V - S$ with the smallest distance $d(p)$
- add p to S
- **for** all nodes $q \in V - S$ that are neighbors of p (i.e., $(p, q) \in F$) **do**

  — using $PARENT$ pointers, get path $\mathcal{P}$ from s to q through p; compute corresponding set $\bar{\mathcal{P}} = \cup_{r \in \mathcal{P}} Q_r$
  — compute a minimum $\mathbf{x}$ of function (22.1) under the constraint $\bar{\mathcal{P}} \subseteq [\mathbf{x}]$
  — if $d(q) > E(\mathbf{x})$, set $d(q) := E(\mathbf{x})$, $PARENT(q) := p$

Figure 22.2
DijkstraGC algorithm.

I1 If $d(p) = +\infty$, then $p \neq s$ and $PARENT(p) = NULL$.

I2 If $d(p) < +\infty$, then $PARENT$ pointers give the unique path $\mathcal{P}$ from s to p, and $d(p) = \min\{E(\mathbf{x}) \mid \bar{\mathcal{P}} \subseteq [\mathbf{x}]\}$ where $\bar{\mathcal{P}} = \cup_{r \in \mathcal{P}} Q_r$.

I3 If $PARENT(q) = p$, then $d(p) \leq d(q) < +\infty$.

I4 $d(p) < +\infty$ for nodes $p \in S$.

Theorem 22.3 *If function $E(\mathbf{x})$ does not have pairwise terms and $Q_p = \{p\}$ for all nodes p (i.e., it is an instance of* **P1**), *then the algorithm in figure 22.2 produces an optimal solution.*

A proof is given in [498].

It is conjectured that the following statement holds:

Conjecture 22.1 *Suppose that $Q_p = \{p\}$ for all nodes p, graph (V, F) is planar, $\mathcal{E} = \mathcal{F}$, all pairwise terms have the form $E_{pq}(x_p, x_q) = c_{pq}|x_q - x_p|$, $c_{pq} \geq 0$, and unary terms for "inner" nodes $p \in V$ (i.e., nodes that do not border the outer face) have no bias or a bias toward label 1, that is, $E_p(1) \leq E_p(0)$. Then the algorithm in figure 22.2 produces an optimal solution.*

If conditions of the theorem are relaxed, then the problem may become NP-hard, as theorem 22.1 states. Not surprisingly, DijkstraGC may then produce a suboptimal solution. Two examples are shown in figure 22.3. Note that in these examples the "direction" of DijkstraGC matters: running DijkstraGC from s to t gives a suboptimal solution, but running it from t to s will give an optimal segmentation.

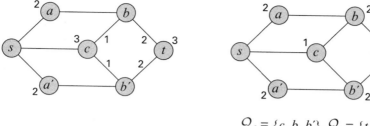

$$\mathcal{Q}_c = \{c, b, b'\}, \ \mathcal{Q}_t = \{t, b, b'\}$$
$$\mathcal{Q}_p = \{p\} \text{ for all other nodes } p$$

(a) Problem **P1**   (b) Problem **P2**, no pairwise terms

Figure 22.3
Suboptimality of DijkstraGC. Examples of problems on which DijkstraGC gives suboptimal results. Graphs shown are the connectivity graphs $(\mathcal{V}, \mathcal{F})$. Number c_p at node p gives the unary term cx_p; number c_{pq} at edge (p, q) gives the pairwise term $c_{pq}|x_q - x_p|$. In both (a) and (b) DijkstraGC will output solution $\{s, a, b, b', t\}$ or $\{s, a', b, b', t\}$ with cost 7, while the optimal solution $\{s, c, b, b', t\}$ has cost 6.

Efficient implementation will be now discussed. One computational component of the algorithm is finding a node $p \in \mathcal{V} - \mathcal{S}$ with the smallest value of $d(p)$ (the same as in the Dijkstra algorithm). A binary heap structure is used for implementing the priority queue that stores nodes $p \in \mathcal{V} - \mathcal{S}$ with $d(p) < +\infty$. The bottleneck, however, is max-flow computations: DijkstraGC requires many calls to the max-flow algorithm for minimizing function (22.1) under the constraints $x_r = 1$ for nodes $r \in \bar{\mathcal{P}}$. These computations are considered in the remainder of this section.

Optimized DijkstraGC   First, a technique that allows reduction of the number of calls to max-flow is described. Consider the step that adds node p to the set of permanently labeled nodes $\mathcal{S}$. Denote $\mathcal{P}$ to be the path from s to p given by *PARENT* pointers, and let $\bar{\mathcal{P}} = \cup_{r \in \mathcal{P}} \mathcal{Q}_r$. Nodes in $\bar{\mathcal{P}}$ are fixed to 1, and a minimum **x** of function (22.1) is computed under these constraints. The segmentation set [**x**] will contain $\bar{\mathcal{P}}$, but it may include many other nodes as well. Then it might be possible to add several nodes to $\mathcal{S}$ using this single computation. Indeed, suppose p has a neighbor $q \in \mathcal{V} - \mathcal{S}$, $(p, q) \in \mathcal{F}$, such that $\mathcal{Q}_q \subseteq$ [**x**]. The algorithm in figure 22.2 would set $d(q) = d(p) = E(\mathbf{x})$ while exploring neighbors of p. This would make the distance $d(q)$ the smallest among nodes in $\mathcal{V} - \mathcal{S}$, so the node q could be the next node to be added to $\mathcal{S}$. Therefore, q can be immediately added to $\mathcal{S}$.

An algorithm that implements this idea is shown in figure 22.4. Before exploring neighbors of q, the algorithm checks which nodes can be added to $\mathcal{S}$ for "free." The set of these nodes is denoted as $\mathcal{A}$; clearly, it includes p. After adding nodes in $\mathcal{A}$ to $\mathcal{S}$, the algorithm explores neighbors of $\mathcal{A}$ that are still in $\mathcal{V} - \mathcal{S}$.

Note that there is a certain freedom in implementing the DijkstraGC algorithm: it does not specify which node $p \in \mathcal{V} - \mathcal{S}$ with the minimum distance to choose if there are several

---

initialize: $\mathcal{S} = \varnothing$, $PARENT(p) = NULL$ for all nodes p,
$\qquad d(s) = \min\{E(\mathbf{x}) \mid \mathcal{Q}_s \subseteq [\mathbf{x}]\}$,
$\qquad d(p) = +\infty$ for $p \in \mathcal{V} - \{s\}$
while $t \notin \mathcal{S}$ and $\mathcal{V} - \mathcal{S}$ contains nodes p with $d(p) < +\infty$

- find node $p \in \mathcal{V} - \mathcal{S}$ with the smallest distance $d(p)$
- using $PARENT$ pointers, get path $\mathcal{P}$ from s to p; compute corresponding set $\bar{\mathcal{P}} = \cup_{r \in \mathcal{P}} \mathcal{Q}_r$
- compute a minimum $\mathbf{x}$ of function (22.1) under the constraint $\bar{\mathcal{P}} \subseteq [\mathbf{x}]$
- add p to $\mathcal{S}$, set $\mathcal{A} = \{p\}$, mark p as "unprocessed"
- **while** $\mathcal{A}$ has unprocessed nodes

  - pick unprocessed node $p' \in \mathcal{A}$
  - **for** all edges $(p', q) \in \mathcal{F}$ with $q \in \mathcal{V} - \mathcal{S}$ **do**

    ◇ if $\mathcal{Q}_q \subseteq [\mathbf{x}]$ set $d(q) := E(\mathbf{x})$, $PARENT(q) := p'$, add q to $\mathcal{S}$ and to $\mathcal{A}$ as an unprocessed node

  - mark p' as "processed"

- **for** all nodes $q \in \mathcal{V} - \mathcal{S}$ that are neighbors of $\mathcal{A}$ (i.e., $(p', q) \in \mathcal{F}$ for some node $p' \in \mathcal{A}$) **do**

  - pick node $p' \in \mathcal{A}$ with $(p', q) \in \mathcal{F}$
  - using $PARENT$ pointers, get path $\mathcal{P}$ from s to q through p'; compute corresponding set $\bar{\mathcal{P}} = \cup_{r \in \mathcal{P}} \mathcal{Q}_r$
  - compute a minimum $\mathbf{x}$ of function (22.1) under the constraint $\bar{\mathcal{P}} \subseteq [\mathbf{x}]$
  - if $d(q) > E(\mathbf{x})$, set $d(q) := E(\mathbf{x})$, $PARENT(q) := p'$

Figure 22.4
Optimized version of the DijkstraGC algorithm.

such nodes. It is not difficult to see that under a certain selection rule DijkstraGC becomes equivalent to the algorithm in figure 22.4.

Flow and Search Tree Recycling The max-flow algorithm in [68] is used, and flows and search trees are reused as described in [244].

In DijkstraGC it is often necessary to fix/unfix nodes in different parts of the graph in a rather chaotic order. This significantly reduces the effectiveness of flow and search tree recycling. Two ideas could potentially be used to overcome this drawback. The first one is based on the observation that different "branches" are often independent in a certain sense. This could allow reordering max-flow computations. Getting the same type of result as DijkstraGC computations will have to be redone if an inconsistency is detected, as in the Bellman–Ford label-correcting algorithm. The second idea is to maintain multiple graphs for performing computations in different parts of the image, so that changes in each graph will be more "local." It could also be feasible to store a small subset of the nodes for each graph, increasing it "on demand." Reduced memory requirements could then allow use of a larger number of graphs. Exploring these ideas is left as future work.

22.3.2 Problem Decomposition Approach

In this section a different technique is proposed for a special case of problem **P1** that will be used for assessing the performance of DijkstraGC.

Overview   On the high level the idea is to decompose the original problem into several "easier" subproblems for which a global minimum (or a good lower bound) can be efficiently computed. Combining the lower bounds for individual subproblems will then provide a lower bound for the original problem. The decomposition and the corresponding lower bound will depend on a parameter vector θ; then the goal is to find a vector θ that maximizes the bound.

This approach is well-known in combinatorial optimization; sometimes it is referred to as "dual decomposition" [35]. In vision the decomposition approach is probably best known in the context of the MAP-MRF inference task. It was introduced by Wainwright et al. [504], who decomposed the problem into a convex combination of trees and proposed message-passing techniques for optimizing the vector θ. These techniques do not necessarily find the best lower bound (see [255] or [520]). Schlesinger and Giginyak [423, 424] and Komodakis et al. [268] proposed using subgradient techniques [435, 35] for MRF optimization, which guarantee a convergence to a vector θ yielding the best possible lower bound.

Solving P1 via Problem Decomposition   This approach is now applied to **P1**. To get tractable subproblems, the following simplifying assumptions are imposed. First, the graph $(\mathcal{V}, \mathcal{F})$ should be planar, and $\mathcal{E} = \mathcal{F}$. Second, the pixels on the image boundary are constrained to be background, that is, their label is 0.

These assumptions represent an important practical subclass of the image segmentation task, and thus can be used for assessing the performance of DijkstraGC for real problems. Note that the second assumption encodes the prior knowledge that the object lies entirely inside the image, which is very often the case in practice.

$C(\mathbf{x})$ denotes the hard constraint term that is 0 if the segmentation $\mathbf{x}$ satisfies the connectivity constraint **C1** and the background boundary condition described above, and otherwise is $+\infty$. Some of these hard constraints will also be included in function $E(\mathbf{x})$ as unary terms, namely, the background boundary constraints and foreground constraints $x_s = x_t = 1$, which follow from **C1**. The parameter vector θ will have two parts: $\theta = (\theta^1, \theta^2)$ where vectors θ^1 and θ^2 correspond to nodes and edges of the graph $(\mathcal{V}, \mathcal{E})$, respectively ($\theta^1 \in \mathbb{R}^{\mathcal{V}}$, $\theta^2 \in \mathbb{R}^{\mathcal{E}}$). Given labeling $\mathbf{x}$, let $\phi(\mathbf{x}) \in \{0, 1\}^{\mathcal{E}}$ be the vector of indicator variables showing discontinuities of $\mathbf{x}$, that is, $\phi_{pq}(\mathbf{x}) = |x_q - x_p|$ for an edge $(p, q) \in \mathcal{E}$.

The first decomposition to be considered was

$$E(\mathbf{x}) + C(\mathbf{x}) = E^0(\mathbf{x} \mid \theta^1) + E^1(\mathbf{x} \mid \theta^1) \qquad (22.2)$$

where

$$E^0(\mathbf{x} \mid \theta^1) = E(\mathbf{x}) - \langle \mathbf{x}, \theta^1 \rangle \qquad (22.2a)$$

$$E^1(\mathbf{x} \mid \theta^1) = C(\mathbf{x}) + \langle \mathbf{x}, \theta^1 \rangle. \qquad (22.2b)$$

It was observed in the experiments that the correspondent lower bound is not tight. To improve tightness, a third subproblem defined the following decomposition, which will be used hereafter:

$$E(\mathbf{x}) + C(\mathbf{x}) = E^0(\mathbf{x} \mid \theta) + E^1(\mathbf{x} \mid \theta) + E^2(\mathbf{x} \mid \theta) \qquad (22.3)$$

where

$$E^0(\mathbf{x} \mid \theta) = E(\mathbf{x}) - \langle \mathbf{x}, \theta^1 \rangle - \langle \phi(\mathbf{x}), \theta^2 \rangle \qquad (22.3a)$$

$$E^1(\mathbf{x} \mid \theta) = C(\mathbf{x}) + \langle \mathbf{x}, \theta^1 \rangle \qquad (22.3b)$$

$$E^2(\mathbf{x} \mid \theta) = C(\mathbf{x}) + \langle \phi(\mathbf{x}), \theta^2 \rangle. \qquad (22.3c)$$

Each subproblem will be discussed below in more detail.

Subproblem 0 Function $E^0(\mathbf{x} \mid \theta)$ consists of unary and pairwise terms. This function should be submodular; it is equivalent to specifying upper bounds on components θ_{pq}^2. Since there are no connectivity constraints, the global minimum $\Phi^0(\theta) = \min_{\mathbf{x}} E^0(\mathbf{x} \mid \theta)$ can be computed using a max-flow algorithm.[4]

Subproblem 1 Function $E^1(\mathbf{x} \mid \theta)$ has only unary terms and the connectivity constraint **C1**. As discussed in the previous section, the global minimum $\Phi^1(\theta) = \min_{\mathbf{x}} E^1(\mathbf{x} \mid \theta)$ can be computed using, for instance, the DijkstraGC algorithm. Note that in this case it is essentially equivalent to the Dijkstra algorithm.

Subproblem 2 The lower bound $\Phi^2(\theta)$ on $E^2(\mathbf{x} \mid \theta^2)$ is computed using a very fast technique whose details are given in [498]. In short, two edge disjoint paths of minimum cost in the dual graph are computed from a set of nodes "behind" node s to a set of nodes "behind" node t. (This is motivated by the fact that an optimal segmentation can be viewed as a simple closed contour going "around" s and t.)

---

4. Instead of restricting function E^0 to be submodular, one could use the roof duality approach [179] to get a lower bound on $E^0(\mathbf{x} \mid \theta)$. For submodular functions this lower bound coincides with the global minimum; therefore the best lower bound on the original function can only become better. This has not yet been implemented.

Maximizing the Lower Bound   The lower bound on problem **P1** can be written as

$$\Phi(\theta) = \Phi^0(\theta) + \Phi^1(\theta) + \Phi^2(\theta) \leq E(\mathbf{x}) + C(\mathbf{x})$$

where θ belongs to a convex set $\Omega = \{(\theta^1, \theta^2 \mid 0 \leq \theta_{pq}^2 \leq \theta_{pq}^{2\,\max}\}$. Clearly, Φ is a concave function of θ. Similar to [423, 424, 268], a projected subgradient method [435, 35] was used for maximizing $\Phi(\theta)$. Details of our implementation and the procedure for choosing solution $\mathbf{x}$ are given in [498].

22.4   Experimental Results

The previous section presented DijkstraGC, a new algorithm that minimizes energy (22.1) under certain connectivity constraints on the segmentation $\mathbf{x}$. In this section both the advantages of including this algorithm in an interactive system for image segmentation and its optimality properties are discussed.

22.4.1   DijkstraGC for Interactive Segmentation

The form of the energy (22.1) follows the approach of previous energy minimization techniques for interactive image segmentation (see chapter 7). $E_p(x_p)$ is a data likelihood term and $E_{pq}(x_p, x_q)$ is a contrast-dependent coherence term, which are defined as follows.

Hard constraints for background and foreground are specified in the form of brush-strokes. Based on this input, a probabilistic model is computed for the colors of background (G_B) and foreground (G_F) using two different Gaussian mixture models. $E_p(x_p)$ is then computed as $E_p(0) = -\log(\Pr(z_p \mid G_B))$ and $E_p(1) = -\log(\Pr(z_p \mid G_F))$ where z_p contains the three color channels of site p (see details in [401], chapter 7). The coherence term incorporates both an Ising prior and a contrast-dependent component, and is computed as

$$E_{pq}(x_p, x_q) = \frac{|x_q - x_p|}{\text{dist}(p, q)} \left(\lambda_1 + \lambda_2 \exp -\beta \|z_p - z_q\|^2\right)$$

where λ_1 and λ_2 are weights for the Ising and contrast-dependent priors, respectively, and $\beta = \left(2 \langle (z_p - z_q)^2 \rangle\right)^{-1}$, where $\langle \cdot \rangle$ denotes expectation over an image sample (as motivated in [401]). A term of this form encourages coherence in regions of similar color and also prevents isolated pixels from appearing in the segmentation (see [66, 401]). In the experiments 5 components for G_B and G_F were used. λ_1 and λ_2 were set to 2.5 and 47.5, respectively (which sums to 50, as in [401]). An 8-neighborhood system for E was used.

It is now discussed how to integrate the DijkstraGC algorithm in an interactive system for image segmentation. After the user has provided scribbles, a segmentation is computed with graph cut. As in [401] this process is iterated to further minimize the energy, where the segmentation of a previous run is used to update color models. It can happen that part of the foreground is missing or that the foreground region is disconnected. Then the user

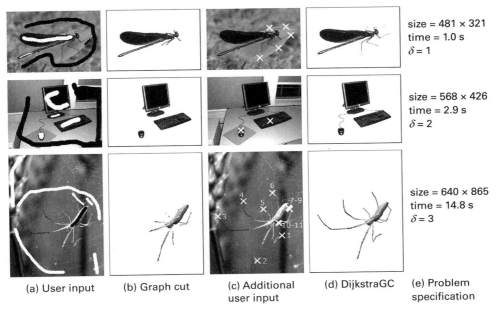

				size = 481 × 321 time = 1.0 s $\delta = 1$
				size = 568 × 426 time = 2.9 s $\delta = 2$
				size = 640 × 865 time = 14.8 s $\delta = 3$
(a) User input	(b) Graph cut	(c) Additional user input	(d) DijkstraGC	(e) Problem specification

Figure 22.5
Results of the DijkstraGC algorithm. (a) Original images with user scribbles; (b) Graph Cut results using [401]; (c) Selection of sites for connectivity, where numbers present the input order; (d) DijkstraGC results; (e) Problem specification: image size, runtime for DijkstraGC (on 2.16 GHz CPU with 2 GB RAM), and minimum width specified by the user.

can specify with one click such a site that should be connected with the current result. The DijkstraGC algorithm is used to compute the new segmentation. In this way the user has to specify only one node (from the two nodes necessary to run DijkstraGC), since the other node is assumed to be contained within the largest connected component of the graph cut segmentation.

This approach was tested on 15 images with a total of 40 connectivity problems (i.e., additional clicks for DijkstraGC). Figures 22.1 and 22.5 show some results: comparing graph cut; using scribbles only; and with DijkstraGC, where the user sets additional clicks after obtaining the graph cut result. Usually graph cut-based algorithms tend to cut off thin, elongated structures in the image. Retrieving these thin structures using brushstrokes can be very difficult, since they may be only one or two pixels wide. To obtain a satisfying result with DijkstraGC, the user needs only some additional clicks and the selection of a width parameter δ, which is a considerable reduction in the number of user interactions needed. For the last example in figure 22.5 the number of clicks necessary to extract the segmentation was 11, since the thin structures to segment (the legs of the spider) intersect each other and the path computed by DijkstraGC goes through the already segmented leg.

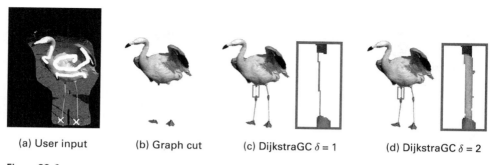

| (a) User input | (b) Graph cut | (c) DijkstraGC $\delta = 1$ | (d) DijkstraGC $\delta = 2$ |

Figure 22.6
Width parameter δ. Two different results obtained with DijkstraGC algorithm for different values of δ (minimum width).

The runtime presented in the last column of figure 22.5 includes all the clicks in the image and is, as to be expected, related to the number of clicks and the image size. The optimized version of DijkstraGC (figure 22.4) improved the runtime over the simple version (figure 22.2) from, for instance, 28.4 to 14.8 seconds for the last image in figure 22.5.

The *width parameter* δ provides the possibility of specifying a minimum desired width of the connection between the two components. This parameter is not included directly in the formulation of the DijkstraGC algorithm. Instead, a set $\mathcal{Q}_p$ is defined for all nodes p according with δ. For $\delta = 1$, $\mathcal{Q}_p = \{p\}$; for $\delta = 2$, $\mathcal{Q}_p$ is the set of four nodes in a 2×2 square that includes node p; and for $\delta = 3$, $\mathcal{Q}_p$ contains p and its neighbors in a 4-connected grid. Figure 22.6 shows that this parameter can be important in a practical system, to avoid the connectivity constraint being is satisfied by a segmentation with a one pixel width only. Note that in general δ does not have to be the exact width of the structure to segment. In figure 22.6 setting the width parameter to $\delta = 2$ was sufficient to recover the thin leg, which has a width larger than five pixels.

Direction of DijkstraGC Swapping the nodes s and t, that is, changing the direction of the DijkstraGC, may lead to two different segmentations, as seen in figure 22.3. However, the two segmentations usually differ by only a small number of pixels (on average less than 1 percent of the number of pixels in set [**x**]), and the difference is often not visually significant.

In contrast, the difference in speed can be substantial. In the examples the runtime was on average reduced by half if the "source" node s was in the smaller component (out of the two components that should be connected). Accordingly, this was chosen as the default option and used for the results presented in figures 22.5 and 22.6.

22.4.2 Optimality of DijkstraGC

The dual decomposition algorithm, described in section 22.3.2, gives both a solution for a special case of **P1** and a lower bound on the optimal value of **P1**. Although this technique

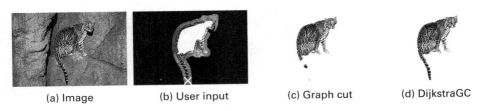

(a) Image   (b) User input   (c) Graph cut   (d) DijkstraGC

Figure 22.7
Optimality of DijkstraGC. A problem for which both DijkstraGC and the decomposition method give the optimal result.

is not useful for a practical system, since the runtime is on average three hours, it can be used to assess the optimality of DijkstraGC.

Forty connectivity problems (i.e., user clicks) where the dual decomposition approach is applicable were considered, that is, all pixels at the image boundary are background. Another restriction for this approach is the use of a planar graph (4-connected 2D grid) for max-flow computations. For 12 out of the 40 problems the dual decomposition algorithm gave the global optimum. It is a positive result that for all these 12 cases DijkstraGC also returned the global optimum.

One such example is shown in figure 22.7. Another example is the first image, in figure 22.5: the global optimum is obtained for all the connectivity constraints. (Note that in this case the result was slightly different from figure 22.5, since for this optimality experiment the graph has to be planar, that is, 4-connected.)

For all the other problems the result provided by DijkstraGC was always better in terms of energy value than the result of the dual decomposition method.

V   Advanced Applications of MRFs

This final part of the book considers applications of complex MRF models, as well as large vision systems where MRFs are an essential component.

The first two chapters consider the extraction of depth from stereo images (chapter 23) and the restoration or denosing of images (chapter 24). These classical vision problems have already been considered in previous chapters (e.g., 11 and 3) by utilizing low-connected, pairwise MRF models. In these two chapters more complex and expressive MRF models are used, which lead to considerably better results. Note that for these applications, highly connected and higher-order models were also discussed in chapters 19 and 11. The next two chapters consider the field of object class recognition and scene understanding, which has gained much attention in recent years in the vision community. MRF models, and in general undirected graphical models, play a dominant role in this field. They are either imposed directly on the pixel level, as in chapter 25, where the result is a pixel-accurate segmentation mask of an object, or the Markov model is on a latent, sparse representation of the object. A very popular sparse representation is called pictorial structure [140], where the object parts (e.g., body limbs), are the latent variables in an MRF that typically takes the form of a tree. Hence efficient and globally optimal inference is tractable (see examples in chapter 21). Many researchers have also combined part-level and pixel-level representations into one MRF model, such as in chapter 25 and OBJCut [281]. Chapter 26 addresses the task of scene understanding in a rather different way. Given a large corpus of images with known properties, such as object labels or motion, scene understanding of a new image can be achieved by simply transferring the properties of the most similar given image to the new one. The underlying MRF describes pixel-accurate matching, as in optical flow, between any two images. Chapter 27, the final chapter of the book, is on a quite different topic: video editing. In this case a generative MRF model is used to express constraints on the mapping from a latent representation, called an unwrapped mosaic, to every pixel in the video sequence. The optimization of this large and complex MRF model is very challenging, but it is shown that high-quality video editing results can be achieved for challenging deformable surfaces.

23 Symmetric Stereo Matching for Occlusion Handling

Jian Sun, Yin Li, Sing Bing Kang, and Heung-Yeung Shum

This chapter addresses the problem of inferring depth and occlusion information from two views of a stereo camera. It is a fundamental and well-studied problem in computer vision and has a large range of applications. Chapters 3, 4, and 11 have already considered simple 4-connected MRF models for this problem, which, however, ignore the occlusion event. Chapter 11 demonstrated the importance of modeling occlusions by comparing a simple 4-connected MRF model with a more complex, highly connected MRF model [265] that implicitly models occlusions. This chapter also focuses on modeling the occlusion event in an explicit way.[1]

23.1 Introduction

Occlusion is one of the biggest challenges in stereo. For two-frame stereo, occluded pixels are visible in only one image. Accurate depth and occlusion information is important for applications in vision and robotics. In certain applications, such as 3D modeling and view interpolation, a stereo algorithm should not only estimate correct depths and detect occlusion at visible areas, but also should provide reasonable guesses of depths at occluded areas.

23.1.1 Previous Work

Classical dense two-frame stereo matching computes a dense disparity or depth map from a pair of images with different viewpoints, under known camera configuration. Currently, the state-of-the-art approaches are based mainly on global energy minimization. For a comprehensive discussion on dense two-frame stereo matching, we refer the reader to the survey by Scharstein and Szeliski [419]. In this section, we review two-frame stereo algorithms that can handle occlusion.

Two kinds of hard constraints are typically used: the ordering constraint and the uniqueness constraint. The ordering constraint preserves ordering along scan lines in both input images. The monotonicity constraint [158] is a variant of the ordering constraint that requires

---

1. This chapter is based on [456].

neighboring pixels to be matched. The uniqueness constraint, on the other hand, enforces a one-to-one mapping between pixels in two images [329].

Most approaches [27, 44, 58, 105, 214] that exploit the ordering or monotonicity constraint use dynamic programming. Stereo matching is formulated as finding a minimum cost path in the matrix of all pairwise matching costs between two corresponding scan lines. The "horizontal" and "vertical" discontinuities of the path correspond to the left and right occlusions, respectively. The uniqueness constraint is usually also applied to simplify the construction of dynamic programming.

The simplest method that uses the uniqueness constraint to detect occlusion is that of cross-checking [134]. An occluded pixel is one that, after being mapped to the other image, does not map back to itself. In [552] and [265] (see also chapter 11), the uniqueness constraint is enforced in the 3D array of the disparity by iterative cooperative algorithm and graph cut optimization, respectively. In [264] stereo is formulated as finding a subset of assignments (pairs of pixels) that may potentially correspond. Using graph cut, the uniqueness constraint can be satisfied when a Potts energy is minimized on the assignments.

Unfortunately, the ordering and uniqueness constraints have significant limitations. The ordering constraint is not always true, in general; it is violated in scenes that contain thin foreground objects or narrow holes. Furthermore, the ordering constraint can be enforced for each scan line only *independently*. Without smoothness assumption between epipolar lines, the results often have streaky artifacts.

Using a discrete representation of disparity, the uniqueness constraint is not appropriate for scenes containing horizontally slanted surfaces (figure 23.1a), which results in correspondence between unequal numbers of pixels. As observed in [354], a horizontally slanted surface will appear more horizontally stretched in one image compared with the other. Figure 23.1b is the output of the graph cuts [264] algorithm. Neither disparity nor occlusion can be recovered correctly using the uniqueness constraint.

23.1.2 Visibility Constraint

For occlusions in more general scenes, the basic visibility constraint is valid. All this constraint requires is that *an occluded pixel must have no match on the other image and a nonoccluded pixel must have at least one match.* The visibility constraint is self-evident because it is derived directly from the definition of occlusion. Unlike the uniqueness constraint, the visibility constraint permits many-to-one matching. Furthermore, the ordering constraint need not be satisfied. As a result, the visibility constraint is a more flexible but weaker constraint. It only enforces consistency between occlusion in one image and disparity in the other.

Applying the visibility constraint is nontrivial because both disparity and occlusion are unknown. In this chapter we propose to enforce the visibility constraint by using an algorithm that iteratively performs two steps: (1) infer the disparity map in one view considering the occlusion map of the other view, and (2) infer the occlusion map in one view from the

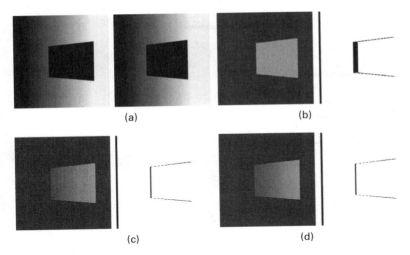

Figure 23.1
Horizontally slanted object. (a) Left and right images. (b) Results using graph cuts [264]. (c) Our results. (d) Ground truth. In (b–d) the disparity map is in the left column and the occlusion map is in the right column. Black means occluded. Here, graph cuts with the uniqueness constraint yield both incorrect disparity and occlusion.

disparity map of the other view. Step (1) improves the disparity map by enforcing piecewise smoothness while using the occlusion maps for both views as constraints. Step (2) improves the occlusion map by using two observations illustrated in figure 23.2.

The first observation is that if pixels on both sides of a discontinuous boundary are visible, their disparities tend to be unambiguous. (As an example, observe the discontinuity between regions C and E in figure 23.2b.) Hence, the occlusion region in the other view can be directly inferred by means of the visibility constraint (using the same example, region D, as in figure 23.2c).

The second observation is that disparities in occlusion regions are usually ambiguous (e.g., the hatched region in figure 23.2b). This observation can be verified by inspecting figure 23.5a, especially the disparities in the occlusion regions. The key is that these pixels rarely affect the occlusion reasoning on the other view. For example, a pixel in region B (no matter what disparity it ends up with inside the hatched region) will not influence the occlusion reasoning, since regions A and C (where the pixel may land after warping) have already been matched.

Our visibility constraint is closely related to another popular "self-occlusion model" used in global optimization frameworks [514, 527] and segmentation-based approaches [56, 200, 314, 467, 553]. In the self-occlusion model, where multiple pixels match to the same pixel in the other view, only the one with the largest disparity is visible and the other pixels are (self-) occluded. Unlike our model it is asymmetric and considers the reference view only. It cannot properly handle a horizontally slanted object because it does not allow many-to-one

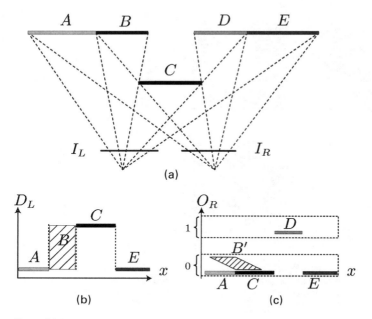

Figure 23.2

Occlusion reasoning. (a) A stereo image pair $\{I_L, I_R\}$ captures a scene with objects A to E. (b) The disparity map of the left image. The disparity for the occlusion region B is ambiguous (usually within a range specified by the hatched area). D_L is the disparity value. (c) The inferred occlusion map of the right image. O_R is the binary occlusion value. The depth discontinuity between C and E in the left image causes the occlusion region D in the right image. The hatched region B' (in the right image) is warped from the region B (in the left image). It does not affect the occlusion reasoning.

matching. In addition, the disparities in the occlusion region can be arbitrary, and the nearby visible pixels are also affected if any smoothness prior is used. Thus, the estimated occlusion using less accurate disparities could be error-prone. In contrast, in our visibility model the occlusion is estimated using more accurate disparities (mainly from the visible pixels) from the other view.

23.2 Symmetric Stereo Model

Given a stereo image pair $I = \{I_L, I_R\}$, we want to compute the disparity $\{D_L, D_R\}$ and occlusion $\{O_L, O_R\}$ for the left view I_L and the right view I_R, respectively. For each pixel s its disparity d_s is in the range $[d_{min}, d_{max}]$ and its occlusion $o_s \in \{0, 1\}$ is a binary variable.

Most local stereo algorithms [419] and global stereo algorithms [72, 457] compute the disparity and occlusion only in the reference view (say, the left image). In addition, most global stereo algorithms are formulated in an energy minimization framework:

$$E(D_L, O_L; I) = E_d(D_L, O_L; I) + E_s(D_L, O_L), \tag{23.1}$$

where the data term $E_d(D_L, O_L; I)$ measures how well the disparity D_L and the occlusion O_L fit the given stereo pair I, and the smoothness term $E_s(D_L, O_L)$ encodes the smoothness assumption made by the algorithm. The occlusion is either considered implicitly or treated as an outlier process. The disparity D_R is computed independently. Here, consistency between the two views is *not* enforced.

The visibility constraint requires occlusion in one image and disparity in the other to be consistent. Hence we embed the visibility constraint within the visibility terms $E_v(O_L, D_R)$ and $E_v(O_R, D_L)$. These terms model the occlusion reasoning depicted in figure 23.2. Next, we formulate the stereo matching problem with two novel visibility terms:

$$E(D_L, D_R, O_L, O_R; I) = E_d(D_L, D_R, O_L, O_R; I) + E_s(D_L, O_L)$$
$$+ E_s(D_R, O_R) + E_v(O_L, D_R) + E_v(O_R, D_L), \tag{23.2}$$

where $E_d(D_L, D_R, O_L, O_R; I)$ is the data term that encodes the intensity consistency of pixel correspondences for hypothesized disparity and occlusion. $E_s(D_L, O_L)$ and $E_s(D_R, O_R)$ are smoothness terms for the left image and the right image, respectively.

23.2.1 Data Term

Because the data terms encode only the intensity consistency, we can factorize it into two independent terms:

$$E_d(D_L, D_R, O_L, O_R; I) = E_d(D_L, O_L; I) + E_d(D_R, O_R; I). \tag{23.3}$$

For a single view the data term $E_d(D, O; I)$ is defined as

$$E_d(D, O; I) = \sum_{s \notin O} \rho_d(F(s, d_s, I)) + \sum_{s \in O} \eta_o, \tag{23.4}$$

where D and O are disparity and occlusion in a single view, either left or right. $F(s, d_s, I)$ is the matching cost function of pixel s with disparity d_s, given observation I. The cost η_o is the penalty for occlusion labeling. This term is necessary to prevent the whole scene from being labeled as occluded. $\rho_d(f)$ is a truncated $L1$ norm function that is robust to noise or outliers: $\rho_d(f) = -\ln((1 - e_d) \exp(-|f|/\sigma_d) + e_d)$, where parameters σ_d and e_d control the shape of the robust function. As matching cost we use the intensity difference between two gray pixels or the Euclidean distance between two color pixels: $F(s, d_s, I) = ||I_L(x_s, y_s) - I_R(x_s + d_s, y_s)||_2$ (for the left view, for example), where (x_s, y_s) are the image coordinates of pixel s.

23.2.2 Smoothness Term

We encode piecewise smoothness on disparity D (given occlusion O) in the smoothness term $E_s(D, O)$. Let $N(s)$ be the neighbors of the pixel s and $C = \{s, t | s < t, t \in N(s)\}$ be the set of all adjacent pixel pairs. The smoothness term of disparity conditioned on the occlusion is

$$E_s(D, O) = \sum_{s,t \in C \backslash B} \rho_p(d_s, d_t), \tag{23.5}$$

where $B = \{s, t | o_s \neq o_t, s, t \in C\}$ is the set of discontinuities at the boundaries between occluded and unoccluded pixels. This term enforces smoothness only within occluded and unoccluded regions. $\rho_p(d_s, d_t)$ is an L1-truncated function and is defined as $\rho_p(d_s, d_t) = \min(\lambda|d_s - d_t|, T)$, where λ is the rate of increase in the cost and T controls the limit of the cost. There are two advantages to using this robust function. First, it preserves discontinuity. And second, we can apply a very efficient implementation [141] of belief propagation to minimize the energy (described in section 23.3).

23.2.3 Visibility Term
In order to enforce the visibility consistency constraint, we define the visibility term $E_v(O_L, D_R)$ as

$$E_v(O_L, D_R) = \sum_s \beta_w |o_s - W_L(s; D_R)| + \sum_{s,t \in C} \beta_o |o_s - o_t|, \tag{23.6}$$

where $W_L(s; D_R) \in \{0, 1\}$ is a binary map defined on the left image. For each pixel s, its binary value in $W_L(s; D_R)$ indicates whether or not there exists one or more pixels matching s from the right view according to the disparity D_R. The value at pixel s is set to 1 if there is no pixel in the right view corresponding to pixel s. The binary map $W_L(s; D_R)$ can be computed by forward warping all the pixels in the right view, using disparity D_R. The parameter β_w controls the strength of the visibility constraint. The last term in (23.6) enforces the smoothness of the occlusion. It is a classical Ising [38] prior that encourages spatial coherence and is helpful in removing some isolated pixels or small holes of the occlusion. The parameter β_o controls the strength of the smoothness. The binary map $W_R(s; D_L)$ and the visibility term $E(O_R, D_L)$ in (23.2) are defined in a similar way.

The combination of (23.3), (23.5), and (23.6) is our basic stereo model. We call it the "symmetric stereo model" because of the symmetric relationship between $\{D_L, O_L\}$ and $\{D_R, O_R\}$ in formulation (23.2). We now describe our iterative optimization algorithm to minimize the energy (23.2).

23.3 Iterative Optimization Using BP

Simultaneously minimizing the energy of disparity and occlusion in (23.2) is difficult. Instead, we propose an iterative optimization algorithm to minimize the energy of disparity and occlusion iteratively, using belief propagation (BP).

23.3.1 Iterative Optimization
The optimization process has two steps: estimate occlusion, given disparity, and estimate disparity, given occlusion.

Estimate Occlusion Given disparity Given the current estimated disparity $\{D_L, D_R\}$, the energy (23.2) can be written as the sum of two functions with respect to O_L and O_R: $E(D_L, D_R, O_L, O_R; I) = E_{O_L} + E_{O_R}$, where

$$E_{O_L} = E_d(D_L, O_L; I) + E_s(D_L, O_L) + E_v(O_L, D_R)$$

$$E_{O_R} = E_d(D_R, O_R; I) + E_s(D_R, O_R) + E_v(O_R, D_L).$$

The occlusion $\{O_L, O_R\}$ is then computed as follows:

$$O_L^* = \arg\min_{O_L} E_{O_L}, \quad O_R^* = \arg\min_{O_R} E_{O_R}. \tag{23.7}$$

Because occlusions are binary variables, $E(D_L, O_L; I)$ can be rewritten as

$$E_s(D_L, O_L; I) = \sum_s ((1 - o_s)\rho_d(F(s, d_s, I)) + o_s\eta_o). \tag{23.8}$$

We ignore $E(D_L, O_L)$ because we cannot recover the disparity of the pixel in the occluded region. It could be worse to arbitrarily guess disparity in the same view. Furthermore, the difference in disparity between adjacent pixels is weak evidence for occlusion. Finally, by combining (23.3), (23.5), and (23.6), we get

$$E_{O_L} = \sum_s ((1 - o_s)\rho_d(F(s, d_s, I)) + o_s\eta_o)$$
$$+ \sum_s \beta_w |o_s - W(s; D_R)| + \sum_{s,t\in C} \beta_o |o_s - o_t|. \tag{23.9}$$

Note that the first two terms on the right-hand side of (23.9) can be viewed as a unary term of a Markov model, and the last term can be viewed as a pairwise term. As a result, we can apply the max-product version of belief propagation to approximately minimize (23.9).

Estimate Disparity Given Occlusion Given the current estimate of occlusion $\{O_L, O_R\}$, the energy (23.2) can be rewritten as the sum of two functions with respect to D_L and D_R: $E(D_L, D_R, O_L, O_R; I) = E_{D_L} + E_{D_R}$, where

$$E_{D_L} = E_d(D_L, O_L; I) + E_s(D_L, O_L) + E_v(O_R, D_L)$$

$$E_{D_R} = E_d(D_R, O_R; I) + E_s(D_R, O_R) + E_v(O_L, D_R).$$

The disparity $\{D_L, D_R\}$ is estimated by minimizing E_{D_L} and E_{D_R}:

$$D_L^* = \arg\min_{D_L} E_{D_L}, \quad D_R^* = \arg\min_{D_R} E_{D_R}. \tag{23.10}$$

The visibility term $E(O_R, D_L)$ encodes the visibility constraint. Actually, the visibility constraint imposes two kinds of constraints on the disparity D_L, given the occlusion O_R. First, for each pixel s in the left image, it should not match the occluded pixels in the right image. In other words, its disparity d_s should be restricted in a range such that $O_R(x_s + d_s, y_s) = 0$. Second, for each nonoccluded pixel in the right image, at least one pixel in the left image should match it. The first constraint is a local constraint on disparity that is easy to encode. On the other hand, the second constraint is a global constraint on disparities of all pixels in the left image, which is implicitly enforced in the matching process. Therefore, in this step we approximate the visibility term $E(O_R, D_L)$ by considering only the local constraint as

$$E_v(O_R, D_L) = \sum_s \beta_w O_R(x_s + d_s, y_s). \tag{23.11}$$

Hence, for the left view, combining (23.3), (23.5), and (23.11), we get

$$E_{D_L} = \sum_{s \notin O} \rho_d(F(s, d_s, I)) + \sum_s \beta_w O_R(x_s + d_s, y_s) + \sum_{s,t \in C \backslash B} \rho_p(d_s, d_t), \tag{23.12}$$

where $O_R(x_s + d_s, y_s)$ indicates whether or not the corresponding pixel of s is occluded, given disparity d_s.

The energy (23.12) can also be interpreted as the Gibbs energy of a Markov network with respect to disparity. The unary terms are contained in the first two parts on the right-hand side of (23.12), and the pairwise terms are in the last part. Again, we can apply belief propagation to minimize (23.12). Although α-expansion-based graph cuts can also be used for the optimization, we empirically found that the results obtained by belief propagation are slightly better than those by graph cuts for the energy defined in this chapter.

In summary, our iterative optimization algorithm alternates between the following two steps:

1. Estimate occlusion $\{O_L, O_R\}$ using (23.7), given the current estimation of disparity $\{D_L, D_R\}$.

2. Estimate disparity $\{D_L, D_R\}$ using (23.10), given the current estimation of occlusion $\{O_L, O_R\}$.

The values of occlusion $\{O_L, O_R\}$ are initially set to zero (all pixels are initially visible).

Figure 23.3 shows the recovered occlusion for four test stereo pairs in the Tsukuba and Middlebury data sets. The iteration number is typically 2 or 3 in our experiments. Our results appear to be very close to the ground truth.

23.4 Segmentation as Soft Constraint

Recently, segmentation-based stereo approaches (e.g., [56, 200, 314, 467, 553, 534]) have demonstrated that the difficulties and ambiguities caused by lack of texture or by occlusion can be handled by assuming no large discontinuities within each segment or region. We call this assumption the "segment constraint" in this chapter. We exploit it by incorporating it into our symmetric stereo model as a *soft* constraint, namely:

$$E_d(D, O; I) = \sum_{s \notin O} \rho_d(F(s, d_s, I)) + \sum_{s \in O} \eta_o + \sum_s \gamma |d_s - (a_s x_s + b_s y_s + c_s)|,$$

Figure 23.3
Occlusion maps. Top: our results. Bottom: ground truth.

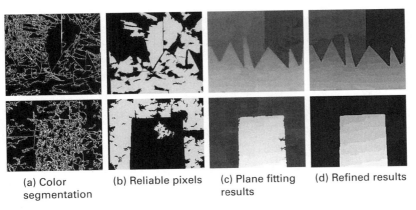

| (a) Color segmentation | (b) Reliable pixels | (c) Plane fitting results | (d) Refined results |

Figure 23.4
Soft segmentation. The top row is the result for the *Sawtooth* input pair and the second row is for the *Map* input pair. In (a) the white lines are the boundaries between segments. The gray pixels in (b) are reliable pixels used for 3D plane fitting. The 3D plane fitting results are shown in (c), and refined results using our symmetric stereo model with soft segmentation are shown in (d). The refined results are an improvement, especially for the *Map* data.

where γ controls the strength of segment constraint and $[a_s\ b_s\ c_s]$ are the 3D plane parameters for the segment containing pixel s. The 3D plane parameter for each segment or region is estimated by a robust fitting algorithm [467].

All previous segmentation-based approaches *commit* to an initial segmentation result prior to 3D plane fitting and stereo processing. This is not ideal because segmentation errors typically cannot be undone, and are thus propagated to the stereo processing stage. Our segmentation-based approach does not suffer from this problem because the segment constraint is soft. This strategy resulted in improvements, as shown in figure 23.4.

Figure 23.4a shows the mean-shift color segmentation results [100] using default parameters. In figure 23.4b, the gray pixels are reliable pixels selected by the robust 3D plane fitting algorithm. These pixels are subsequently used for 3D plane estimation. The black regions are ignored for robust 3D plane parameter estimation. Figure 23.4c shows 3D plane fitting results. The disparity of the *Sawtooth* data is significantly improved, especially around the occlusion boundaries. However, the disparity is worse for the *Map* data because the segment constraint is violated. No previous segment-based approaches [56, 200, 314, 467, 553, 534] were to handle this image well. By using the segment constraint as a soft constraint, we obtained better results, as shown in figure 23.4d. The improvement is more dramatic for the *Map* data; here, the errors caused by the violation of the segment constraint have been significantly reduced.

Table 23.1
Parameters for *Tsukuba* and *Middlebury* data sets

T	η_o	σ_d	e_d	β_w	β_o	γ
2	2.5	4.0	0.01	4.0	1.4	2.0

Table 23.2
Comparisons

Algorithm	Tsukuba		Sawtooth		Venus		Map	
	bad	disc.	bad	disc.	bad	disc.	bad	disc.
Symm. BP with Seg.	0.97	5.45	0.19	2.09	0.16	2.77	0.16	2.20
Symmetric BP	1.01	5.79	0.57	3.46	0.66	x8.72	0.14	1.97
One way BP	1.42	8.01	1.18	7.71	1.21	15.22	0.15	1.85
Segm.-based GC [201]	1.23	6.94	0.30	3.24	0.08	1.39	1.49	15.46
Segm.+glob.vis. [56]	1.30	7.50	0.20	2.30	0.79	6.37	1.63	16.07
Layered [315]	1.58	8.82	0.34	3.35	1.52	2.62	0.37	5.24
Belief prop [457]	1.15	6.31	0.98	4.83	1.00	9.13	0.84	5.27
MultiCam GC [266]	1.85	6.99	0.62	6.86	1.21	5.71	0.31	4.34
GC+occl. [265]b	1.19	6.71	0.73	5.71	1.64	5.41	0.61	6.05
Improved Coop. [334]	1.67	9.67	1.21	6.90	1.04	13.68	0.29	3.65
GC+occl. [265]a	1.27	6.90	0.36	3.65	2.79	2.54	1.79	10.08
Disc. pres. [10]	1.78	9.71	1.17	5.55	1.61	9.06	0.32	3.33
Graph cuts [419]	1.94	9.49	1.30	6.34	1.79	6.91	0.31	3.88
Graph cuts [72]	1.86	9.35	0.42	3.76	1.69	5.40	2.39	9.35
Bay. diff. [419]	6.49	12.29	1.43	9.29	3.89	18.17	0.20	2.49
. . .								

The underlined number is the best for each data set. Our algorithm "Symmetric BP with Seg." consistently outperforms most of the other algorithms listed. The complete set of results is at http://vision.middlebury.edu/~schar/stereo/web/results.php. The latest evaluation results (including more images and new features) can be found at http://vision.middlebury.edu/stereo/.

23.5 Experimental Results

All experiments were performed on a 2.8 GHz Pentium 4 PC. Table 23.1 lists the values for the symmetric stereo model parameters used in *Tsukuba* and *Middlebury* data.

To evaluate the performance of our approach, we followed the methodology proposed by Scharstein and Szeliski [419]. The quality is measured by the percentages of bad matching (where the absolute disparity error is greater than 1 pixel) in the image ("bad"), in the textureless region ("untex."), and in the discontinuity region ("disc.").

The quantitative comparison in table 23.2 and the depth map in figure 23.5 demonstrate the high-quality performance of our approaches. "One-way BP" is the result without the visibility term, and "Symmetric BP" has the term. "Symmetric BP with Seg." is the result with both visibility and segment constraints. The disparities of occluded pixels are produced by a postprocessing method (e.g., for the left image, assign the disparity next to the right boundary of the occluded region). For the *Tsukuba* and *Map* data, "Symmetric BP" yields the

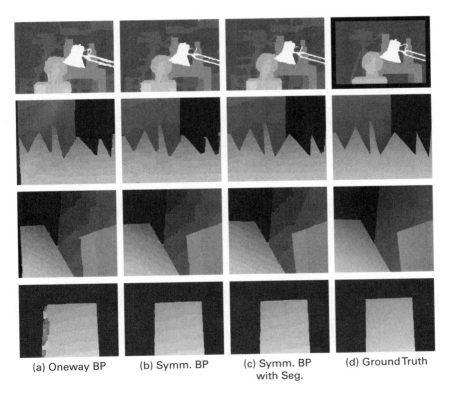

| (a) Oneway BP | (b) Symm. BP | (c) Symm. BP with Seg. | (d) Ground Truth |

Figure 23.5
Results for *Tsukuba*, *Sawtooth*, *Venus*, and *Map* image pairs.

Table 23.3
Occlusion Detection Rates

	Tsukuba	Sawtooth	Venus	Map
False negatives	29.9%	17.0%	25.4%	8.7%
False positives	0.7%	0.2%	0.2%	0.3%

most significant improvements using the visibility constraint. For the *Sawtooth* and *Venus* data, both "Symmetric BP" and "Symmetric BP with Seg." give significant improvements using both visibility and segment constraints. Note that "Symmetric BP with Seg." is ranked at or very close to first place among more than two dozen stereo algorithms.

To evaluate the accuracy of the occlusion detection, we also show the incidence of false negatives and false positives in table 23.3. The false negative rate is measured by the percentage of missed occluded pixels in occluded regions, and the false positive rate is expressed as the percentage of detected occluded pixels in nonoccluded regions. Figure 23.3 shows the visual comparison of our occlusion maps with ground truth.

23.6 Conclusions

In this chapter we have described a symmetric stereo matching model to handle occlusion using the visibility constraint. The visibility constraint is a general constraint that allows correct recovery of horizontally slanted surfaces and thin foreground objects. Our iterative optimization algorithm, in conjunction with the soft segment constraint, is validated by state-of-the-art results.

24 Steerable Random Fields for Image Restoration

Stefan Roth and Michael J. Black

24.1 Introduction

Markov random fields (MRFs) are used to perform spatial (or spatiotemporal) regularization by imposing prior knowledge on the types of admissible images, depth maps, flow fields, and so on. While such models have proven useful for regularizing problems in computer vision, MRFs have mostly been limited in three respects: (1) They have used very simple neighborhood structures. Most models in low-level vision are based on pairwise graphs, where the potential functions are formulated in terms of pixel differences (image derivatives) between neighboring sites (see chapter 1). (2) In many cases, potentials have remained hand-defined and hand-tuned. Consequently, many MRFs do not necessarily reflect the statistical properties of the data. (3) MRF models have typically not been spatially adaptive, that is, their potentials do not depend on the spatial location within the image. The first two shortcomings have been addressed by a number of recent approaches [306, 397, 549] (also chapter 19). This chapter describes a spatially adaptive random field model that addresses the third limitation as well.

In particular, in the steerable random field (SRF) [396] model described here, the potentials are adapted to the local image structure. This formulation builds on the idea of defining MRF clique potentials in terms of linear filter responses [397, 549] and connects MRF models with the literature on steerable filters [149]. Instead of using a fixed set of filters, such as derivative filters in the pairwise case, or some other fixed set of filters in the high-order case [397, 549], the filters are *steered* to the local structure of the input image. Specifically, the horizontal and vertical image derivatives are rotated based on the predominant orientation of the image structure, resulting in derivatives that are orthogonal to, and aligned with, the local image orientation (figure 24.1).[1] The image derivatives are computed using spatially extended filters (i.e., not a pairwise approximation). Consequently, the SRF is a high-order random field based on extended cliques (see [397, 549] and chapter 1).

---

1. This steering can be based on the output of the model (images, depth maps, flow fields, etc.) or on the input. SRFs that are steered to the input, such as the model defined here, are conditional models (i. e.,conditional random fields (CRFs)) that directly model the posterior distribution of the output, given the input image.

Figure 24.1
Example image and steered derivatives. The derivative response orthogonal to the local structure is shown in the middle, and the response aligned with the image structure is on the right.

The local orientation is computed using the structure tensor approach [238], which has a long history in continuous-space anisotropic regularization methods (see, e. g., [516]). SRFs combine and connect ideas from MRFs, steerable filters, and anisotropic diffusion, and specifically introduce the idea of steering into the domain of spatially discrete random field models. Doing so has several advantages: First, the empirical statistics of the steered filter responses are used to motivate the model. Second, SRF models are learned from training data, which gives steerable (or anisotropic) regularization a statistical foundation and avoids parameter tuning by hand.

Additionally, analysis of the marginal statistics of steered derivative filter responses (figure 24.2) reveals that while both are heavy-tailed, the derivative orthogonal to the image structure has a much broader histogram than the aligned derivative. The SRF potentials model these steered filter responses using a Gaussian scale mixture (GSM) [508], which is more flexible than many previous potential functions and is able to capture their heavy-tailed characteristics.

The SRF model is illustrated in image restoration applications, but note that, as with any MRF, it applies much more generally, such as to stereo and image motion [455]. The results show that SRFs substantially outperform pairwise MRF models (as well as higher-order, but unsteered, models) in image denoising and inpainting. One particular advantage of SRF models is that by focusing the model on oriented image structure, they lead to a better restoration of image edges.

24.2 Related Work

While steered derivatives [149] have been used in a variety of contexts including image restoration [516] and image coding [238], the statistics of steered derivative responses in generic scenes are not widely studied. Sidenbladh and Black [438] explored the "object specific" statistics of steered filter responses at locations in the image corresponding to the limbs of people. In generic scenes Konishi et al. [272] studied the statistics of gradient responses and eigenvalues on, and off, image edges. Finally, Scharr et al. [417] modeled the statistics of the eigenvalues of the structure tensor in natural scenes and used these marginal statistics in a diffusion denoising method.

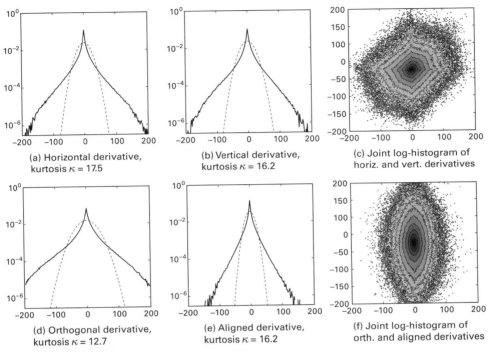

Figure 24.2
Marginal filter response statistics (log scale) of standard derivatives (top row) and steered derivatives (bottom row), as well as their joint log-histograms. The histograms are shown in solid lines; a fit with a Gaussian is shown in dashed lines. Note the difference between the orthogonal and the aligned cases of the steered derivatives.

The SRF is quite closely related to anisotropic [516], as well as classical edge-preserving [89], regularization techniques. In anisotropic diffusion, smoothing depends on the orientation of the local image structure. While the orientation may be computed using the structure tensor, as in the SRF model, the amount of smoothing depends on the eigenvalues of the structure tensor or on the gradient magnitude, whereas in the SRF the amount of smoothing depends on steered image derivatives. Scharr et al. [417] showed that these eigenvalues are smoothed versions of the (squared) steered derivatives. This is an important difference, because an energy function based on eigenvalues introduces a smoothing term in the corresponding diffusion algorithm, which leads to inferior results [417]. Moreover, the model from [417] is based on learning marginals of the eigenvalues, while the SRF uses full discriminative learning. Standard anisotropic diffusion is motivated in *algorithmic* terms and not through an energy function, and cannot be directly interpreted as being an approximate inference technique for a probabilistic model. Steerable random fields, on the other hand, are derived as a generic *probabilistic model* of images (or other dense scene representation), which admits a wide range of uses beyond diffusion-based smoothing.

Related to SRFs, there is work by Lyu and Simoncelli [327], that performs image denoising by modeling oriented wavelet responses using an MRF. In contrast to what is presented here, they used a fixed set of orientations and did not explicitly adapt the potentials to the local structure orientation. Hammond and Simoncelli [180] modeled wavelet responses in an orientation adaptive way, but did not propose a spatial model such as an MRF. Like the SRF model proposed here, these works use Gaussian scale mixtures to capture heavy-tailed image statistics.

Levin et al. [306] performed image inpainting in the gradient domain, which allowed them to regularize the image by penalizing changes in the gradient magnitude and orientation. In contrast to the SRF, they formulated a pairwise MRF in this gradient magnitude and orientation domain. For inpainting applications they learned the model from the local image statistics, whereas the model defined here is generic since it is trained on a large database.

24.3 Steered Filter Responses and Their Statistics

The statistics of horizontal and vertical image derivatives in natural scenes have been extensively studied (see, e. g., [448]). These derivatives are found to have heavy-tailed marginal statistics that arise from the fact that while neighboring pixels often have similar intensities, significant discontinuities arise quite frequently. Heavy-tailed distributions are characterized by large values of the kurtosis $\kappa = E[(x - \mu)^4]/E[(x - \mu)^2]^2$, where $E[\cdot]$ represents expectation. Figure 24.2a,b show marginal log-histograms of horizontal and vertical image derivatives. The histograms were computed from a set of 25 natural images taken from the Berkeley segmentation data set [331] (only the luminance was considered). Simple first-order derivative filters ($(1, -1)$ and $(1, -1)^T$) were used. The histograms have much tighter peaks and heavier tails than a Gaussian with the same mean and variance.

The first step in steering the derivatives is to estimate the orientation of the local image structure; this is achieved using the structure tensor [238]:

$$S = G_\rho * \nabla \mathbf{z} \cdot \nabla \mathbf{z}^T = G_\rho * \begin{bmatrix} (\partial_x^{5\times5}\mathbf{z})^2 & \partial_x^{5\times5}\mathbf{z} \cdot \partial_y^{5\times5}\mathbf{z} \\ \partial_x^{5\times5}\mathbf{z} \cdot \partial_y^{5\times5}\mathbf{z} & (\partial_y^{5\times5}\mathbf{z})^2 \end{bmatrix}. \tag{24.1}$$

Here $\partial_x^{5\times5}\mathbf{z}$ denotes the horizontal derivative of image $\mathbf{z}$ computed with a 5×5 filter $D_x^{5\times5}$ [416], $\partial_y^{5\times5}$ denotes the vertical derivative, and G_ρ is a Gaussian smoothing kernel with standard deviation ρ.

After estimating the structure tensor, an eigendecomposition gives the eigenvectors $(\cos\theta, \sin\theta)^T$ orthogonal to, and $(-\sin\theta, \cos\theta)^T$ aligned with, the local orientation. If a strong edge is present, the local orientation is the orientation of the edge. The derivative orthogonal to the local orientation, ∂_O, and the aligned derivative, ∂_A, are now given as

$$\partial_O = \cos\theta \cdot \partial_x + \sin\theta \cdot \partial_y \tag{24.2}$$

$$\partial_A = -\sin\theta \cdot \partial_x + \cos\theta \cdot \partial_y. \tag{24.3}$$

Here, ∂_x and ∂_y are the horizontal and vertical image derivatives, respectively, which are computed using 2×3 and 3×2 filters (see below). Figure 24.1 shows an example image along with its steered derivatives. Notice that the derivative orthogonal to the local orientation shows continuous edgelike structures, while the aligned derivative has much less spatial structure.

The empirical steered derivative histograms are shown in figure 24.2d,e. The log-histogram of the derivative orthogonal to the local (e. g., edge) orientation has much broader tails than the aligned derivative; this indicates that, as expected, large intensity changes orthogonal to the edge orientation occur more frequently. While both log-histograms are heavy-tailed, the kurtosis of the aligned derivative is much higher.

These findings lead to two observations. First, the steered marginal statistics provide a statistical motivation for anisotropic diffusion methods. Standard anisotropic diffusion performs relatively strong linear smoothing along edges, as well as nonlinear smoothing that allows for large intensity jumps orthogonal to the edges. The tight marginal histogram of the aligned derivative suggests that there is a benefit to performing stronger smoothing aligned with edges than orthogonal to them. Second, and in contrast to what is done in standard anisotropic diffusion, the non-Gaussian characteristics of the histograms indicate that nonlinear smoothing should be employed even aligned with the edges.

Finally, comparing the joint log-histogram of steered derivatives in figure 24.2f with that of standard derivatives in figure 24.2c is revealing. The log-histogram of horizontal and vertical derivatives exhibits polygonal isocontours as previously noted in the study of natural images [448], but the joint log-histogram of the steered responses has much more elongated, elliptical contour lines.

24.4 Steerable Random Field Model

The steerable random field model exploits statistical properties of steered derivatives to define a random field model of natural images that can be automatically learned from training data, for example, using a discriminative variant of contrastive divergence [193]. As is standard for Bayesian approaches, the goal is to recover an artifact-free, true, or "hidden" image $\mathbf{x}$ from a corrupted or "noisy" observation $\mathbf{z}$ using the posterior distribution $P(\mathbf{x} \mid \mathbf{z})$. Typically, the posterior is then rewritten as $P(\mathbf{x} \mid \mathbf{z}) \propto P(\mathbf{z} \mid \mathbf{x}) \cdot P(\mathbf{x})$, where the likelihood $P(\mathbf{z} \mid \mathbf{x})$ describes the observation process for the noisy observation $\mathbf{z}$, given the true image $\mathbf{x}$, and the prior $P(\mathbf{x})$ models the a priori probability density of having a particular underlying true image $\mathbf{x}$ among all possible images. Such priors are often formulated as Markov random fields. The approach here is slightly different and models the posterior distribution directly, while still breaking it into two components:

$$
\begin{aligned}
P(\mathbf{x} \mid \mathbf{z}, \omega) &= \frac{1}{Z(\mathbf{z}, \omega)} \exp\{-E(\mathbf{x}, \mathbf{z}, \omega)\} \\
&= \frac{1}{Z(\mathbf{z}, \omega)} F_L(\mathbf{z}; \mathbf{x}) \cdot F_S(\mathbf{x}; \mathbf{z}, \omega).
\end{aligned}
\tag{24.4}
$$

Here, $F_L(\mathbf{z}; \mathbf{x})$ is a distribution (unnormalized) that models the observation process, $F_S(\mathbf{x}; \mathbf{z}, \omega)$ is a steerable image model (unnormalized), ω represents the model parameters, and $Z(\mathbf{z}, \omega)$ is the partition function that ensures the posterior is normalized. Since applications of the model involve maximizing the posterior w. r. t.$\mathbf{x}$, the partition function need not be known during inference and, for the most part, can be ignored. Observation models suitable for different problems will be described in section 24.5. It is important to notice here that neither the observation model nor the image model by itself is a good model of the posterior distribution. Only their combination results in a good Bayesian model, for instance, for image restoration.

Basic Model

The steerable image model $F_S(\mathbf{x}; \mathbf{z}, \omega)$ intuitively takes the role of the prior in that it assesses how "natural" the true image $\mathbf{x}$ is. In contrast to the standard approach, the image model is not truly a prior distribution here, because it depends on the image observation $\mathbf{z}$. The SRF thus has a conditional random field (CRF) structure (cf. [186, 285, 288, 474]). As in a standard MRF-based formulation, image pixels correspond to nodes in a graph. Instead of describing the factorization structure of the image model via the edges of the graph, the factorization is explicitly represented as a factor graph [507] (see chapter 1). The true image $\mathbf{x}$ is subdivided into overlapping patches of $m \times n$ pixels and $\mathbf{x}_c$ denotes the vector of all pixels in the cth patch. The steerable image model is then defined as a product over all patches (cliques) in the image:

$$F_S(\mathbf{x}; \mathbf{z}, \omega) = \prod_c F_{S,c}(\mathbf{x}_c; \mathbf{z}, \omega). \tag{24.5}$$

Disregarding the dependence on $\mathbf{z}$, each factor corresponds to a clique in a classical MRF prior on images. But unlike a standard pairwise prior, which models each factor using either horizontal or vertical image derivatives, and unlike the Field of Experts (FoE) (chapter 19), which models each factor using filter responses from a set of learned filters, the SRF models each factor using responses from steered filters. For that, let $\theta_c = \theta_c(\mathbf{z})$ denote the orientation of the image structure at position c (i. e.,the center of the patch $\mathbf{x}_c$) as determined from the eigendecomposition of the structure tensor of $\mathbf{z}$. Each factor of the SRF model is then written as

$$F_{S,c}(\mathbf{x}_c; \mathbf{z}, \omega) = f_O(\cos\theta_c \cdot \partial_x \mathbf{x} + \sin\theta_c \cdot \partial_y \mathbf{x}, \omega)$$
$$\cdot f_A(-\sin\theta_c \cdot \partial_x \mathbf{x} + \cos\theta_c \cdot \partial_y \mathbf{x}, \omega), \tag{24.6}$$

where $f_O(\cdot)$ is a model of the derivative response orthogonal to the structure orientation, and $f_A(\cdot)$ models the derivative aligned with the structure. $\partial_x \mathbf{x}$ and $\partial_y \mathbf{x}$ denote the horizontal and vertical image derivatives evaluated at position c and computed from the patch $\mathbf{x}_c$.

The potentials are represented using a Gaussian scale mixture (GSM) [508], which has been employed in various models of natural images (e. g., [180]). GSM models are computationally relatively easy to deal with, yet flexible enough to represent heavy-tailed distributions such as the ones shown in figure 24.2. In particular, the model for the orthogonal derivative is

$$f_O(r, \omega) = \sum_{k=1}^{K} \omega_{O,k} \cdot \mathcal{N}(r; 0, \sigma_O^2/s_k). \qquad (24.7)$$

In this formulation $\omega_{O,k}$ is the mixture weight for the kth Gaussian component with mean 0, base variance σ_O^2, and scale s_k. The model for the aligned derivative is equivalent (but uses $\omega_{A,k}$ and σ_A). The implementation here assumes that the base variance and scales are fixed and $\omega = (\omega_{O,k}, \omega_{A,k} \mid k = 1, \ldots, K)$ represents the set of parameters to be estimated. Details are provided below.

Practical Considerations

It may now be tempting to define the model using factors on overlapping 3×3 patches, and to use standard derivative filters of the type $(1/2, 0, -1/2)$ (with possible smoothing in the orthogonal direction). Doing so, however, leads to checkerboard-like artifacts in image restoration, as has been observed in [417]. The problem is that standard 3×1 derivative filters effectively decouple directly neighboring pixels (because of the 0 center coefficient), leading to artifacts. This could be corrected using an additional smoothing term, as suggested in [417], but it could produce oversmoothing of image boundaries. An alternative would use $(1, -1)$-type derivative filters to avoid this problem, but then the x- and y-derivatives are not computed at the same spatial location.

The solution adopted here is to define *two* kinds of filters, one pair of 2×3 derivative filters and one pair of 3×2 derivative filters:

$$D_x^{2\times3} = \tfrac{1}{2} \begin{pmatrix} 1 & 0 & -1 \\ 1 & 0 & -1 \end{pmatrix} \qquad D_y^{2\times3} = \begin{pmatrix} 0 & 1 & 0 \\ 0 & -1 & 0 \end{pmatrix} \qquad (24.8)$$

$$D_x^{3\times2} = \left(D_y^{2\times3}\right)^{\mathsf{T}} \qquad D_y^{3\times2} = \left(D_x^{2\times3}\right)^{\mathsf{T}}. \qquad (24.9)$$

These filters have the advantage that they do not have a 0 center coefficient in one of the directions, but each pair estimates x- and y-derivatives at the same spatial location. These filters are combined in the SRF framework by having *two* kinds of factors with their corresponding image patches: one consists of all overlapping patches of 2×3 pixels; the other one, of all overlapping 3×2 patches. Depending on which patch size $\mathbf{x}_c$ has, the factor $F_{S,c}(\mathbf{x}_c; \mathbf{z}, \omega)$ uses the appropriate derivative filters. Figure 24.3a shows the corresponding factor graph with both types of factors.

Learning

To estimate the model parameters (i. e., the GSM mixture weights) from data, one could simply fit the empirical marginals of the steered derivatives, using an expectation maximization

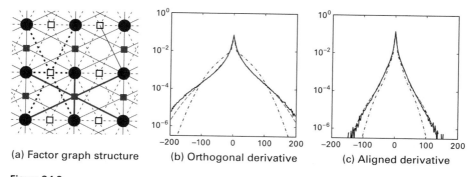

(a) Factor graph structure   (b) Orthogonal derivative   (c) Aligned derivative

Figure 24.3
Steerable random field: *(a)* Factor graph representation of the SRF model (only nodes of **x** are shown). The hollow factor nodes and dashed edges indicate the 3×2 factors; the solid nodes and lines, the 2×3 factors. One factor each is highlighted with bold edges. *(b)*, *(c)* Fit of GSM model with four scales (dashed) to filter response statistics (solid) and the GSM model learned with contrastive divergence (dash-dotted).

(EM) procedure. Figure 24.3 shows how the steered marginal derivative statistics are fitted well by GSM models with four scales. In each case the base variance σ_O^2 is chosen to be the variance of the respective empirical marginal, and scales $s = (1/\sigma_O) \cdot (0.008, 0.04, 0.2, 1)^{\mathrm{T}}$ are used. Since in random fields, particularly in high-order ones, marginals and potentials generally do not correspond [549], this learning approach is suboptimal.

It is thus preferable to use a more rigorous learning procedure, such as maximum likelihood (see chapter 1). Because of the conditional nature of the SRF model, training needs to be done in the context of a particular application represented by a suitable observation model. The aim is to maximize the conditional log-likelihood of the training data $X = \{\mathbf{x}^{(1)}, \ldots, \mathbf{x}^{(t)}\}$, given the "noisy" observation data $Z = \{\mathbf{z}^{(1)}, \ldots, \mathbf{z}^{(t)}\}$ with respect to the model parameters (mixture weights) ω. Unfortunately, maximizing the (conditional) likelihood in loopy graphical models is difficult because the partition function cannot easily be computed. Learning thus needs to rely on approximations, often using Markov chain Monte Carlo (MCMC) methods [549], which tend to be very slow. An alternative is the contrastive divergence (CD) algorithm [193], which has been applied to a number of random field models in vision [186, 397]. A discriminative variant for training CRF models is used here (see [186] for details). The advantage of CD over (conditional) maximum likelihood is that the Markov chain does not have to be run until convergence, but only for a small number of steps. As suggested in [397], a hybrid Monte Carlo sampler is used with 30 leaps, $l = 1$ MCMC step, and a learning rate of 0.01. CD was run for 2000 iterations, after which the mixture parameters did not change significantly. The derivation of the gradient of the posterior energy with respect to the mixture weights is relatively straightforward, and is omitted due to space constraints.

24.5 Applications to Image Restoration

Image denoising and inpainting are used to compare the steerable random field model with traditional pairwise MRF models. The denoising method assumes that the image observation $\mathbf{z}$ is corrupted with additive $i.i.d.$ Gaussian noise ($\sigma_L = 20$), and thus the observation model is formulated as $F_L(\mathbf{z}; \mathbf{x}) = \prod_{i=1}^{N} \mathcal{N}(x_i; z_i, \sigma_L^2)$ where the product is taken over all N pixels. This observation model is combined with the SRF model ($\rho = 1$) from (24.5), and the parameters of the SRF model are trained discriminatively, using contrastive divergence. The training data consist of 25 "clean" training images, X, used in section 24.3, and a set of noisy training images, Z, obtained by adding Gaussian noise to X. The actual training procedure proceeds on 20,000 image patches of 9×9 pixels, which have been randomly cropped from the training images. Note that the structure tensor was computed on the full images to avoid boundary artifacts. figure 24.3b, c shows the GSM response models determined by this procedure. Note that the shape of the learned potentials differs noticeably from the marginal distributions (cf. [549]), but that the denoising performance of this model improves compared to fitting the potentials to the marginals.

Due to the difficulties of inference in high-order random field models (see chapter 1), simple continuous local optimization methods are used for both the SRF and the baseline models. In particular, the posterior energy $E(\mathbf{x}, \mathbf{z}, \omega)$ is maximized w. r. t.$\mathbf{x}$ using a conjugate gradient method [385]. Denoising quality can typically be improved by using a weighted regularization term $F_S(\mathbf{x}; \mathbf{z}, \omega)^\alpha$ (see, e. g., [397]); here α is estimated to maximize the denoising performance on ten training images. Weights are learned individually for all models compared here.

Denoising performance is evaluated on a set of 68 test images, using the peak signal-to-noise ratio (PSNR) as well as the perceptually based structural similarity index (SSIM) [513]. The results are compared with a traditional pairwise MRF model, using GSM potentials (see (24.7)). To clearly separate the contribution of the steerable filters versus the high-order cliques, the comparison also includes a high-order, nonsteerable MRF based on 2×3 and 3×2 derivative filters. In both cases the EM algorithm is used and the scale parameters are as described in section 24.4. Full experimental details are given in [396].

The SRF substantially outperforms the traditional pairwise MRF model in terms of PSNR (28.32 dB (SRF) versus 27.73 dB) and SSIM (0.788 (SRF) versus 0.767), despite using the same number of filters. The SRF also substantially outperforms the high-order, nonsteered MRF, illustrating the importance of using steerable filters (27.71 dB and SSIM of 0.770). Figure 24.4 shows representative denoising results for one of the test images, where it can be noted that the SRF does a good job of recovering continuous edge structures while also preserving detail (e. g., the lines on the wall in the background).

Despite its discriminative nature, the SRF generalizes to different image applications. In particular, the model trained on a denoising task can be applied to image inpainting.

(a)	(b)	(c)	(d)

Figure 24.4
Image denoising using an SRF. (a) Original image. (b) Gaussian noise added ($\sigma = 20$, PSNR = 22.49 dB, SSIM = 0.528). (c) Denoised with a pairwise MRF (PSNR = 27.60 dB, SSIM = 0.810). (d) Denoised with an SRF (PSNR = 28.63 dB, SSIM = 0.836). The bottom row shows a cropped version of the image above.

(a)	(b)	(c)	(d)

Figure 24.5
Image inpainting using an SRF. (a) Masked image (white regions are to be filled in). (b) Inpainting with a pairwise MRF (PSNR = 37.83 dB, SSIM = 0.980). (c) Inpainting with an SRF (PSNR = 41.08 dB, SSIM = 0.983). (d) Detail of results. Top row: Original image, masked image. Bottom row: Inpainting with pairwise MRF (left), inpainting with SRF (right).

Inpainting assumes that a mask of pixels to be inferred is given by the user. A uniform likelihood is assumed in regions to be inpainted [397], and conjugate gradient is used for inference. To reliably estimate the local orientation in areas with missing pixels, a larger structure tensor is used with $\rho = 4$ in (24.1). The inpainting performance of the SRF on a data set with 68 inpainting tasks shows that the SRF model performs substantially better than a pairwise MRF model (31.58 dB vs. 30.79 dB; see [396] for details). Figure 24.5 shows one of the test images that illustrates how the steered derivatives help to smoothly complete image contours.

24.6 Summary and Outlook

The steerable random field model combines steerable filters with spatially discrete random field models of images. Such a model is applicable to a wide range of dense scene-modeling problems. In contrast to previous MRF models, which formulate clique potentials based on fixed sets of filters, the SRF uses steered filter responses computed using a structure tensor. The statistics of steered filter responses suggest the formulation of the potentials as Gaussian scale mixtures used here. The parameters of the model are learned from training data with a discriminative version of contrastive divergence. The presented model thus unifies ideas from random fields and anisotropic regularization with structure tensors, and puts the latter on a statistical foundation.

The SRF can be used in image restoration applications with substantial performance gains over pairwise MRFs and other nonsteered models. In particular, edgelike structures are restored much more cleanly when using the SRF. Furthermore, by connecting algorithmic anisotropic diffusion techniques with probabilistic MRF models, the SRF opens the possibility of employing new learning and inference methods, such as belief propagation [376], in these problems.

There are several other avenues for future work. For example, instead of modeling the responses to orthogonal and aligned derivatives separately, as in (24.6), they may be modeled jointly in order to capture their residual dependencies. It is also interesting to observe that Fields of Experts (chapter 19) still outperform SRFs in terms of denoising results, likely due to their larger cliques and their use of more filters. This motivates research on whether these two kinds of models can be combined to learn filters sensitive to the local image orientation, and whether more complex models with many filters, such as the FoE, can be steered as well.

Acknowledgments

This work was supported by NSF grants IIS-0534858 and IIS-0535075. We thank Siwei Lyu for interesting discussions related to SRFs.

25 Markov Random Fields for Object Detection

John Winn and Jamie Shotton

This chapter describes how Markov random fields can be used to detect and segment objects of a known category in an image. A key advantage of random fields over, for example, sliding window object detection is that they allows detection and segmentation to be achieved simultaneously, rather than as separate algorithmic stages.

One of the earliest applications of random fields for object detection [284] applied a multiscale conditional random field to the problem of detecting man-made structures in natural images. In this approach the latent variables of the random field are the *class labels* of a pixel: here, "man-made" or "Background." The random field encourages the class labeling to be smooth, that is, to favor connected regions of pixels being given the same class label. Hence, in this approach the random field acts as a prior over the shape of the detected object or objects in the image. Using such a field of class labels has proven very successful for multiclass segmentation [186, 437] and for inferring the geometry and depth of image scenes [197, 415].

The ability of the random field to detect structured objects can be much enhanced by changing the labeling to include the *part* of the object as well as its class. For example, the label could now be "car wheel" or "car door" rather than just "car." The use of such part labels has several advantages. First, recognizing parts of an object allows for object detection under partial occlusion. Second, there are local spatial interactions between parts that can help with detection; for example, we expect to find the nose just above the mouth on a face. Hence, we can exploit local part interactions to exclude invalid detections at a local level. Third, knowing the location of one part highly constrains the locations of other, more distant parts. For example, knowing the locations of wheels on a car constrains where the rest of the car can be detected. Thus, we can improve object detection by incorporating long-range spatial constraints on the parts. Fourth, by subdividing an object into parts, we restrict the variability in appearance corresponding to a label, and so improve detection accuracy. For example, the appearance of an image region labeled "car wheel" is much less variable than an image region labeled "car," which could contain any part of a car. Finally, by considering the layout of parts we can determine the number of instances of an object class present in an image, even if these instances occlude each other.

When using part labels, an important question is how to define what the parts of an object are. The most straightforward method is to manually define a set of parts, as in [107], though this requires considerable human effort for each new object class. Alternatively, parts can be learned based on their appearance, such as by clustering visually similar image patches [5, 296]. However, this approach does not fully exploit the spatial layout of the parts in the training images and can struggle to distinguish, for example, the front and back wheels of a car. OBJCut by Kumar et al. [278] uses a discriminative model for detection and a separate generative model for segmentation, but requires that the parts be learned in advance from video. Others have used generative models to learn spatially coherent parts in an unsupervised manner. For example, the constellation models of Fergus et al. [142] learn parts that occur in a particular spatial arrangement. However, the parts correspond to sparsely detected interest points and thus are limited in size, cannot represent untextured regions, and do not provide a segmentation of the image. Winn and Jojic [524] use a dense generative model to learn a partitioning of the object into parts, along with an unsupervised segmentation of the object. Their method does not learn a model of object appearance (only of object shape) and so cannot be used for object detection in cluttered images.

In this chapter we will focus on the layout consistent random field (LayoutCRF) as an example parts-based model for object detection [525]. The approach uses an automatically defined part labeling that densely covers the object, and models the label distribution using a conditional random field. The LayoutCRF model was motivated by the hidden random field (HRF) [465] (see also chapter 1), which classifies handwritten ink by automatically learning parts of diagram elements (boxes, arrows, etc.) and models the local interaction between them. The LayoutCRF also extends the located HRF model [225] that allows for multiple object instances and interobject occlusion.

A key aspect of the LayoutCRF model is the use of asymmetric pairwise potentials to capture the spatial ordering of parts (e.g., car wheels must be below the car body, not vice versa. These asymmetric potentials allow propagation of long-range spatial dependencies using only local interactions, and are carefully constructed to distinguish between various types of occlusion, such as object occluding background, background occluding object[1], and object occluding object. The model is capable of representing multiple object instances that interocclude, and infers a pairwise depth ordering.

25.1   Layout Consistent Random Field Model

The LayoutCRF model aims to take the image $\mathbf{z}$ and infer a label for each pixel indicating both the part of the object and the instance of the object that the pixel belongs to. Figure 25.1 gives an overview of the approach.

---

1. Note that throughout the chapter, "background" is used to mean pixels not belonging to an identified object class and "foreground" is used to mean pixels that do belong to the class. Hence it is possible to have background objects in front of foreground ones, as illustrated by a person (background) occluding a car (foreground) in figure 25.4.

Part labels   Input image   Unary potentials   Inferred part labels

Figure 25.1
LayoutCRF Overview. A set of dense parts, denoted by shades of gray, is defined over the object. For a given input image, local information alone is not enough to infer a good part labeling of an input image (unary potentials, best viewed in the online color version of this figure). By adding pairwise potentials that enforce a consistent layout of the part labels, a reliable detection is achieved along with an object segmentation.

Let the set of all image pixels be denoted V. Each pixel $i \in V$ has an instance label $y_i \in \{0, 1, \ldots, M\}$ where the background label is indicated by $y_i = 0$, and M foreground instances by $y_i \in \{1, \ldots, M\}$. Here we will describe the case where only one nonbackground class is considered at a time, though the model extends naturally to multiple classes, in which case y_i labels pairs of (class, instance).

The random field is defined not on these instance labels, but on a hidden layer of *part labels* h_i, as introduced in the hidden random field (HRF) model of [465]. Each object instance has a separate set of H part labels so that $h_i \in \{0, 1, \ldots, H \times M\}$. These hidden variables represent the assignment of pixels to parts and, unlike the instance labels, are not observed during training.

The layout consistent random field (LayoutCRF) is a hidden random field with asymmetric pairwise potentials extended with a set of discrete-valued instance transformations $\{T_1, \ldots, T_M\}$. Each transformation T represents the translation and left/right flip of an object instance by indexing all possible integer pixel translations for each flip orientation. As described in section 25.4.4, the transformation variable T can also be extended to handle multiple viewpoints. Each of these transformation variables is linked to every part label h_i. This aspect of the model extends the work of [225] to cope with multiple object instances.

Figure. 25.2 shows the graphical model corresponding to the LayoutCRF. Note that the local dependencies captured are between parts rather than between instance labels. The edges from part labels h_i to instance labels y_i represent the unique deterministic mapping from part labels to instance labels, which we denote as $y_i = y(h_i)$.

The conditional distribution for the label image $\mathbf{y}$ and part image $\mathbf{h}$ is defined as

$$P(\mathbf{y}, \mathbf{h}, \{T\} \mid \mathbf{z}; \boldsymbol{\theta}) \propto \prod_{i \in V} \phi_i(h_i, \mathbf{z}; \boldsymbol{\theta}) \delta(y_i = y(h_i)) \lambda_i(h_i, \{T\}; \boldsymbol{\theta})$$

$$\times \prod_{(i,j) \in E} \psi_{ij}(h_i, h_j, \mathbf{z}; \boldsymbol{\theta}),$$

(25.1)

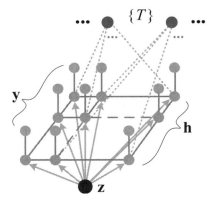

Figure 25.2
The layout consistent random field. All part label nodes **h** are conditioned on the image **z**, and connected 4-wise with their neighbors. These pairwise potentials are set up to favor consistent layouts of the part labels, as discussed in the text. A deterministic mapping links **h** to class labels **y**. A set of instance transformations $\{T\}$ are optionally connected to all of the part labels.

where $\boldsymbol{\theta}$ represents the learned parameters of the model and E is the set of all 4-wise neighbors between pairs of part labels. The *unary* potentials $\phi_i(h_i, \mathbf{z}; \boldsymbol{\theta})$ use only local image information and, as described below, take the form of randomized decision trees. The *asymmetric pairwise* potentials $\psi_{ij}(h_i, h_j, \mathbf{z}; \boldsymbol{\theta})$ encourage local and, to a certain extent long-range, compatibility between the part labels. The *instance* potentials $\lambda_i(h_i, \{T\}; \boldsymbol{\theta})$ encourage the correct long-range spatial layout of parts for each object instance. Finally, the potentials $\delta(y_i = y(h_i))$ enforce the deterministic mapping from part labels to instance labels.

25.1.1   Layout Consistent Pairwise Potentials

The most important feature of the LayoutCRF is the form of the pairwise potentials ψ_{ij}. A common choice in CRF models [465, 225] is to use only symmetric pairwise potentials, whereas the LayoutCRF uses *asymmetric* potentials. These allow the relative layout (above/below/left/right) of parts to be modeled, and hence can propagate long-range spatial information using only local pairwise interactions. Further, by distinguishing types of transitions in these pairwise potentials, the LayoutCRF can achieve a local depth ordering of objects in the image.

A neighboring pair of labels is defined to be *layout consistent* if both labels could plausibly belong to the same object instance. More precisely, a part label is defined to be layout consistent with itself and with those labels that are adjacent in the grid ordering, as defined in figure 25.3. Neighboring pixels whose labels are not layout consistent are assumed to belong to different object instances (or the background), and thus must have an occluding boundary between them.

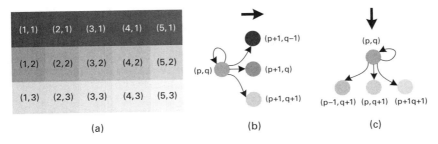

Figure 25.3
Layout consistency. Colors represent part labels. (a) A subsection of the regular grid with label numbers overlaid as pairs (p, q). (b, c) Layout-consistent label pairs for pairwise links of left-to-right and top-to-bottom. Right-to-left and bottom-to-top are defined analogously. Note that slight deformations from the regular grid are still considered layout consistent.

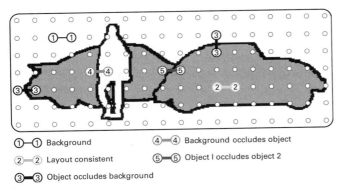

①—① Background   ④—④ Background occludes object

②—② Layout consistent   ⑤—⑤ Object I occludes object 2

③—③ Object occludes background

Figure 25.4
Distinguished transitions. The distinguished types of transitions between neighboring part label nodes in the graph. See text for definitions. Note that a pairwise depth ordering is implicit in these types.

Hence, a pair of neighboring labels h_i and h_j must be in one of the following states (illustrated in figure 25.4):

Background Both h_i and h_j are background labels.

Layout Consistent Both h_i and h_j are *layout consistent* foreground labels. Note the asymmetry here: for example, if $h_i = a$ to the left of $h_j = b$ is layout consistent, then (assuming $a \neq b$) $h_i = b$ to the left of $h_j = a$ is not layout consistent (see figure 25.3).

Object Occludes Bg The object occludes the background. One label is background, and the next is a part label *that lies on the object edge*. Treating this type of transition specially is used to encourage object-background transitions at the true object boundary.

Bg Occludes Object The "background" occludes the object. One label is an *interior* foreground label, and the next is the background label.

Obj. Occludes Obj.   One instance of an object occludes another instance. Both are foreground labels but are not layout consistent, with at least one label being an object edge.

Inconsistent   Both labels are interior foreground labels that are not layout consistent. This can occur only due to transparency or self-occlusion, and hence this case should not occur frequently.

The pairwise potentials are set up to assign different values to each of these states as follows:

$$-\log \psi_{ij}(h_i, h_j, \mathbf{z}; \boldsymbol{\theta}) = \begin{cases} \beta_{\mathrm{bg}} & \text{Background} \\ 0 & \text{Layout consistent} \\ \beta_{\mathrm{ob}}.e_{ij} & \text{Object occludes background} \\ \beta_{\mathrm{bo}}.e_{ij} & \text{Background occludes object} \\ \beta_{\mathrm{oo}}.e_{ij} & \text{Object 1 occludes object 2} \\ \beta_{\mathrm{inc}} & \text{Inconsistent} \end{cases} \qquad (25.2)$$

where cost e_{ij} is an image-based edge cost to encourage object edges to align with image boundaries, and is set to $e_{ij} = e_0 + \exp(\gamma \|z_i - z_j\|^2)$. The contrast term γ is estimated separately for each image as $(2 < \|z_i - z_j\|^2 >)^{-1}$ where $<>$ denotes a mean over all neighboring pairs of pixels.

25.1.2 Instance Potentials

The instance potentials are lookup tables indicating where each object part is expected to be, given the object's position and orientation T.

$$\lambda_i(h_i, \{T_1, \ldots, T_M\}; \boldsymbol{\theta}) = \widetilde{P}(h_i | \mathrm{loc}(T_{y(h_i)}, i))^{\nu} \qquad (25.3)$$

where $\mathrm{loc}(T_m, i)$ returns position i inverse-transformed by the transformation T_m, and ν is a parameter to weight the strength of the potential. This potential encourages the correct spatial layout of parts for each object instance by gravitating parts toward their expected positions, given the transformation $T_{y(h_i)}$ of the instance.

25.2 Inference

Inference in the LayoutCRF is achieved using a modified version of the alpha-expansion move algorithm (chapter 3).[2] The modification involves the use of an annealing procedure to help the alpha-expansion escape from local minima. A three-step refinement algorithm then employs this expansion move algorithm to infer the number of object instances and the instance level labeling.

---

2. To be precise, the alpha-expansion move algorithm is performed in a transformed label space; hence, the move making algorithm uses the more general fusion move procedure 18.

25.2.1 Expansion Move Algorithm

An annealed expansion move algorithm is used for approximate MAP inference of the part labels. The standard expansion move algorithm reduces the problem of maximizing a function $f(\mathbf{h})$ of multiply valued labels $\mathbf{h}$ to a sequence of binary-valued maximization problems. These subproblems are called α-*expansions*, and for *submodular* energies can be efficiently solved using graph cuts (see [66, 266] for details and chapter 2).

Suppose that we have a current configuration (set of labels) $\mathbf{h}$ and a fixed label $\alpha \in U$ where U is the set of possible label values. In the α-expansion operation, each pixel i makes a binary decision: it can either keep its old label or switch to label α. The expansion move algorithm starts with an initial configuration $\mathbf{h}^0$. Then it computes optimal α-expansion moves for labels α in some order, accepting the moves only if they increase the objective function.

The LayoutCRF aims to discover contiguous regions of part labels that are layout consistent. Since any part of a regular grid is guaranteed to be layout consistent, the expansion move used is the move to a repeating grid of labels at a fixed offset (see figure 25.5). The total set of expansion moves is the set of possible offsets of this repeating grid (though for efficiency these are quantized to be only every 3×3 pixel). At each iteration any of the pixels can choose to adopt this new labeling, and a region that does so will form a rigid grid structure. Deformations in the grid can be handled over a number of expansion moves by using labels at nearby offsets. The resultant regions will be layout consistent and will form a deformed, rather than a rigid, grid. This process is illustrated in figure 25.5, which shows two expansion moves with slightly different offsets being used to label a car with a deformed grid. This label grid expansion algorithm can be considered an instance of the more recent fusion move algorithm (see chapter 18).

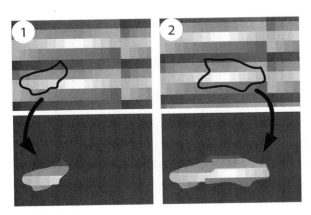

Figure 25.5
Expansion move algorithm. During inference, at each iteration of the expansion move algorithm a repeated regular grid relabeling is permitted. Hence, an object can be labeled with a deformed grid over several iterations. Note that the offsets of the grid are different in the two iterations illustrated.

The set of expansion moves corresponding to all grid offsets (typically several hundred offsets) is applied in a random order. Additionally, these expansion moves are interspersed with standard α-expansion moves for changing to the background label. The pairwise potentials are not guaranteed to be submodular [61], but in the rare cases where they are not submodular (typically < 0.5 percent of cases) the potential is truncated to the closest submodular potential. Note that alternatively the BHS algorithm can be utilized, which handles nonsubmodular terms, as in many other applications that use fusion move (see chapter 18).

Despite this careful choice of expansion move, the algorithm is vulnerable to getting stuck in local minima due to the strong interaction terms that are present in the model. Highly deformed objects are particularly affected, as it takes more expansion moves to reach the optimal labeling. To ameliorate this, an annealing schedule is used: during early rounds of the expansion move algorithm, the pairwise potential is weakened (by raising to a power less than 1). Experimentally, the annealing gives a minor but noticeable improvement in performance for fairly rigid classes (such as cars, faces). For more deformable objects such as horses, annealing becomes more important.

25.2.2 Inferring Object Instances

A three-step algorithm infers the number of object instances and their locations, as follows.

Step 1   Initially the number of objects is unknown, so different instances are not distinguished. Thus all the part labels are collapsed together across instances, that is, $h_i \in \{0, 1, \ldots, H\}$. Additionally, all the instance labels are merged together so that $y_i \in \{0, 1\}$, and the edges in the graphical model from the instance transformation nodes $\{T\}$ to the part labels $\mathbf{h}$ are removed. MAP inference is performed on this simplified model, resulting in a part labeling image $\mathbf{h}^*$.

Step 2   The number of layout consistent regions in the labeling $\mathbf{h}^*$ is determined using connected component analysis, where two pixels are considered connected if they have layout consistent part labels. This yields an initial estimate of the number of object instances M and an initial instance labeling.

It is then necessary to estimate the transformations $T_1 \ldots T_M$ for each instance label. These are estimated as $\arg \max_{\{T\}} \prod_i \lambda_i(h_i, \{T\}; \boldsymbol{\theta})$, which can be computed separably for each instance label. To capture two possible modes corresponding to left/right flips of the object, two instance labels are created for each connected component. When estimating T for each label, the first is constrained to have T facing left, and the second has T facing right. Thus, M is equal to twice the number of connected components.

Step 3   The full model is now used, with label set $h_i \in \{0, 1, \ldots, H \times M\}$, $y_i \in \{0, 1, \ldots M\}$ and including the links from $\{T\}$ to $\mathbf{h}$. Using this model, the MAP inference is rerun to obtain $\hat{\mathbf{h}}$, which now distinguishes between different object instances. Typically, $\hat{\mathbf{h}}$ contains part labels for only a subset of the instances. For example, normally only one of each pair of left-facing and right-facing instances is retained. In section 25.4.4 we add a further penalty to minimize the number of instances.

If desired, steps 2 and 3 can be iterated to refine the instance transformation and the instance labeling, though this was not found to be necessary for the experiments discussed in this chapter.

25.3 Learning

The potentials in the LayoutCRF model are learned using a supervised algorithm that requires a foreground/background segmentation for each training image, though not for the part labelings.

25.3.1 Unary Potentials

The LayoutCRF uses randomized decision trees [302] for the unary potentials since these are both straightforward to implement and very efficient. Using a set of decision trees, each trained on a random subset of the data, increases the efficiency of learning and improves generalization performance over using a single decision tree. For position i in image $\mathbf{z}$, decision tree t_k returns a distribution over the part labels, $\phi_i^k(y_i, \mathbf{z}; \theta)$. The set of K such decision trees is combined by simply averaging these distributions, so that $\phi_i(y_i, \mathbf{z}; \theta) = \frac{1}{K} \sum_{k=1}^{K} \phi_i^k(y_i, \mathbf{z}; \theta)$.

Each decision tree t_k is a binary tree where each nonterminal node evaluates a binary test based on one image feature. Two types of feature are used, chosen for speed: pixel intensity differences and absolute pixel intensity differences. Each is evaluated relative to the position of pixel i being classified. Both features are constrained to use only pixel information within a box of side D, centered on pixel i. A small D value is important for achieving good recognition results of occluded objects, since this ensures invariance to occlusions that are farther than $D/2$ pixels away. Having two types of features allows the classifier to detect both image edges and smooth image regions. The intensity difference is compared with a learned threshold, and the left or right branch of the node is taken accordingly. At each terminal node a distribution over part labels is learned as the histogram of all the training image pixels that have reached that node. Inferring $\phi_i^k(y_i, \mathbf{z}; \theta)$ simply involves traversing the tree, evaluating features relative to position i in image $\mathbf{z}$, and taking the learned distribution at the terminal node reached.

The trees are built in a simple, greedy fashion, where nonterminal node tests are chosen from a set of candidate features together with a set of candidate thresholds to maximize the expected gain in information. This process is halted when the best expected gain in information falls below a threshold ϵ. The time taken to learn the decision trees is dominated by feature calculations, and hence is almost independent of the number of labels. This becomes important as the number of object classes and part labels increases.

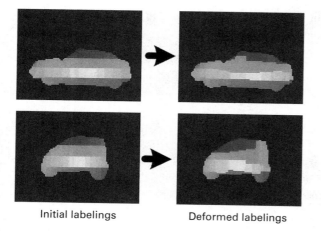

Initial labelings   Deformed labelings

Figure 25.6
Deforming the part labelings of training data. Left: Two examples of initial labelings, based on a tight-fitting regular grid. Different shades of gray represent different part labels; since the initial labeling is scan line ordered, the gray values vary slowly along rows and jump between rows. Right: The resulting labelings after deformation. Note that corresponding parts (e.g., wheels, rear) are now given corresponding labelings, and hence the unary classifier will learn a tighter appearance model for each part, as desired. This figure is bested viewed in the online color version.

Deformed Labelings   In order to build the unary classifier, a part labeling is required for each training image. To avoid needing hand-labeled part positions, and yet have a unary classifier that can learn consistent appearance models for each part despite object deformations, the LayoutCRF employs an iterative learning scheme, as follows.

The part labeling for the training images is initialized based on a dense regular grid that is sized to tightly fit the bounding box of the object and then masked with the given object segmentation (see figure 25.6, left). The dense grid is spatially quantized such that a part covers several pixels (on average an 8×8 pixel square). The unary classifiers are learned as described above, after which a new labeling is inferred for all the training images (illustrated in figure 25.6, right). The deformed labeling is then used to relearn the unary classifier, which can now learn a much tighter appearance distribution for each part. Two iterations of this process were found to be sufficient for good results.

25.3.2 Pairwise Potentials

The parameters for the pairwise potentials, β_{bg}, β_{ob}, β_{bo}, β_{oo}, β_{inc}, ν, and e_0 are learned using cross-validation, by a search over a sensible range of positive values. For the experiments in this chapter, the size of the data set made gradient-based maximum likelihood learning of the parameters too slow to be used in practice.

25.3.3 Instance Potentials

The instance potential lookup tables $\widetilde{P}(h|w)$ for label h at position w are learned as follows. The deformed part labelings of all training images are aligned on their segmentation mask centroids. A bounding box is placed relative to the centroid around the part labelings, just large enough to include all nonbackground labels. For each pixel within the bounding box, the distribution over part labels is learned by histogramming the deformed training image labels at that pixel. A count of 1 (corresponding to a weak Dirichlet prior) is added to ensure nonzero probabilities.

25.4 Evaluation

The capabilities of the LayoutCRF model are demonstrated in the experiments below. The model is evaluated on the UIUC car database [296] for both detection and segmentation performance, and on the Caltech and AR face databases [142, 332] for tolerance of partial occlusion. Further results on multiclass segmentation and on an extension to 3D objects are also given.

25.4.1 UIUC Car Database

The training set comprised 46 segmented images from the TU Darmstadt database [296] (for the purposes of this work the car windows were labeled as part of the car), and also a subset of 20 images from the UIUC car database [296] containing one completely visible car instance. These training images were segmented by hand. To learn the pairwise potential parameters by cross validation, the training set was divided into halves, and the parameters were hand-optimized against one half. The unary potentials were then retrained on the entire training set. The final parameters used were $\beta_{ob} = 6$, $\beta_{bo} = 12$, $\beta_{oo} = 12$, $\beta_{inc} = 30$, $\nu = 0.2$, $e_0 = 0.2$, and $D = 15$.

Detection Accuracy To test detection accuracy, the system was evaluated on the remaining 150 previously unseen images. These contain cars under considerable occlusions and rotations, facing both left and right.

Figure 25.7 shows example detections (and the simultaneously achieved segmentations) achieved by the model. The LayoutCRF detects multiple instances jointly and does not involve any detection mechanisms such as sliding windows, thresholding, or postprocessing merging. One disadvantage of the unified LayoutCRF method is that generating a full recall precision curve is extremely slow, as the entire inference procedure must be rerun for each point on the curve, using a different value of the background prior β_{bg}. Hence results of the method are shown at four points (at $\beta_{bg} \in \{1.65, 1.70, 1.75, 1.80\}$) on the recall precision axes alongside competing methods [436, 142, 5, 296] for comparison (figure 25.8). The point closest to equal error rate on the recall precision curve achieved is recall $= 96.1\%$ at precision $= 89.6\%$. Note that these figures are not directly comparable with the other

Figure 25.7

Example detections and segmentations on the UIUC Database. In each pair the left shows the test image with detected object segmentations illustrated with dark (red) outline, and the right shows the corresponding instance labeling for each pixel, where colors denote different instances. Note tolerance of partial occlusions, detection of multiple instances, detections facing both left and right, and very accurate segmentations. The bottom right result is an example failure case where a false positive has been detected.

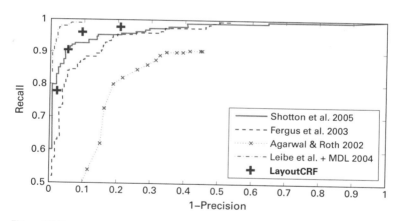

Figure 25.8

Recall precision curves for the UIUC Database. Note that the unified algorithm does not have a simple threshold that can be varied to generate the whole curve efficiently. Hence we show only four points on the curve for comparison.

techniques, as the method was tested on only 150 of the 170 test images; moreover, the 20 images removed from the test set and used for training were clean, single-instance images, and so the performance over the 150 remaining test images would therefore be expected to be slightly lower than for the whole database. Also, car instances with fewer than 70% of parts detected were discounted, as the supplied ground truth data do not include labelings of partially occluded cars.

Ignoring these differences, the detection performance of the LayoutCRF exceeds or is highly competitive with all competing methods, bar that of [296], when the minimum description length criterion is used (without this the LayoutCRF recall precision points lie above their performance). Note that the LayoutCRF also solves a harder problem than the compared methods: allowing occluded cars gives more degrees of freedom, and hence a higher error rate than if the model were constrained to detect only unoccluded cars. For example, the false positive in figure 25.7 is unlikely to have been detected had the model been able to assume there was no occlusion.

Segmentation Accuracy Segmentation accuracy was evaluated on a randomly chosen subset of 20 of the UIUC test images containing a total of 34 car instances. These were segmented by hand to produce ground truth instance labels. Averaged across all image pixels, the model achieved a per-pixel figure ground segmentation accuracy of 96.5%. To get a measure of the segmentation accuracy per instance, the ratio of the intersection to the union of the detected and ground truth segmentations areas was computed for each car instance. The average of this measure across all 34 instances was 0.67. Some example segmentations are shown in figure 25.7. Note that the LayoutCRF produces segmentations that accurately delineate the true object boundary and cope with occlusions correctly.

25.4.2 Face Databases
The performance of the LayoutCRF was investigated on the Caltech face database [142] under artificial partial occlusion, using 20 segmented face images for training and evaluating the same trained model on images from the AR face database [332] containing real occlusions. Shown in figure 25.9 are some example results of detection and segmentation where randomly the top, bottom, left, or right half of images was occluded by a uniform gray rectangle. Note the excellent detection and segmentation despite significant occlusion; many sparse feature-based approaches (which rely heavily on, say, the presence of both eyes) would fail under such occlusion.

25.4.3 Multiple Classes
The LayoutCRF can be extended to recognize multiple object classes by enlarging the label set to include a set of part labels for each class. The number of parts used can vary between classes, and this allows detection of both structured objects (e.g., cars) and unstructured textural objects (e.g., grass, sky) by using a single part for unstructured object classes.

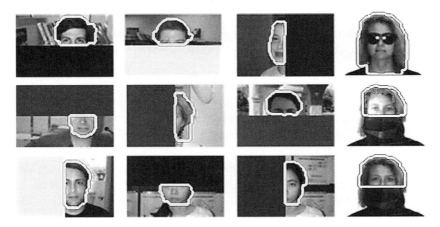

Figure 25.9
Detection and segmentations on the Caltech face database with artificial occlusions (left three columns) and the AR face database with real occlusions (right column). Notice that faces are detected correctly even when significant features (such as eyes) are occluded.

Figure 25.10
Multiclass detection and segmentation. One structured class (building) and three unstructured classes (sky, tree, grass) are accurately detected and segmented using a multiclass LayoutCRF. Left: Input image. Middle: Inferred parts labelings. Unstructured classes are assigned only one part label (shown as different shades of red in the online color version of this figure), while structured classes have a grid of part labels. Right: Output segmentations given by deterministic mapping from the part labelings, with inferred class labels superimposed.

Figure 25.10 shows example results for a multiclass LayoutCRF trained using multiple part labels for buildings and a single part label for tree, grass, and sky classes.

25.4.4 Multiple Viewpoints

The LayoutCRF assumes that the object appears from a fixed viewpoint, for example, that cars are seen only from the side. However, it can be extended to form the 3D LayoutCRF model [198], which can detect objects from multiple viewpoints. The 3D LayoutCRF works by defining part labels over the entire surface of an object. The key idea is that, for convex objects, any projection of such a 3D surface of part labels into an image will still satisfy the layout consistency constraints. The object transformation variable T is extended to include the viewpoint information, and the appearance models (unary potentials) are specialized to model the appearance of a part within a $45°$ viewing range. The 3D LayoutCRF also adds a per-instance cost, to give an equivalent to the minimum description length criterion of [296]. Figure 25.11 gives examples of applying the 3D LayoutCRF to test images containing cars from the PASCAL VOC 2006 data set.

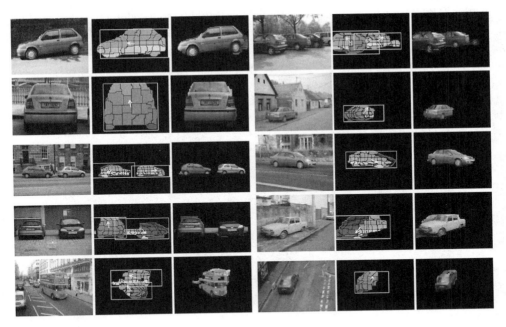

Figure 25.11
Detection from multiple viewpoints. For convex 3D objects, layout consistency constraints still apply when parts labels on the surface of the object are seen from any viewpoint. This allows the LayoutCRF to be extended into a viewpoint invariant form called the 3D LayoutCRF. The figure shows example detections and segmentations achieved by applying the 3D LayoutCRF to images from the Pascal VOC 2006 data set.

25.5 Conclusions

The use of random field models holds much promise for solving multiclass detection and segmentation problems. In particular, the LayoutCRF is an example of a discriminative random field model that infers consistent part labelings to achieve simultaneous object detection and segmentation while explicitly handling partial occlusions.

However, many interesting problems remain unsolved. The number of labels of the LayoutCRF grows approximately linearly in the number of classes to be recognized. For tens of thousands of classes, this number of labels would make the cost of inference prohibitive for practical applications. An approach that may overcome this is to share part labels between objects, such as sharing wheel parts between all wheeled vehicles. Part sharing in this way would require a much more complex definition of layout consistency. Even with part sharing, inference with high cardinality labels is an expensive operation, and there is need for more efficient inference algorithms if models such as the LayoutCRF are to see real-time application.

The LayoutCRF does not exploit context [122], scene geometry [197], or depth information [199]. A very promising future direction would be to develop integrated random field models to combine these various cues into a coherent latent representation. Such an integrated model has the potential to significantly improve detection accuracy while also providing a more complete interpretation of the image.

26 SIFT Flow: Dense Correspondence across Scenes and Its Applications

Ce Liu, Jenny Yuen, Antonio Torralba, and William T. Freeman

This chapter introduces SIFT flow, a method to align an image to its nearest neighbors in a large image corpus containing a variety of scenes. The SIFT flow algorithm consists of matching densely sampled, pixelwise SIFT features between two images while preserving spatial discontinuities. Based on SIFT flow, we propose an alignment based large database framework for image analysis and synthesis, where image information is transferred from the nearest neighbors to a query image according to the dense scene correspondence. This chapter is based on [319, 320].

26.1 Introduction

Image alignment, registration, and correspondence are central topics in computer vision. For example, aligning different views of the same scene has been studied for the purpose of image stitching and stereo matching [461], (see figure 26.1a. The considered transformations are relatively simple (e.g., parametric motion for image stitching and 1D disparity for stereo), and images to register are typically assumed to have the same pixel value after applying the geometric transformation.

Image alignment becomes more complicated for dynamic scenes in video sequences, such as optical flow estimation [202, 326, 78]. The correspondence between two adjacent frames in a video is often formulated as an estimation of a 2D flow field. The extra degree of freedom (from 1D in stereo to 2D in optical flow) introduces an additional level of complexity. Typical assumptions in optical flow algorithms include brightness constancy and piecewise smoothness of the pixel displacement field [48].

Image alignment becomes even more difficult in the object recognition scenario, where the goal is to align different instances of the same object category, as illustrated in figure 26.1b. Sophisticated object representations [28, 140] have been developed to cope with the variations of object shapes and appearances (see also chapter 25). However, these methods still typically require objects to be salient and similar, and to have limited background clutter.

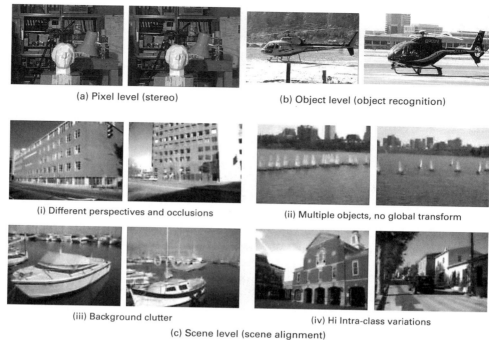

(a) Pixel level (stereo)   (b) Object level (object recognition)

(i) Different perspectives and occlusions   (ii) Multiple objects, no global transform

(iii) Background clutter   (iv) Hi Intra-class variations

(c) Scene level (scene alignment)

Figure 26.1
Image alignment resides at different levels. Researchers used to study image alignment problems at the pixel level, where two images are taken at the same scene at a slightly different time or at a different perspective [461] (a). Recently, correspondence has been extended to the object level (b) for object recognition [30]. We are interested in image alignment at the scene level, where two images come from different 3D scenes but share similar scene characteristics (c). SIFT flow is proposed to align the examples in (c) for scene alignment.

In this work we are interested in a new, higher level of image alignment: aligning two images that come from different 3D scenes but share similar scene characteristics. Image alignment at the scene level is thus called *scene alignment*. As illustrated in figure 26.1c, the two images to be matched may contain object instances captured from different viewpoints, placed at different spatial locations, or imaged at different scales. The two images may also contain different quantities of objects of the same category, and some objects present in one image may be missing in the other. Due to these issues, scene alignment can be extremely challenging.

Ideally, in scene alignment we want to build correspondence at the semantic level, that is, matching at the object class level, such as buildings, windows, and sky. But current object detection and recognition techniques are not robust enough to detect and recognize all objects in images. Therefore, we take a different approach for scene alignment by matching local, salient, and transform invariant image structures. We hope that semantically meaningful correspondences can be established through matching these image structures. Moreover, we want to have a simple, effective, object-free model to align all the pairs in figure 26.1c.

Recent advances in image features suggest that image correspondences can be established beyond the pixel level. Representations such as scale invariant feature transform (SIFT) [325], shape context [28, 30], and histogram of oriented gradients (HOG) [115] have been introduced to account for large appearance changes, and have proven to be effective in applications such as visual tracking [16] and object recognition [325]. Nevertheless, little has been investigated for establishing dense, pixelwise correspondences at the scene level using these features.

Inspired by optical flow methods, which are able to produce dense, pixel-to-pixel correspondences between two images, we propose *SIFT flow*, adopting the computational framework of optical flow but matching SIFT descriptors instead of raw pixels. In SIFT flow a SIFT descriptor [325] is extracted at each pixel to characterize local image structures and encode contextual information. A discrete, discontinuity-preserving, flow estimation algorithm is used to match the SIFT descriptors between two images. The use of SIFT features allows robust matching across different scene/object appearances, and the discontinuity-preserving spatial model allows matching of objects located at different parts of the scene.

Optical flow is applied only to two adjacent frames in a video sequence in order to obtain meaningful correspondences; likewise, we need to define the *neighborhood* for SIFT flow. Motivated by the recent progress in large image database methods [183], we define the neighbors of SIFT flow as the top matches retrieved from a large database. The chance of obtaining semantically meaningful correspondence increases as the database grows and the nearest neighbors are more likely to share the same scene characteristics as a query.

We propose an alignment based large database framework for image analysis and synthesis. The information to infer for a query image is transferred from the nearest neighbors in a large database according to the dense scene correspondence estimated by SIFT flow. Under this framework we apply SIFT flow to two applications: *motion prediction from a single static image* and *face recognition*. More applications in image retrieval, registration, and object recognition can be found in [320] and [318]. Through these examples we demonstrate the potential of SIFT flow for broad applications in computer vision and computer graphics.

26.2 The SIFT Flow Algorithm

26.2.1 Dense SIFT Descriptors and Visualization

SIFT is a local descriptor to characterize local gradient information [325]. In [325] the SIFT descriptor is a sparse feature representation that consists of both feature extraction and detection. In this chapter, however, we use only the feature extraction component. For

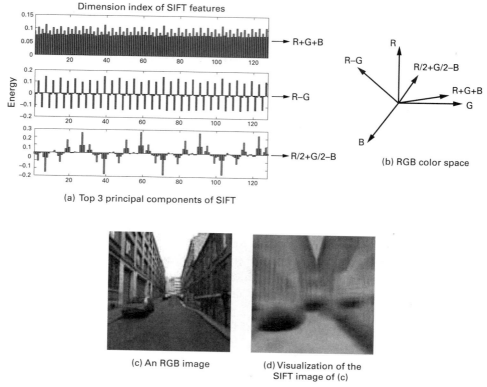

(a) Top 3 principal components of SIFT

(b) RGB color space

(c) An RGB image

(d) Visualization of the
SIFT image of (c)

Figure 26.2

Visualization of SIFT images. To visualize SIFT images, we map the top three principal components of SIFT descriptors (a) to the principal components of the RGB space (b). For an image in (c), we compute a 128D SIFT feature for every pixel, project the SIFT feature to 3D color space, and visualize the SIFT image in (d). Intuitively, pixels with similar colors share similar structures.

every pixel in an image, we divide its neighborhood (e.g., 16×16) into a 4×4 cell array, quantize the orientation into 8 bins in each cell, and obtain a $4 \times 4 \times 8 = 128$D vector as the SIFT representation for a pixel. We call this per-pixel SIFT descriptor *SIFT image*.

To visualize SIFT images, we compute the top three principal components of SIFT descriptors from a set of images, then map these principal components to the principal components of the RGB space, as shown in figure 26.2. Through projecting a 128D SIFT descriptor to a 3D subspace, we are able to visualize a SIFT image as shown in fig. 26.2d, where pixels with similar colors share similar local image structures. Note that this projection is only for visualization; in SIFT flow all 128 dimensions are used for matching.

Now that we have per-pixel SIFT descriptors for two images, our next task is to build dense correspondences to match these descriptors.

26.2.2 Matching Objective

We design an objective function similar to that of optical flow to estimate SIFT flow from two SIFT images. Similar to optical flow [78], we want SIFT descriptors to be matched along the flow vectors, and the flow field to be smooth, with discontinuities agreeing with object boundaries. Based on these two criteria, the objective function of SIFT flow is formulated as follows. Let $\mathbf{p} = (x, y)$ be the grid coordinate of images, and $\mathbf{w}(\mathbf{p}) = (u(\mathbf{p}), v(\mathbf{p}))$ be the flow vector at $\mathbf{p}$. We allow $u(\mathbf{p})$ and $v(\mathbf{p})$ to be only integers, and we assume that there are L possible states for $u(\mathbf{p})$ and $v(\mathbf{p})$, respectively. Let s_1 and s_2 be two SIFT images that we want to match. Set $\mathcal{E}$ contains all the spatial neighborhoods (a 4-neighbor system is used). The energy function for SIFT flow is defined as

$$
E(\mathbf{w}) = \sum_{\mathbf{p}} \min\left(\left\|s_1(\mathbf{p}) - s_2(\mathbf{p} + \mathbf{w}(\mathbf{p}))\right\|_1, t\right) + \eta\left(|u(\mathbf{p})| + |v(\mathbf{p})|\right)
$$
$$
+ \sum_{(\mathbf{p},\mathbf{q})\in\mathcal{E}} \min\left(\alpha|u(\mathbf{p}) - u(\mathbf{q})|, d\right) + \min\left(\alpha|v(\mathbf{p}) - v(\mathbf{q})|, d\right). \tag{26.1}
$$

In this objective function, truncated L1 norms are used in both the data term and the smoothness term to account for matching outliers and flow discontinuities, with t and d as the threshold, respectively. An L1 norm is also imposed on the magnitude of the flow vector as a bias toward smaller displacement when no other information is available. This energy function can be directly optimized by running sequential belief propagation (BP-S) [463] on a dual layer setup [433].

However, directly optimizing (26.1) may scale poorly with respect to the image size. In SIFT flow, a pixel in one image can literally match to any other pixel in another image. Suppose the image has n pixels; then the time and space complexity of the BP algorithm to estimate the SIFT flow is $O(n^2)$. As reported in [319], the computation time for 145×105 images with an 80×80 searching neighborhood is 50 seconds. In practice we do a coarse-to-fine approach, as discussed in detail in [320], which reduces runtime from 50 seconds to 5 seconds.

26.2.3 Neighborhood of SIFT Flow

In theory, we can apply optical flow to two arbitrary images to estimate a correspondence, but we may not get a meaningful correspondence if the two images are from different 3D scenes. In fact, even when we apply optical flow to two adjacent frames in a video sequence, we assume dense sampling in time so that there is significant overlap between two neighboring frames. Similarly, in SIFT flow we define the neighborhood of an image as the nearest neighbors when we query a large database with the input. Ideally, if the database is large and dense enough to contain almost every possible image in the world, the nearest neighbors will be close to the query image, sharing similar local structures. This motivates the following analogy with optical flow:

$$\text{Dense sampling in time : optical flow}$$
$$\text{Dense sampling in space of all images : SIFT flow}$$

As dense sampling of the time domain is assumed to enable tracking, dense sampling in (some portion of) the space of world images is assumed to enable scene alignment. In order to make this analogy possible, we collect a large database consisting of 102,206 frames from 731 videos, mostly from street scenes. Analogous to the time domain, we define the "adjacent frames" to a query image as its N nearest neighbors in this database. SIFT flow is then established between the query image and its N nearest neighbors.

For a query image we use a fast indexing technique to retrieve its nearest neighbors that will be further aligned using SIFT flow. As a fast search we use spatial histogram matching of quantized SIFT features [293]. First, we build a dictionary of 500 visual words [442] by running K-means on 5000 SIFT descriptors randomly selected from all the video frames in our data set. Then, histograms of the visual words are obtained on a two-level spatial pyramid [293], and histogram intersection is used to measure the similarity between two images.

26.3 Experiments on Dense Scene Correspondence

Experiments are conducted to test the SIFT flow algorithm on our video database. One frame from each of the 731 videos was selected as the query image, and histogram intersection matching was used to find its 20 nearest neighbors, excluding all other frames from the query video. The SIFT flow algorithm is then used to estimate the dense correspondence (represented as a pixel displacement field) between the query image and each of its neighbors. The best matches are the ones with the minimum energy defined by (26.1). Alignment examples are shown in figures 26.3–26.5. The original query image and its extracted SIFT descriptors are shown in columns (a) and (b) of 26.3. The minimum energy match (out of the 20 nearest neighbors) and its extracted SIFT descriptors are shown in columns (c) and (d) of 26.3. To investigate the quality of the pixel displacement field, we use the computed displacements to warp the best match onto the query image. The warped image is shown in column (e) of 26.3. The visual similarity between (a) and (e) demonstrates the quality of the matching. Last, the displacement field, visualized using the color coding in [21], is shown in column (f) (omitted in figures 26.4 to 26.6 to save space).

Figure 26.3 shows examples of matches between frames coming from exactly the same (3D) scene but different video sequences. The almost perfect matching in (1) demonstrates that SIFT flow reduces to classical optical flow when the two images are temporally adjacent frames in a video sequence. In (2) and (3) the query and the best match are more

Figure 26.3
SIFT flow for image pairs depicting the same scene/object. (a) shows the query image, and (b) its densely extracted SIFT descriptors. (c) and (d) show the best (lowest energy) match from the database and its SIFT descriptors, respectively. (e) shows (c) warped onto (a). (f) shows the estimated displacement field.

distant within the video sequence, but the alignment algorithm can still match them reasonably well.

Figure 26.4 shows more challenging examples, where the two frames come from different videos but contain the same types of objects. SIFT flow attempts to match the query image by reshuffling the pixels in the candidate image. Notice significant changes of objects between the query and the match in these examples. The large number of discontinuities in the flow field is due to (1) the coefficient on spatial regularization α is small, and (2) the content of the two images is too different to produce smooth matches (compare to the examples in figure 26.3). The square shaped discontinuities are a consequence of the decoupled regularizer on the horizontal and vertical components of the pixel displacement vector.

Figure 26.5 shows alignment results for examples with no obvious visual correspondences. Despite the lack of direct visual correspondences, SIFT flow attempts to rebuild the house (10), change the shape of the door into a circle (11), and reshuffle boats (12).

Some failure cases are shown in figure 26.6, where the correspondences are not semantically meaningful. Typically, the failures are caused by the lack of visually similar images in the video database for the query image. It shows that our database is not dense enough in the space of images.

We find that SIFT flow improves the ranking of the K-nearest neighbors retrieved by histogram intersection, as illustrated in figure 26.7. This improvement demonstrates that image similarities can be better measured by taking into account displacement, an idea that will be used for later applications of SIFT flow.

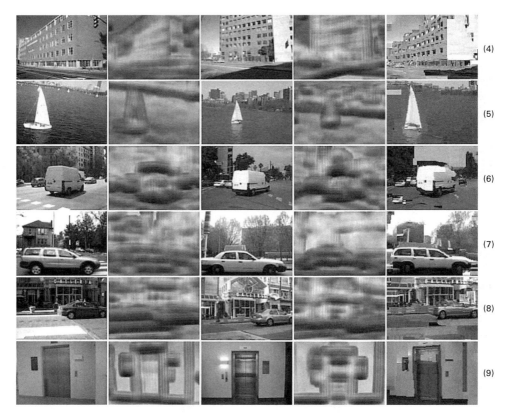

(4)

(5)

(6)

(7)

(8)

(9)

Figure 26.4
SIFT flow computed for image pairs depicting the same scene/object category where the visual correspondence is obvious.

26.4 Alignment-Based Large Database Framework for Image Analysis and Synthesis

Using SIFT flow as a tool for scene alignment, we design an alignment-based large database framework for image analysis and synthesis, illustrated in figure 26.8. For a query image we retrieve a set of nearest neighbors in the database, apply SIFT flow to establish dense scene correspondence between the query and its nearest neighbors, and transfer information such as motion, geometry, and labels from the nearest neighbors to the query. This framework is implemented in *motion prediction from a single image* (section 26.4.1) and *face recognition* (section 26.4.2).

26.4.1 Predicting Motion Fields from a Single Image

We are interested in predicting motion fields from a single image, namely, in knowing which pixels can move and how they move. This adds potential temporal motion information

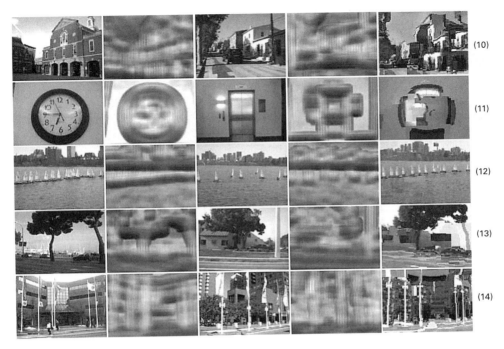

Figure 26.5
SIFT flow for challenging examples where the correspondence is not obvious.

Figure 26.6
Some failure examples with semantically incorrect correspondences. Although the minimized SIFT flow objectives are low for these samples (compared with those in figure 26.5), the query images are rare in the database and the best SIFT flow matches do not belong to the same scene category as the queries. However, these failures can be overcome through increasing the size of the database.

(a) Query image

(b) Top three ranking from histogram intersection

(c) Top three ranking from the matching of SIFT flow. Left: original; right: warped

Figure 26.7
SIFT flow typically improves ranking of the nearest neighbors. For a query image in (a), we display the top three nearest neighbors found by histogram intersection [293] in (b) and the top three nearest neighbors by SIFT flow in (c). Clearly, SIFT flow returns more meaningful matches due to image warping.

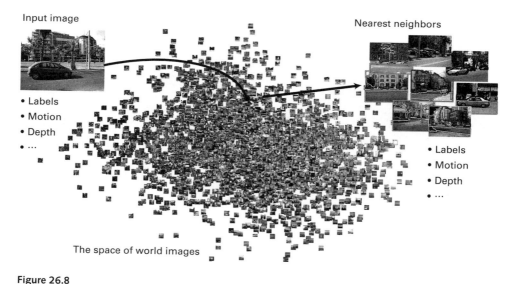

Input image

Nearest neighbors

• Labels
• Motion
• Depth
• ...

• Labels
• Motion
• Depth
• ...

The space of world images

Figure 26.8
A large database-driven framework for image analysis and synthesis. Under this framework an input image is processed through transferring the information such as labels, motion, and depth from its nearest neighbors in a large database to the input image according to the dense correspondence.

Figure 26.9
Motion from a single image. (a) The original image. (b) The matched frame from the video data set. (c) Motion of (b). (d) Warped and transferred motion field from (b). and (e) Ground truth for (a). Note that the predicted motion in (d) is inferred from a single input still image, that is, no motion signal is available to the algorithm. The predicted motion is based on the motion present in other videos with image content similar to the query image.

onto a singe image for further applications, such as animating a still image and event analysis.

A scene retrieval infrastructure is established to query still images over a database of videos containing common moving objects. The database consists of sequences depicting common events, such as cars driving along a street and kids playing in a park. Each individual frame was stored as a vector of word-quantized SIFT features, as described in section 26.2.3. In addition, we store the temporal motion field estimated using [78] between every two consecutive frames of each video.

The model for predicting motion fields from a single image is designed as follows. First, using the SIFT-based histogram matching in section 26.2.3, we retrieve nearest neighbors (similar video frames) that are roughly spatially aligned with the query. Then, dense correspondences are estimated between the query and the nearest neighbors using SIFT flow, and the temporally estimated motions of the nearest neighbors are warped to the query according to the estimated SIFT flow fields. Figure 26.9 shows examples of predicted motion fields directly transferred from the top five database matches and the warped motion fields.

A still image may have multiple plausible motions: a car can move forward, back up, turn, or remain static. This is handled by retrieving multiple nearest neighbors from the video database. Figure 26.10 shows an example of five motion fields predicted using our video database. All the motion fields are different but plausible.

26.4.2 Face Recognition
Aligning images with respect to structural image information contributes to building robust visual recognition systems. We design a generic image recognition framework based on SIFT flow and apply it to face recognition, since face recognition can be a challenging problem when there are large pose and lighting variations for a large corpus of subjects.

Figure 26.10
Multiple motion field candidates. A still query image with its temporally estimated motion field (top left) and multiple motion fields predicted by motion transfer from a large video database.

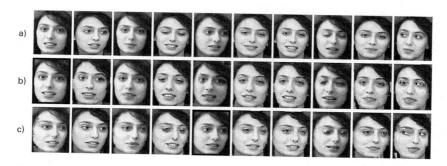

Figure 26.11
SIFT flow can serve as a tool to account for pose, expression, and lighting changes for face recognition. (a) Ten samples of one subject in ORL database [410]. Notice pose and expression variations of these samples. (b) We select the first image as the query, apply SIFT flow to align the rest of the images to the query, and display the warped images with respect to the dense correspondence. The poses and expressions are rectified to that of the query after the warping. (c) The same as (b) except for choosing the fifth sample as the query.

We use the ORL database [410], which contains 40 subjects and 10 images for each subject with some pose and expression variations, as the data for the experiment. In figure 26.11 a female sample is selected as an example to demonstrate how dense registration can deal with pose and expression variations. We select the first image as the query, apply SIFT flow to align the rest of the images to the query, and display the warped images with respect to the SIFT flow field in figure 26.11b, where the poses and expressions of other images are rectified to that of the query. We can also choose a different sample as query and align the rest of the images to this query, as demonstrated in 26.11c. Distances established on images after the alignment will be more meaningful than the distances directly on the original images.

In order to compare with the state of the art, we conduct experiments for both original size (92×112) and downsampled (32×32) images. We randomly split a γ ($\gamma \in (0, 1)$)

portion of the samples for each subject for training, and use the rest $(1 - \gamma$ portion) for testing. For each test image we first retrieve the top nearest neighbors (maximum 20) from the training database using GIST matching [356], and then apply SIFT flow to find the dense correspondence from the test to each of its nearest neighbors by optimizing the objective function in (26.1). We assign the subject identity associated with the best match, that is, the match with the minimum matching objective, to the test image.

The experimental results are shown in figure 26.12. We use the nearest neighbor classifier based on pixel-level Euclidean distance (Pixels + NN + L2), and nearest neighbor classifier using the L1-norm distance on GIST [356] features (GIST + NN + L1) as the benchmark. Clearly, GIST features outperform raw pixel values because the GIST feature is invariant to lighting changes. SIFT flow further improves the performance as SIFT flow is able to align images across different poses. We observe that SIFT flow boosts the classification rate significantly, especially when there are few samples (small γ). In table 26.1 we compare the performance of SIFT flow with the state of the art [81], where facial components are explicitly detected and aligned. Our recognition system based on SIFT flow is comparable with the state of the art when there are few samples for training.

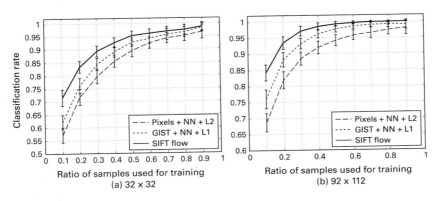

Figure 26.12
SIFT flow is applied to face recognition. The curves in (a) and (b) are the performance plots for low-res and high-res images in the ORL face database, respectively. SIFT flow significantly boosted the recognition rate, especially when there are not enough training samples.

Table 26.1
Our face recognition system based on nearest neighbors and SIFT flow outperforms the state of the art [82] when there are few training samples

Test Errors	1 Train	2 Train	3 Train
S-LDA [82]	N/A	17.1 ± 2.7	8.1 ± 1.8
SIFT flow	28.4 ± 3.0	16.6 ± 2.2	8.9 ± 2.1

26.5   Conclusion

We introduced the concept of dense scene alignment to estimate the dense correspondence between images across scenes. We proposed SIFT flow to match salient local image structure SIFT with spatial regularities, and conjectured that matching in a large database using SIFT flow leads to semantically meaningful correspondences for scene alignment. Extensive experiments verified our theory, showing that SIFT flow is able to establish dense scene correspondence despite significant differences in appearances and spatial layouts of matched images. We further proposed an alignment-based large database framework for image analysis and synthesis, where image information is transferred from the nearest neighbors in a large database to a query image according to the dense scene correspondence estimated by SIFT flow. This framework is concretely realized in motion prediction from a single image and face recognition. The preliminary success on these experiments suggested that scene alignment using SIFT flow can be a useful tool for various applications in computer vision and computer graphics.

Acknowledgments

Funding for this work was provided by NGA NEGI-1582-04-0004, MURI Grant N00014-06-1-0734, NSF Career award IIS 0747120, NSF contract IIS-0413232, a National Defense Science and Engineering Graduate Fellowship, and gifts from Microsoft and Google.

27   Unwrap Mosaics: A Model for Deformable Surfaces in Video

Alex Rav-Acha, Pushmeet Kohli, Carsten Rother, and Andrew Fitzgibbon

In this chapter we describe a generative model for video that represents the motion of 3D surfaces under nonrigid motion and possible occlusion. The model is based on a 2D latent image, coupled with a per-frame 2D-to-2D warp field and occlusion mask, yielding a parameterization of the image sequence with the number of parameters being of the order of the number of pixels. Adding regularizers to encourage smooth deformations and assuming a smooth 3D surface lead to a formulation in terms of energy minimization. This minimization is effected by alternation over subsets of parameters, leading to a novel view of nonrigid reconstruction as a nonlinear embedding into $\mathbb{R}^2$. The chapter is based on work previously reported by Rav-Acha et al. [387].

27.1   Introduction

We are given a video sequence captured in the real world. Our model of the world is a collection of deforming 3D surfaces viewed by a moving camera. A common goal of computer vision is to recover a 3D representation of the scene, most concretely expressed (and demonstrated) by exhibiting 3D mesh models with texture maps. However, such models are not readily obtained from a priori unseen and uncalibrated footage: the state of the art in the recovery of 3D information from images is briefly as follows. The extraction of *sparse* 3D information from image sequences of rigid scenes is by now well understood, and software packages are available that can recover 3D camera trajectories and sparse 3D point clouds from uncalibrated image sequences [1, 478]. The mathematical extensions to *nonrigid* scenes are understood [75, 73, 481], but their estimation is somewhat less reliable under occlusion. For *dense* reconstruction from video, however, we are firmly restricted to rigid scenes [429]. Some classes of dense models can be built using interactive tools [118, 490], which aid in the recovery of polyhedral surface models from video, but again, these are restricted to rigid scenes. Triangulation of the sparse points from nonrigid structure may be expected to be at least as difficult as it is from rigid structure, which has proved surprisingly troublesome [297].

    We introduce a technique that overcomes these difficulties to a large extent, generating a representation that is in some ways equivalent to a deforming 3D surface model, but can be

Figure 27.1
Representing nonrigid motion of a 3D surface. (Left) Three input frames from a video of a talking head. (Right)
The extracted "unwrap mosaic," the latent image underlying our generative model for video.

extracted directly from video. The key difference is that we recover a 2D representation in
the form of a latent image akin to a computer graphics "texture map." Accompanying the
recovered latent image are a 2D-to-2D mapping describing its projection to the images, and
a sequence of binary masks modeling occlusion. The combination of texture map, 2D-to-2D
mapping, and occlusion masks is what we call the *unwrap mosaic*, illustrated in figure 27.1
A video will typically be represented by an assembly of several unwrap mosaics: one per
object, and one for the background.

27.1.1   Previous Work

Even the name "unwrap mosaics" reveals that some of the ideas in this chapter have a
long history. The works of Wang and Adelson [511] on layered representations and of Irani
et al. [207] are clear precursors of the present chapter. In fact, it was thinking about how
layers might apply to self-occludng objects that inspired the current model. Two important
differences exist with our model. First is structural: Wang and Adelson's layers do not
allow the visible portion of the mosaic to vary over time, and so they cannot model a 3D
object that rotates with respect to the camera. Second, although it is suggested that a dense
nonparametric flow field might be associated with the mosaic, in practice the mapping was
restricted to an affine transformation per layer. Indeed, almost all developments of layers
have used some form of whole-image parametric motion estimate.

Many authors have reported developments of the ideas in [510, 207], for example, dealing
with nonopaque layers, computing superresolution mosaics, computing summary mosaics,
and other representations such as layered depth images [431]. An excellent recent overview
is included in the work on transferring information from still photos to mosaics [40]. The
latter paper shows how, for rigid scenes, dense 3D reconstruction can give motion fields
and occlusion masks that extend the homography-based work to scenes containing *rigid*
3D objects.

For nonrigid scenes 3D structure may be computed from sparse point tracks [481]. These
techniques are based on the observation that Tomasi–Kanade factorization extends to multiple motions and deformable models if the factorization rank r is taken to be higher than 3.

This amounts to saying that each track is a linear projection of a point in $\mathbb{R}^r$, effectively finding an embedding of the tracks into r-dimensional space. In our case, the embedding is not constrained to be linear, so it can map from a lower dimensional space—indeed, it maps from 2D space, the natural domain of the latent image. The difficulty with moving from sparse to dense structure with these methods is that some 2D neighborhood system must be defined either in the r-D space in which the latent coordinates are defined, or in the image. The latter cannot be propagated through occlusions, and the former introduces considerable difficulties when the density of reconstructed points is not very close to uniform. Because we embed directly into 2D, we avoid both issues.

Frey et al. [152] derive a probabilistic analogue of [511] that converges from a wide range of starting positions, but is practical only for short low-resolution sequences with relatively simple motion models. In contrast, our energy is specifically designed so that a good initialization can be computed, meaning that conventional optimizers can be brought to bear. Kannan et al. [222, 223] extend this model to deforming surfaces, increasing the complexity of the permitted motion models, but the restriction to short low-resolution sequences remains. An approach of particular interest is the Jigsaw model of Kannan et al. [224], which contains the key components of our model—a latent image and a per-frame mapping—but with the key difference that the mapping is defined in reverse: from the video frames to the latent image, rather than from the mosaic to the video frames. This representation yields a very compact representation of the video on which a number of interesting edits can be made, but the primary goal of the work is to develop a patch-based model of appearance rather than a representation suitable for video editing.

27.2   The Unwrap Mosaic Model

We assume that the sequence has been presegmented into independently moving objects, most likely using an interactive system, such as "video cut and paste" [311], that allows accurate segmentation maps to be obtained with relatively little effort.

Derivation of the algorithm will comprise three stages: image generation model, energy formulation, and minimization. First, the *image generation model* defines how an image sequence is constructed from a collection of unwrap mosaics. The model is introduced in the continuous domain, and then its discrete analogue is derived. Given such a model, extracting it from a supplied image sequence becomes a fitting problem, albeit a nonlinear and underconstrained one. The bulk of the chapter deals with this fitting problem. It is expressed as a problem of *energy minimization*, which can be implemented via nonlinear optimization. The key to the unwrap mosaic model we develop is that a good *initial estimate* for the 2D-to-2D mapping, and hence for the texture map, can be obtained from sparse 2D tracking data.

In order to explain the model and its recovery from video, the next several paragraphs will assume a greatly simplified scenario. Although this ignores many complexities, such as model topology and lighting, it will be enough to motivate the technique. The more detailed model is described in [386].

Despite the difficulties alluded to above of recovering 3D models from video, let us proceed as if to solve the general 3D surface reconstruction problem. Let the world be a collection of 3D surfaces represented as geometry images [177]; that is, each surface is represented as a function $\mathbf{S} : \mathcal{Q} \mapsto \mathbb{R}^3$ where $\mathcal{Q} \subset \mathbb{R}^2$ is the unit square. The surface is also accompanied by a texture map $\mathbf{C} : \mathcal{Q} \mapsto \mathbb{C}$, where $\mathbb{C}$ represents the color space in use, such as RGB. Thus, each point $\mathbf{u} = (u, v) \in \mathcal{Q}$ is associated with the 3D point $\mathbf{S}(u, v)$ and the color $\mathbf{C}(u, v)$.

A generalized camera is a function $\boldsymbol{\pi} : \mathbb{R}^3 \mapsto \mathbb{R}^2$, which induces the 2D-to-2D mapping $\mathbf{w}(\mathbf{u}) = \boldsymbol{\pi}(\mathbf{S}(\mathbf{u}))$. The function $\mathbf{w}$ now maps from the unit square in the surface's parameter space to the image domain. Let us assume for the moment a trivial lighting model where texture map colors $\mathbf{C}$ are simply copied to the image plane. Let the point-spread function (PSF) of the imaging camera [428] be the function $\rho : \mathbb{R}^2 \mapsto \mathbb{R}$.

If every point on the surface were visible, the rendered image $\mathbf{I}(\mathbf{x})$ would be defined by

$$\mathbf{I}(\mathbf{x}) = \int \rho(\mathbf{w}(\mathbf{u}) - \mathbf{x})\mathbf{C}(\mathbf{u})\mathrm{J}(\mathbf{u})d\mathbf{u} \qquad (27.1)$$

where $\mathrm{J}(\mathbf{u})$ is the determinant of the mapping Jacobian.

In practice, of course, parts of the surface are facing backward, or hidden by other surfaces, or self-occluded by the surface itself. We encapsulate all of these processes into an object-space visibility map $b(\mathbf{u})$, defined as

$$b(\mathbf{u}) = \begin{cases} 1 & \text{if } \mathbf{S}(\mathbf{u}) \text{ is visible} \\ 0 & \text{otherwise,} \end{cases} \qquad (27.2)$$

yielding the complete imaging function

$$\mathbf{I}(\mathbf{x}) = \int \rho(\mathbf{w}(\mathbf{u}) - \mathbf{x})\mathbf{C}(\mathbf{u})b(\mathbf{u})\mathrm{J}(\mathbf{u})d\mathbf{u}. \qquad (27.3)$$

This is a key step in deriving the new model: the link between b and the 3D geometry is relaxed. Essentially we will not enforce geometrically correct hidden surface relationships, thus simplifying the recovery of b from images, but the recovered b will nonetheless usefully encapsulate the occlusion geometry. Figure 27.2 illustrates this relaxed model. When recovering the model from video, a Markov random field prior on b will replace 3D occlusion reasoning to constrain and regularize the model. Conversely, fitting the model can return a $\mathbf{w}$ and b that are not consistent with any 3D geometry, but if the sequence is correctly rerendered by the returned parameters, many editing tasks will not suffer.

The first extension of the model is to sequences. The object's colors remain the same for each frame of video, but the mapping $\mathbf{w}$ and the visibility map b will change. Thus a video sequence of T frames $\{\mathbf{I}(\mathbf{x}, t)\}_{t=1}^{T}$ is defined by

$$\mathbf{I}(\mathbf{x}, t) = \int \rho(\mathbf{w}(\mathbf{u}, t) - \mathbf{x})\mathbf{C}(\mathbf{u})b(\mathbf{u}, t)\mathrm{J}(\mathbf{u}, t)d\mathbf{u}. \qquad (27.4)$$

Occlusion mask $[b(\mathbf{u},t)]_{\mathbf{u}}$ (modulating $\mathbf{C}$)	2D–2D mapping $[\mathbf{w}(\mathbf{u},t) - \mathbf{u}]_{\mathbf{u}}$ (modulated by b)	Image $[\mathbf{I}(\mathbf{x},t)]_{\mathbf{x}}$

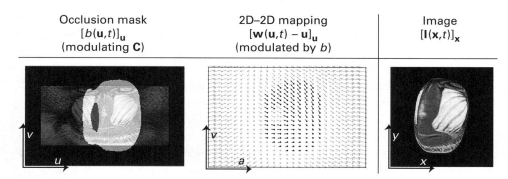

Figure 27.2
The image generation model. At each time t the model is parameterized by a binary visibility map $b(\mathbf{u}, t)$ (white overlay, left column) and the 2D–2D mapping $\mathbf{w}(\mathbf{u}, t)$ (center column). To aid visualization, the visibility map is shown modulating the latent image $\mathbf{C}(\mathbf{u})$ (which is constant throughout the sequence). The mapping $\mathbf{w}$ is represented by arrows showing how the texture map is warped to produce each image. Although only the values of $\mathbf{w}$ where b is nonzero are used in order to render each frame, we emphasize that $\mathbf{w}$ is defined for *all* values of $\mathbf{u}$ and t, and it is shown in gray for occluded surface points.

Figure 27.3
Reconstruction results, synthetic sequence. (Left) One frame from the synthetic sequence. (Middle) Point tracks extracted fom the sequence. (Right) The latent image recovered by embedding point tracks into 2D.

Now the *trajectory* of the point at parameter-space position $\mathbf{u}$ is the sequence of 2D points $\mathbf{w}(\mathbf{u}, :) = [\mathbf{w}(\mathbf{u}, 1); \mathbf{w}(\mathbf{u}, 2); \ldots; \mathbf{w}(\mathbf{u}, T)]$. Figure 27.3 shows the sparse trajectories acquired by tracking on the input images.

The final modification is to deal with multiple objects in the sequence. Let the number of surfaces (including the background) be L, with each object represented by the tuple of functions $(\mathbf{C}^l, \mathbf{w}^l, b^l)$. Image formation then becomes

$$\mathbf{I}(\mathbf{x}, t) = \sum_{l=1}^{L} \int \rho(\mathbf{w}^l(\mathbf{u}, t) - \mathbf{x})\mathbf{C}^l(\mathbf{u})b^l(\mathbf{u}, t)\mathbf{J}^l(\mathbf{u}, t)\mathrm{d}\mathbf{u} \tag{27.5}$$

where the visibility masks b are now encoding interobject occlusions as well as self-occlusions. Figure 27.2 illustrates the model.

27.2.1 Discrete Energy Formulation

The above description is in terms of continous functions $\mathbf{C}$, b, $\mathbf{w}$, and $\mathbf{I}$. In computation we adopt a discretization onto a regular grid. The images $\mathbf{I}(\mathbf{x}, t)$ are received in discrete form, as grids of size $W \times H$. We choose a discretization of the parameter space $\mathcal{Q}$ into a $w \times h$ grid, where w and h are chosen as described in section 27.3.1. For a sequence of T RGB frames, the variables to be recovered are then the $w \times h \times 3$ texture map $\mathbf{C}(\hat{\mathbf{u}})$, the $w \times h \times T \times 2$ mapping $\mathbf{w}(\hat{\mathbf{u}}, t)$, and the $w \times h \times T$ mask sequence $b(\hat{\mathbf{u}}, t)$.

The caret notation means that the indicated variable can take only integer values. The notation $\tilde{\mathbf{C}}$ will refer to the table of values $\{\mathbf{C}(\hat{u}, \hat{v}), \hat{u} \in 0..w, \hat{v} \in 0..h\}$. There is a rescaling of axes implicit in the (u, v) discretizations, as the unit square is mapped to a $w \times h$ rectangle, but we ignore this by redefining $\mathcal{Q}$ to be the rectangle $[0, w] \times [0, h]$ in the continuous domain. Any such reparameterization of the model does not affect the generated sequence.

The goal of this chapter is to recover the unknown variables $\tilde{\mathbf{C}}$, $\tilde{\mathbf{w}}$, and $\tilde{b}$ from the given data $\tilde{\mathbf{I}}$. At first sight this task seems poorly defined: if we assume w and h are approximately equal to W and H, the number of unknowns to be estimated is of the order of the video size: the images provide $3whT$ measurements, and the unknowns number $3wh + whT \times (2 \text{ scalars} + 1 \text{ bool})$. However, by casting the problem as energy minimization, the decomposition into color and motion allows strong regularizers to be placed on $\mathbf{C}$, $\mathbf{w}$, and b. The energy measures the accuracy with which the parameters explain the input frames, as well as the a priori plausibility of the parameters.

The energy, like the image generation process above, is naturally described in a continuous formulation, with conversion to discrete form involving a number of simple but tedious integrals. It may appear that some of the terms will be difficult to optimize, but the alternating optimization strategy presented in section 27.3 means that only a subset of the variables appears in each optimization step.

27.2.2 Data Cost

The first term in the energy is the data cost, encouraging the model to predict the input sequence, and in particular to explain every input image pixel. If the input frames are $\tilde{\mathbf{I}}(\hat{\mathbf{x}}, t)$, the basic form of the data cost is the sum

$$E_{\text{data}} = \sum_t \sum_{\hat{\mathbf{x}}} \|\tilde{\mathbf{I}}(\hat{\mathbf{x}}, t) - \mathbf{I}(\hat{\mathbf{x}}, t)\|_\tau. \tag{27.6}$$

The robust norm $\|e\|_\tau = \min(\|e\|, \tau)$ deals with outlier pixels due to lighting or small unmodeled occlusions.

This cost is a discrete sum over the point samples in $\tilde{\mathbf{I}}$ but contains a continuous integral in the evaluation of $\mathbf{I}(\hat{\mathbf{x}}, t)$. Evaluating the integral yields the discrete model

$$\mathbf{I}(\mathbf{x}, t) = \frac{\sum_{\hat{\mathbf{u}}} A(\hat{\mathbf{u}}, \mathbf{x}, t) b(\hat{\mathbf{u}}) \mathbf{C}(\hat{\mathbf{u}})}{\sum_{\hat{\mathbf{u}}} A(\hat{\mathbf{u}}, \mathbf{x}, t) b(\hat{\mathbf{u}})}, \tag{27.7}$$

where the weights $A(\hat{\mathbf{u}}, \mathbf{x}, t)$ are a function of the mapping $\mathbf{w}$, its Jacobian, and the PSF. They measure the contribution of each $\hat{\mathbf{u}}$ point to pixel $\mathbf{x}$, and will be zero at all but a few points $\hat{\mathbf{u}}$. The data cost is then

$$\sum_t \sum_{\hat{\mathbf{x}}} \left\| \tilde{\mathbf{I}}(\hat{\mathbf{x}}, t) - \frac{\sum_{\hat{\mathbf{u}}} A(\hat{\mathbf{u}}, \mathbf{x}, t) b(\hat{\mathbf{u}}) \mathbf{C}(\hat{\mathbf{u}})}{\sum_{\hat{\mathbf{u}}} A(\hat{\mathbf{u}}, \mathbf{x}, t) b(\hat{\mathbf{u}})} \right\|_\tau . \tag{27.8}$$

At points in the implementation we shall use an approximation to the correct integrals that is given by

$$A(\hat{\mathbf{u}}, \mathbf{x}, t) = \begin{cases} \mathrm{J}(\hat{\mathbf{u}}) & \text{for } \hat{\mathbf{u}} \in U(\mathbf{x}, t) \\ 0 & \text{otherwise} \end{cases} \tag{27.9}$$

where $U(\mathbf{x}, t)$ is the set of all texture map pixels that project to a given image pixel defined by $U(\mathbf{x}, t) = \{\hat{\mathbf{u}} | \rho(\mathbf{w}(\hat{\mathbf{u}}, t) - \mathbf{x}) > 0\}$, that is, "the points $\mathbf{u}$ that map to nonzero values of the point-spread function at $\mathbf{x}$."

27.2.3 Constraints

Simply minimizing the data term can yield a reconstruction that maps every latent pixel to a single image pixel. Thus we should restrict the search for models to those that explain every pixel. This is imposed as a soft penalty based on a "count of contributing pixels" $C(\mathbf{x}, t) = \sum_{\hat{\mathbf{u}} \in U(\mathbf{x}, t)} b(\hat{\mathbf{u}})$. This yields an energy term

$$\sum_t \sum_{\hat{\mathbf{x}}} \tau_c [C(\mathbf{x}, t) = 0] \tag{27.10}$$

where the threshold τ_c is a parameter of the algorithm, and the operator $[p]$ is 1 if p is true, and 0 otherwise. This formulation may then be tractably optimized using graph cut.

27.2.4 Mapping Smoothness

The mapping $\mathbf{w}$ is a proxy for the projection of a 3D surface that we assume to be undergoing smooth deformations over time. We might further assume a relatively smooth camera motion. However, these assumptions are not sufficient to ensure that $\mathbf{w}$ is smooth, so conventional smoothness terms, such as thin-plate splines, are not appropriate.

Instead, we wish to encourage the recovered texture map to be sampled such that each texture pixel is taken from the input frame in which it is most frontoparallel. Equivalently, the mapping is encouraged to be frontoparallel in at least one frame. Without camera roll or zoom this could be expressed as the energy

$$\sum_{\hat{\mathbf{u}}} \min_t \| \mathrm{J}(\hat{\mathbf{u}}) - \mathrm{I} \|_F^2 , \tag{27.11}$$

saying that, for each $\mathbf{u}$, the mapping Jacobian should be close to the identity (in Frobenius norm) in at least one frame. As written, it does not account for rotation about the camera optical center or zoom, so in practice we estimate an overall affine transformation for each frame, called H_t, and minimize

$$E_w = \sum_{\hat{\mathbf{u}}} \min_t \|J(\hat{\mathbf{u}}) - H_t\|_F^2. \tag{27.12}$$

Although this appears to offer no spatial smoothing, it can be argued that in combination with a temporal coherence term of the form

$$E_t = \sum_{\hat{\mathbf{u}},t} \|\mathbf{w}_t(\hat{\mathbf{u}}, t)\|^2, \tag{27.13}$$

it leads to a spatial regularizer akin to a weak membrane [54]. The compelling feature of this regularizer is that it leads to an excellent way to initialize the parameterization, as will be discussed in section 27.3.1.

27.2.5   Visibility Smoothness

We recall that the visibility map b is used to represent the effects of hidden surface removal without explicitly modeling the 3D geometry. Instead, we observe that discontinuities in b are rare, and define a Potts energy that counts discontinuities, as used in image segmentation [66]:

$$E_b = \sum_{(\hat{\mathbf{u}},\hat{\mathbf{u}}')\in\mathcal{N},t} [b(\hat{\mathbf{u}}, t) \neq b(\hat{\mathbf{u}}', t)] \tag{27.14}$$

where $\mathcal{N}$ is the set of 2×1 neighborhoods. A similar term is applied temporally, taking the mapping into account:

$$E_{bt} = \sum_{\hat{\mathbf{u}},t} [b(\hat{\mathbf{u}}, t) \neq b(\hat{\mathbf{u}} + \Delta\mathbf{u}(\hat{\mathbf{u}}, t), t)] \tag{27.15}$$

where $\Delta\mathbf{u}(\mathbf{u}, t) = J(\mathbf{u}, t)^{-1}(\mathbf{w}(\mathbf{u}, t+1) - \mathbf{w}(\mathbf{u}, t))$, using the Jacobian to convert local displacements in the image into displacements on the mosaic.

27.2.6   Texture Prior

A final regularizing term encourages the texture map $\tilde{\mathbf{C}}$ to have the same texture statistics as the input sequence. Following [528], we encourage neighboring pixels in the texture map to come from the same input image.

27.3 Minimizing the Energy

A linear combination of the above terms yields the overall energy. The energy is written as a function of the discrete variables $\tilde{\mathbf{C}}$, $\tilde{\mathbf{w}}$, $\tilde{b}$, giving $E(\tilde{\mathbf{C}}, \tilde{\mathbf{w}}, \tilde{b}) = E_{\text{data}}(\tilde{\mathbf{C}}, \tilde{\mathbf{w}}, \tilde{b}) + \lambda_1 E_{\text{w}}(\mathbf{w}) + \lambda_2 E_{\text{wt}}(\mathbf{w}) + \lambda_3 E_{\text{b}}(b) + \lambda_4 E_{\text{bt}}(b)$.

Minimizing the energy by alternation comprises two main steps. First, $\tilde{\mathbf{w}}$ is recovered by computing latent image coordinates $\mathbf{u}$ for sparse tracks to minimize $\lambda_1 E_{\text{w}}(\mathbf{w}) + \lambda_2 E_{\text{wt}}(\mathbf{w})$. Given $\tilde{\mathbf{w}}$, minimization with respect to $\tilde{\mathbf{C}}$ and $\tilde{b}$ yields a process closely related to panoramic stitching [7].

27.3.1 Finding $\tilde{\mathbf{w}}$: Reparameterization and Embedding

An important variable that does not appear as an explicit parameter of the energy functional relates to the parameterization of $\mathbf{u}$ space. The data cost E_{data} is—by construction—invariant to reparameterization, but the warp costs (27.12), (27.13) are not. It turns out that addressing this question leads to the crucial step in initializing the energy minimization, as we now show.

The initialization of the overall algorithm consists in obtaining sparse point tracks. The ith track is the set $\{\tilde{\mathbf{x}}(\mathbf{u}_i, t) \mid t \in T_i\}$ where T_i is the set of frame indices in which the point is tracked, and $\mathbf{u}_i$ is the *unknown* pre-image of the track in parameter space. Finding these $\mathbf{u}_i$ will anchor all other computations.

Finding the optimal parameterization then consists in assigning the $\mathbf{u}_i$ values such that the warp terms $E_{\text{w}}(\mathbf{w}) + E_{\text{wt}}(\mathbf{w})$ are minimized. For a given pair of tracks with coordinates $\mathbf{u}_i$ and $\mathbf{u}_j$, we wish to know the energy of the mapping that minimizes the regularizer subject to the mapping being consistent with the tracks. Specifically, we require the value of

$$\min_{\mathbf{w}} \quad E_{\text{w}}(\mathbf{w}) + E_{\text{wt}}(\mathbf{w})$$

$$\text{such that} \quad \mathbf{w}(\mathbf{u}_i, t) = \tilde{\mathbf{x}}(\mathbf{u}_i, t) \quad \forall t \in T_i \tag{27.16}$$

$$\mathbf{w}(\mathbf{u}_j, t) = \tilde{\mathbf{x}}(\mathbf{u}_j, t) \quad \forall t \in T_j.$$

Note that only the value of the minimizing energy is required, not the mapping itself. It can be shown that the minimal energy in the pairwise case, as a function of $\mathbf{u}_i$ and $\mathbf{u}_j$, is

$$\left(\frac{\| (\tilde{\mathbf{x}}(\mathbf{u}_i, t_{ij}^*) - \tilde{\mathbf{x}}(\mathbf{u}_j, t_{ij}^*)) - (\mathbf{u}_i - \mathbf{u}_j) \|}{\| \mathbf{u}_i - \mathbf{u}_j \|} \right)^2 \| \mathbf{u}_i - \mathbf{u}_j \| \tag{27.17}$$

where $t_{ij}^* = \underset{t \in T_i \cap T_j}{\operatorname{argmax}} \| \tilde{\mathbf{x}}(\mathbf{u}_i, t) - \tilde{\mathbf{x}}(\mathbf{u}_j, t) \|$.

Given several tracks as above, the $\mathbf{u}_i$ are chosen to minimize the sum of weighted distances

$$\sum_{ij} \| \mathbf{d}_{ij} - (\mathbf{u}_i - \mathbf{u}_j) \|^2 \frac{1}{\| \mathbf{u}_i - \mathbf{u}_j \|} \tag{27.18}$$

where $\mathbf{d}_{ij} := \tilde{\mathbf{x}}(\mathbf{u}_i, t_{ij}^*) - \tilde{\mathbf{x}}(\mathbf{u}_j, t_{ij}^*)$.

Note that this is analogous to embedding via multidimensional scaling [106], but with a distance weighting term $\frac{1}{\|\mathbf{u}_i - \mathbf{u}_j\|}$. The minimization is implemented as an iterated reweighted least squares problem [386]. In practice, to avoid numerical issues when $\mathbf{u}_i$ and $\mathbf{u}_j$ become close during optimization, we use an exponential weighting $\exp(-(\|\mathbf{u}_i - \mathbf{u}_j\|/\tau_3)^2)$. The affine transformation H_t is estimated from sparse tracks and applied before embedding.

The mosaic size is naturally selected by this process: because distances in (u, v) space are measured in pixels, and because pairs of points are encouraged to be as far apart as their longest separation in the input sequence, a simple bounding box of the recovered coordinates is ideally sized to store the model without loss of resolution.

27.3.2 Minimizing over w: Dense Mapping

Before optimizing for $\tilde{\mathbf{C}}$, it is necessary to obtain a dense mapping $\mathbf{w}$, which is obtained given the tracks and their embedding coordinates. In this case (27.16) is minimized with one constraint per track, and the resulting $\mathbf{w}$ can be shown in 1D to be a linear interpolation of the sparse track data. Although the 2D case has not, to our knowledge, been characterized, we assume an analogous situation and simply use MATLAB's `griddata` to interpolate. Although this unvalidated assumption means that there is no guarantee of minimizing the original energy, it is a simple matter to check that the overall energy has reduced at each iteration, and to reject iterations where the energy increases. Indeed, to adumbrate the discussion in [386], this is a useful general principle: energy minimization approaches are attractive because all the system tuning parameters are clearly defined and visible in the energy, but it is difficult to find closed-form minimizers for each energy component. However, using ad hoc optimizers, even when they may have their own tuning parameters, will affect only rate of convergence, not correctness, if reduction of the original energy is verified at each stage.

27.3.3 Minimizing over w and b: Dense Mapping with Occlusion

Given an initial approximation to $\mathbf{w}$ as above, we may solve simultaneously for b and a refined mapping. By solving for an update $\Delta\mathbf{w}$ to the initial estimate, the problem may be cast as one of optical flow computation. The minimization is now over all energy terms, since all terms depend on $\mathbf{w}$ and b.

The energy for the update is implemented as a variant of robust optical flow [77], alternating search for $\Delta\mathbf{w}$ and b on a multiresolution pyramid.

Let $\tilde{\mathbf{C}}$ be the current estimate of the texture map and let $\mathbf{w}^0$ be the current mapping estimate. Then we wish to determine the update $\Delta\mathbf{w}$ that minimizes

$$E_{\text{data}}(\Delta\mathbf{w}) = \sum_{\hat{\mathbf{u}}} b(\hat{\mathbf{u}}) \|\tilde{\mathbf{C}}(\hat{\mathbf{u}}) - \tilde{\mathbf{I}}(\mathbf{w}^0(\hat{\mathbf{u}}) + \Delta\mathbf{w}, t)\|^2 \qquad (27.19)$$

under the local regularizers

$$E_{\Delta\mathbf{w}} = \lambda_{\text{wl}} \sum_{\hat{\mathbf{u}}} \|\mathbf{w}_{uu}^0 + \Delta\mathbf{w}_{uu}\|^2 + \|\mathbf{w}_{vv}^0 + \Delta\mathbf{w}_{vv}\|^2, \qquad (27.20)$$

with E_b and E_{bt} as above. Linearizing (27.19) gives a linear system in $\Delta\mathbf{w}$ that is readily solved.

Temporal smoothness is imposed via a forward/backward implementation where the mapping $\mathbf{w}$ and the mask b of the previous frame are transformed to the coordinate system of the current frame, using the image domain optic flow between frames, and are added as a prior to the current estimate, as follows:

$$E_t = \sum_{\hat{\mathbf{u}}} \|\mathbf{w}_{\text{prev}}(\hat{\mathbf{u}}) - \mathbf{w}(\hat{\mathbf{u}})\|^2 + \|b_{\text{prev}}(\hat{\mathbf{u}}) - b(\hat{\mathbf{u}})\|^2.$$

27.3.4 Minimizing over C: Stitching

Given the mapping $\mathbf{w}$ and the occlusion mask b, we must solve for the texture map $\mathbf{C}$. Notice that only the E_{data} term of the energy depends on $\mathbf{C}$, so for fixed $\mathbf{w}$ and b, the minimization is simply $\mathbf{C} = \arg\min_{\mathbf{C}} E_{\text{data}}$. Minimization under the robust norm (27.8) can be cast as a graph cut problem by restricting the choice of $\mathbf{C}$. Specifically, an integer label $s(\hat{\mathbf{u}})$ is associated with each texture map pixel $\hat{\mathbf{u}}$, which indicates one of the input frames from which $\mathbf{C}(\hat{\mathbf{u}})$ is to be chosen. The input images are warped by the inverse of $\mathbf{w}$, to generate registered images $\mathbf{I}^w(\hat{\mathbf{u}}, t)$, from which $\mathbf{C}$ is optimized at any pixel $\hat{\mathbf{u}}$ by computing

$$s^* = \arg\min_s \sum_t \|\mathbf{I}^w(\hat{\mathbf{u}}, t) - \mathbf{I}^w(\hat{\mathbf{u}}, s)\|_\tau \qquad (27.21)$$

and setting $\mathbf{C} = \mathbf{I}^w(\hat{\mathbf{u}}, s^*)$. At this point it is easy to add a texture prior to the original energy, which encourages adjacent pixels in the texture map to be taken from the same input images, yielding an energy of the form

$$E(\tilde{s}) = \sum_{\hat{\mathbf{u}}} \sum_t \|\mathbf{I}^w(\hat{\mathbf{u}}, t) - \mathbf{I}^w(\hat{\mathbf{u}}, s(\hat{\mathbf{u}}))\|_\tau +$$

$$+ \lambda_{\text{texture}} \sum_{\{\hat{\mathbf{u}}, \hat{\mathbf{u}}'\} \in \mathcal{N}} \mu(\hat{\mathbf{u}}, \hat{\mathbf{u}}')[s(\hat{\mathbf{u}}) \neq s(\hat{\mathbf{u}}')] \qquad (27.22)$$

where $\mu(\cdot, \cdot)$ measures patch overlap as in [7].

27.3.5 Process Summary

One cycle of the above steps, beginning with the embedding, gives a reasonable mosaic that is improved slightly by one or two more iterations. Of course the above process offers no guarantee of globally minimizing the overall energy, and depends on the quality of the initial estimate of $\tilde{\mathbf{w}}$ produced in the first iteration of embedding. However, as the results below indicate, it has been found to work well on various sequence types. We hope that further research will yield better guarantees.

27.4 Results

In testing the algorithm a number of success criteria present themselves, but for video editing the primary criterion is obviously the range and quality of effects that are enabled by the model. As it is rather difficult to evaluate these on the printed page, the reader is referred to the accompanying video, which should be studied in conjunction with the text below. Computation times for all of these sequences are of the order of a few hours.

It is interesting to note that there is no concept of a "ground truth" model to be recovered, even with synthetic data. The synthetic sequence is generated by texture mapping a deforming 3D surface rendered over a static background. As shown in figure 27.2 the surface exhibits considerable self-occlusion, with about 30 percent of mosaic pixels visible in any one frame. There is also some more subtle self-occlusion near the nose. The texture coordinates obey a roughly equal area parameterization, but this does not constitute ground truth, because the minimum energy parameterization of the mosaic minimizes the rather different metric (27.12). We can, however, visually evaluate the recovered mosaic (figure 27.3), confirming that it is approximately a diffeomorphic reparameterization of the model texture map, with compression at the top and bottom, where the model was seen only obliquely, and some overall twists and warps. This is effectively a perfect result, as one would hope from a noiseless sequence, but also illustrates the expected performance of the model fitting.

The "Giraffe" and "Boy" sequences (figures 27.4 and 27.5, respectively) are more realistic tests of the method. The "Giraffe" sequence contains two layers. The background would easily succumb to conventional homography-based mosaic estimation, but it is interesting

Figure 27.4
Giraffe sequence. (Top) Several images from the sequence. (Bottom) The recovered mosaic for the background layer (including a static giraffe) and the foreground giraffe.

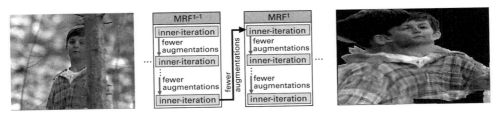

Figure 27.5
(Left) Two images from the "Boy" sequence. (Right) The recovered mosaic.

that the much less constrained embedding-based estimate produces a mosaic of essentially equivalent quality. The foreground layer contains a small amount of nonrigid 2D motion, as well as the turning head, which is correctly laid out in the mosaic. The "Boy" sequence shows a reasonable result (however, the ear is duplicated) on a more 3D object with occlusion.

27.5 Discussion

This chapter presents a new representation for deforming 3D objects in image sequences. Explicit 3D shape recovery is replaced by an essentially 2D process, yielding several advantages. The topology of the underlying 3D points is explicitly computed, whereas previous algorithms have either had to discover it as a postprocess, or have been limited to simple shapes such as quadrics and planes. It might be thought that the embedding would be unstable, especially given that more constrained models (such as factorization) have difficulties with the large amounts of missing data that self-occlusion causes. In practice, it is possibly the most robust component of the system, because the linear algorithm at its core scales to large amounts of data. This means that it may use all the information in the input tracks, particularly the information in the very many short tracks.

Acknowledgments

Discussions with many people contributed to the unwrap mosaics chapter. The work was developed over two internships at Microsoft Research Cambridge, first Pushmeet Kohli, then Alex Rav-Acha, and during that time the contributions of John Winn and Andrew Blake were particularly inspiring. The SIGGRAPH reviewers provided a healthy dose of scepticism which caused us to test the system on many more examples, greatly enhancing the paper.

Bibliography

[1] 2d3 Ltd. Boujou 4: The virtual interchangeable with the real, 2008. http://www.2d3.com.

[2] R. Adams and L. Bischof. Seeded region growing. *IEEE Trans. Pattern Analysis and Machine Intelligence*, 16(6):641–647, 1994.

[3] Adobe Systems Inc. *Adobe Photoshop User Guide*. 2002.

[4] S. Agarwal, M. K. Chandraker, F. Kahl, D. J. Kriegman, and S. Belongie. Practical global optimization for multiview geometry. In *Proc. European Conf. Computer Vision*, part 1, pages 592–605, 2006.

[5] S. Agarwal and D. Roth. Learning a sparse representation for object detection. In *Proc. 7th European Conf. Computer Vision*, part 4, pages 113–130, 2002.

[6] A. Agarwala, M. Agrawala, M. Cohen, D. Salesin, and R. Szeliski. Photographing long scenes with multiviewpoint panoramas. *Proc. ACM Siggraph*, 25(3):853–861, 2006.

[7] A. Agarwala, M. Dontcheva, M. Agrawala, S. Drucker, A. Colburn, B. Curless, D. Salesin, and M. Cohen. Interactive digital photomontage. *Proc. ACM Siggraph*, 23(3):294–302, 2004.

[8] A. Agarwala, C. Zheng, C. Pal, M. Agrawala, M. Cohen, B. Curless, D. Salesin, and R. Szeliski. Panoramic video textures. *Proc. ACM Siggraph*, 24(3):821–827, 2005.

[9] M. Agrawal and L. Davis. Window-based, discontinuity preserving stereo. In *Proc. IEEE Conf. Computer Vision and Pattern Recognition*, volume 6, pages 66–73, 2004.

[10] R. Ahuja, T. Magnanti, and J. Orlin. *Network Flows*. Prentice Hall, Englewood Cliffs, NJ, 1993.

[11] F. Alizadeh and A. V. Goldberg. Implementing the push-relabel method for the maximum flow problem on a connection machine. In *Network Flows and Matching*, pages 65–96, 1993.

[12] Y. Altun, I. Tsochantaridis, and T. Hofmann. Hidden Markov support vector machines. In *Proc. 20th Int. Conf. Machine Learning*, 2003.

[13] D. Amit. *Modeling Brain Function: The World of Attractor Neural Networks*. Cambridge University Press, 1992.

[14] D. Anguelov, B. Taskar, V. Chatalbashev, D. Koller, D. Gupta, G. Heitz, and A. Ng. Discriminative learning of Markov random fields for segmentation of 3D scan data. In *Proc. IEEE Conf. Computer Vision and Pattern Recognition*, volume 2, pages 169–176, 2005.

[15] G. Aronsson, M. G. Crandall, and P. Juutinen. A tour of the theory of absolutely minimizing functions. *Bulletin of the American Mathematical Society*, n.s. 41(4):439–505, 2004.

[16] S. Avidan. Ensemble tracking. *IEEE Trans. Pattern Analysis and Machine Intelligence*, 29(2):261–271, 2007.

[17] S. Avidan and A. Shamir. Seam carving for content-aware image resizing. *Proc. ACM Siggraph*, 26(3), 2007.

[18] X. Bai and G. Sapiro. A geodesic framework for fast interactive image and video segmentation and matting. In *Proc. 11th IEEE Int. Conf. Computer Vision*, pages 1–8, 2007.

[19] X. Bai and G. Sapiro. Geodesic matting: A framework for fast interactive image and video segmentation and matting. *Int. J. Computer Vision*, 82(2):113–132, 2009.

[20] S. Baker and T. Kanade. Limits on super-resolution and how to break them. *IEEE Trans. Pattern Analysis and Machine Intelligence*, 24(9):1167–1183, 2002.

[21] S. Baker, D. Scharstein, J. P. Lewis, S. Roth, M. J. Black, and R. Szeliski. A database and evaluation methodology for optical flow. In *Proc. 11th IEEE Int. Conf. Computer Vision*, pages 1–8, 2007.

[22] F. Barahona. On the computational complexity of Ising spin glass models. *J. Physics A: Mathematical and General*, 15(10):32–41, 1982.

[23] F. Barahona, M. Jünger, and G. Reinelt. Experiments in quadratic 0–1 programming. *Mathematical Programming*, 44:127–137, 1989.

[24] A. Barbu and S. C. Zhu. Graph partition by Swendsen-Wang cuts. In *Proc. 9th Int. Conf. Computer Vision*, volume 1, pages 320–327, 2003.

[25] A. Barbu and S. C. Zhu. Generalizing Swendsen-Wang to sampling arbitrary posterior probabilities. *IEEE Trans. Pattern Analysis and Machine Intelligence*, 27(8):1239–1253, 2005.

[26] S. Barnard. Stochastic stereo matching over scale. *Int. J. Computer Vision*, 3(1):17–32, 1989.

[27] P. N. Belhumeur. A Bayesian-approach to binocular stereopsis. *Int. J. Computer Vision*, 19(3):237–260, August 1996.

[28] S. Belongie, J. Malik, and J. Puzicha. Shape matching and object recognition using shape contexts. *IEEE Trans. Pattern Analysis and Machine Intelligence*, 24(4):509–522, 2002.

[29] J. L. Bentley. Multidimensional binary search trees used for associative searching. *Commun. ACM*, 18(9):509–517, 1975.

[30] A. Berg, T. Berg, and J. Malik. Shape matching and object recognition using low distortion correspondence. In *Proc. IEEE Conf. Computer Vision and Pattern Recognition*, volume, pages 26–33, 2005.

[31] J. Bergen, P. Burt, R. Hingorani, and S. Peleg. A three-frame algorithm for estimating two-component image motion. *IEEE Trans. Pattern Analysis and Machine Intelligence*, 14(9):886–896, 1992.

[32] J. Berger. *Statistical Decision Theory and Bayesian Analysis*, 2nd edition. Springer-Verlag, 1985.

[33] M. Bertalmío, G. Sapiro, V. Caselles, and C. Ballester. Image inpainting. In *Proc. ACM Siggraph*, pages 417–424, 2000.

[34] D. Bertismas and J. Tsitsiklis. *Introduction to Linear Optimization*. Athena Scientific, 1997.

[35] D. P. Bertsekas. *Nonlinear Programming*, 2nd edition. Athena Scientific, 1999.

[36] D. P. Bertsekas. *Dynamic Programming and Optimal Control*, 2nd edition. Athena Scientific, 2000.

[37] J. Besag. Statistical analysis of non-lattice data. *The Statistician*, 24(3):179–195, 1975.

[38] J. Besag. On the statistical analysis of dirty pictures. *J. Royal Statistical Society B*, 48(3):259–302, 1986.

[39] A. Besbes, N. Komodakis, G. Langs, and N. Paragios. Shape priors and discrete MRFs for knowledge-based segmentation. In *Proc. IEEE Conf. Computer Vision and Pattern Recognition*, pages 1295–1302, 2009.

[40] P. Bhat, C. L. Zitnick, N. Snavely, A. Agarwala, M. Agrawala, M. Cohen, B. Curless, and S. B. Kang. Using photographs to enhance videos of a static scene. In *Proc. Eurographics Symposium on Rendering*, pages 327–333, 2007.

[41] A. Billionnet and M. Minoux. Maximizing a supermodular pseudo-Boolean function: A polynomial algorithm for supermodular cubic functions. *Discrete Applied Mathematics*, 12(1):1–11, 1985.

[42] S. Birchfield. *Depth and Motion Discontinuities*. Ph.D. thesis, Stanford University, 1999.

[43] S. Birchfield, B. Natarjan, and C. Tomasi. Correspondence as energy-based segmentation. *Image and Vision Computing*, 25(8):1329–1340, 2007.

[44] S. Birchfield and C. Tomasi. A pixel dissimilarity measure that is insensitive to image sampling. *IEEE Trans. Pattern Analysis and Machine Intelligence*, 20(4):401–406, 1998.

[45] S. Birchfield and C. Tomasi. Multiway cut for stereo and motion with slanted surfaces. In *Proc. 7th Int. Conf. Computer Vision*, pages 489–495, 1999.

[46] C. Bishop. *Pattern Recognition and Machine Learning*. Springer, 2006.

[47] M. Black and A. Rangarajan. On the unification of line processes, outlier rejection, and robust statistics with applications in early vision. *Int. J. Computer Vision*, 19(1):57–91, 1996.

[48] M. J. Black and P. Anandan. The robust estimation of multiple motions: Parametric and piecewise-smooth flow fields. *Computer Vision and Image Understanding*, 63(1):75–104, January 1996.

[49] A. Blake. Comparison of the efficiency of deterministic and stochastic algorithms for visual reconstruction. *IEEE Trans. Pattern Analysis and Machine Intelligence*, 11(1):2–12, 1989.

[50] A. Blake, R. Curwen, and A. Zisserman. Affine-invariant contour tracking with automatic control of spatio-temporal scale. In *Proc. Int. Conf. Computer Vision*, pages 66–75, 1993.

[51] A. Blake and M. Isard. *Active Contours*. Springer-Verlag, 1998.

[52] A. Blake, C. Rother, and P. Anandan. Foreground extraction using iterated graph cuts. U.S. patent 7660463 (filing date 2004), 2009.

[53] A. Blake, C. Rother, M. Brown, P. Perez, and P. Torr. Interactive image segmentation using an adaptive GMMRF model. In *Proc. European Conf. Computer Vision*, volume 1, pages 428–441. Springer-Verlag, 2004.

[54] A. Blake and A. Zisserman. *Visual Reconstruction*. MIT Press, 1987.

[55] M. Blaschko and C. Lampert. Learning to localize objects with structured output regression. In *Proc. European Conf. Computer Vision*, part 1, pages 2–15, 2008.

[56] M. Bleyer and M. Gelautz. A layered stereo algorithm using image segmentation and global visibility constraints. In *Proc. Int. Conf. Image Processing*, volume 5, pages 2997–3000, 2004.

[57] M. Bleyer, C. Rother, and P. Kohli. Surface stereo with soft segmentation. In *Proc. IEEE Conf. Computer Vision and Pattern Recognition*, 2010.

[58] A. F. Bobick and S. S. Intille. Large occlusion stereo. *Int. J. Computer Vision*, 33(3):181–200, 1999.

[59] J. S. De Bonet. Multiresolution sampling procedure for analysis and synthesis of texture images. In *Proc. ACM Siggraph*, pages 361–368, 1997.

[60] E. Borenstein and J. Malik. Shape guided object segmentation. In *Proc. IEEE Conf. Computer Vision and Pattern Recognition*, pages 969–976, 2006.

[61] E. Boros and P. Hammer. Pseudo-Boolean optimization. *Discrete Applied Mathematics*, 123(1–3):155–225, 2002.

[62] E. Boros, P. L. Hammer, and X. Sun. Network flows and minimization of quadratic pseudo-Boolean functions. Technical Report RRR 17–1991, RUTCOR, May 1991.

[63] E. Boros, P. L. Hammer, and G. Tavares. Preprocessing of unconstrained quadratic binary optimization. Technical Report RRR 10–2006, RUTCOR, 2006.

[64] S. Boyd and L. Vandenberghe. *Convex Optimization*. Cambridge University Press, 2004.

[65] Y. Boykov and M.-P. Jolly. Interactive organ segmentation using graph cuts. In *Proc. Medical Image Computing and Computer-Assisted Intervention*, pages 276–286, 2000.

[66] Y. Boykov and M.-P. Jolly. Interactive graph cuts for optimal boundary and region segmentation of objects in n-d images. In *Proc. Int. Conf. Computer Vision*, volume 1, pages 105–112, 2001.

[67] Y. Boykov and V. Kolmogorov. Computing geodesics and minimal surfaces via graph cuts. In *Proc. 9th Int. Conf. Computer Vision*, volume 2, pages 26–33, 2003.

[68] Y. Boykov and V. Kolmogorov. An experimental comparison of min-cut/max-flow algorithms for energy minimization in vision. *IEEE Trans. Pattern Analysis and Machine Intelligence*, 26(9):1124–1137, September 2004.

[69] Y. Boykov and O. Veksler. Graph cuts in vision and graphics: Theories and applications. In N. Paragios, Y. Chen, and O. Faugeras, editors, *Handbook of Mathematical Models in Computer Vision*, pages 79–96. Springer-Verlag, 2006.

[70] Y. Boykov, O. Veksler, and R. Zabih. Markov random fields with efficient approximations. In *Proc. Conf. Computer Vision and Pattern Recognition*, pages 648–655, 1998.

[71] Y. Boykov, O. Veksler, and R. Zabih. Fast approximate energy minimization via graph cuts. In *Proc. Int. Conf. Computer Vision*, volume 1, pages 377–384, 1999.

[72] Y. Boykov, O. Veksler, and R. Zabih. Fast approximate energy minimization via graph cuts. *IEEE Trans. Pattern Analysis and Machine Intelligence*, 23(11):1222–1239, 2001.

[73] M. Brand. Morphable 3D models from video. In *Proc. IEEE Conf. Computer Vision and Pattern Recognition*, volume 2, pages 456–463, 2001.

[74] M. Bray, P. Kohli, and P. H. S. Torr. Posecut: Simultaneous segmentation and 3D pose estimation of humans using dynamic graph-cuts. In *Proc. European Conf. Computer Vision*, pages 642–655, 2006.

[75] C. Bregler, A. Hertzmann, and H. Biermann. Recovering non-rigid 3D shape from image streams. In *Proc. IEEE Conf. Computer Vision and Pattern Recognition*, volume 2, pages 690–696, 2000.

[76] X. Bresson, S. Esedoglu, P. Vandergheynst, J.-P. Thiran, and S. Osher. Fast global minimization of the active contour/snake model. *J. Mathematical Imaging and Vision*, 28(2):151–167, 2007.

[77] T. Brox, A. Bruhn, N. Papenberg, and J. Weickert. High accuracy optical flow estimation based on a theory for warping. In *Proc. 8th European Conf. Computer Vision*, pages 25–36, 2004.

[78] A. Bruhn, J. Weickert, and C. Schnörr. Lucas/Kanade meets Horn/Schunck: Combining local and global optical flow methods. *Int. J. Computer Vision*, 61(3):211–231, 2005.

[79] A. Buades, B. Coll, and J.-M. Morel. A review of image denoising algorithms, with a new one. *SIAM Multiscale Modeling and Simulation*, 4(2):490–530, 2005.

[80] C. Buehler, S. J. Gortler, M. F. Cohen, and L. McMillan. Minimal surfaces for stereo. In *Proc. 7th European Conf. Computer Vision*, pages 885–899, 2002.

[81] D. Cai, X. He, Y. Hu, J. Han, and T. Huang. Learning a spatially smooth subspace for face recognition. In *Proc. IEEE Conf. Computer Vision and Pattern Recognition*, pages 1–9, 2007.

[82] P. Carr and R. Hartley. Solving multilabel graph cut problems with multilabel swap. In *Digital Image Computing: Techniques and Applications*, pages 532–539, 2009.

[83] M. E. Carreira-Perpignan and G. E. Hinton. On contrastive divergence learning. In *Proc. 10th Int. Work. Artificial Intelligence and Statistics*, pages 33–40, 2005.

[84] V. Caselles, R. Kimmel, and G. Sapiro. Geodesic active contours. In *Proc. 5th Int. Conf. Computer Vision*, pages 694–699, 1995.

[85] A. Chambolle. Total variation minimization and a class of binary MRF models. In *Energy Minimization Methods in Computer Vision and Pattern Recognition*, pages 136–152, 2005.

[86] A. Chambolle, D. Cremers, and T. Pock. A convex approach for computing minimal partitions. Technical report, Ecole Polytechnique, Paris, 2008.

[87] T. Chan, S. Esedoglu, and M. Nikolova. Algorithms for finding global minimizers of image segmentation and denoising models. *SIAM J. Applied Mathematics*, 66(5):1632–1648, 2006.

[88] T. F. Chan and L. A. Vese. Active contours without edges. *IEEE Trans. Image Processing*, 10(2):266–277, 2001.

[89] P. Charbonnier, G. Aubert, L. Blanc-Féraud, and M. Barlaud. Deterministic edge-preserving regularization in computed imaging. *IEEE Trans. Image Processing*, 6(2):298–315, 1997.

[90] C. Chekuri, S. Khanna, J. Naor, and L. Zosin. Approximation algorithms for the metric labelling problem via a new linear programming formulation. In *Proc. 12th Anne ACM-SIAM Symp. Discrete Algorithms*, pages 109–118, 2001.

[91] A. Choi and A. Darwiche. A variational approach for approximating Bayesian networks by edge deletion. In *Proc. 22nd Conf. Uncertainty in Artificial Intelligence*, pages 80–89, 2006.

[92] S. Chopra and M. R. Rao. The partition problem. *Journal of Mathematical Programming* 59:87–115, 1993.

[93] P. Chou and C. Brown. The theory and practice of Bayesian image labeling. *Int. J. Computer Vision*, 4(3):185–210, 1990.

[94] Y.-Y. Chuang, A. Agarwala, B. Curless, D. H. Salesin, and R. Szeliski. Video matting of complex scenes. In *Proc. ACM SIGGRAPH*, 21(3):243–248, 2002.

[95] Y.-Y. Chuang, B. Curless, D. H. Salesin, and R. Szeliski. A Bayesian approach to digital matting. In *Proc. IEEE Conf. Computer Vision and Pattern Recognition*, volume 2, pages 264–271, 2001.

[96] H. Chui and A. Rangarajan. A new point matching algorithm for non-rigid registration. *Computer Vision and Image Understanding*, 89(2–3):114–141, 2003.

[97] J. Clausen. Branch and bound algorithms—principles and examples. In *Parallel Computing in Optimization*. Prentice-Hall, 1997.

[98] P. Clifford. Markov random fields in statistics. In G. Grimmett and D. Welsh, editors, *Disorder in Physical Systems: A Volume in Honour of John M. Hammersley*, pages 19–32. Oxford University Press, 1990.

[99] M. Collins. Discriminative training methods for hidden Markov models: Theory and experiments with perceptron algorithms. In *Proc. ACL-02 Conf. Empirical Methods in Natural Language Processing*, pages 1–8, 2002.

[100] D. Comaniciu and P. Meer. Mean shift: A robust approach toward feature space analysis. *IEEE Trans. Pattern Analysis and Machine Intelligence*, 24(5):603–619, 2002.

[101] W. J. Cook, W. H. Cunningham, W. R. Pulleyblank, and A. Schrijver. *Combinatorial Optimization*. Wiley-Interscience, 1998.

[102] J. Coughlan and S. Ferreira. Finding deformable shapes using loopy belief propagation. In *Proc. 7th European Conf. Computer Vision*, part 3, pages 453–468, 2002.

[103] J. Coughlan and H. Shen. Shape matching with belief propagation: Using dynamic quantization to accommodate occlusion and clutter. In *Proc. IEEE Conf. Computer Vision and Pattern Recognition Workshop*, volume 12, page 180, 2004.

[104] R. G. Cowell, A. P. Dawid, S. L. Lauritzen, and D. J. Spiegelhalter. *Probabilistic Networks and Expert Systems*. Springer, 1999.

[105] I. J. Cox, S. L. Hingorani, S. B. Rao, and B. M. Maggs. A maximum likelihood stereo algorithm. *Computer Vision and Image Understanding*, 63(3):542–567, 1996.

[106] T. F. Cox and M. A. A. Cox. *Multidimensional Scaling*, 2nd edition. Chapman and Hall, 2001.

[107] D. Crandall, P. Felzenszwalb, and D. Huttenlocher. Spatial priors for part-based recognition using statistical models. In *Proc. IEEE Conf. Computer Vision and Pattern Recognition*, volume 1, pages 10–17, 2005.

[108] D. Cremers, S. Osher, and S. Soatto. Kernel density estimation and intrinsic alignment for shape priors in level set segmentation. *Int. J. Computer Vision*, 69(3):335–351, 2006.

[109] D. Cremers, M. Rousson, and R. Deriche. A review of statistical approaches to level set segmentation: Integrating color, texture, motion and shape. *Int. J. Computer Vision*, 72(2):195–215, 2007.

[110] D. Cremers, F. R. Schmidt, and F. Barthel. Shape priors in variational image segmentation: Convexity, Lipschitz continuity and globally optimal solutions. In *Proc. IEEE Conf. Computer Vision and Pattern Recognition*, pages 1–6, 2008.

[111] D. Cremers, F. Tischhäuser, J. Weickert, and C. Schnorr. Diffusion snakes: Introducing statistical shape knowledge into the Mumford–Shah functional. *Int. J. Computer Vision*, 50(3):295–313, 2002.

[112] A. Criminisi, G. Cross, A. Blake, and V. Kolmogorov. Bilayer segmentation of live video. In *Proc. IEEE Conf. Computer Vision and Pattern Recognition*, pages 53–60, 2006.

[113] T. S. Criminisi T. Sharp, and A. Blake. GeoS: Geodesic image segmentation. In *Proc. European Conf. Computer Vision*, pages 99–112, 2008.

[114] P. Dagum and M. Luby. Aproximating probabilistic inference in Bayesian networks is NP hard. *Artificial Intelligence*, 60(1):141–153, 1993.

[115] N. Dalal and B. Triggs. Histograms of oriented gradients for human detection. In *Proc. IEEE Conf. Computer Vision and Pattern Recognition*, volume 10, pages 886–893, 2005.

[116] J. Darbon. Global optimization for first order Markov random fields with submodular priors. In *Proc. 12th Int. Workshop on Combinatorial Image Analysis*, 2008.

[117] J. Darbon and M. Sigelle. Image restoration with discrete constrained total variation. Part I: Fast and exact optimization. *J. Mathematical Imaging and Vision*, 26(3):261–276, 2006.

[118] P. E. Debevec, C. J. Taylor, and J. Malik. Modeling and rendering architecture from photographs. In *Proc. ACM Siggraph*, pages 11–20, 1996.

[119] J. DeLeeuw. Applications of convex analysis to multidimensional scaling. In J. R. Barra et al., editors, *Recent Developments in Statistics*, pages 133–146, 1977.

[120] A. Delong and Y. Boykov. A scalable graph-cut algorithm for N-D grids. In *Proc. IEEE Conf. Computer Vision and Pattern Recognition*, 2008.

[121] A. P. Dempster, N. M. Laird, and D. B. Rubin. Maximum likelihood from incomplete data via the EM algorithm. *J. Royal Statistical Society, B*, 39(1):1–38, 1977.

[122] C. Desai, D. Ramanan, and C. Fowlkes. Discriminative models for multi-class object layout. In *Proc. 12th IEEE Int. Conf. Computer Vision*, pages 229–236, 2009.

[123] T. Deschamps and L. D. Cohen. Fast extraction of minimal paths in 3D images and applications to virtual endoscopy. *Medical Image Analysis*, 5(4):281–299, 2001.

[124] J. Deutscher, A. Blake, and I. Reid. Articulated body motion capture by annealed particle filtering. In *Proc. IEEE Conf. Computer Vision and Pattern Recognition*, volume 2, pages 21–26, 2000.

[125] M. M. Deza and M. Laurent. *Geometry of Cuts and Metrics*. Springer-Verlag, 1997.

[126] E. A. Dinic. Algorithm for solution of a problem of maximum flow in networks with power estimation. *Soviet Math. Dokl.*, 11:1277–1280, 1970.

[127] C. Do, C.-S. Foo, and A. Ng. Efficient multiple hyperparameter learning for log-linear models. In J. Platt, D. Koller, Y. Singer, and S. Roweis, editors, *Advances in Neural Information Processing Systems volume 20*, pages 377–384. MIT Press, Cambridge, MA, 2007.

[128] C. Domb and M. S. Green, editors. *Phase Transitions and Critical Phenomena*, volume 1. Academic Press, London, 1972.

[129] O. Duchenne, J.-Y. Audibert, R. Keriven, J. Ponce, and F. Ségonne. Segmentation by transduction. In *Proc. IEEE Conf. Computer Vision and Pattern Recognition*, 2008.

[130] R. O. Duda and P. E. Hart. *Pattern Classification and Scene Analysis*. John Wiley & Sons, 1973.

[131] R. Durbin, R. Szeliski, and A. L. Yuille. An analysis of an elastic net approach to the travelling salesman problem. *Neural Computation*, 1:348–358, 1989.

[132] A. Efros and W. Freeman. Image quilting for texture synthesis and transfer. In *Proc. ACM Siggraph*, pages 341–346, 2001.

[133] A. Efros and T. Leung. Texture synthesis by non-parametric sampling. In *Proc. IEEE Int. Conf. Computer Vision*, pages 1033–1038, 1999.

[134] G. Egnal and R. Wildes. Detecting binocular half-occlusions: Empirical comparisons of five approaches. *IEEE Trans. Pattern Analysis and Machine Intelligence*, 24(8):1127–1133, 2002.

[135] R. Fattal. Image up-sampling via imposed edges statistics. In *Proc. ACM Siggraph*, pages 95–102, 2007.

[136] O. Faugeras and R. Keriven. Variational principles, surface evolution, PDE's, level set methods, and the stereo problem. *IEEE Trans. Image Processing*, 7(3):336–344, 1998.

[137] J. Feldman, D. Karger, and M. J. Wainwright. LP decoding. In *Proc. 41st Ann. Allerton Conference on Communication, Control, and Computing*, 2003.

[138] P. Felzenszwalb and D. Huttenlocher. Efficient graph-based image segmentation. *Int. J. Computer Vision*, 59(2):167–181, 2004.

[139] P. Felzenszwalb, D. McAllester, and D. Ramanan. A discriminatively trained, multiscale, deformable part model. In *Proc. IEEE Conf. Computer Vision and Pattern Recognition*, 2008.

[140] P. F. Felzenszwalb and D. P. Huttenlocher. Pictorial structures for object recognition. *Int. J. Computer Vision*, 61(1):55–79, 2005.

[141] P. F. Felzenszwalb and D. P. Huttenlocher. Efficient belief propagation for early vision. *Int. J. Computer Vision*, 70(1):41–54, 2006.

[142] R. Fergus, P. Perona, and A. Zisserman. Object class recognition by unsupervised scale-invariant learning. In *Proc. IEEE Conf. Computer Vision and Pattern Recognition*, volume 2, pages 264–271, 2003.

[143] M. A. T. Figueiredo. Bayesian image segmentation using Gaussian field priors. In *Proc. Conf. Energy Minimization Methods in Computer Vision and Pattern Recognition*, pages 74–89, 2005.

[144] T. Finley and T. Joachims. Training structural SVMs when exact inference is intractable. In *Proc. 25th Int. Conf. Machine Learning*, pages 304–311, 2008.

[145] A. Fitzgibbon, Y. Wexler, and A. Zisserman. Image-based rendering using image-based priors. In *Proc. 9th IEEE Int. Conf. Computer Vision*, volume 2, pages 1176–1183, 2003.

[146] L. Ford and D. Fulkerson. *Flows in Networks*. Princeton University Press, 1962.

[147] D. Freedman and P. Drineas. Energy minimization via graph cuts: Settling what is possible. In *Proc. IEEE Conf. Computer Vision and Pattern Recognition*, volume 2, pages 939–946, 2005.

[148] D. Freedman and T. Zhang. Interactive graph cut based segmentation with shape priors. In *Proc. IEEE Conf. Computer Vision and Pattern Recognition*, volume 1, pages 755–762, 2005.

[149] W. T. Freeman and E. H. Adelson. The design and use of steerable filters. *IEEE Trans. Pattern Analysis and Machine Intelligence*, 13(9):891–906, September 1991.

[150] W. T. Freeman, E. C. Pasztor, and O. T. Carmichael. Learning low-level vision. *Int. J. Computer Vision*, 40(1):25–47, 2000.

[151] W. T. Freeman, J. B. Tenenbaum, and E. C. Pasztor. Learning style translation for the lines of a drawing. *Proc. ACM Siggraph*, 22:33–46, 2003.

[152] B. J. Frey, N. Jojic, and A. Kannan. Learning appearance and transparency manifolds of occluded objects in layers. In *Proc. IEEE Conf. Computer Vision and Pattern Recognition*, volume 1, pages 45–52, 2003.

[153] B. J. Frey, R. Koetter, and N. Petrovic. Very loopy belief propagation for unwrapping phase images. In *Neural Information Processing Systems*, volume 14. MIT Press, 2002.

[154] B. J. Frey and D. Mackay. A revolution: Belief propagation in graphs with cycles. In *Neural Information Processing Systems*, volume 10, pages 479–485, 1997.

[155] S. Fujishige. *Submodular Functions and Optimization*. North-Holland, Amsterdam, 1991.

[156] M. R. Garey and D. S. Johnson. *Computers and Intractability*. W. H. Freeman, San Francisco, 1979.

[157] D. Gavrila and V. Philomin. Real-time object detection for "smart" vehicles. In *Proc. 7th IEEE Int. Conf. Computer Vision*, volume 1, pages 87–93, 1999.

[158] D. Geiger, B. Ladendorf, and A. Yuille. Occlusions and binocular stereo. *Int. J. Computer Vision*, 14:211–226, 1995.

[159] D. Geiger and A. L. Yuille. A common framework for image segmentation. *Int. J. Computer Vision*, 6(3):227–243, 1991.

[160] D. Geman and G. Reynolds. Constrained restoration and the recovery of discontinuities. *IEEE Trans. Pattern Analysis and Machine Intelligence*, 14(3):367–383, 1992.

[161] S. Geman and D. Geman. Stochastic relaxation, Gibbs distributions, and the Bayesian restoration of images. *IEEE Trans. Pattern Analysis and Machine Intelligence*, 6(6):721–741, 1984.

[162] S. Geman and C. Graffigne. Markov random field image models and their applications to computer vision. In *Proc. Int. Cong. Mathematicians*, pages 1496–1517, 1986.

[163] C. J. Geyer. Markov chain Monte Carlo maximum likelihood. In *Computer Science and Statistics. Proc. 23rd Symp. on the Interface*, pages 156–163, 1991.

[164] J. Gil and M. Werman. Computing 2-D min, median, and max filters. *IEEE Trans. Pattern Analysis and Machine Intelligence*, 15(5):504–507, 1993.

[165] W. Gilks, S. Richardson, and D. Spiegelhalter. *Markov Chain Monte Carlo in Practice*. Chapman and Hall, 1996.

[166] T. Gisy. *Image Inpainting Based on Natural Image Statistics*. Diplom thesis, Eidgenössische Technische Hochschule, Zürich, Switzerland, September 2005.

[167] D. Glasner, S. Bagon, and M. Irani. Super-resolution from a single image. In *Proc. IEEE Int. Conf. Computer Vision*, 2009.

[168] B. Glocker, N. Komodakis, G. Tziritas, N. Navab, and N. Paragios. Dense image registration through MRFs and efficient linear programming. *Medical Image Analysis*, 12:731–741, 2008.

[169] M. Goemans and D. Williamson. Improved approximation algorithms for maximum cut and satisfiability problems using semidefinite programming. *J. Association for Computing Machinery*, 42(6):1115–1145, 1995.

[170] A. V. Goldberg. *Efficient Graph Algorithms for Sequential and Parallel Computers*. Ph.D. thesis, MIT, January 1987.

[171] A. V. Goldberg and R. E. Tarjan. A new approach to the maximum-flow problem. *J. Association for Computing Machinery*, 35(4):921–940, October 1988.

[172] R. Gonzalez and P. Wintz. *Digital Image Processing*. Addison-Wesley, 1987.

[173] S. Gould, F. Amat, and D. Koller. Alphabet soup: A framework for approximate energy minimization. In *Proc. IEEE Conf. Computer Vision and Pattern Recognition*, pages 903–910, 2009.

[174] L. Grady. Multilabel random walker image segmentation using prior models. In *Proc. IEEE Conf. Computer Vision and Pattern Recognition*, volume 1, pages 763–770, 2005.

[175] L. Grady. Random walks for image segmentation. *IEEE Trans. Pattern Analysis and Machine Intelligence*, 28(11):1768–1783, 2006.

[176] D. Greig, B. Porteous, and A. Seheult. Exact maximum a posteriori estimation for binary images. *J. Royal Statistical Society, B*, 51(2):271–279, 1989.

[177] X. Gu, S. J. Gortler, and H. Hoppe. Geometry images. *Proc. ACM Siggraph*, pages 355–361, 2002.

[178] V. Gulshan, C. Rother, A. Criminisi, A. Blake, and A. Zisserman. Geodesic star convexity for interactive image segmentation. In *Proc. IEEE Conf. Computer Vision and Pattern Recognition*, 2010.

[179] P. L. Hammer. Some network flow problems solved with pseudo-Boolean programming. *Operations Research*, 13:388–399, 1965.

[180] D. K. Hammond and E. P. Simoncelli. Image denoising with an orientation-adaptive Gaussian scale mixture model. In *Proc. IEEE Int. Conf. Image Processing*, pages 1433–1436, 2006.

[181] X. Han, C. Xu, and J. L. Prince. A topology preserving level set method for geometric deformable models. *IEEE Trans. Pattern Analysis and Machine Intelligence*, 25(6):755–768, 2003.

[182] R. Hartley and A. Zisserman. *Multiple View Geometry in Computer Vision*, 2nd edition. Cambridge University Press, 2004.

[183] J. Hays and A. A. Efros. Scene completion using millions of photographs. *Proc. ACM Siggraph*, 26(3), 2007.

[184] T. Hazan and A. Shashua. Convergent message-passing algorithms for inference over general graphs with convex free energies. In *Proc. 24th Ann. Conf. Uncertainty in Artificial Intelligence*, pages 264–273, 2008.

[185] X. He, R. Zemel, and D. Ray. Learning and incorporating top-down cues in image segmentation. In *Proc. European Conf. Computer Vision*, pages 338–351, 2006.

[186] X. He, R. S. Zemel, and M. A. Carreira-Perpiñán. Multiscale conditional random fields for image labeling. In *Proc. IEEE Conf. Computer Vision and Pattern Recognition*, volume 2, pages 695–702, 2004.

[187] D. J. Heeger and J. R. Bergen. Pyramid-based texture analysis/synthesis. In *Proc. ACM Siggraph*, pages 229–236, 1995.

[188] M. R. Henzinger, P. Klein, S. Rao, and S. Subramanian. Faster shortest-path algorithms for planar graphs. *J. Computer and System Sciences*, 55:3–23, 1997.

[189] J. Hertz, K. A., A. Krogh, and P. R. Palmer. *Introduction to the Theory of Neural Computation*, volume 1. Westview, 1991.

[190] T. Heskes. Convexity arguments for efficient minimization of the Bethe and Kikuchi free energies. *J. Artificial Intelligence Research*, 26:153–190, 2006.

[191] T. Heskes, K. Albers, and B. Kappen. Approximate inference and constrained optimization. In *Proc. 19th Conf. Uncertainty in Artificial Intelligence*, pages 313–320, 2003.

[192] G. E. Hinton. Products of experts. In *Proc. 19th Int. Conf. Artificial Neural Networks*, volume 1, pages 1–6, 1999.

[193] G. E. Hinton. Training products of experts by minimizing contrastive divergence. *Neural Computation*, 14(8):1771–1800, 2002.

[194] D. S. Hochbaum, editor. *Approximation Algorithms for NP-Hard Problems*. PWS Publishing Co., 1996.

[195] D. S. Hochbaum. The pseudoflow algorithm for the maximum flow problem. Manuscript, UC Berkeley, 2002, revised 2003. Extended abstract in The pseudoflow algorithm and the pseudoflow-based simplex for the maximum flow problem. In *Proc. IPCO98*, pages 325–337, June 1998.

[196] D. Hoiem, A. Efros, and M. Hebert. Automatic photo pop-up. *Proc. ACM Siggraph*, 24(3):577–584, 2005.

[197] D. Hoiem, A. Efros, and M. Hebert. Geometric context from a single image. In *Proc. IEEE Int. Conf. Computer Vision*, volume 1, pages 654–661, 2005.

[198] D. Hoiem, C. Rother, and J. Winn. 3D Layout CRF for multi-view object class recognition and segmentation. In *Proc. 11th IEEE Conf. Computer Vision and Pattern Recognition*, pages 1–8, 2007.

[199] D. Hoiem, A. Stein, A. A. Efros, and M. Hebert. Recovering occlusion boundaries from a single image. In *Proc. 11th IEEE Int. Conf. Computer Vision*, pages 1–8, 2007.

[200] L. Hong and G. Chen. Segment-based stereo matching using graph cuts. *Proc. IEEE Conf. Computer Vision and Pattern Recognition*, volume 1, pages 74–81, 2004.

[201] J. J. Hopfield and D. W. Tank. Neural computation of decisions in optimization problems. *Biological Cybernetics*, 52(3):141–152, 1985.

[202] B. K. P. Horn and B. Schunck. Determining optical flow. *Artificial Intelligence*, 17:185–203, 1981.

[203] http://research.microsoft.com/en-us/projects/i3l/default.aspx.

[204] J. Huang and D. Mumford. Statistics of natural images and models. In *Proc. IEEE Conf. Computer Vision and Pattern Recognition*, pages 1541–1547, 1999.

[205] A. Hyvärinen. Estimation of non-normalized statistical models by score matching. *J. Machine Learning Research*, 6:695–709, 2005.

[206] S. Ikeda, T. Tanaka, and S. Amari. Stochastic reasoning, free energy, and information geometry. *Neural Computation*, 16(9):1779–1810, 2004.

[207] M. Irani, P. Anandan, and S. Hsu. Mosaic based representations of video sequences and their applications. In *Proc. 5th Int. Conf. Computer Vision*, pages 605–611, 1995.

[208] M. Isard. PAMPAS: Real-valued graphical models for computer vision. In *Proc. IEEE Conf. Computer Vision and Pattern Recognition*, vol. 1, pages 613–620, 2003.

[209] M. Isard and A. Blake. Condensation—conditional density propagation for visual tracking. *Int. J. Computer Vision*, 29(1):5–28, 1998.

[210] M. Isard, J. MacCormick, and K. Achan. Continuously-adaptive discretization for message-passing algorithms. In *Neural Information Processing Systems*, pages 737–744, 2008.

[211] H. Ishikawa. Exact optimization for Markov random fields with convex priors. *IEEE Trans. Pattern Analysis and Machine Intelligence*, 25(10):1333–1336, October 2003.

[212] H. Ishikawa. Higher-order clique reduction in binary graph cut. In *Proc. IEEE Conf. Computer Vision and Pattern Recognition*, pages 2993–3000, 2009.

[213] H. Ishikawa. Higher-order gradient descent by fusion-move graph cut. In *Proc. 10th IEEE Int. Conf. Computer Vision*, pages 568–574, 2009.

[214] H. Ishikawa and D. Geiger. Occlusions, discontinuities, and epipolar lines in stereo. *Proc. 5th European Conf. Computer Vision*, pages 232–248, 1998.

[215] S. Iwata, L. Fleischer, and S. Fujishige. A combinatorial strongly polynomial algorithm for minimizing submodular functions. *J. Association for Computing Machinery*, 48(4):761–777, 2001.

[216] F. Jensen. *An Introduction to Bayesian Networks*. Springer, 1997.

[217] I. Jermyn and H. Ishikawa. Globally optimal regions and boundaries as minimum ratio weight cycles. *IEEE Trans. Pattern Analysis and Machine Intelligence*, 23(10):1075–1088, October 2001.

[218] H. Jiang and D. R. Martin. Global pose estimation using non-tree models. In *Proc. IEEE Conf. Computer Vision and Pattern Recognition*, pages 1–8, 2008.

[219] N. Jojic and B. Frey. Learning flexible sprites in video layers. In *Proc. IEEE Conf. Computer Vision and Pattern Recognition*, volume 1, pages 199–206, 2001.

[220] M. Jordan, Z. Ghahramani, T. Jaakkola, and L. Saul. An introduction to variational methods for graphical models. *Machine Learning*, 37:183–233, 1999.

[221] O. Juan and Y. Boykov. Active graph cuts. In *Proc. IEEE Conf. Computer Vision and Pattern Recognition*, volume 1, pages 1023–1029, 2006.

[222] A. Kannan, B. J. Frey, and N. Jojic. A generative model for dense optical flow in layers. In *Proc. Workshop on Spatial Coherence for Visual Motion Analysis, in Conjunction with ECCV 2004*, pages 104–114, 2004.

[223] A. Kannan, N. Jojic, and B. Frey. Layers of appearance and deformation. In *Proc. 10th Int. Workshop Artificial Intelligence and Statistics*, 2005.

[224] A. Kannan, J. Winn, and C. Rother. Clustering appearance and shape by learning jigsaws. In *Neural Information Processing Systems*, vol. 19, 2006.

[225] A. Kapoor and J. Winn. Located hidden random fields learning discriminative parts for object detection. In *Proc. European Conf. Computer Vision*, volume 3, pages 302–315, 2006.

[226] D. R. Karger. Random sampling in cut, flow, and network design problems. *Mathematics of Operations Research*, 24(2):383–413, May 1999.

[227] M. Kass, A. Witkin, and D. Terzolpoulos. Snakes: Active contour models. *Int. J. Computer Vision*, 1(4):321–331, 1988.

[228] E. J. Keogh, L. Wei, X. Xi, S.-H. Lee, and M. Vlachos. Lb-keogh supports exact indexing of shapes under rotation invariance with arbitrary representations and distance measures. In *Proc. 32nd Int. Conf. Very Large Data Bases*, pages 882–893, 2006.

[229] S. Kichenassamy, A. Kumar, P. J. Olver, A. Tannenbaum, and A. J. Yezzi. Gradient flows and geometric active contour models. In *Proc. 5th IEEE Int. Conf. Computer Vision*, pages 810–815, 1995.

[230] J. Kim, J. W. Fisher, A. Yezzi, M. Çetin, and A. Willsky. Nonparametric methods for image segmentation using information theory and curve evolution. In *Proc. Int. Conf. Image Processing*, volume 3, pages 797–800, 2002.

[231] S. Kim and M. Kojima. Second order cone programming relaxation of nonconvex quadratic optimization problems. *Optimization Methods and Software*, 15(3):201–224.

[232] R. Kimmel and A. M. Bruckstein. On regularized Laplacian zero crossings and other optimal edge integrators. *Int. J. Computer Vision*, 53(3):225–243, 2003.

[233] C. L. Kingsford, B. Chazelle, and M. Singh. Solving and analyzing side-chain positioning problems using linear and integer programming. *Bioinformatics*, 21(7):1028–1039, 2005.

[234] S. Kirkpatrick, C. D. Gelatt, Jr., and M. P. Vecchi. Optimization by simulated annealing. *Science*, 220(4598):671–680, 1983.

[235] J. Kittler and J. Föglein. Contextual classification of multispectral pixel data. *Image Vision Comput.*, 2(1):13–29, 1984.

[236] J. Kleinberg and E. Tardos. Approximation algorithms for classification problems with pairwise relationships: Metric labeling and Markov random fields. In *40th Ann. Symp. Foundations of Computer Science*, pages 14–23, 1999.

[237] M. Klodt, T. Schoenemann, K. Kolev, M. Schikora, and D. Cremers. An experimental comparison of discrete and continuous shape optimization methods. In *Proc. European Conf. Computer Vision*, pages 332–345, October 2008.

[238] H. Knutsson, R. Wilson, and G. H. Granlund. Anisotropic nonstationary image estimation and its applications: Part 1—Restoration of noisy images. *IEEE Trans. Comput. Commun.*, 31(3):388–397, 1983.

[239] C. Koch, J. Marroquin, and A. Yuille. Analog neuronal networks in early vision. *Proc. National Academy of Sciences*, 83:4263–4267, 1986.

[240] P. Kohli, M. P. Kumar, and P. Torr. P^3 and beyond: Solving energies with higher order cliques. In *Proc. IEEE Conf. Computer Vision and Pattern Recognition*, pages 1–8, 2007.

[241] P. Kohli, L. Ladicky, and P. Torr. Robust higher order potentials for enforcing label consistency. In *Proc. IEEE Conf. Computer Vision and Pattern Recognition*, pages 1–8, 2008.

[242] P. Kohli, J. Rihan, M. Bray, and P. Torr. Simultaneous segmentation and pose estimation of humans using dynamic graph cuts. *Int. J. Computer Vision*, 79(3):285–298, 2008.

[243] P. Kohli, A. Shekhovtsov, C. Rother, V. Kolmogorov, and P. Torr. On partial optimality in multilabel MRFs. In *Proc. 25th Int. Conf. Machine Learning*, pages 480–487, 2008.

[244] P. Kohli and P. H. Torr. Efficiently solving dynamic Markov random fields using graph cuts. In *Proc. 10th Int. Conf. Computer Vision*, pages 15–21, 2005.

[245] P. Kohli and P. H. S. Torr. Measuring uncertainty in graph cut solutions—efficiently computing min-marginal energies using dynamic graph cuts. In *Proc. European Conf. Computer Vision*, pages 30–43, 2006.

[246] P. Kohli and P. H. S. Torr. Dynamic graph cuts for efficient inference in Markov random fields. *IEEE Trans. Pattern Analysis and Machine Intelligence*, 29(12):2079–2088, 2007.

[247] K. Kolev and D. Cremers. Integration of multiview stereo and silhouettes via convex functionals on convex domains. In *Proc. European Conf. Computer Vision*, 2008.

[248] K. Kolev and D. Cremers. Anisotropic minimal surfaces for the integration of multiview stereo and normal information. Technical report, Department of Computer Science, University of Bonn, June 2009.

[249] K. Kolev and D. Cremers. Continuous ratio optimization via convex relaxation with applications to multiview 3D reconstruction. In *Proc. IEEE Conf. Computer Vision and Pattern Recognition*, pages 1854–1864, 2009.

[250] K. Kolev, M. Klodt, T. Brox, and D. Cremers. Continuous global optimization in multview 3D reconstruction. *Int. J. Computer Vision*, 84(1):80–96, 2009.

[251] K. Kolev, M. Klodt, T. Brox, S. Esedoglu, and D. Cremers. Continuous global optimization in multiview 3D reconstruction. In *Proc. of EMMCVPR*, pages 441–452, 2007.

[252] D. Koller, U. Lerner, and D. Angelov. A general algorithm for approximate inference and its application to hybrid Bayes nets. In *Proc. Conf. Uncertainty in Artificial Intelligence*, pages 324–333, 1999.

[253] D. Koller, J. Weber, and J. Malik. Robust multiple car tracking with occlusion reasoning. In *Proc. 3rd European Conf. Computer Vision*, pages 189–196, 1994.

[254] V. Kolmogorov. Convergent tree-reweighted message passing for energy minimization. In *Proc. Int. Workshop Artificial Intelligence and Statistics*, 2005.

[255] V. Kolmogorov. Convergent tree-reweighted message passing for energy minimization. *IEEE Trans. Pattern Analysis and Machine Intelligence*, 28(10):1568–1583, October 2006.

[256] V. Kolmogorov and Y. Boykov. What metrics can be approximated by geo-cuts, or global optimization of length/area and flux. In *Proc. 10th IEEE Int. Conf. Computer Vision*, volume 1, pages 564–571, 2005.

[257] V. Kolmogorov, Y. Boykov, and C. Rother. Applications of parametric maxflow in computer vision. In *Proc. 11th Int. Conf. Computer Vision*, pages 1–8, 2007.

[258] V. Kolmogorov, A. Criminisi, A. Blake, G. Cross, and C. Rother. Bi-layer segmentation of binocular stereo video. In *Proc. IEEE Conf. Computer Vision and Pattern Recognition*, vol. 25 pages 407–414, 2005.

[259] V. Kolmogorov, A. Criminisi, A. Blake, G. Cross, and C. Rother. Probabilistic fusion of stereo with color and contrast for bilayer segmentation. *IEEE Trans. Pattern Analysis and Machine Intelligence*, 28(9):1480–1492, 2006.

[260] V. Kolmogorov and C. Rother. Comparison of energy minimization algorithms for highly connected graphs. In *Proc. European Conf. Computer Vision*, pages 1–15, 2006.

[261] V. Kolmogorov and C. Rother. Minimizing non-submodular functions with graph cuts—a review. *IEEE Trans. Pattern Analysis and Machine Intelligence*, 29(7):1274–1279, 2007.

[262] V. Kolmogorov and A. Shioura. New algorithms for convex cost tension problem with application to computer vision. *Discrete Optimization*, 6(4):378–393, 2009.

[263] V. Kolmogorov and M. J. Wainwright. On the optimality of tree-reweighted max-product message-passing. In *Proc. 21st Ann. Conf. Uncertainty in Artificial Intelligence*, pages 316–323, 2005.

[264] V. Kolmogorov and R. Zabih. Computing visual correspondence with occlusions using graph cuts. In *Proc. IEEE Int. Conf. Computer Vision*, pages 508–515, 2001.

[265] V. Kolmogorov and R. Zabih. Multi-camera scene reconstruction via graph cuts. In *Proc. 7th European Conf. Computer Vision*, pages 82–96, 2002.

[266] V. Kolmogorov and R. Zabih. What energy functions can be minimized via graph cuts?. *IEEE Trans. Pattern Analysis and Machine Intelligence*, 26(2):147–159, 2004.

[267] N. Komodakis and N. Paragios. Beyond loose LP relaxations: Optimizing MRFs by repairing cycles. In *Proc. European Conf. Computer Vision*, pages 806–820, 2008.

[268] N. Komodakis, N. Paragios, and G. Tziritas. MRF optimization via dual decomposition: Message-passing revisited. In *Proc. 11th IEEE Int. Conf. Computer Vision*, pages 1–8, 2007.

[269] N. Komodakis and G. Tziritas. Approximate labeling via graph cuts based on linear programming. *IEEE Trans. Pattern Analysis and Machine Intelligence*, 29(8):1436–1453, 2007.

[270] N. Komodakis, G. Tziritas, and N. Paragios. Fast, approximately optimal solutions for single and dynamic MRFs. In *Proc. IEEE Conf. Computer Vision and Pattern Recognition*, pages 1–8, 2007.

[271] N. Komodakis, G. Tziritas, and N. Paragios. Performance vs computational efficiency for optimizing single and dynamic MRFs: Setting the state of the art with primal dual strategies. *Computer Vision and Image Understanding*, 112(1):14–29, 2008.

[272] S. M. Konishi, A. L. Yuille, J. M. Coughlan, and S. C. Zhu. Fundamental bounds on edge detection: A information theoretic evaluation of different edge cues. In *Proc. IEEE Conf. Computer Vision and Pattern Recognition*, pages 573–579, 1999.

[273] A. Koster, S. P. M. van Hoesel, and A. Kolen. The partial constraint satisfaction problem: Facets and lifting theorems. *Operations Research Letters*, 23(3–5):89–97, 1998.

[274] U. Köster, J. T. Lindgren, and A. Hyvärinen. Estimating Markov random field potentials for natural images. In *Proc. 8th Int. Conf. Indep. Comp. Analysis*, pages 515–522, 2009.

[275] A. V. Kozlov and D. Koller. Nonuniform dynamic discretization in hybrid networks. In *Proc. 13th Int. Conf. Uncertainty in Artificial Intelligence*, pages 314–325, 1997.

[276] F. R. Kschischang, B. J. Frey, and H.-A. Loeliger. Factor graphs and the sum–product algorithm. *IEEE Trans. Information Theory*, 47(2):498–519, 2001.

[277] M. P. Kumar and P. Torr. Improved moves for truncated convex models. In *Proc. 22nd Conf. Neural Information Processing Systems*, pages 889–896, 2008.

[278] M. P. Kumar, P. Torr, and A. Zisserman. OBJ cut. In *Proc. IEEE Conf. Computer Vision and Pattern Recognition*, volume 1, pages 18–25, 2005.

[279] M. P. Kumar and D. Koller. MAP estimation of semi-metric MRFs via hierarchical graph cuts. In *Proc. 25th Ann. Conf. Uncertainty in Artificial Intelligence*, pages 313–320, 2009.

[280] M. P. Kumar, V. Kolmogorov, and P. H. S. Torr. An analysis of convex relaxations for MAP estimation. In *Neural Information Processing Systems*, 2007.

[281] M. P. Kumar, P. Torr, and A. Zisserman. OBJ cut. In *Proc. IEEE Conf. Computer Vision and Pattern Recognition*, volume 1, pages 18–25, 2005.

[282] M. P. Kumar, P. H. S. Torr, and A. Zisserman. Solving Markov random fields using second order cone programming relaxations. In *Proc. IEEE Conf. Computer Vision and Pattern Recognition*, pages 1045–1052, 2006.

[283] S. Kumar, J. August, and M. Hebert. Exploiting inference for approximate parameter learning in discriminative fields: An empirical study. In *Energy Minimization Methods in Computer Vision and Pattern Recognition*, pages 153–168. Springer, 2005.

[284] S. Kumar and M. Hebert. Discriminative random fields: A discriminative framework for contextual interaction in classification. In *Proc. 9th Int. Conf. Computer Vision*, volume 2, pages 1150–1157, 2003.

[285] S. Kumar and M. Hebert. Discriminative random fields. *Int. J. Computer Vision*, 68(2):179–201, June 2006.

[286] D. Kurtz, G. Parker, D. Shotton, G. Klyne, F. Schroff, A. Zisserman, and Y. Wilks. CLAROS—bringing classical art to a global public. In *5th IEEE Int. Conference on e-Science*, 2009.

[287] V. Kwatra, A. Schödl, I. Essa, G. Turk, and A. Bobick. Graphcut textures: Image and video synthesis using graph cuts. *Proc. ACM Siggraph*, 22(3):277–286, July 2003.

[288] J. Lafferty, A. McCallum, and F. Pereira. Conditional random fields: Probabilistic models for segmenting and labeling sequence data. In *Proc. 18th Int. Conf. on Machine Learning*, pages 282–289. Morgan Kaufmann, San Francisco, 2001.

[289] C. H. Lampert, M. B. Blaschko, and T. Hofmann. Beyond sliding windows: Object localization by efficient subwindow search. In *Proc. IEEE Conf. Computer Vision and Pattern Recognition*, pages 1–8, 2008.

[290] X. Lan and D. P. Huttenlocher. Beyond trees: Common-factor models for 2D human pose recovery. In *Proc. 10th IEEE Int. Conf. Computer Vision*, volume 1, pages 470–477, 2005.

[291] X. Lan, S. Roth, D. Huttenlocher, and M. Black. Efficient belief propagation with learned higher-order Markov random fields. In *Proc. European Conf. Computer Vision*, pages 269–282, 2006.

[292] J. Lasserre, A. Kannan, and J. Winn. Hybrid learning of large jigsaws. In *Proc. IEEE Conf. Computer Vision and Pattern Recognition*, pages 1–8, 2007.

[293] S. Lazebnik, C. Schmid, and J. Ponce. Beyond bags of features: Spatial pyramid matching for recognizing natural scene categories. In *Proc. IEEE Conf. Computer Vision and Pattern Recognition*, volume 2, pages 2169–2178, 2006.

[294] Y. LeCun, L. Bottou, Y. Bengio, and P. Haffner. Gradient-based learning applied to document recognition. *Proc. IEEE*, 86(11):2278–2324, November 1998.

[295] Y. LeCun, S. Chopra, R. Hadsell, M. Ranzato, and F. Huang. A tutorial on energy-based learning. In G. Bakir, T. Hofmann, B. Schölkopf, A. Smola, and B. Taskar, editors, *Predicting Structured Data*. MIT Press, 2006.

[296] B. Leibe, A. Leonardis, and B. Schiele. Combined object categorization and segmentation with an implicit shape model. In *ECCV'04 Workshop on Statistical Learning in Computer Vision*, pages 17–32, May 2004.

[297] V. Lempitsky and D. Ivanov. Seamless mosaicing of image-based texture maps. In *Proc. Int. Conf. Computer Vision and Pattern Recognition*, pages 1–6, 2007.

[298] V. Lempitsky, P. Kohli, C. Rother, and T. Sharp. Image segmentation with a bounding box prior. In *Proc. Int. Conf. Computer Vision*, 2009.

[299] V. Lempitsky, S. Roth, and C. Rother. FusionFlow: Discrete-continuous optimization for optical flow estimation. In *Proc. IEEE Conf. Computer Vision and Pattern Recognition*, pages 1–8, 2008.

[300] V. Lempitsky, C. Rother, S. Roth, and A. Blake. Fusion moves for Markov random field optimization. *IEEE Trans. Pattern Analysis and Machine Intelligence*, 32(8):1392–1405, 2010.

[301] V. S. Lempitsky, A. Blake, and C. Rother. Image segmentation by branch- and mincut. In *Proc. European Conf. Computer Vision*, part 4, pages 15–29, 2008.

[302] V. Lepetit, P. Lagger, and P. Fua. Randomized trees for real-time keypoint recognition. In *Proc. IEEE Conf. Computer Vision and Pattern Recognition*, volume 2, pages 775–781, 2005.

[303] M. E. Leventon, W. E. L. Grimson, and O. D. Faugeras. Statistical shape influence in geodesic active contours. In *Proc. IEEE Conf. Computer Vision and Pattern Recognition*, volume 1, pages 316–323, 2000.

[304] A. Levin, R. Fergus, F. Durand, and W. T. Freeman. Image and depth from a conventional camera with a coded aperture. In *Proc. ACM Siggraph*, 26(3), 2007.

[305] A. Levin and Y. Weiss. Learning to combine bottom-up and top-down segmentation. In *Proc. European Conf. Computer Vision*, pages 581–594, 2006.

[306] A. Levin, A. Zomet, and Y. Weiss. Learning how to inpaint from global image statistics. In *Proc. 9th IEEE Int. Conf. Computer Vision*, volume 1, pages 305–312, 2003.

[307] A. Levin, A. Zomet, and Y. Weiss. Learning to perceive transparency from the statistics of natural scenes. In *Proc. Conf. Neural Information Processing Systems*, pages 1247–1254, 2002.

[308] S. Z. Li. *Markov Random Field Modelling in Computer Vision*. Springer-Verlag, 1995.

[309] S. Z. Li. *Markov Random Field Modeling in Image Analysis*. Springer, 2001.

[310] Y. Li and D. P. Huttenlocher. Learning for optical flow using stochastic optimization. In *Proc. European Conf. Computer Vision*, pages 379–391, 2008.

[311] Y. Li, J. Sun, and H.-Y. Shum. Video object cut and paste. In *Proc. ACM Siggraph*, 24(3):595–600, 2005.

[312] Y. Li, J. Sun, C.-K. Tang, and H.-Y. Shum. Lazy snapping. *Proc. ACM Siggraph*, 23(3):303–308, 2004.

[313] L. Liang, C. Liu, Y. Xu, B. Guo, and H. Shum. Real-time texture synthesis by patch-based sampling. *Proc. ACM Siggraph*, 20(3):127–150, 2001.

[314] M. Lin and C. Tomasi. *Surfaces with Occlusions from Layered Stereo*. Ph.D. thesis, Stanford University, 2002.

[315] C. Liu, H. Shum, and C. Zhang. A two-step approach to hallucinating faces: Global parametric model and local non-parametric model. In *Proc. IEEE Conf. Computer Vision and Pattern Recognition*, volume 1, pages 192–198, 2001.

[316] C. Liu, H.-Y. Shum, and W. T. Freeman. Face hallucination: Theory and practice. *Int. J. Computer Vision*, 75(1):115–134, 2007.

[317] C. Liu, A. B. Torralba, W. T. Freeman, F. Durand, and E. H. Adelson. Motion magnification. *Proc. ACM Siggraph*, 24(3):519–526, 2005.

[318] C. Liu, J. Yuen, and A. Torralba. Nonparametric scene parsing: Label transfer via dense scene alignment. In *Proc. IEEE Conf. Computer Vision and Pattern Recognition*, pages 1972–1979, 2009.

[319] C. Liu, J. Yuen, A. Torralba, J. Sivic, and W. T. Freeman. SIFT flow: Dense correspondence across different scenes. In *Proc. European Conf. Computer Vision*, 2008.

[320] C. Liu, J. Yuen, A. Torralba, and W. T. Freeman. SIFT flow: dense correspondence across scenes and its applications. *IEEE Transactions on Pattern Analysis and Machine Intelligence* (to appear).

[321] J. Liu, J. Sun, and H.-Y. Shum. Paint selection. *Proc. ACM Siggraph*, 28(3), 2009.

[322] X. Liu, O. Veksler, and J. Samarabandu. Graph cut with ordering constraints on labels and its applications. In *Proc. IEEE Conf. Computer Vision and Pattern Recognition*, pages 1–8, 2008.

[323] H. Lombaert, Y. Sun, L. Grady, and C. Xu. A multilevel banded graph cuts method for fast image segmentation. In *Proc. 10th Int. Conf. Computer Vision*, volume 1, pages 259–265, 2005.

[324] L. Lovasz. Submodular functions and convexity. In *Mathematical Programming: The State of the Art*, pages 235–257. Springer, 1983.

[325] D. G. Lowe. Object recognition from local scale-invariant features. In *Proc. Int. Conf. Computer Vision*, pages 1150–1157, 1999.

[326] B. D. Lucas and T. Kanade. An iterative image registration technique with an application to stereo vision. In *Proc. 7th Int. Joint Conf. Artificial Intelligence*, pages 674–679, 1981.

[327] S. Lyu and E. P. Simoncelli. Statistical modeling of images with fields of Gaussian scale mixtures. In *Proc. Conf. Neural Information Processing Systems*, pages 945–952, 2006.

[328] D. MacKay. *Information Theory, Inference, and Learning Algorithms*. Cambridge University Press, 2003.

[329] D. Marr and T. Poggio. Cooperative computation of stereo disparity. *Science*, n.s. 194(4262):283–287, 1976.

[330] J. L. Marroquin, S. K. Mitter, and T. A. Poggio. Probabilistic solution of ill-posed problems in computational vision. *J. Amer. Statistics Association*, 82(397):76–89, March 1987.

[331] D. Martin, C. Fowlkes, D. Tal, and J. Malik. A database of human segmented natural images and its application to evaluating segmentation algorithms and measuring ecological statistics. In *Proc. 8th Int. Conf. Computer Vision*, volume 2, pages 416–423, 2001.

[332] A. Martinez and R. Benavente. The AR face database. CVC Technical Report 24, June 1998.

[333] L. Matthies, T. Kanade, and R. Szeliski. Kalman filter-based algorithms for estimating depth from image sequences. *Int. J. Computer Vision*, 3:209–236, 1989.

[334] H. Mayer. Analysis of means to improve cooperative disparity estimation. *Proc. ISPRS Conf. on Photogrammetric Image Analysis*, 34(20):16–18, 2003.

[335] J. J. McAuley, T.S. Caetano, A. J. Smola, and M. O. Franz. Learning high-order MRF priors of color images. In *Proc. 23rd Int. Conf. Machine Learning*, pages 617–624, 2006.

[336] A. McCallum. Efficiently inducing features of conditional random fields. In *Proc. 19th Conf. Uncertainty in Artificial Intelligence*, pages 403–410, 2003.

[337] R. J. McEliece, D. J. C. MacKay, and J. F. Cheng. Turbo decoding as an instance of Pearl's belief propagation algorithm. *IEEE J. Selected Areas in Communication*, 16(2):140–152, 1998.

[338] T. Meltzer, C. Yanover, and Y. Weiss. Globally optimal solutions for energy minimization in stereo vision using reweighted belief propagation. In *Proc. 10th IEEE Int. Conf. Computer Vision*, volume 1, pages 428–435, 2005.

[339] R. Memisevic and G. E. Hinton. Unsupervised learning of image transformations. In *Proc. IEEE Conf. Computer Vision and Pattern Recognition*, pages 1–8, 2007.

[340] G. Miller and J. Naor. Flows in planar graphs with multiple sources and sinks. In *Proc. 30th IEEE Symp. on Foundations of Computer Science*, pages 112–117, 1989.

[341] T. Minka. Expectation propagation for approximate Bayesian inference. In *Proc. 17th Conf. Uncertainty in Artificial Intelligence*, pages 362–369, 2001.

[342] T. Minka. Divergence measures and message passing. Technical Report MSR-TR-2005-173. Microsoft Research, Cambridge, UK, 2005.

[343] E. Mortensen and W. Barrett. Intelligent scissors for image composition. *Proc. ACM Siggraph*, pages 191–198, 1995.

[344] D. Mumford and J. Shah. Optimal approximations by piecewise smooth functions and associated variational problems. *Comm. Pure Appl. Math.*, 42:577–685, 1989.

[345] M. Muramatsu and T. Suzuki. A new second-order cone programming relaxation for max-cut problems. *J. Operations Research Japan*, 46:164–177, 2003.

[346] I. Murray, Z. Ghahramani, and D. MacKay. MCMC for doubly-intractable distributions. In *Proc. 22nd Conf. Uncertainty in Artificial Intelligence*, pages 359–366. 2006.

[347] R. M. Neal. Probabilistic inference using Markov chain Monte Carlo methods. Technical Report CRG-TR-93-1. Dept. of Computer Science, University of Toronto, September 1993.

[348] R. M. Neal and G. E. Hinton. A view of the EM algorithm that justifies incremental, sparse, and other variants. In *M.I. Jordan, editor, Learning in Graphical Models*, pages 355–368. MIT Press, Cambridge, MA, 1999.

[349] M. H. Nguyen, J.-F. Lalonde, A. A. Efros, and F. de la Torre. Image based shaving. *Computer Graphics Forum Journal (Eurographics 2008)*, 27(2):627–635, 2008.

[350] H. Nickisch, C. Rother, P. Kohli, and C. Rhemann. Learning an interactive segmentation system. In *Proc. Indian Conference on Computer Vision*, 2010 (to appear).

[351] F. Ning, D. Delhomme, Y. LeCun, F. Piano, L. Bottou, and P. E. Barbano. Toward automatic phenotyping of developing embryos from videos. *IEEE Trans. Image Processing*, 14(9):1360–1371, September 2005.

[352] M. Norouzi, M. Ranjbar, and G. Mori. Stacks of convolutional restricted Boltzmann machines for shift-invariant feature learning. In *Proc. IEEE Conf. Computer Vision and Pattern Recognition*, pages 2735–2742, 2009.

[353] S. Nowozin and C. H. Lampert. Global connectivity potentials for random field models. In *Proc. IEEE Conf. Computer Vision and Pattern Recognition*, pages 818–825, 2009.

[354] A. S. Ogale and Y. Aloimonos. Stereo correspondence with slanted surface: Critical implication of horizontal slant. *Proc. IEEE Conf. Computer Vision and Pattern Recognition*, volume 1, pages 568–573, 2004.

[355] M. Ohlsson, C. Peterson, and A. L. Yuille. Track finding with deformable templates—the elastic arms approach. *Computer Physics Communications*, 71:77–98, 1992.

[356] A. Oliva and A. Torralba. Modeling the shape of the scene: A holistic representation of the spatial envelope. *Int. J. Computer Vision*, 42(3):145–175, 2001.

[357] B. A. Olshausen and D. J. Field. Sparse coding with an overcomplete basis set: A strategy employed by V1? *Vision Research*, 37(23):3311–3325, December 1997.

[358] J. Orlin. A faster strongly polynomial time algorithm for submodular function minimization. In *Proc. Conf. Integer Programming and Combinatorial Optimization*, pages 240–251, 2007.

[359] M.R. Osborne. *Finite Algorithms in Optimization and Data Analysis*. John Wiley, 1985.

[360] S. Osher and J. A. Sethian. Fronts propagating with curvature-dependent speed: Algorithms based on Hamilton-Jacobi formulations. *J. Computer Physics*, 79(1):12–49, 1988.

[361] R. Paget and I. Longstaff. Texture synthesis via a noncausal nonparametric multiscale Markov random field. *IEEE Trans. Image Processing*, 7(6):925–931, 1998.

[362] C. Pal, C. Sutton, and A. McCallum. Sparse forward-backward using minimum divergence beams for fast training of conditional random fields. In *Proc. IEEE Int. Conf. Acoustics, Speech, Signal Processing*, 2006.

[363] C. H. Papadimitriou and K. Steiglitz. *Combinatorial Optimization: Algorithms and Complexity*. Prentice Hall, 1982.

[364] N. Papenberg, A. Bruhn, T. Brox, S. Didas, and J. Weickert. Highly accurate optic flow computation with theoretically justified warping. *Int. J. Computer Vision*, 67(2):141–158, April 2006.

[365] G. Parisi. *Statistical Field Theory*. Addison-Wesley, Reading, MA, 1988.

[366] M. Pawan Kumar, P. H. Torr, and A. Zisserman. Learning layered motion segmentations of video. *Int. J. Computer Vision*, 76(3):301–319, 2008.

[367] J. Pearl. *Probabilistic Reasoning in Intelligent Systems*. Morgan Kaufmann, San Francisco, 1988.

[368] P. Pérez, M. Gangnet, and A. Blake. Poisson image editing. *ACM Trans. Graph.*, 22(3):313–318, 2003.

[369] C. Peterson and J. R. Anderson. A mean field theory learning algorithm for neural networks. *Complex Systems*, 1(5):995–1019, 1987.

[370] S. D. Pietra, V. D. Pietra, and J. Lafferty. Inducing features of random fields. *IEEE Trans. Pattern Analysis and Machine Intelligence*, 19(4):380–393, April 1997.

[371] T. Pock, A. Chambolle, D. Cremers and H. Bischof. A convex relaxation approach for computing minimal partitions. In *Proc. IEEE Conf. Computer Vision and Pattern Recognition*, pages 810–817, 2009.

[372] T. Pock, D. Cremers, H. Bischof, and A. Chambolle. An algorithm for minimizing the piecewise smooth Mumford-Shah functional. In *Proc. Int. Conf. Computer Vision*, 2009.

[373] T. Pock, T. Schoenemann, G. Graber, H. Bischof, and D. Cremers. A convex formulation of continuous multi-label problems. In *Proc. European Conf. Computer Vision*, pages 792–805, 2008.

[374] T. Poggio, E. B. Gamble, and J. J. Little. Parallel integration of vision modules. *Science*, 242(4877):436–440, 1988.

[375] J. Portilla, V. Strela, M. J. Wainwright, and E. P. Simoncelli. Image denoising using scale mixtures of Gaussians in the wavelet domain. *IEEE Trans. Image Processing*, 12(11):1338–1351, November 2003.

[376] B. Potetz. Efficient belief propagation for vision using linear constraint nodes. In *Proc. IEEE Conf. Computer Vision and Pattern Recognition*, pages 1–8, 2007.

[377] R. Potts. Some generalized order-disorder transformations. *Math. Proc. Cambridge Philosophical Society*, 48:106–109, 1952.

[378] W. Press, B. Flannery, S. Teukolsky, and W. Vetterling. *Numerical Recipes in C*. Cambridge University Press, 1988.

[379] Y. Qi, M. Szummer, and T. P. Minka. Bayesian conditional random fields. In *Proc. 10th Int. AI & Statistics*, pages 269–276, 2005.

[380] Y. Qi, M. Szummer, and T. P. Minka. Diagram structure recognition by Bayesian conditional random fields. In C. Schmid, S. Soatto, and C. Tomasi, editors, *Proc. Int. Conf. Computer Vision and Pattern Recognition*, volume 2, pages 191–196, 2005.

[381] L. Rabiner and J. Bing-Hwang. *Fundamentals of Speech Recognition*. Prentice Hall, 1993.

[382] L. Rabiner and B. Juang. A tutorial on hidden Markov models. *Proc. IEEE*, 77(2):257–286, 1989.

[383] A. Rabinovich, S. Belongie, T. Lange, and J. Buhmann. Model order selection and cue combination for image segmentation. In *Proc. IEEE Conf. Computer Vision and Pattern Recognition*, pages 1130–1137, 2006.

[384] S. Ramalingam, P. Kohli, K. Alahari, and P. Torr. Exact inference in multi-label CRFs with higher order cliques. In *Proc. IEEE Conf. Computer Vision and Pattern Recognition*, pages 1–8, 2008.

[385] C. E. Rasmussen. Code:minimize.m. http://www.kyb.tuebingen.mpg.de/bs/people/carl/code/minimize/. 2006.

[386] A. Rav-Acha, P. Kohli, C. Rother, and A. Fitzgibbon. Unwrap mosaics. Microsoft Research, Technical Report MSR-TR-2008-94, 2008. http://research.microsoft.com/unwrap.

[387] A. Rav-Acha, P. Kohli, C. Rother, and A. Fitzgibbon. Unwrap mosaics: A new representation for video editing. *Proc. ACM Siggraph*, 27(3), 2008.

[388] P. Ravikumar and J. Lafferty. Quadratic programming relaxations for metric labeling and Markov random field MAP estimation. In *Proc. 23rd Int. Conf. Machine Learning*, pages 737–744, 2006.

[389] X. Ren and J. Malik. Learning a classification model for segmentation. In *Proc. 9th IEEE Int. Conf. Computer Vision*, volume 1, pages 10–17, 2003.

[390] C. Rhemann, C. Rother, P. Kohli, and M. Gelautz. A spatially varying PSF-based prior for alpha matting. In *Proc. IEEE Conf. Computer Vision and Pattern Recognition*, 2010.

[391] T. Roosta, M. J. Wainwright, and S. S. Sastry. Convergence analysis of reweighted sum-product algorithms. *IEEE Trans. Signal Processing*, 56(9):4293–4305, 2008.

[392] M. Rosen-Zvi, M. I. Jordan, and A. L. Yuille. The DLR hierarchy of approximate inference. In *Proc. Conf. Uncertainty in Artificial Intelligence*, pages 493–500, 2005.

[393] S. Roth. *High-Order Markov Random Fields for Low-Level Vision*. Ph.D. dissertation, Dept. of Computer Science, Brown University, Providence, RI, May 2007.

[394] S. Roth and M. Black. Fields of experts: A framework for learning image priors. In *Proc. IEEE Conf. Computer Vision and Pattern Recognition*, volume 2, pages 860–867, 2005.

[395] S. Roth and M. J. Black. On the spatial statistics of optical flow. *Int. J. Computer Vision*, 74(1):33–50, 2007.

[396] S. Roth and M. J. Black. Steerable random fields. In *Proc. 11th IEEE Int. Conf. Computer Vision*, pages 1–8, 2007.

[397] S. Roth and M. J. Black. Fields of experts. *Int. J. Computer Vision*, 82(2):205–229, April 2009.

[398] S. Roth, V. Lempitsky, and C. Rother. Discrete-continuous optimization for optical flow estimation. In D. Cremers et al., editors, *Statistical and Geometrical Approaches to Visual Motion Analysis*, LNCS vol. 5604:1–22. Springer, 2009.

[399] C. Rother, L. Bordeaux, Y. Hamadi, and A. Blake. AutoCollage. *Proc. ACM Siggraph*, 25(3), 2006.

[400] C. Rother, P. Kohli, W. Feng, and J. Jia. Minimizing sparse higher order energy functions of discrete variables. In *Proc. IEEE Conf. Computer Vision and Pattern Recognition*, pages 1382–1389, 2009.

[401] C. Rother, V. Kolmogorov, and A. Blake. GrabCut—interactive foreground extraction using iterated graph cuts. In *Proc. ACM Siggraph*, 23(3), August 2004.

[402] C. Rother, V. Kolmogorov, Y. Boykov, and A. Blake. Interactive foreground extraction using Graph Cut. In MSR Technical Report: MSR-TR-2010-71, 2010.

[403] C. Rother, V. Kolmogorov, V. Lempitsky, and M. Szummer. Optimizing binary MRFs via extended roof duality. In *Proc. IEEE Conf. Computer Vision and Pattern Recognition*, 2007.

[404] C. Rother, S. Kumar, V. Kolmogorov, and A. Blake. Digital tapestry. In *Proc. IEEE Conf. Computer Vision and Pattern Recognition*, pages 589–596, 2005.

[405] S. Rowe and A. Blake. Statistical mosaics for tracking. *J. Image and Vision Computing*, 14:549–564, 1996.

[406] S. Roy and V. Govindu. MRF solutions for probabilistic optical flow formulations. In *Proc. Intl. Conf. Pattern Recognition*, vol. 3, pages, 1041–1047, 2000.

[407] B. Russell, W. Freeman, A. Efros, J. Sivic, and A. Zisserman. Using multiple segmentations to discover objects and their extent in image collections. In *Proc. IEEE Conf. Computer Vision and Pattern Recognition*, pages 1605–1614, 2006.

[408] J. Rustagi. *Variational Methods in Statistics*. Academic Press, 1976.

[409] M. Ruzon and C. Tomasi. Alpha estimation in natural images. In *Proc. IEEE Conf. Computer Vision and Pattern Recognition*, pages 18–25, 2000.

[410] F. Samaria and A. Harter. Parameterization of a stochastic model for human face identification. In *Proc. 2nd IEEE Workshop on Applications of Computer Vision*, 1994.

[411] K. G. G. Samuel and M. F. Tappen. Learning optimized MAP estimates in continuously-valued MRF models. In *Proc. IEEE Conf. Computer Vision and Pattern Recognition*, pages 477–484, 2009.

[412] S. Sanghavi, D. Shah, and A. S. Willsky. Message passing for max-weight independent set. In *Neural Information Processing Systems*, 2007.

[413] S. Sarawagi and R. Gupta. Accurate max-margin training for structured output spaces. In *Proc. 25th Int. Conf. Machine Learning*, pages 888–895, 2008.

[414] L. Saul and M. Jordan. Exploiting tractable substructures in intractable networks. *Advances in Neural Information Processing Systems*, 8:486–492, 1996.

[415] A. Saxena, S. Chung, and A. Ng. Learning depth from single monocular images. In *Neural Information Processing Systems*, vol. 18, 2005.

[416] H. Scharr. Optimal filters for extended optical flow. In *Proc. 1st Int. Workshop on Complex Motion*, LNCS 3417, pages 14–29. Springer, 2004.

[417] H. Scharr, M. J. Black, and H. W. Haussecker. Image statistics and anisotropic diffusion. In *Proc. IEEE Int. Conf. Computer Vision*, volume 2, pages 840–847, 2003.

[418] D. Scharstein and C. Pal. Learning conditional random fields for stereo. In *Proc. IEEE Conf. Computer Vision and Pattern Recognition*, pages 1–8, 2007.

[419] D. Scharstein and R. Szeliski. A taxonomy and evaluation of dense two-frame stereo correspondence algorithms. *Int. J. Computer Vision*, 47(1–3):7–42, April 2002.

[420] D. Schlesinger. Exact solution of permuted submodular min-sum problems. *Proc. of the 6th International Conference on Energy Minimization Methods in Computer Vision and Pattern Recognition*, pages 28–38, 2007.

[421] D. Schlesinger and B. Flach. Transforming an arbitrary min-sum problem into a binary one. Technical Report TUD-FI06-01, Dresden University of Technology, April 2006.

[422] M. Schlesinger. Syntactic analysis of two-dimensional visual signals in noisy conditions. *Kybernetika*, 4:113–130, 1976 (in Russian).

[423] M. I. Schlesinger and V. V. Giginyak. Solution to structural recognition (MAX,+)-problems by their equivalent transformations. Part 1. *Control Systems and Computers*, 1:3–15, 2007.

[424] M. I. Schlesinger and V. V. Giginyak. Solution to structural recognition (MAX,+)-problems by their equivalent transformations. Part 2. *Control Systems and Computers*, 2:3–18, 2007.

[425] T. Schoenemann and D. Cremers. Introducing curvature into globally optimal image segmentation: Minimum ratio cycles on product graphs. In *Proc. 11th IEEE Int. Conf. Computer Vision*, pages 1–6, 2007.

[426] W. F. Schreiber and D. E. Troxel. Transformation between continuous and discrete representations of images: A perceptual approach. *IEEE Trans. Pattern Analysis Machine Intelligence*, 7(2):176–178, 1985.

[427] A. Schrijver. A combinatorial algorithm minimizing submodular functions in strongly polynomial time. *J. Comb. Theory, ser. B*, 80(2):346–355, 2000.

[428] H. Seetzen, W. Heidrich, W. Stuerzlinger, G. Ward, L. Whitehead, M. Trentacoste, A. Ghosh, and A. Vorozcovs. High dynamic range display systems. *Proc. ACM SIGGRAPH*, 23(3):760–768, 2004.

[429] S. M. Seitz, B. Curless, J. Diebel, D. Scharstein, and R. Szeliski. A comparison and evaluation of multiview stereo reconstruction algorithms. In *Proc. IEEE Conf. Computer Vision and Pattern Recognition*, volume 1, pages 519–526, 2006.

[430] A. Sha'asua and S. Ullman. Structural saliency: The detection of globally salient structures using a locally connected network. In *Proc. 2nd Int. Conf. Computer Vision*, pages 321–327, 1988.

[431] J. Shade, S. Gortler, L. He, and R. Szeliski. Layered depth images. *Proc. ACM Siggraph*, 1998.

[432] E. Sharon, A. Brandt, and R. Basri. Segmentation and boundary detection using multiscale intensity measurements. In *Proc. IEEE Conf. Computer Vision and Pattern Recognition*, volume 1, pages 469–476, 2001.

[433] A. Shekhovtsov, I. Kovtun, and V. Hlavac. Efficient MRF deformation model for non-rigid image matching. In *Proc. IEEE Conf. Computer Vision and Pattern Recognition*, pages 1–6, 2007.

[434] J. Shi and J. Malik. Normalized cuts and image segmentation. *IEEE Trans. Pattern Analysis and Machine Intelligence*, 22(8):888–905, 2000.

[435] N. Z. Shor, K.C. Kiwiel, and A. Ruszcaynsk. *Minimization Methods for Nondifferentiable Functions*. Springer-Verlag, 1985.

[436] J. Shotton, A. Blake, and R. Cipolla. Contour-based learning for object detection. In *Proc. 10th Int. Conf. Computer Vision*, volume 1, pages 503–510, 2005.

[437] J. Shotton, J. Winn, C. Rother, and A. Criminisi. Textonboost: Joint appearance, shape and context modeling for multi-class object recognition and segmentation. In *Proc. European Conf. Computer Vision*, pages 1–15, 2006.

[438] H. Sidenbladh and M. J. Black. Learning the statistics of people in images and video. *Int. J. Computer Vision*, 54(1–3):183–209, 2003.

[439] L. Sigal, S. Bhatia, S. Roth, M. J. Black, and M. Isard. Tracking loose-limbed people. In *Proc. IEEE Conf. Computer Vision and Pattern Recognition*, volume 1, pages 421–428, 2004.

[440] D. Singaraju, L. Grady, and R. Vidal. P-brush: Continuous valued MRFs with normed pairwise distributions for image segmentation. In *Proc. IEEE Conf. Computer Vision and Pattern Recognition*, pages 1303–1310, 2009.

[441] A.K. Sinop and L. Grady. A seeded image segmentation framework unifying graph cuts and random walker which yields a new algorithm. *Proc. 11th Int. Conf. Computer Vision*, pages 1–8, 2007.

[442] J. Sivic and A. Zisserman. Video Google: A text retrieval approach to object matching in videos. In *Proc. 9th IEEE Int. Conf. Computer Vision*, volume 2, pages 1470–1477, 2003.

[443] D. Snow, P. Viola, and R. Zabih. Exact voxel occupancy with graph cuts. In *Proc. IEEE Conf. Computer Vision and Pattern Recognition*, volume 1, pages 345–352, 2000.

[444] D. Sontag and T. Jaakkola. New outer bounds on the marginal polytope. In *Proc. 21st Ann. Conf. Neural Information Processing Systems*, 2007.

[445] D. Sontag, T. Meltzer, A. Globerson, Y. Weiss, and T. Jaakkola. Tightening LP relaxations for MAP using message passing. In *Proc. 24th Conf. Uncertainty in Artificial Intelligence*, 2008.

[446] A. Sotiras, N. Komodakis, B. Glocker, J.-F. Deux, and N. Paragios. Graphical models and deformable diffeomorphic population registration using global and local metrics. In *Proc. 12th Int. Conf. Medical Image Computing and Computer-Assisted Intervention*, pages 672–677, 2009.

[447] B. K. Sriperumbudur and G. R. G. Lanckriet. On the convergence of the concave-convex procedure. In *Proc. 23rd Ann. Conf. Neural Information Processing Systems*, 2009.

[448] A. Srivastava, A. B. Lee, E. P. Simoncelli, and S.-C. Zhu. On advances in statistical modeling of natural images. *J. Mathematical Imaging and Vision*, 18(1):17–33, January 2003.

[449] T. Starner, J. Weaver, and A. Pentland. Real-time American Sign Language recognition using desk and wearable computer based video. *IEEE Trans. Pattern Analysis and Machine Intelligence*, 20(12):1371–1375, 1998.

[450] C. Stauffer and W. Grimson. Adaptive background mixture models for real-time tracking. In *Proc. IEEE Conf. Computer Vision and Pattern Recognition*, pages 246–252, 1999.

[451] L. Stewart, X. He, and R. S. Zemel. Learning flexible features for conditional random fields. *IEEE Trans. Pattern Analysis and Machine Intelligence*, 30(8):1415–1426, August 2008.

[452] M. Stiglmayr, F. Pfeuffer, and K. Klamroth. A branch & bound algorithm for medical image registration. In *Proc. Int. Combinatorial Image Analysis*, pages 217–228, 2008.

[453] E. Sudderth, A. Ihler, W. Freeman, and A. Willsky. Nonparametric belief propagation. In *Proc. IEEE Conf. Computer Vision and Pattern Recognition*, volume 1, pages 605–612, 2003.

[454] E. Sudderth, M. Mandel, W. Freeman, and A. Willsky. Distributed occlusion reasoning for tracking with nonparametric belief propagation. In *Neural Information Processing Systems*, pages 1369–1376, 2004.

[455] D. Sun, S. Roth, J. P. Lewis, and M. J. Black. Learning optical flow. In *Proc. European Conf. Computer Vision*, volume part 3, LNCS 5304, pages 83–97, 2008.

[456] J. Sun, Y. Li, S.-B. Kang, and H.-Y. Shum. Symmetric stereo matching for occlusion handling. *Proc. IEEE Conf. Computer Vision and Pattern Recognition*, volume 2, pages 399–406, 2005.

[457] J. Sun, H.-Y. Shum, and N.-N. Zheng. Stereo matching using belief propagation. In *Proc. European Conf. Computer Vision*, volume 2, pages 510–524, 2002.

[458] J. Sun, W. Zhang, X. Tang, and H.-Y. Shum. Background cut. In *Proc. European Conf. Computer Vision*, volume 2, pages 628–641, 2006.

[459] C. Sutton and A. McCallum. Piecewise training for undirected models. In *Proc. Conf. Uncertainty in Artificial Intelligence*, pages 568–575, 2005.

[460] R. Szeliski. Bayesian modeling of uncertainty in low-level vision. *Int. J. Computer Vision*, 5(3):271–301, December 1990.

[461] R. Szeliski. Image alignment and stitching: A tutorial. *Foundations and Trends in Computer Graphics and Computer Vision*, 2(1):1–104, 2006.

[462] R. Szeliski. Locally adapted hierarchical basis preconditioning. *Proc. ACM Siggraph*, 25(3):1135–1143, 2006.

[463] R. Szeliski, R. Zabih, D. Scharstein, O. Veksler, V. Kolmogorov, A. Agarwala, M. Tappen, and C. Rother. A comparative study of energy minimization methods for Markov random fields. In *Proc. European Conf. Computer Vision*, part 2, pages 18–29, 2006.

[464] R. Szeliski, R. Zabih, D. Scharstein, O. Veksler, V. Kolmogorov, A. Agarwala, M. Tappen, and C. Rother. A comparative study of energy minimization methods for Markov random fields with smoothness-based priors. *IEEE Trans. Pattern Analysis and Machine Intelligence*, 30(6):1068–1080, 2008.

[465] M. Szummer. Learning diagram parts with hidden random fields. In *Proc. 8th Int. Conf. Document Analysis and Recognition*, volume 2, pages 1188–1193, August 2005.

[466] M. Szummer, P. Kohli, and D. Hoiem. Learning CRFs using graph cuts. In *Proc. European Conf. Computer Vision*, 2008.

[467] H. Tao, H. S. Sawhney, and R. Kumar. A global matching framework for stereo computation. In *Proc. 9th IEEE Int. Conf. Computer Vision*, volume 1, pages 532–539, 2001.

[468] M. Tappen and W. Freeman. Comparison of graph cuts with belief propagation for stereo, using identical MRF parameters. In *Proc. Int. Conf. Computer Vision*, volume 2, pages 900–907, 2003.

[469] M. Tappen, C. Liu, E. H. Adelson, and W. T. Freeman. Learning Gaussian conditional random fields for low-level vision. In *Proc. IEEE Conf. Computer Vision and Pattern Recognition*, pages 1–8, 2007.

[470] M. F. Tappen. Utilizing variational optimization to learn Markov random fields. In *Proc. IEEE Conf. Computer Vision and Pattern Recognition*, pages 1–8, 2007.

[471] M. F. Tappen, K. G. G. Samuel, C. V. Dean, and D. M. Lyle. The logistic random field—a convenient graphical model for learning parameters for MRF-based labeling. In *Proc. IEEE Conf. Computer Vision and Pattern Recognition*, pages 1–8, 2008.

[472] B. Taskar, V. Chatalbashev, and D. Koller. Learning associative Markov networks. In *Proc. 21st Int. Conf. Machine Learning*, 2004.

[473] B. Taskar, V. Chatalbashev, D. Koller, and C. Guestrin. Learning structured prediction models: A large margin approach. In *Proc. 22nd Int. Conf. Machine Learning*, pages 896–903, 2005.

[474] B. Taskar, C. Guestrin, and D. Koller. Max-margin Markov networks. In *Neural Information Processing Systems*, 2003.

[475] S. Tatikonda and M. I. Jordan. Loopy belief propogation and Gibbs measures. In *Proc. 18th Ann. Conf. Uncertainty in Artificial Intelligence*, pages 493–500, 2002.

[476] Y. W. Teh, M. Welling, S. Osindero, and G. E. Hinton. Energy-based models for sparse overcomplete representations. *J. Machine Learning Research*, 4(7–8):1235–1260, December 2003.

[477] D. Terzopoulos and R. Szeliski. Tracking with Kalman snakes. In A. Blake and A. Yuille, editors, *Active Vision*. MIT Press, 1992.

[478] T. Thormählen and H. Broszio. Voodoo camera tracker: A tool for the integration of virtual and real scenes, 2008. http://www.digilab.uni-hannover.de/docs/manual.html (version 1.0.1 beta).

[479] P. H. S. Torr. Solving Markov random fields using semidefinite programming. In *Proc. 9th Int. Work. Artificial Intelligence and Statistics*, 2003.

[480] P. H. S. Torr, R. Szeliski, and P. Anandan. An integrated Bayesian approach to layer extraction from image sequences. *IEEE Trans. Pattern Analysis and Machine Intelligence*, 23(3):297–303, 2001.

[481] L. Torresani, A. Hertzmann, and C. Bregler. Non-rigid structure-from-motion: Estimating shape and motion with hierarchical priors. *IEEE Trans. Pattern Analysis and Machine Intelligence*, 30(5):878–892, 2008.

[482] L. Torresani, V. Kolmogorov, and C. Rother. Feature correspondence via graph matching: Models and global optimization. In *Proc. European Conf. Computer Vision*, 2008.

[483] W. Trobin, T. Pock, D. Cremers, and H. Bischof. Continuous energy minimization via repeated binary fusion. In *Proc. 10th European Conf. Computer Vision*, part 4, pages 677–690, 2008.

[484] I. Tsochantaridis, T. Joachims, T. Hofmann, and Y. Altun. Large margin methods for structured and interdependent output variables. *J. Machine Learning Research*, 6:1453–1484, 2005.

[485] Z. Tu, X. Chen, A. L. Yuille, and S. C. Zhu. Image parsing: Unifying segmentation, detection, and recognition. *Int. J. Computer Vision*, 63(2):113–140, 2005.

[486] Z. Tu and S. Zhu. Image segmentation by data-driven Markov chain Monte Carlo. *IEEE Trans. Pattern Analysis and Machine Intelligence*, 24(5):657–673, 2002.

[487] J.K. Udupa and P. K. Saha. Fuzzy connectedness and image segmentation. *Proc. of the IEEE* 91(10):1649–1669, 2003.

[488] M. Unger, T. Mauthner, T. Pock, and H. Bischof. Tracking as segmentation of spatial-temporal volumes by anisotropic weighted TV. In *Proc. 7th Int. Conf. Energy Minimization Methods in Computer Vision and Pattern Recognition*, pages 193–206, 2009.

[489] M. Unger, T. Pock, W. Trobin, D. Cremers, and H. Bischof. TVSeg—interactive total variation based image segmentation. In *Proc. British Machine Vision Conf.*, September 2008.

[490] A. vanden Hengel, A. Dick, T. Thormählen, B. Ward, and P. H. S. Torr. VideoTrace: Rapid interactive scene modelling from video. *ACM Trans. Graphics*, 20(3), 2007.

[491] M. van Herk. A fast algorithm for local minimum and maximum filters on rectangular and octagonal kernels. *Pattern Recognition Letters*, 13(7):517–521, 1992.

[492] A. Vasilevskiy and K. Siddiqi. Flux maximizing geometric flows. *IEEE Trans. Pattern Analysis and Machine Intelligence*, 24(12):1565–1578, December 2002.

[493] V. Vazirani. *Approximation Algorithms*. Springer, 2001.

[494] O. Veksler. *Efficient Graph-Based Energy Minimization Methods in Computer Vision*. PhD thesis, Cornell University, July 1999. Available from http://www.csd.VWO.ca.

[495] O. Veksler. Graph cut based optimization for MRFs with truncated convex priors. In *Proc. IEEE Conf. Computer Vision and Pattern Recognition*, pages 1–8, 2007.

[496] O. Veksler. Multi-label moves for MRFs with truncated convex priors. In *Proc. of the 7th International Conference on Energy Minimization Methods in Computes Vision and Pattern Recognition*. pages 1–13, 2009.

[497] S. Vicente, V. Kolmogorov, and C. Rother. Graph cut based image segmentation with connectivity priors. In *Proc. IEEE Conf. Computer Vision and Pattern Recognition*, 2008.

[498] S. Vicente, V. Kolmogorov, and C. Rother. Graph cut based image segmentation with connectivity priors. Technical Report, Dept. of Computer Science, University College London, 2008.

[499] S. Vicente, V. Kolmogorov, and C. Rother. Joint optimization of segmentation and appearance models. In *Proc. Int. Conf. Computer Vision*, 2009.

[500] P. Viola and M. Jones. Rapid object detection using a boosted cascade of simple features. In *Proc. IEEE Conf. Computer Vision and Pattern Recognition*, vol. 1, 2001.

[501] S. Vishwanathan, N. Schraudolph, M. Schmidt, and K. Murphy. Accelerated training of conditional random fields with stochastic meta-descent. In *Proc. 23rd ACM Int. Conf. Machine Learning*, pages 969–976, 2006.

[502] S. V. N. Vishwanathan, N. N. Schraudolph, M. W. Schmidt, and K. P. Murphy. Accelerated training of conditional random fields with stochastic gradient methods. In *Proc. 23rd ACM Int. Conf. Machine Learning*, pages 969–976, 2006.

[503] G. Vogiatzis, P. Torr, and R. Cipolla. Multi-view stereo via volumetric graph-cuts. In *Proc. 5th IEEE Conf. Computer Vision and Pattern Recognition*, vol. 2, pages 391–398, 2005.

[504] M. Wainwright, T. Jaakkola, and A. Willsky. Map estimation via agreement on trees: Message-passing and linear programming. *IEEE Trans. Information Theory*, 51(11):3697–3717, 2005.

[505] M. Wainwright and M. Jordan. Treewidth-based conditions for exactness of the Sherali-Adams and Lasserre relaxations. Technical Report 671, Dept. of Statistics, University of California, Berkeley, 2004.

[506] M. J. Wainwright, T. S. Jaakkola, and A. S. Willsky. Tree-based reparameterization framework for analysis of sum-product and related algorithms. *IEEE Trans. Information Theory*, 49(5):1120–1146, 2003.

[507] M. J. Wainwright and M. I. Jordan. Graphical models, exponential families, and variational inference. *Foundations and Trends in Machine Learning*, 1(1–2):1–305, December 2008.

[508] M. J. Wainwright and E. P. Simoncelli. Scale mixtures of Gaussians and the statistics of natural images. In *Neural Information Processing Systems*, pages 855–861, 2000.

[509] C. Wang, Q. Yang, M. Chen, X. Tang, and Z. Ye. Progressive cut: In An image algorithm that models user intentions, *Proc. 14th Ann. ACM Conf. Multimedia*, pages 251–260, 2006.

[510] J. Y. A. Wang and E. H. Adelson. Layered representation for motion analysis. In *Proc. IEEE Conf. Computer Vision and Pattern Recognition*, pages 361–366, 1993.

[511] J. Y. A. Wang and E. H. Adelson. Representing moving images with layers. *IEEE Trans. Image Processing Special Issue: Image Sequence Compression*, 3(5):625–638, September 1994.

[512] Y. Wang and L. H. Staib. Boundary finding with correspondence using statistical shape models. In *Proc. IEEE Conf. Computer Vision and Pattern Recognition*, pages 338–345, 1998.

[513] Z. Wang, A. C. Bovik, H. R. Sheikh, and E. P. Simoncelli. Image quality assessment: From error visibility to structural similarity. *IEEE Trans. Image Processing*, 13(4):600–612, April 2004.

[514] Y. Wei and L. Quan. Asymmetrical occlusion handling using graph cut for multi-view stereo. *Proc. IEEE Conf. Computer Vision and Pattern Recognition*, volume 2, pages 902–909, 2005.

[515] J. Weickert. A review of nonlinear diffusion filtering. In *Proc. 1st Int. Scale-Space Theory in Computer Vision*, LNCS 1252, pages 1–28, Springer, Berlin, 1997.

[516] J. Weickert. *Anisotropic Diffusion in Image Processing*. Teubner, Stuttgart, 1998.

[517] Y. Weiss and W. Freeman. On the optimality of solutions of the max-product belief-propagation algorithm in arbitrary graphs. *IEEE Trans. Information Theory*, 47(2):736–744, 2001.

[518] Y. Weiss and W. T. Freeman. What makes a good model of natural images? In *Proc. IEEE Conf. Computer Vision and Pattern Recognition*, pages 1–8, 2007.

[519] Y. Weiss, C. Yanover, and T. Meltzer. MAP estimation, linear programming and belief propagation with convex free energies. In *Proc. 23rd Ann. Conf. Uncertainty in Artificial Intelligence*, pages 416–425, 2007.

[520] T. Werner. A linear programming approach to max-sum problem: A review. *IEEE Trans. Pattern Analysis and Machine Intelligence*, 29(7):1165–1179, 2007.

[521] J. Wills, S. Agarwal, and S. Belongie. What went where. In *Proc. IEEE Conf. Computer Vision and Pattern Recognition*, pages I volume 1, pages 37–40, 2003.

[522] A. Wilson and A. Bobick. Parametric hidden Markov models for gesture recognition. *IEEE Trans. Pattern Analysis and Machine Intelligence*, 21(9):884–900, 1999.

[523] G. Winkler. *Image Analysis, Random Fields And Dynamic Monte Carlo Methods*. Springer, 1995.

[524] J. Winn and N. Jojic. Locus: Learning object classes with unsupervised segmentation. In *Proc. 10th IEEE Int. Conf. Computer Vision*, volume 1, pages 756–763, 2005.

[525] J. Winn and J. Shotton. The layout consistent random field for recognizing and segmenting partially occluded objects. In *Proc. IEEE Conf. Computer Vision and Pattern Recognition*, volume 1, pages 37–44, 2006.

[526] O. Woodford, I. Reid, P. Torr, and A. Fitzgibbon. Fields of experts for image-based rendering. In *Proc. British Machine Vision Conf.*, 2006.

[527] O. Woodford, P. Torr, I. Reid, and A. Fitzgibbon. Global stereo reconstruction under second order smoothness priors. In *Proc. IEEE Conf. Computer Vision and Pattern Recognition*, pages 1–8, 2008.

[528] O. J. Woodford, I. D. Reid, and A. W. Fitzgibbon. Efficient new-view synthesis using pairwise dictionary priors. In *Proc. IEEE Conf. Computer Vision and Pattern Recognition*, pages 1–8, 2007.

[529] O. J. Woodford, I. D. Reid, P. H. S. Torr, and A. W. Fitzgibbon. On new view synthesis using multiview stereo. In *Proc. British Machine Vision Conf.*, 2007.

[530] O. J. Woodford, P. H. S. Torr, I. D. Reid, and A. W. Fitzgibbon. Global stereo reconstruction under second order smoothness priors. In *Proc. IEEE Conf. Computer Vision and Pattern Recognition*, pages 1–8, 2008.

[531] J. Xiao and M. Shah. Motion layer extraction in the presence of occlusion using graph cut. In *Proc. IEEE Conf. Computer Vision and Pattern Recognition*, volume 2, pages 972–979, 2004.

[532] J. Xiao and M. Shah. Motion layer extraction in the presence of occlusion using graph cuts. *IEEE Trans. Pattern Analysis and Machine Intelligence*, 27(10):1644–1659, October 2005.

[533] J. Yang, J. Wright, T. Huang, and Y. Ma. Image super-resolution as sparse representation of raw image patches. In *Proc. IEEE Conf. Computer Vision and Pattern Recognition*, 2008.

[534] Q. Yang, L. Wang, R. Yang, H. Stewenius, and D. Nister. Stereo matching with color-weighted correlation, hierarchical belief propagation and occlusion handling. *IEEE Trans. Pattern Analysis and Machine Intelligence*, 31(3):492–504, 2009.

[535] C. Yanover, T. Meltzer, and Y. Weiss. Linear programming relaxations and belief propagation—an empirical study. *J. Machine Learning Research*, 7:1887–1907, 2006.

[536] C. Yanover, T. Meltzer, and Y. Weiss. MAP estimation, linear programming and belief propagation with convex free energies. In *Proc. 23rd Ann. Conf. Uncertainty in Artificial Intelligence*, 2007.

[537] C. Yanover and Y. Weiss. Approximate inference and protein folding. In *Neural Information Processing Systems*, volume 15, pages 84–86, 2002.

[538] J. Yedidia, W. Freeman, and Y. Weiss. Understanding belief propagation and its generalizations. In *Proc. Int. Joint Conf. Artificial Intelligence*, 2001.

[539] J. Yedidia, W. Freeman, and Y. Weiss. Constructing free energy approximations and generalized belief propagation algorithms. *IEEE Trans. Information Theory*, 51:2282–2312, 2004.

[540] J. S. Yedidia, W. T. Freeman, and Y. Weiss. Generalized belief propagation. In *Neural Information Processing Systems*, volume 13, pages 689–695. MIT Press, 2001.

[541] C.-N. Yu and T. Joachims. Learning structural SVMs with latent variables. In *Proc. 26th Int. Conf. Machine Learning*, 2009.

[542] A. L. Yuille. Energy functions for early vision and analog networks. *Biological Cybernetics*, 61:115–123, June 1987.

[543] A. L. Yuille. CCCP algorithms to minimize the Bethe and Kikuchi free energies: Convergent alternatives to belief propagation. *Neural Computation*, 14(7):1691–1722, 2002.

[544] A. L. Yuille and N. M. Grzywacz. A mathematical analysis of the motion coherence theory. *Int. J. Computer Vision*, 3(2):155–175, 1989.

[545] A. L. Yuille and J. J. Kosowsky. Statistical physics algorithms that converge. *Neural Computation*, 6(3):341–356, 1994.

[546] A. L. Yuille and A. Rangarajan. The concave-convex procedure (CCCP). *Neural Computation*, 15(4):915–936, 2003.

[547] C. Zach, M. Niethammer, and J.-M Frahm. Continuous maximal flows and Wulff shapes: Application to MRFs. In *Proc. IEEE Conf. Computer Vision and Pattern Recognition*, pages 1911–1918, 2009.

[548] Y. Zeng, D. Samaras, W. Chen, and Q. Peng. Topology cuts: A novel min-cut/max-flow algorithm for topology preserving segmentation in N-D images. *Computer Vision and Image Understanding*, 112(1):81–90, 2008.

[549] S. Zhu, Y. Wu, and D. Mumford. Filters, random fields and maximum entropy (FRAME). *Int. J. Computer Vision*, 27(2):107–126, 1998.

[550] S. C. Zhu and D. Mumford. Prior learning and Gibbs reaction-diffusion. *IEEE Trans. Pattern Analysis and Machine Intelligence*, 19(11):1236–1250, November 1997.

[551] S. C. Zhu and A. Yuille. Region competition: Unifying snakes, region growing, and Bayes/MDL for multi-band image segmentation. *IEEE Trans. Pattern Analysis and Machine Intelligence*, 18(9):884–900, September 1996.

[552] C. L. Zitnick and T. Kanade. A cooperative algorithm for stereo matching and occlusion detection. *IEEE Trans. Pattern Analysis and Machine Intelligence*, 22(7):675–684, July 2000.

[553] C. L. Zitnick and S. B. Kang. Stereo for image-based rendering using image over-segmentation. *Int. J. Computer Vision*, 75(1):49–65, 2007.

Contributors

Aseem Agarwala   Adobe Systems, aseem@agarwala.org

Michael J. Black   Brown University, black@cs.brown.edu

Andrew Blake   Microsoft Research, ablake@microsoft.com

Yuri Boykov   University of Western Ontario, Canada, yuri@csd.uwo.ca

Antonin Chambolle   Ecole Polytechnique, antonin.chambolle@polytechnique.fr

Daniel Cremers   Technical University of Munich, daniel.cremers@in.tum.de

Antonio Criminisi   Microsoft Research, antcrim@microsoft.com

Geoffrey Cross   Microsoft Research

Andrew Fitzgibbon   Microsoft Research, awf@microsoft.com

William I. Freeman   MIT, billf@mit.edu

Leo Grady   Siemens Corporate Research, leo.grady@siemens.com

Derek Hoiem   UIUC, dhoiem@cs.uiuc.edu

Michael Isard   Microsoft Research, misard@microsoft.com

Hiroshi Ishikawa   Waseda University, Tokyo, Japan, hfs@ieee.org

Sing Bing Kang   Microsoft Research, sbkang@microsoft.com

Pushmeet Kohli   Microsoft Research, pkohli@microsoft.com

Kalin Kolev   University of Bonn, kolev@cs.uni-bonn.de

Vladimir Kolmogorov   University College London, v.kolmogorov@cs.ucl.ac.uk

Nikos Komodakis   University of Crete, komod@csd.uoc.gr

M. Pawan Kumar   Stanford University, pawan@cs.stanford.edu

Lubor Ladicky   Oxford Brookes University, lladicky@brookes.ac.uk

Victor Lempitsky   University of Oxford, vilem@robots.ox.ac.uk

Yin Li   Microsoft Research

Ce Liu   Microsoft Research, celiu@microsoft.com

Talya Meltzer   CS HUJI, talyam@cs.huji.ac.il

Thomas Pock   Graz University of Technology, pock@icg.tugraz.at

Alex Rav-Acha   Weizmann Institute of Science, ravacha@gmail.com

Stefan Roth   Department of Computer Science, TU Darmstadt, Germany, sroth@cs.tu-darmstadt.de

Carsten Rother   Microsoft Research, carrot@microsoft.com

Daniel Scharstein   Middlebury College, schar@middlebury.edu

Jamie Shotton   Microsoft Research, jamie@shotton.org

Heung-Yeung Shum   Microsoft Research

Dheeraj Singaraju   Johns Hopkins University, dheeraj@cis.jhu.edu

Ali Kemal Sinop   Carnegie Mellon University, asinop@cs.cmu.edu

Jian Sun   Microsoft Research, jiansun@microsoft.com

Richard Szeliski   Microsoft Research, szeliski@microsoft.com

Martin Szummer   Microsoft Research, szummer@microsoft.com

Marshall F. Tappen   University of Central Florida, mtappen@cs.ucf.edu

Philip H. S. Torr   Oxford Brookes University, philiptorr@brookes.ac.uk

Antonio Torralba   MIT, torralba@csail.mit.edu

Olga Veksler   University of Western Ontario, London, Canada, olga@csd.uwo.ca

Sara Vicente   University College London, svicente@cs.ucl.ac.uk

René Vidal   Johns Hopkins University, rvidal@cis.jhu.edu

Yair Weiss   CS HUJI, yweiss@cs.huji.ac.il

John Winn   Microsoft Research, john@johnwinn.org

Chen Yanover   FHCRC, cyanover@fhcrc.org

Jenny Yuen   MIT, jenny@csail.mit.edu

Alan Yuille   Dept. Statistics, UCLA, yuille@stat.ucla.edu

Ramin Zabih   Cornell University, Ithaca, USA, rdz@cs.cornell.edu

Index